from

The Japan Foundation

Democratizing Japan

Contributors

Amakawa Akira
Yokohama National University

Hans H. Baerwald
University of California, Los Angeles

Theodore H. McNelly
University of Maryland

Ota Masahide
University of the Ryūkyūs

Ōtake Hideo
Tōhoku University

T. J. Pempel
Cornell University

Susan J. Pharr
Harvard University

Sakamoto Yoshikazu
Tokyo University

Kurt Steiner
Stanford University

Takemae Eiji
Tokyo Keizai University

Tanaka Hideo
Tokyo University

Uchida Kenzō
Hōsei University

Robert E. Ward
Stanford University

This book is based on a conference sponsored by both the Japan Society for the Promotion of Science and the Joint Committee on Japanese Studies of the American Council of Learned Societies and the Social Science Research Council with support from the National Endowment for the Humanities.

Democratizing Japan

The Allied Occupation

Edited by
Robert E. Ward
and
Sakamoto Yoshikazu

UNIVERSITY OF HAWAII PRESS

HONOLULU

Library of Congress Cataloging-in-Publication Data

Democratizing Japan.

   Based on papers presented at a conference
sponsored by both the Japan Society for the
Promotion of Science and the Joint Committee
on Japanese Studies of the American Council
of Learned Societies and the Social Science
Research Council with support from the National
Endowment for the Humanities.
   Includes bibliographies and index.
   1.   Japan—Politics and government—1945–
2.   Japan—Constitutional history.   3.   Political
planning—Japan—History.   4.   Japan—History—
Allied occupation, 1945–1952.   I.   Ward,
Robert Edward.   II.   Sakamoto, Yoshikazu.
III.   Nihon Gakujutsu Shinkōkai.   IV.   Joint
Committee on Japanese Studies.   V.   Social Science
Research Council (U.S.)
JQ1624.D46   1987   940.53'144'0952   86–25023
ISBN 0–8248–0883–5

Contents

Abbreviations

The following abbreviations are used throughout the text and notes.

CAA	Civil Affairs Administration
CAC	Country and Area Committee
CAD	Civil Affairs Division (U.S. Army)
CI&E	Civil Information and Education Section (of SCAP)
CINCAFPAC	Commander-in-Chief, American Forces in the Pacific
ESS	Economic and Scientific Section (of SCAP)
FEAC	Far Eastern Advisory Commission
FEC	Far Eastern Commission
GHQ	General Headquarters
GS	Government Section (of SCAP)
JCP	Japan Communist party
JCS	Joint Chiefs of Staff
JSP	Japan Socialist party
PWC	Postwar Programs Committee
SANACC	State-Army-Navy-Air Coordinating Committee
SCAP	Supreme Commander for the Allied Powers (refers also to the complex bureaucratic structure set up under the commander)
SCAPIN	Instruction by the Supreme Commander to the Government of Japan
SWNCC	State-War-Navy Coordinating Committee

Introduction

Robert E. Ward and Sakamoto Yoshikazu

There have been very few occasions in history when major modern nations have undergone revolutionary changes in their political and social systems as a result of foreign influence and pressure and subsequently, once the foreign pressure was withdrawn, freely elected to maintain these new institutions basically intact for substantial periods of time. Although some of the more successful colonial experiences might seem to meet these criteria, the societies concerned were not by Western standards either major or modern. Similarly, whereas the satellite states of Eastern Europe undoubtedly underwent types and degrees of sociopolitical change at the hands of an external agency that may well be regarded as revolutionary, it is questionable that their decision to maintain them has been freely taken.

The case seems different, however, where Japan and the Federal Republic of Germany are concerned. Both nations are indubitably major and modern. Both were occupied by foreign troops after their defeat in World War II. In each case the occupying authorities played a determining role in the introduction of political and other changes that may well be viewed as revolutionary by contrast to the institutions that had preceded them. And both have freely chosen to maintain the essential institutions involved for upwards of thirty years since their occupations ended.

A historical event of this magnitude and novelty cries out for explication. How does one account for it? What actually happened during the ostensibly critical years of the foreign occupation? What was the role of the occupiers and what the role of the occupied in determining these results? Have the postwar changes really proven durable? Or are they subject to mounting challenges and piecemeal erosion?

These are important and fascinating questions—especially to the Japanese and Germans, but to Americans as well—since it was the armed forces of the United States that played the leading role in both occupations and American military and political leaders, interests, views, and values that critically influenced the actual outcomes. In this sense it might seem surprising that more numerous, systematic, and authoritative attempts have not been made in any of these countries to respond to the preceding questions. In fact, there is no dearth of relevant literature. But it is largely episodic in nature, limited in perspective, polemic in intent, or restricted in its access to the essential primary sources of information. A number of the participants on both sides of both occupations have described their personal experiences and views, sometimes with eloquence and insight, sometimes in controversial terms. A number of Japanese and Germans who might, if they chose, have shed very substantial light on these years from 1945 to 1952 have delayed or refrained from doing so for the sake of their own, their friends', or their country's interests. Practically all authors have been seriously disadvantaged by the official declassification system of the three governments primarily involved —the United States, Japan, and the Federal Republic of Germany—and of sundry other states less directly involved. It was only in the latter 1970s that the official U.S. documentation began to become publicly available in sufficient depth and completeness to make definitive studies for the years before 1950 feasible. More recently the comparable Japanese archival materials have begun to surface, especially those of the ministries of Foreign Affairs and Finance.

These were the circumstances in the late 1970s under which the present group of authors, both Japanese and American, decided to explore the possibilities of binational research and publication on the fascinating conjoining of American and Japanese national history that is known somewhat misleadingly as "the Allied Occupation of Japan, 1945–1952." The background and rationale for this undertaking were as follows.

Few qualified observers comparing Japan today with the Japan of the 1930s would deny that the society has undergone revolutionary changes in politics, economics, tastes, and life-styles. Practically all would also agree that the most intensively seminal period for such changes is to be found in the years 1945 to 1952, when American forces, masquerading under the title of an Allied Occupation of Japan, were in effective, if diminishing, control of the Japanese government. At that point, agreement ceases. The consequent polarities can be symbolized by the following quotations. The first is from a column in the editorial section of the *New York Times* entitled "Please, Japan, Return the Favor: Occupy Us."

After World War II Americans spent 80 months in Japan building a peace-loving, democratic, and self-supporting society. It was the most ambitious large-scale exercise of peacetime diplomacy in American history. Now is the time for the Japanese to reciprocate. The United States needs renewal, a

new beginning in the words of President Reagan. Japanese leadership, supported by American hard work, could accomplish this noble purpose. Without a preliminary war, we should ask the Japanese to come here, occupy us,
and do exactly those things we did for them from 1945 to 1952.[1]

Although facetious in intent, the passage captures accurately the views
of most American and some Japanese students of the Occupation. In
brief, it was an unprecedented success.

Other Americans—and Japanese too—would take strong exception to
such a conclusion. The following passage from the introduction to
America's Asia: Dissenting Essays on Asian-American Relations represents one such viewpoint.

> More than two decades ago the Occupation of Japan set the course for the
> militarist and anti-popular character of American intervention in Asia. John
> Dower explores the failure of the Occupation to live up to its promise to
> democratize and demilitarize Japan. With the seizure of Pacific island bases
> and the "reverse course" of the Occupation, the banner of an Asian *Pax
> Americana* was unfurled. A decade earlier Japan had marched through Asia,
> bombed Pearl Harbor, and carved out an empire justified by anti-Commu-
> nist politics and the promise of independence and development. That
> empire was brought to its knees by a combination of American technology,
> United States Marine human wave assaults, the fire-bombing of Tokyo,
> nuclear holocaust in Hiroshima and Nagasaki, and heroic efforts of guer-
> rilla fighters in China and other parts of rural Asia. But the end of European
> and Japanese colonialism brought neither genuine independence nor auton-
> omous development to the nations of "Free Asia." American military and
> economic power swept in to fill the void left by the departing colonial
> powers—achieving for America many of the dreams of empire it had denied
> a vanquished Japan, its rationale then as now the necessity to crush Com-
> munist aggression.[2]

Between these poles one encounters a gamut of intermediate viewpoints and interpretations most of which, despite a variety of qualifications, reach a favorable verdict on the Occupation. Adverse judgments
on this score have, however, existed from the beginning, especially in
Japan. But one heard relatively little about these until the last five or six
years, when increasing attention has been paid to Japanese writers of the
so-called nationalist school. The American equivalent on the negative
side is perhaps best represented by the work of a group of revisionist
scholars who emphasize in critical terms the Cold War and strategic
aspects of the planning and conduct of the Occupation.

In its conception, though not in its publication, the present volume
antedates the beginning of the recent "Occupation boom" of writings in
Japan. It derives ultimately from an earlier joint Japanese-American
study of the literature relating to the Allied Occupation of Japan. This
was sponsored on the Japanese side by the Japan Society for the Promo-

tion of Science (Nihon Gakujutsu Shinkōkai) and on the American by the
Joint Committee on Japanese Studies of the Social Science Research
Council and the American Council of Learned Societies.[3] These bibliographic explorations led quite naturally to a similarly sponsored plan for
a binational study of the Occupation itself jointly chaired by the chief
editors of the earlier bibliographic project: Sakamoto Yoshikazu* of
Tokyo University's Faculty of Law and Robert E. Ward of Stanford University's Department of Political Science. On the American side the new
Occupation project was financed by a generous grant to the Social Science Research Council from the National Endowment for the Humanities, and, on the Japanese side, by a similar grant from the Japan Society
for the Promotion of Science. The editors would like to acknowledge
their gratitude and indebtedness to both agencies.

The binational group involved in this study consists of six American
and seven Japanese members. They are

> Amakawa Akira, Political Science, Faculty of Economics, Yokohama
>   National University
> Hans H. Baerwald, Political Science, University of California (Los
>   Angeles)
> Theodore H. McNelly, Political Science, University of Maryland
> Ota Masahide, Sociology, Faculty of Law and Letters, University of
>   the Ryūkyūs
> Ōtake Hideo, Political Science, Faculty of Law, Tōhoku University
> T. J. Pempel, Political Science, Cornell University
> Susan J. Pharr, Government and Reischauer Institute for Japanese
>   Studies, Harvard University
> Sakamoto Yoshikazu, International Politics, Faculty of Law, Tokyo
>   University
> Kurt Steiner, Political Science, Stanford University
> Takemae Eiji, Political Science, Faculty of Economics, Tokyo Keizai
>   University
> Tanaka Hideo, Anglo-American Law, Faculty of Law, Tokyo Univer-
>   sity
> Uchida Kenzō, Political Science, Faculty of Law, Hōsei University
> Robert E. Ward, Political Science, Stanford University.

The entire group convened on two occasions to plan the book and to
review first drafts of the chapters. The Americans have written in
English, the Japanese in Japanese. The Japanese-authored chapters that
follow have been translated from the original by The Asia Foundation's

---

* All Japanese personal names are given in Japanese style, that is, with surname first.

Translation Service Center in Tokyo. The book will also be published in a Japanese-language version.[4]

The authors' basic interest in designing the book was to bring to bear both American and Japanese scholarship on and interpretations of what was after all an intimately shared historical experience. Even with our two meetings, we found trans-Pacific research collaboration to be an extraordinarily time-consuming and patience-requiring endeavor. Without exception, however, we are convinced in both scholarly and personal terms that this perseverance was eminently worthwhile.

On balance we agree among ourselves that the Occupation, judged in terms of historical precedent or realistic possibilities, was in many ways remarkably and unexpectedly successful. But we differ widely—and along national lines—as to the degree to which it realized its full potential in some critical respects, especially where democratization is concerned. The principal issue that divides us here is the "reverse course" phase of the Occupation, that is, the period during which the Occupation authorities are alleged for several reasons, involving primarily the onset of the Cold War, to have abandoned or severely modified their earlier efforts during the so-called New Deal phase of the Occupation to reform Japan along truly democratic lines and to have substituted for these a new set of more conservative, repressive, discriminatory, and democratically retrogressive policies and programs. Frequent differences on this score will be encountered in the chapters that follow. We should emphasize, however, that they are essentially differences of degree and interpretation. All contributors acknowledge readily that at some point between 1947 and 1949 there occurred a series of incremental changes in SCAP (Supreme Commander for the Allied Powers, i.e., General MacArthur and, at the end, General Ridgway) policy that substantially changed the Occupation authorities' attitudes and programs with respect to left-wing political parties, the labor unions, and the treatment of Japanese individuals and groups suspected of promoting what came to be viewed as radical causes. The disagreements relate to such matters as the underlying causes for this shift, the dating of its initiation, the justification for it or lack thereof, and the interpretation of just what the United States government and SCAP meant in practice by that abstract phrase "the democratization of Japan."

Such differences aside, the authors see the value of the book as residing essentially in the interweaving of Japanese and American scholarship and viewpoints. The research phase of the work coincided with the long-delayed opening of the SCAP and State Department archives through the year 1949. This made available an enormous mass of extremely valuable documentation hitherto unavailable to scholars. Most members of both groups made extensive use of these new materials either in the U.S. National Archives or through microfilm copies. Two members of the

American group—Steiner and Baerwald—had served as Occupation officials. Most members of both groups had conducted extensive interviews
with former high-ranking members of the Occupation and their Japanese
counterparts. All made use of the increasing Japanese literature on the
Occupation. A great deal of new and important information was, therefore, available.

It was not our intention to produce an overall study of the Occupation
of Japan. Because of the inaccessibility until recently of many of the basic
official records, the existing state of research on the subject is not yet sufficiently advanced or complete to substantiate such an endeavor. Our
purpose was to select a number of aspects of the total occupation experience that (1) seemed to us of critical importance in any historical explanation of its accomplishments or shortfalls; (2) possessed an adequate
data base, especially with respect to the availability of new primary
sources; and (3) were of professional interest to one of our group of Japanese and American scholars. On the basis of these criteria we made the
choices that have in turn determined the structure of this volume.

We felt, first, the need to provide a proper context for a study of the
Occupation period proper in two different senses: (1) the presurrender
planning that lay behind and in some measure determined the actual policies of SCAP (chapter 1, Ward), and (2) the overall international context
in which the Occupation was set (chapter 2, Sakamoto). Against this
background we felt that the new constitution of 1946–1947 was the
most fundamental institutional change wrought by the Occupation and
have, therefore, devoted two chapters to it. The first, by Professor
McNelly (chapter 3), provides a definitive account of the emergence of
this basic document and the policies and problems attending its adoption. The second, by Professor Tanaka (chapter 4), sheds new light on
the fascinating but neglected problem of why the Matsumoto Committee, which was officially charged by the Japanese cabinet with the
responsibility of recommending changes in the Meiji Constitution, had
no influence on the actual process of constitutional revision. If this committee had perceived its mission and the political circumstances in which
it was operating in more realistic terms, the so-called MacArthur Constitution probably would never have been written.

Thereafter we take up sequentially several of the Occupation's major
programs of institutional and procedural reform. This section begins
with Professor Baerwald's treatment of the rehabilitation of the National
Diet (chapter 5) and continues with Professor Pempel's account of
SCAP's relatively ineffectual efforts to reform the Japanese bureaucracy
(chapter 6), Professor Steiner's study of the revision of the Japanese Civil
Code (chapter 7), and Professor Pharr's account of the politics of
women's rights during the Occupation (chapter 8). Included also are Professor Amakawa's analysis of the complexities of local governmental

reform (chapter 9) and Professor Ota's views of the manner in which the quite separate and special occupation of Okinawa related to postwar reform programs in Japan (chapter 10). A further section treats the formation and early development of the conservative (chapter 11, Uchida) and reformist parties (chapter 12, Takemae). A penultimate section describes an important but little-known aspect of business-labor relations during the Occupation, the managerial councils for dealing with labor problems (chapter 13, Ōtake). The final chapter, by Professor Ward, highlights and comments on some of the more important themes and findings of the preceding chapters.

Notes

1. John Curtis Perry (March 4, 1981), p. A27.

2. Edward Freidman and Mark Selden, eds. (New York: Vintage Books, 1971), p. xi.

3. This resulted in the publication of two sizeable annotated bibliographies on the Japanese and Western language literature on the Occupation: Sakamoto Yoshikazu, ed., *Nihon senryō bunken mokuroku* [A bibliography of the Allied Occupation of Japan] (Tokyo: Japan Society for the Promotion of Science, 1972), xxiv, 349 pp.; and Robert E. Ward and Frank Joseph Shulman, eds., *The Allied Occupation of Japan, 1945–1952: An Annotated Bibliography of Western Language Materials* (Chicago: American Library Association, 1974), xx, 867 pp.

4. Sakamoto Yoshikazu, ed., *Nihon senryō no kenkyū* [Studies in the Occupation of Japan] (Tokyo: University of Tokyo Press, 1987).

Presurrender Planning: Treatment of the Emperor and Constitutional Changes

Robert E. Ward

It is often difficult to date with precision either the beginning or the end of a planning process. It may, and often does, commence as a dawning awareness on the part of one or several individuals that they or the agency or interest that they represent is faced with an emerging problem about which someone should be more systematically concerned. At the other end, planning merges with the execution of plans and, if it persists thereafter, it does so in more complex shapes where it interacts with and is affected by the results of action on prior plans.

Additionally, the planning procedure is often ill-documented, especially in its earlier stages, and thus difficult for historians to recapture in adequate detail. Even in times allegedly characterized by a greater degree of rationality and foresight in our larger social and governmental undertakings, it is remarkable how little planning and foresight is often given to even the most consequential problems. The circumstances of the United States following World War I provide a good example. Generalities aside, the government of the United States had done little planning about the type of peace settlement it would like to see negotiated at Versailles or how the terms of such a settlement might best be carried out.

Against such a background the Allied Occupation of Japan (1945–1952) is quite remarkable. Planning began early in the war, was organized in formal and readily identifiable fashion at the outset, was carried on systematically throughout the war, and was documented in extensive reports that are now largely available for scrutiny and analysis. Most remarkable of all, these wartime plans were in large part carried out by the American authorities who controlled the allegedly "Allied" Occupation, and many of the changes that they effected survive more or less intact in Japan today.

The entire episode is of great historical and social scientific interest. It revolves about the systematic and planned attempt of a victorious power, the United States, to ensure the fruits of its victory. First, the victor disarmed and demilitarized its enemy. Second, steps were taken calculated to produce lasting alterations in Japan's political, economic, and social institutions and in the behavior and values of Japanese society to render them more compatible with American practices and beliefs and, it was hoped, to produce a Japan more disposed toward friendly relations with the United States in the future. These plans in turn gave rise to a predominantly American military occupation of Japan. In the course of its six years and eight months a Supreme Commander for the Allied Powers (SCAP) was vested with total authority over the Japanese government and people; the population of Japan was almost completely cut off from any but SCAP-approved external contacts or communications; domestic censorship was imposed; and the Occupation authorities were given orders and virtually plenary powers to bring about "the democratization of Japan."

Fundamentally, the Occupation was an exercise in "planned political change." Several things made it unusual. First, the planning was on a grand scale; its subject was an entire nation. Second, the planning agencies and immediate agents of change were foreigners, not Japanese. Third, the degree of control they exercised over the subjects of change, that is, the Japanese, was extraordinary in its scope and authority (although in this connection it should be emphasized that the Japanese role was far from passive; in fact the history of the Occupation is in part one of steadily increasing Japanese assertiveness and influence vis-à-vis their occupiers). Fourth, the relationship between occupiers and the occupied involved important racial and cultural differences. Finally, the Occupation authorities had an appreciable, if not necessarily optimal, amount of time in which to carry out their plans—almost seven years—although in fact the outbreak of the Korean War in June 1950 largely diverted their attention to external developments during the last twenty-two months of the Occupation.

Although unusual, such circumstances are not unique. There were somewhat similar Allied occupations of Germany, Italy, and Austria following World War II, and the Soviet Union also occupied a number of its border states for varying periods of time. At a somewhat greater remove and usually with less intensity, the historical efforts of earlier imperialist powers to alter the institutions and ways of their colonies were also exercises in "planned political change" by external agencies.

If one can for analytic purposes refer to this class of events as "experiments in externally directed planned political change," it should be instructive to examine them in retrospect to determine the original intentions and expectations of the planners and thus to lay the foundations for achieving a better understanding of the postwar emergence of what is often called "the New Japan."

Let us begin with an examination of plans relating either to the treatment of the reigning emperor or, in more general terms, of the imperial system.[1] Thereafter we will group a variety of other postwar political plans under the rubric of "constitutional change" and describe these in some detail. It should be understood that where presurrender political planning for Japan is concerned we are dealing largely with the Department of State, since, for planning purposes at least, the military were usually willing to accept the primacy of the State Department.

Planning for the Treatment of the Emperor

No political issue concerning the postwar treatment of Japan received more attention or proved more controversial than the question of what was to be done about the emperor. Among the planners and their colleagues within the Department of State the treatment of the emperor became almost a shorthand symbol for the more general problem of the democratization of Japan. Views ranged from a belief that no durable or reliable liberalization of Japanese politics could be achieved until the imperial system had been abolished to the conviction that only by working through the emperor could the United States hope to democratize Japan. Thus the American planners of both persuasions may be said to have shared the traditional Japanese view of the Japanese political system: that at its heart lay the imperial institution. Let us see how American planning doctrines in this respect developed.

The State Department planners began to give serious consideration to the imperial problem in 1943. It is first mentioned in a paper of the Subcommittee on Political Problems of the Advisory Committee on Postwar Foreign Policy, dated March 10, 1943, where it is simply identified as one among a series of major problems relating to the "Treatment of Japan": "To what degree should the United States be concerned with the internal political development of Japan? Should the continuance of the Imperial Household be favored?"[2] Thus posed, the question served to launch a series of papers and discussions that continued well into the early stages of the Occupation proper.

From there the planners moved on May 25, 1943, to their first formal paper "Status of the Japanese Emperor." A twelve-page summary of the historical, legal, constitutional, political, and psychological roles and powers of the emperor, it concludes by outlining the principal policy alternatives available to the United States with respect to his postwar treatment—either terminate the emperorship or continue it. It provides arguments for both choices. The case for termination rests upon its efficacy as a means of curbing future Japanese nationalism and aggression and denying to proponents of such causes the opportunity once again to take control of the government by exploiting the imperial mystique and authority. The case for continuation is more extensively and persuasively presented.

> The survival of the emperorship would be a potential asset of great utility, as an instrument not only for promoting domestic stability, but also for bringing about changes desired by the United Nations in Japanese policy. The very fact that the power to initiate amendments to the Japanese constitution is reserved to the emperor makes orderly constitutional change more readily feasible if the approach is through the emperor. A non-militaristic governing group would be in a better position to make reforms effective if it could speak in the name and with the authority of the emperor.[3]

Although the paper offers no policy preference, the majority of the State Department planners—four-fifths or nine-tenths of all Japan experts, Blakeslee once claimed—obviously favored continuation of the emperorship. Members of the various departmental committees that received and criticized the planners' papers and, at still higher levels of the department, most notably Assistant Secretary Dean Acheson, voiced opposition to it.

By September 27, 1943, the State Department planners are saying: "If the decision which now seems to be acceptable is to continue to prevail that the Emperor as an individual and the Emperorship as an institution should not be destroyed but should continue as a part of a reformed government, then some provision should appear in the terms of surrender concerning the attitude of the United Nations towards this problem and the protection of the Emperor."[4] This assertion represents an early effort by the planners to have their conclusions in this respect incorporated in much higher-level and more meaningful documents, in this case the projected terms of surrender for Japan. For those familiar with the later controversy over whether or not to incorporate into the terms of the Potsdam Declaration some explicit assurance of the Allies' intentions with respect to the emperor, this assertion may also represent the earliest antecedent of what became a vexatious policy issue.

Later documents indicate that the planners somewhat overreached in their claim that the decision to continue the emperorship was "acceptable."[5] An Army Civil Affairs Division document of the same vintage, entitled "Draft Directive for Military Government of Japan," produced by the School of Military Government at Charlottesville, Virginia, provides in its relative simplicity an interesting contrast: "Government officials, the Emperor, members of the Imperial Family, the premier, high court officials, elder statesmen, Privy Council members, Imperial Conference members, Cabinet ministers, Governors of Prefectures, and other high political functionaries of Japan, found within the occupied territory, will be arrested and held as prisoners of war pending further instructions."[6]

Toward the end of 1943 a new and more explicit note begins to appear in the continuing argument about the emperor. We find the proponents of continuing the emperorship now normally prefacing their case by statements such as: "In case the Japanese people at the end of the war desired to abolish the institution of the emperor, the United States should not raise any objection."[7] Although this scenario obviously represents a concession to the opposition, it was also a contingency that the planners regarded as highly unlikely. It does, however, account for the convoluted nature of that portion of Section 2, Part II (Relationship to Japanese Government) of the U.S. Initial Postsurrender Policy for Japan that relates to policy toward the emperor.

During 1944 the subject of how to treat the emperor and the imperial system continued to provoke interest and controversy among the State Department planners. The earliest 1944 papers in the Notter Files summed up the options available for U.S. policy and conveyed to higher authorities the recommendations of the Interdivisional Area Committee on the Far East.[8] Of this series the definitive paper is H-114a of February 23 by Dr. Hugh Borton.[9] It describes the background in terms of the positive and negative potentials of the imperial position from the U.S. standpoint, notes that the British government is opposed to the abolition of the imperial position and that Chiang Kai-shek is thought to favor leaving this decision to the Japanese people, and indicates that the existing U.S. policy of not criticizing the emperor in its propaganda releases has recently been attacked by the American press as being tantamount to a policy of indirect support for the emperorship. H-114a then poses five alternative policies for consideration by the U.S. government: (1) On the assumption that the Japanese will desire its retention, the adoption for the present of a policy of contributing to reformation of the institution of the emperor; (2) on the assumption that the Japanese will desire its elimination, the adoption for the present of a policy of contributing to the elimination of the institution of the emperor; (3) the adoption of a policy of refraining from criticizing the emperor or the emperorship; (4) the adoption of a policy of active support of the emperor by the United Nations; and (5) the adoption of a policy of forceful elimination of the institution of the emperor as a prerequisite for a reformed Japan.

Option 1 was the obvious favorite of the planners. They argued that this solution accorded with the high-level promise of self-determination of forms of government set forth in the Atlantic Charter, that the Japanese people would almost certainly wish to retain the emperorship, that it would be practically impossible to achieve its permanent elimination under these circumstances, that such a solution would enable U.S. propaganda to emphasize the extent to which the Japanese military had corrupted and exploited the emperor for their selfish ends, that this policy would facilitate the emperor's signing the terms of surrender—if this seemed advisable—and would also be helpful in the formation of a stable and acceptable government in Japan after the war. Practically no serious disadvantages to such a policy were perceived. The advantages attaching to options 2 and 3 were seen as fewer and less significant, while options 4 and 5 were rejected as unfeasible and counterproductive to American interests. These then were the planners' recommendations with respect to the treatment of the emperor at the outset of 1944.

Shortly after the completion of the above policy summary, consideration of the problem of the emperorship escalated to a much higher level of review and decision within the Department of State. The relevant planning papers are of two series: (1) CAC, papers of the Country and Area Committees, in this case the Interdivisional Area Committee on the Far East; and (2) PWC, papers of the Postwar Programs Committee which, together with the Secretary's Policy Committee, was the highest body for the determination of policy within the Department of State.

In the first relevant paper of the new series the problem of the emperor is viewed in a different and more operational light: "Should the occupation authorities suspend the exercise of all, none, or some of the emperor's functions?" After citing the arguments for each of these alternatives, the PWC made a number of policy recommendations. If politically practicable and physically possible

> the emperor and his immediate family should be placed under protective custody. They should be removed from the Imperial Palace in Tokyo and be taken to a location which is comparatively easy to guard, such as the Hayama Palace on the seacoast south of Tokyo. The emperor should be kept in seclusion but his personal advisors should be allowed to have access to him so that the people would have assurance as to his welfare and safety. Courtesy and deference due his rank should be accorded him.[10]

The committee went on to recommend that, while all the functions of sovereignty of the emperor would devolve on the theater commander, "in order to facilitate the use of Japanese government officials by CAA [Civil Affairs Administration], certain functions of government should be exercised, if possible, through the emperor or in his name with the approval of the occupation authorities." The functions involved would relate to the delegation of administrative duties to subordinate officials and would not include those stipulated in articles V, VI, VII, XI, and XII of the Meiji Constitution. "CAA would then be in a position to use a maximum number of Japanese officials directly under its supervision and would be able to leave the operation of administration to the Japanese themselves." These provisions clearly anticipate the sort of indirectly administered occupation that later came to pass.

The remainder of the paper notes simply that if it should become apparent that the preceding arrangements would be of "comparatively little benefit to CAA," then it might be advantageous "to suspend all of the functions of the emperor." The Occupation authorities should then be prepared "to take charge of both the direction and the actual operation of the basic functions of Japanese government." Provision was also made for the direct administration of any parts of Japan proper occupied by American forces prior to the unconditional surrender of the entire country.

Three statements considered by the Postwar Programs Committee on April 26, 1944, express very well the views of the Japan specialists among the postwar planners. Their authors were Julius W. Pratt, Joseph W. Ballantine, and Joseph C. Grew.[11] All three papers stress the essential neutrality of the imperial institution, its recent exploitation by the military, and the availability of suppressed liberal elements and a liberal tradition in Japan. Pratt well summarizes the views of all when he says: "As a symbol, the Emperor can be used for either good or evil ends. The objectives of United Nations policy should be the liquidation of the military class which has controlled the symbol and the upbuilding of new groups which will use it in support of a policy of moderation and international cooperation."

On May 9, 1944, the following provision was added to the basic paper of March 21:

> The occupation authorities should in all of their treatment of and their contacts with the emperor refrain from any action which would imply recognition of or support for the Japanese concept that the Japanese emperor is different from and superior to other temporal rulers, that he is of divine origins and capacities, that he is sacrosanct or that he is indispensable. They should permit absolute freedom of discussion, except where there may be incitement to breaches of the peace, of political as well as other subjects.[12]

In July 1944 a CAC paper distinguished between the treatment of the imperial institution as such and that of the reigning emperor, Hirohito.[13] The issue was "whether or not the military government should insist on the deposition of Hirohito even though recognizing the institution of the emperor." The recommendation was that it should not, for reasons of international law and the absence of agreement as yet on this point by the United Nations. Similarly, an August 2, 1944, paper poses the question whether, during the period of Allied military government, the United Nations should attempt to bring about the abdication of Hirohito.[14] The authors saw many reasons why such a development might be useful: the frequency of imperial abdication in the past, the lack of personalized relationship between a particular emperor and the Japanese people, the public acceptance of responsibility entailed in such a gesture, and the predominant sense of public opinion among the United Nations that Hirohito bore some responsibility for the war and that he should atone for it. It was also felt that, since the crown prince was still a minor and a regency would therefore have to be established, the military government might well be in a position to bring about the selection of regents disposed to collaborate with the United Nations. Despite such considerations the paper recommends that the military government refrain from any actions calculated to bring about the emperor's abdication or the transfer of the throne to anyone else. If, however, "properly qualified Japanese should take the initiative to effect by recognized Japanese processes the transfer of the throne from Hirohito to another person, the military government should not interfere with such transfer. If a regency should be required, the military government should use its influence to assure the appointment of regents from among those Japanese who may be expected to collaborate with the military government."

At roughly the same time the State Department planners were also asked to consider how imperial property should be treated by the Occupation authorities.[15] Their answer was that "in principle the Imperial Household properties be treated as though they were Japanese Government property," but that "only those properties which are substantially useful for the purposes of the military occupant be confiscated" and that "property of the Imperial Family which is dedicated to religion, charity, and education, the arts and sciences is entitled to the immunities of private property."[16]

Finally, between August and November 1944, the planners considered the role of the emperor with respect to what were termed the "underlying principles of the terms of surrender."[17] The question involved was "What Japanese authority should sign the surrender instrument?" Feeling that "the most conclusive and therefore the most desirable form of acknowledgment of unconditional surrender would be a document to that effect signed by the emperor," the planners recommended that the document "should receive the emperor's official signature and privy seal, should be countersigned by the highest available representative of the Japanese High Command, and should be delivered to the Allied Theater Commander. This document will constitute the instrument of unconditional surrender of Japan."

The papers cited thus far represent the state of U.S. planning with respect to the treatment of the emperor at the end of 1944. The year had been one of more or less continuous action on this score. It had also brought many refinements to the relatively simple and straightforward planning papers of 1943 in respect to such matters as the reformation and constructive use of the imperial institution by the Allies, the supervision of some imperial functions, the attitude to be adopted by the Occupation authorities toward the imperial institution, the deposition or abdication of the emperor, the treatment of imperial property, and the role of the emperor where the instrument of surrender was concerned. It remained now to transform these decisions from policies devised and formally accepted by the Department of State through its Postwar Programs

Committee to the status of policies adopted by the government of the United States. In most cases this meant securing the approval of the State-War-Navy Coordinating Committee (SWNCC), which is to say persuading the War and Navy departments to accept the policies recommended by the Department of State. The initial reactions from the military were not favorable. For example, on January 19, 1945, in a memorandum to Colonel Marcus of the army's Civil Affairs Division (CAD), Herbert Feis, a special consultant to the Secretary of War, wrote with respect to the State Department papers on Japan: "In general, they seem to me slightly saturated with a Sunday School flavor—somewhat out of keeping with the nature of the enemy, his past behavior, and anticipatable future behavior. Regard for the forms of action is too preponderant as compared with the conception of control." Feis went on to say, "While I am not suggesting that we should undertake to destroy the institution of the emperor, or even directly proceed to bring about constitutional reform, I certainly think we should not take any steps to make it easier for the present system to continue into the future fundamentally unchanged. Fifty years of aggression should be sufficient proof of its inevitable tendencies."[18]

Major General Hull, Assistant Chief of Staff, in commenting on the same papers, had even more basic reservations. He noted that the suggestion that in certain circumstances it may be found desirable to abolish the institution of the emperor by fiat would be "a fundamental change in the constitution of Japan beyond the authority of a military occupant to make. If desired, the elimination of this institution would preferably be accomplished by placing in power those liberal Japanese who would proceed to do it by lawful means, or by providing for it in the treaty of peace." General Hull also thought it admirable to treat the emperor courteously but that "care should be taken that nothing be done which would preclude holding the emperor as a war criminal."[19]

It is apparent from a number of documents in the Civil Affairs Division files that CAD became more actively engaged in planning for the military government of Japan during January and February 1945.[20] These papers, however, allude to the treatment of the emperor as a problem to be solved by SWNCC, not by CAD.

Consequently, on March 13, 1945, SWNCC inaugurated its 55 Series: "Politico-Military Problems in the Far East: Treatment of the Emperor of Japan."[21] This is a procedural paper requesting the Department of State to prepare a draft paper on the subject "The Treatment of the Japanese Emperor by Military Government following Unconditional Surrender or Collapse." It was to encompass the treatment to be accorded the emperor and his immediate household, the attitude to be taken by military government toward the institution of the emperor, and policies to be followed if the emperor escaped, disappeared, or abdicated.

At this point the State Department would normally have quickly submitted a composite version of its 1944 PWC papers on this subject, which would have been presented to SWNCC's Subcommittee for the Far East (SFE) for discussion and preliminary agreement among the State, War, and Navy departments, and the SFE report would then have gone forward to SWNCC for final approval as official United States policy. In fact, this was not the case. There is no further version of a SWNCC-55 paper until September 25, 1945, more than a month after the end of the war, and this (SWNCC-55/1/D) was informational rather than substantive. Similarly, SWNCC-55/2 of October 4, 1945, was procedural. Only with SWNCC-55/3 of October 6, 1945, does one encounter a substantive SWNCC paper—"Treatment of the Person of Hirohito, Emperor of Japan." How can one account for this gap of more than six months in the official planning for the treatment of the emperor, especially after it had been a subject of continuous interest and attention throughout 1943–1944 and because an extensive series of planning papers already existed —approved at the highest levels of the State Department?

No available evidence permits a conclusive answer. It seems probable, however, that the following factors were relevant. First, during the early months of 1945, SWNCC was just getting underway, having been established in December 1944, and its Subcommittee for the Far East dated only from January 13, 1945. Inevitably, it took time to organize properly, assemble a staff, establish procedures, and determine a working agenda. It is also far more difficult and time-consuming to orchestrate policies among three departments than to do so within a single department. Second, until the summer of 1945 few, even among the planners, anticipated an early surrender by Japan. Third, other aspects of the planning for the occupation of Japan commanded a higher priority than did the treatment of the emperor. Fourth, influential elements in the military were seriously dissatisfied with the State Department's views on treatment of the emperor. Herbert Feis's and General Hull's opinions have already been noted. Perhaps more important is the fact that General Hilldring, director of the Civil Affairs Division, shared this dissatisfaction. In a memorandum of June 30, 1945, to Assistant Secretary of War McCloy, the army representative on SWNCC, Hilldring said, speaking of the State Department planning papers, that they "do not touch upon such issues of central importance as whether the emperor is to be treated as a war criminal or whether the property holdings of the Imperial Family are to be confiscated. Until these questions have been settled, it is impossible to say that basic policy of the United States has been established."[22] Finally, it is conceivable that the army—knowing that with the establishment of the Occupation both its influence and its freedom of action with respect to policy problems in Japan would be greatly enhanced—was in no hurry to press such matters to an early decision or even, perhaps, to permit one.

Finally, when in the fall of 1945, well after Japan's surrender, the SWNCC-55 Series resumed, the results are interesting and demand at least brief notice. SWNCC-55/1/D of September 25, 1945, simply transmits to SWNCC for information the text of U.S. Senate Joint Resolution 94 of the 79th Congress, First Session (introduced by Mr. Russell on September 18). This declares it to be the policy of the United States that Emperor Hirohito of Japan be tried as a war criminal. SFE-55/2 of October 4 and SWNCC-55/4 of October 8 conclude that SWNCC should not make a formal reply to the Senate's Committee on Military Affairs with respect to this joint resolution.

Despite this decision, the issue of the emperor's possible war guilt was now squarely before SWNCC, whereas before, while mentioned in a number of contexts, it had not really been confronted. Against this background SFE, with what one is inclined to regard as suspicious celerity, on October 6, 1945, produced SWNCC-55/3—the substantive report, "Treatment of the Person of Hirohito, Emperor of Japan," requested by SWNCC more than six months earlier. The paper concludes that "Hirohito is subject to arrest, trial, and punishment as a war criminal"; that under strict security safeguards all available evidence should be assembled and transmitted to the Joint Chiefs of Staff by General MacArthur together with his recommendation as to the initiation of proceedings against Hirohito as a war criminal; that "Hirohito should be removed from office and arrested for trial as a war criminal when the U.S. Government decides that he can be removed without substantial prejudice to the accomplishment of our general purposes in Japan"; and that "administrative convenience gained by retention of Hirohito in office will not justify a failure to try him as a war criminal."[23]

The starkness of this formulation, as well as its difference from earlier State Department views, is in considerable part mitigated by the attached "Discussion," which explains in some detail the problems and dangers of proceeding along the lines recommended. Among these is the statement:

> At this time, and with the limited information now available, it is impossible to determine whether or not the trial of Hirohito at some future date would prejudice our objectives. For the moment it appears that his continuance in office serves the purpose of the Supreme Commander. It would accordingly be inappropriate for the Joint Chiefs of Staff [JCS] to direct General of the Army MacArthur at the present time to institute proceedings against Hirohito, or for this government to announce that it intended to do so. If proceedings ought to be instituted during the period of the Supreme Commander's responsibility, he should make recommendation as to the appropriate time for such proceedings, and a decision on the matter be made at that time by this government.

The obvious internal contradictions as well as the timing of this document lead to the suspicion that elements, presumably outside the State

Department and sensitive to American and much foreign opinion on the emperor's guilt, hastily produced this version in response to the Senate's initiative. Apparently Robert A. Lovett, Assistant Secretary of War for Air, shared this view, since in SWNCC-55/5/D of October 15, 1945, he urged that SWNCC itself consider 55/3 before the Joint Chiefs did and said at one point:

> The tone of the discussion . . . seems to me to be susceptible of the interpretation that Hirohito should be tried regardless of what the available evidence may be, if that is desirable as a matter of policy. I feel that the principle should be regarded as firmly settled that the trial of war criminals, so far as participated in by the United States, should be a judicial matter, and that proceedings should be initiated only where the evidence warrants. In a paper which recommends collecting the evidence, it seems to me to be premature to decide what will be the action taken when the evidence is collected. Thus far, I am aware of no adequate collection of the evidence with respect to Hirohito's actions, and certainly no dispassionate appraisal of any such evidence has been made.[24]

Assistant Secretary Lovett's intervention was effective. It led on October 26, 1945, to SWNCC-55/6 (Revised), a new formulation by SFE of U.S. policy on the treatment of the emperor. The critical parts state:

> In reconsidering the problem posed in SWNCC-55/3, it has become apparent that the treatment of Hirohito as a war criminal cannot be divorced from our overall objectives in Japan. These include particularly the objective of encouraging the Japanese to establish a representative, democratic government fully responsive to the people. This may involve the abolition by the Japanese themselves of the institution of the emperor or its complete alteration along lines which would make its existence consistent with that objective. Final decision as to the treatment of Emperor Hirohito cannot therefore be made until the agreed policy has been obtained regarding this government's attitude toward the Emperor institution. A study to formulate such policy is in process.

Pending the development of such a policy, 55/6 concluded that Hirohito was not immune from arrest, trial, and punishment as a war criminal, and that all available evidence should be quietly gathered by SCAP and transmitted to JCS with his recommendations. This is a formulation very close in effect to that of the State Department planners at the end of 1944. It was sent by JCS to SCAP for his guidance on November 29, 1945.

The final paper in this series is SWNCC-55/7 of June 12, 1946, which simply removes 55/3 from the agenda and cancels the directive to SFE requiring a further report on this subject. Thereafter any evidence relating to the emperor's possible war guilt was simply to be transmitted by SCAP to JCS for submission to SWNCC. The issue was effectively dead by this time.

The terms of the SWNCC-55 series obviously related more to the treatment of Hirohito personally than to U.S. policies toward the institution of the emperorship. The members of SWNCC felt, therefore, that something should be done to develop a formal policy on this larger issue and, at their meeting of October 11, 1945, instructed the Subcommittee for the Far East to prepare a comprehensive policy statement on the treatment of the institution of the Japanese emperorship as distinguished from the treatment of the person of Hirohito. This statement was to consider the imperial institution as an element, favorable or unfavorable, in the attainment of ultimate U.S. objectives in Japan, and also as an element in Japanese religious beliefs, in the democratic reform of the Japanese government, and in the control of Japan by the Occupation forces. These instructions to SFE were incorporated in a new series, SWNCC-209/D of October 18, 1945.[25]

SFE prepared such a report and on March 6, 1946, sent it to SWNCC as 209/1.[26] The report concludes that, although the United States as a republic would favor the creation of a republican form of government in Japan, it is apparent that the great majority of Japanese were unwilling to eliminate the imperial system. The Supreme Commander should not force an immediate decision on the ultimate role of the monarchy in Japan since more time for consideration was apt to lead to more liberal results. The report also advocates certain specific reforms, in addition to the political reforms set forth in SWNCC-228, which SCAP should "call to the attention of the Japanese government." He should not, however, order the Japanese government to effect any of these, "unless the Japanese government has clearly shown its unwillingness to act in these matters." The specific reforms envisaged were (1) changes in articles I, III, and IV of the Meiji Constitution to "eliminate the implications that the imperial line is divine and . . . to have it made clear that the emperor is under the constitution"; (2) the elimination of all forms of "emperor worship" from the school system; and (3) the end of "extensive measures to keep the person of the emperor mysteriously distant from the public and veiled in awesome secrecy." Finally, the report concludes:

> It is considered desirable for the emperor to demonstrate to his people that he is a human being not different from other Japanese, that he himself, as stated in the imperial rescript of January 1, 1946, does not believe in the divine origin of the imperial line or the mystical superiority of Japan over other lands, and that there is no such thing as the "imperial will" as distinct from governmental policy. Insofar as these objectives have not been completely realized, the Supreme Commander should influence the emperor to continue voluntarily to demonstrate these points to his people. Specific measures the emperor could take would be to mix more freely and on terms of greater equality with foreigners and Japanese and to make whatever further pronouncements regarding the origin of the imperial line, the equality of all

races, and the true nature of the "imperial will" that he is willing to make. Any attempt to persuade the emperor to participate in his own "debunking" should be made in such a manner as to be unknown to the Japanese people and should be handled with such diplomacy as to give no suggestion of compulsion.

Although the version of SWNCC-209/1 published in *Foreign Relations of the United States, 1946* does not so indicate, it is clear from other sources that a copy of this paper was sent to SCAP for informational purposes.[27]

To those familiar with the background of the present Japanese constitution it will be apparent that the timing of the principal paper in the SWNCC-209 series, that is, 209/1, coincided precisely with General MacArthur's public statement of March 6, 1946, unveiling for the first time the text of the new draft constitution of Japan that his headquarters had prepared and induced the Japanese government to accept. The terms of the new constitution in regard to the imperial position and powers accomplished, or in some respects exceeded, the requirements of the Washington planners. Thus, the entire matter of reforming the imperial institution became largely moot insofar as SWNCC was concerned, although it did, of course, continue to be of interest to SCAP, the Far Eastern Commission, and the Japanese government and people—at least until the formal adoption of the new constitution on November 3, 1946.

That the final version of SWNCC-209/1 did not reach MacArthur until after the drafting of the new constitution does not necessarily mean that SCAP was ignorant of its contents. Normally, the Joint Chiefs of Staff would informally request MacArthur's views on a proposed SWNCC paper between the time it was drafted by the Subcommittee for the Far East and its submission to SWNCC. In the case of SWNCC-209/1, SFE was ordered to prepare such a paper on October 18, 1945. SFE papers usually went through several drafts, any one of which might be sent to JCS for comment and, in turn, be forwarded by them to SCAP with a request for his views. If this occurred with 209/1, the messages involved have not been located. Nevertheless, the condition and complexity of the message files and available channels prevent one from concluding definitely that MacArthur did not receive informal advance notice of the contents of SWNCC-209/1.

It should also be noted that additional instructions with respect to the treatment of the emperor were incorporated in other sources, specifically the U.S. Initial Postsurrender Policy for Japan (August 29, 1945) and the Basic Directive for Postsurrender Military Government in Japan Proper (November 3, 1945). General MacArthur was consulted on the terms of these, and one section of an exchange he had with General Marshall on July 27, 1945, is of particular interest. In it General MacArthur explained:

> Limitation in occupation forces dictates a maximum utilization of existing
> Japanese governmental agencies and organizations. Control of the popula-
> tion by these agencies is highly effective and under favorable circumstances
> it is believed they can be employed to our material advantage. Premature
> dislocation of governmental machinery would involve an undesirable aug-
> mentation of forces and multiplication of the difficulties of control.[28]

As the person charged with the actual administration of the Occupation,
General MacArthur obviously valued highly any local cooperation that
might be forthcoming and had little inclination to render this difficult by
premature intervention in the Japanese political sphere. His later conduct
and views regarding the emperor suggest that he was not anxious either
to bring him before a war crimes court or to abolish the imperial institution. The preceding message suggests that he may well have felt this way
from the beginning.

Both the initial postsurrender policy and the basic directive make clear
that, for the time at least, the emperor was to be used, not eliminated.
The former says: "In view of the present character of Japanese society
and the desire of the United States to obtain its objectives with a minimum commitment of its forces and resources, the Supreme Commander
will exercise his authority through Japanese governmental machinery
and agencies, including the emperor, to the extent that this satisfactorily
furthers United States objectives." The terms of the basic directive are
similar: "You will exercise your supreme authority through the emperor
and Japanese governmental machinery, national and local."

Both documents go on to make clear, however, that these instructions
carry with them potentially important qualifications. The postsurrender
policy continues:

> This policy, moreover, does not commit the Supreme Commander to sup-
> port the emperor or any other Japanese governmental authority in opposi-
> tion to evolutionary changes looking toward the attainment of United States
> objectives. The policy is to use the existing form of government in Japan,
> not to support it. Changes in the form of government initiated by the Japa-
> nese people or government in the direction of modifying its feudal and
> authoritarian tendencies are to be permitted and favored.

The words of the basic directive are almost identical.

Despite this decision to preserve and use the emperor for the time
being, there remained, of course, the possibility that American or Allied
public opinion would ultimately oblige the Occupation authorities to
charge the emperor with the commission of war crimes and thus bring
about a trial. Consequently, on November 29, 1945, the Joint Chiefs of
Staff radioed General MacArthur the terms of SWNCC-55/6 and instructed him to gather information and evidence relating to the emperor's
possible war guilt. MacArthur did not respond to this directive until Jan-

uary 25, 1946.[29] His reply was couched in terms so extravagantly dis-
couraging to any endeavor on the part of the United States or the Allies
to bring criminal charges against the emperor that they merit quotation.

> Since receipt of WX 85811 investigation has been conducted here under the
> limitations set forth with reference to possible criminal actions against the
> emperor. No specific and tangible evidence has been uncovered with regard
> to his exact activities which might connect him in varying degree with the
> political decisions of the Japanese Empire during the last decade. . . .
>
> If he is to be tried great changes must be made in occupational plans and
> due preparation therefor should be accomplished in preparedness before
> actual action is initiated. His indictment will unquestionably cause a tre-
> mendous convulsion among the Japanese people, the repercussions of which
> cannot be over-estimated. . . .
>
> The whole of Japan can be expected, in my opinion, to resist the action
> either by passive or semi-active means. They are disarmed and therefore will
> represent no special menace to trained and equipped troops; but it is not
> inconceivable that all government agencies will break down, the civilized
> practices will largely cease, and a condition of underground chaos and dis-
> order amounting to guerrilla warfare in the mountainous and outlying
> regions result. I believe all hope of introducing modern democratic methods
> would disappear and that when military control finally ceased some form of
> intense regimentation probably along communistic lines would arise from
> the mutilated masses. This would represent an entirely different problem of
> occupation from the one now prevalent. It would be absolutely essential to
> greatly increase the occupational forces. It is quite possible that a minimum
> of a million troops would be required which would have to be maintained
> for an indefinite number of years. In addition a complete civil service might
> have to be recruited and imported, possibly running into a size of several
> hundred thousand. An overseas supply service under such conditions would
> have to be set up on practically a war basis embracing an indigent civil pop-
> ulation of many millions. . . .
>
> The decision as to whether the emperor should be tried as a war criminal
> involves a policy determination upon such a high level that I would not feel
> it appropriate for me to make a recommendation; but if the decision by the
> heads of states is in the affirmative, I recommend the above measures as
> imperative.

If there were any surviving inclinations in U.S. military circles to try
the emperor for war crimes, they were probably obliterated by this message. Questions of justice aside, even the possibility that such a move
might entail the stationing of "a minimum of a million troops" in Japan
"for an indefinite number of years" was calculated to strike terror into
the hearts of the American military leadership, which was already under
the strongest political and public pressure to repatriate and demobilize
America's armed forces with the greatest possible speed.

So ends the story of the planning for the postwar treatment of the
emperor and the imperial institution. It is long and complex. It began in

early 1943 and reached a peak during the last part of 1944 with the elaboration and approval within the Department of State of a series of plans that recommended policies for almost every aspect of this complex issue. Thereafter, however, for a variety of reasons that have been suggested, these plans were put aside and not considered or acted upon by SWNCC until some months after the end of the war. Even then, legal action against the reigning emperor for criminality under the terms of the SWNCC-55 series went no further than the above-noted request to General MacArthur to assemble relevant evidence under strict security safeguards. MacArthur's reply to this request on January 25, 1946, apparently laid to rest the entire matter of war crime proceedings against the emperor, at least so far as SWNCC was concerned. The announcement of the new constitution in March was an additional reason for not proceeding further. Finally, on June 12, 1946, the SWNCC-55 series was removed from the agenda.

The SWNCC-209 series in effect accepted the basic premise of the earlier State Department plans, that is, that the United States should make use of the emperor as a means of achieving its national objectives in Japan. But in this case the series was overtaken by events; specifically, the basic paper was issued on the very day, March 6, 1946, that MacArthur was informing the Joint Chiefs of Staff of the existence of a new draft constitution of Japan, the terms of which effectively took care of practically all of the recommendations of SWNCC-209/1.

The question of the degree and nature of precise influence exercised by the Washington plans and planners on the formulation by SCAP of Chapter I (The Emperor) of the Japanese constitution of 1946–1947 remains, therefore, somewhat unclear. General MacArthur, on November 29, 1945, was sent, for his information and "guidance"—not as a JCS directive—the text of SWNCC-55/6. It is quite possible that he also had seen some preliminary version of SWNCC-209/1 prior to February 3, 1946, when he wrote out and gave to General Whitney, chief of SCAP's Government Section, his personal instruction as to the three major points he wanted to have incorporated in the text of the model constitution that he ordered Whitney and the Government Section to prepare. In addition to these two SWNCC papers that addressed specifically the problem of the treatment of the emperor personally and as an institution, General MacArthur also had available to him the more general provisions of SWNCC-228 with respect to "Reform of the Japanese Governmental System" (this will be discussed below) and the terms of the U.S. Initial Postsurrender Policy and the Basic Directive.

It seems probable that these five documents, or at least four of them, provide the background against which General MacArthur penned his February 3, 1946, instructions to General Whitney about the treatment of the emperor in the so-called model constitution:

The Emperor is at the head of the State.

His succession is dynastic.

His duties and powers will be exercised in accordance with the Constitution and responsible to the basic will of the people as provided therein.[30]

These instructions conform in substance to the intent and desire of the State Department planners. They are also in substantial accord with most of the provisions of SWNCC-55/6 and 209/1. They possibly deviate from these in only the following respects: (1) They assume at least provisionally, that is, subject to the subsequent ratification of the constitution, that the Japanese people desired the continuance of the imperial institution, and (2) they are open to the construction that either the emperor was guilty of no war crimes and should not, therefore, be subject to trial, or that his importance to the accomplishment of the United States' ultimate objectives in Japan was so crucial that his trial for war crimes was inadvisable. It could quite reasonably be contended, however, that in a legal sense the terms of the new constitution were neutral with respect to any subsequent decision on the part of SCAP or the United States to bring the emperor to trial on war crimes charges. Practically speaking, however, it should be obvious that by explicitly providing for the continuance of the imperial institution and simultaneously for the continuation of Hirohito in that office, General MacArthur was making it far more difficult, if not impossible, for the United States government or the United Nations thereafter to bring any charges.

Planning for Constitutional Change

From the outset—at least as early as the Atlantic Charter of August 14, 1941—fairly clear, authoritative, and oft-repeated indications were given that the Axis powers after their defeat would be required to adopt more liberal and more peacefully inclined forms of government. The statements involved were, however, uniformly vague and general as to what precisely would be involved in such a liberalization and what particular forms of governance would be deemed acceptable by the victorious powers.

The State Department planners began to come to grips with this problem in early 1943. The first relevant document is an agenda paper for a meeting on March 10, 1943, of the Subcommittee on Political Problems of the Advisory Committee on Postwar Foreign Policy.[31] This simply poses problems for discussion. Among them was the question

Should the United States . . . favor changes in Japanese political institutions to assure such objectives as limitation of the power of the military, development of parliamentary government, extension of civil rights, and the decentralization of administrative authority? To what extent should it participate in measures to secure a change in Japanese political philosophy through supervision of the educational system and of other media of indoctrination?

If the decision to the first question proved to be affirmative, the probability was that such changes would require sweeping alterations in the Meiji Constitution as well as in existing Japanese political practices. By May 1943 one finds the Territorial Subcommittee of the same advisory committee writing background papers preparatory to trying to answer the questions posed.[32]

In July 1943 the debate on the political reformation of Japan was seriously launched within the membership of the Territorial Subcommittee. At this time Dr. George Blakeslee, the senior Japanese specialist, first suggested a series of five principles as a means of organizing their discussions. The fourth of these related to the Allies' postwar political objectives in Japan. By September 1943 it had acquired the following form:

IV. The political objective in the postwar settlement should be a government in Japan which will fulfill Japan's international obligations and respect the rights of other states.

This principle implies a government free from military dominance and under the control of civilian elements which aim to keep the peace. The means which appear most likely to facilitate the establishment of such a government are constitutional and administrative changes which will deprive the military of its special political privileges, freedom of intellectual communication with democratic countries through press and radio, and other measures which will strengthen the moderate political elements in Japan.[33]

This principle obviously required extended consideration of how the goals might best be achieved. In October 1943 a paper by Dr. Hugh Borton began to spell out a way.[34] This is a truly remarkable document. In it are to be found the ultimate intellectual roots of many of the basic political changes realized in postwar Japan under Occupation auspices, as well as the rationale and grand strategy involved. Consider the principal points made in the paper.

1. Constitutional change is desirable.
2. If possible, it should not be imposed by the Occupation; but the occupying authorities should in all possible ways, including educational means and economic pressures, stimulate the Japanese to accomplish this themselves.
3. Such constitutional changes should include
   a. maintenance of the imperial institution with curtailed authority;
   b. elimination of the privileges and practices that have enabled the military to control important spheres of political policymaking in Japan and discredit of the military by saddling them with the responsibility for both the war and the defeat;

    c. establishment of cabinet responsibility to the Diet;

    d. establishment of Diet control of the budget;

    e. introduction of a far broader and more effective Bill of Rights with particular attention to freedom of speech, assembly, and worship and judicial safeguards.

4. The unprecedented experience of defeat and occupation will probably make Japan unusually susceptible to political changes of a basic sort.

5. There is sound reason to believe that the emergence of new and more liberal political leadership elements is distinctly possible in postwar Japan.

6. Not a great deal can be expected from the Japanese populace at large by way of new political initiatives.

7. The economic circumstances of postwar Japan are apt to have a determining effect on the possibility of effectuating liberal political changes.

Although there is no evidence to establish that this paper had a direct effect on the strategy or policies actually adopted by SCAP in 1945–1946, it does encapsulate in a remarkably accurate and prescient form most of the basic principles subsequently incorporated in SWNCC-228 and 228/1, "Reform of the Japanese Governmental System," in November and December 1945. It also coincides in all respects save one with what actually happened in postwar Japan. The one certain exception is the degree of suasion finally resorted to by SCAP to secure the timely adoption of the new constitution. Despite such qualifications, however, a planning paper of this sort—at a point during the war when Japanese fortunes were still much in the ascendancy and written almost two years in advance of the surrender—is a most impressive achievement.

The debate engendered by Blakeslee's five principles for the postwar treatment of Japan and Borton's elaborations thereon continued for the remainder of 1943 in the Territorial Subcommittee. On October 22, for example, Ballantine gave his opinion that "there was no way in which we could remake the Japanese people by changing their institutions or by telling them what to do. As for convincing them of their defeat, he was quite certain that one week of military occupation in Tokyo would have greater effect than any revision of the constitution which we might think of." Later in the same meeting Ballantine went on to say that once the generals had signed the terms of surrender

> we should then tell the moderates what our aims were. We should not try to control their conduct of affairs but we should let them know that when their educational system and their political aims had developed in such a way as to approach the objectives which we had considered, we would give them a greater amount of confidence and respect. In this fashion we would be

able to win their confidence and make the necessary reforms without direct intervention. . . . an imposed government would be of only short-term duration.[35]

The same sort of argument was advanced by some and rejected by others with respect to whether or not the Occupation should try to impose a Bill of Rights upon a defeated Japan.

Early in 1944 the locus of this discussion shifted to the Postwar Programs Committee. The first paper relating to constitutional change dates from March 9 and simply notes that, with the disbanding of Japan's prewar political parties in 1940 and the formation of the reactionary Imperial Rule Assistance Association, no political parties existed with which the Occupation authorities could usefully deal. It recommends, therefore, that the latter work "with individuals who formerly held high positions in Japanese governmental, financial and commercial circles and who have not been closely identified with the formulation of the policies of the present regime."[36]

Until May 1944 practically all of the planners' designs for constitutional change in postwar Japan had focused exclusively at the national level. On May 1, however, one encounters the first high-level paper devoted specifically to the local levels of government in Japan.[37] This sets forth the collective view of the Interdivisional Area Committee for the Far East. It begins by noting the basic dilemma involved for the Occupation authorities:

> It is true that whatever is done in this direction [i.e., toward decentralization] will tend to reduce Japan's effective military capacity, but on the other hand decentralization would militate against the maintenance of organization, which is essential if the Japanese people are to live under the conditions with which they will be faced. . . . Without such organization and discipline as only a centralized administration can give them their position might well nigh be hopeless.

The paper goes on to argue:

> The objectives sought in the suggestion offered for administrative decentralization are, of course, admirable, but it seems to us that the decentralization of the functions of the Japanese Government has been confused with the decentralization of *political power* in the Japanese Government, which all of us agree is an essential. . . .
>
> It is believed that our objectives can be attained most effectively by directing our efforts to laying the foundations for a diffusion of *political power* among the Japanese people. It is believed that the most important steps that could be taken would lie in the direction of the strengthening of prefectural and municipal assemblies and other organs of local government, in the building up of the authority and dignity of the legislative branch of the national government, and above all, in the awakening of the electorate to a consciousness of their rights and responsibilities so as to make elections

expressive of the will of the people rather than exercises in manipulation by bureaucratic or militaristic elements of the population.

Fundamental reforms in Japan's political structure would have to be accomplished through changes in the Japanese constitution and laws duly adopted by the Japanese. In other words they would be brought about in connection with the establishment, recognition, and subsequent support of a provisional Japanese government. They would not be carried out by the military government. In fact, an attempt to impose such drastic changes through obvious outside means would defeat its own purpose.

In early May 1944 also a series of three papers entitled "Japan: Abolition of Militarism and Strengthening Democratic Processes" took up this and a variety of other problems in a more general context.[38] Its final version contained an outline called "Steps to Prevent Revival of Militarism." In addition to sections on the nullification of obnoxious laws, the elimination of ultranationalistic influences, and the creation of internal economic conditions favorable to the growth of democracy, an important section was devoted to the "Encouragement of Liberal Forces." This first identified the liberal elements through whom it was hoped to build a new Japan, describing them as "the group of statesmen of the so-called Anglo-American school who held political offices in the 1920s and who have been conspicuous among the personal advisers of the emperor, a considerable sprinkling of business leaders whose prosperity was based on world trade rather than on the Greater East Asia Co-Prosperity Sphere, Christian leaders such as Kagawa, a limited but courageous group of educators and social and political reformers, etc." Thereafter it enumerates seven ways in which liberal thought and democratic processes might be strengthened:

1. Freedom of the press, radio, and motion pictures except for ideas subversive of the aims of the United Nations.
2. Freedom of discussion except as it might endanger security.
3. Elimination of restrictions on liberal education.
4. Explanation through press, radio, and motion pictures of the meaning of personal liberties in a democracy.
5. Encouragement of political parties, labor unions, credit unions, consumer cooperatives and other organizations of the people.
6. Widespread use of municipal and prefectural assemblies.
7. Preparation of the people for and, if necessary, supervision of an election, or some other means, whereby the people may express without prejudice, their will as to their own future form of government.

A further section of the paper notes:

In connection with the establishment of a Japanese Government acceptable to the United Nations, it may be possible to insist upon certain basic governmental reforms which should include:

1. A national legislature with full powers over the national budget and with the right to initiate amendments to the constitution. . . .
2. If, notwithstanding the wide consensus which now exists that Japan should not be permitted in the postwar period to retain an army, navy, or air force, Japan should later be permitted to maintain some form of military establishment, such permission should envisage as an essential condition the elimination of existing statutes and ordinances that stipulate that ministers of war and of the navy shall be high-ranking military and naval officers. . . .
3. Increased civil rights and emphasis upon the status of the individual . . .
4. The freeing of the judiciary from the control of the Minister of Justice and of the police, by election to the bench or by other well-tried devices, along with other necessary reforms, should be an essential feature of any program for the democratization of the Japanese.

These prescriptions will readily be recognized as a somewhat elaborated version of Borton's recommendations in his October 6, 1943, paper "Japan: Postwar Political Problems" (T-381). It is no surprise, therefore, to find that Borton was also the author of this PWC-152 series. Between the two papers, progressively more detailed and specific insights into the sorts of political and constitutional changes anticipated for a defeated Japan were emerging. Ambiguity about one point of great importance continued, however. Just how and by whom were these changes to be effected? The papers frequently protest that changes should be accomplished by the Japanese, not by fiat of the Occupation authorities, but the issue was not really that simple. Clearly, some degree of duress was apt to be involved, through economic pressures, for example, or, more frequently, through withholding recognition—and presumably other even more basic benefices as well—from whatever provisional Japanese government would eventually be established in postwar Japan. This would simply remove the Occupation by one degree from the role of directly initiating postwar political changes to that of recommending, scrutinizing, and approving or withholding approval for Japanese initiatives in this area. It should be understood, however, that—depending on the manner of implementation—this one-step removal could confer upon the Japanese a far greater degree of initiative and freedom for maneuver than they would have under direct control.

Given the long history and salience of the postwar argument over the antecedents of Article IX of the new Japanese constitution, the precise language used with respect to the demilitarization of Japan, as quoted above, should be noted. It clearly anticipates a situation in which Japan has no armed forces, accepting this as a circumstance about which there existed a "wide consensus." If so, General MacArthur's instructions to General Whitney on this score—"No Japanese Army, Navy, or Air Force will ever be authorized"[39]—may be less idiosyncratic than has often been thought.

Between September and December 1944 the Postwar Programs Committee approved the recommendations of the above-noted papers and early in 1945 sent them on to SWNCC and its Subcommittee for the Far East. As with planning for the postwar treatment of the emperor, there was a long hiatus in substantive planning activities. One procedural paper was produced on April 7, 1945—SWNCC-90, "Japanese Political Structures under Military Government during the Postsurrender Period."[40] In July "Positive Policy for Reorientation of the Japanese" appeared; this very perceptive paper by Artemus L. Gates, undersecretary of the navy and Navy representative on SWNCC, concerned the psychological preparation of the Japanese people for the acceptance of a more democratic system of government[41] and suggested a number of steps to assist in this endeavor.

Neither the Initial Postsurrender Policy (August 29, 1945) nor the Basic Directive, issued later in the same year, specifically mentioned or mandated constitutional change in postwar Japan. They both, however, made completely clear the American preference for a far more democratic form of government. Many of the particular changes noted as desirable strongly suggested that Japan would in fact be obliged to change the Meiji Constitution if it hoped to persuade the victorious powers that it had become a "peaceful and responsible government."

Not until upwards of three months after the cessation of hostilities did the SWNCC Subcommittee for the Far East finally reach agreement on the text of its basic report, "Reform of the Japanese Governmental System,"[42] even though work had been under way on it for some time. In the meantime, however, a number of developments looking toward constitutional change had been initiated by the Japanese themselves, partially as a result of suggestions made by General MacArthur to the first two postwar Japanese prime ministers—Prince Higashikuni and Baron Shidehara. The earliest substantive move of this sort was begun by the Lord Keeper of the Privy Seal, Prince Konoe, on October 4, 1945, as a result of his second meeting with General MacArthur.

In the absence of any agreed-upon U.S. policy statement regarding constitutional reform the Japanese initiatives were both tempting and embarrassing to George Atcheson, General MacArthur's political advisor, who could not be certain what advice he should give either MacArthur or the Japanese on this score. Seeking instructions, he radioed the secretary of state on October 4, 1945, saying: "As there appears to be considerable discussion among politically minded Japanese in regard to the question of revision of the Japanese constitution, it is suggested that completion of the directive on this subject be expedited as much as possible. Meanwhile please telegraph outline of draft so that we may know direction which American government thought is taking in this matter."[43]

The secretary replied to this request on October 16, 1945, providing Atcheson—and, since all telegraphic communications with Japan were routed through the Pentagon, the Joint Chiefs and General MacArthur as well—with the first specific information about official policy on constitutional change in Japan.

> The Secretary of State to the Acting Political Advisor in Japan (Atcheson): Washington, October 16, 1945—8 p.m.
>
> 38. Urtel 18, October 4. Attitude of Departmental officers who have been giving consideration to this matter may be summarized as follows:
>
> There should be assurance that the Japanese constitution is amended to provide for government responsible to an electorate based upon wide representative suffrage. Provision should be made that executive branch of government derive its authority from and be responsible to the electorate or to a fully representative legislative body. If Emperor institution is not retained, constitutional safeguards against that institution will obviously not be required but provision should be made for:
>
> (1) Complete control by an elected congress of financial and budgetary matters,
>
> (2) Guarantee of fundamental civil rights to all persons within Japanese jurisdiction, not to Japanese only, and
>
> (3) Action be [by] head of state only pursuant to authority expressly delegated to him.
>
> If Emperor is retained, following safeguards in addition to those enumerated above would be necessary:
>
> (1) A cabinet to advise and assist the Emperor should be chosen with advice and consent of and responsible to representative legislative body,
>
> (2) No veto over legislative measures should be exercised by other bodies such as House of Peers or Privy Council,
>
> (3) Emperor should be required to initiate amendments to constitution recommended by cabinet and approved by legislative body,
>
> (4) Legislative body should be permitted to meet at will, and
>
> (5) Any ministers for armed forces which may be permitted in future should be civilians and all special privileges of direct access to throne by military should be eliminated.
>
> We concur in general in the views summarized in your CA-53137, October 11 [telegram No. 31, October 10, 1945], and desire that you continue your discussions and keep the Department informed.
>
> It is hoped that a full report of the Government's views can be sent to you in the near future.[44]

To anyone familiar with the earlier planning papers of 1943–1944, it is at once apparent that these instructions from Washington are simply a more specific and operational version of the recommendations and reasoning set forth in Borton's two basic papers of October 6, 1943, and

May 9, 1944. It should be noted, however, that item 5 of the list of safeguards to be invoked if the emperor is retained does specifically envisage
the possibility of Japan's maintaining armed forces at some future time. It
will be recalled that some of the earlier papers did not agree on this score.
The earlier message from Atcheson mentioned in the telegram summarizes the advice that he, in a personal capacity, had given Prince Konoe
on the subject of constitutional reform.[45] This, too, conforms with the
1944 plans in basic conception but is also more specific and pointed in its
recommendations.

Two further developments during November and December 1945 provide insights into official U.S. policy with respect to constitutional
reform. Both concern the activities of George Atcheson. The first involves an extraordinarily frank and alarmed message sent by Atcheson in
Japan to Dean Acheson, the Undersecretary of State, on November 7,
1945, via diplomatic mail pouch and thus, unlike telegraphic communications, not accessible to SCAP. The message notes that Atcheson has
been ordered by General MacArthur to break off his discussions of constitutional reform with Prince Konoe and his associates; complains that
MacArthur and his chief of staff, or the "Bataan Club," who act as
MacArthur's "privy council" or *genro,* want to keep the State Department out of the matter of constitutional reform in Japan; and claims that
several days earlier MacArthur asked Atcheson to draw up a press statement about constitutional revision "partially for the purpose of clearing
the air in the matter but primarily with a view to meeting recent Soviet
and British criticism of him."[46] Atcheson felt that MacArthur implied
that he preferred Atcheson to issue the release rather than doing so himself since this would give it a less formal character and not seem to be in
the nature of a directive to the Japanese government. But SCAP decided
against issuing the press statement at all. Atcheson's message urges that
the Department of State issue the release from Washington in order to let
the Japanese government know clearly and in advance of a formal
endorsement by the emperor or Japanese cabinet of any Japanese proposal for constitutional reform just what sort of constitutional changes
would be acceptable to the United States.

The press release that Atcheson had drafted is a remarkable document. It sets forth the foundations in the Potsdam Declaration, the U.S.
Initial Postsurrender Policy for Japan, and other official statements for
the American expectation that the Japanese government and people
would basically revise their constitution and then lists in quite specific
detail—far more than does SWNCC-228, for example—the particular
changes that the United States wanted to have accomplished. The draft
press release was given to General MacArthur and may have been shared
by him with others on his staff. The State Department, however, did not
choose to follow Atcheson's advice. The reason may well have been a

telegram from Atcheson to the Secretary of State on November 8, 1945
—the day after sending the draft press release by mail—formally notifying the Secretary that he had been advised by SCAP to discontinue all further constitutional discussions with Prince Konoe and that he was com-
plying with this advice.

Atcheson, however, continued to doubt that the Japanese government,
voluntarily and without more explicit U.S. guidance, would make acceptable proposals for constitutional reform, and he continued to make
his concerns known to the Department of State.[47] Acknowledging these
communications, the Department, on or about December 13, 1945, sent
Atcheson the texts of two preliminary reports by SWNCC's Subcommittee for the Far East that constituted the basis for SWNCC-228.[48] These
were very similar to the actual text of SWNCC-228 of November 27,
1945, which was formally approved by SWNCC on January 7, 1946,
and sent to General MacArthur on January 11, 1946. Upon receiving
them, Atcheson promptly (on December 13, 1945) informed both General MacArthur and his Chief of Staff of their nature and contents and
provided them with copies of the amended conclusions of SFE 142/1. In
transmitting these Atcheson also indicated that both officers—SCAP and
the Chief of Staff—were already familiar with the substance of the State
Department's earlier telegram of October 16, 1945 (cited in full above).

In the body of his December 13 memorandum to MacArthur, Atcheson once more set forth in clear and strong terms his grounds for concern
about the process of constitutional reform. To his knowledge no American source had provided the Japanese government with further guidance
or advice on acceptable terms of constitutional change since early
November, when he had been ordered to discontinue his conversations
with Prince Konoe and his associates. In the meantime, published statements by the prime minister, by Home Minister Dr. Matsumoto, who
was charged by the cabinet with drafting a revised version of the Meiji
Constitution, and by other constitutional authorities clearly indicated
that the changes being considered by the Japanese government would fall
far short of meeting minimal requirements of the United States. Atcheson
thought there was a real danger that the Japanese government, in the
absence of American guidance, might publicly proclaim an unacceptable
draft and thereby oblige SCAP formally to reject it and order the government to make extensive changes. To avoid so difficult and mutually
embarrassing a situation, Atcheson strongly recommended that the contents of SFE-142/1 be informally communicated to Dr. Matsumoto, possibly by SCAP's Government Section. General MacArthur did not choose
to act upon this recommendation.

These developments are of very substantial historical interest. The
procedures Atcheson was recommending to MacArthur probably were
the only practicable way in which it might have been possible to emerge

with a new constitution that was at the same time authored by Japanese and couched in terms acceptable to the United States and the Far Eastern Commission. Once SCAP decided against Atcheson's suggestions, it became almost inevitable that the Japanese would produce an unacceptable document, thus making it necessary for SCAP to intervene massively and in far more dogmatic and offensive terms in the development of a new Japanese constitution. Given the time constraints involved, the only real alternative would have been to turn the entire matter over to the Far Eastern Commission, which was then organizing in Washington, D.C. Needless to say, neither General MacArthur nor the Japanese government was prepared to do this.

So far as is now known and with the possible exceptions noted below, the State Department's telegram of October 16, 1945, to Atcheson plus the above-described interchanges among Atcheson, MacArthur, and the Chief of Staff represent the only insights into official U.S. policy on this matter available to the Occupation authorities in Japan prior to January 11, 1946, when the official text of SWNCC-228 was sent to MacArthur for his information.

The first possible exception to the preceding generalization involved Robert Fearey, private secretary to Ambassador Grew at the outbreak of war and, following his repatriation, a prominent and active member of the Interdivisional Area Committee for the Far East for the duration of hostilities. In the latter capacity Fearey was continuously and closely involved with practically all of the State Department planning for the postwar treatment of Japan. When George Atcheson was assigned to serve as MacArthur's political advisor in late September 1945, Fearey accompanied him to Tokyo as a member of his staff. Fearey took a selection of postwar planning documents for Japan that included some relating to constitutional reform. These were made available to Atcheson and possibly, through Atcheson, to MacArthur.[49]

The second possible exception involves Colonel Charles L. Kades, Deputy Chief of the Government Section, who, prior to his arrival in Tokyo in September 1945, had been assigned to the Joint Chiefs of Staff in a capacity that gave him access to the postwar planning documents for Japan. When Colonel Kades learned of his assignment to Tokyo he collected all available postwar planning papers for Japan and assembled them in a black binder that has occasionally been referred to by others in the Government Section as "Kades's bible."[50] This was kept in Kades's office safe and seems not to have been available to other staff members, with the possible exception of General Whitney. Colonel Kades was, however, chairman of the small steering committee that actually put the Government Section draft of the new Japanese constitution into its final form before it was shown to the representatives of the Japanese cabinet on February 13, 1946. His influence on the terms of that draft at least equaled, and quite probably exceeded, that of any other of its primary authors. He was, through his so-called bible, well informed on the state and terms of the Washington plans at least up to the time of his departure from the United States in September 1945.

Slightly more than a month after the mid-October telegram summarizing the contents of SWNCC-228 was sent to Atcheson, the final text of the entire document became available in Washington in the form of an SFE report circulated for consideration by SWNCC.[51] It is the definitive statement of official U.S. policy on constitutional and governmental change in postwar Japan. It was approved with no substantive changes by SWNCC on January 7, 1946, almost a month before Government Section began to write the so-called MacArthur Draft of the new Japanese constitution. It was formally transmitted to General MacArthur—for "information," not as a JCS "directive"—on January 11, 1946, three weeks before Government Section began work on its draft, but, as we have seen, Atcheson had provided SCAP with detailed information about its contents at least as early as December 13, 1945.

SWNCC-228 is a fascinating document. It represents the culmination of State Department plans for constitutional and governmental changes in postwar Japan that extend back to at least mid-1943. There is little evidence of significant influence upon its terms by agencies other than the Department of State. Viewed as a possible progenitor of the MacArthur Draft of the new Japanese constitution, it is of interest in two senses.

The first is substantive and is best explained by considering the relevant portions of SWNCC-228 itself. These occur primarily in the "Conclusions" and, incidentally, in the "Discussion" section of the document.

It is completely clear from both the wording and the fundamental nature of the changes recommended in the "Conclusions" that extensive constitutional revision would be required. When one considers these recommendations in the light of earlier State Department plans for changes in Japan's postwar political and imperial systems, it seems obvious that the paper is a lineal descendant of the 1943–1944 planning papers. For example, items "a" 1 through 7 and many others as well are specifically treated in similar terms in the earlier papers. In fact, particular provisions aside, the rationale underlying the conclusions of SWNCC-228 is identical with that which came to prevail in the earlier planning papers by the end of 1944.

Specific differences can, however, be pointed out. The paper is considerably more specific in stipulating precise governmental mechanisms to achieve its goals—for example, the provisions that no body shall have more than a temporary veto over legislative measures or that the legislative body may meet at will. The treatment of the Imperial Household's private income is harsher than anticipated in the earlier papers. And one misses the constant earlier emphasis on measures to achieve and ensure the demilitarization of Japan. This last is probably attributable, however, to the fact that by November 1945 the process of actual demilitarization was well under way and Japan's armed forces were actively being abolished. Furthermore, the "Discussion" section of SWNCC-228 makes clear the importance of permanently subordinating any military forces to civilian control. Such minor variations aside, however, there would seem to be no doubt about the paternity of the substantive provisions of SWNCC-228.

The paper also contains important procedural provisions. Section 1 of the "Discussion" part of the paper confronts the point raised by the Joint Chiefs of Staff in SWNCC-228/1 of December 19, 1945, that the Potsdam Declaration in effect guarantees that the ultimate form of government in Japan is to be determined by "the freely expressed will of the Japanese people." The somewhat facile answer given by 228 is that "the Allies, in accordance with the above provisions and as a part of their overall program for the demilitarization of Japan, are fully empowered to insist that Japanese basic law be so altered as to provide that in practice the government is responsible to the people, and that the civil is supreme over the military branch of the government."

This argument has a distinctly Orwellian flavor to it. It claims in effect that some parts of the Potsdam terms of surrender are "more equal than others," in other words that the right of the Japanese people freely to determine their ultimate form of government—at least during the Occupation—is subordinate to the Allies' right to insist that the form of government selected is democratic in nature.

Section 7, of equal interest and importance, expresses the hope that the Japanese themselves will initiate the constitutional and administrative reforms essential for democratization. Absent such a constructive initiative by the Japanese, the Supreme Commander should, first, "indicate the reforms which this Government considers necessary" and, second, if this does not work, only then "as a last resort" should a formal instruction be issued to the Japanese government. These provisions are, of course, of the highest interest in light of the subsequent preparation and presentation to the Japanese by SCAP's Government Section of the so-called MacArthur Draft and its later imposition on the Japanese government under circumstances that actually left both that government and the Japanese people very little freedom of choice.[52]

Were Generals MacArthur and Whitney still alive and asked to respond to a charge that they had in effect exceeded their instructions by these actions, their reply would doubtless be somewhat as follows.[53] First, SCAP had no orders on this score. SWNCC-228 was sent to MacArthur only for "information," not as a "directive" from the Joint Chiefs of Staff. It was, therefore, completely within his normal powers as theater commander to use his own discretion in interpreting and applying it. Second, he did in fact give the Japanese government an opportunity from September 1945 to February 1946 to take the initiative in introducing acceptable constitutional reforms, but it failed to do so. Third, SCAP at no time issued "a formal instruction" to the Japanese government specifying in detail the reforms to be effected. Finally, MacArthur and Whitney would doubtless claim that they had simply followed alternative 2—they had indicated through a device that they called a "model constitution" the sorts of reforms that the U.S. government considered necessary.

Such an argument has much technical and legal force. Practically speaking, however, it is hard to see a substantial difference between what actually transpired and the issuance of a "formal instruction" by SCAP to the Japanese government. George Atcheson's unsuccessful efforts to persuade General MacArthur to provide informal guidance on constitutional reform to the Japanese government through the Matsumoto Committee on Constitutional Revision marked the last occasion upon which it might have been possible to avoid the sort of massive intervention by Government Section that finally took place.

Enough has been said at this point to demonstrate a close relationship between the State Department plans of 1943–1944 and the provisions of SWNCC-228. Only two further points require comment. The first relates to our still unclear understanding of why MacArthur, after paying only episodic attention to the question of constitutional revision from September 1945 to February 1, 1946, suddenly took drastic action. The second concerns the relationship between SWNCC-228 and the terms of both the MacArthur Draft and the final version of the new constitution.

Where the first question is concerned, we have long speculated on the basis of several well-known circumstances that the principal motivating factors were probably (1) the *Mainichi* "scoop" of February 1, 1946, revealing publicly the inadequacies of the Matsumoto Draft, (2) the imminence of the organization of the Far Eastern Commission, which, once operational, would acquire preemptive authority in the field of constitutional reform, and (3) General Whitney's memorandum to SCAP of February 1, 1946, showing how MacArthur could, if he acted before the Far Eastern Commission actually organized and asserted its authority in this area, legitimately induce Japanese constitutional reform.[54] All of these factors, however, pertain to events, perceptions, and decisions taking place in Japan. In other words, the decision to initiate constitutional reform in Japan has been seen as solely attributable to General MacArthur and Whitney, perhaps with marginal assistance from a few staff members.

This may well be a correct and sufficient explanation, but at least two documents in the National Archives indicate the existence of somewhat similar concerns in Washington at critical times in December 1945 and

January 1946. The first is a draft memorandum for the Secretary of SWNCC from Dr. Hugh Borton dated December 5, 1945.

> It is reported from Tokyo that the Japanese press states that the Cabinet Constitutional Revision Committee (i.e., the Matsumoto Committee) arrived at general conclusions on November 24 and plans to complete its draft by the middle of January for submission to the new Diet. Furthermore, there is considerable interest on the parts of the governments represented on the Far Eastern Advisory Commission. It would be much more difficult for the Japanese to include any suggestions for governmental reform in their own program if such suggestions are submitted after rather than prior to formal issuance by the Japanese of their proposed reforms in government.
>
> In view of this situation, it is recommended that SWNCC request the Joint Chiefs of Staff to forward to SWNCC, as a matter of priority, their report on SWNCC-228, Reform of the Japanese Governmental System, so that the paper may be approved by SWNCC in the near future and transmitted to the Supreme Commander as official U.S. policy.[55]

Borton apparently sent this through John Carter Vincent, then his section chief. It may well have been stimulated by Atcheson's telegrams from Japan, which Borton routinely saw. Whether it was then forwarded to SWNCC is uncertain.

The second possibly relevant document is a memorandum of January 4, 1946, from General Hilldring, Director of CAD, to John J. McCloy, Assistant Secretary of War and the army's representative on SWNCC.[56] This provides essentially the same information as the Borton memorandum.

The importance of these two documents is suggestive, not probative. The Borton memorandum of December 5, 1945, was obviously intended to support Atcheson and to put pressure on the Joint Chiefs of Staff to act rapidly on SWNCC-228 so that its terms might be transmitted to SCAP and passed on to the Japanese by him as "suggestions" or "guidance" on the nature of U.S. expectations about the terms of a new constitution before the Japanese preempted such a move by themselves announcing constitutional reforms without benefit of U.S. "advice." It does, however, indicate serious concern on this score at high working levels in the Department of State and may well have been part of the developments that led to sending Atcheson the preliminary versions of SWNCC-228 on or about December 13, 1945. Where the Hilldring memorandum to McCloy is concerned, its terms are quite neutral and seem to be aimed primarily at ensuring that the reservations of the Joint Chiefs about the original text of SWNCC-228—set forth in SWNCC-228/1[57]—be incorporated in the final document and that this then constitute the negotiating instructions of the American delegate (Dr. Borton) to the Far Eastern Commission's Working Committee on Constitutional Reform. But the memo also makes it quite clear to Assistant Secretary McCloy, first, that the Japanese may themselves very soon act on constitutional reform and, second, that the terms of the Moscow Agreement of December 27, 1945 (agreed upon by the foreign ministers of the United States, the Soviet Union, and the United Kingdom) prevent any unilateral action by the United States in the area of constitutional reform in Japan and, in effect, give to the Far Eastern Commission—which included, of course, the Soviet Union—a veto over American initiatives. It also does this at precisely the time that, following several years of planning and several months of negotiation on the text, the United States government had just succeeded in reaching internal agreement on the specific sorts of constitutional and political changes it wanted to see made in Japan.

This particular conjunction of circumstances was certainly not auspicious from the U.S. standpoint. One can, however, only speculate about its consequences. On the one hand, Assistant Secretary McCloy or his colleagues may have done nothing beyond arrange for the incorporation of the Joint Chiefs' reservations into the final text of SWNCC-228. We know that this was done. Or, between January 4 and the end of the month, someone may have transmitted the text of the Hilldring memorandum or its equivalent to General MacArthur or General Whitney through any one of numerous available channels for their "information." Should this have been the case, then General Whitney's memorandum to General MacArthur of February 1, 1946, explaining in detail the nature and limitations of his authority to act in the matter of Japanese constitutional reform, was very much the sort of reaction that might have been expected in Tokyo.[58] There is, however, no presently available evidence to indicate that such a message was transmitted from Washington to SCAP. In the absence of such evidence, it is completely plausible that SCAP and General Whitney acted entirely on their own initiatives in this matter.

Finally, we turn to the question of probable relationships between the terms of SWNCC-228 as transmitted to General MacArthur on January 11, 1946, and the terms of the MacArthur Draft of the new Japanese constitution completed by Government Section on February 10 and approved by General MacArthur with only one significant change on February 12. If one takes the explicit changes in the Japanese constitutional and political system stipulated in SWNCC-228 and compares them with the provisions of either the MacArthur Draft or the constitution of 1946–1947, it is at once evident that they are in almost complete conformity. Every one of the changes advocated by 228 is found in the other two texts. The differences that do occur are additions and elaborations attendant upon making specific, operational, and secure the quite general injunctions of SWNCC-228.

The most notable addition to the terms of 228 is, of course, SCAP's initiative in building the imperial institution firmly into the framework of the new constitution. Although not without warrant in 228 or in the objective circumstances of Japanese popular opinion and desires insofar as these were then manifest, SCAP's action in this respect does seem calculated to preempt the possibility of any other course of action or, really, of any serious public discussion of alternative decisions about the throne. This may in many respects be a technicality, however, since there seem to be almost no grounds for believing that the Japanese would have preferred to eliminate the imperial institution. The only serious objections would probably have come from those who would have preferred to give greater dignity and status to the emperor than was provided by the new constitution. Such persons were both numerous and influential.

The second major exception is the sweeping nature of Article IX, particularly in its early formulations. This went beyond anything anticipated by SWNCC-228, which, indeed, has relatively little to say on the score of demilitarization. Only Section 10 of the "Discussion" treats the matter in prospective terms: "Although the authority and influence of the military in Japan's governmental structure will presumably disappear with the abolition of the Japanese armed forces, formal action permanently subordinating the military services to the civil government by requiring that the ministers of state or the members of a cabinet must, in all cases, be civilians would be desirable." This formulation does leave open the possibility of an eventual reemergence of Japanese armed forces. It can readily be argued on this basis, therefore, that the "Renunciation of War" chapter in the MacArthur draft constitution (Article VIII in that document) exceeds the intent of SWNCC-228 in two important respects. First, it incorporates demilitarization provisions in the constitution rather than in the peace treaty or statutory law. SWNCC-228 nowhere contemplates such an action. Neither does it forbid it. Second, the MacArthur Draft seems to preclude eternally any resurrection of Japan's armed forces. The relevant passage is: "No army, navy, air force or other war potential will ever be authorized and no rights of belligerency will ever be conferred upon the State." Little reason exists to doubt that these provisions are the work of General MacArthur and his staff.

Where the final text of the constitution of 1946–1947 is concerned, the first of the above-noted discrepancies still exists. Demilitarization is provided for by constitutional means. With the addition of the Ashida Amendment, however, and its subsequent interpretation along lines that permit the maintenance of armed forces for defensive purposes, the second discrepancy has vanished.

In a way one might also argue that the treatment of the composition of the new upper house of the national Diet marks a substantial elaboration on the intent of SWNCC-228. The Washington planners paid no specific attention to this issue and provided no guidelines for SCAP. SWNCC-228 does not even mention the matter except indirectly in its provisions that the legislative body must be "fully representative of the electorate" and that the electorate must be "based upon wide representative suffrage"; Section 5a of the discussion part of the document mentions the subject more directly but very generally. These provisions obviously ruled out the existing House of Peers. The MacArthur Draft solved the problem very simply by providing (in Article XLI) that "the Diet shall consist of one House of elected representatives with a membership of not less than 300 nor more than 500." In no way violating the terms of SWNCC-228, this nevertheless represents a bold and sweeping innovation that seems never to have been contemplated in Washington. The same is true of the type of upper house that emerged in the final version of the new constitution. Indeed, it is even conceivable that the above-quoted provisions from SWNCC-228 about a "fully representative" legislative body and an electorate "based upon wide representative suffrage" may have been one reason why SCAP's representative so strongly resisted Japanese efforts to introduce a corporative upper house.

Despite such deviations from and elaborations on the provisions of SWNCC-228, the most important fact is the degree of conformity between it on the one hand and the MacArthur Draft and the new constitution on the other. This is so marked it leads one to conclude that, prima facie, the latter ineluctably flowed from the former; in other words that SWNCC-228 was clearly a model for the Japanese constitution.

Another and even more probative way of approaching this problem exists: asking what is known about the chain of causality involved. Can it be demonstrated (1) that MacArthur received SWNCC-228, (2) that he made its contents known at least to General Whitney or the small group in Government Section that determined the contents of the MacArthur Draft or, alternatively, that they had independent knowledge of SWNCC-228 or its equivalent from some unknown source in Washington, and (3) that, if so, SWNCC-228 was the dominant model followed in writing the MacArthur Draft?

It is known that the text of SWNCC-228 was sent to General MacArthur by the Joint Chiefs of Staff for his information—not as a directive or order—on January 11, 1946.[59] The official Government Section account of the making of the new constitution, however, makes no mention of 228 and, indeed, clearly states that General MacArthur gave "full discretion to the Government Section" with respect to the terms of the MacArthur draft constitution save that he wanted three major points included in it.[60] It is quite certain, however, that this was not the only guidance provided to Government Section with respect to the terms of the MacArthur Draft of the new constitution—although the accounts made public by Government Section and its chief, General Whitney, notably fail to mention any other form of external guidance beyond a passing reference to the need to bear in mind the principles of the United Nations.[61] The most authoritative source on the production of the MacArthur Draft by Government Section is the official notes taken at the time of the drafting by Miss Ruth A. Ellerman. These make completely clear that SWNCC-228 was not only available to Government Section drafters but also that they were under orders to conform to its provisions. The actual words employed were as follows:

> 6. *Conformity with SWNCC-228:*
> SWNCC-228 must be used as a control document. Each Subcommittee Chief is responsible for checking his committee's proposals for conformity.[62]

Under these circumstances there can be no doubt as to the basic paternity of the MacArthur Draft. It was clearly SWNCC-228 where most of the basic principles were concerned. To these General MacArthur and Government Section added a number of important ideas of their own plus the all-important details and specification that made a constitution out of what had been merely a vague and abstract set of principles.

Conclusion

In the light of the preceding sections what can be said in more general terms about the process of presurrender planning for the Allied Occupation of Japan? Several thoughts occur.

First, it is astonishing how early the planning began and how consistently and thoroughly it was carried on. No other major war has been characterized by postwar planning activities with this degree of forethought, depth, continuity, and completeness.

Second, the plans were unusual in their scope. Modern wars have frequently involved wartime planning for postwar transfers of territory, for reparations payments, for military occupations, and the like. Before World War II, however, in no modern case did the postwar planners conceive of their mission as requiring the total restructuring of the defeated nation's basic values, behavior, and political, economic, and social institutions with the goal of eventually restoring to that nation a status of independence and equality in the international community.

Third, the quality of the planning for the postwar treatment of Japan was remarkably good. The planners successfully identified the major problems requiring attention—often several years in advance of their materialization. They were able to formulate these problems in researchable and increasingly practical terms and to emerge with recommendations that, given the bitterness of the war, were surprisingly objective, humane, and wise. The ultimate credit belongs primarily to a small group of eight or ten intelligent men, knowledgeable about Japan, in the Department of State and, secondarily, to an even smaller group in the army's Civil Affairs Division and General Staff. The planners' numbers were small, their service in a planning capacity was continuous, and postwar planning for Japan took place in a relatively inconspicuous backwater free of much of the political controversy, rivalry, and publicity that afflicted their European counterparts. These characteristics had a great deal to do with the high quality of the operation.

Fourth, the morphology of the postwar planning process is of interest. It starts with no guidance beyond a few vague and general pronouncements of principle by presidents, prime ministers, and international conferences. It then dissects these and applies them to an increasing number of specific postwar problems at which point the planning process acquires a life and vitality of its own. It begins to clothe the generalities of the national leaders with proposed solutions to specific anticipated postwar needs and circumstances and, in so doing, gives real substance to postwar policy. In the case of Japan this process began in a single department—State—that seized upon it with unusual vigor and interest because the outbreak of war had stripped the department of so many of its normal functions and activities and, in so doing, dangerously diminished its stature in the bureaucratic community. For some time State developed its plans without serious rivalry. But as victory in Europe approached and victory in the Pacific became a more real and imminent prospect, the War Department in particular became more active and in certain fields—especially those affecting the operational structure, composition, authority, and security of the Occupation of Japan—began increasingly to challenge and sometimes supersede the primacy of the State Department planners. In this sense the end of hostilities and the actual beginning of the Occupation also marked an abrupt end to the State Department's predominance and the beginning of the period of military ascendancy. In practice, however, it turned out to be not the Joint Chiefs of Staff in Washington but the field commander, General MacArthur, to whom this ascendancy passed.

Fifth, because of the obstacles that invariably intervene between planning and implementation, it does not by any means follow that good plans will in fact be followed. True, what happened to the structure and operations of the Japanese government in the almost seven years of the Allied Occupation in many important respects resembled very closely what the State Department planners had envisaged. It is not clear in all cases, however, that as the Occupation progressed the presurrender plans were normally the models used by SCAP in exerting its influence for change on the Japanese. This does not, however, lead to the conclusion that the original planning activities were futile and, therefore, dispensable. In fact they seem to have penetrated military as well as State Department thinking. They are known to have affected the thinking and practice of a number of highly placed members of the Occupation either directly or indirectly. One suspects that they influenced General Mac-

Arthur's own thinking. In short, they helped to create among the occupiers a climate of opinion with respect to the postwar treatment of Japan that was both intelligent and effective.

Finally, it is very easy to overestimate the ultimate influence of the American plans in any attempt to account for the extensive and dramatic changes that have occurred in postwar Japan. Whatever their authorship, the fundamental importance of the plans was in stimulating, reinforcing, and giving direction and form to forces for change that were endogenous to Japan. Major changes may have occurred as a result of Occupation initiatives, but none would have endured had they not elicited critical and continuing support from new leadership groups in Japan. In this sense the most profound insight achieved by any of the American planners was undoubtedly the recognition that Japanese society was ripe for change and that a new leadership was available in Japan that would see many of the changes envisaged by the American planners as being to its own and the country's long-term advantage.

Notes

1. Because of limitations of time and space the present chapter will be restricted to those aspects of official United States planning for the postwar treatment of Japan that relate to projected changes in the structure and operations of the Japanese government and, more particularly, to what I will call major "positive" plans for political change, excluding "negative" plans such as provisions for the trial of war criminals, the abolition of obnoxious laws, or the purging from public office of certain suspect segments of the Japanese population, which represent U.S. efforts to remove obstacles from the path of democratization more than they do attempts positively to foster the development of new political institutions. Although the primary focus of the chapter is on "presurrender" planning (i.e., prior to September 2, 1945), in a number of cases the planning phase carries on beyond the point of the formal surrender. Any narrative that failed to take this extension into account would be seriously incomplete. The present chapter will, therefore, in some instances treat developments occurring as late as March 1946.

2. National Archives, Diplomatic Section, Notter Files, Box 57, P-213, "Agenda for the Meeting of March 13, 1943," Appendix, p. 2. The Notter Files are the principal repository of presurrender planning documents held by the Department of State. They are named after Harley R. Notter, a State Department official who was deeply and continuously involved in the wartime planning operations.

3. Notter Files, Box 63, T-315 of May 25, 1943, "Status of the Japanese Emperor."

4. Notter Files, Box 64, T-366 of September 27, 1943, "Political and Economic Aspects of the Terms of Surrender for Japan," p. 7.

5. See, for example, Notter Files, Box 64, T-357a of September 29, 1943, "General Principles Applicable to the Postwar Settlement with Japan," p. 2; or Box 65, T-381 of October 6, 1943, "Japan: Postwar Political Problems," p. 5.

6. National Archives, Modern Military Records Section, Record Group 165, Box 34, "Memorandum for Chief," CAD of October 8, 1943.

7. Notter Files, Box 58, T-Minutes 58 of December 3, 1943, p. 10.

8. The structure of the wartime planning agencies operating in the Department of State and elsewhere in the federal government was extraordinarily complex and variable. A description of their origins and development would be of inordinate length. As a substitute, Appendix 2 attempts to chart the evolution of these central planning agencies.

9. The principal individuals involved in the State Department's postwar planning for Japan and their dates of entry into the department in 1942 were Dr. John W. Masland, Jr. (June 29), Dr. George H. Blakeslee (August 23), Dr. Amry Vandenbosch (September 8), Clarence J. Spiker (September 23), Cabot Coville (September 30), Robert A. Fearey (October 7), and Dr. Hugh Borton (October 19). Coville and Spiker were assigned from the Foreign Service and returned to Foreign Service posts in February and March 1943, respectively. Masland left the group in September 1943, and Vandenbosch was reassigned to another unit in January 1944.

10. Notter Files, PWC-116 (CAC-93) of March 21, 1944.

11. Notter Files, PWC-147 of April 4, 1944, by Pratt; PWC-145 of April 26, 1944, by Ballantine; and PWC-146 of April 26, 1944, by Grew. There was also a fourth paper of this sort by Earl R. Dickover, but it was missing from the Diplomatic Section files (CAC-179 of April 25, 1944).

12. Department of State, *Foreign Relations of the United States, 1944* (Washington, D.C.: GPO, 1965), vol. 5, pp. 1250–1255. The paper (PWC-116d or CAC-93c) was by Hugh Borton. This source hereafter cited as *FRUS*.

13. CAC-251 Preliminary of July 12, 1944. Notter Files, Box 113. The paper is by Hugh Borton.

14. Notter Files, Box 113, CAC-265 Preliminary.

15. PWC-301 of August 16, 1944, in a letter from Major General Hilldring, Director of CAD, to James C. Dunn, Acting Director of the Office of Special Political Affairs in the State Department. Notter Files, Box 144.

16. PWC-294 (CAC-283) of September 13, 1944. Notter Files, Box 144.

17. The papers involved are PWC-284 (CAC-262) of August 30, 1944, and PWC-284a of November 13, 1944. The former may be found in the Notter Files, Box 144, the latter in *FRUS, 1944*, vol. 5, pp. 1275–1285.

18. CAD Files, CAD-321 (12-21-42) (1), sec. 7.

19. CAD Files, Hull to Hilldring of January 19, 1945. CAD-321 (12-21-42) (1), sec. 7.

20. See, for example, two papers by Lt. Col. Daniel C. Fahey, Jr., on January 26, 1945, "Basic Assumptions underlying concept of Military Government for Japan," or Col. Marcus's comment of February 6, 1945, on "There is no basis in fact for Assumptions made below—Planning for Military Control of Japan." CAD Files, Japan-General.

21. National Archives, Diplomatic Section, Record Group 353, Box 15.

22. Record Group 165, Box 34, CAD-014 Japan (7-8-42) (1), sec. 3.

23. Record Group 353, Box 15.

24. Record Group 353, Box 15.

25. Record Group 353.

26. The basic Report was SFE-141/1, which, on submission to SWNCC became SWNCC-209/1 of March 7, 1946. With minor revisions this was approved by SWNCC on April 11, 1946. The text has been published in substantial part in *FRUS, 1946*, vol. 8, pp. 199–201. The basic and complete text, including "Facts Bearing on the Problem" and "Discussion" sections, may be found in Record Group 353.

27. See General Headquarters, SCAP, "SWNCC-SANACC Documents pertaining to the Activities of SCAP," November 1, 1948, p. 7. The reference radio number involved was W80789, and the paper was referred to the Government Section of SCAP. It is curious in the light of the despatch of SWNCC 55/6 (Revised) of October 26, 1945, to General MacArthur by the JCS on November 29, 1945 (see Record Group 218, Box 117, CCS 091.11 Japan, sec. 1, message no. WARX-85811), that there is no mention in the index of "SWNCC-SANACC Documents pertaining to the Activities of SCAP" of SWNCC-55 ever being received by SCAP either as a directive or for guidance or of its contents being assigned to any section of SCAP's headquarters for action. I know of no explanation for this.

28. MacArthur Memorial Library, Norfolk, Va., War Department Messages: 1001 to 1094 from April 29 to August 2, 1945.

29. The radiograms involved are JCS to MacArthur, WARX-85811 of November 29, 1945, and MacArthur to WARCOS-JCS, CA 57235 of January 25, 1946. These may be found in National Archives, Record Group 218, Box 117, CCS 091.11 Japan, sec. 1.

30. Government Section, Supreme Commander for the Allied Powers, *Political Reorientation of Japan, September 1945 to September 1948* (Washington, D.C.: GPO, n.d.), vol. 1, p. 102.

31. Notter File, Box 57, P-213.

32. Notter File, Box 63, a sixteen-page paper dated May 22, 1943, "Japan: Administration and Structure of Japanese Government." This provides a succinct but thorough description of the structure and operations of the Japanese government before and after the centralizing measures of 1937.

33. Notter File, Box 64, T-357a, September 29, 1943, "General Principles applicable to the Postwar Settlement with Japan—Revision."

34. Notter File, Box 65, T-381, October 6, 1943, "Japan: Postwar Political Problems."

35. Notter File, Box 59, T-Minutes 54, October 22, 1943.

36. Notter File, Box 109, CAC-108 Preliminary, March 9, 1944.

37. Notter File, Box 142, PWC-153, May 1, 1944, "Decentralization of Japanese Administration."

38. Notter File, Box 142, PWC-152 (CAC-185) of May 1, 1944; PWC-152a (CAC-185a) of May 4, 1944; and PWC-152b (CAC-185b) of May 9, 1944. The last item is reprinted in *FRUS, 1944*, vol. 5, pp. 1257–1260.

39. *Political Reorientation of Japan*, vol. 1, p. 102.

40. Record Group 353, Box 20. There are no further papers in the SWNCC-90 Series. The 228 Series replaces it.

41. Record Group 353, Box 27, SWNCC-162/D of July 19, 1945. The series has four additional papers between August 30, 1945, and February 13, 1946.

42. Record Group 353, Box 40, SWNCC-228 of November 27, 1945. There are some fourteen additional papers in the series but only one of these, SWNCC-228/1 of December 19, 1945, ibid., predates the publication of the first draft of the new constitution in Japan. Paper 228/1 sets forth the comments of the Joint Chiefs of Staff and—after noting the "freely expressed will of the Japanese people" clause from the Potsdam Declaration, stating that the primary short-term interest of the military is that the proposed governmental reform not foment unrest in Japan, and indicating the diminished capacity of the military to cope with such unrest because of demobilization—approves the basic paper, SWNCC-228.

43. *FRUS, 1945,* vol. 6, p. 736.

44. *FRUS, 1945,* vol. 6, pp. 757–758. The State Department's only direct and private way of communication with Atcheson was by mail pouch.

45. Atcheson's telegram No. 31 of October 10, 1945, may be found in *FRUS, 1945,* vol. 6, p. 739.

46. *FRUS, 1945,* vol. 6, pp. 837–841. This includes the text of the proposed press release.

47. *FRUS, 1945,* vol. 6, pp. 854–856 and 870–871.

48. These were "Reform of the Japanese Governmental System," SFE-142, October 22, 1945, and a similarly titled paper slightly revising the conclusions of SFE-142 numbered SFE-142/1 of November 14, 1945. National Archives, Records of SWNCC, Subcommittee for the Far East, Microfilm Series T-1205. See also *FRUS, 1945,* vol. 6, pp. 882–884.

49. Personal letter from Mr. Fearey to the author, July 15, 1978.

50. See Columbia University, Oral History Files, Charles L. Kades, p. 4.

51. Record Group 353, Box 40, SWNCC-228, November 27, 1945, "Reform of the Japanese Governmental System."

52. See chapter 3 by Theodore McNelly for a full account of the MacArthur Draft and the making of the present Japanese constitution.

53. Justin Williams, "Making the Japanese Constitution: a Further Look," *American Political Science Review,* vol. 59 (September 1965), pp. 665–679, makes this argument most persuasively.

54. See chapter 3 of this volume for additional information.

55. Record Group 353, Box 40.

56. Ibid.

57. See footnote 42.

58. *Political Reorientation of Japan,* vol. 2, pp. 622–623.

59. Record Group 353, Box 40, Memorandum for the Commander in Chief, U.S. Army Forces, Pacific, Tokyo, Japan (OPD 014.1 TS, 11 Jan. '46).

60. *Political Reorientation of Japan,* vol. 1, p. 102.

61. Ibid., pp. 102–105; and Courtney Whitney, *MacArthur, His Rendezvous with History* (New York: Knopf, 1946), p. 249.

62. See Ellerman Notes on Minutes of Government Section, Public Administration Division Meetings and Steering Committee Meetings between 5 February [1946] and 12 February inclusive, Summary Report on Meeting of the Government Section, 6 February 1946, p. 2. Copies of the Ellerman Notes are held by the Stanford and University of Michigan libraries. Commander Hussey's personal copy is in the possession of the National Diet Library of Japan.

2

The International Context of the Occupation of Japan

Sakamoto Yoshikazu

Japan's defeat in 1945 led to another "opening of the country." During the six and one-half years of the Allied Occupation, Japanese society was permeated by "international society." Politically, the national border separating inside from outside vanished as outside powers superimposed their authority within Japan on the local power structure. Japanese society had earlier experienced various forms of interaction with international society, but the Occupation period represents an extreme form, characterized by the overwhelming dominance of the latter. It was the polar opposite to the extreme that prevailed before the Occupation of Japan when the Japanese Empire penetrated the outside region in the form of the Greater East Asian Co-Prosperity Sphere.

This chapter is concerned with the political significance of the Occupation when seen as a process of interaction between Japanese society and international society. I am particularly interested in exploring the political meaning of the process that we identify with the Occupation for, as it developed, Allied policy, formulated and carried out according to a well-prepared plan before and during the early phase of the Occupation, was disfigured by a factor that did not enter into the original plan—the Cold War confrontation. This had irreversible ramifications for, while the impact of the Occupation itself on Japanese politics, the economy, society, and culture was enormous, this impact was doubled when Allied policy changed course in midstream. This dual impact of the Occupation elicited a dual response in Japan, compounding the complexity of its significance for the postwar history of this Asian nation.

A series of policy changes, which later were to be called the "reverse course," took place in the latter phase of the Occupation. These were not minor readjustments of initial Occupation policies, but far-reaching modifications affecting, and being perceived by the Japanese as affecting, the fundamental principles of demilitarization and democratization.

For instance, the purge policy of the Occupation brought about a profound impact on the Japanese power structure. Conversely, as a former general headquarters (GHQ) official in charge of the purge admitted, the reversal of policy shifted the goal of the purge from that of eliminating militarists and ultranationalists to that of purging Communists and fellow travelers. The purge policy, which was to have eliminated those militarist Japanese leaders responsible for the aggressive war, was now applied to those who had been imprisoned during the war because of their opposition to the war. The "Red purge" coincided with the depurge of militarists and ultranationalists, thus creating the image that the Occupation forces, preoccupied with giving priority to Cold War considerations, had lost interest in the demilitarization and democratization of Japan.[1]

Furthermore, although the Occupation policy changes were largely a consequence of the evolution of the Cold War, they did not exactly correspond to the specific events involved in the outbreak and intensification of the Cold War between the United States and the USSR. The Cold War is such a broad concept that it encompasses disputes and conflicts of divergent characters in varying contexts that came to be entangled in the rivalry between the two superpowers at various moments in history. Thus, while we shall demonstrate the significant, occasional absence of correspondence between the development of the Cold War on one hand and the Occupation policy shifts on the other, we shall also point out that the absence of correspondence does not mean that they were unrelated.

To appreciate the complex processes that link the evolution of the Cold War and the shift in Occupation policy, our analysis must comprise the following three levels: (1) the macro-historical context of Japan's defeat and occupation; (2) the spread of the Cold War from its original arena, Europe, to East Asia, affecting Occupation policy toward Japan in a complicated way; and (3) the response of the Japanese people to the external impact—a response that was a component of the Occupation process.

As (2) encompasses at least three distinguishable dimensions, let us examine the question under the following five headings:

1. the macro-historical context of the Occupation
2. the Cold War between the U.S. and the USSR over Europe
3. the Cold War in Asia
4. the Cold War and the shift in Occupation policy, that is, extension of the Cold War to Japanese domestic politics
5. Japanese resistance to the Cold War and the subsequent indigenization of reforms

Although we deal with these five dimensions separately for purposes of identification and exposition, they are intricately interrelated as the component parts of the Occupation process.

Macro-historical Context of the Occupation

The "ultimate objective" of the initial postsurrender policy of the United States was to demilitarize and democratize Japan to "insure that Japan will not again become a menace to the United States or to the peace and security of the world." The main goal of Occupation policy was to disarm and demilitarize Japan, to eliminate totally the "authority of the militarists and the influence of militarism . . . from her political, economic, and social life."[2]

At that time and in later studies of postwar history Japanese militarism was treated as a phenomenon unique to Japan. During the Occupation period in particular, both occupiers and occupied tended to share the view that this type of militarism was a distinctly Japanese characteristic. Militarism in a larger sense, of course, is by no means unique to Japan.

The term "militarism" was first used in nineteenth century Europe particularly with reference to the political regime under Napoleon III and then later almost exclusively, and with negative connotations, to the German empire.[3] In the twentieth century, World War I was characterized by Anglo-Saxon nations as a war of democracy against "militarism." World War II was defined by the United Nations as a war of democracy against "Nazism" or "fascism"; the term "militarism" generally referred to Japan alone among the Axis powers, in part because under German "Nazism" and Italian "fascism" political power was primarily wielded by militarized political parties, while in wartime Japan it was the politicized military that came to power. Hence there was a tendency among both the victors and the vanquished to consider "militarism" peculiar to Japan as distinct from other Axis powers.

While the distinction between Japan's militarism on the one hand and German Nazism and Italian fascism on the other should not be underrated,[4] there are significant differences between Japan's militarism and militarism under the second German empire. Thus it is not only permissible but also useful from a macro-historical perspective to shed light on features common to "militarism," "Nazism," and "fascism." A crucial common feature is the militarization of the political regime and its basic policies—namely, a high probability that the regime would rely on coercion as a mode of allocating values, internally and internationally.

It is precisely these militarized regimes of the Axis powers that the United Nations, particularly Western nations, identified as the enemy of democracy and the source of legitimation for the war they were fighting. Seen in this broader context, militarism was not a problem peculiar to Japan. By reconceptualizing militarism as a more general problem in this way, we shall also be able to identify the characteristics and limitations of the Occupation policy of demilitarization.

To make this point clear from a macro-historical point of view, let us look briefly at the process of "modernization," which consists of a dynamic dialectic between unequal economic development and equalizing political development.

"Take-off time lag" (TOTIL) is the major indicator of unequal economic development. Modes of development can be divided into "capitalist" and "socialist." Thus, we can classify the countries of the world as in Table 1. The classification is illustrative, not exhaustive, but for heuristic purposes includes representative countries in each category. It is not intended as a "grand theory" such as world system analysis, which employs three basic categories—that is, cores, semiperipheries and peripheries. Historical realities are too complex to be subsumed under these categories. The major criterion used in our analysis is the moment in his-

Table 1
Time Lags in Economic Development

		Capitalist Countries		Socialist Countries
1800s	E M P I R E S	I: Great Britain France United States	I':	
1830s		II: Germany Japan Italy	II':	Russia
1930s	C O L O N I E S	III: Brazil Argentina South Korea India	III':	China North Korea Vietnam
1980s(?)		IV: Nepal Bangladesh Haiti Chad	IV':	Angola Mozambique Ethiopa Cambodia Laos

NOTE: I = early-starting advanced capitalist countries
         II = late-starting advanced capitalist countries
        III = early-starting developing capitalist countries
        IV = late-starting developing capitalist countries
        I' = early-starting advanced socialist countries
       II' = late-starting advanced socialist countries
      III' = early-starting developing socialist countries
      IV' = late-starting developing socialist countries

tory when a society has largely fulfilled the initial conditions for basically self-sustaining capital accumulation and growth on the basis of industrial and/or agricultural development. Moreover, the term "take-off" used here has nothing to do with the Rostowian idea of the stages of linear growth, as it takes into consideration the structural problem of "dependency and underdevelopment" that has emerged in the process of development.

As the table shows, there is a time lag in take-off between different categories of capitalist countries, between socialist countries, and also between capitalist and socialist countries, and this time lag is closely related to the worldwide structure of unevenness and disparities in development. Most notably, countries in categories I, II, and II′ have all experienced an "empire" phase in the history of the state system in the modern period, while all those in remaining categories have been "colonies" of at least one other nation in the same period. A lag in time, in this case, gave rise to a structural gap in power.

The dialectics of modernization involve, besides uneven economic development, a dynamic orientation to political equality. This has manifested itself in the struggle, on the international level, for "sovereign equality," that is, the "equality of states" or the "equality of nations" and, on the domestic level, in the struggle for "equal rights" that underlies the popular demand for "democracy" or "socialism." As a general rule, assertions of equality on the international level have preceded those on the domestic level, thus giving rise to nationalism in its various forms. It is also noteworthy that in the process by which category II countries closed the gap with category I countries in their search for equality, World War II broke out.[5] In this sense, World War II involved an element of contest over imperial hegemony. Similarly, when nations in category III sought to attain international equality vis-à-vis categories I and II, wars of national liberation and colonial independence were often inevitable. Herein resides the problem of the militarization that accompanied the efforts of late-comers to close in on the early starters and to oppose their policy of preserving their vested interests even by force of arms.

To put this in macro-historical terms, the early starting advanced capitalist countries of category I have acquired, in the course of their economic development, the status of major military powers through their domination of colonies. Thus, while they were militarized externally, a democratic regime was established internally in the early days of their modern history. External militarization and internal democratization went hand in hand. In contrast, the late starting advanced capitalist countries of category II embarked on systematically accelerated economic development challenging the vested interests of category I countries. Their internal militarization gave rise to authoritarian political regimes internally as well as to external militarization. As a result of this combination of internal and external militarization, category II countries are considered classic examples of militarism. In similar vein, Russia in category II´ can be characterized as militarist as the term is defined here.[6]

Category II is of particular relevance to our inquiry, for it contains the three primary Axis powers—Japan, Germany, and Italy. Despite a number of significant differences among the three, we may focus on the internal authoritarian regimentation, which was coupled with external military expansion. If we do, the several proclivities of militarism shared by all three become clear. All three were anti–liberal-democratic (as distinct from merely non–liberal-democratic), anticommunist, and colonialist or imperialist. Clearly, the quality of anti–liberal-democracy came out most strongly in the relationship between categories II and I; anticommunism, in the relationship between II and II´; and imperialism, in the relation between II and III and III´ (during World War II the countries in III´ were in category III). Looked at in this way, the Allies' (category I) justification for the war against Japan (the Axis) was the safeguarding of democracy, while the Soviet Union (II´) fought the Axis in defense of the socialist homeland, and anti-Japanese or antiimperialist movements in China and other Asian countries (III) aimed at national liberation. Thus, militarism contained within it a triple negation and stimulated a triple opposition. For category II countries, World War II was a three-front war.[7]

These three aspects of militarism also provide important clues to the significance of Japan's demilitarization. Above all else, demilitarization involved the infiltration of "Western liberalism and democracy" from category I into category II. On the other hand, with respect to its relationship with the developing Asian countries of categories III and III´, Japan was forced to abandon its colonies as stipulated in Section 8 of the Potsdam Declaration. In this context demilitarization meant the termination of infiltration of those countries by the Japanese empire. But in terms of Japan's relations with the Soviet Union, demilitarization by the Allied forces meant basically a continuation, albeit modified, of anticommunism and an anti-Soviet stance.

Thus the basic framework of postwar Japanese international relations was shaped during the Occupation and built on closer ties with the Western advanced capitalist nations, on a break in imperial relations with the developing Asian countries, and on anticommunism. As a consequence, the response of postwar Japan to international affairs differed markedly in one important respect from those of the Western advanced capitalist countries of category I. It was similar in that, when the Cold War began to intensify around 1947–1948, Japan's leaders, such as Ashida Hitoshi and Yoshida Shigeru, quickly decided to follow the lead of the advanced Western countries. There was little time differential between the decision by the Western countries to adopt a hardline policy toward the Soviet Union and adaptation to this major shift on the part of Japanese elites. If there was some delay, it was less because of the elites' response than other factors which will be discussed later. But in their awareness of and response to North-South problems, Japan's elites lagged far behind those of the Western advanced countries—mainly because Japan's political and economic relations with the newly independent nations were severed through the defeat primarily by the advanced countries and, during the Occupation, actually by the United States. One result of being "forced out of Asia" by the advanced countries was to heighten the prewar aspirations of the Japanese to "leave Asia and enter the West."

We have seen that militarism in the broad sense of authoritarian militarist regimentation quite often appears in late-starting capitalist countries when they begin to "take off," stimulated by the need of catching up with the early-starting capitalist countries.[8] Opposition to liberal democracy, anticommunism, and colonialism or imperialism are all common to militarism, but the process or mode by which militarism is dismantled or disintegrates is not necessarily uniform. The process could not possibly be the same, particularly in nations in categories II and III. The demilitarization of countries in category II—including Japan, Germany, and Italy —was accomplished through their military defeat and occupation and the infiltration of liberalism and democracy by nations in category I.

This constitutes a macro-historical framework for analyzing the long-term meaning of the Allied Occupation of Japan.

Generally speaking, when a country takes off on the basis of a capitalist model, it is a structural inevitability that tensions arise in relations between that country and those which take off on the socialist model. Historically, it was also virtually inevitable that democracy from the advanced Western nations (I) would infiltrate into the late-starting advanced capitalist countries (II) through war and subsequent occupation. But how and to what degree these latter countries remain necessarily anti-Soviet and anticommunist is determined not by democratization itself but by the relationship between the Soviet Union and the promoters of democratization, that is, the Western advanced nations and especially the United States. In this sense, the anticommunism of countries in category II is a function of the relationship between the nations in categories I and II'. Let us then examine the impact of the Cold War on the Occupation of Japan.

The Cold War between the U.S. and USSR

There are many ways to interpret the origins of the Cold War. Despite the divergence of views, we can safely argue that before World War II, the Soviet Union posed no actual threat to the security of the United States. On the contrary, it was the Bolshevik regime that was threatened, for example, by the dispatch of American troops to Siberia. And it was during those formative years of the Soviet Union that the basic pattern of

the conclusion of peace with the adversaries in Eastern Europe in
During these two years Soviet-American mutual distrust spiraled
The Soviets, their country severely weakened by extensive war
and their leaders worried about a possible revival of Germany,
to shore up their national security by setting up pro-Soviet re-
Eastern Europe. But the measures they employed were interpret-
he United States as an "export of revolution" and a sign of an
sionist drive." This U.S. response, in turn, amplified Soviet dis-
d fear of the United States. This vicious circle of distrust was not
out in the context of a symmetrical power relationship; the Soviet
was in an incomparably weaker position. But the United States
hed the Soviet Union as if their relationship were intrinsically
rical—which in itself worked to increase Russian anxiety.

ng to play up Russian "control" over Eastern Europe and to mag-
Soviet "threat" to the Western nations, the United States ex-
the propaganda value of the large number of Russian troops
ng in East European countries after the war.

oteworthy, however, that the dominant view held by the West,
arly the U.S. government, has been questioned not only by revi-
but also by main stream historians.

isionist view was expounded by Joyce and Gabriel Kolko. Ac-
to them, it was U.S. Naval Intelligence that in early 1946 esti-
at the large number of Russian troops still in Europe was par-
result of necessity; several million Soviet soldiers would have
lace to live and no food to eat if they had gone back to the Soviet
Naval Intelligence concluded that the Soviet Union was in a state
mic exhaustion.[11] This was perhaps a reasonable assessment of
t situation, but there was no chance that it would receive much
from the U.S. government. The atmosphere of hostility had
rown too strong.

Ulam, a main stream historian, citing the statistics given by
nev on the size of the Soviet armed forces at the beginning of the
r, said: "The legend of massive Soviet armies ready to march to
ish Channel still persists among many Western writers. . . .
ev's figures tell a different story: the Soviet armies . . . now
erform police duties over vast areas of Eastern Europe, in the
where passive acceptance of Moscow-imposed regimes could
ken for granted." In short, Stalin and his clique "expected
pressure on the Soviet Union, economic and psychological in
ter, to make her surrender some of her wartime gains. Once
radoxical though it sounds, one of the main reasons for the
Soviet posture between 1945 and 1950 was the awareness of
s of her weakness and vulnerability."[12]

event the continued stationing of the Red Army in Eastern

conflict between the U.S. and the USSR
claim that the decisive framework of the
the Russian Revolution and World War II
stream" and "revisionist" schools wou
between the United States and the Sovie
exception in the history of Soviet-Americ
Even this wartime cooperation was bes
cions. The Soviet Union grew more war
tions when the opening of a second fro
the United States and Britain were a
might conclude a separate peace with C
in point.[9] One can fault the United Sta
opening the second front in Europe,
heavily on it; at the same time, tha
dilemma of Americans and British co
Soviet Union and Germany might conc
the war against Japan, the Anglo-Ame
card its neutrality and help by opening
sians complied, but their role on the A
their fulfillment of the promise cost th
far too much.

In sum, while there was nothing in
made the later occurrence of the Cold
strenuous efforts by both sides to avc
tionship that could all too easily lead
thermore, the relationship between th
ric. More active initiatives to avoid a (
been taken by the United States and
Western powers in category I, were
advanced than the USSR and in the
Given the fact, recognized by Georg
the Soviet Union, unlike Nazi Germ
long-term rationality,[10] systematic ef
ain to prevent intensification of the (
How, then, has the crisis mounted?

Between the latter phase of World
years, there arose three major issues
West or, more properly, between the
They were the Eastern Europe issue
energy issue. Let me touch briefly u
and their implications for the Occup

The Eastern

The Eastern Europe issue took sha
Poland's boundaries and sovereign

Europe was an indication not of Soviet power but of weakness, and yet the American image of exaggerated Soviet strength persisted. Thus the "Soviet threat" was inflated and the American overestimation of Russian power accelerated the vicious circle of distrust.

On the other hand, the gap between the American perception and reality was not totally baseless. The stationing of Russian troops in Eastern Europe may have stemmed from weakness but, whatever the reason, their presence in the region nullified U.S. influence there once and for all. "National self-determination," a principle inherited from the Wilsonian era, was one of the basic pillars of U.S. policy toward Eastern Europe at that time. But the kind of "self-determination" envisioned by the United States was not easy to achieve. It may well be that, as Isaac Deutscher and others have pointed out, Eastern Europe could become socialist only as a consequence of its indigenous forces choosing socialism;[13] but this did not accord with the American definition of self-determination which was derived from Western liberal traditions. It is doubtful that any kind of indigenous liberal-centered system could have been established in Eastern Europe at that time, for in many parts of the region there was not much to build on except a semifeudalistic social structure that remained largely intact until the end of the war. Aside from that, however, the presence of Soviet troops greatly curtailed any chance that a Western pattern of self-determination might have prevailed in the region.

In sum, the East European issue caused the United States to overestimate Soviet strength and created a sense of frustration and powerlessness vis-à-vis the USSR. The conflict in U.S.-Soviet relationships that arose at that juncture eventually spread to other issues and other regions. At the same time the bitter "lesson" learned from the experience of allowing Soviet troops to remain in Eastern Europe would later affect U.S. policy toward other regions. Besides Japan, Germany was a prime example.

The German Issue

Basic U.S. Occupation policy toward Germany was set by the Joint Chiefs of Staff directive of May 1945 (JCS-1067), a somewhat modified version of the Morgenthau Plan. The Allies had divided the country into occupation zones, set up a direct military government in each zone, and dissolved the German central government. Two factors influenced the division of Germany into four occupation zones: first, the idea that the centralized power structure of Germany should be dismantled and, second, the fait accompli that Soviet troops already occupied the area east of the Oder-Neisse line. Thus unlike in Eastern Europe, an Allied Control Council was established composed of representatives from the United States, the Soviet Union, Britain, and France. Each occupation zone retained considerable independence concerning reparations but, as spelled out in the Potsdam Agreement, there was a consensus among the four powers regarding the importance of maintaining the unity of the German economy. For these reasons the U.S. position in Germany was far more symmetrical with that of the USSR than was the case in Eastern Europe. The United States tried to capitalize on the "economic unity of all Germany" to extend American influence into the Soviet zone; but the attempt failed in the face of unbending opposition from the USSR, whose own economic reconstruction depended heavily on reparations from its occupation zone in Germany.[14] Once more, weakness in the Soviet economy contributed to the closed nature of its policy.

The unification of all Germany was at that time a symbol advantageous not only to the United States but to the Soviet Union as well. In June 1945, two months before the Western powers took similar moves, the Soviet Union authorized freedom of organization for political parties within its occupation zone, and very quickly the Social Democrats (SPD), the Christian Democrats (CDU), and the Liberal Democrats (LDP) as well as the Communists (KPD) were legally established. The Soviet Union then drove a political wedge into the other occupation zones by supporting a national united front of the Communist party and the SPD.[15] In view of the fact that in early postwar Germany—and Western Europe as a whole for that matter—leftist forces were generally strong, this was a very good political tactic. If a unified government had been formed in Germany right after the war, that government would certainly have been leftist.[16] In short, the Soviet Union could possibly have had a political advantage concerning the unification of Germany.

The Soviet-American parity in Germany was conditioned by the interplay of U.S. superiority in the economic realm and Soviet advantage in the political realm. But such a "symmetrical" relationship between the two powers, both of which aimed at German unity, could not possibly be stable. The very parity intensified the confrontation and made cooperative coexistence more difficult. On September 6, 1946, Secretary of State James F. Byrnes declared in a speech that the United States should "do everything in [its] power to secure maximum possible unification"— which in effect meant unification only of the British and American zones —and that the United States did "not want Germany to become a satellite of any power."[17] At that point, the United States having made clear its intent to discard the principle of the economic unity of Germany including the Russian zone, the Cold War between the United States and the Soviet Union over Germany became overt.

The Atomic Energy Issue

The United States consistently retained superiority over the Soviet Union in atomic power, but its policies raised questions as to how to deal with that power. In the joint declaration of November 15, 1945, of the United States, Great Britain, and Canada, the United States enunciated the principle of international control of atomic energy. Several moves followed, including the so-called Acheson-Lilienthal Report of March 1946 addressed to the president in preparation for deliberations at the United Nations. Then in June, the Baruch Plan was presented by the United States to the U.N. Atomic Energy Commission. Although there were points of significant difference between the two documents named, consistent in all the American actions was the intent to place not just atomic weapons but all fissionable materials (such as uranium) under complete international control and to make certain that their ownership, management, processing, and research would be controlled by an international authority. Moreover, in the Baruch Plan it was proposed that violations of the control agreement should be met with "condign punishment" and that action against serious breaches of the agreement should be taken by the U.N. Security Council, where the veto power would be abolished insofar as the issue of atomic power was concerned.[18]

Obviously there was some ambivalence behind these American moves. On the one hand, the United States had actually used an atomic weapon and was, therefore, all too aware of its formidable destructive power. Americans knew that such weapons would have to be totally banned through international cooperation. On the other hand, the United States wanted to strip all other countries, particularly the Soviet Union, of any capability to develop atomic weapons at the earliest possible stage, and it wanted the United Nations, where American influence was still dominant, to have definitive authority over international atomic energy control in order to be able to monopolize both the world's atomic weapons and its nuclear development capability. Generally speaking, the former attitude was relatively strong right after the war, but as time went by, the latter came to dominate American thinking.[19]

From the outset the United States was far ahead in the production and use of atomic energy, and its attempts to consolidate this advantage reinforced the threat already felt by the Russians. In the words of Daniel Yergin, "Even Baruch was willing to acknowledge that fear was their [Russians'] dominating emotion."[20] Internationally isolated since the days of the Bolshevik Revolution, the Soviet Union had long resorted to a non-Marxist symbol—"national sovereignty"—as an ideological weapon to protect its independence and security. For the Soviet Union the international atomic energy control plan presented by the United States meant an infringement on national sovereignty through exposing its armaments to the surveillance of Western powers and limiting its freedom to develop atomic energy even for peaceful purposes. Because such a plan also allowed the Western powers to meddle in the Soviet socialist planned economy, the American proposal was a double "threat"—militarily to the state and economically to the system.[21]

It is important to remember that the "Soviet threat" the United States perceived in the nuclear issue was not an actual but a potential threat based on U.S. government projections of Soviet capability to develop atomic weapons five to twenty years later.[22] Such calculations compelled the United States to try to secure permanent and absolute superiority in atomic energy before the USSR could develop it. This attempt naturally increased Soviet distrust of the United States even more.

The three major issues that served to intensify the U.S.-USSR confrontation of 1945–1946—Eastern Europe, Germany, and atomic energy—generated conflicts each of which had a distinct structure. But underlying all of them was the weakness of the Soviet Union with its war-ravaged economy. This weakness existed not only in atomic energy (where the American superiority was unquestionable), but also in relation to the German issue (where the United States and the Soviet Union appeared to be equal), and even in Eastern Europe (where the Soviet Union seemed dominant). Despite these realities, it was during this period that Americans formed their image of the Soviet Union as a "threat." There was a crucial gap between image and reality, and the American perception of the confrontation with the USSR became in itself an important factor affecting their relations. On the one hand, Americans had a considerable leeway in interpreting the confrontation, but on the other, that leeway created confusion in the American interpretations.

By mid-1945 the U.S. government had moved away from Roosevelt's policy of accommodation with the Soviet Union during the war and had begun to question the interpretation that the Soviet Union's first priority was national security. Once more Moscow came to be seen as the headquarters of world revolution, bent on exporting the most aggressive kind of Communist subversion to other countries. This thinking emerges clearly in a number of documents including a State Department memorandum of June 1945[23] and a statement by Undersecretary of State Grew in July.[24] From the latter half of 1945 through the early months of 1946 confusion dominated U.S. government perceptions of the Soviet Union. Forrestal and others fully recognized the need for a new, definitive viewpoint that would provide a rational basis for America's policy toward the USSR.[25] Then came George Kennan's memorandum to Byrnes on February 22, 1946, which had a virtually decisive influence on shaping the U.S. government's view of the Soviet Union for years thereafter.[26] The message of the memorandum was almost the same as that of the now famous "X" article in *Foreign Affairs* which appeared in July 1947. Kennan asserted, in effect, that the Soviet Union relied on ideology and foreign policy as the chief means of maintaining its dictatorial regime and that the Kremlin leaders sought to stabilize their regime by strengthening their military power and at the same time causing disturbances in the political and economic systems of the West through the international

Communist movement. Accordingly, Kennan prescribed determined resistance by the West to the world revolutionary movement, but he also advised the necessity of patience until the internal nature of the Soviet system had evolved into something else. The memorandum offered U.S. policy makers a timely and reasoned conceptual frame to justify abandoning Roosevelt's conciliatory posture and adopting a tough, new policy reformulated and justified on the grounds that a stiff anti-Soviet, anti-Communist stand would lead to salutory internal changes in the USSR. It was at that point that an image of the Soviet Red Army as out to invade the West, joined by Communist parties throughout the world, took root among U.S. policy makers.

This seemed to end the wavering in the U.S. government's view of the Soviet Union. But Kennan himself, among others, objected to this new, hard-line position. He had written in his memorandum that Marxist-Leninist ideology was necessary to rationalize the oppressive, dictatorial Russian system; but he did not believe, nor did he state, that there was any element in that system pushing the Soviet Union to set up Communist regimes throughout the world. Much less did he believe in the possibility of an invasion of the West by the Red Army. The regimes the Russians wanted to establish in surrounding countries had to be friendly toward, or subordinate to, the USSR; the Russians did not necessarily demand that they be Communist regimes. As Kennan pointed out at the time, there had been no attempt so far in Poland, for example, to establish a regime that could be called a Communist government.[27]

If Kennan presented his views accurately, then the U.S. government leaders misunderstood them. It is more likely that, given the circumstances, American elites and public opinion needed an "objective" basis to justify a hard-line Soviet policy, and that Kennan's views were to perform a certain political function independent of his intention. In any case, while Kennan's analyses appeared to have helped the U.S. government to establish an unambiguous policy, they actually added to the confusion in its understanding of Soviet intentions and behavior. This episode demonstrates how wide a margin existed at the time in the United States' interpretation of the Soviet Union, and how the American image of the USSR could affect the way the Cold War would develop.[28]

It is important to recognize the role of American domestic politics and public opinion in the decision to adopt a tough anti-Soviet line somewhat removed from Kennan's policy recommendations. For instance, many still accept the view that wrangling over Poland started the Cold War. But why, if Russian behavior toward Poland was based on the perceptions and intentions Kennan described, did the United States take a hard-line policy on this issue? One important reason is that more than six million Polish-Americans were among the decisive voters in several key states at the time of the 1944 presidential election.[29] This kind of political demography has often produced irrational distortions in the formation of American foreign policy, and what happened in the case of Poland also happened in U.S. relations with other East European countries—and it resembles the role played by Jewish-Americans in American Middle East policy. The interests of immigrant groups were naturally exploited by a Republican party trying to get back in power, challenging the government in the Congress, particularly in the Senate. Such constraints even compelled the administration to adopt a proposal for international atomic control that was impossible for the Soviet Union to accept, because the administration was more concerned with winning congressional support than with acceptability to the Kremlin.[30]

It is true that the Soviet Union was by no means at a total disadvantage vis-à-vis the United States. Soviet dominance on the issue of the political unification of Germany has already been discussed. But this political advantage did not in the least reflect Soviet superiority in its national capabilities; it stemmed simply from objective conditions—the opportunity created by Germany's political disarray and economic impoverishment for a possible leftist united front to stay on top. The United States, however, misunderstood the real source of Soviet influence in Germany and instead interpreted it as part of a deliberate Russian strategy for world revolution. This tendency to regard every spontaneous revolutionary movement as the result of instigation and support by an external force, and to intensify the Cold War by acting on the basis of such a perception, was particularly pronounced in U.S. policy toward Asia, especially China.

The Cold War in Asia

The basic pattern of the Cold War as it intensified in Europe was pretty well established by the latter half of 1946, but the inception and development of the Cold War in Asia indicated that there it would take a very different course. Its focus was China. There, completely unlike its Cold War moves in Europe (particularly Eastern Europe), the Soviet Union did not, even after World War II, withdraw its support for the Nationalist regime, which the United States also supported. On that point the Soviet Union and the United States had parallel positions. At the Yalta Conference the Soviet Union showed willingness to conclude a treaty of friendship and alliance with the Kuomintang. As presidential advisor William Leahy stated, to have gained at the conference Stalin's consent for the support of Chiang Kai-shek was an achievement extremely favorable to the United States.[31] On August 14, 1945, a treaty of friendship and alliance was signed between the Soviet Union and Nationalist China. In December at a foreign ministers' conference in Moscow, Molotov reaffirmed Russian support of the Chiang Kai-shek regime.[32] From Stalin's comments at Yalta, it seems clear that he saw China and Japan as part of the American sphere of influence.[33] The main Soviet interest regarding China at that time was to secure the industrial facilities in Manchuria and transport them into Soviet territory. Then on May 3, 1946, all Russian troops were withdrawn from China and Manchuria, again in marked contrast to Soviet actions in its occupied areas in Eastern Europe and Germany.

Moreover, with the consent of Great Britain and the Soviet Union, the United States ordered the Japanese troops in China to surrender only to the Nationalists (General Order No. 1, issued on August 14, 1945), and on September 30, 53,000 U.S. marines began landing in northern China with the task of disarming the Japanese troops. This was scheduled to be finished by the end of November, but on November 5 Chiang Kai-shek requested the United States to postpone the withdrawal of the marines. The number of American military personnel in China had grown to 113,000 by the end of that year. U.S. forces remained in China until 1949. In the meantime, they conveyed weapons taken from the Japanese troops to the Nationalist forces and helped in restraining the power of the Chinese Communist forces.

U.S. policy regarding China was based on two assumptions in particular that distinguished it from U.S. policy in Europe. First, the immediate enemy was the Chinese Communists, not the Soviet Union; the United States aimed, therefore, at containing Chinese communism by assisting the Nationalist regime on the one hand, and by obtaining Soviet cooperation, or at least neutrality, on the other. The policy of isolating the Chinese Communists came about partly because the United States judged that the communization of China was not desirable. But that was not the sole reason. Another important reason stemmed from the second assumption: that if the Chiang regime fell apart, the Soviet Union would probably enter Manchuria, an event that eventually would lead to the division of China into Communist and anti-Communist parts.[34] A divided China would mean the collapse of one pillar of U.S. postwar planning in which a strong, non-Communist China was to become one of five major powers upholding a new world order and maintaining a stable, pro-American force in Asia.[35] American operations to bring the Nationalist and Communist forces together in a coalition, starting in December 1945 and led by Special Envoy George Marshall, were an unambiguous expression of the aims and assumptions of U.S. policy in Asia. By containing the Chinese Communists within a system controlled by the Kuomintang, the Marshall mission attempted to remove the possibilities of Soviet intervention and to establish the integrity of a pro-American China. The effect, however, was that while trying to appear as a neutral third party and with Marshall increasingly reluctant to take sides with the corrupt Nationalists, the United States played a substantial role in assisting Chiang Kai-shek. This was in striking contrast to the Russians who, while publicly pro-Nationalist, actually withdrew from China, and supported neither side. In fact during 1945–1946, Washington's policy makers did not seriously think that the Soviet Union was giving active support to the Chinese Communists.[36]

That did not mean that Washington leaders recognized no essential relationships between the Soviets and the Chinese Communists. In their judgment the Chinese Communists were linked, if not subordinate, to the Russians and, as long as the Soviet Union was neutral, Chinese communism would wane. But the fact was that without Russian assistance the Chinese Communists survived the period between mid-1946 and early 1947 when the Nationalists were militarily stronger. U.S. policy makers were not able to see the reality of "indigenous, nationalistic communism" or to appreciate its stubborn strength without external support.

President Harry Truman, in fact, noted that "in the early stages" of General Marshall's mission (December 1945–February 1946), when the Communists were still militarily weaker, "the Communist representatives appeared more tractable to Marshall than the leaders of the Central Government, and it was his [Marshall's] impression that they could win their battle on political grounds more easily than on tactical fighting grounds."[37] But the United States was already committed; under Lend-Lease it had provided military assistance amounting to some $600 million to the Chiang regime during the period from August 15, 1945, to February 1946, and it could not possibly be a good neighbor to the Communists. With U.S. aid, the Nationalists were able to stay on top militarily until about the time they captured the Communist headquarters in Yenan in March 1947. Then deep-seated corruption within the regime, terrible inflation, and other economic and social problems began to undermine what popular support Chiang's government had been able to retain. Well-timed counterattacks by the Communists begun in the spring of 1947 were effective; and by autumn they began to overthrow Nationalist military control. By mid-1948 all major areas north of the Yangtze River were under Communist rule.

On March 11, 1948, Truman announced the U.S. decision to oppose any form of inclusion of the Communists in the Chinese Government, thus shifting American policy into open hostility toward the Communists.[38] This was a turning point that led toward the Cold War in Asia. The regional environment thus underwent a portentous change that was to affect all Asia, including the Allied Occupation of Japan.[39] In this connection, three points may be noted.

First, the change in U.S. policy toward China in March 1948 did not come about until a year and a half after the U.S. government shifted to a nonconciliatory stance toward the Soviet Union's activities in Europe. Nor was it an isolated event. In another development, in late February

1948 the United Nations Assembly approved, as a result of an American initiative, a proposal for national elections in South Korea alone, thus bypassing the deadlocked U.S.-USSR Joint Commission in Korea. This virtually determined and consolidated the partition of Korea into north and south. Also in February 1948 a decision was made at the Southeast Asia Youth Conference held in Calcutta to launch a determined armed resistance to imperialism in the region. As in the Chinese Communist case, it is doubtful how far this effort in Southeast Asia was authorized or overtly encouraged by the Soviet Union. It is more likely that the motivation was strongly indigenous. From the American perspective this new self-assertion in Southeast Asia was an important turning point toward the Cold War in Asia, and the U.S. response here was the same as it had been toward Chinese communism. And although the coup in Czechoslovakia also took place in February 1948, any linkage was only in time. The Czechoslovakian coup was an "indirect invasion" by the Soviet Union crossing the confrontation line already established between East and West; confrontation in China and Southeast Asia was between indigenous Communist forces and the United States, and did not take full-fledged form until 1948. Thus, in political terms, the pivotal events in Asia did not coincide with the Czechoslovakian coup. We must recognize, therefore, a significant political time lag in the development of the Cold War in Europe and in Asia.[40]

Second, starting in late 1947, when the U.S. government began seriously to question a viable future for Chiang Kai-shek's regime, the idea of giving up on China and making Japan the pillar of America's Asian policy began to surface.[41] The American response here, too, was quite different from what it had been in Europe. While the degree of perceived threat or impact from the Soviet Union or from Soviet-dominated Communist forces determined U.S. European policy and tactics, the emergence of Japan as a vital strategic area for the United States was based on other factors and considerations. It was the disintegration from within of the Nationalist regime despite extravagant U.S. assistance that provided the impetus to turn toward Japan. How far did the new, Japan-oriented policy reflect this difference? To what degree did U.S.—and by extension, Japanese—policy recognize the special political context of Asia? How did the U.S. and Japanese policies function politically in the special context of Asia, which was so unlike the European situation? In discussing these questions and their answers, we should always remember that, while the postwar rehabilitation of Japan and Germany was carried out in each case in a Cold War context, the perceptions and framework of international politics governing each situation were different.

Third, during the summer of 1947, when the U.S. leadership had come around to believing that the decline of Chiang Kai-shek's regime was impossible to arrest, a mission led by General Albert Wedemeyer was dispatched to China. One of its main tasks was to persuade Chiang of the necessity for social reform and in so doing to push the creation of a new kind of leadership that was neither Nationalist nor Communist. A statement by Truman in March 1948 reflected this U.S. goal. Besides declaring open hostility toward the Chinese Communists, Truman also expressed U.S. hope that "liberals would be taken into the Government."[42] But there was no such third "liberal" force that was politically viable in China. If the United States sought to encourage a new force in China, then perhaps we can assume that when the United States turned its attention from China to Japan, there, too, it was directed not at "Japan" but at a "third force" within Japan, a middle group between right and left.

Just as U.S. interest in Japan was growing, however, the liberal third group that did exist in Japan suffered a series of setbacks. Both the Katayama Tetsu and Ashida Hitoshi cabinets, upon which SCAP had pinned great hopes, were short-lived. Who would play the role of that middle force the United States sought was contingent upon domestic politics, as demonstrated by GHQ's unrealized preference for Yamazaki Takeshi, secretary-general of the Democratic-Liberal party, to replace Ashida Hitoshi as prime minister in October 1948. But at the same time we must remember that one of the factors that lay behind the U.S. efforts to cultivate a third force in Japan was the bitter experience in China. Whether this effort was appropriate and consistent or not is a different question.

The Cold War and Occupation Policy

Allied Occupation policy in Japan transfused the Cold War confrontations of Europe and of Asia into Japan, but it did not directly reflect the international confrontation. It was "deflected" through the General Headquarters of the Allied Powers, General Douglas MacArthur in particular.

D. C. James said of the authoritarian personality of MacArthur: "He will demand the utmost loyalty and obedience from his subordinates, yet will be continuously critical of the decisions of his superiors, the President and the Joint Chiefs of Staff, and will sometimes defy their directive."[43] MacArthur was likened to Caesar by John Gunther, and the general himself seemed to enjoy making the same comparison.[44] MacArthur also had an institutional guarantee that strengthened his independence. On the one hand, as CINCAFPAC (Commander-in Chief, Army Forces, Pacific)—later CINCFE (CINC, Far East)—he was bound to obey the commands of the U.S. president, secretary of war, chairman of the Joint Chiefs of Staff, and chief of the General Staff. This, coupled with the

U.S. government's rights to veto the decisions of, and to issue "interim directives" for, the Far Eastern Commission, put MacArthur in a position to execute what Washington policy makers decided. On the other hand, as Supreme Commander for the Allied Powers he was not necessarily restrained by Washington. This strengthened his independence. MacArthur's autonomy from the Far Eastern Commission was displayed when SCAP prepared and announced the draft of the new Constitution of Japan even before the commission had gotten fully underway, while the Department of State's inability to open a direct communication channel with the Office of Political Advisors (POLAD), its outlet in Japan, demonstrated his independence from Washington.[45] MacArthur never changed his style, and Truman finally relieved him of command at the time of the Korean War.

MacArthur was a crucial figure in the Occupation and figured importantly in the way the Cold War influenced Occupation policy. To measure that influence, let us turn to the circumstances of the October 1948 decision by the National Security Council (NSC 13/2).

George Kennan, then director of the Policy Planning Staff (PPS) of the State Department, met MacArthur three times while he was in Japan, on March 1, 5, and 21, 1948. These meetings were the basis for the staff's proposal PPS 28/2 prepared on May 26 for the National Security Council. Kennan had already exerted decisive influence on Washington's policy makers in 1946 through his interpretation of the Soviet-American Cold War in Europe, and now, having visited Japan in March 1948, he once more played a leading part in Washington's reexamination of policy, this time centered on Japan and the Occupation in the context of the Cold War in Asia.

The heart of PPS 28/2 was a recommendation to halt the Occupation reforms and purges and end the trials of war criminals so that "the prime objective" could be switched to economic recovery. Projecting ahead to a peace treaty, the proposal also emphasized the necessity of strengthening the Japanese police, securing U.S. military bases in Okinawa, Yokosuka, and elsewhere, and gradually transferring SCAP authority to the Japanese government.[46] This indicated a momentous shift in the very assumptions on which the Occupation had been launched; the initial reform-oriented policy in force since the end of the war would be superseded by a Cold War–oriented policy. MacArthur did not easily consent to the implementation of this policy shift, as the meetings between MacArthur and Kennan in March demonstrate.

MacArthur knew the strategic importance of the American military base in Okinawa, and he also recognized the necessity to expand trade if Japan's economy were to revive. He even supported a peace treaty without a Soviet signature. This was clearly a Cold War thought pattern.[47] But at the same time he opposed Japan's rearmament even after the con-

clusion of a peace treaty, insisting that a nonmilitary Japan be upheld by
international agreement. On that point his position and Kennan's were
very different. If MacArthur's perceptions of Japan's position were so
congruous with the Cold War frame of reference, why did he oppose its
post-treaty rearmament?

MacArthur himself cited five factors to explain his opposition. First,
Japan's rearmament would be directly contrary to solemn American
international commitments in the Occupation; it would alienate Asian
nations which were still mortally fearful of a remilitarized Japan. Second,
and especially noteworthy, Japan's rearmament would be incompatible
with most of the fundamental principles of SCAP. On the basis of these
principles SCAP had eliminated militarism and the armament industries.
MacArthur feared that abandonment of these principles would dangerously weaken the prestige of America in Japan and "would place us in a
ridiculous light before the Japanese people." Third, even if Japan re-
armed, it would still never be able to defend itself. Fourth, rearmament
would put a fatally heavy pressure on Japan's economy. And fifth, the
Japanese people had sincerely and unconditionally renounced war. There
was no chance that they would voluntarily rearm their country.[48] All
these factors—except the second—were also pointed out and discussed
by a number of later analysts.

It is interesting to speculate that probably only one of those factors
was of vital importance to MacArthur himself. His talks with Kennan in
March 1948 concerned Japan *after* the peace treaty, which was expected
to be signed several years thereafter. As will be discussed later, MacArthur conceded to Kennan that the Cold War was intensifying. His own
Cold War mentality made it very unlikely that he would continue to insist
on the validity of the points he made—except the second—if the U.S.
position in the East-West confrontation were to deteriorate seriously.
Four of those factors could change depending on MacArthur's policies
and actions. It is impossible, indeed, to assume that a man with such confidence in his own power believed certain factors to be unchangeable pos-
tulates given the anticipated intensification of the Cold War. However, on
the second factor, which directly related to the immediate postwar
reforms engineered by MacArthur, he had no choice but to be adamant,
for his own reputation was involved. Rearmament would open him, personally, to ridicule by the Japanese people as a reformer with miserable
lack of insight and foresight. Such humiliation would have been intolerable, even if it were to happen several years later. MacArthur had what
amounts to a "politico-psychological vested interest" in the postwar
reforms he initiated and supervised in the early phase of the Occupation.

The differences between MacArthur and Kennan cannot be explained
in terms of MacArthur's World War II thought patterns premised on
U.S.-Soviet cooperation versus Kennan's Cold War thought patterns. As
a matter of fact, when he met Kennan in March 1948, MacArthur

explained himself as follows: When he proposed a peace treaty for Japan the previous year (1947), there was a good chance it would be concluded because "United States-Soviet international differences had not yet been aired publicly," and also because the Russians knew that a peace treaty would mean the dissolution of SCAP—which would work to the advantage of the Japan Communist party. But as of March 1948, said MacArthur, the Soviet Union would obstruct America's Asian policy and was interested primarily in weakening the U.S. leadership in the region; therefore, the Russians would resist signing a peace treaty "which would establish Japan as an economic entity oriented toward the United States."[49] MacArthur was very conscious of the rapid intensification of the Cold War and accordingly he changed his views on, among other things, the peace treaty, which reflected the circumstantial awareness of the Cold War in his thinking.

MacArthur was also notoriously anti-Communist. In his talks with Kennan he justified Occupation policy by saying that "the greatest significance of this occupation lay in the fact that it was bringing to the Japanese people two great appreciations which they had never before possessed and which were destined to revolutionize their thinking, namely democracy and Christianity."[50] MacArthur's awareness of international circumstances and his Cold War thinking pattern were girded by a sense of mission. His politico-psychological "vested interest" in the Occupation and its reforms satisfied this sense of mission. Thus, his opposition to Japan's rearmament and his anti-Communist Cold War thinking were two sides of the same coin.

How much this politico-psychological need influenced his thinking regarding the Occupation comes out even more clearly in his reaction to the NSC 13/2 decision. In preparation for the peace treaty, NSC 13/2 called on SCAP to reduce its control over Japan, cut down its personnel, increase the authority of the Japanese government, and receive an ambassador sent from the State Department. MacArthur vehemently opposed the directive.[51] His recalcitrance in this case had less to do with the gathering storm of the Cold War or with the conditions in Japan than with the simple fact that he could not permit a reduction of the "kingdom" he had built in Japan. That would have meant conceding the heavy politico-psychological vested interest in the Occupation that he himself ran.

On December 1, 1948, the Joint Chiefs of Staff conveyed the NSC 13/2 decision to SCAP. Stubbornly insisting on the preservation of the reforms and Occupation authority, MacArthur replied that he had no intention of implementing the directive.[52] The Department of the Army and the Department of State made every effort to persuade MacArthur, but he would not yield, sometimes threatening to resign. NSC 13/2 remained inoperative until the Korean War broke out and altered the circumstances entirely.

One of the proposals of NSC 13/2 that did not go against or threaten

MacArthur's position was the one concerning economic recovery. Mac-Arthur had no objection to rebuilding Japan's capitalist economy, but he would make no concessions to any proposal that might affect the basic policies of the reforms, including rearmament and strengthening the police. It would be totally inaccurate to attribute that attitude to his rejection of Cold War thinking. But because of his personal stake in the postwar reform, what we have called his "politico-psychological vested interest," because of the authoritative power he had, and also because of his authoritarian character, the transfusion of the Cold War into Japan was delayed. If MacArthur had not resisted Kennan's ideas, Occupation policy would have changed in 1948. As it was, any major change was delayed until the period from 1949 to the outbreak of the Korean War in 1950.

"Indigenization" of Reforms

The involvement of Japan in the international tensions and conflict of the late forties was delayed not because of MacArthur's commitment to the principles of the postwar reforms as they affected Japanese politics and society, but because of his personal stake in Occupation policy. This had two important consequences later.

First, MacArthur's sense of mission symbolized by "democracy and Christianity" was easy to link with the aggressive anti-Communist policy and strategy the U.S. adopted as the Cold War intensified, especially when war broke out in Korea. Further reforms in Japan were sacrificed and, in these circumstances, MacArthur did not feel that his convictions and work were betrayed. During the Korean War he consistently demon-strated a zealous, crusader-like, Cold War thinking, a mindset that impelled his northern advance beyond the 38th parallel, the bombing of Supung Dam between Manchuria and Korea, and his proposal for an attack on the Chinese mainland. His aggressiveness on the Korean front may seem to belie the image of the man who had pushed the Occupation reforms and who opposed Kennan's proposal for Japan's rearmament. But these two apparently conflicting aspects were, in fact, perfectly con-sistent. For MacArthur, the most important value was embodied in an "ideal society" built on "democracy and Christianity" as he saw them, not necessarily on a democracy that could be rooted in Japanese social and political soil. So in 1949–1950 MacArthur was able to accept poli-cies that led to a "reverse course" with anticommunism as their main objective, endangering the achievements of the postwar reforms.

The other consequence of MacArthur's politico-psychological vested interest in the Occupation was that the continuation and rooting of the reforms as they took hold in Japanese politics and society had to be car-ried on not *by* SCAP but *against* SCAP by the popular movements and reformist forces within Japan that had benefited most from the postwar reforms. Ironically, but inevitably, "peace" and "democracy" became the symbols of resistance to a Cold War policy in international relations and to a reverse course in domestic policy. A case in point regarding "peace" was the campaign led by intellectuals pursuing "overall peace" which came to open political controversy after Tokyo University president Nambara Shigeru's statement in the United States in December 1949. The campaign grew into a labor union–led mass movement in mid-1951. "Democracy" was the rallying cry for the movement of students and intellectuals opposing the "Red purge." This became a heated political issue as a result of a speech made in November 1949 by W. C. Eells. As Civil Information and Education Section advisor Eells called for the purge of left-oriented faculty members from Japanese universities. The public, including unionists, was swept up in the movement in the latter half of 1950 just when the depurging of right-wingers and militarists got underway.[53]

Behind these movements lay deep doubts as to whether a policy or system that refused to accept the participation, or even the existence, of Communists was really democratic or even liberal in the *Japanese political and social context*. Underlying the series of protest movements against SCAP at that time was the widespread consciousness that *Japanese* democracy and peace could not possibly be attained without accepting coexistence with Communist forces on both the domestic and international levels.[54]

To appreciate the meaning of these views, one would only have to recall the prewar history of Japan where the repression of Communists was a prelude to the repression of liberals. The latter found themselves totally isolated when they in turn faced the violent assault of right-wingers and militarists. One may also refer to the experience of many Third World nations in the contemporary world where the policy of Western countries supporting reactionary or authoritarian anti-Communist forces has not led to the blossoming of liberal-democracy, but instead to the polarization of society to the detriment of democratic values.

Did these movements have any political effect in the way the Cold War influenced Japan? In Japan's international relations popular movements were almost powerless to prevent the Cold War from spreading to Japan in the sense that an overall peace did not come about. Domestically, however, mass movements did succeed in preventing or restraining the adoption of a Cold War–oriented, reactionary policy. Japan's conservative government, despite its nondemocratic thinking and predisposition, had to take public opinion and popular rights into account. Strong resistance against the "Red purge," widespread opposition to increased pressure on the labor movement, and objections to rearmament were deep-seated, native forces that had to be reckoned with.

It is true that as the Occupation's reverse course surfaced, public opinion was divided and polarized. But any bipolarity in public opinion or in the political lineup was different from the bipolarity that wracked international politics. Bipolarity within Japan was a reflection of the conflict between reactionary elements whose primary concern was anticommunism on one side and, on the other, liberals or democrats in the broad sense who, despite their sharp ideological difference from or even opposition to the Communists, regarded coexistence with the Communists as the touch-stone of liberalism and democracy to be rooted in Japanese soil. A powerful Communist force comparable to the Communist bloc on the international level did not exist in Japan on the domestic level. Nor was there strong popular support for it. Its influence, which was considerable in the very early days of postwar Japan, declined primarily as a result of the successful social reforms undertaken by SCAP. Coexistence with the Communists was not a mere reaction to their impact; it was a process through which democratic ideas and behavior forged themselves into those viable in the Japanese context. When SCAP ceased to function as the proponent of reforms in the late 1940s and to serve as a dam keeping out the Cold War tide from Japan in 1950, Japanese democratic forces originally sponsored by GHQ took over that role. Because they assumed that function, SCAP's achievements during the early phase of the Occupation were not totally eradicated by the waves of the East-West confrontation.

Conclusion

From what has been said, we can formulate three hypothetical propositions.

First, in any treatment of how the international Cold War changed Occupation policy and distorted the reforms one must bear in mind that the phenomenon referred to here as "international Cold War" in fact contained at least five different levels of historical processes and political behavior. The variables of the Cold War were many, ranging from a first level characterized by a high degree of structural constraint to a fourth level that refers to leadership personality, that is, MacArthur, and even to a fifth level of voluntary mass participation and action. When and how the Cold War influenced Occupation policy becomes a very complex issue, chiefly because of the way the question is posed. The question usually comes up without any specification of the different levels of the Cold War concept. Another factor is a lack of sufficient research based on adequate resources that accurately traces the concrete process whereby the Cold War was transfused into Japan. But to carry out this type of research, it is necessary to clearly delineate the levels of the Cold War concept and to clarify the relationships among these levels.

Second, by specifying the different levels of the Cold War and identifying the forces that resisted the Cold War and its influence on Japan, we can pinpoint how and by whom the Occupation reforms were continued after SCAP withdrew from that function. This task assumes tackling the related question of locating areas of continuity or discontinuity in the development of Japanese society as it received the impact of the occupation. Here it is again necessary to specify. To analyze society in terms of the continuity or discontinuity brought about by the Occupation, we must specify the periods under comparison. Whether the comparison is between the prewar and postwar periods or between the early years of the Occupation and the later years must be made clear.[55] In general, the Occupation reforms served as a strong force for discontinuity. Not one of the basic reforms carried out under the Occupation could have been achieved without the best efforts of SCAP. In the case of the land reform, however, scholars sometimes regard it as representing continuity between the prewar and postwar periods, insofar as many elements in the reform had been conceptually prefigured. They argue that landowner-tenant disputes had frequently broken out as early as the 1920s; that, under the controlled wartime economy, farm rents were lowered considerably and, as a consequence, the power of the landlords was devoid of substance by the end of the war.[56] Nonetheless, these scholars tend to underestimate the perhaps disproportionate weight the landowners held in the Japanese power structure. Look at the developing capitalist countries of the postwar era; almost none, except Taiwan, has carried out a smooth agricultural reform. No matter how contradictory to economic rationality, and no matter how obstructive to high productivity, the old, traditional landownership system stubbornly persisted. Only a very powerful force could break that continuity and lay the groundwork for a permanent land reform. The example of the developing countries testifies to the impossibility of Japan's land reform without the force exerted by the Occupation.

Probably more complex and more important is the question of continuity or discontinuity between the reform period and the period following the Occupation's reverse course. Japan's conservative forces experienced sharp discontinuity from the prewar period when they faced the reforms of the early years of the Occupation. Then, however, the discontinuity brought about by the Cold War—the reverse course in Occupation policy—restored to the conservatives considerable continuity from prewar times. What about the reformist forces? They, too, went through some degree of discontinuity from the prewar period in the sense that the great majority of socialists, Communists excluded, found SCAP's reforms more radical than their own position. But they became the chief beneficiaries of the reforms and, when SCAP set out on its reverse course, they found themselves up against SCAP, the U.S. government, and the domestic conservatives in their attempts to maintain continuity in the postwar reforms. Their efforts to inherit and preserve SCAP's legacy of reforms threw them into confrontation with SCAP during which they took the initiative to indigenize the postwar reforms in opposition to SCAP's reverse course. Thus, the reformist forces, which would be expected to have encouraged discontinuity, became the vanguard of supporters of continuity in the very reforms wrought by SCAP and the United States.

This paradox is true not only in postwar Japan. Generally when a certain ideology spreads from early-starting Nation A to late-starting Nation B, the group in Nation B that assumes and inherits Nation A's ideology in more concrete form than any other is often those people who advocate anti–Nation A policies and actions. For instance, the elite of the British colonies who studied in Great Britain and absorbed the British value system often became the vanguard of anti-British movements after returning home. Individuals from Latin American countries who went to the United States and absorbed the North American value system frequently went home to become activists and leaders in anti-U.S. campaigns. There is no end to the list of such cases. The same is true with socialism and socialist countries. Mao Tse-tung, who led the realization of a concrete form of Marxism and Leninism in his country, eventually embraced a vehement anti-Russian position. As in the phrase, "the many roads to socialism," the further the Russian socialist ideology spreads into other nations, and the more indigenized that ideology becomes there, the stronger the demand for independence from Russian influence. As a consequence, tension and even confrontation arises between the Soviet Union and these countries. Examples of this, too, are too many to enumerate.

On the other hand, when the ideology of Nation A, which never went through such a process, is directly imported intact into Nation B, it will probably begin to lose substance as it is transferred to Nation B. It is not necessary to elaborate on how "liberalism" was robbed of its substance by some countries, especially non-Western countries, of the "Free World." Thus, the continuity-discontinuity question in postwar Japan has implications of much wider significance. That the apparently anti-U.S. forces of the reformists became the successors to SCAP's reforms (they were the ones who most adamantly fought to preserve the new Constitution, for example) is a phenomenon not unique to Japan.

That brings us to the third hypothetical proposition: that post-reform Occupation policy and planning were only partially formulated, if at all, in the presurrender and early Occupation stage and that this lack of long-term planning was one reason for the reverse course. To begin with, in making and executing plans for the reforms, what group of Japanese did the American government and SCAP expect to take over and indigenize the reforms?[57] That there was no consensus on that is certain. The conservative liberals represented by Joseph C. Grew and Eugene H. Dooman held the notion that, if those responsible for Japanese militarism and aggressive acts of war were removed, "liberal" elites would reappear in politics and in business. The American conservative liberals definitely did not envisage the "left wing" taking the lead in carrying on the reforms. On the other hand, the so-called New Deal group of liberals expected organized workers and self-employed farmers to play a leading role. The two views did not always conflict, but neither were they ever totally reconciled to each other. In general, however, did the U.S. government and SCAP have certain agents in mind who would and could take over the planning and implementation of reforms? A definite answer eludes us but, from the outset, neither the U.S. government nor SCAP aimed at a long-term occupation of Japan. That being true, how much did they expect to accomplish during a limited period? By whom and in what way did they think the reforms would be carried on, advanced, and indigenized after the Occupation was over?

The authorities had a plan for the Occupation, but did they ever create a viable or even rough post-Occupation plan? If not, it is possible that their planning ended with the completion of all the reforms and objectives of the Occupation per se. A large number of officials, including General MacArthur, seem to have judged that all the necessary reforms had been completed by around 1947.[58] If by that time the authorities concerned had begun to lose their vitality in approaching the task of reforms, and if adequate policy and planning for the postreform period were lacking, that in itself could have been a reason for the stagnation mid-stream in the entire reform program and for the reaction that followed. This casts serious doubt on the validity of the generally accepted assumption that the only factor in the reverse course in Occupation policy was the intensification of the Cold War. The Cold War certainly figured importantly in SCAP's decision to take the reverse course, but other factors must also be taken into account. The reverse course would seem to have been equally, or at least partially, attributable to the lack of postreform policy and planning for the Occupation.[59] Given that possibility the reverse course was likely even if there had been no Cold War.

Notes

1. Hans H. Baerwald, *The Purge of Japanese Leaders under the Occupation* (Berkeley and Los Angeles: University of California Press, 1959), p. 99.

2. "United States Initial Postsurrender Policy for Japan," September 24, 1945.

3. A classic study of militarism is Alfred Vagts, *A History of Militarism* (New York: Meridian Books, 1959), which deals chiefly with the nations of continental Europe. But its emphasis is on the organizational aspects of militarism; it does

not give a historical analysis of the political and economic functions of militarism.

4. For example, see Maruyama Masao, *Thought and Behavior in Modern Japanese Politics* (New York: Oxford University Press, 1963); and Juan J. Linz, "Some Notes Toward a Comparative Study of Fascism in Sociological Historical Perspective," in Walter Laqueur, ed., *Fascism: A Reader's Guide* (Berkeley and Los Angeles: University of California Press, 1976).

5. Similarly, World War I broke out when Germany closed in on Great Britain, the earliest of the category I countries.

6. Table 1 clearly indicates the absence of a category I′, namely, early-starting advanced socialist countries. This accounts for the structural asymmetry that exists between the capitalist world and the socialist world in terms of economic development. The Cold War may be seen as a process through which the USSR, incapable of qualifying for category I′ economically, has desperately attempted to gain a symmetrical relationship with category I countries by military means, particularly in the area of nuclear arms. An intriguing question results. By what means will the USSR be liberalized, given the impossibility for category I countries, particularly the U.S., of resorting to war as they did earlier toward category II countries?

7. This complex nature of the Pacific War explains why it is inappropriate to characterize the International Military Tribunal for the Far East as merely "victors' justice." To ignore Japan's imperialist domination over Asian nations is as misleading as to overlook the interimperialist war that Japan waged. At the height of its military power in the early 1940s, Japan, posing as the liberator of Asian nations, expelled the Western imperial powers from Asia, while in fact it was simply replacing Western imperialism with late-starting Japanese imperialism.

8. With Japanese militarism coming to an end, "militarism" as distinct from the military receded from the main scope of political studies with few exceptions until the late 1960s and 1970s when "militarism," now "transferred" to the Third World, again became a focus of political analysis, as illustrated by the works of Robin Luckham. See his "Militarism," *IDS Bulletin,* vol. 8 (1977), and "Militarism: Force, Class and International Conflict," in Mary Kaldor and Asbjørn Eide, eds., *The World Military Order* (London: Macmillan, 1980).

9. John L. Gaddis, *The United States and the Origins of the Cold War, 1941–1947* (New York: Columbia University Press, 1972), pp. 63ff. and 73.

10. George F. Kennan, "The Sources of Soviet Conduct" (originally published in *Foreign Affairs,* July 1947), in *American Diplomacy, 1900–1950* (Chicago: University of Chicago Press, 1951), pp. 116–117; and "Telegraphic Message from Moscow of February 22, 1946 (excerpts)," in his *Memoirs, 1925–50* (Bantam ed., 1967), p. 595.

11. Thomas B. Inglis, "Soviet Capabilities and Intentions . . . ," memorandum, January 12, 1946, cited in Joyce and Gabriel Kolko, *The Limits of Power* (New York: Harper, 1972), p. 33.

12. Adam B. Ulam, *Expansion and Coexistence* (New York: Praeger, 1968), pp. 404, 438.

13. Isaac Deutscher, *Stalin,* 2d ed. (New York: Oxford University Press, 1963), p. 554.

14. It must also be noted that "any move to reunify Germany was abhorrent to French voters. So every time the British or Americans suggested fresh ideas for nationwide agencies in Germany to operate railways, power grids, and the like, the French Government would invoke its veto to block our plans." Robert Murphy, *Diplomat among Warriors* (London: Collins, 1964), p. 371.

15. Lewis J. Edinger, *Kurt Schumacher—A Study in Personality and Political Behavior* (Stanford: Stanford University Press, 1965), pp. 97–98. Otto Grotewohl and his associates in the Central Committee of the Social Democrats "were encouraged . . . by the great popularity of the resurrected S.P.D. in the Soviet zone. . . . They hoped, it seems, that the S.P.D. would emerge far stronger than the K.P.D., not only in the Soviet zone but throughout Germany, and that therefore its leaders would dominate any united front or merger of the two parties."

16. Gaddis, *The United States and the Cold War,* p. 328. The referendum of the S.P.D. in West Berlin held on March 31, 1946, showed that, although 82% opposed amalgamation with the K.P.D., 62% favored close collaboration. One of the reasons for the strong support for the united front was their reading of the "lessons of the past" that a united working-class movement could have prevented Hitler from coming to power. The weight carried by the S.P.D. in West Berlin can be understood if one remembers that in those days Berlin was considered the center of politics and the capital of Germany. Further, according to the results of elections held from 1946 to 1947 at the level of Land and other local governments in the U.S. and British zones, the S.P.D. obtained over 40% to close to 50% and the K.P.D. over 10% except in Bavaria and some other localities. Edinger, *Kurt Schumacher,* pp. 332–335.

17. *Department of State Bulletin,* XV, September 15, 1946, pp. 496–501; James F. Byrnes, *Speaking Frankly* (New York: Harper, 1947), pp. 188–192. The Stuttgart speech also had significant implications for the German people and the U.S. occupation forces (OMGUS). See John Gimbel, *The American Occupation of Germany* (Stanford: Stanford University Press, 1968), pp. 71–87.

18. Bernhard C. Beckhoefer, *Postwar Negotiation for Arms Control* (Washington, D.C.: Brookings Institute, 1961), p. 41ff.

19. The former views were represented by Stimson's September 1945 memorandum to the president in which he expressed his grave concern about the destructive power of atomic bombs and put forward an agreement with the Soviet Union under the terms of which the Soviet Union would refrain from efforts to develop an atomic bomb while the West would freely make available information on the peaceful application of atomic energy. Another example is the "Oppenheimer plan" in which Oppenheimer proposed that the fissionable materials should be "denatured" by the international authority and then be left in national hands for peaceful uses—the policy he called "security through cooperative development." Gregg Herken, *The Winning Weapon* (New York: Alfred Knopf, 1980), pp. 24–25 and pp. 155–156. The latter views were represented by the Baruch plan.

20. Daniel Yergin, *Shattered Peace* (Boston: Houghton Mifflin, 1977), p. 239.

21. "Even if atomic energy had been entirely devoid of military significance, it still would have been impossible for the Soviets to agree to an international agency prying and probing into their economy, maintaining or sending inspectors into the U.S.S.R., etc." Ulam, *Expansion and Coexistence,* p. 416. It is notewor-

thy that objection to an international authority was raised by Americans, too. For instance, John M. Hancock, Baruch's businessman associate, feared that "the Authority envisioned would be 'the first start to an international socialized State.' " Accordingly, the Baruch plan shifted the responsibility for the mining and refining of fissionable materials back to private industry. Herken, *The Winning Weapon,* p. 164. There was a strange coincidence between the socialist state and the capitalist entrepreneur in their opposition to the intervention of an international authority.

22. In mid-May 1945 James Conant voiced the almost unanimous opinion of those who had built the bomb that the Russians would catch up with the United States in three to five years. General Groves, who was the sole dissenter, claimed that it would take the Soviets up to a generation. Herken, *The Winning Weapon,* pp. 98–99. The President's Air Policy Commission forwarded its (Finletter) report to the government on January 1, 1948, in which the earliest practical date to expect a Russian nuclear attack upon the United States was set for January 1, 1953. Ibid., pp. 243–244. Early in 1949 the Joint Chiefs of Staff turned their attention to the drafting of a plan, code-named Dropshot, for a possible war with the USSR occurring as late as 1957, by which time the Russians would have some atomic bombs. Ibid., pp. 280–284.

23. "Memorandum by Raymond E. Murphy, June 2, 1945," Department of State, *Foreign Relations of the United States, The Conference of Berlin (The Potsdam Conference), 1945,* 1, pp. 267–280. This source hereafter cited as *FRUS.*

24. "Grew to Kennan, July 25, 1945," *FRUS 1945,* 5, pp. 872–873.

25. *The Forrestal Diaries,* ed. W. Millis (New York: Viking, 1951), p. 72 (Diary, June 30, 1945).

26. "Kennan to Byrnes, February 22, 1946," *FRUS 1946,* 6, pp. 696–709. Also, his *Memoirs,* pp. 309–311.

27. Gaddis, *The United States and the Cold War,* pp. 322–323.

28. "More important than the observable nature of external reality, when it comes to the determination of Washington's view of the world, is the subjective state of readiness on the part of Washington officialdom to recognize this or that feature of it." Kennan, *Memoirs,* p. 310.

29. Gaddis, *The United States and the Cold War,* p. 138ff., and pp. 166–167.

30. Ibid., p. 332.

31. William D. Leahy, *I Was There* (New York: Whittlesey House, 1950), p. 318.

32. *FRUS 1945,* 2, pp. 666–668.

33. Herbert Feis, *The China Tangle* (Princeton: Princeton University Press, 1953), pp. 426–427.

34. Harry S. Truman, *Memoirs,* vol. 2 (New York: Doubleday, 1956), pp. 68–72. *Forrestal Diaries,* p. 175. Feis, *The China Tangle,* pp. 420–421.

35. Tang Tsou, *America's Failure in China* (Chicago: University of Chicago Press, 1963), pp. 153–156.

36. Kolko, *The Limits of Power,* p. 264. Lyman P. Van Slyke, ed., *The China White Paper, August 1949* (1967), vol. 1, pp. 357–358.

37. Truman, *Memoirs,* vol. 2, p. 74.

38. Secretary of State Marshall made his comment at a regular press confer-

ence on March 10, 1948, when asked if the United States still favored a coalition government in China with the Communists included; but because of the obscurity of his remarks, he was misinterpreted by the media. On March 11, the Department of State supplemented Marshall's comment by saying that "he [Marshall] replied that this matter [the determination of whether the Communists should be included in the Chinese Government] was for the Chinese to decide, not for the United States Government to dictate." Thus the State Department attempted to coordinate American views on China. However, on the same day, President Truman stated at a press conference: "We did not want any Communists in the Government of China or anywhere else if we could help it." This brought out his anti-Communist attitude even more clearly. Van Slyke, *The China White Paper,* pp. 271–273.

39. "In mid-December 1948 someone in the Pentagon, State Department, or more likely, on MacArthur's staff in Tokyo, apparently leaked the contents of an 'urgent' sixteen-page message from MacArthur to the Joint Chiefs of Staff 'which gave our top men a historic shock.' Reportedly, MacArthur told the JCS 'that the Communist victories in China have gravely jeopardized U.S. security.' MacArthur claimed that 'the Soviet Union will soon be in a position to seize Okinawa and Japan and to sweep the U.S. from the western Pacific.'" Lisle A. Rose, *Roots of Tragedy* (Westport, Conn.: Greenwood Press, 1976), p. 202.

40. It may be noted that "Mao and his comrades were desirous of avoiding the impression that they were turning to the Soviet Union for aid, precisely as they accused the Nationalists of relying on American support. Actually, the Communists seem to have been concerned lest a continued American presence in China should bring about Soviet counteraction, thus causing direct confrontation between the two super-powers on Chinese soil. . . . As the Marshall mission came to an end in January 1947, therefore, the Communists not surprisingly emphasized that chances of war between the United States and the Soviet Union were subsiding." Iriye Akira, *The Cold War in Asia* (Englewood Cliffs, N.J.: Prentice-Hall, 1974), p. 144.

41. *Forrestal Diaries,* p. 341 (Diary, November 7, 1947).

42. Van Slyke, *The China White Paper,* p. 273.

43. D. Clayton James, *The Years of MacArthur* (Boston: Houghton Mifflin, 1975), vol. 2, p. ix.

44. "General MacArthur's Remarks at Lunch, March 1, 1948," *FRUS 1948,* 6, p. 697. MacArthur stated that the only case in world history when a military occupation met with true success, marking a genuinely constructive and durable achievement, was Julius Caesar's military occupation after conquering the barbarian regions.

45. Interview with John K. Emmerson, October 27, 1978. Emmerson also wrote: "MacArthur never held the Department [of State] in high esteem and had accepted a political adviser only reluctantly." Emmerson implied that MacArthur's advice to George Atcheson, the political adviser, not to associate with Prince Konoe in regard to constitutional reform might have an element of bureaucratic politics. John K. Emmerson, *Arms, Yen & Power* (New York: Dunellen, 1971), pp. 42–47. Also, *FRUS 1948,* 6, pp. 322–323. This describes how, prior to the peace treaty, MacArthur vehemently opposed the establishment of a diplomatic mission which would have a communication channel with the

State Department on the grounds that dual channels of command were unnecessary.

46. *FRUS 1948,* 6, pp. 775–781.

47. Ibid., pp. 707–708.

48. Ibid., pp. 708–709.

49. Ibid., p. 707.

50. Ibid., p. 697. MacArthur's emphasis on the importance of Christianity as a pillar of reformed Japan was spelled out by Ray A. Moore in his paper, "Soldier of God: MacArthur's Attempt to Christianize Japan," presented at the Amherst conference on the Occupation of Japan, held in August 1980.

51. "MacArthur to Draper," *FRUS 1948,* 6, pp. 819–823.

52. "SCAP (MacArthur) to Draper (c 66402), December 18, 1948," JCS file. Cited in Hata Ikuhiko, "Amerika no tai-Nichi senryō seisaku" [U.S. Occupation policy in Japan], Financial History Office, Ministry of Finance, ed., *Shōwa zaiseishi* (Tokyo, 1976), p. 406.

53. SCAP's policy against "left-wing" forces came to the fore first in its relations to the labor movement. Following SCAP's order prohibiting a general railway strike scheduled for February 1, 1947, "with increasing frequency, as overly energetic strikers and labor demonstrators clashed with the Japanese police, American military police in jeeps and occasionally even American combat troops with tanks maneuvered conspicuously into supporting positions behind the Japanese police to exercise an overawing effect. In [July] 1948 when General MacArthur personally ordered Prime Minister Hitoshi Ashida to impose severe restrictions on the union activities of employees in government-owned enterprises, the respected chief of SCAP's Labor Division, who had had a distinguished career in the American trade union movement, resigned in protest." Kawai Kazuo, *Japan's American Interlude* (Chicago: University of Chicago Press, 1960), p. 164. The term "democratization of public service" shifted its emphasis from the "reform of traditional, privileged bureaucracy" to the "elimination of Communist-affiliated elements." A large-scale "red-purge" began in 1950.

54. Heiwa Mondai Danwakai (Peace Problems Discussion Circle), consisting of more than fifty leading intellectual figures, developed the most persuasive logic of peaceful coexistence in the context of Japanese democracy. See its statement, "Mitabi heiwa ni tsuite" [On peace, for the third time], *Sekai,* December 1950.

55. Iriye Akira holds the view that the coming of the Cold War did not matter since the United States, throughout the war and postwar periods, consistently pursued the policy of maintaining its dominant position exercising control over Japan and of keeping a "stable, reformist, peaceful Japan" integrated into an international order "defined in liberal terms." Iriye Akira, "Continuities in U.S.-Japanese Relations, 1941–49," in Nagai Yōnosuke and Iriye Akira, eds., *The Origins of the Cold War in Asia* (Tokyo: University of Tokyo Press, 1977), p. 405. It is true that the United States consistently sought to keep Japan within the American sphere of influence. But the crucial question concerns the means adopted to attain that goal. For instance, to ensure Japan's "Western orientation," would the United States focus its efforts on the political elimination of "militarist, ultranationalist elements" or allow reactionary forces to regain influence by concentrating on the elimination of "Communist-affiliated elements"? Would the United States confine Japan's "Western orientation" to economic and political coopera-

tion with the West, or extend it to military collaboration? These are points that obviously have had implications of great importance for the politics and diplomacy of postwar Japan.

56. Continuity between the prewar and postwar periods in this respect was pointed out by Ōuchi Tsutomu and Nakamura Takafusa, within different analytical frameworks. An overview of the debate among Marxist schools of thought on the "continuity-discontinuity" issue is presented in Ōishi Kaichiro, "Sengo kaikaku to nihon shihonshugi no kōzō henka" [Postwar reforms and the structural transformation of Japanese capitalism], Institute of Social Sciences, The University of Tokyo, ed., *Sengo Kaikaku,* vol. 1 (1974), pp. 63–97.

57. In October 1943, Hugh Borton prepared a list of candidates who would lead a reformist, liberal government. He mentioned Matsudaira Tsuneo, Kido Kōichi, Wakatsuki Reijiro, and Konoe Fumimaro. Iriye, "Continuities," p. 382. Of these "moderate and liberal" leaders, Kido and Konoe were included in the list of war criminals at an early stage of the Occupation. One notable difference between Japan and Germany was that in the latter's case there was a sizeable number of refugees in the United States who helped the U.S. Occupation authorities identify the right postwar leaders. Edinger, *Kurt Schumacher,* p. 95n.

58. Interview with Frank Rizzo, April 27, 1976. Even as early as May 1946, General MacArthur wrote that "the sweeping measures which the United States of necessity alone has taken . . . in the occupation of Japan have been largely accomplished." Iriye, *Cold War,* p. 399. He then said on March 21, 1947, that "it is my considered view that the Japanese nation and people are now ready for the initiation of negotiations leading to a Treaty of Peace—ready in the sense that Japan's war-making power and potential is destroyed, the framework to democratic government has been erected, reforms essential to the reshaping of Japanese lives and institutions to conform to democratic ideals have been instituted, and the people have been accorded the fundamentals of human liberty." *FRUS 1947,* 6, pp. 454–455.

59. The United States, taking into consideration the stern policy of the West toward defeated Germany in the post–World War I period which had proved counterproductive, generally adopted a milder occupation policy vis-à-vis the former Axis nations. Accordingly, it was not very likely that a "reverse course" based on anti-American "revanchist" feelings would emerge among the Japanese people in general against the reform measures taken by SCAP. On the contrary, one of the achievements of the Occupation was the creation of a large number of "beneficiaries" of initial reforms among the populace. But precisely because the initial reform measures brought about drastic changes to Japan's political regime giving birth to new constituents, it was natural that the "victims of reforms," particularly the purged militarists and ultranationalists, should stage a "reverse course" sooner or later.

3

"Induced Revolution":
The Policy and Process
of Constitutional Reform
in Occupied Japan

Theodore H. McNelly

General MacArthur said that the enactment of the postwar Japanese constitution was "probably the single most important accomplishment of the occupation."[1] Many students of the Occupation concur in this evaluation of Japan's new basic law, which prescribes the system of democratic government and guarantees the basic liberties enjoyed by Japanese today. The fundamental reform of the constitution was described by one Occupation official as an "induced revolution."[2]

During the war the U.S. State Department officials who formulated policy on the surrender and postwar occupation of Japan determined that its governmental system needed to be drastically reformed to end the dominance of the military and to protect political liberties. They disagreed bitterly, however, on what to do with the emperor system and about the extent of social and economic reform required. Decisions on specific reforms and the manner of their implementation were deferred until after the Allied forces actually set foot in Tokyo.

In its first formal offer to surrender, the Japanese government indicated its willingness to accept the provisions of the Potsdam Declaration with the understanding that the prerogatives of the emperor as sovereign ruler would not be prejudiced. The Allied reply did not accept this proviso, but indicated that the emperor and government of Japan would be subject to the orders of the Allied Supreme Commander, who would enforce the surrender terms, and that "the ultimate form of government" would be "established by the freely expressed will of the Japanese people." When Japan surrendered three days later, the emperor, in a recorded statement broadcast to the Japanese people, said that in ending the war, the government had preserved the "structure of the Imperial State *(kokutai),*" which implied that the sovereign status of the emperor had not been impaired. This imperial statement may have represented wishful thinking and was probably intended to calm the military, who might not have laid down their arms without such an assurance.

The timely surrender helped save the monarchy. If the land war had been carried to the main islands of Japan, the emperor's usefulness in saving lives by ordering a surrender would have ended, although he would still have been useful as a means of controlling a defeated Japan. After the surrender, the Allies applied the system of indirect rule in Japan, preserving the Imperial Japanese Government, which enforced directives it received from the Supreme Commander for the Allied Powers (SCAP). If it had been found that indirect rule was not working satisfactorily, SCAP could have abandoned it in favor of direct military government. But indirect rule made it possible in effect to carry out Occupation reforms in the name of the emperor, thus greatly facilitating the Allied administration.

The most controversial substantive issue in Japanese constitutional reform was the question of the future of the monarchy. The continuing utility of the emperor to SCAP as a means of controlling Japan meant that his abdication or trial as a war criminal and/or the abolition of the monarchy, widely advocated in the Allied countries, would have to be foregone or at least delayed.

Initial Efforts

Officials in the Japanese cabinet's Bureau of Legislation were mindful that fulfillment of the Potsdam terms might require some changes in the imperial constitution, and after the surrender ceremony they began a discreet preliminary study of what amendments might be necessary.[3] The surrender was not regarded as contractual by the Allies, who reserved to themselves the right to interpret the nature and scope of Japan's unconditional surrender, and who believed that they had full authority to order Japan to carry out specific reforms. On October 4, 1945, General MacArthur suggested to Prince Konoe Fumimarō, vice premier of the Higashikuni cabinet, that he take the lead in democratizing the Japanese constitution.[4] In a subsequent conference, MacArthur's political advisor, George C. Atcheson, Jr., informally suggested to Konoe those points in the constitution needing revision, most notably the need to strengthen the authority of the Diet. Konoe obtained a commission from the emperor to investigate, within the Office of the Lord Privy Seal, the matter of constitutional revision.

On October 11, 1945, General MacArthur suggested to the new prime minister, Shidehara Kijurō, that the accomplishment of needed political and social reforms would "unquestionably involve a liberalization of the Constitution." Shidehara, however, publicly asserted that the constitution did not need amending. Like most Japanese moderates he believed that the militarists had "abused" the imperial constitution. All that was now required to achieve democracy was the proper interpretation and application of the existing constitution; political reform could be achieved by the enactment of appropriate legislation.

Strong public criticism both in Japan and abroad of Konoe's involvement with constitutional reform was grounded in his alleged responsibility for causing the war. At the same time, Matsumoto Jōji, minister of state without portfolio, publicly asserted that constitutional revision was a matter of state to be handled by the cabinet rather than by the Office of the Lord Privy Seal. Matsumoto was appointed by the prime minister to head an informal committee of experts to make recommendations to the cabinet on possible constitutional revision. On November 1, 1945, after a number of conferences between Konoe and his staff and representatives of SCAP's political advisor, General MacArthur's headquarters denied that the general had asked Konoe to revise the constitution. MacArthur's repudiation of the Konoe effort seems to have been in part an aspect of the general's effort to eliminate any direct involvement in Japanese internal politics by the State Department, represented in Tokyo by the Office of the Political Advisor.[5] Nevertheless, American newspaper criticism of his choice of Konoe appears to have been MacArthur's primary consideration. Although deeply offended by the SCAP statement, Konoe and his principal collaborator, Professor Sasaki Sōichi, separately reported their findings and recommendations to the emperor on November 22 and 24.

Nothing concrete seems to have resulted from the Konoe and Sasaki recommendations, but the attendant publicity provoked public discussion of constitutional reform and may have stimulated Washington planners to clarify their policies on constitutional amendment.[6] On January 1, 1946, the emperor publicly renounced the traditional notion of his divinity. This famous New Year's rescript facilitated the rehabilitation of the throne and its current incumbent, both of which MacArthur and the more influential State Department planners wished to preserve. Also, the rescript weakened the principle of divine right asserted in Article 1 of the imperial constitution. From December 1945 through February 1946, political parties, private groups, and individuals published proposals for constitutional reform. The drafts of the governing Liberal and Progressive parties stressed emphatically their support of the "national structure." The Communists were the only political party to advocate a republican system of government.

The SCAP Initiative

In Washington the interdepartmental State-War-Navy Coordinating Committee adopted its "Reform of the Japanese Governmental System" (SWNCC-228) on January 7, 1946.[7] This secret document, about which more will be said later, was transmitted to SCAP headquarters, where no immediate action was taken on it. In mid-January 1946 the members of the Far Eastern Advisory Commission (FEAC, predecessor of the Far Eastern Commission, which represented the principal Allied powers) visited Tokyo. MacArthur had protested the decision made at the Moscow conference of foreign ministers in December 1945 to set up the Far Eastern Commission to make policy for the Occupation of Japan. The FEAC representatives expressed great interest in the reform of the Japanese constitution. On January 30 MacArthur told them that this matter had been taken out of his hands by the Moscow agreement establishing the Far Eastern Commission and that SCAP headquarters "was not then working on it."[8] The interest of the FEAC may have stimulated SCAP headquarters to concern itself further with constitutional revision.

On February 1, 1946, the *Mainichi Shinbun* published a draft constitution produced by the Matsumoto committee. Staff members of SCAP's Government Section (GS), comparing its provisions with SWNCC-228, found that it fell far short of SWNCC requirements. Also, on the same day General Courtney Whitney, chief of SCAP's Government Section, forcefully indicated to General MacArthur the need and legality of prompt action by SCAP on revising the constitution before the newly organized Far Eastern Commission could remove the matter from MacArthur's authority.

On February 4 General Whitney called a meeting of Government Section personnel and said that MacArthur had entrusted them with drafting a new Japanese constitution. The Supreme Commander had directed that three major points be incorporated in the draft: (1) the emperor is at the head of the state, (2) war as a sovereign right is abolished and is renounced by Japan "even for preserving its own security. No army, navy, or air force is authorized," and (3) the feudal system is abolished, and the rights of peerage, except those of the emperor's family, would not extend beyond the lives of those now holding them. Finally, the budget would be patterned after the British system.[9] It is the "guess" of Charles L. Kades, Whitney's chief aide, that the "MacArthur Notes," on which the constitution was to be based, had been dictated by MacArthur to Whitney.[10] But it seems possible that the ideas had originated with Whitney, who then obtained MacArthur's assent to them. In later years, MacArthur repeatedly stated that the no-war, no-arms provision had originally been suggested to him by Prime Minister Shidehara on January 24, 1946, but some scholars question the general's accuracy on this point.

While a student at Harvard, Charles Kades had been deeply impressed with the Kellogg-Briand pact renouncing war. He was also impressed by the reference in the emperor's January 1, 1946, rescript to Japan's "being thoroughly pacific." In January, as General Whitney and Colonel Kades were driving to a meeting with Prime Minister Shidehara to discuss the purge, Kades "blurted out" to General Whitney, "Do you think that the Emperor could issue an imperial rescript renouncing war, which might also help remake the Japanese international image and help carry out the Potsdam declaration?"

At the close of the Shidehara-Whitney-Kades meeting, Whitney "said casually that some consideration might be given to a rescript renouncing war." Thus, Shidehara's reported suggestion to MacArthur that the Japanese constitution renounce war may have stemmed indirectly from Kades's initiative.[11] In any event, it is clear that key figures in Tokyo were thinking along very similar lines. The General Treaty for the Renunciation of War (Kellogg-Briand pact), which Japan had repeatedly violated, represented a potential problem for the emperor's defenders, as it might be cited in an indictment of the emperor as a war criminal. The treaty's language, however, might be used to embellish a new constitution that would preserve the monarchy.

It seems unlikely that the specific provisions of SWNCC-228 directly inspired the MacArthur Notes since the SWNCC paper stressed the importance of civilian control over the military rather than perpetual disarmament and the importance of responsible government and a more powerful legislature and cabinet that would take over powers hitherto included in the emperor's prerogatives. The MacArthur Notes did not even mention the Diet and the cabinet. With respect to the emperor, SWNCC-228 had stated as a basic policy that "the Japanese should be encouraged *to abolish* the Emperor Institution *or to reform* it along more democratic lines" (emphasis added). According to Hugh Borton, the principal author of SWNCC-228, however, paragraph 4d3 of the paper "clearly implies" an expectation that the imperial institution would continue.[12] MacArthur's first point gave the Japanese no choice in the matter, but dictated the preservation of the throne. It seems doubtful that, even had he wanted to, MacArthur at any time had the personal authority to encourage the Japanese to abolish the emperor system, suggested as an option in SWNCC-228, since he had been previously directed not to "take any steps toward his [the emperor's] removal" without first consulting the Joint Chiefs of Staff and "to take no action against the Emperor as a war criminal pending receipt of a special directive concerning his treatment."[13]

Because the status of the emperor was the topic of Point One of the MacArthur Notes, it would appear that the preservation of the imperial throne was uppermost in his mind in regard to constitutional revision. Only a week and a half earlier (on January 25), MacArthur had cabled Washington urging against trying the emperor as a war criminal and warning that to do so would probably require the maintenance in Japan of a minimum of a million troops "for an indefinite number of years."[14]

Very possibly because of SCAP's attitude, on or shortly before February 5, 1946, the United States ambassador to the United Kingdom, John G. Winant, discussed the matter of the war criminal lists with Prime Minister Attlee and obtained his agreement that "no action ought to be taken by War Crimes Commission that might result in *publicity on the possibility* of the Emperor being charged as a war criminal" (emphasis added).[15]

MacArthur's Point One, which also referred to the "powers" of the emperor, did not call for the explicit statement of the principle that sovereignty resided with the people. As before, the monarchy would continue to be based on the hereditary principle. Point One alone might not have been enough to save the throne from the clamor in some Allied circles for its abolition. But Point Two, the renunciation of war and arms, might reinforce Point One. The main argument for abolishing the emperor system was that it might again be used to support militarism and aggression. A radical disarmament provision of this sort largely negated that argument.

For the purpose of drafting a model Japanese constitution, the Public Administration Division of Government Section was divided into eight subject-matter committees, each concerned with one chapter of the constitution, and a steering committee that gave final approval to the drafts prepared by the other committees. In civilian life General Whitney and all three members of the steering committee had been lawyers. Other constitution drafters included a former university professor specializing in Chinese legal history, a sociologist with prewar teaching experience in Japan, a former congressman, two specialists in public administration, and three women, including one who had lived for ten years in Japan and was fluent in Japanese. Several of the drafters had formally studied the Japanese language, and they were assisted by a fairly competent team of translators. Colonel Charles L. Kades, a New Deal lawyer well briefed in Occupation policies before going to Japan, was chairman of the steering committee. The Americans were much influenced by a draft constitution recently proposed by a group of prominent Japanese liberals, which enunciated the principles that sovereignty resided with the people and that the emperor's functions were purely ceremonial.[16] Using the MacArthur Notes as the basis and SWNCC-228 as one of their references, the twenty-one Americans wrote the constitution within a week. MacArthur personally approved it with one change on February 11: deletion of a provision prohibiting amendments to the constitution that would impair or alter the bill of rights.

Although neither SWNCC-228 nor the MacArthur Notes prescribed an explicit statement of the principle of popular sovereignty, the authors of the draft constitution believed that the Potsdam Declaration required it. The declaration had demanded that there be "established in accordance with the freely expressed will of the Japanese people a peacefully inclined and responsible government." GS officers believed that "this means that sovereignty is to rest with the people."[17]

The SCAP draft constitution provided that "the emperor shall be the symbol of the State and of the Unity of the People, deriving his position from the sovereign will of the people, and from no other source. He shall have no governmental powers." Again, "war as a sovereign right of the nation is abolished. . . . No army, navy, air force, or other war potential will be authorized." The document protected the rights of the accused in criminal trials, guaranteed basic civil liberties, enumerated certain social and economic rights (including social security), and banned discrimination on the basis of "race, creed, sex, social status, caste, or national origin." The Diet would be "the highest organ of state power." The legislature would be unicameral, but the drafters felt that this issue could be used as a "bargaining lever" with the Japanese to be compromised if necessary to obtain some more important principle.[18]

On February 13, 1946, General Whitney, accompanied by three members of his staff, personally delivered fifteen mimeographed English-language copies of the draft to Foreign Minister Yoshida Shigeru and Minister of State Matsumoto. Whitney said that the Matsumoto draft was wholly unacceptable whereas the document he proposed "represents the principles which the Supreme Commander and the Allied Powers are willing to accept as a basis for the government of Japan because the principles enunciated in this document provide a basis for free democratic government in Japan and for carrying out the terms of the Potsdam Declaration."[19] The Americans stressed the need to adopt the SCAP draft constitution in order to save the emperor from trial as a war criminal. This statement was interpreted by Matsumoto as a threat,[20] but it was probably intended as friendly advice.[21] Whitney also suggested that if the cabinet did not sponsor SCAP's draft constitution, MacArthur would present it directly to the people, who were already dissatisfied with the published version of the Matsumoto draft. The cabinet had a reactionary reputation and, to save itself, it had best adopt this draft constitution, Whitney stressed. The Japanese had expected the Government Section officials to discuss the Matsumoto draft and appeared flabbergasted by the boldness of the Americans in presenting this model constitution.

It seems possible that some of the unpleasantness of the February 13 meeting might have been averted if during the preceding months SCAP headquarters had played a more active role in counseling the Shidehara government about the Allied criteria for constitutional reform, which had been fairly well understood in GHQ ever since Secretary of State Byrnes' message to SCAP's political advisor on October 16, 1945. The Japanese might then have formulated an acceptable draft and a confrontation could have been averted.[22]

Japanese Response

Matsumoto reported on the meeting to the prime minister and made a renewed effort to persuade GHQ to approve his committee's draft. The prime minister conferred with General MacArthur, and Matsumoto met with GS officers to work out a compromise. The only major concession made to the Japanese was an agreement to a bicameral legislature (the members of both houses being democratically chosen) rather than a unicameral body as called for in the SCAP draft. On February 22, following a meeting of the cabinet, Prime Minister Shidehara had an audience with the emperor, in which the premier (according to the best Japanese sources) evidently reported on the recent negotiations with GHQ and the cabinet's decision to formulate a constitution embodying the principles of the SCAP draft.[23]

Japanese officials hastily prepared a document based on the outline and text of that draft but substantially modified in details. The new Japanese draft provided for a bicameral legislature. The provision in the SCAP document that "the ultimate fee to the land and to all natural resources reposes in the state" was thought by Matsumoto to provide for communism and was eliminated. On March 4 at 10:00 A.M., Matsumoto and four other Japanese officials brought to Government Section their adaptation in Japanese of the Government Section draft. A bitter argument over the text developed between Matsumoto and GS officers, and the former departed at 2:30 P.M., leaving the other Japanese at Government Section headquarters. After 6:00 P.M. the Americans announced that the definitive draft would have to be agreed upon that night. Informed of this, Matsumoto told the Japanese already there, including Satō Tatsuo, of the Bureau of Legislation, to work on the draft. At about 8:30 P.M. an article by article discussion of the document began, lasting overnight until about 1:00 P.M. on March 5. Throughout the day, batches of final text were sent to the cabinet for its study.

The Americans insisted on retaining unchanged the democratic preamble of the SCAP draft, which the Japanese had hoped to eliminate as inconsistent with the emperor's legal role in initiating constitutional amendments. Except for the provision for a bicameral legislature in the Japanese draft, which the Americans accepted, there were no substantive differences between the original SCAP draft and the document finally agreed upon.[24] GHQ forwarded ten copies of the final English version to the Shidehara cabinet and asked whether they would accept it before the day was over. The cabinet members believed that if they did not accept the draft, GHQ would publish it anyway. In that case, the newspapers would probably approve it and the cabinet would have to resign in favor of a leftist government that would support the document. In an emotionally charged meeting, the cabinet decided that it had no choice but to accept the text before it.

Article 73 of the Meiji Constitution required that in amending the constitution the emperor assume "the initiative right" and that the amendment project be submitted to the Diet by "imperial order." If it was the intent of SCAP and the Japanese government to follow legal procedure in amending the constitution, the emperor's formal participation was essential. On March 6 the government published the Japanese version of the proposed basic law as an "outline" together with an imperial rescript dated March 5. The rescript referred to the acceptance of the Potsdam Declaration, which had provided that the ultimate form of government be decided by the people, and commanded the government to undertake the revision of the constitution.

Also on March 6, MacArthur announced his satisfaction with the "decision of the Emperor and Government of Japan to submit to the Japanese people a new and enlightened constitution which has my full approval." The emperor had successfully ordered the surrender of the Japanese military and naval forces in August, he had renounced his divinity in January, and in March he became an official sponsor of the democratic constitution written in MacArthur's headquarters. MacArthur had publicly praised the emperor's actions in January and March. It was now most unlikely that the monarchy, thoroughly reformed in the draft constitution based on SWNCC guidelines and approved by SCAP, would be abolished.

MacArthur's Civil Censorship Detachment forbade any references in the Japanese press to the fact that the proposed constitution had been written by Occupation officials.[25]

Shortly after the publication of the outline constitution on March 6, representatives of the People's National Language Movement League proposed to the government that the draft constitution be written in colloquial style *(kōgotai)* rather than the archaic literary style *(bungotai)* hitherto used in Japanese laws and the imperial constitution. The suggestion was well received by the cabinet, and as a result the postwar constitution, the laws implementing it, and all subsequent legislation have been written in the colloquial style. A principal advantage of *kōgotai* is that it is readily understood by people of average education. In addition, the government thought that the *kōgotai* text would have less of the odor of translation widely noted in the first published Japanese version of the draft.

Procedural Problems

The Japanese government's publication of its draft constitution took completely by surprise the delegates to the Far Eastern Commission, which had just begun its meetings in Washington. During their visit to Tokyo in January MacArthur had told them that his headquarters was not working on constitutional reform, and they were bitter that they had purposely been kept ignorant of SCAP activities. Even the United States government had not been informed of Government Section's activities. When the draft constitution was published in Tokyo, no copies of it were immediately available in Washington.[26]

On March 20, 1946, the Far Eastern Commission suggested to SCAP that the general election (scheduled for April 10) be postponed to give more time for liberal elements to organize and to give more consideration to the issue of constitutional amendment. MacArthur replied that the purge had already removed reactionaries from consideration and that all of the political parties except the Communist "overwhelmingly favor the proposed constitution, which represents the work of men from many different groups and many different affiliations." The election was held as planned. Also on March 20, the FEC indicated its apprehension that MacArthur's approval of the government's March 6 draft might preclude consideration of other proposals for constitutional revision. The commission wanted SCAP to make clear to the Japanese government that the FEC must be give an opportunity to pass on the final draft of the constitution before the Diet voted on it in order to determine whether it was consistent with the Potsdam Declaration and any other controlling documents.

The cabinet formally presented its proposed constitutional amendment to the privy council on April 17, as required by the imperial ordinance on the organization of that body. Prime Minister Shidehara told the councillors that the new constitution would establish the throne on a more solid basis. The president of the council, Suzuki Kantarō, who had been prime minister at the time of the decision to surrender, said that the national structure had been preserved in the surrender and that the proposed constitution would also preserve the national structure. Privy Councillor Minobe Tatsukichi, the famous liberal interpreter of the imperial constitution and advisor to the defunct Matsumoto committee, raised the fundamental issue of the government's procedure for constitutional amendment. According to Minobe, Japan's acceptance of the Potsdam provision that the ultimate form of government be determined by the freely expressed will of the people had rendered invalid Article 73 of the imperial constitution, which assigned the initiative for constitutional revision to the emperor. At the same time, the preamble of the draft constitution stated that the people establish the constitution. Because Article 73 was invalid, he said, the appropriate procedure for the enactment of a democratic constitution would be to convoke a representative assembly that would draft a constitution and submit it to a popular referendum.

In reply, the president of the Bureau of Legislation expressed doubts that Article 73 had been invalidated by the acceptance of the Potsdam Declaration and said that free deliberation in the Diet, which represented the people, was one of various ways in which the people's will could be freely expressed.[27] Actually, in the light of the radical nature of the draft constitution, the Shidehara cabinet had already considered the possibility of first amending Article 73 of the imperial constitution and later submitting the proposed constitution to a constituent assembly or a constituent Diet. On March 12, 1946, the cabinet decided that this idea was too idealistic.[28] If it took too long to amend the constitution, unpredictable changes might occur internationally, and it was deemed necessary to move as rapidly as possible. In this matter the cabinet obtained the concurrence of GHQ.

The privy councillors dealt at length with points in the draft that made them unhappy, such as the unclear locus of sovereignty, the problem of defending a permanently demilitarized Japan, the nationalization of imperial household property, and confusion about the composition of the House of Councillors. The hope was that further changes by the government and suitable implementing legislation might alleviate some of the numerous shortcomings of the draft. The new prime minister, Yoshida Shigeru, emphasized Japan's obligations under the terms of the Potsdam Declaration to remove obstacles to democracy and to establish a government inclined toward peace as prerequisites for the withdrawal of the occupying forces.

The emperor and his brother Prince Mikasa were present at the June 8, 1946, meeting of the Privy Council, at which the council's investigating committee presented its report recommending approval of the government's Constitutional Revision Bill. Prince Mikasa pointed out that if the emperor was removed from political affairs, as provided in the proposal, he would naturally tend to social work: "Unless the people come to revere the Imperial House not only religiously as they used to do but also materially, *even the Emperor system may become a subject of discussion,* and if the Imperial Household expenditure is reduced his intention for social work may become difficult to realize" (emphasis added). The prince also expressed unhappiness that according to the proposed constitution the new Imperial House Law would be determined by the Diet independently of the imperial family, which had a strong desire to participate in revising the law. He urged that the present session of the Diet limit itself to revising Article 73 of the imperial constitution and leave the work of making the new constitution to the next session. Refusing either to oppose or approve the government's Constitutional Revision Bill, the prince chose to abstain from voting and withdrew from the meeting. When the vote was taken on the Constitutional Revision Bill, "a large number stood up," but Minobe Tatsukichi did not. The president ruled that the bill had been passed by a majority. The record does not indicate that the emperor said anything at the meeting.[29]

In the meantime, the political left in Japan organized mass demonstrations on May Day and Food May Day (May 19, 1946). Some foreign journalists and Far East experts favored a violent revolution in Japan in which the "people" themselves would thoroughly destroy the militarists, monopolists, and reactionary monarchy. The basic postsurrender directive to SCAP (November 1, 1945) had stated that changes in the government to make it less feudal and authoritarian were to be permitted and favored: "In the event that the effectuation of such changes involves the use of force by the Japanese people or government against persons opposed thereto, you as Supreme Commander should intervene only where necessary to ensure the security of your forces and the attainment of all other objectives of the occupation."

After the Food May Day demonstration, MacArthur issued a statement cautioning the Japanese people that "the growing tendency to mass violence and physical processes of intimidation, under organized leadership, present a grave menace to the future development of Japan . . . the physical violence which undisciplined elements are now beginning to practice will not be permitted to continue."

Clearly, MacArthur would not permit basic political reform in Japan to be carried out by a revolution; constitutional change would have to be brought about peacefully and legally. Thus, as General Whitney has stressed, the constitution was reformed without resort to bloodshed.[30]

Policies of the Far Eastern Commission

Some members of the Far Eastern Commission doubted that the draft constitution expressed the free will of the Japanese people and feared that it would be pushed through the Diet without sufficient deliberation. On April 10 the FEC asked SCAP whether the Japanese were seriously considering alternative constitutional drafts and various democratic procedures for the enactment of a new constitution—including a constitutional convention or a plebiscite. They also asked that MacArthur dispatch a member of his staff to inform them of the plans of the Japanese government and SCAP and to relay FEC views on the constitution to SCAP. MacArthur's reply, received six weeks later, was that he could not send an officer because he was giving his personal attention to the constitution, no officer was in a position to express in detail his views, and the release of an officer would effect an impairment of his command. Both the U.S. delay in relaying the message and MacArthur's attitude offended the FEC.[31]

On May 13 the FEC adopted its "Criteria for the Adoption of a New Constitution," which called for (1) adequate time for full discussion, (2) "complete legal continuity" from the 1889 constitution to the new constitution, and (3) the adoption of the new constitution "in such a manner as to demonstrate that it affirmatively expresses the free will of the Japanese people." This policy statement was designed in part to aid the American effort to avert a FEC veto of the MacArthur draft constitution. Widely supported proposals in the FEC that the proposed constitution be deliberated on by a new Diet to be elected later or by a constituent assembly and then be submitted to a popular referendum were successfully resisted by the United States representative.

Legal continuity was necessary to prevent subsequent invalidation of the constitution. This would seem to imply adherence to the amendment procedure prescribed in the Meiji Constitution, which required, among other things, the emperor's formal initiative. Thus, the FEC apparently wanted to preserve the throne, at least for the time being, to facilitate the democratization of Japan. Indeed, on April 3, 1946, the FEC adopted a policy on the trial of war criminals in the Far East (FEC 007/3) with the understanding that the directive to MacArthur be "so worded as to exempt the Japanese Emperor from indictment as a war criminal without direct authorization."[32] As Whitney had told the Japanese on February 13, "the acceptance of the provisions of this new Constitution would render the Emperor practically unassailable."[33] At the time of the Japanese government's submission of the draft constitution to the Diet on June 21, General MacArthur issued a public statement closely paraphrasing the procedural criteria established by the FEC but not mentioning the commission or the possibility of a referendum. MacArthur pointed out that constitutional revision had already been publicly discussed for more than eight months and specified that Article 73 of the Meiji Constitution would be complied with, thus assuring legal continuity.

Japanese legal scholars differed as to whether under Article 73 the Diet had the power to do more than either pass or reject a constitutional revision bill presented to it by the emperor. SCAP and the Japanese government held that deletions, changes, and additions could be made by the Diet. Such a procedure would seem necessary in view of the Allied policy that a new constitution reflect the freely expressed will of the people. Government Section took the view that the substantive scope of the Emperor's authority to initiate constitutional amendments was unlimited: "He is not bound to retain the fundamental principles of Japanese government, usually referred to as the national polity," because the Meiji Constitution contained no such limitation and because "the acceptance of the Potsdam Declaration has altered the national polity."

The emperor's direct role in the implementation of the provisions of the Potsdam proclamation by formally initiating constitutional change was made clear in his message *(chokusho)* of June 20, 1946, in which he submitted to the Diet the imperial project for the amendment of the constitution. The imperial message referred to the elimination of obstacles to democratic tendencies and the revision of the constitution by the freely expressed will of the people. It was understood that any proposed changes in the draft required the concurrence of SCAP headquarters, and the necessary clearances were requested and often obtained by government officials and Diet members. The assumption at the beginning of the parliamentary session was that the Diet would not reject the draft constitution because the governing parties had a majority and that the Socialists would support the suprisingly progressive document.

Throughout the Diet deliberations, Prime Minister Yoshida repeatedly made it clear that the early enactment of the new democratic constitution would fulfill a basic precondition for the withdrawal of the Occupation forces, that is, the establishment of a democratic form of government as provided in paragraph 12 of the Potsdam Declaration. It also was evident that to delay or defeat a draft that had MacArthur's approval and was presumably acceptable to the Allied powers might prolong or aggravate the Occupation.

At the outset of the debate in the House of Representatives on the Constitutional Revision Bill, which began late in June 1946, a Communist member urged that the deliberations be postponed because there had been no participation by the people in the preparation of the text presented to the Diet. The Communists and some Socialists advocated that a constitutional convention be held for the purpose of formulating a draft. This view, however, rapidly lost support because of the feeling that the international situation required expeditious action and that the content of the bill was in basic respects as progressive as the Socialists' own draft constitution. The five Communists in the House of Representatives remained opposed to the draft and advocated a constitution that would establish a Japanese People's Republic.

On June 28 the draft was referred to a special committee of seventy-two members representing all political parties. On July 23 the bill was sent to a fourteen-man subcommittee representing all parties except the small Communist party. Deliberating until August 20, the subcommittee kept its proceedings secret and often, when references to SCAP demands were made, stenographic note-taking was suspended. In the subcommittee it was possible to iron out discrepancies between the Japanese and English versions of the constitution, to make interparty agreements on a set of revisions to be recommended, and to incorporate changes asked for by SCAP. SCAP requests were not made directly to the Diet but through the government, and were never conveyed in writing.[34] To ensure the necessary two-thirds majority vote in favor of the bill, the government parties found it expedient to concur with some of the opposition's proposals.

Popular Sovereignty and the National Polity

On July 2, 1946, the Far Eastern Commission adopted its "Basic Principles for a New Constitution," which was based on SWNCC-228. Although the general tenor of the FEC document resembled that of the SWNCC paper, it contained one significant difference: FEC policy called for recognition in the constitution that "sovereign power resides in the people." On July 10 Government Section officers drafted a four-page memorandum, finding that "in every respect, the English translation

Government Draft of the Japanese Constitution conforms to the Basic Principles of the Far Eastern Commission." Although no specific provision of the draft constitution required that the ministers of state be civilians as prescribed by the FEC, "inasmuch as article 9 denounces [*sic*] the right of waging war and forbids the maintenance of land, sea, and air forces, as well as other war potential, the existence of any Japanese military officers of any character is prohibited under the Constitution."[35]

The FEC originally intended to publish its July 2 policy statement, but out of deference to MacArthur's strong opposition to this plan did not do so. MacArthur asserted that its publication at that time "would tend to provoke a revulsion of the Japanese people against any such reform, irrespective of its terms, as *the voluntary character of the work now in progress would instantly become clothed with the taint of Allied force*" (emphasis added).[36] In light of MacArthur's strong views on the importance of keeping SCAP and FEC influence on the constitution secret, it seems astonishing that in 1949, when the constitution was scarcely three years old and the Occupation was still in force, Government Section published virtually the whole story—amply documented—in its *Political Reorientation of Japan.* Commander A. Rodman Hussey, the author of the account of the constitution in that compilation, was himself very much surprised that General Whitney permitted its publication.[37]

The governing Liberal and Progressive parties were committed, along with the Yoshida coalition cabinet, to the support of the proposed constitution, but their members had been elected on platforms emphatically advocating the preservation of the national polity, which was generally understood to mean that the emperor ruled by divine right. Kanamori Tokujirō, the cabinet minister then in charge of constitutional revision, stressed to the Diet that the draft constitution would not alter the national polity, but would preserve it. On the other hand, the Socialists in the political opposition pressed for clarification of the principles that sovereignty would reside in the people and that the reactionary national polity would be changed. They were mollified by Kanamori's statements that sovereignty would reside in the nation, which included the emperor.

At meetings with Kanamori on July 17 and 23, Colonel Kades complained that Kanamori's statements that the draft constitution would not alter the national structure were undermining the determined efforts of MacArthur to preserve the emperor and the throne. If the Japanese did not make the necessary corrections in the ambiguous Japanese text and in their interpretations of this text, there would not be any essential difference between the present draft and the reactionary Matsumoto document. MacArthur was "not almighty"; he had to defend the new constitution to the Allied powers, who were extremely critical of the emperor and the throne, and the Japanese were making it very difficult for MacArthur to do this. According to Kades, popular sovereignty in the new constitution would mean that, if they wished, the Japanese could at some time in the future amend it so as to abolish the emperor system.[38] Kanamori prepared for Kades a memorandum clarifying his views, which, he explained, had been distorted by newspaper headlines. The national polity—in the sense that the emperor was legally sovereign— *would* change. The national polity as Kanamori understood it, however, did not mean that the emperor was a legal or political figure; he was a moral figure, the center of national "adoration" *(akogare)*. *Kokutai* in this sense would remain unaltered by the new constitution. The *political* structure *(seitai)* would change in that sovereignty would rest with the people.[39] Thus, Kanamori's unusual, but not completely original, definition of *kokutai* permitted him to reassure the conservatives that the *kokutai* would not change in spite of any shift in the location of sovereignty.

Both Government Section and the Yoshida cabinet were seriously embarrassed by a widely noted discrepancy between the published English and Japanese versions of the draft constitution.[40] The English text of the preamble stated that the Japanese people "proclaim the sovereignty of the people's will," whereas the Japanese version avoided the usual equivalents for sovereignty and stated *"kokumin no sōi ga shikō na mono de aru koto o sengen shi,"* which has the much vaguer meaning of "declare that the general will of the people is supreme." Likewise, Article 1 in English stated that the emperor derives "his position from the sovereign will of the people," but in Japanese the words *shikō no sōi* (supreme general will) were used.

While the Constitutional Revision Bill was being debated in the subcommittee, the conservatives suddenly gave up their efforts to enhance the emperor's authority and instead proposed amendments that would clarify the principle of popular sovereignty. In both the preamble and Article 1, the Japanese text was altered from *shikō no sōi* to *shuken* to render the English "sovereignty." Thus, Article 1 in the Japanese much more unequivocally meant "the Emperor shall be the symbol of the State and the unity of the people, deriving his position from the will of the people with whom resides sovereign power." The conservatives reversed their view on this issue at the insistence of SCAP headquarters, which was under pressure from the press and the FEC, both of which called for a clear statement of popular sovereignty. It should, however, be noted that *kokumin* was not changed to *jinmin* for "people." *Kokumin* refers to the Japanese people and carries a very strong connotation of "nation." Thus, the constitution could be interpreted to mean that sovereignty resides in the Japanese *nation*.[41]

Another concern of GS officers was the possible implication in the Japanese version of Article 4 that the emperor had substantive powers that could be delegated by law. This, it was feared, might permit the establishment of an imperial affairs ministry that would enjoy a special status in the cabinet and would be able to exercise a powerful veto power over other organs of government. At the request of GS, the text was amended to specify that the emperor would have no powers related to government.

The subcommittee adopted amendments proposed by the Socialists that provided for the people's right to "minimum standards of whole-some and cultured living," the "right and obligation to work," and the fixing by law of standards for working conditions. Also adopted was the Socialist proposal that "peerage shall not be recognized." This went beyond the milder original text, which would have prevented future creation of peers and the inheritance of existing titles and would have deprived peers of governmental authority. This immediate abolition came as a pleasant surprise to SCAP officers, who had not been pressing for it.

The Socialists advocated that the principle of popular sovereignty be clearly stated in a separate chapter preceding the chapter on the emperor, that the provision on the inviolability of private property be modified to permit socialist take-over without compensation, and that the emperor's functions be further limited. These proposals were defeated successively in the subcommittee, in the special committee, and, finally, in the plenary session of the House of Representatives.

The subcommittee adopted a provision insisted upon by the FEC and relayed to the Japanese by SCAP that provided that a majority of the ministers of state had to be appointed from among the members of the Diet. (At the same time a provision in the original bill that the appointment of the individual cabinet members required Diet approval was deleted.)

The subcommittee also made changes (the "Ashida amendments")— generally regarded at the time as of a minor nature—in the provisions renouncing war and arms. These changes in Article 9 attracted little attention in Japan at the time, but they became the object of very bitter controversy after the Occupation ended.

The final version of Article 9 (with the Ashida amendments shown in italics) reads as follows:

> *Aspiring sincerely to an international peace based on justice and order,* the Japanese people forever renounce war as a sovereign right of the nation and the threat or use of force as means of settling international disputes.
>
> *In order to accomplish the aim of the preceding paragraph,* land, sea, and air forces, as well as other war potential will never be maintained. The right of belligerency of the state will not be recognized.

Paragraph 1 of Article 9 as amended may be interpreted to mean that war and the threat or use of force are renounced only *as a means of settling international disputes.* War and force might therefore be permissible for self-defense. The phrase at the beginning of paragraph 2, "in order to accomplish the aim of the preceding paragraph," could be interpreted as qualifying the renunciation of land, sea, and air forces. Thus, although armaments for settling international disputes are banned, armaments for other purposes, such as self-defense, are not renounced.[42] When Ashida Hitoshi brought this amendment to Colonel Kades for approval (all proposed amendments had to be cleared with GHQ), Kades made no objection. Kades interpreted the proposed modification in language as intended to clarify the sincerity of the Japanese commitment to peace and believed that any flexibility implied in the text would permit Japanese participation in a United Nations force. When Ashida pointed out the importance of his amendments and asked if they should not be approved by MacArthur, Kades said no. He was under orders to permit changes that did not involve basic principles.[43] Dr. Cyrus Peake, another Government Section officer, pointed out to General Whitney that these textual modifications would permit Japan to maintain defense forces. Whitney concurred in this interpretation and agreed that this change in the text was "acceptable."[44]

The Nationalization of Imperial Properties

As originally written, Article 88 provided that all property of the Imperial Household, other than the hereditary estates, would belong to the state and that the income from the estates would be paid into the national treasury. The allowances for the expenses of the Imperial Household would be appropriated by the Diet in the annual budget. These provisions conformed with SWNCC-228. In the House of Representatives subcommittee the conservatives strongly advocated deleting the provision that income from imperial estates be paid to the national treasury. They believed that the revenue from the estates should go to the imperial family to assure the economic security of the dynasty. The Socialists, on the other hand, defended the measure as it stood, claiming that the Diet appropriations for the imperial family should prove adequate. The subcommittee, however, responding to strong SCAP pressure to bring this provision of the constitution into conformity with the FEC policy of July 2, 1946, eliminated the phrase that exempted hereditary estates from being taken over by the state and deleted the reference to income from the hereditary estates: all property of the Imperial Household would belong to the state. The government made it clear, however, that the individual members of the imperial family could own personal effects and that the palaces and appurtenances used by the emperor in his capacity as symbol of the state would continue to be at his disposal.

The speaker of the House of Representatives, Higai Senzō, and several other leading conservatives tried to prevent the subcommittee from adopting this change concerning the imperial properties by appealing to Prime Minister Yoshida. Before the House of Representatives began deliberation on the special committee's report, the Socialists introduced a no-confidence resolution against Higai. Although the resolution was defeated, within a few days he had to resign in the face of a possible Socialist boycott of further proceedings.

The special committee approved the amendments recommended by the subcommittee but no other proposed amendments. On August 24 the House of Representatives passed by a vote of 421 to 8 the Constitutional Revision Bill with the amendments recommended by the special commit- tee together with a supplementary resolution, or rider, which had origi- nated in the subcommittee. The four-paragraph rider expressed the mem- bers' dissatisfaction with aspects of the procedure and substance of the constitutional reform. It pointed out that even the outlines of the new Imperial House Law, the House of Councillors Law, and the Cabinet Law, among others, were not yet clear, making it impossible to deliberate thoroughly on the constitution. Social and economic reform was inade- quately provided for in the new constitution. The members hoped that the composition of the House of Councillors, left unclear in the draft constitution, would not merely duplicate the House of Representatives, but would include persons of knowledge and experience from each spe- cialty and occupation as members.[45] The supplementary resolution may have represented more accurately than the constitution itself the real thinking of the Japanese legislators.

The Constitutional Revision Bill was now sent to the House of Peers for its decision. This aristocratic body had been decimated by the purge. Moreover, a number of eminent constitutional scholars had been ap- pointed to membership to bring their expertise to bear on the delibera- tions. The views presented in the Peers' debates were thus those of the individual speakers rather than those of political parties. The Peers' inter- pellations, which reflected a high level of theoretical sophistication, focused especially on the status of the emperor in the proposed constitu- tion.

The Civilian Ministers Clause

The Chinese delegate to the Far Eastern Commission was outraged by the changes in the disarmament clause made in the House of Representa- tives. In an FEC meeting on September 21 he asserted that Article 9, as now altered, was a trick by the Japanese militarists to deceive the world into thinking that Japan was absolutely renouncing military forces when actually they planned to rearm the country using the loopholes created by the textual changes in the constitution.[46] If Japan was permitted to rearm under the new constitution, it was essential that civilian control over the military be established. A provision that all cabinet ministers had to be civilians, although called for by SWNCC-228, had not been included in the SCAP draft constitution—evidently because Article 9 seemed to mean that Japan would not possess a military establishment. Prime Minister Yoshida had objected to the requirement that ministers of state be civilians (as embodied in the July 2 FEC policy statement previously cited and passed on to the Japanese by SCAP officers), holding that it was unsuitable because there would be no military men in Japan in the future as the result of Article 9. Sympathizing with Yoshida's view, General MacArthur had agreed not to require the insertion of such a provision.[47] On September 25 the FEC passed another policy reiterating its requirements of July 2 that all cabinet members be civilians and that the proposed House of Councillors not have dominance over the House of Representatives.

By this time the Constitutional Revision Bill was being debated in the House of Peers. In response to the FEC's repeated insistence on the principle that all ministers of state be civilians, General Whitney and Colonel Kades asked Prime Minister Yoshida to see to the insertion of this provision in the draft constitution. GHQ officers admitted that although they had previously agreed with the Japanese that such a provision was not necessary in the light of Article 9, SCAP could not counter the FEC's insistence.

No Japanese word corresponded precisely with the English "civilian." The cabinet's Legislative Bureau, speculating that the provision was designed to perpetuate the purge, suggested the expression "persons without records as military officers." Subcommittee members rejected this phrase as too restrictive, as it would ban from the cabinet even civilians who had once studied in a military academy. The subcommittee regarded the civilian-ministers requirement as essentially meaningless since all Japanese would be civilians as a result of Article 9. In order to meet but not go beyond the FEC requirement it was necessary to devise a Japanese word signifying "civilian," no more and no less. After considerable discussion the subcommittee agreed upon a word that they coined as the closest approximation to "civilian": *bummin* (lit., literary person).[48]

Notwithstanding the Ashida amendments and the civilian-ministers amendment, Prime Minister Yoshida and his government maintained their interpretation that Article 9 forbade even defensive war and arms. It would have been disastrous for the image of Japan as a new convert to peace to announce that the proposed new "peace constitution" had been amended to permit rearmament. On October 6, 1946, the amended Constitutional Revision Bill was passed by a standing vote in the House of Peers with only three or four members opposed.[49] The bill as amended by the Peers was passed without debate by the lower house on October 7, and the Privy Council approved the amended bill on October 29. The

constitution was promulgated in the form of an amendment of the imperial constitution on November 3, 1946 (the anniversary of the birth of
the Meiji emperor) to become effective on May 3, 1947.

Immediately after the emperor had sanctioned the text of the edict of
promulgation that had been prepared by the cabinet, Colonel Kades
requested that the edict include the following: "As from the date of the
enforcement of the Constitution on May 3, 1947, the Imperial Constitution together with the Edict of Promulgation should be abrogated." The
Japanese government believed that the Meiji Constitution had not been
abolished, but rather had been amended. All along, GHQ had stressed
the legal continuity between the two constitutions. Besides, the purport
of Kades's text was already implied in the body of the new constitution.
In the face of Japanese objections, Kades withdrew his proposal.[50]

Review by the FEC

Throughout the summer of 1946 some members of the Far Eastern Commission—especially representatives of the Soviet Union and New Zea-
land—had been demanding that the FEC have the opportunity to vote on
the text of the draft constitution before its final approval by the Diet.
MacArthur strongly opposed this procedure not only because the substance of the draft already conformed to Allied policy but also because
this procedure would constitute a flagrant foreign intervention into a
process that the Allies had already decided should reflect the freely
expressed will of the Japanese people.[51] The War Department successfully upheld MacArthur's position in this matter.[52]

It was essential that the Soviet Union not be given an opportunity to
veto the proposed constitution. The United States, supported by a majority of the members, was able to "get on the right side of the veto," that is,
prevent a formal vote on a policy approving the constitution, which
would invite a Soviet veto.[53] Consequently, the commission never formally voted for or against the new constitution either before or after its
enactment. As we have noted, however, the FEC had successfully insisted
on certain amendments to the text before it was finally voted on in the
House of Peers.

On October 17, 1946, the FEC adopted a policy calling for review of
the new constitution *after* its enactment and enforcement. Not sooner
than one year and not later than two years after the constitution went
into effect, "the situation with respect to the new Constitution should be
reviewed by the Diet," and furthermore, the commission itself would
review the constitution within this period. In addition, the FEC might
require a referendum or some other procedure to ascertain Japanese
opinion concerning the new basic law. At the request of the American

representative, the FEC approved the review policy with the understanding that the "time and manner of issuance" of the decision would be subject for further consideration by the commission.

MacArthur indicated to the FEC his view that, in light of the constitutional provision for its amendment and of the continuing authority of the Allied powers, the purposes of the review policy were unclear. Besides, the publication of the review policy "would be instantly viewed in the public mind as a display of force by the Allied powers." On December 12 the FEC nevertheless directed that the terms of the review policy "be formally communicated to the Government of Japan" and indicated that "the time and manner of the public announcement of this policy decision" were still being considered by the commission.[54] General MacArthur then wrote a very informal letter to Prime Minister Yoshida on January 3, 1947, conveying to him the substance of the FEC policy, referring simply to the "Allied powers," without mentioning the commission by name.

On March 20, 1947, the FEC made public the text of its review policy. Four days later, however, SCAP Government Section asked the Civil Censorship Detachment of MacArthur's G-2 to "withhold from press or radio publication in Japan all reports that the Japanese constitution is to be reviewed by the Far Eastern Commission or by the Japanese people in compliance with a FEC directive."[55] General MacArthur, in his message to the Japanese people of May 3, 1948, commemorating the first anniversary of the enforcement of the new constitution, made no reference to a review of it by the Diet, by the Far Eastern Commission, or by the people in a plebiscite. During the review period (May 3, 1948, to May 3, 1949) Prime Minister Ashida Hitoshi and the speakers of the two houses of the Diet considered naming a Diet committee to deliberate on the possible revision of the constitution. After discussing the problem with political leaders, they decided against attempts to revise the new document, as such an effort in the first few years of its existence could undermine the constitution's prestige in the minds of the public.[56]

The FEC formally began its review on December 9, 1948, with less than six months left of the specified review period. The American attitude was that the FEC should "as inconspicuously as possible and with a minimum of debate review promptly the Constitution," and that the FEC should determine that the constitution met all FEC requirements and needed no further investigation or action, such as a referendum.[57] MacArthur completely agreed with this American position. The new constitution, the general informed the FEC in January 1949, was "now universally accepted as an indigenous product," and there was, he said, "no slightest question but that the Japanese people with practical unanimity would vote to preserve the document unaltered were the matter referred for popular action." He recommended that the Allies not force upon the Japanese people "a review of their constitution with the view to its modification."⁵⁸

Although the FEC transmitted to MacArthur the opinions of various members regarding possible specific amendments to the constitution, it did not extend the review period or enact a new policy on review. It is essentially correct to say that, following the publication of the FEC's review policy on March 20, 1947, "no later action based on this policy was taken . . . either by the Commission or by the Diet."⁵⁹

MacArthur had moved rapidly on constitutional reform in early February 1946 to avoid interference by the FEC. The adoption of the new constitution, MacArthur wrote, "would never have been accomplished had the occupation been dependent on the deliberation of the Far Eastern Commission—with the Soviet power of veto!"⁶⁰

The New Constitution in Theory and Practice

The new constitution invalidated the provisions of many of Japan's existing laws and necessitated a substantial overhaul of the legal codes. Government Section's *Political Reorientation of Japan* includes forty-five laws that were hastily enacted to implement the new constitution. Among them are the new Imperial House Law, the Diet Law, the Cabinet Law, the Civil Service Law, electoral laws, the Impeachment of Judges Law, the Police Law, the Law Abolishing the Home Ministry, the Law on the People's Examination of Supreme Court Judges, the Habeas Corpus Act, the Labor Standards Law, laws amending the Code of Civil Procedure and the Code of Criminal Procedure, and an amended Civil Code. All of these laws either were already being debated or had already been passed by the Diet before the FEC had an opportunity to examine them, and FEC influence was consequently nonexistent.

The fundamental principles of the new constitution usually cited by Japanese writers are (1) popular sovereignty, (2) pacifism, and (3) the guarantee of fundamental human rights. Chapter III, the "bill of rights," is notable for its very detailed provisions for the protection of the accused in criminal trials. It also includes a few rather general statements of social and economic rights and forbids virtually all forms of discrimination. The new basic law prescribes a parliamentary-cabinet form of democratic government similar to that of England and explicitly provides for judicial review of the constitutionality of legislation as in the United States.

The constitution stipulates that, if the lower house votes no confidence in the government, within ten days the cabinet must either resign or the lower house must be dissolved (Article 69). The text does not make absolutely clear, however, whether or not the emperor may dissolve the lower house on the cabinet's advice (Article 7) without the cabinet's first being defeated in a vote of confidence. During the Occupation, SCAP authorities insisted that such a vote be arranged in 1948 when the Yoshida cabinet wanted a dissolution. In 1952, after the end of the Occupation, the Yoshida cabinet brought about dissolution without such a vote and an appeal by a Diet member to invalidate the dissolution was rejected by the Supreme Court as not justiciable. Thus, the new constitution does not protect the Diet, "the highest organ of state power," from arbitrary dissolution by the cabinet, which—as in other parliamentary democracies—can time the dissolution in the light of political considerations.

Since 1950 the most hotly debated provision of the constitution has been Article 9 on the renunciation of war and arms. Although Premier Yoshida stated, as the draft constitution was being debated, that Article 9 banned armament even for defense, the government has since asserted that defensive armament is permissible. The Self-Defense Forces, now consisting of some 250,000 men, have since their inception been attacked by the Socialists as unconstitutional; and the laws creating them were finally declared unconstitutional by a district court in 1973. This suit, the Naganuma Nike case, was appealed to the Sapporo High Court, and the lower court ruling was quashed on the ground that the original plaintiffs lacked status to sue. The high court also stated in an *obiter dictum* that the matter of the constitutionality of the Self-Defense Forces was a political question not susceptible to judicial review. The case is currently under consideration by the Supreme Court.

In recent years the majority of the public has supported the existence of the Self-Defense Forces (partly because of their usefulness in times of natural disasters) at the same time that it has opposed amending Article 9. If the Supreme Court rules definitively that Article 9 bans the Self-Defense Forces, a very unlikely possibility, the public would have to choose between either abolishing the SDF or amending the constitution. The already bitter political confrontation between the right and left would intensify. The controversy over the meaning of Article 9 is the most explosive question of constitutional interpretation and raises the most serious doubts as to the practicality of a central feature of the new constitution.

After the Occupation ended in 1952, the conservatives began to advocate constitutional amendments to raise the status of the emperor and clarify the legality of defensive forces. In 1956 the Diet created the Commission on the Constitution to investigate the enactment, operation, and possible amendment of the basic law. The Socialist party boycotted the commission, asserting that its creation violated the constitutional procedure for constitutional amendment and that the conservative majority (Liberal Democratic) of the members had already made up their minds to recommend constitutional revision.

When the commission finished its massive investigation in 1964, the majority held that the constitution had been imposed on Japan by the Occupation and that basic amendments should be made. By this time, however, conservative strength among the voters and in the Diet had substantially declined, and the Liberal Democrats did not have the two-thirds majorities in the houses of the Diet and the simple majority among the voters needed to amend the constitution. No proposals for amendment were, therefore, introduced.

Conclusion

It was the judgment of the Allied powers and of the Japanese government, under SCAP prodding, immediately after the war that a completely new or drastically amended constitution was necessary to accomplish the objectives set forth at Potsdam—removing obstacles to democracy and establishing a government inclined toward peace. Constitutional reform in postwar Japan was thus largely the product of both presurrender and postsurrender planning. The text of the new constitution was originally drafted in Tokyo by MacArthur's staff using guidelines from Washington as a reference, and the Allied powers were able to insist on minor modifications. The substance of the new constitution, except for Article 9 and a number of economic and social provisions, was essentially the product of American planning. The procedure used by SCAP headquarters, however, in bringing about the sponsorship of the draft by the Japanese cabinet and its passage by the Diet fell short of what officials in the State Department and the Allied countries believed was desirable. Although MacArthur's headquarters insisted that the end product resulted from the freely expressed will of the Japanese people, the view became widespread that the new constitution was "imposed on Japan."

MacArthur followed the American policies of maintaining American dominance in the Allied Occupation, of indirect control of Japan through the imperial Japanese government, and of preserving the monarchy in order to carry out the surrender and to democratize the country. In executing these policies, MacArthur's staff assumed dynamic leadership in urging the Japanese cabinet to sponsor a democratic constitution drafted in GHQ before the Far Eastern Commission could intervene. Washington on the whole tolerated and even defended in the FEC MacArthur's initiatives because they conformed essentially with American policies.

What if MacArthur had not taken the initiative in February 1946 and waited for a policy statement on constitutional reform from the FEC? Conceivably the FEC, if able to agree on a policy, might have involved itself publicly in supervising or reviewing the drafting of a constitution in the Diet or a constituent assembly. The text might then have been submitted to a popular referendum. The constitution emerging from such a process would likely have been somewhat similar to the one actually adopted. It seems doubtful that the document could have avoided the stigma of alien imposition any better than the MacArthur constitution did. In view of Soviet opposition to the monarchy and the Soviet power of veto, however, it seems quite possible that the FEC would have been unable to agree on a definite policy. The Meiji Constitution and other institutions might then have been reformed only on a piecemeal basis in response to a series of interim policies from SWNCC and the FEC and guidance from SCAP in the face of continuous resistance by conservative Japanese governments and Allied criticism. If MacArthur had not taken the initiative, the achievement of basic Potsdam objectives would probably have been considerably delayed, and it seems doubtful that these objectives would have been as effectively accomplished. I do not, of course, mean to imply that the constitution adopted does not bear the onus of appearing to be imposed, but this was probably the best that could have been done under the circumstances.

Even if MacArthur had used other procedures, the presence of Allied forces in Japan would necessarily have raised doubts about whether or not the Japanese were freely expressing their will. There is no evidence to suggest that in the absence of an Allied Occupation force the Japanese on their own initiative would have reformed their constitution. The presumption would seem to be that the new constitution was indeed imposed. On the other hand, progressives in Japan supported the SCAP draft from the beginning and, after the Occupation ended in 1952, the Japanese chose not to amend a single word of their constitution, although they were perfectly free to do so and there was much agitation among conservatives to modify the document. No doubt the preservation of the new basic law owes much to the constitution-protection movement launched by Japanese progressives in the late 1950s and 1960s.

Two principal themes emerge when one considers the matter of historical continuity in postwar constitutional reform: the perpetuation of the monarchy and the strengthening of existent democratic tendencies.

It is generally known that a principal concern of Prime Minister Shidehara was the preservation of the incumbent emperor and the monarchy and that the cabinet's acceptance of the MacArthur draft constitution was largely motivated by a desire to save the imperial institution. The ancient throne was saved by both the procedure and the substance of postwar constitutional reform. The Allied policy that constitutional amendment follow legal procedures, that is, the procedures required by the imperial constitution, made the emperor an indispensable participant in the process. During the spring and summer of 1946, while the purges and war crimes trials were just getting under way, the emperor assumed formal leadership in the democratization of Japan. His Imperial Majesty's trial as a war criminal in such a situation would have been incongruous to say the least, and the question of his war guilt had become virtually a dead issue by the time the Tokyo war crimes trial opened on May 3, 1946, with the emperor conspicuously absent from the dock.

The two essential provisions of the draft constitution, MacArthur told Shidehara on February 21, 1946, were the symbolic position of the emperor and the renunciation of war and arms. A principal objection to the emperor system among the Allies was that the throne had been used to justify militarism and aggression. By banning war and arms, the draft constitution would remove this objection to the perpetuation of the monarchy. Under the new constitution the emperor would no longer exercise military prerogatives; rather he would be the symbol of a pacifist state. On the basis of the logic of the situation and statements made by some of the formulators of the new constitution, I incline to the view that a principal purpose of Article 9 was the preservation of the monarchy.[61]

The view that the ancient monarchy should be abolished was held by some, as was the view that the emperor should have been more respected in the new constitution. The position of the emperor under the new constitution seems to me to accord adequately both with the practice of democracy and the centuries-old Japanese monarchical tradition in which the emperor was normally a powerless monarch who fostered political stability while legitimizing change.

Democracy had roots in Japan before the reforms effected under Occupation leadership or direction. The Japanese parliament, established in 1889, is the oldest national legislature in Asia. In the 1920s political parties, whose leaders served as prime ministers, began to assert a dominant voice in Japanese politics, and a parliamentary-cabinet system of democracy, patterned after the British model, seemed in course of establishment. Japanese democracy, however, was not firmly enough established to survive a major economic depression. The eclipse of political parties and of the Diet by the military in the 1930s was facilitated by ambiguities and defects in the imperial constitution. These shortcomings of the old basic law were corrected by the enactment of the postwar constitution.

After the Occupation ended, sweeping changes occurred in Japan's economy and society. Whereas before the war the majority of Japanese were farmers and villagers, today most of the people live in cities and are employed in industry and services. Most Japanese today believe that they belong to the middle class, a class regarded by political scientists since Aristotle's time as an essential stabilizing force in democratic societies. To a measure undreamed of by SCAP reformers, Japan has become a prosperous welfare state governed by bureaucrats. Conservative political parties have ruled without interruption since 1949. The issues of concern today are the administration of affluence rather than the management of poverty. The monarchy, an exotic anachronism in today's democratic and scientific age, seems vastly less relevant than it did in 1946, and its continued eclipse in Japan seems likely. Japan's postwar democratic constitution, despite earlier predictions that it would not outlast the Occupation, is now one-third of a century old. It remains to be seen how usefully it serves the Japanese people in the postindustrial era, but it has done well so far.

Notes

The writer is deeply indebted to the late Dr. Cyrus Peake and Messrs. Hugh Borton, John K. Emmerson, Osborne Hauge, Inumaru Hideo, Charles L. Kades, Satō Isao, and Justin Williams for their very generous assistance.

1. Douglas MacArthur, *Reminiscences* (Greenwich, Conn.: Fawcett, 1964), p. 436.

2. SCAP, Government Section, *Political Reorientation of Japan,* 2 vols. (Washington, D.C.: GPO, n.d. [1949?]), 2, pp. 622–666. The researcher should consult these volumes for sources quoted or mentioned but not documented in this chapter.

3. Satō Tatsuo, *Nihonkoku kenpō seiritsu shi* [Establishment of the Japanese constitution] (Tokyo: Yūhikaku, 1962), 1, pp. 162–168.

4. On the Konoe effort, see ibid., pp. 177–244. Also, Theodore McNelly, "Domestic and International Influences on Constitutional Revision in Japan, 1945–46" (Ph.D. diss., Columbia University, 1952), pp. 22–61; and Theodore McNelly, "Civil-Military Relations in Tokyo, August-December, 1945: The Konoe-Atcheson-MacArthur Triangle and the Japanese Constitution," in *Proceedings of the Fourth International Symposium on Asian Studies* (Hong Kong: Asian Research Service, 1982).

5. Interview with Mr. John K. Emmerson, January 4, 1969. Mr. Emmerson was a member of the Political Advisor's staff in 1945–1946.

6. Minutes of the Subcommittee for the Far East, State-War-Navy Coordinating Committee, October 23, 1945, Microfilm T1198, National Archives.

7. Text in Theodore McNelly, ed., *Sources in Modern East Asian History and Politics* (New York: Appleton-Century-Crofts, 1967), pp. 177–187.

8. *Foreign Relations of the United States, 1946,* 8, pp. 124–125. Hereafter *FRUS.*

9. Takayanagi Kenzō, Ohtomo Ichiro, and Tanaka Hideo, eds., *Nihonkoku kenpō seitei no keika* [Development of the Japanese constitution], 2 vols. (Tokyo: Yūhikaku, 1972), 1, pp. 100–107.

10. Letter from Kades to McNelly, March 3, 1977.

11. Theodore McNelly, "General Douglas MacArthur and the Constitutional Disarmament of Japan," *Transactions of the Asiatic Society of Japan* Third Series, vol. 17 (October 1982), pp. 1–33; and Charles L. Kades, "Discussion of Professor McNelly's Paper . . . ," in the same issue, pp. 35–52.

12. In a telephone conversation with me, June 20, 1978.

13. *FRUS, 1945,* 6, pp. 926–936.

14. *FRUS, 1946,* 8, pp. 395–397.

15. *FRUS, 1946,* 8, p. 401.

16. Theodore McNelly, "The Role of Monarchy in the Political Moderniza-tion of Japan," *Comparative Politics,* vol. 1, no. 3 (April 1969), pp. 366–381.

17. Takayanagi, Ohtomo, and Tanaka, *Nihonkoku kenpō,* 1, p. 82.

18. Ibid., pp. 120–122.

19. Ibid., pp. 320–336; *Gendai tennōsei* [The contemporary imperial system] (Tokyo: Nihon Hyōronsha, 1977), p. 135.

20. Robert E. Ward, "The Origins of the Japanese Constitution," *American Political Science Review,* vol. 50, no. 4 (December 1956), pp. 980–1006.

21. Letter from General Courtney Whitney to Takayanagi Kenzō, December 18, 1958 (author's files).

22. *FRUS, 1945,* 6, pp. 757–758 and 882–884.

23. Takayanagi, Ohtomo, and Tanaka, *Nihonkoku kenpō,* 1, pp. 390–392; 2, pp. 96–97; and Irie Toshio, *Kenpō seiritsu no kei-i to kenpōjō no shomondai* [The making of the constitution and some constitutional problems] (Tokyo: Irie Toshio Zenshū Kenkōkai, 1976), p. 203.

24. For a detailed summary of the negotiations, see Satō Tatsuo, "Nihonkoku kenpō" [The constitution of Japan], serialized in *Jurisuto,* 1, July 15, and August 8, 12, 1955.

25. Robert M. Spaulding, quoted in *The Occupation of Japan: Impact of Legal Reform* (Norfolk, Va.: The MacArthur Memorial, n.d.), p. 58; and Eto Jun, "The Constraints of the 1946 Constitution," *Japan Echo,* vol. 8, no. 1 (1981), pp. 44–59.

26. Hugh Borton, *Japan's Modern Century* (New York: Ronald Press, 1955), p. 424.

27. "Proceedings of the Examination Committee of the Privy Council on Revi-sion Bill of Imperial Constitution" (in English). Government Section, SCAP, Record Group (RG) 331, Washington National Records Center (Suitland, Md.). Hereafter WNRC.

28. Irie, *Nihonkoku kenpō,* p. 311.

29. Record of the Privy Council (in English). Government Section, SCAP, RG 331, WNRC.

30. Courtney Whitney, *MacArthur: His Rendezvous with History* (New York: Knopf, 1956), p. 257.

31. George Hubbard Blakeslee, *The Far Eastern Commission: A Study in International Cooperation: 1945–52* (Washington, D.C.: GPO, 1953), pp. 51–53.

32. *FRUS, 1946,* 8, p. 428.

33. Takayanagi, Ohtomo, and Tanaka, *Nihonkoku kenpō,* 1, p. 328.

34. Satō Tatsuo, *Kenpō tanjōki* [The birth of the constitution] (Tokyo: Okurasho Insatsukyoku, 1957), p. 156; the proceedings of the subcommittee in English are available in RG 331, WNRC.

35. Kenneth Colegrove, T. A. Bisson, Frank E. Hays, Cyrus H. Peake, "Memorandum for the Record: FEC Basic Principles for the New Japanese Con-stitution" (W-93298), File Constitution, Government Section, SCAP, RG 331, WNRC.

36. *FRUS, 1946,* 8, pp. 266–267.

37. Hussey told me this on November 30, 1961.

38. *Gendai tennōsei,* pp. 139–142.

39. Satō Tatsuo, *Jurisuto,* January 15, 1957, pp. 38–39.

40. Cyrus Peake et al., "Memorandum for the Chief, Government Section, 11 July 1946." File Constitution, Government Section, SCAP, RG 331, WNRC.

41. Genji Okubo, *The Problems of the Emperor System in Postwar Japan* (Tokyo: Nihon Taiheiyō Mondai Chōsakai, 1948), p. 52.

42. Ashida Hitoshi, "Japan, Communists' Temptation," *Contemporary Japan,* vol. 20, nos. 1–3 (January-March 1951), pp. 15–24.

43. Interview with Charles L. Kades in Omori Minoru, *Sengo hishi* [Secret history of postwar times] (Tokyo: Kodansha, 1975), 5, p. 246. Also *Sandē Mainichi,* 15 (June 1976), pp. 60–64; Satō Tatsuo, *Kenpō tanjōki,* p. 136.

44. Cyrus H. Peake, "Reflections on the Occupation of Japan and the Drafting of the New Constitution," in Laurence G. Thompson, ed., *Studia Asiatica: Essays in Asian Studies in Felicitation of the Seventy-Fifth Anniversary of Professor Ch'en Shou-ui* (San Francisco: Chinese Materials Center, 1975), pp. 413–424.

45. *Nihonkoku kenpō kaisetsu to shiryō* [Records relating to the establishment of the Japanese constitution] (Tokyo: Jiji Tsūshinsha, 1946), pp. 103–104.

46. Verbatim record of the 27th meeting of the Far Eastern Commission (September 21, 1946), National Archives, Washington, D.C.

47. *Sandē Mainichi,* June 15, 1976, pp. 62–63.

48. Miyazawa Toshiyoshi, *Nihonkoku kenpō* [The constitution of Japan] (Tokyo: Nihon Hyōronsha, 1955), supplementary volume, pp. 328–332.

49. *Kenpō seitei no keika ni kansuru shō-i-inkai hōkokusho* [Subcommittee records on the making of the constitution] (Tokyo: Kenpō chōsakai jimukyoku, December 1961), p. 552; Yoshida Shigeru, *Kaisō jūnen* [Reflections on a decade] (Tokyo: Shinchosha, 1957), II, 48. General Whitney reported to Washington that the House of Peers passed the Constitutional Revision Bill by a standing vote of 298 to 2. (CINCAFPAC to WARCOS, 7 October 1946. File Constitution, GS, SCAP, RG 331, WNRC.)

50. Irie, *Nihonkoku kenpō,* pp. 429–431. Mr. Kades told me in June 1978 that he did not recall this incident.

51. *FRUS, 1946,* 8, pp. 200–226.

52. Hugh Borton, "Preparation for the Occupation of Japan," *Journal of Asian Studies,* vol. 26, no. 2 (February 1966), pp. 203–212, esp. p. 211.

53. Blakeslee, *Far Eastern Commission,* p. 56.

54. *FRUS, 1946,* 8, pp. 352–353, 375.

55. Daily Action Report, GHQ, SCAP, December 31, 1947–January 1, 1948, in GS, SCAP, RG 133, WNRC.

56. *Mainichi Shinbun* (Osaka) August 16, 1948, cited in SCAP, *History of the Nonmilitary Activities of the Occupation, 1945 through December 1951,* vol. 3, *Political and Legal,* Part B, *Constitutional Revision,* p. 77. See also message from General MacArthur to FEC, quoted in Minutes of FEC 138th Meeting, January 27, 1949.

57. Message CSCAD ICO to CONCPE, December 17, 1948. Blue Binders, FEC file, RG 9, MacArthur Archives. (FEC 438, as indexed by MacArthur Archives.)

58. *FRUS, 1949,* 7, pp. 626–627.

59. F. C. Jones, Hugh Borton, and B. R. Pearn, *The Far East, 1942–1946* (London: Oxford University Press, 1955), p. 351.

60. MacArthur, *Reminiscences,* p. 346.

61. Satō Isao, "Kenpō kaisei" [Revision of the constitution], in *Kataritsugu shōwashi* [A family history of the Shōwa period] (Tokyo: Asahi Shinbunsha, 1977), 6, pp. 5–58, esp. pp. 45–46.

4

The Conflict between
Two Legal Traditions in Making
the Constitution of Japan

Tanaka Hideo

Matsumoto Jōji was chairman of the Shidehara cabinet's Constitutional Problem Investigation Committee (Naikaku Kempō Mondai Chōsa Iinkai), popularly known as the Matsumoto Committee. He was a central figure in the government's efforts in 1945–1946 to revise the Meiji Constitution. Matsumoto's recollections provide invaluable insights on his views.

> According to the Potsdam Declaration and the other documents [exchanged with the Allies] just before Japan accepted the Declaration as a basis for our render, Japan's national polity would be decided . . . according to the will of the Japanese people. Therefore, I thought it would probably be better [to revise the constitution] after a peace settlement. However, since in any case research would have to be done, the feeling was that a Committee to Investigate Constitutional Problems should be organized. . . . Since the Allies were saying they would leave [constitutional reform] to Japan, we thought we could handle the matter as we pleased. We even thought it might be all right to leave it as it was.[1]

This attitude about constitutional reform had a decisive effect on the process by which the Constitution of Japan was made. Had the Japanese government correctly understood what kind of new constitutional system was expected—which was indicated in the Potsdam Declaration, the fundamental document about how postsurrender Japan would have to change—and taken a more positive attitude toward constitutional reform, the General Headquarters, Supreme Commander for the Allied Powers (GHQ, SCAP) might not have drawn up its own draft constitution and presented it to the Japanese government. Hence, there might not have been a fundamental revision of the constitution along GHQ lines.

Many people today may find the Matsumoto Committee's attitude incomprehensible. Yet it arose from Japan's legal tradition since the Meiji period. In that sense, the making of the postwar constitution was a conflict between two different legal cultures.

Several studies have previously appeared on the adoption of the postwar constitution.[2] I have coauthored one study with Takayanagi Kenzō and Ōtomo Ichirō and have written several articles on the subject.[3] There is also an excellent account by Professor McNelly in this book. Drawing upon these works, this essay attempts to examine the establishment of the constitution as a clash between two different legal traditions.

Developments Prior to February 1946

Two sections of the Potsdam Declaration relevant to Japan's political system state:

> 10. . . . The Japanese Government shall remove all obstacles to the revival and strengthening of democratic tendencies among the Japanese people. Freedom of speech, of religion, and of thought, as well as respect for the fundamental human rights shall be established. . . .

> 12. The occupying forces of the Allies shall be withdrawn from Japan as soon as these objectives have been accomplished and there has been established in accordance with the freely expressed will of the Japanese people a peacefully inclined and responsible government.

To those trained in the American intellectual tradition, it was obvious that a sweeping revision of the Meiji Constitution was necessary to carry out these provisions. The Americans believed that constitutional reform should be done on Japanese initiative and that the Allied role should be limited to determining whether the Japanese government's proposals fully carried out the provisions of the Potsdam Declaration. SWNCC-228 states: "Only as a last resort should the Supreme Commander order the Japanese Government to effect the above listed reforms, as the knowledge that they had been imposed by the Allies would materially reduce the possibility of their acceptance and support by the Japanese people for the future."[4] The GHQ, which had primary responsibility for carrying out Occupation policy and the Potsdam Declaration, followed this policy. GHQ's attitude is seen in an exchange at a meeting on January 17, 1946, between Charles L. Kades, Government Section, GHQ, and a member of the Far Eastern Advisory Commission (FEAC) Tomas Confesor (Republic of the Philippines), who asked if GHQ was considering amendments to the constitution. Kades's reply was: "No. The Government Section has understood that this is a long-range problem concerning fundamental changes in the Japanese constitutional structure which is within the province of your Commission."[5]

GHQ was not, however, totally inactive on constitutional reform. First, the necessity for constitutional revision was suggested to the government of Japan. When Konoe Fumimaro, deputy prime minister in the Higashikuni cabinet, visited General Douglas MacArthur on October 4, 1945, the latter made a suggestion about constitutional revision.[6] On

October 8, 1945, George C. Atcheson, SCAP's political adviser, explained to Konoe the basic points needing reform. During the formal courtesy call by the newly designated prime minister, Shidehara Kijūrō, on October 9, 1945, General MacArthur again indicated that constitutional revision was required.

Second, GHQ had begun preparatory work to review the draft it expected the government of Japan to submit. The purpose of the review was to determine if the proposal satisfied the provisions of the Potsdam Declaration and other directives. This review was done almost single-handedly by Milo E. Rowell of the Government Section,[7] and several documents resulted from his preliminary work. Rowell prepared a "Report of Preliminary Studies and Recommendations of Japanese Constitution," dated December 6, 1945; and when a private group, the Kempō Kenkyūkai (Constitutional Research Association),[8] published on December 26, 1945, its "Draft Outline of the Constitution," Rowell commented on it in a memorandum dated January 11, 1946.[9]

Third, in connection with the January 17, 1946, meeting with the FEC, a staff study was made of the Supreme Commander's authority regarding constitutional revision. It was compiled as a "Memorandum for the Supreme Commander—Subject: Constitutional Reform," dated February 1, 1946.[10]

GHQ continued to wait for a Japanese draft, however, until the end of January, 1946. It may seem strange that after Rowell's report on January 11, with the exception of the study of the Supreme Commander's authority, nothing was done about constitutional revision. However, according to Kades and Rowell, they were both busy in January implementing the purge directive and with other work.[11] Since the Public Administration Division of the Government Section had a staff of only between a dozen and twenty members,[12] their preoccupation with other duties is believable.

It is evident from the way the drafting work was actually carried out from February 4 to 12, once the Supreme Commander had decided to go ahead on his own, that until the beginning of February, MacArthur had no intention of preparing a draft constitutional revision and presenting it to the Japanese government. The work assignments were hastily made; later there were jurisdictional conflicts; and only very general instructions were given to the subcommittees that did the initial drafting.[13] The result was that there were many stylistic inconsistencies about the length of the articles and how they should be divided into paragraphs.[14]

The Matsumoto Draft Constitution

The official account of GHQ's change of policy states: "[T]he Supreme Commander . . . finally came to the conclusion that the most effective method of instructing the Japanese Government on the nature and application of these principles he considered basic would be to prepare a draft constitution embodying those principles."[15] The change of policy occurred on February 1 when the *Mainichi Shinbun* published a tentative draft constitution which indicated the contents of the Matsumoto draft.

The Japanese government had informed GHQ of the progress of the Matsumoto Committee's work in very general terms. In response to a question from Nakatani Takeyo in the House of Representatives Budget Committee, Chairman Matsumoto had explained to the Diet on December 8, 1945, his basic approach to reform, dubbed Matsumoto's "Four Principles." They included no change in the basic principle that the emperor retains the rights of sovereignty; broadening of the sphere of matters that must be approved by the Diet and consequent reduction in imperial prerogatives; extension of responsibility of ministers of state, who will be responsible to the Diet, with no interference by imperial advisors, who have no constitutional authority; and strengthening of the protection of the people's freedoms and rights, including provision for satisfactory means of redressing violations of freedoms and rights. From these and other sources, GHQ officials knew that the committee would be conservative, although they do not seem to have had information about the details of its work.

Then the *Mainichi Shinbun* scored a journalistic coup by publishing one of the committee's draft constitutions.[16] GHQ judged the document to be "Chairman Matsumoto's own draft" and regarded the scoop as "[Foreign Minister] Yoshida's trial balloon."[17] One GHQ official's reaction was typical: "We expected to receive a conservative draft, but not as conservative as that."[18]

GHQ concluded that there was no prospect of a satisfactory revision coming from the Japanese government and that if such a conservative draft were made public, dire results would follow. On the one hand, the SCAP's policy of respecting the initiative of the government of Japan as far as possible regarding postwar reforms would come under fire. On the other hand, disclosure would lead to difficulties with the Far Eastern Commission, which was scheduled to begin functioning in February 1946. General MacArthur decided, therefore, to have the Government Section prepare a draft constitution as a model to show what GHQ thought the Potsdam Declaration required.[19]

The Matsumoto Committee's final drafts were no more than a touching-up of the Meiji Constitution.[20] This was certainly the case with the final committee draft and the Plan A; it was also true of the Plan B draft, which the committee regarded as a "document with wide-ranging revisions."[21] The group's basic outlook is most apparent in the reaction to a draft by Nomura Junji, an adviser to the committee. He submitted a sweeping set of changes which included the adoption of a presidential system, national ownership of land and large factories, and government operation of banking, insurance, and other industries. Nomura included a detailed explanation with his proposals. Matsumoto's response was "This involves too great a change. I cannot accept this approach." The committee did not consider the Nomura proposal.[22]

The Matsumoto draft, unlike proposals put forth by political parties and by private groups, would be reported to the cabinet and in due course be enacted into law. The Matsumoto Committee, therefore, had to work out a viable draft revision. Since, in the committee's judgment at least, public opinion was not demanding extensive reform, the committee had to devise a revision compatible with this public will. Yet another factor impeded a fundamental examination of the chapter on the emperor in the Meiji Constitution. Only a few months before, national sentiment had been agreed on "ending the war" *(shūsen)* on the basis of a definite promise by the Japanese government that the "national polity would be preserved" *(kokutai goji)*. Still, a tendency to maintain the status quo is conspicuous in every one of these drafts. The drafts did strengthen the position of the legislative branch, particularly the lower house of the Diet. For example, they granted the Diet the power to initiate constitutional amendments. It is fair to say that the drafts did try to correct the defects of the Meiji Constitution in this respect. However, in their treatment of human rights, the fundamental rights of citizens and how they would be guaranteed, the drafts broke very little new ground. Under the Meiji Constitution most of the suppression of freedom was done through legislation enacted by the Imperial Diet. Despite that bleak record, these drafts relied on the Diet to take human rights into account in performing its legislative function.[23]

The Matsumoto Committee draft (Draft A) retained the Privy Council and made only one slight change in the first four articles of the constitution, which concerned the crucial elements of the emperor system. Article III had stated: "The person of the Emperor is *sacred*." The Matsumoto draft changed this to: "The person of the Emperor is *supreme*."

In the Matsumoto Committee's deliberations, problems were almost always discussed in terms of whether article so-and-so was to be revised. Extenuating circumstances notwithstanding, Matsumoto Committee members clearly believed that the Meiji Constitution just needed to be touched up a little here and there.

Given the nature of the Matsumoto Committee draft, what would have happened if it had been made public in early February 1946 as the Japanese had intended? Almost certainly there would have been two results. First, the Allied countries insisting upon tougher policies toward Japan would have reacted strongly. Second, GHQ and the Japanese government would have been placed in a very difficult position.

General Courtney Whitney, chief, Government Section, accurately described the political situation in a letter to Shirasu Jirō, Councilor, Shū-sen Renraku Jimukyoku (Central Liaison Office) after the GHQ draft was presented to the Japanese government.

> [I]t must be realized that the matter of constitutional reform in Japan is not confined to the exclusive interest of the Japanese people or even to them jointly with the Supreme Commander, but rather it is the opinion of the world which must be fully satisfied before the Allied Forces will release their complete control over Japan. In the final analysis, unless this issue is met forthrightly by the Japanese Government or the Supreme Commander him-self takes action, it is quite possible that a constitution might be forced upon Japan from the outside which would render the term "drastic" as used by you in your letter to describe the document submitted by me on the 13th, far too moderate a term with which to describe such new constitution—a con-stitution which well might sweep away even those traditions and structures which the Supreme Commander by his instrument makes it possible to pre-serve.[24]

The Japanese Tradition of Constitutional Scholarship

Assuming that my analysis is correct to this point, I would like to ask another hypothetical question and hazard an answer. What would have happened if the Matsumoto Committee had drawn up a draft constitu-tion with liberal changes? I think it would have been adopted, even if there were some changes at the suggestion of GHQ and the other Allies. Therefore, why the Matsumoto Committee thought such an extremely conservative draft would be satisfactory is an important key to under-standing how the new constitution was made.

To state my conclusions in advance, the tradition of constitutional scholarship in Japan prevented an adequate understanding of the require-ments of the Potsdam Declaration. To GHQ, operating in the American legal tradition, the need for extensive revision of the constitution was self-evident, but it was not so obvious to the Japanese. The adoption of the postwar constitution proceeded in a maze of mutual misunderstand-ing attributable to deep-rooted differences in legal culture.

The Matsumoto Committee was an extraordinarily distinguished group. Chairman Matsumoto was a state minister without portfolio in the Shidehara cabinet, and he had been the leading authority on Japan's Commercial Code when he taught at Tokyo Imperial University. He was one of the top legal minds of his generation. Nor were his experiences confined to the campus. He had served as vice-president of the South Manchuria Railway, director general of the Cabinet Legislation Bureau, a member of the House of Peers, and minister of commerce and industry. It was rare for a scholar to have such extensive experience in political and economic affairs.

The committee members were also a very distinguished group. A few leading legal experts had been left out, such as Kyoto Imperial University's Sasaki Sōichi, who had been deeply involved in the study of constitutional problems in the office of the Lord Keeper of the Privy Seal under Prince Konoe,[25] but with a few such exceptions, nearly every authority on constitutional law was on the committee.

The Matsumoto Committee held its first plenary session on October 27, 1945. In addition to plenary sessions, there were 15 "investigative meetings." The committee completed its work in its seventh plenary session on February 1, 1946. Meetings varied in length. Shorter sessions ran three to four hours, while longer meetings consisted of morning and afternoon sessions for a total of five to six hours.[26]

The Matsumoto draft was produced by the nation's leading authorities on constitutional law after ample time for deliberation. It reflects the nature of Japanese constitutional scholarship under the Meiji Constitution in the following respects.

1. Japan's legal scholarship began early in the Meiji period, when efforts were made to transplant Western legal systems to facilitate "modernization." The legal systems of advanced countries, particularly those of England, France, and Germany, were enthusiastically studied. The adoption of Western legal systems was also unavoidable if the unequal treaties were to be revised, and treaty revision was a very high priority for the Meiji government. Consequently a new legal system was adopted in great haste; little attention was paid to differences in tradition and social structure.

After the various legal codes were adopted in mid-Meiji, the new legal profession devoted its energies to their interpretation and application. Emphasis was on "usefulness," on a narrow utilitarianism. This approach deeply affected the study of foreign legal systems as well. Even matters that were theoretically of major significance were rarely discussed if they did not bear directly upon an interpretation of the legal codes. Some scholars occasionally published research on some aspects of foreign law that had no immediate relevance to the interpretation of Japanese codes and other statutes, but academic circles ignored their work.

The same basic approach prevailed in the field of constitutional law. Although many draft revisions of the constitution were published from the time of Japan's surrender on August 15, 1945, until March 6, 1946, when the government announced the "General Outline of the Draft Revision of the Constitution," which was based on the GHQ draft, none of those by constitutional scholars went beyond partial amendment of the Meiji Constitution. This was also true of the Matsumoto Committee. They were content to delete an article here, change an article there. Neither the draft by Konoe Fumimaro nor that by Sasaki Sōichi went beyond this mode of thought. Miyasawa Toshiyoshi later argued that the acceptance of the Potsdam Declaration should be regarded, in a legal sense, as a kind of revolution and emphasized that Japan's postwar constitution was a "new" constitution rather than an amendment to the Meiji Constitution. But in a talk at the Foreign Ministry on September 28, 1945, entitled "Major Points of the Constitution and Related Laws and Ordinances to be Revised on the Basis of the Potsdam Declaration,"[27] Miyasawa showed himself satisfied with relatively minor revisions. Under the section on "Strengthening Democratic Tendencies," Miyasawa mentioned reorganization of the House of Peers, extending the length of Diet sessions, and strengthening the power of the Court of Administrative Litigation (Administrative Court). The fact that he made only these modest proposals is significant.

Some draft constitutions showed a real understanding that a new age was dawning for Japan and confronted fundamental questions unfettered by the Meiji Constitution. They were written by those outside the field of constitutional law. The draft revision by the Kempō Kenkyūkai was read by GHQ officials and influenced the GHQ draft. Except Suzuki Yasuzō, those who worked on this draft—Takano Iwasaburō, Morito Tatsuo, Murobushi Kōshin, Sugimori Kōjirō, and Iwabuchi Tatsuo—were not constitutional law specialists. Even Suzuki's experience was limited. He was a student in the economics department at Kyoto Imperial University, and his official experience with constitutional law was limited to a 1942–1943 stint on the compilation committee for a parliamentary history of the House of Representatives.

The one constitutional reform project that could have influenced the Japanese government restricted itself to the framework of the Meiji Constitution. This made it remarkably inadequate in the area of human rights in spite of the demands of the Potsdam Declaration. Constitutional scholarship under the Meiji Constitution was concerned with the study of a German-style "theory of state structure" *(Staatsrechtslehre),* the "national polity" *(kokutai),* the "political system" *(seitai),* and the structure of government—legislative and administrative powers. Little attention was paid to human rights and their protection. Chapter II of the Meiji Constitution on Rights and Duties of Subjects had 15 articles. Almost all the rights acknowledged there, however, were expressly qualified by a statement "within the limits of law." Legislation that restricted the freedoms guaranteed by the constitution was constitutional. Therefore, in the prewar period scholars gave insufficient consideration to the problems of basic human rights. For example, Minobe Tatsukichi, a typical liberal interpreter of the Meiji Constitution, in his *Kempō satsuyō* (Essentials of the constitution), a 626-page tome, devoted only 27 pages to the rights and duties of subjects. His explanation was perfunctory: "Freedom of speech, writing, publication, public meetings and associations" were disposed of in ten lines. Miyasawa Toshiyoshi's 304-page

Kempō ryakusetsu (Summary of the constitution) gives only 16 pages to rights and duties. By comparison, the 704-page *Kempō jutsugi* (The constitution truly explained) by the leader of the conservative school of legal scholars, Uesugi Shinkichi, covers rights and duties in 42 pages.[28]

This style of constitutional analysis and commentary, given the state-centered structure of the Meiji Constitution, may have been quite natural. But even in theoretical legal studies, scholars were remiss regarding basic human rights.

This tendency is apparent in the research on the U.S. Constitution by Japanese scholars before World War II. Two early works may be cited as examples: Minobe Tatsukichi's *Beikoku kempō no yurai oyobi tokushitsu* (The origins and special characteristics of the American constitution), published in 1918, and Fujii Shin'ichi's *Beikoku kempō-ron* (The American constitution), published in 1926. These books dealt chiefly with the form of government and said very little about the protection of fundamental rights by the courts. Minobe cited federalism, democracy, and the separation of powers as the special features of the U.S. Constitution, and he explained each in detail. The Bill of Rights was treated in eight pages in the section on democracy; the explanation was sketchy and incomplete. Fujii's huge work ran to 808 pages; he described not only the federal constitution but also state constitutions. He spent 320 pages on the individual states' governments. But Fujii gave only six pages to human rights, and his explanation was fragmentary and full of mistakes.

2. Liberal academic theorists had concentrated their efforts on strengthening the popularly elected lower house of the Diet rather than a system of judicial review or the creation of constitutional courts.

There are two principal methods of determining whether a law passed by a legislature is constitutional or not. European countries have established constitutional courts with the authority to decide questions of constitutionality. Another method is the American practice of granting regular courts the power to review legislation for constitutionality. Since there was no explicit provision for a constitutional court in the Meiji Constitution, it could not be established. Thus the latter method was debated by legal scholars.

Opinions were divided on whether the Meiji Constitution gave the courts the authority to review the substance of laws. In the early years the majority of specialists held that the courts should have such power.[29] About the middle of the Taishō period (1912–1926), the conservative Uesugi Shinkichi advocated such authority for the courts, while the liberal Minobe Tatsukichi opposed judicial review.[30] From that point the lines were drawn. Not surprisingly, the liberals showed little concern for a system of constitutional review. Since the Meiji Constitution as a whole was a conservative document in which human rights were hedged by "limitations imposed by law," judicial review of legislation might well

have worked under the Meiji Constitution more to maintain the emper-
or-centered governmental structure than to safeguard human rights. It is
thus also understandable that the conservatives supported such a review.
In practice the courts consistently ruled that they did not have the authority to review the constitutionality of an act of the Diet.[31]

The American system of judicial review was first studied in detail in
Japan by Takayanagi Kenzō, who returned from five years of study
abroad in 1920. In 1921 he published a long essay entitled "Beikoku kensei ni okeru shihōken no yūi o ronzu" (Discourses upon judicial supremacy in the American constitutional system).[32] He later published *Shihōken no yūi* (Judicial supremacy), a collection of his essays on the subject.
However, as Takayanagi himself has related,[33] his research attracted very
little attention until after World War II. The conservatives probably
found the American-style guarantee of human rights irrelevant, and the
liberals regarded the judicial review system as pernicious.

Freedom was suppressed under the Meiji Constitution primarily
through laws enacted by the Imperial Diet. This having been the case, it
would have seemed appropriate, when the constitution was under scrutiny, to consider whether the system of judicial review should be introduced. But in fact it was hardly discussed in the Matsumoto Committee.
For example, after the committee's first investigative meeting, Miyasawa
Toshiyoshi drew up a detailed list of thirty-seven "items to be researched."[34] A judicial review system was not among them. Its absence is
attributable to the fact that the committee drew up the research agenda
according to the views of scholars who favored a liberal interpretation of
the Meiji Constitution. As we have seen, these scholars had no interest in
a judicial review system.

The Potsdam Declaration's statement about "the revival and strengthening of democratic tendencies" meant only one thing to these scholars:
enhancing the legislature's authority; specifically, increasing the power of
a popularly elected lower house.

At the Matsumoto Committee's first plenary session Minobe Tatsukichi said that it would be sufficient if the constitution included one article regarding human rights stating that the rights and duties would be
specified by law.[35] This was the logical conclusion of the Minobe school's
concept of democracy. But the Potsdam Declaration had made another
demand: "Freedom of speech, of religion, and of thought, as well as
respect for the fundamental human rights shall be established." Could
this have been achieved in a country like Japan where there was no tradition of respect for individual rights simply by adopting a system of legislative supremacy? The Matsumoto Committee did not seriously debate
the question. Several proposals called for certain rights not restricted by
law. But there was no discussion of how this objective would actually be
realized if the proposals were adopted. The *Seifu kisō kempō kaisei ni*

taisuru ippanteki setsumei (General explanation of the constitutional revision drafted by the government), written by Matsumoto Jōji, was submitted to GHQ along with the *Kempō kaisei yōkō* (Gist of the revision of the constitution) (the Matsumoto draft). Matsumoto's explanation was extremely sanguine.

> Despite provisions in the present constitution which should have provided reasonable safeguards for freedom of speech, religion, and thought and basic human rights for the Japanese people, in practice these rights were not fully respected and in some cases were widely violated. This happened because the constitution was established under an antidemocratic government and because laws were flagrantly abused. The draft constitutional revisions envision, as previously stated, the establishment of a democratic government and greater powers for the legislature. Therefore, in sharp contrast with the past, the freedom and human rights of the Japanese people should be fully respected by just legislation and the fair application of such just laws.

That democracy was equivalent to respect for a popularly elected legislature was an article of faith.

3. The legislative-superiority approach may be seen in the frequent attempts by the liberals to ameliorate the conservatism of the Prussian-style Meiji Constitution by seeking a model in the English system.

The influence of the British system of government on the Matsumoto Committee may also be found in the *Kempō kaiseian setsumei hojū* (Supplementary explanation of the constitution revision proposal) written by Matsumoto and submitted to GHQ on February 18, 1946. "The new draft constitution submitted the other day may seem outwardly meagre in bulk and of a rather neutral character . . . [T]he revised constitution marks, in practice, a big step forward toward parliamentary democracy after the English pattern."[36]

Japanese liberals naturally felt an affinity for England, which had established a liberal political system revered as the mother of modern parliamentary government while maintaining the same ruling dynasty from the Middle Ages. But here as well, their understanding of the English system was often superficial.

English parliamentary sovereignty rests on two principles. First, laws enacted by parliament are the supreme law of the land, and no organ or agency can legally overthrow them. Second, parliament can legislate on any subject whatsoever; matters concerning the Crown are no exception. Thus it is possible for parliament to change the order of royal succession, as was done in the Act of Settlement (1701) and His Majesty's Declaration of Abdication Act (1936). Under the Meiji Constitution, however, the Imperial House Law had equal status with the constitution. This law stipulated succession to the imperial throne, rules for a regency, and other matters related to the imperial family, including provisions concerning jurisdiction over cases among members of the royal family and cases brought by ordinary subjects against them.[37] Modifications of the Imperial House Law did not have to be submitted to the Imperial Diet.[38] This was a fundamental difference from the English principle of parliamentary sovereignty.

The Matsumoto Committee was aware that the Imperial House Law's equal standing with the constitution posed a problem. But perhaps because the committee did not fully appreciate the importance of this issue, the only change proposed regarding the emperor and the imperial family was one word in Article III of the Meiji Constitution. The emperor's status was revised from "sacred" to "supreme."[39] At the first plenary session of the committee on October 27, Minobe cited the relationship between the constitution and the Imperial House Law as a question that should be researched to determine if revision was necessary.[40] At the investigative meeting on October 30, it was decided that "while there is an opinion that several provisions of the Imperial House Law should be included in the constitution, no action is necessary at present."[41] This conservative way of thinking prevailed throughout the committee's deliberations.[42]

How were these issues treated in the various drafts prepared before the Japanese government announced its official draft on March 6, 1946? Let us look first at the drafting undertaken by Konoe Fumimaro, who believed he had been assigned the job by General MacArthur. Konoe was assisted by his chief adviser Sasaki Sōichi.[43] Konoe and Sasaki both produced drafts; neither made the Imperial House Law subject to the Diet's legislative power. And both envisioned only very modest changes regarding fundamental human rights and their protection. Konoe's draft stated, "The impression that subjects' fundamental freedoms can be abrogated by the law shall be removed." But Konoe said nothing about constitutional guarantees for such fundamental freedoms. Sasaki's draft established a constitutional court with authority to rule upon the constitutionality of legislation. Yet the section on fundamental rights provided only that they were guaranteed within the scope fixed by law.

The draft revisions made by political parties and private groups[44] and the deliberations within the government showed the same blind spots.[45] Among the more than a dozen separate drafts, those by Inada Masatsugu, the Kempō Kenkyūkai, and the Kempō Kondankai (Constitution Consultation Association) called for the Imperial House Law to be decided by the Diet. Three drafts, those by Inada Masatsugu, the Kempō Kondankai, and the Nihon Shimpo-tō, proposed a system of judicial review. None of the three (at least explicitly), however, proposed to change the provisions that allowed the legislature to limit human rights. The Takano Iwaburō and the Japan Communist party drafts both advocated a republican system. But concern for human rights was even less noticeable in these two drafts than in the others. This approach to sovereignty and human rights reflects Japan's legal tradition at the end of World War II.

Matsumoto's Early Failure to Consult SCAP Opinion

The Matsumoto Committee also displayed a lack of sensitivity about the significance of Japan's acceptance of the Potsdam Declaration and the ensuing Allied Occupation. Matsumoto's memoirs, quoted above, attest to this.

Despite an opinion filed by Dr. Nomura,[46] most of the committee members, including Chairman Matsumoto as we have seen, rested their hopes on a statement in the Allied reply to the Japanese government's offer to surrender. The crucial line was "The ultimate form of government of Japan shall, in accordance with the Potsdam Declaration, be established by the freely expressed will of the Japanese people." As we have seen, Matsumoto thought that, depending on circumstances, it might not be necessary to revise the constitution at all.[47]

This optimism bordering on wishful thinking led to a lack of interest in American constitutional thought and the American system of government, although the United States was the most important of the Allied powers and was primarily responsible for the Occupation. There were very few authorities on the U.S. Constitution in Japan in 1945. That the views of one of the few, Takagi Yasaka, were not sought may be explained by Matsumoto's antipathy to the work being done under Konoe, in which Takagi participated. However, the views of another highly competent specialist on American law, Takayanagi Kenzō, were not solicited, and there is no record that the opinions of other specialists were sought either.

Chairman Matsumoto strictly adhered to his policy that it was not necessary for the committee to ascertain GHQ's views.[48] Konoe Fumimaro and his advisers Takagi Yasaka, Matsumoto Shigeharu, and Ushiba Tomohiko followed exactly the opposite tack. Feeling that if they wasted time by working in a political vacuum, the Allied powers would impose a constitution, the Konoe group had unofficial consultations and negotiations with U.S. officials.[49]

Why did Matsumoto never doubt his interpretation of the Potsdam Declaration? The first reason was probably his personality; he was known as a supremely confident man. This confidence was doubtless reinforced by the fact that he had assembled the best legal minds of the day on the committee. I suspect, however, that another reason was Japan's tradition of legal scholarship that was concerned only with the "law on the books" and rarely evinced any interest in the sociological facts behind the law. Although some scholars had advocated sociological studies of law from the 1920s, until 1945 research in the sociology of law was almost exclusively in the field of civil law. Moreover, even in civil law only a few individuals recognized the value of this work.

The Japanese had been cut off from accurate information about international developments since the start of World War II. They had no way of knowing the complex relationships among the Allied powers. It was quite natural that members of the Matsumoto Committee could not appreciate a situation that now, with the benefit of hindsight, seems obvious to us. Nevertheless, if they had taken a little broader view of revision, the committee draft would have been somewhat different, and the whole process of enacting a new constitution would have been significantly altered.

The day after the *Mainichi Shinbun* published the Matsumoto Committee draft, February 2, 1946, the paper's "Kenteki" (Reflections) column commented:

> We believe most people are deeply disappointed at the draft document prepared by the Constitutional Problem Investigation Committee. The draft is too conservative and simply seeks to preserve the status quo. The committee has defined its mandate narrowly as "amendment of the Constitution"; its draft resembles a document drawn up by law clerks. It is devoid of the vision, statesmanship, and idealism needed for a new state structure. Revision of the constitution at this time is not just a legal problem. Changing the constitution is a supremely political act. To establish a constitutional revision committee headed by a legal specialist, State Minister Matsumoto, and proceed as if they were studying changes in the Civil Code or the Commercial Code shows no understanding that Japan is in a revolutionary period. We should recall that the present [Meiji] Constitution was drawn up under the direction of the foremost statesman of the age, Itō Hirobumi.[50]

It was trenchant criticism of the weaknesses of the draft produced by the Japanese government.

Negotiations with the Government Section

On February 13, 1946, General Whitney, together with Kades, Rowell, and Rodman Hussey, met with Foreign Minister Yoshida, State Minister Matsumoto, and others at the foreign minister's official residence. The Japanese thought the meeting was to discuss the Matsumoto draft submitted to GHQ on February 8 and had come prepared to explain it. They were astounded to receive GHQ's totally new draft.[51]

In subsequent contact between the GHQ staff and Japanese officials until the cabinet made public its "General Outline of Draft Revision of the Constitution" on March 6, basic differences in approach emerged on many points. These led to a number of misunderstandings.

1. There is no doubt that one major reason why GHQ decided to draft

its own revision and submit it to the Japanese government was its concern about the attitudes of other Allied nations, in particular the Far Eastern Commission (FEC), which was to begin functioning in February 1946.[52] General MacArthur's apprehensiveness about the FEC is apparent in the account by Ashida Hitoshi, minister of health and welfare, of Prime Minister Shidehara's report to the cabinet about his meeting with General MacArthur on February 21. According to Ashida, MacArthur told Shidehara that "I understand that the discussions of the Far Eastern Commission held in Washington . . . were very tough in tone against Japan."[53] However, other GHQ officials endeavored only indirectly to explain how dangerous the international situation was for Japan. This reticence was because GHQ considered it absolutely essential to maintain the appearance vis-à-vis the other Allies that a new constitution was drawn up at Japanese initiative and that GHQ's role was to offer suggestions and indicate approval.

The government of Japan was not adequately informed by these guarded warnings. That ignorance was due in part to a dearth of background information. There was an unavoidable intelligence gap about the international situation. A second reason was the ivory-tower approach adopted by the Matsumoto Committee. Chairman Matsumoto was particularly unable to understand why GHQ was in such a hurry to amend the constitution which would form the legal basis of the nation.[54] He thought GHQ's attitude was arbitrary and high-handed.

2. For the same reasons that the GHQ staff did not adequately explain the international situation, Japanese officials were not informed of General MacArthur's decision on February 3 to prepare a GHQ draft after learning the contents of the Matsumoto draft from the *Mainichi Shinbun* article two days earlier.

When the GHQ draft was presented to the Japanese government on February 13, General Whitney said, "The draft of constitutional revision, which you submitted to us the other day, is wholly unacceptable to the Supreme Commander as a document of freedom and democracy."[55] Japanese officials, for their part, were shocked to receive the draft. They believed that the fundamental law of the nation should first be subjected to careful scholarly research and only then should there be debate over revisions. These deliberate stages were an essential process in enacting a new constitution, as far as the Japanese were concerned. It was inconceivable to them that GHQ could have drafted a constitution in just a few days. The Japanese thought that GHQ had previously prepared its own draft, had waited until the Matsumoto Committee finally finished its work, and was now asking Japan to accept the American document. Given this perception of events, the strong sentiment among the Matsumoto Committee and other Japanese officials against GHQ action is quite understandable.[56]

3. There were also differences of opinion over the individual chapters

and articles of the Constitution. The following exchange about the emperor's status, for example, occurred at the discussion on February 22.

> MATSUMOTO: Is it essential that the Imperial House Law be enacted by the Diet? Under the present Japanese Constitution the Imperial House Law is made up by members of the Imperial Household. The Imperial Household has autonomy.
>
> WHITNEY: Unless the Imperial House Law is made subject to approval by the representatives of the people, we pay only lip service to the supremacy of the people.
>
> KADES: We have placed the Emperor under the law, as in England.
>
> ROWELL: At present the Imperial House Law is above the Constitution.
>
> WHITNEY: Unless the Imperial House Law is enacted by the Diet the purpose of the Constitution is vitiated. This is an essential article.
>
> MATSUMOTO: Is this, control of the Imperial House Law by the Diet, a basic principle?
>
> WHITNEY: Yes.[57]

GHQ staff members had been worried about Matsumoto's attitude toward the emperor system as indicated by his preference for only slight changes in the provisions concerning the emperor. Matsumoto's questions about the above point strengthened their concern about his conservatism. On the other hand, the Americans tended to regard the emperor as a ruler with the actual authority of the U.S. president and consequently to have exaggerated the conservatism of the Matsumoto draft.[58]

A second disagreement concerned the constitutional relationship between the Diet and the cabinet. GHQ favored the superiority of the legislative branch and seemed to regard the cabinet as a kind of executive committee subordinate to the legislature. This preference can be seen in various articles in the GHQ draft: Article XL stipulated that "the Diet shall be the highest organ of state power"; Article LVII stipulated that the Diet could be dissolved only when a nonconfidence resolution was passed (or when a confidence resolution was rejected); and Article LXIII required that even in the case of a general election won by the ruling party, the cabinet still had to resign en masse and the Diet select a new prime minister. Given their experience with a parliamentary cabinet system, there were many points in these proposals that the Japanese found difficult to accept.

4. The Japanese side argued that there was no essential difference between the GHQ and the Japanese drafts: both documents sought to achieve a democratic political system. They tried to persuade GHQ to let them use the Matsumoto draft, which reflected Japanese tradition and

national conditions, as the basic working text. One example of such an attempt was the letter (known as the "Jeep way letter") dated February 15, 1946, from Shirasu Jirō to General Whitney.

> [Matsumoto] and his colleagues in the cabinet feel that yours and theirs aim at the same destination but there is this great difference in the routes chosen. Your way is so American in the way that it is straight and direct. Their way must be Japanese in the way that it is round about, twisted, and narrow. Your way may be called an airway and their way a Jeep way over bumpy roads.[59]

Matsumoto made a similar attempt at persuasion in the "Supplementary Explanation of Constitutional Revision,"[60] dated February 18, 1946, and sent to General Whitney. Matsumoto repeated the same theme at the meeting with General Whitney and his associates on February 22 when he began his statement by saying, "We have accepted the ideas set forth in the [GHQ] draft of a new constitution . . . "[61]

The chief motive in these overtures was, of course, to persuade GHQ officials. But it might not have been just guile. As I have shown above, the Japanese understanding of democracy was such that they might not have thought there was a great difference between the two positions.

At the meeting with General Whitney on February 22, Matsumoto stated: "[F]irst, how many of the articles in the new Constitution do you consider basic and unalterable? I want to advise the Cabinet what and how many of the Articles are absolutely necessary."[62]

GHQ officers must have found this a very trying question. They had waited for the government of Japan to submit a liberal draft revision (or at least one that would fulfill the minimum demands of the Potsdam Declaration). They had finally received the Matsumoto draft, only to find their expectations betrayed. The GHQ staff must have feared that if they said certain provisions were fundamental, the rest of the draft would be ignored. A realistic assumption was that the GHQ draft would be "revised," that is, emasculated, and the final document would be very conservative. The GHQ representatives replied as follows:

> WHITNEY: We feel that the whole Constitution as written is basic. We accept the fact that in presentation our language will be subject to modification in order to make it better understood by the Japanese people, and the form will be subject to modification in those instances where the procedure set forth, is in your opinion, unworkable in terms of the Japanese situation. But in general, we regard this document as a unit.

> ROWELL: The new Constitution was written as an interwoven unit, one section fitting into another, so there is no one section or chapter that can be cut out.[63]

This reply shocked the Japanese. They had been trained, in the practice prevalent since the codification in the Meiji era, to discuss every legal problem simply as a matter of how to apply the articles in codes or other statutes. They tended to examine each article individually without paying adequate attention to the general structure of law. In a note entitled "Record of the Meeting on the Afternoon of February 22," made immediately after the session, Matsumoto summarized the GHQ reply as, "In short, you are allowed to make only small changes."[64]

Because of this misunderstanding, Matsumoto, who, lacking information about the international situation, did not perceive the reasons why GHQ had presented its own draft, believed that the Americans were taking a tough attitude: Japan had to accept the GHQ draft virtually as it was written.

That was not GHQ's intention. Its position was that the final decision on whether the GHQ draft was followed or not was up to Japan. If the GHQ draft was accepted as the basis for the revision work and deliberations, GHQ would allow any modification that did not violate its basic spirit. This position was explained to the Japanese many times.[65] And in fact, GHQ did agree to a fairly large number of changes, foremost among them its assent to a bicameral legislature instead of the unicameral system first proposed. GHQ's policy was acknowledged by Satō Tatsuo, who negotiated with the Government Section on specific provisions of the draft. In his memoirs Satō states:

> They [GHQ staff] were very strict about the Preface and the chapter on the Emperor. They would make no concessions. Only a few minor wording changes were allowed. But they granted a great many of our points and objections about other parts of the draft. . . . unlike their attitude at the stage when we were preparing the government draft [based upon the GHQ draft] the GHQ applied hardly any direct pressure on the Diet's deliberations on the constitution. Indeed, they seemed to have great respect for the Diet as the supreme representative of the people. With the revisions as well, they needed SCAP's approval, but 80 or 90 percent of our changes were allowed to stand."[66]

The Matsumoto Committee's misreading of GHQ's policy may well have led them to think that it would be useless even to request adjustments in the GHQ draft. It may well have been because of this misunderstanding that the Japanese government attempted to revise the GHQ document only within a relatively narrow scope.

Conclusion

Two different legal traditions clashed in the making of the postwar Japanese constitution. After the constitution was enacted, however, despite controversy over its genesis and merits, it has not once been revised. Not only has the document survived unscathed but since the late 1960s, the adversaries in political and social disputes have accepted the fundamental concepts of the new constitution.

Why have ideas that were totally foreign to Japanese tradition taken root and become part of Japan's political culture? I would like to conclude this essay with a few personal comments on this question.

1. There was a rapid change of public opinion in the postwar period. When Japan emerged from the shock of defeat, from physical and psychological "collapse," the public became very critical of the old political system. The government had assumed that the public supported the basic philosophy of the Meiji Constitution and that partial adjustments in that document would suffice for constitutional revision. But the shift in public opinion undermined that assumption.

In the conference on February 13, 1946, General Whitney stated:

> The Supreme Commander has directed me to offer this Constitution to your government and party for your adoption and your presentation to the people with his full backing if you care to do so, yet he does not require this of you. He is determined, however, that the principles therein stated shall be laid before the people—rather by you, but, if not, by himself . . . I cannot emphasize too strongly . . . that the Supreme Commander is determined that the people of Japan shall be free to choose between this Constitution and any form of Constitution that does not embody these principles.[67]

Whitney made this statement without prior approval from MacArthur.[68] It was a bluff, and it worked. At the cabinet meeting on February 19, Minister of Health and Welfare Ashida Hitoshi stated:

> If the American draft is made public, the newspapers will trumpet its line and endorse the draft. It is clear that if the Shidehara Cabinet resigns to avoid responsibility for this draft, a group of political leaders will take over who will accept it as it is. Whitney is even saying that the Constitution should tilt to the left, thus we can imagine what the political character of the next cabinet will be like. When we consider the outcome of the next general election, we certainly should be very careful about the future.[69]

When the government announced its "General Outline of Draft Revision of the Constitution" on March 6, the public reaction was generally favorable. Of course, the news media and public discussion were subject to GHQ censorship; militaristic or extremely nationalistic views were banned. Under these circumstances, many opportunistic and sycophantic statements were made. To say that the draft constitution was well received is not to ignore this expediency. Nevertheless, it is wrong to regard the enthusiasm for the new constitution as merely a mindless popular fad. Most of the populace had suffered from the arbitrary rule of the military, the police, and the bureaucracy for more than a decade. They were now offered a new intellectual framework, a fresh set of ideas and values. The experiences of the 1930s and early 1940s were seen in a new perspective and deeply regretted. The new constitution symbolized the break with an oppressive past.

2. With the enactment of the new constitution, most legal scholars accepted it as a fact and began to analyze and comment on it. This behavior can probably be partially explained by the prewar tradition of textual exegesis as the main work of legal scholars. It should be noted, however, that the new constitution was favorably received by scholars from other fields, men not so constricted by the tradition of constitutional scholarship. There was a sharp break with the prewar narrow provincialism of legal experts who stuck to their own specialities and avoided other legal problems. During this period there was extensive cooperation in analyzing the problems that would follow the adoption of the new constitution among specialists in administrative law, private law, criminal law, comparative law, and other fields.[70]

Despite the difficult economic and social conditions in the wake of defeat, public meetings and lectures about the new constitution were held throughout Japan, and many commentaries and explanations of the new law were published.

3. The great efforts to teach democracy and civics in the primary and secondary schools were highly significant in inculcating the new values. The schools, of course, could only teach the basic principles of the new constitution. There were limits to what the educators could do, and there was controversy about how some did it. The teachers' union was influential in deciding what was taught about the constitution; the teachers were criticized for presenting the material in an oversimplified way that reflected their "progressive" views.[71] Nevertheless, it is undeniable that educating the population about the constitution early in life meant that the basic concepts became a common ground for analyzing and discussing social issues. More than half the electorate today have graduated from primary school since the new constitution was adopted. It is irrefutable that its concepts have become part of our *Zeitgeist* to such an extent that people often think in terms of this value system without being consciously aware of it.

Notes

1. On August 10, 1945, Japan offered to surrender on the basis of the Potsdam Declaration "with the understanding that the said declaration does not comprise any demand which prejudices the prerogatives of His Majesty as a Sovereign Ruler." On August 11 the Allies replied: "The ultimate form of government of Japan shall, in accordance with the Potsdam Declaration, be established by the freely expressed will of the Japanese people." For Matsumoto's recollections see "Matsumoto Jōji-shi ni kiku" [Interview with Matsumoto Jōji] (Kempō Chōsakai Jimukyoku, 1960). This document is a reprint of the interview of Matsumoto Jōji at the Tokyo Daigaku Senryō Taisei Kenkyūkai (Study Group on the Occupation,

University of Tokyo) meeting held on November 23, 1950. For the convenience of readers I have cited the materials of the Kempō Chōsakai (Commission on the Constitution). The quotation is from pp. 67–68.

2. Major works include Satō Tatsuo, *Nihonkoku kempō seiritsu-shi* [History of the formulation of the constitution of Japan], 2 vols. (1962, 1964); Irie Toshio, *Kempō seiritsu no keii to kempōjō no shomondai* [The formulation of the constitution and some constitutional problems] (1976); and the reports, materials, and proceedings of the Commission on the Constitution.

3. My articles include: "Nihonkoku kempō seitei no katei ni arawareta kempōgaku no tsishitsu" [Characteristics of Japanese constitutional scholarship as seen in the making of the constitution of Japan], *Jurisuto* (1973), 528, p. 100; " 'Keikoku' to 'kyōhaku'—oshitsuke kempō-ron ni tsuite" [On the "Imposed Constitution"—"Warning" and "Threat"], *Jurisuto* (1973), 530, p. 110; "Kempō seiritsushi" [A history of the formulation of the constitution], *Jurisuto* (1973), 638, p. 27; "Kempō seitei katei arekore" [Episodes in the making of the constitution], *Jurisuto* (1978), 673–680; (1979) 682–683. These articles have been compiled in book form in *Kempō seitei katei oboegaki* [Notes on the process of the making of the constitution] (1979). See also my *The Japanese Legal System* (1976), pp. 642–685.

4. The State-War-Navy Coordinating Committee officially approved SWNCC-228 on January 7, 1946, but discussion of the document had begun much earlier; it was in nearly final form by mid-October 1945.

5. Minutes of Conference with Far Eastern [Advisory] Commission held 17 January [19]46 (January 18, 1946), Hussey Papers, File 20-A, p. 31 (extracts of this record can also be found at the Washington National Record Center, Record Group [RG] 331, Box 2229). See also Tanaka, *Kempō seitei katei oboegaki*, pp. 55–57.

6. *Political Reorientation of Japan*, vol. 1, p. 91, states: "In September, then, Prince Higashikuni, Prime Minister of the so-called Surrender Cabinet, was informed that the Supreme Commander regarded revision of the constitution as a matter of first importance." There is no Japanese record of a direct response to this. In September 1945 there was an unofficial discussion in a cabinet meeting about whether constitutional revision was necessary. (On that occasion, those opposed to taking action prevailed.) See Commission on the Constitution, *Sixteenth Session of the Subcommittee on the Formation of the Constitution*, statement by Yamazaki Iwao, p. 14. However, there is no mention of a suggestion from SCAP. In Higashikuni Naruhiko, *Watakushi no kiroku* [My record] (1947), p. 242, there is an account of a discussion about constitutional reform with state ministers Konoe Fumimaro and Ogata Taketora immediately after the cabinet was formed. But no suggestion from GHQ is mentioned.

7. Interview with Milo E. Rowell, August 28, 1974; and interview with Charles L. Kades, January 8, 1975.

8. For a memoir by a member of this research group, see Suzuki Yasuzō, *Kempō seitei zengo* [When the constitution was adopted] (1977).

9. Takayanagi Kenzō, Ōtomo Ichirō, and Tanaka Hideo, *Nihonkoku kempō seitei no katei* [The making of the constitution of Japan], 1972, vol. 1, p. 2ff. and p. 26ff.

10. Ibid., vol. 1, p. 90ff.

11. Interviews with Rowell, August 28, 1974, and Kades, January 8, 1975; and Tanaka, *Kempō seitei katei oboegaki,* pp. 67–69.

12. General Headquarters, SCAP, Government Section, Administrative Memorandum No. 17, Subject: Personnel Assignments (January 2, 1946), Washington National Record Center, RG 331, Box 2187, which lists 15 names, and ibid., No. 19 (February 4, 1946), which lists 21 names.

13. Handwritten Memo by Rowell Making Suggestions on the Organization of the Office in Preparing the Constitution, in Takayanagi, Ōtomo, and Tanaka, *Nihonkoku kempō seitei no katei,* vol. 1, pp. 115, 134–141, and 105–106.

14. When the Government Section began drafting its own version, the only preparatory work that had been done was the report by Rowell dated December 6, 1945. There was no general outline, not even a rough draft of individual chapters. No decision had been made on how many chapters there would be or on their headings. Interview with Rowell, August 28, 1974.

15. *Political Reorientation of Japan,* vol. 1, p. 102.

16. On January 31, 1946, Nishiyama Ryūzō of the *Mainichi Shinbun* "borrowed" the draft constitution from the office of the Matsumoto Committee without authorization. He took it to the newspaper offices, where the binding was removed and pages were distributed to staff members and copied by hand. The copying completed, the pages were put back in the binding and the document was returned to the committee office. Interview with Nishiyama Ryūzō, February 9, 1973. A newspaper reporter's instinct for an exclusive story decisively influenced the fate of Japan's constitution. For details, see Tanaka, *Kempō seitei katei oboegaki,* pp. 39–49.

17. Takayanagi, Ōtomo, and Tanaka, *Nihonkoku kempō seitei no katei,* vol. 1, pp. 42–43.

18. Interview with Rowell, August 28, 1974. The Government Section's strong negative reaction to the draft printed in the *Mainichi Shinbun* is recorded in "Memorandum for the Supreme Commander—Subject: Constitutional Reform (Matsumoto draft)," in Takayanagi, Ōtomo, and Tanaka, *Nihonkoku kempō seitei no katei,* vol. 1, pp. 40–75. For the Government Section's critical comments on the "Kempō kaisei yōkō" [Gist of the revision of the constitution] formally submitted to SCAP on February 8, 1946, see "Comments on the Document, 'Gist of the Revision of the Constitution,' " dated February 12, 1946, in ibid., vol. 1, pp. 80–90.

19. Interview with Kades, January 8, 1975.

20. My point here is not whether revision procedures should have followed Article 73 of the Meiji Constitution to preserve legal continuity. I am concerned with the attitudes prevalent during the deliberations.

21. The complete texts of Plan A and Plan B are in Commission on the Constitution, *Report of the Subcommittee on the Formation of the Constitution,* p. 679ff.; and Satō, *Nihonkoku kempō seiritsu-shi,* vol. 2, pp. 550ff. and 567ff. Until midway through the deliberations, what later corresponded to Plan A was called Plan B and vice versa. Caution is advised.

22. For details on the Nomura Memorandum and how it was treated, see Satō, *Nihonkoku kempō seiritsu-shi,* vol. 2, pp. 326–333.

23. During the deliberations there was no discussion about the establishment of a constitutional court or the adoption of a judicial review system or other machinery to perform that function.

24. Letter from General Whitney to Mr. Shirasu, February 16, 1946, in Takayanagi, Ōtomo, and Tanaka, *Nihonkoku kempō seitei no katei,* pp. 346–347.

25. The possibility of adding Sasaki Sōichi to the Matsumoto Committee was considered. But Minobe Tatsukichi objected on the grounds that there could be no approval of the office of the Lord Keeper of the Privy Seal officially engaging in research on constitutional reform and that the inclusion of Sasaki would constitute such approval (Satō, *Nihonkoku kempō seiritsu-shi,* vol. 1, pp. 261–262). Matsumoto requested that Sasaki join but he declined, saying that he would have too many irons in the fire (ibid., and interview with Sasaki Sōichi, Tokyo, November 26, 1954).

26. All members except advisers were on the "investigative committee." Eight sessions, the seventh to fourteenth meetings, were held by a three-man subcommittee to draw up a draft. The subcommittee members were Miyasawa Toshiyoshi, Irie Toshirō, and Satō Tatsuo. For details on the deliberations of the Matsumoto Committee, see Satō, *Nihonkoku kempō seiritsu-shi,* vol. 1, pp. 252–374; vol. 2, pp. 485–627; and Irie, *Kempō seiritsu no keii to kempōjō no shomondai,* pp. 19–196.

27. Foreign Ministry Document R. No. 92 *no* 2–1, A'3.0.0.2–2 *dai* 1, nine pages.

28. Reference to *Kempō satsuyō* is to the fifth edition (1932; the first edition was published in 1923). Reference to *Kempō ryakusetsu* is to the 1942 edition. Reference to *Kempō jutsugi* is to the 1924 edition.

29. See Takayanagi Kenzō, "Shihōteki kempō hoshōsei" [Guarantee of constitutional rights through the judiciary], *Kokka gakkai zasshi* (1929), vol. 43, no. 9, p. 1378, note 3.

30. Uesugi Shinkichi, *Kempō jutsugi* [The constitution truly explained] (1924), pp. 601–606. For a representative work by the latter, see Minobe Tatsukichi, *Kempō satsuyō* [Essentials of the constitution] (5th ed., 1932), pp. 567–569. This was Minobe's position from his first work, *Kempō kōwa* [Lectures on the constitution] (1912).

31. Great Court of Judicature, Judgment, March 3, 1937, *Keishū* [Great Court of Judicature reports, criminal cases], vol. 16, p. 193. The administrative courts took the same position. Administrative Court Judgment, December 27, 1927, *Gyōroku* [Records of judgments of the administrative court], vol. 38, p. 1330.

32. *Hōgaku kyōkai zasshi,* vol. 39, no. 1, p. 19; no. 2, p. 208; no. 4, p. 514; and no. 9, p. 1477.

33. Takayanagi Kenzō, *Shihōken no yūi* [Judicial supremacy] (Rev. ed., 1958), preface, p. 1, and text, pp. 2–3.

34. Satō, *Nihonkoku kempō seiritsu-shi,* vol. 1, pp. 273–278.

35. Irie, *Kempō seiritsu no keii to kempōjō no shomondai,* p. 25.

36. For the original and the translation submitted to SCAP, see Takayanagi, Ōtomo, and Tanaka, *Nihonkoku kempō seitei no katei,* vol. 1, pp. 359–360.

37. (Prewar) Imperial House Law, Arts. 49, 50.

38. The Imperial Constitution of Japan, Art. 74 and the (prewar) Imperial House Law, Art. 62.

39. "Gist of the Revision of the Constitution," Art. 1.

40. Satō, *Nihonkoku kempō seiritsu-shi,* vol. 1, p. 262; and Irie, *Kempō seiritsu no keii to kempōjō no shomondai,* p. 25.

41. Satō, *Nihonkoku kempō seiritsu-shi,* vol. 1, p. 266.

42. For example, see Commission on the Constitution, *Fifth Plenary Meeting,* December 22, vol. 1, p. 355.

43. The original Konoe and Sasaki drafts are in Kempō Chōsakai Jimukyoku, *Teikoku kempō daisei shoan oyobi kankei bunsho* [Drafts and related documents on the reform of the Imperial Constitution], vol. 6, *Naidaijinfu gawa kankei bunsho* [Lord Keeper of the Privy Seal office documents] (Kenshi, Sō No. 26) (1958). For the project under Konoe carried out at the office of the Lord Keeper of the Privy Seal, see Satō, *Nihonkoku kempō seiritsu-shi,* vol. 1, pp. 177–244.

44. The drafts submitted by Inada Masatsugu, Kiyose Ichirō, Kempō Kenkyū-kai, Kempō Kondankai, Satomi Kishio, Dai Nihon Bengoshi Rengōkai, Takano Iwasaburō, Nihon Kyōsan-tō, Nihon Shakai-tō, Nihon Jiyu-tō, Nihon Shimpo-tō, Fuse Tatsuji, etc. See Kempō Chōsakai Jimukyoku, *Teikoku kempō kaisei shoan oyobi kankei bunsho,* vol. 2 (Kenshi, Sō No. 10) (1957).

45. For the discussions in the Cabinet Legislation Bureau, see Irie, *Kempō seiritsu no keii to kempōjō no shomondai.*

46. See n. 22 above.

47. That this statement did not change the meaning of the Potsdam Declaration is apparent from its tone and content and the explicit phrase "in accordance with the Potsdam Declaration."

48. Takagi Yasaka recalled:

> I believe it was January 26. I visited Matsumoto-*sensei* in his office in the prime minister's official residence. I said to him: "Our feeling is that an attempt to limit reforms to the very minimum will not resolve the problem. Thus, well, we wonder if it wouldn't be better to listen to the views of GHQ and take them into consideration before you make the final draft. As we understand the situation, for example, the idea of retaining most of the present constitution as it is will not work." Matsumoto-*sensei* replied: "Constitutional reform is to be done spontaneously and independently. Therefore, I see no need to find out American intentions or reach preliminary understandings." (Commission on the Constitution, "Takagi Yasaka meiyo kyojū danwaroku" [Record of interview with Professor Emeritus Takagi Yasaka], in *1953 nen 10 gatsu 26 nichi ni Tokyo Daigaku Senryō Taisei Kenkyūkai ga okonatta intavū* [Interview conducted by the Tokyo Daigaku Senryō Taisei Kenkyūkai on October 26, 1953])

Ōtomo Ichirō, then a young administrative assistant attached to the cabinet, recalled that Takagi Yasaka's shoulders were stooped as he left Matsumoto's office that day completely discouraged. Conversation with the author.

49. See Yabe Teiji, *Konoe Fumimaro,* vol. 2 (1952), p. 591; and the Commission on the Constitution, *Ninth Session of the Subcommittee on the Formation of the Constitution,* statement by Tomita Kenji, pp. 8, 596. Ushiba Tomohiko has stated: "Dr. Takagi and Matsumoto [Shigeharu] and I, together or individually, visited the office of Atcheson, the Political Adviser [to the Supreme Commander]. We usually met with Bishop and Emmerson and we tried to find out American

views on constitutional reform." Commission on the Constitution, *Ninth Session of the Subcommittee on the Formation of the Constitution,* pp. 15–16. See also Takagi Yasaka's statement in ibid., pp. 17, 19–20.

50. These materials are in Satō, *Nihonkoku kempō seiritsu-shi,* vol. 2, pp. 661–662.

51. The GHQ officers—Kades, Hussey, and Rowell—jointly prepared a report of the discussions within an hour after returning from the meeting. See "Records of Events on 13 February 1946 When Proposed New Constitution for Japan Was Submitted to the Foreign Ministry, Mr. Yoshida, on Behalf of the Supreme Commander." For the original and a translation, see Takayanagi, Ōtomo, and Tanaka, *Nihonkoku kempō seitei no katei,* vol. 1, pp. 320–336.

52. The Government Section prepared a memorandum for General MacArthur on his authority for constitutional reform after the FEC had come into existence: "Memorandum for the Supreme Commander, Subject: Constitutional Reform" (February 1, 1946). The document is included in ibid., pp. 90–98.

53. Shidehara Heiwa Zaidan, comp., *Shidehara Kijurō* (1955), p. 688. However, the FEC had not yet begun to function, and there is considerable doubt about the authenticity of this account. Nevertheless, there does seem to have been some kind of concrete explanation of the international situation.

54. Even after the GHQ draft was presented, Matsumoto remained unconcerned about the international situation. See Commission on the Constitution, "Matsumoto Jōji-shi ni kiku" [Interview with Matsumoto Jōji], *Record of Conversation with Tokyo University Senryō Taisei Kenkyūkai on November 23, 1950* (1960), pp. 68–70. By contrast, career diplomat Yoshida adopted a different position relatively early after February 13.

55. Takayanagi, Ōtomo, and Tanaka, *Nihonkoku kempō seitei no katei,* vol. 1, pp. 322–323.

56. Conversation with Ōtomo Ichirō.

57. Takayanagi, Ōtomo, and Tanaka, *Nihonkoku kempō seitei no katei,* vol. 1, pp. 394–395.

58. Tanaka, *Kempō seitei katei oboegaki,* pp. 112–116. For example, see the comment on the provisions concerning the emperor in the Matsumoto draft. See "Comments on the Document, 'Gist of the Revision of the Constitution,'" in Takayanagi, Ōtomo, and Tanaka, *Nihonkoku kempō seitei no katei,* vol. 1, pp. 82–87.

59. Takayanagi, Ōtomo, and Tanaka, *Nihonkoku kempō seitei no katei,* pp. 338–339.

60. The original and an English translation are in ibid., pp. 354–364.

61. Ibid., pp. 380–381.

62. Ibid., pp. 388–389.

63. Ibid.

64. Matsumoto Bunsho [Matsumoto documents], in the possession of the Tokyo Daigaku Hōgakubu [Tokyo University Law Faculty], p. 791.

65. At the outset of the meeting on February 22, General Whitney said:

We have set forth principles, in this new constitution, and defined procedures that tie these basic principles together and will make them work. As far as matters of procedure are concerned we will discuss them with you. We have great respect for your experience and I know that you can draft an instrument more in tune with Japanese forms than I or my staff can. As General MacArthur told your Prime Minister yesterday, it is the basic principles and structure that we are insistent upon. (Takayanagi, Ōtomo, and Tanaka, *Nihonkoku kempō seitei no katei,* vol. 1, pp. 380–383)

66. Satō, *Nepāru no Itō Hirobumi* [An Itō Hirobumi from Nepal] (1972), pp. 206, 219. See also Tanaka, *Kempō seitei katei oboegaki,* pp. 79–80.

67. Takayanagi, Ōtomo, and Tanaka, *Nihonkoku kempō seitei no katei,* vol. 1, pp. 327–329.

68. Courtney Whitney, *MacArthur, His Rendezvous with History* (1956), pp. 250–252.

69. Commission on the Constitution, *Seventh Plenary Session,* statement by Ashida Hitoshi, p. 75.

70. In the early literature about the constitution several works were produced through the cooperation of a large number of legal scholars from diverse fields of specialization. For example, see Kokka Gakkai, *Shin kempō no kenkyū* [Research on the new constitution] (1947); Hōgaku Kyōkai, *Chūkai Nihonkoku kempō* [Commentary on the constitution of Japan] (1948–1950; rev. ed., 1953); Kempō Fukyūkai, ed., *Shin kempō soshō* [Series on the new constitution] (1947–1948).

71. There was also a tendency to describe prewar politics and administration more negatively than the facts warranted.

5

Early SCAP Policy
and the Rehabilitation
of the Diet

Hans H. Baerwald

National legislatures are in bad repute these days, and the Japanese Diet is no exception. Forty years ago, however, both the Occupation authorities, principally Government Section of the Supreme Commander for the Allied Powers (SCAP), and certain segments of the Japanese government sought to strengthen the powers of Japan's supreme legislative body. Attempting to lift the Diet to a position of preeminence within the Japanese legal framework was of course not without moments of failure as well as of success.

Interestingly enough, neither the Potsdam Declaration, which had set forth the terms of surrender, nor the United States State-War-Navy Coordinating Committee (SWNCC) Instructions, nor the Joint Chiefs of Staff Directive to Supreme Commander Douglas MacArthur directly mentions the Japanese parliamentary body.[1] To be sure, the need to encourage the Japanese to establish a democratic form of self-government was discussed at length, with the admonition that they should not be forced to adopt a form of government against their freely expressed will. It was assumed by Occupation and by Japanese policy makers alike that a democratic system of government would perforce include a vastly strengthened publicly elected national legislature. Yet this assumption, which was incorporated into the process of constitutional revision and the law governing parliamentary procedure, was never explicitly set forth in the basic policy documents that guided the initial reform phase of the Occupation.

In the latter half of September 1945, less than a month after the beginning of the Occupation, the Diet became the subject of informal discussions between SCAP's Political Affairs Advisor George Atcheson and Prince Konoe Fumimaro. Ambassador Atcheson suggested a number of points that later would be accepted as axiomatic; possibly the most important of these points was that the House of Representatives have a larger share of authority, particularly in formulating the national budget, and that the House of Peers no longer have veto power over legislation passed by the House of Representatives.[2] Throughout the fall of 1945 and early winter of 1946, the Japanese seemed generally to agree that some revision of the Meiji Constitution was inevitable. Political party proposals were freely discussed and circulated. Most important, the so-called Matsumoto Committee on Constitutional Revision was established in October 1945. Even that committee's minimal suggested amendments included replacing the House of Peers (Kizokuin) with a more broadly representative chamber.

By and large, however, the Matsumoto Committee's minimalist approach occasioned dismay within General Headquarters and led to the decision that Government Section be constituted as the agency to draft a new model constitution for Japan. The results, of course, were far-reaching.

The question of whether Japan's parliament should have one chamber or two was the first issue raised. That it would almost immediately become one of the most emotional of issues and that the results of the decision would be controversial even today were problems not anticipated in early Government Section meetings. Initial Government Section discussions included the idea that the Diet should be unicameral rather than bicameral.

> At the first meeting, it was made known that General MacArthur favored a unicameral legislature and the general opinion was strongly in support of this position, primarily because it was felt that the House of Peers should be done away with, and nothing should be established that in any way resembled it. Furthermore, there was strong objection to any form of a corporate or functional upper house, a favorite proposition of the Japanese.[3]

When the new draft of the Japanese constitution was presented to the Japanese government on the morning of February 13, 1946, the "Report" of Government Section notes, the only item raised for discussion was the notion of the Diet becoming unicameral. "The Japanese appeared visibly surprised and disturbed and said they would have to consider the matter and discuss it with the Cabinet before any definite answer could be given."[4]

Satō Tatsuo, who at the time of the drafting of the new constitution was councillor of the Bureau of Legislation and who served as one of the principal go-betweens in his government's negotiations with Government Section, writes that Committee Chairman Matsumoto included bicameralism in the March 2, 1946, draft and insisted that the electorate be based on occupational groups. General Courtney Whitney, chief of Government Section, and his deputy, Colonel Charles Kades, had obviously failed to persuade Matsumoto that "Japan is different from the United States, which consists of many states. Hence an upper house is not required [in Japan]. Furthermore, unicameralism is simpler than bicameralism."[5] Satō also quotes from an explanatory document attached to the Japanese draft in which Matsumoto set out his ideas on the differences between the House of Peers and the proposed House of Councillors.

> The *Sangiin* (House of Councillors) should be organized in order to reflect the best of public opinion. This goal will be achieved by having representatives who are men of knowledge and wisdom within the community or who reflect occupational groups. Thus the House of Councillors, unlike the old House of Peers, will be able to reflect the soundest opinion among all the residents of the nation. It is for these reasons that some of the members of the House of Councillors should be appointed by the Cabinet, because sometimes difficulties may arise in finding an appropriate electorate for certain types of occupational groups.[6]

Professor Matsumoto's draft provision regarding the House of Councillors proved to be "absolutely unacceptable" to Government Section officials. After overnight discussions, in which Satō was the principal negotiator, it was finally agreed that a new provision in the draft constitution would read: "Both Houses shall consist of representatives of all of the residents of the nation and shall be elected."[7] It was also agreed that the terms of the members of the House of Councillors should be six years with half of them elected every three years. Satō credits Matsumoto with this innovative electoral system. It was also during these negotiations that the Japanese government representatives put forth their idea that the House of Councillors remain in session after the House of Representatives had been dissolved and while it was awaiting a new election. Satō reports that Government Section officials initially were reluctant to accept this idea and finally agreed to a provision stating that the House of Councillors can continue to function on behalf of the Diet in case of emergency, providing that at soon as it is again operational the House of Representatives approves the actions taken by the House of Councillors.[8]

Although there seemed to be general agreement in both the House of Representatives and the House of Peers that bicameralism was preferable to unicameralism, from the outset there was considerably uncertainty about the role of the second chamber, the projected House of Councillors. Sasaki Sōichi reflected these concerns in his remarks at a plenary session of the House of Peers.

> It is strange for us to have two organs that represent all residents of the nation. It is also absurd that the House of Representatives has greater power, but that it can also be dissolved while both houses are supposedly representing the same people. Insofar as the House of Councillors is concerned, it should perform duties that are different from the House of Representatives and should also be organized differently.[9]

In a discussion of the Diet law after the constitution was framed, Viscount Okōchi Kikō of the House of Peers expressed his bitterness over proposals for a decrease in power for the successor of that chamber: "Under the Imperial Diet Law the two houses were at least equal in terms of having the right to request a conference between the two chambers. Under this new Diet Law, the proposed House of Councillors may not even be able to request such a joint meeting."[10] Satō Tatsuo, of the House of Representatives Secretariat, responded to the Viscount's remarks by stating:

> I can understand your contention that the House of Councillors also should have the right to request a conference between the two chambers. However, the Diet Law must not conflict with Article 59 of the [new] constitution. The new Diet Law must observe the superiority of the House of Representatives. Hence, the House of Councillors cannot be entitled to request a conference between the two chambers without paying attention to what the House of Representatives desires.[11]

Decades later it is still not entirely clear why it was that Japanese officials (exemplified by Professor Matsumoto) so vociferously supported retention of a second chamber when there was no consensus on what that chamber should do or whom it should represent. Maeo Shigesaburō, who in 1977 had just retired from the speakership of the House of Representatives after a particularly turbulent session of the Diet, surprised me by the vehemence of his statement that "our government's representatives made a very serious mistake when they insisted that the Diet should be bicameral and that the House of Councillors should be created to replace the House of Peers. We would have been much better off at the present time if the second chamber did not exist."[12] Echoing these sentiments a year later Uchida Kenzō remarked: "If there is disagreement between the two chambers, the management of politics becomes difficult. If there is no disagreement between the two chambers, then what is the use of having the House of Councillors?"[13]

Some modern observers believe bicameralism in Japan reflects the theme of form over substance (*tatemae* versus *honne*). Other Japanese colleagues have suggested that the themes of continuity and tradition may help to explain the Japanese position at that time: unicameralism would have been too abrupt a break with tradition, and furthermore, the Japanese tend to prefer a system of dispersed political power. Except for the bureaucracy, competing centers of authority had been either reduced to virtual impotence, such as the imperial institution, or completely abolished, as in the case of the Privy Council (Sūmitsuin). Hence a unicameral parliament would be too strong. A third possibility is that the bureaucracy itself felt threatened by a strong unicameral legislature. Whatever the reason or reasons, bicameralism as a doctrine triumphed over unicameralism.

The question also arises, why did SCAP give in on this issue? It is conceivable that the retention of bicameralism in the new constitution was a price SCAP had to pay for the Japanese government's adoption of some far-reaching revisions affecting the powers of the House of Representatives. The constitutional doctrine of parliamentary supremacy as opposed to the imperial sovereignty that had existed under the Meiji Constitution was a far more important matter to SCAP. Naturally, there was some confusion about this doctrine. From the Japanese perspective, the shift from imperial prerogative to Diet supremacy created uneasiness. From the American perspective, there was the contradiction between the Diet's role as the "sole law-making organ of the State" and the newly established Supreme Court's authority to determine the constitutionality of any law, as under the American doctrine of separation of powers. To resolve these and other problems and to create a constitutional framework fundamentally at variance with the existing one required a concentrated effort. That this effort succeeded was no mean achievement. It is well known that Government Section played a controlling role in the process of constitutional revision. Without external intervention in Japanese politics at the highest level it is possible that the House of Peers might have been retained, and it is certain that the new constitution would not have provided that "the Diet shall be the highest organ of state power and shall be the sole law-making organ of the State."[14]

A brief review of some of the major steps that led to the Diet's prominence within Japan's new constitutional order will provide perspective for an analysis of the actions taken to change the new doctrine into political reality. First, as indicated in Professor Ward's chapter in this volume, presurrender planning in Washington, D.C., had given consideration to strengthening the national representative assembly. Second, both the SWNCC and JCS directives to SCAP had included general admonitions to upgrade the position of the Diet, especially vis-à-vis the cabinet and with reference to the budget. Third, these requirements had been discussed by SCAP Political Advisor George Atcheson in his meeting with Prince Konoe Fumimaro in early fall 1945. Fourth, this goal formed the background for, but not necessarily the substance of, the Matsumoto Committee's work in drafting amendments to the Meiji Constitution. Finally, the presurrender planning that was reflected in the Washington directives to General MacArthur became central to Government Section's writing of the "model" constitution. All this prior work provided the general policy framework to guide SCAP's Government Section in preparing the constitutional provisions that were to govern the Diet.

There were differences in priorities at different times in Government Section as elsewhere. In his book on the Occupation, Justin Williams brings out some crucial points regarding priorities affecting the Diet.[15] First, and possibly most important, no specific policy guidelines from Washington or anywhere else had been sent to SCAP regarding the organization or operations of the Diet under the constitution. Dr. Williams' immediate predecessor as Chief of the Legislative Branch, Commander Guy Swope, had served as a congressman and was presumed able to communicate to the Japanese his knowledge of legislative procedure. Furthermore, while very early in the Occupation SCAP had sent an order to the Japanese government[16] requesting that Occupation authorities be kept informed of the Diet's activities, which was done by having the "Diet Record" *(Kampō)* translated into English, other than that translation the Diet was left pretty much on its own day-to-day workings for the first year of the Occupation, especially from March to September 1946. This was so even during those months when the constitution was being redrafted to make the Diet the "highest organ of state power" and during the period when a Diet committee was considering revisions in the Diet law.

By and large, Government Section officials were activists in their dealings with the Japanese government. Even so, and primarily because of differences in priorities, it was not until September 1946 that Justin Williams undertook his campaign within Government Section to focus on the Diet as the key to Japan's democratization under the new constitution. There is some ambiguity about how much direct SCAP supervision of the Diet took place during the late spring and summer of 1946. Williams' recollections indicate that the interaction was minimal, but Japanese sources tend to reflect fairly constant tutoring by Government Section officials. Williams recounts that before he could undertake to persuade Diet leaders to overhaul Japan's half-century-old legislative system he had to sell the specifics of a comprehensive reform plan to his superiors, General Whitney and Colonel Kades. This he did in a lengthy memorandum dated September 10, 1946, initially drafted September 3, then informally and unofficially examined by Professor Harold S. Quigley. Professor Quigley was a recognized authority on prewar Japanese politics serving with SCAP's Civil Information (Intelligence) Section, and the collaboration between the two men was significant in that it indicated at least some cooperation between the two SCAP agencies.

In the memorandum Williams set forth certain weaknesses of the Diet: first, a lack of dignity and prestige; second, internal machinery that was insufficient to direct the affairs of a modern state; third, the possibility that the increase of power under the new constitution might be curtailed by subsequent legislation; and fourth, that the current leadership of the Diet did not seem to be willing to act against the "feudalistic bureaucracy which dominates the national government."[17] All these generalizations came to be part of Government Section's "conventional wisdom," but the one that has the loudest overtones thirty years later is the fourth. I can vividly recall the feelings of frustration that all of us in Government Section at the time felt toward the immense power of the Japanese bureaucracy in comparison to the elected politicians in the national Diet and, despite the "Purge,"[18] toward our limited tools for dealing with Japan's governmental officials.

After setting forth the weaknesses of the Diet and providing a good deal of supporting evidence, Williams turned to the whole matter of how the Diet might best be strengthened. Because there is no reference to meetings with the Japanese committees working on Diet law reform it must be assumed that Dr. Williams prepared these materials without interaction with the Japanese at this stage. He made fourteen recommendations: (1) that the members receive appropriate pay, (2) that each member have adequate secretarial assistance, (3) that each member have an office, (4) that each member be provided with franking privileges, (5) that each house of the Diet have an independent contingency fund that was to be included in the Diet's budget (rather than be under the control of the Ministry of Finance), (6) that a Diet library be established, (7) that each house have adequate legislative reference services, (8) that a legislative council of the houses be established to iron out differences between them, (9) that a standing committee for each ministry be established in each house, (10) that these committees employ qualified experts, (11) that the committees have public hearings, (12) that there be provision for "free discussion" by the members, (13) that interpellations have a time limit, and (14) that all practices degrading to members be eliminated.[19]

This memorandum was vetted inside Government Section and ultimately received the approval of Deputy Chief Charles L. Kades. Having obtained the concurrence of his colleagues as well as the approval of General Courtney Whitney, chief of Government Section, Williams' next task was to convince the leadership of the Diet to accept his far-reaching reorganization plan. In this effort he had the active support of some Diet members as well as of officials in the Diet's Secretariat.

At this point we must go back to the period immediately after the new draft of the constitution had been publicized in the spring of 1946. Williams' effort to alter the Diet law occurred primarily in the fall of 1946. Nishizawa Tetsushirō, who at the time was deputy secretary general of the House of Representatives Secretariat, recalls that shortly after the publication of the new constitution—long before it was promulgated officially—Secretariat members discussed the need to alter the Diet law itself as well as the "Rules" of the House of Representatives.[20] He recalls that, in discussions with Government Section officials in late spring and summer 1946, doubt was expressed about the need for revising the Diet law itself and that possibly only the "Rules" of the respective houses would have to be altered. Having received little encouragement from SCAP officials on this score, however, Mr. Nishizawa and his colleagues in the House of Representatives Secretariat drew up a list of changes needed for the Diet to perform its functions as envisaged by the new constitution.

Inside Government Section the whole question of revising the Diet law was far less important, apparently, than trying to replace the newly elected Speaker of the House of Representatives, Higai Senzō, whose opposition to change was manifest. In characteristically stinging style former congressman Guy J. Swope, then chief of the Legislative Branch of Government Section, wrote a memorandum to General Whitney in which he reported on a meeting that he and some of his colleagues had had with Speaker Higai. Commander Swope's memorandum deserves reproduction as it reflects the attitudes toward the Diet prevailing at the highest levels of the Occupation. After noting that the organization and procedures then in effect in the Diet were designed for a weak and subservient legislature, Swope goes on:

> If the Diet is to meet its heavy responsibilities under the proposed Constitution as the "highest organ of state power and the supreme law-making authority of the State," its machinery must be adequate to permit the full and efficient discharge of those responsibilities. A Diet incompetent to discharge these duties will discredit representative government.
>
> Under present circumstances, the Diet requires vigorous, devoted leadership to pilot it through the period during which the Diet must assume effective control of government, strengthen its machinery, and establish its prestige. The new Speaker, Higai Senzō, is tragically unfit for this responsibility.
>
> Because of long experience in the Japanese bureaucracy, the new Speaker looks upon government with bureaucratic eyes. He shares the prevailing attitude of the professional bureaucrats who regard legislation as a subordinate function of government and look upon Members of the House of Representatives as half-educated, incompetent boors and ignoramuses. With the formal legalism that characterizes Japanese bureaucrats, he persistently interposes trivial obstructions to important measures necessary to establish the new Diet on a solid foundation. A typical instance was his hesitation to agree to a select committee of House Members to study organizational and procedural reform because of possible difficulty in securing funds for that purpose and because members might be "too busy" during the coming session.
>
> It is most unfortunate that at this critical moment the Diet should be burdened with a leader who is both: (a) too weak to press the interest of the Diet through forceful and constructive leadership, and (b) unwilling because of a bureaucratic cast of thought even to concede to the Diet a pre-eminent role in Government.[21]

In due course, Speaker Higai was forced to resign at the request of the members of the House of Representatives, not through Government Section intervention. Higai was replaced by Speaker Yamazaki Takeshi, who proved to be much more amenable to fundamental change.

Throughout the summer and fall of 1946 two separate Japanese committees were involved in trying to devise a Diet law establishing a new set of ground rules. The second section of the Provisional Legislative Investigating Committee (Rinji Hōsei Chōsakai) reflected the government's viewpoint—that is, it did the cabinet's and bureaucracy's bidding. The second group was appointed by the Inter-Party Negotiating Conference (Kaku-ha Kōshō-Kai) within the House of Representatives and was called the Representatives' Law Investigation Committee (Giin Hōki Chōsa Iinkai). Nakamura Kōichi, a member of the committee, explained its task in these terms:

> We devoted particular attention to the following matters. Under the new constitution the operation of the individual houses should be in the hands of the Diet even though under the Meiji constitution the Diet had been subordinate to the government [the imperial institution and the bureaucracy]. We eliminated all sections of the old "Imperial Law of the Houses" in which the government would be in a position of superiority over the Diet. In this sense, the new "Diet Law" is centered in the houses instead of in the government. We have either revised or discarded faults which we found in the operation of the old "Imperial Law of the Houses." For example, the Committee of the Whole [Zen-in Iinkai] and the system of having three readings for each bill [sandokukaiseidō] were discarded.[22]

Ultimately this committee's views prevailed over those of the cabinet and bureaucracy.

The Inter-Party Negotiating Conference had agreed on June 18 to establish the committee, and the selection of its members was concluded by July 1, 1946. Its principal period of activity was from August 9 through September 7[23] (the last week roughly corresponding with the inception of Williams' campaign within Government Section to focus attention on the Diet). One of the first tasks that the committee undertook was to translate the then newly adopted "Congressional Reorganization Act of 1946." Ōike Makoto, who at the time was director general of the House of Representatives Secretariat and who also played a central role in drafting the new Diet law, reported the following:

> Government Section of GHQ rendered every assistance throughout this period [that is, the drafting of the law], supplying us with the "Reorganization Act of 1946" as passed by the United States Senate, encouraging the committee to frame a genuinely democratic Diet law, and offering suggestions on numerous occasions for increasing the authority of the National Diet, for which the entire membership of this committee is most grateful.[24]

It is noteworthy that although neither the Far Eastern Commission nor the Allied Council for Japan sanctioned the use of the act as a guide for the reorganization of the national Diet, and this purpose certainly was not a consideration in its fashioning, the new internal procedures of Congress had a profound impact on the sister institution in Japan.

The fourteen specific points that Government Section had recommended to strengthen the powers of the Diet under the new constitution were boiled down to eleven, and these were submitted to Speaker Yamazaki on November 5, 1946.[25] On the basis of the available record, including recollections of those involved, this is the only written memorandum with specific suggestions on legislative reform made to the Japanese government by Government Section. It must be emphasized that the document is "informal" in the sense that it is not a SCAPIN, that is to say, an official order from the Occupation to the Japanese government. On the other hand, it is "formal" in contrast to the other suggestions that flowed from Government Section to members of the House of Representatives Secretariat, which were oral with very few records having been kept.

At the top of the Government Section list and representing the core of the recommendations made was the suggestion that a system of standing committees be created. These were to be subject-matter committees, intended to cover all major fields of legislative activity rather than one-to-one, paralleling the ministries. They were also to be provided with adequate assistance at government expense. Particularly noteworthy is one change made during the course of discussions between Dr. Williams and Speaker Yamazaki regarding the Government Section suggestions. The original typed manuscript indicates that members of a standing committee, once they had been selected, were to remain on it from session to session or as long as they desired. This was altered so that the members would remain "for term"—presumably so that the membership would revolve, although this is not clearly indicated. It was also suggested that specific parliamentary rules be drawn up to govern the conduct of committee deliberations, including the holding of public hearings and the calling of witnesses.

Of all the changes in the Diet law the establishment of subject-matter committees was the most fundamental. To be sure, as will be noted in greater detail below, members of the imperial Diet during the 1930s had discussed the possibility or feasibility of creating "standing committees." However, efforts to do so had been abortive.[26]

> The most significant part of the Diet law, the chapter dealing with standing committees, parallels in several important respects the "United States Legislative Reorganization Act of 1946." The system of standing committees more than anything else differentiates the House of Representatives from the British House of Commons and gives the Diet a strong resemblance to the United States Congress. Whether the Diet becomes "the highest organ of state power and the sole law-making organ" will depend, in the last analysis, upon the degree to which the standing committees use the powers conferred upon them and the skill with which they employ the legislative aids and devices provided in the Diet law.[27]

This retrospective commentary in the official "Report" of Government Section reflects the importance placed by Dr. Williams and his associates on this particular innovation in the Diet's structure. For them, and in all probability for the Japanese participants in the drafting of the new rules, this shift in emphasis was to be the fundamental building block that would support the Diet's ability to live up to its new, constitutionally pre-scribed mandate. In this connection it must be remembered that the imperial Diet that was gradually being phased out of existence had con-ducted most of its business in plenary session, a natural state of affairs under a parliamentary system of government in which the cabinet was the center of power with the members of the legislative assembly re-sponding to initiatives of the executive branch. There is almost no indica-tion in the records of Government Section, in the debates in the Diet, or in the recollections of the participants involved in negotiations between the Diet and Government Section that this change, the creation of sub-ject-matter committees, would become one of the most difficult struc-tural problems facing the new Diet. Instead, everyone hoped that the members of the Diet would somehow be able to resolve the major prob-lems inherent in such a marriage of convenience between parliamentary and congressional systems of government. In assessing this and other American innovations, Dr. Williams notes the following:

> [The Diet] was restructured with no other thought than to strengthen it vis-à-vis the Japanese bureaucracy for the more responsible role it was to play under the democratic Constitution. Both the new Constitution and the National Diet Law contain features borrowed from the British and Ameri-can systems of government. To those Japanese leaders who were dubious about mixing parliamentary and presidential democracy, SCAP's advice was always the same, "Try the new system, keep what is good, discard what is unworkable."[28]

In addition it was suggested that all committee hearings and plenary sessions be freely open to the public and that executive sessions be per-mitted only under exceptional circumstances. Since most members of the Diet and the Secretariat were not familiar with congressional procedure, the term "executive session" created some difficulty and required expla-nation. It was also proposed that a Legislative Council be created, to consist of members of both houses with the functions of advising the cab-inet and both chambers on legislative needs and problems as well as studying and proposing revisions of the Diet law and the "Rules" of both houses. This Legislative Council caused considerable difficulties and was one of the first provisions stricken from the Diet law in the aftermath of the Occupation.

Implicit in all the suggestions was the desire that Diet members be allowed to participate freely in making national policy. To that end it was proposed that a free discussion period be allowed once every two weeks. All members could question the government on any aspect of national policy. This free discussion period and the traditional "interpellations" of the government—that is, formal questions on government policy that had been a traditional element in Diet procedure even in the prewar period—would, however, be subject to a time limit. The rationale behind this suggestion was that more members should be encouraged to participate. In his exegesis on these suggestions, Dr. Williams notes that the recommendation regarding free and open discussion was intended to safeguard minority rights. There is no question in my mind that all of these proposals were made with the best of intentions. They were also made with the clear purpose of strengthening the Diet vis-à-vis the government, especially the national bureaucracy, which—as has already been noted—was the *bête noire* of Government Section.

I have not been able to determine from the available records why the political parties and their role were disregarded. It seemed to be assumed in all the recommendations that the members of the Diet would act as individual legislators who would not have loyalties to anything other than their role as autonomous law-givers and, possibly, their relationship with their constituents. Yet, as is well known, in Japan it is the group that predominates. Somehow this feature of Japanese society was neglected both by Government Section officials and, even more incomprehensibly, by the Japanese who participated in the drafting of the new Diet law. For the Japanese, it is conceivable that the neglect lies in the fact that so many of the participants in the ad hoc negotiations with Government Section officials were not themselves members of the Diet but officials attached to the Diet Secretariat. In other words they, too, were bureaucrats rather than members of political parties who would be involved in the daily parliamentary maneuvering of a Diet session.

This omission is curious given the fact that much time had been devoted by Government Section and by Japanese officials, particularly those in the Diet Secretariat, to studying the old imperial "Diet Record," which had given parties a role—the Inter-Party Negotiating Conference being a particularly salient feature. A quirk in the internal organization of Government Section may have been partially responsible for the omission on the American side. The Legislative Branch was separate from the Political Parties Branch.[29] Since political parties were thus under another jurisdiction, it is understandable that they were not uppermost in the minds of those concerned with reorganizing the Diet. To be sure, political parties were overlooked—probably deliberately—in drafting the American constitution, and many of the American suggestions for reform seemed to reflect the notion that the members of the Diet would act as individuals in the same sense that members of Congress are first and foremost individuals rather than disciplined members of political parties. However, some of the wholly unanticipated consequences of the suggestions are, in my opinion, due to this neglect of the political party system in Japan.[30]

It will be recalled that two Japanese committees had been working on revising the "Imperial Law of the Houses" since the early summer of 1946. The House of Representatives committee, drawn from all political parties, ultimately was far more important than that representing the bureaucracy. Technically the new Diet law was produced by the committee, but it should be noted that the House of Representatives Secretariat did the actual drafting in detail—a not unusual circumstance.

Mr. Nishizawa, in his recollections for the Constitutional Investigation Commission,[31] stated that the new Diet law was based on the "Imperial Law of the Houses" and on the outline that had been prepared by the House of Representatives' committee. Its draft, presented to Government Section on October 31, 1946, furnished the occasion for Dr. Williams to submit his suggestions in return, in the first week of November. As might have been anticipated, given its innovative character, the standing-committee system created the greatest difficulties in the ensuing negotiations between the Diet, whose representatives included Speaker Yamazaki and officials of the Diet Secretariat, and Government Section, represented by Dr. Williams. The development of Chapter 5 of the new Diet law, "Committees and Their Membership,"[32] will be used to illustrate the kind of working relationship that came into existence between Government Section and its Japanese government counterparts.

Committees had existed in the imperial Diet. That system, patterned after the Westminster model, had consisted of a Committee of the Whole, standing committees (jōnin iinkai), and special or ad hoc committees (tokubetsu iinkai). Standing committees, which were, of course, most closely related to those that Dr. Williams and his associates in Government Section sought to introduce into the Diet, had been few. They included committees on qualifications, on the budget, on disciplinary measures, and on petitions. Under special circumstances the House could establish a standing committee to deal with a particular legislative bill. In addition, the House of Representatives had sought to incorporate the idea that committees could function even during recesses of the imperial Diet. That is, certain committees could continue (keizoku suru) from one session to the next. This proposal was not realized because the government (that is, cabinet) sanction it required was never forthcoming.

Nishizawa also recollected that the imperial Diet, especially the House of Representatives, had three times sought to establish a system of standing committees—jōchi iinkai—during the 1930s. Jōchi iinkai were distinguished from jōnin iinkai because they incorporated both the idea of being standing committees during a particular session and that of being allowed to continue (keizoku suru) to operate during recesses of the Diet. Each attempt to establish the jōchi iinkai system in the 1930s had been killed by the House of Peers.[33] Memories of these efforts lingered in the minds of the members as they were drafting the new Diet law.

In retrospect it seems that terminological confusion arose between the Japanese and SCAP negotiators over the distinctions between the two types of standing committees, the *jōchi* and the *jōnin iinkai*. According to the Japanese negotiators, Williams initially disapproved of the whole notion of the *jōchi* form of standing committees. It was his contention that such continuing committees might supersede the authority of the Diet when the latter was not in session because they would remain active between Diet sessions. He is further reported to have told the Japanese that all activities of the Diet should be carried out only when it was in session, which would cause all committee activity to cease as soon as the Diet went into recess.[34]

Considerable consternation among the Japanese resulted from Williams' opposition to committees sitting during Diet recesses. A meeting of secretaries-general of all political parties was convened to discuss the refusal of GHQ to accept the creation of the *jōchi* form of standing committees. Apparently, further negotiations took place between representatives of the Diet and SCAP, because at a second meeting (December 6) GHQ gave its approval. A compromise worked out between the negotiators is evidenced in the provisions of Article 47 of the new Diet law: "Standing Committees and Special Committees shall examine matters entrusted to them only during the term of a session. During adjournment, however, Standing Committees and Special Committees may, by decision of each House, examine matters especially entrusted to them."[35] The inclusion of the second sentence was a clear-cut victory for the Japanese negotiators. Battles of the 1930s between the Representatives and the Peers had now been decided with SCAP's Government Section, in exquisite irony, serving as proxy for the defeated Peers.

Each standing committee's sphere of jurisdiction proved to be another nettlesome issue. Initially, members of the House of Representatives' Law Investigation Committee, as well as Nishizawa and his associates in the House of Representatives Secretariat, had conceived of the standing committees within a parliamentary framework of proceedings. They had postulated that an existing standing committee would be assigned jurisdiction over a pending piece of legislation depending on each committee's current workload. The whole idea of standing committees with fixed jurisdictions was alien to the Japanese way of thinking and to the procedures to which they had been accustomed under the imperial Diet.

Williams' memo of November 5, 1946, had recommended that standing committees be established for "each major field of activity." In the law adopted in spring 1947 twenty committees were named and given specified areas of activity. Sixteen had jurisdiction over major subject areas; the remaining four—the committees on the budget, on audit, on house management, and on disciplinary measures—had much broader jurisdictions.[36] Almost from the outset the matter of jurisdictions for the standing committees created problems. Subject areas were not as clearly defined as the drafters had hoped. Consequently, after some experimentation the Diet amended the new Diet law (in July 1948) to make the standing committees conform more closely to Japanese practice. Each of the major subject-matter committees was accorded a sphere of activity that corresponded to one of the major ministries in the Japanese government. This system, with minor exceptions, has prevailed to this day.

Despite all the attention devoted to the creation of the new committee system, certain provisions of the new Diet law remain curiously vague. Article 41, for example, provided: "Standing committee members shall be selected by each House at the beginning of the first session of their term of office as Diet Members and shall serve during their term."[37] Article 25 provided: "Chairmen of Standing Committees shall be elected in each House from among the membership of the respective standing committees."[38] Neither of these articles spelled out the procedures to be followed. Furthermore, little in the "Diet Record" of the discussions regarding the new Diet law indicates that the members themselves were concerned about such matters at the time that the law was pending their approval. There was, however, one relatively illuminating exchange between a member of the House of Peers, Nakamura Tōbei, and Minister of State Uehara Etsujirō, who was explaining the Diet law to the Peers at the time.

> According to Article 25, committee chairmen are to be elected by the House, not by the committee members. Since the committee members are not involved in the selection, it gives me the impression of *amakudari iinchō* [committee chairmen who descend from heaven]. I fear that this process may create difficulties for committee discussions.[39]

Minister of State Uehara Etsujirō responded:

> The characteristics of the committee system under the new Diet law need to be emphasized. Legislative bills will be referred to the committee first, and deliberations inside the committee will be considered as being far more substantial than in plenary session. In my opinion, *a committee chairman should be a man of knowledge in the field over which the committee has jurisdiction* and should also be elected from among those who are most qualified. Hence, they should not necessarily be drawn from among the members of a committee. We must remember that a committee chairman will serve for four years once he is elected and if the Diet is not dissolved. There is also the possibility that he can continue to serve in the same position were he to be re-elected. I believe that it is entirely appropriate for the House to select the chairmen of committees, since the functions of the committees are quite different [from the functions of committees in the imperial Diet]. (my italics)[40]

State Minister Uehara's response did not really address itself to the crux of the matter: what would be the impact on committee proceedings if the chairman of that committee "descended" on it from "heaven"? Furthermore, Minister of State Uehara's contention that a committee chairman should be a person qualified in the field over which that committee had jurisdiction was an intelligent hope, but certainly no guarantee provided that the selection process—whatever it might be—would result in such appointments. Finally, as far as SCAP officials were concerned, nothing in the available material indicates why consideration was not given to adopting a seniority system for the selection of committee chairmen. Posing this alternative is not to suggest that seniority of service on a committee would necessarily be preferable. Instead, it is to ask what the basis was for determining which features of the United States congressional model were to be grafted onto the new Diet. It is regrettable that available records are silent on this point.

Ultimately, the members of the Diet themselves, with the help of the secretariats attached to each chamber, unscrambled the procedures that would ultimately be followed. They utilized a traditional mechanism of the imperial Diet for determining procedures. Many of the daily housekeeping functions of the imperial Diet had been performed by the Inter-Party Negotiating Conference. Its reputation at Government Section was somewhat blemished, primarily because it was viewed as extralegal and secondarily because it was reputed to be the home of political party "bosses."[41] Despite Government Section's disapprobation, Nishizawa recounts, the Inter-Party Conference decided that committee chairmen should be distributed in accordance with the ratio of seats held by each party in each house.[42] One may also infer that the respective committee chairmen were actually selected by the Inter-Party Conference. This arrangement was not in accordance with the wishes of Government Section, which suggested instead that all committee chairmen be representatives of the governing majority party or coalition of parties.[43] In this instance, although not in others, the interrelation between the majority party or parties and the actual coordination of committee efforts was given primacy by Government Section in recognition of the role that the political parties themselves played in the day-to-day work of the Diet. This change in emphasis from predominant concern with formal structure to a much greater interest in the actual operations of the Diet reflects the changed SCAP-Diet relationship that came into existence once the new constitution had been formally adopted and the Diet law had been approved by both houses of the imperial Diet.

During the course of the first year of the new Diet a subtle change that was occurring resulted in the diminution of the Inter-Party Negotiation Conference's powers. The Diet law provided for a new standing committee in each chamber to assist the presiding officer in regulating its affairs. This new committee, the Standing Committee on House Management (Giin Un'ei Iinkai, or Giun), had originally been conceived of as a kind of replica of the Committee on Rules in the United States Congress. Gradually, the Giun began to exercise the prerogatives of the Inter-Party Conference. This shift in authority was more apparent than real in that the old party leaders gradually gravitated to membership in the Committee on House Management in order to continue to exercise their leadership. This, too, is a system that has continued to the present day. As was to be true of so many other provisions of the new Diet law, this shift reflected the gradual naturalization process taking place as the members of the Diet began to apply the provisions of the new rules under which they were operating.

Government Section's official "Report" and Williams' more informal recollections emphasize that the new Diet law was largely a product of Japanese endeavor. There is little evidence on the Japanese side to suggest that this is an inaccurate observation. Government Section officials did, however, intervene in the process with respect to certain crucial issues, such as the committee system. In all probability the Japanese, had they been left to their own devices, would have established a *jōchi* system of standing committees rather than one based on the congressional model. I am not convinced, however, that the insertion of this alien form into the Japanese parliamentary system was either necessary or beneficial.[44]

To summarize: In this essay I have concentrated on constitutional and procedural changes introduced during the initial reform-minded era of the Occupation. During the initial two years of the Occupation, SCAP policy did emphasize reform, and much was done to strengthen the powers of the Diet. Constitutionally, instead of the emperor, it was the Diet that became "the highest organ of state power, and . . . the sole law-making organ of the State." This provision came close to incorporating the doctrine of parliamentary supremacy into the Japanese system of government. In addition, even though bicameralism was retained, in effect the House of Representatives was assigned greater powers than the House of Councillors. The Representatives were accorded final determination of the selection of the prime minister, of the nation's budget, of treaties, and ultimately, of legislation in general. These constitutional changes dramatically altered the relationship between the two houses.

Inasmuch as the adoption of the new Diet law strengthened the institution and reflected the initial intention of the Occupation authorities to give the Diet greater prominence within the Japanese governmental system, and inasmuch as one is hard-pressed to find any indication in the initial SWNCC and JCS postsurrender policy directives to General MacArthur that Washington envisaged these specific changes, the question arises: who determined that the Diet should become the preeminent law-making institution in the Japanese government? In one sense the answer seems to be simple: the decision was made by Government Section personnel. In another sense the answer is more complex, because—

as has been noted throughout this paper—the policy-making process involved both officials in the Occupation and officials in the Japanese government, including leading members of the Diet. A more realistic answer, then, would be that both sides, in their almost daily contacts with each other, determined the new shape of the Diet.

One of my working hypotheses prior to doing the research for this essay was that most of the changes regarding the Diet were the result of ad hoc negotiations between Occupation officials and the Diet Secretariat. Implicit in this hypothesis was the belief that most of these changes were suggested by my former colleagues in Government Section and were subsequently either adopted or partially rejected by Japanese government officials. This assumption was drastically altered during the research.

As early as the middle of September 1945, for example, discussions were held within the Japanese government concerning the need to reorganize the House of Peers, the principle of equality between the two chambers, and the requirement that the prime minister henceforth be a member of the Diet.[45] This process of policy planning within the Japanese government was complemented by the creation of the Constitutional Revision Committee under Professor Matsumoto. Although most of the committee's work was not designed to enhance the powers of the Diet, and indeed seemed at times to obstruct that effort, its ability to anticipate certain changes made it possible for Japanese government representatives to react effectively to the suggestions that subsequently flowed from Government Section.

The primary case in point is the very strong position taken by Japanese officials on behalf of the retention of bicameralism in the newly restructured Diet. Furthermore, much of the "Law for the Election of Members of the House of Councillors" was initially prepared by Japanese officials. They did the spadework, while officials in Government Section merely reacted positively or negatively to provisions of the new legislation. Crucial in all of this is that frequently the initiative lay with the Japanese rather than—as I had supposed—with Government Section officials.

Japanese authorities also took the initiative in revising the Diet law. Dr. Williams refers to a memorandum that had been written in May 1946 by two officials in the Legislative Division of Government Section: "Reform of Diet structure and procedures should not endeavor to create a model legislature and should be left to develop under native auspices resulting from experience gained in meeting the daily problems of legislation."[46] In part this position reflected the lack of policy guidance from Washington, D.C., or from any of the international organizations that were supposed to supervise basic policy for the Occupation of Japan. Apparently Government Section officials felt some constraint regarding the degree to which they should (or could) intervene in the internal processes of the Japanese government. That they had no specific authority to act had not prevented them from playing a crucial role in drafting the new Japanese constitution; nonetheless, at least some of them believed it would be better for the Japanese themselves to work out the specific details of internal Diet procedures.[47]

Japanese officials did not reflect a single viewpoint with one set of premises. Individuals associated with the House of Representatives and its Secretariat had long sought an opportunity to redress the balance of power between it and the House of Peers. Understandably, the House of Representatives' committee on the new Diet law wished to insure that the Representatives' powers would be superior to those of the other chamber. Members of the House of Peers, understandably enough, were particularly bitter about provisions that would accord their successors less prominence. In my opinion, that chamber's negative influence was overcome only by counterpressure from Occupation authorities, although this interpretation is partially conjectural.

Both the cabinet's Provisional Legislative Investigating Committee and the House of Representatives' Law Investigation Committee utilized the old "Imperial Law of the Houses" as the basis for their drafts of the new Diet law. On only two issues did the Occupation authorities make a substantial contribution to the law. The first—and by far the most important—was the introduction of a subject-matter standing committee system in both chambers of the Diet. The second was the insistence that the members of the Diet as individuals and the separate chambers—including their committees—be provided with substantially increased assistance, including reference services, private secretaries, and private offices. One unsuccessful innovation of the Americans was the suggestion that a Legislative Council be established to facilitate cooperation between the two chambers of the Diet. This council never really functioned and was abolished by the Japanese in 1955.

It is fair to state that the goal of "democratization" was uppermost in the minds of Government Section officials and their Japanese government counterparts, at least until the summer of 1947.[48] For the Occupation authorities, basic to the achievement of this goal was the creation of a national representative assembly that would be able to grapple with that traditional source of power in the Japanese government, the bureaucracy. How well, then, did all concerned do their handiwork? In terms of constitutional doctrine as it relates to the Diet, at least, the answer is a simple, "Very well, indeed." The Diet did replace the imperial institution and government as the central organ of state power. Furthermore, the elimination of all appointed and hereditary seats in the national legislature and the creation of a system whereby all members were to be publicly elected—no matter what reservations one might have about the House of Councillors Election Law—was a major break with the past. Similarly, that members would have status, measured in terms of pay scales, equal to the highest-ranking bureaucrats in the government created a situation very different from that which had prevailed under the Meiji Constitution. Also, many of the procedural changes incorporated into the new Diet law strengthened the authority of members as individuals as well as that of the institution as an entity vis-à-vis the nation's bureaucracy. Finally, the introduction of a congressional-style committee system, while probably not necessary, was intended to enhance the Diet's independence from bureaucratic control.

Possibly the greatest weakness of the Diet reforms was the disjunction between procedural changes and the role that the political parties would come to play in the day-to-day operations of the Diet. Nowhere is this more clearly indicated than in the transformation of the Standing Committee on House Management into a vehicle that would allow the individual political parties to have a dominant voice in the operations of the Diet, much as the old Inter-Party Conference had in the imperial Diet. From another perspective, this disjunction between procedural reform and the activities of political parties may have had a salutary outcome. Diet reform never became a political football among the parties. All of them, particularly in the House of Representatives, were dedicated to strengthening their role and that of their chamber in the overall scheme of the Japanese government. Basic disagreements surfaced only when the new legislation was introduced into the House of Peers for its approval.

In conclusion, it must be added that the Diet has not in practice lived up to the high hopes and expectations of those who helped to draft the new constitution and the new Diet law.[49] Weaknesses in the Diet's performance have not necessarily been due either to the constitutional provisions under which it operates or to the Diet law itself. Rather, these weaknesses are to be found in the manner in which the political parties have evolved in the intervening years and in the fact that, at least until the middle 1970s, a fundamental ideological chasm separated the majority Liberal-Democratic party from its opposition parties. This gap reflected deep fissures within the fabric of Japanese society. These were not necessarily inevitable nor could they have been reasonably anticipated. Hence, in terms of the achievement of the broadly defined policy objective, democratization, the reform of the Diet must be counted as one of the successes of the early Occupation, a success that could be counted as jointly achieved with the very substantial initiative and assistance of most of the Japanese authorities concerned.

Notes

Acknowledgments are due Mr. James Hastings, who was unfailingly courteous in helping me find my way through the mountain of documentary material stored at the Suitland National Record Center, and Dr. Justin Williams, who gave me the benefit of his thoughtful reflections. Many colleagues in Japan were more than generous with their time in helping me collect written records there, including Professor Hashimoto Akira of Meiji University, Professor Kobayashi Katsumi of the National Defense College, Dr. Hata Ikuhiko, then Chief of the Finance Ministry Postwar Economic History Collection Room (which contains much more than the title implies), and Mr. Hirano Sadao of the Diet Secretariat, and private secretary to then House of Representatives Speaker Maeo Shigesaburō. Miss Minoura Yasuko has my undying gratitude for painstakingly reading all of the Japanese-language materials that were given to me and organizing them for my use.

One negative note must be added. For the Occupation side of the story, I have relied almost exclusively on former Government Section officials and documents, in part because Government Section was the center of SCAP activity as far as the Diet was concerned, and in part because the files of the Civil Information (Intelligence) Section (CIS), which also played a limited role, are not presently available. Of course, writing the Occupation side of the story from Government Section's perspective was congenial in that it allowed me to deal with material that I will always associate with my youth. Nonetheless, I am aware that the full story of the Occupation's manipulations of Japanese politics cannot be recounted until the CIS—and possibly Counter-Intelligence Corps (CIC)—files become part of the public domain.

1. For texts of the Potsdam Declaration, the SWNCC Instructions, and the JCS Directive, see Government Section, *Political Reorientation of Japan* (hereafter *PRJ*), vol. 2 (Washington, D.C.: GPO, n.d. [1949?]), pp. 413, 423–426, 428–439.

2. *PRJ*, "The New Constitution of Japan," vol. 1, p. 91. Also Sato Tatsuo, "Kempō 'Dai yon Sho: Kokkai' no seiritsu katei" [The process of creating the constitution, Chapter IV, the Diet], in *Reference (Refuarensu)*, no. 52 (May 1955), pp. 1–26.

3. *PRJ*, "The New Constitution of Japan," vol. 1, p. 103.

4. Ibid., p. 105.

5. This is based on the Satō Tatsuo essay in *Reference*, no. 52.

6. Ibid., pp. 11–12.

7. The final version of the Japanese constitution's Article 43 reads: "Both Houses shall consist of elected members, representative of all the people."

8. The Constitution of Japan, Chapter IV, Article 54, paragraphs 2 and 3.

9. Satō Tatsuo, "Sangiin Zenkokku-sei no seiritsu katei" [The process of creating the House of Councillors' national constituency (electoral) system], in *Reference*, no. 83 (December 1957), p. 15.

10. *Dai Kyūjūikkai Teikoku Gikai, Shūgiin* [91st Imperial Diet, House of Representatives], *Kokkai Hōan Tokubetsu Iinkai Gijiroku Kiroku* [Records of Proceedings of the Special Committee on the Diet Law], no. 1, p. 17.

11. 91st Imperial Diet, House of Representatives, Diet Law Committee, No. 3, p. 17. The Constitution of Japan, Chapter IV, Article 59, states "A bill becomes a law on passage by both Houses, except as otherwise provided by the Constitution."

12. Interview with Maeo Shigesaburō, June 28, 1977. Former Speaker Maeo may also have had in mind the possibility that the Liberal-Democratic party (of

which he was a member) might lose its majority in the House of Councillors in the imminent election on July 10, 1977. Former Government Section officials who fought for unicameralism in 1946 might be pleased to learn that they finally gained support at a senior level of the House of Representatives.

13. Mr. Uchida made this comment while discussing an earlier draft of this essay presented at the Maui Conference in July 1978.

14. The Constitution of Japan, Chapter IV, Article 41.

15. Justin Williams, *Japan's Political Revolution Under MacArthur,* chap. 8, "SCAP's Role in Restructuring the Diet," pp. 144–163. It is interesting to compare this chapter with his much earlier "The Japanese Diet under the New Constitution," Part I of "Postwar Politics in Japan," *The American Political Science Review* 42 (October 1948), pp. 927–939. The latter was written while he was Chief, Legislative Branch, Government Section, SCAP. Moreover, both of these essays should also be compared with "The National Diet" in *PRJ,* vol. 1, pp. 145–185.

16. "Proceedings of the Diet," SCAPIN 179, 22 October 1945: "In order that the Supreme Commander may be informed of the activities of the Diet, it desired that the Japanese Government establish a procedure by which this headquarters will be furnished with copies, *in English* [my italics], of proposed laws and reports on the progress of proposed legislation from the time the bills come before the Bureau of Legislation throughout the entire legislative process and enacted into law," in *PRJ,* vol. 2, p. 695.

17. Williams, "SCAP's Role," p. 145.

18. Hans H. Baerwald, *The Purge of Japanese Leaders under the Occupation* (University of California Press, 1959, and Greenwood Press, 1977).

19. Williams, "SCAP's Role," pp. 147–148.

20. Interview with Mr. Nishizawa Tetsushirō on April 19, 1976. (Verbatim minutes were taken by Professor Hashimoto Akira of Meiji University.) The main points made by Mr. Nishizawa were checked against his testimony before the Constitutional Investigation Commission (Kempō Chōsa-Kai Dai-ni Iinkai; hereafter KCK, Second Committee), *Dai-yon, go, roku, nana Kaigi Gijiroku* [Proceedings of Sessions 4, 5, 6, and 7], February–May 1959. Mr. Nishizawa's recollections were in accordance with his lengthy testimony.

21. *PRJ,* vol. 1, p. 148. Swope's memorandum was written in late March 1947.

22. 91st Imperial Diet, House of Representatives, Diet Law Committee, No. 1, p. 10.

23. Interview with Mr. Hirano Sadao, member of the House of Representatives Secretariat's Committee Section, March 29, 1978. Mr. Hirano had been kind enough to consult several of his Secretariat colleagues and had prepared a memorandum of reflections, concerning an earlier draft of this essay, for my use.

24. *PRJ,* vol. 1, p. 158.

25. Dr. Justin Williams graciously provided me with a photocopy of this set of suggestions. Because of its historical significance, an exact reproduction of the content of this document is attached as Appendix 1 to this volume. The date on the note prepared by Dr. Williams is November 4, but in the recollections of Mr. Nishizawa the date given is November 5.

26. See Hans Baerwald, "The Committee System of the National Diet," in John Lees and Malcolm Shaw, eds., *Committees in National Legislatures* (Duke University Press, 1979).

27. *PRJ*, vol. 1, p. 164.

28. Williams, "SCAP's Role," p. 162.

29. "Roster of Assignments," Public Administration Division of Government Section, 1 August 1946. *PRJ*, vol. 2, p. 814. Dr. Williams, in his letter to me of February 25, 1978, asserts that I am wrong on this point.

This surmise is not correct. There was no demarcation line between the Political Parties Division (not Branch) and the Legislative Division. Where [Dr. Pieter K.] Roest [chief of the Political Parties Division] sought to make the parties more democratic and less corrupt, and to have a political party law enacted to eliminate splinter parties and require the printed ballot, I worked with party leaders regularly in their capacity as power brokers. The Negotiating Conference, and later the Standing Committee for House Management, continued to operate the House in the traditional way, that is, as party agents. It was taken for granted that the respective political parties would provide policy guidance for their Diet members. Party leaders envisaged a dominant role for the body to which they belonged, and, without splitting hairs over parliamentary versus congressional models, regarded strong standing committees as their ace-in-the-hole vis-à-vis the pre-Occupation system of rule.

I am ever more puzzled that none of the Diet reforms mentions political parties.

30. For further elaboration, see Hans Baerwald, *Japan's Parliament: An Introduction* (Cambridge University Press, 1974), chaps. 3 and 4.

31. KCK, Second Committee, *Dai-yonkai Kaigi Gijiroku* [Proceedings, Session 4], p. 15.

32. For full text, see *PRJ*, vol. 2, pp. 968–976.

33. KCK, Second Committee, *Dai-gokai Kaigi Gijiroku* [Proceedings, Session 5], pp. 7–8.

34. KCK, Second Committee, *Dai-yonkai Kaigi Gijiroku*, p. 21. Dr. Williams, in his February 25, 1978, letter to me, discusses the issue of

committees carrying on during Diet recess or between sessions. This type of committee was urged before the war when Diet sessions were short and when regular or special sessions were arbitrarily prorogued by imperial prerogative. This practice ceased when the new Constitution became effective. To stipulate, therefore, that a permanent committee would carry on between sessions was not only unnecessary but raised the specter of Diet interference with the Cabinet's execution of the law. This was considered administratively unsound. The solution that was adopted accorded with sound parliamentary practice.

35. *PRJ*, vol. 2, p. 971.

36. Ibid., p. 970.

37. Ibid.

38. Ibid., p. 969.

39. "Remarks of Nakamura Tōbei," in *Dai Kyūjūikkai Teikoku Gikai, Kizo-kuin* [91st Imperial Diet, House of Peers], *Kokkai Hōan Tokubetsu Iinkai Gijiroku Kiroku* [Records of Proceedings of the Special Committee on the Diet Law], no. 2, p. 15.

40. Ibid. Dr. Williams, in his letter of comment, adds the following: "How the government party would select committee chairmen was a matter in which GS was wise not to meddle. And we couldn't have cared less about any method selected by the Japanese."

41. There are hints of this antagonistic feeling in "Development of Legislative Responsibility," pp. 31–32. This declassified essay is Part 3 of Volume V, "Political," of GHQ, SCAP, *History of the Nonmilitary Activities of the Occupation of Japan, 1945 through October 1950.* (Photocopy was obtained from Dr. Hata Ikuhiko's Finance Ministry Postwar Economic History Collection Room.)

42. KCK, Second Committee, *Dai-gokai Kaigi Gijiroku,* p. 12.

43. Nishizawa Tetsushirō testimony in ibid., p. 13.

44. Dr. Williams disagrees with my presentation. He notes:

Without the power exercised by the opposition parties in the standing committees between 1952 and 1960, thanks to the existence of such committees, I shudder at what Prime Minister Kishi and his predecessors might have done to Japan's budding democracy. Such power does not exist for the opposition parties in the House of Commons. If standing committees are out of place in Japan's parliamentary system, why has there not been a movement to eliminate them in favor of the British model? Since the Diet Law was enacted, the Diet has changed a number of SCAP-suggested procedures.

For an elaboration of my own position, see my "Committee System of the National Diet."

45. *"Hōritsu"* [Law], vol. 3 of *Shiryō: Sengo Nijūnen-shi* [Postwar 20-year history: documents] (Tokyo: Nippon Hyōronsha, 1967), p. 59.

46. Williams, "SCAP's Role," p. 145.

47. Professor Kurt Steiner of SCAP's Legal Section has made the point that noninterference in the Diet's legislative machinery was SCAP policy "in principle." He also suggested that SCAP officials would not normally interfere if the proposed legislation had been vetted and approved by the relevant SCAP staff section *prior* to its submission to the Diet—as in the case of the Diet law. Assuming that the proposed bill would not be amended during the legislative process, there would be no reason for SCAP to interfere. Professor T. J. Pempel, however, has noted that government (cabinet)-initiated bills had a higher "success" rate under the Occupation than ever since, suggesting that the Diet then operated under the hidden control of SCAP. This crucial issue of Diet autonomy or lack thereof remains an unfinished item of research. It deserves elaboration and I hope to turn to it in a future essay.

48. All discussions of the "reverse course" in Occupation policy really start in the latter half of 1947. For one case study, see my *Purge of Japanese Leaders under the Occupation.*

49. For further details regarding this assessment, see Hans Baerwald, *Japan's Parliament: An Introduction,* especially chap. 5.

6

The Tar Baby Target:
"Reform" of the Japanese Bureaucracy

T. J. Pempel

One of the most striking characteristics of Japanese politics from the late nineteenth century until the end of World War II was the strength and political influence of its national bureaucracy. As a latecomer to the industrial revolution, Japan was under fierce pressures to "catch up" with the technically more sophisticated nation-states of the West. A strong state bureaucracy was an essential instrument in efforts to reach this goal. In areas such as finance, economic management, education, public works, local government, and domestic social control, the bureaucracy had a wide array of powers in public policy formation. Throughout the period it worked closely with key sectors of finance and industry to generate the economic and social conditions for rapid industrialization. In war as well the mobilization capabilities of the central bureaucracy were critical to national unity and success. With respect to the individual citizen, the executive organs of state were also extremely powerful: guarantees of civil liberties were minimal, and the balance of power between official and citizen was well capsulized in the pungent phrase *"kanson minpi"* ("revere officials and the public be damned").

Although civil liberties have been significantly expanded for Japan's citizenry since the end of World War II, the political power of the state bureaucracy seems not to have been as drastically affected. One of the most readily agreed upon features of contemporary Japan is the power of its national bureaucracy.[1] It appears to be one of the few sectors of prewar Japan that emerged rather minimally scathed by the seven years of U.S. military occupation. Indeed, some have argued that vis-à-vis other political institutions, the postwar bureaucracy has even more relative power than it enjoyed during the prewar period.[2] If true, the fact is puzzling in light of the overall American approach to Japan during and after the war.

Official American analysis of the causes of World War II did not rest primarily on conflicts of international interests. Rather, in accord with a long-standing liberal tradition in American foreign policy and also as a device for mobilizing the American public, the war was attributed to fundamental flaws in the social, economic, and political character of the countries against which America fought.[3] America's enemies were not Germany, Italy, and Japan, but rather Hitler and Nazism, Mussolini and fascism, Tojo, the emperor, and Japanese authoritarianism. Ostensibly to obliterate such conditions and hence to prevent future aggression, the United States pressed for the unconditional surrender and the subsequent social and political revamping of these countries.[4] Extensive efforts were devoted to presurrender planning for the eventual occupation of Germany and Japan, and the postwar occupations of both countries, unlike virtually all prior military occupations, were directed not only at military goals but also at ensuring sweeping social, political, economic, and cultural changes.

In many areas the impact of the American Occupation was sharp and unmistakable. In others, the American efforts achieved less success. Yet even where success was comparatively limited, many important changes occurred. One is hard pressed to find many significant areas in which the U.S. Occupation left little impact.[5]

Given this orientation, plus the extent of prewar bureaucratic power, one would suspect that the bureaucracy would have been subjected to intense scrutiny by the Americans and that major efforts would have been made to reduce its overwhelming political powers. Yet the historical record suggests that this was not wholly the case.

Numerous changes in other political institutions restructured the context of Japanese politics. A new constitution drastically recalibrated the balance between the rights and duties of citizens, legitimating a wide range of civil liberties easily breached by prewar government officials. The power and influence of the Diet, the courts, and local governments were bolstered. The emperor, who had provided the legitimation for prewar bureaucratic activities, saw his powers reduced to the purely symbolic. The military was completely disbanded, and the police force was restructured. These were all measures that weakened the power of the bureaucracy. Other changes affected the bureaucracy more directly.

Several ministries were dissolved and new ones were created. A serious, albeit unsuccessful, effort went into the decentralization of many important functions of the national government. A National Personnel Law was passed to alter various features of the civil service, and a retrenchment program aimed at cutting back the size of the civil service was implemented. But when the total picture is examined, the central conclusion that emerges is that the overall structure and character of the Japanese bureaucracy itself was minimally affected: most bureaucrats were still drawn from the same social background and training as previously; administrative discretion remained wide; direct control by elected officials over administrators remained low; and the powers of the various bureaucratic agencies vis-à-vis the rest of the political organs of state remained high. The question is why so little direct change occurred.

One of the classic answers is that the Americans simply had no choice. The Occupation was indirect, and having to work through the Japanese bureaucracy the Americans, in effect, guaranteed that the bureaucracy would retain substantial power.[6] So parsimonious an explanation is attractive: the Americans would have ensured reforms if only they had been able, but force of circumstances prevented them; hence they made the most pragmatic adjustment possible to an undesirable situation. Given the wide scale of the reforms the Americans sought to make and the limited number of Americans capable of effectively functioning linguistically, culturally, and politically within Japan, they had little choice but to work through the existing organs of state. If the bureaucracy, as a result, was targeted for only minimal reforms and if it in fact emerged from the Occupation in a position of relative strength, this might be unfortunate but it was essentially inevitable.

Unfortunately for parsimony, such an explanation does not hold up well. Since the Americans operated through the Japanese bureaucracy, the latter obviously retained important powers. But the Americans *were* at the top of a genuine hierarchy of authority, and the power relationships between occupier and occupied were stark, particularly during the early years of the Occupation when young lieutenants and captains wielded real power over the most senior echelons of the Japanese civil service. To overstress American dependency is to ignore such realities of power.

Even more compelling is the comparative evidence. The West German Occupation, for example, was "direct," but there too the central bureaucracy was the focal point of only limited reform efforts, and it is generally conceded to have emerged from the Allied Occupation in a position of strength not dissimilar to that enjoyed during the prewar period.[7] In contrast, the East German Occupation under the Soviet Union was not dramatically different from that of either Japan or West Germany in terms of the important role assigned to domestic bureaucratic forces, but within a very short period a dramatic overhaul took place in the sociopolitical character of key members of the central bureaucracy. Soviet-trained German cadres were installed in critical positions in all agencies, and the entire bureaucratic apparatus was subjected to the dictates of the Communist party. Hence the implementational role assigned to the Japanese bureaucracy in the American Occupation appears to explain little.

The historical record shows that little direct effort at bureaucratic reform was ever considered by the United States. By the time the Occupation began, for example, rather detailed guidelines for SCAP outlined changes to be made in Japanese politics, economics, and society; strikingly absent in any of these planning documents, however, is any mention of the need for a direct reorganization of administrative or bureaucratic structures. Nor is there reason to suspect that attention had been devoted to the problem only to be dropped, either out of frustration or political exigency. Hugh Borton, one of the key State Department planners during this period, indicates that the subject simply did not come up for any serious attention.[8]

This lack of attention is reflected as well in all of the early SCAP directives and in the initial recommendations for various changes in Japanese political, social, and economic organizations. Throughout, no mention is made of the need for fundamental changes in the character of the national bureaucracy, whether in personnel, internal organization, relations with other political bodies, or relations with individual citizens. Whereas directives cite "the militarists" or "monopoly capitalists" as explicitly responsible for the undemocratic nature of the prewar state and hence as central targets of reform efforts, no comparable mention is made of "the bureaucrats."[9] Although broad categories of individuals allegedly in policy-making positions were subjected to a purge from public office in accord with directives issued in the first months of the Occupation, the bureaucracy as a category was in fact provided with a special appeals procedure "to avoid the disruption of essential governmental functions."[10] Under this program, approximatley 90 percent of the bureaucrats technically covered by the purge were eventually exempted from its provisions.[11]

Furthermore, in the American-inspired constitution only two explicit references are made to the civil service. Article 15 states in part that "all public officials are servants of the whole community and not of any special group." Article 73 states in part that the cabinet shall "administer the civil service." Aside from these brief provisions, there is no further mention of the political powers or limits thereon of the central bureaucracy. Indeed, as early as June 13, 1946, the top levels of SCAP's Government Section decided explicitly to resist pushing the Japanese government to reorganize the central bureaucracy.[12]

Why was the bureaucracy not initially targeted for more fundamental reforms by the Americans? Why did the activities that operated under the label of "bureaucratic reform" take the peculiar shape that they did? Why did many of the reforms that were attempted fail to reshape the political powers of the Japanese bureaucracy in any fundamental way? The answers to these questions would seem to lie, not in the extent to which the Americans were forced to rely on Japanese governmental agencies during the actual Occupation, but far more demonstrably in preexisting American conceptions of the political role of bureaucracies and in American practices of bureaucratic-political interaction. It is such perceptions and the policies they generated that provide a clue as to why such limited bureaucratic transformations took place not only in Japan but in West Germany as well. By implication they also shed light on the contrast with the far more substantial transformations that occurred in East Germany.

The American Administrative Heritage

Two dominant and somewhat conflicting traditions can be identified in American administrative practice during the mid-twentieth century. On the one hand was the ideal of hierarchically based efficiency and scientific management—bureaucracy viewed as a depersonalized and automated machine, processing and implementing decisions made somewhere "above." On the other hand was the reality of fragmentation by function and the dominance and penetration of particular government agencies by special interests.[13] These two traditions played a major role in the eventual evolution of bureaucratic reform efforts within Japan, both in the early conceptualization of what "bureaucratic reform" came to mean, and, particularly from about 1947 on, in the utilization of "bureaucratic reform" as a tool with which to bolster the strength of conservative forces within Japan.

Thinking about bureaucracy *qua* bureaucracy was almost nonexistent at the time of the founding of the American republic. Only with Jacksonian democracy did the bureaucracy force its way to the level of political consciousness. Starting with President Jackson, thousands of jobs came to be doled out as rewards for personal or party loyalty with each change of administration. With the assassination of President Garfield by a disappointed office-seeker and the subsequent passage of the Pendleton Act in 1883, however, the so-called Mugwumps began a drive for the replacement of party loyalists with nonpartisans chosen for proven competence in some particular field of endeavor. Thus began the first of the two key elements in the American administrative tradition, the search for the separation of "politics" and "administration" and for the creation of an efficiency-based civil service.

The Mugwumps were not fully successful in their efforts, however, and until nearly the end of the century the number of positions outside civil service restrictions at both state and national levels continue to expand faster than the number controlled by civil service regulations. Slightly later, though, the Progressives proved to be far more successful in introducing efficiency-based administrative reforms. Neutral competence rather than political dependability, the Progressives successfully maintained, should be the key criterion in the selection of administrators.

These moves received official presidential sanction in the form of Theodore Roosevelt's Committee on Department Methods (the Keep Commission) and William Taft's Commission on Economy and Efficiency. Outside the political arena they were bolstered by the scientific management theories of Frederick Taylor and Leonard White and the development of a core of political scientists and public administrators dedicated to the same principles—such as Frederick A. Cleveland, Luther Gulick, Louis Brownlow, Edwin Godkin, Charles Merriam, and Frank L. Goodnow.[14] All came to exercise substantial influence over both the theories and practices of public administration in America in the early to middle twentieth century.

A second major element in public administration had also developed in the United States during the Progressive era, however—namely, the trend toward functionally specific public oversight commissions. Taking aim at the railroads, the trusts, and other "special interests," the Progressives demanded that such private groups be made increasingly responsive to the public interest. In that political parties and the electoral mechanism could not be counted upon to guarantee such responsiveness, nonpartisan regulation through independent appointive governmental commissions was to provide the needed check.[15] The administrative ideals of impersonality, independence, and expertise were thus enlisted in the service, not only of governmental efficiency itself, but also of public control over a wide variety of private interests hitherto thought to be outside public control. Particular interests would, through efficient administration and regulation, be subjugated to the general interest.[16]

Reality, however, proved to be incompatible with vision. Although independent commissions sprang up throughout virtually all areas of government, and although the functional expert and the specialized bureau or agency came to be viewed as more competent than the politician to make judgments about the regulation and administration of particular technical fields such as aviation, radiowave regulation, interstate commerce, occupational safety, securities and exchange transactions, and the like, true oversight was more promised than practiced. With time, most of these specialized agencies, bureaus, and commissions forged close personal and organizational links with the private groups most affected by their decisions and with the legislative committees charged with oversight responsibilities in the same areas. The regulators became allies of the regulated.

These two strands in American administration—the search for apolitical efficiency, order, and expertise and the reality of entrenched functional alliances among agencies, congressional committees, and private interests—can best be appreciated by a brief examination of President Franklin D. Roosevelt's efforts at governmental reorganization from 1936 to 1939.[17] Seeking to institutionalize a scientifically managed bureaucracy responsive to strong executive discretion, Roosevelt appointed the Presidential Committee on Administrative Management, composed of three strong advocates of scientific management—Louis Brownlow, Charles Merriam, and Luther Gulick. The committee's recommendations were wide-ranging, but central to its report was the goal of increased efficiency through the managerial norm of nonpartisanship, so much a part of the Progressive rhetoric: "Good management will promote in the fullest measure the conservation and utilization of our national resources. . . . The adjustments and arrangements we suggest have no other purpose or justification than better public service for our people through administrative management. . . . Management is a servant, not a master—a means, not an end, a tool in the hands and for the purpose of the Nation."[18]

Yet such principles and ideals foundered on the realities that had come to dominate American politics. FDR's efforts at governmental reorganization went down to ignominious defeat. As Polenberg describes it: "A phalanx of war veterans, labor unions, civil service reformers, doctors, and business organizations opposed the measure. They were joined by spokesmen for various government agencies. For the most part, these groups sympathized with the broader aims of reorganization, they merely wanted exemption for the particular function of special interest to them."[19] The result was a sound drubbing for the proposals for administrative reorganization and a reaffirmation of the sovereignty of functional fiefdoms and bureaucratic satrapy. As ideals, the merit system and the apolitical civil service were not crushed by this effort; in fact, they were strengthened by its failure. But the principles of efficiency and expertise remained parceled out to specific arenas of power and never came fully under the control of a monolithic executive.

For the U.S. military, despite many important differences from civilian organization, the same two key trends were organizational realities. If any institution is based on theories of hierarchy, rationality, efficiency, clarity of command, and "scientific management," it is the military. Never purporting to be democratic and never as suffused with "politics" as its civilian counterpart, the American military administration had enshrined the very same Weberian and Progressive principles of rational bureaucratic organization.[20] America's victory in World War II, based, as it was seen to be, on the successful application of such principles, further elevated the respect they commanded within the military. Still, internal disputes among branches of the military and among component elements of any single branch have constantly divided the unity of military command just as functional fiefdoms had done in civilian administration. The attempt to overcome such intraservice rivalries led to the creation of the Department of Defense following World War II; and the inability of the department to override intra- and interservice rivalries lay behind the Pentagon reforms attempted under Robert MacNamara in the 1960s.

These two broad trends, efficiency and scientific management plus functional feudalism, influenced deeply Occupation efforts to reform the Japanese bureaucracy. The search for efficiency tended to shape official definitions of the *problematique* of bureaucratic reform in Japan; functional feudalism tended to dominate the actual working out of many of the attempted reforms.

Early Reform Efforts

Democratization during the Occupation in many areas meant doing things the way they were done in the United States. Yet the two administrative trends described above were not particularly salient during the earliest months of the Occupation. They began to unfold only as the Occupation wore on. In evaluating the Occupation and its impact on Japan, policy actions during the years following the dramatic landing of MacArthur and his occupationaires must be given weight at least equal to those of the first days and months when rhetoric and enthusiasm tended to be at least as prominent as actual changes. At the outset not all members of the Occupation operated on the assumption that politics and administration were as separable as the Progressive heritage would have it. There were those who doubted that the Japanese bureaucracy had been, or deserved to be, treated as a politically neutral agent. They saw an organic linkage between the Japanese bureaucracy and the overall nature of the prewar Japanese regime, which demanded a thoroughgoing "democratization" of prewar bureaucratic structures, personnel, and relations to other political bodies.

Such attitudes were particularly prevalent within Government Section. A memo of January 30, 1946, from Lieutenant Milton Esman of the Public Administration Division of Government Section is very strong on this point.

> Of all the major bulwarks of feudal and totalitarian Japan, only the bureaucracy remains unimpaired. . . . As yet, there are no signs of reform in the bureaucratic structure. . . . The present Japan bureaucracy [*sic*] is incompetent to manage a modern democratic society. Only relentless pressure from this Headquarters will induce the Japanese to make these essential and fundamental changes. . . . Unless a thoroughgoing democratization and modernization of the civil service is [*sic*] carried out, it is difficult to see how the objectives of this occupation can be fully realized. In my opinion, civil service reform should continue as an active interest and a major priority of the Government Section.[21]

In early 1946 a memo was sent to the Chief of Staff over the signature of Courtney Whitney, Chief of Government Section, also calling for fundamental changes in the powers of the civil service.[22] The appendix to the memo offers a blistering analysis intimately linking the bureaucracy with the antidemocratic nature of the prewar state.

> The Imperial bureaucracy has been one of the mainstays of totalitarian Japan. Now that the military clique is broken and the financial clique is tot-

tering, the bureaucracy alone remains unimpaired, its power relatively greater than ever before. In the turmoil of politics, it has successfully outlasted its erstwhile allies, military and economic. . . . the formal legalism and the technical backwardness of the Japanese Civil Service contributed markedly to the modern development of the Japanese police state.[23]

Additionally, in Government Section's official report entitled *Political Reorientation of Japan,* the justification for reform of the bureaucracy also quite explicitly links bureaucratic strength to the overall undemocratic nature of the prewar regime.

> Before the Occupation . . . the Japanese bureaucracy was a key instrument in the totalitarian regimentation of the people's life. . . . Undemocratic by composition and conviction, the bureaucracy was a natural ally of both the militarists and the Zaibatsu, a ready, willing and effective instrument for carrying out the policies of these groups. . . . A successful reformation of the Japanese civil service will not only enhance governmental efficiency but will break up one of the ruling cliques of presurrender Japan—the tightly knit, exclusive and self-perpetuating bureaucracy which exercised the powers of government over the people in the feudal concept of dynastic rule by divine right—and will substitute therefore a body of democratically selected officials who will administer the laws in the concept of service to the people.[24]

Such attacks occurred with some frequency during the first year of the Occupation. Yet they were not matched by any comparable pressures from Washington for bureaucratic revamping. Nor do they appear with much frequency in Occupation documents after late 1947 or early 1948. Despite the absence of any major political commitment to bureaucratic reform at the top levels of the U.S. government, certain changes in the Japanese bureaucracy were in fact effected during the earliest phase of the Occupation. At the time of surrender Japan had twelve cabinet-level ministries—Foreign, Home Affairs, Finance, Army, Navy, Justice, Education, Welfare, Greater East Asia, Agriculture and Forestry, Munitions, and Communications. As part of the overall demilitarization of the Occupation, both the Greater East Asia Ministry and the Munitions Ministry were reduced to the first and second demobilization ministries on December 1, 1945; these two subsequently were combined as the Board of Demobilization under the prime minister.[25] In addition, individual bureaus within agencies were added, subtracted, or combined to meet other specific functional goals of SCAP. One SCAP calculation in April 1949 indicated that sixteen reorganizations were directly or indirectly authorized by specific SCAP documents; another twenty-three were established by the Japanese government to perform functions and activities officially directed by SCAP; twenty are presumed to have emerged as a consequence of oral or informal memoranda, while one was apparently established simply by an oral suggestion from SCAP.[26]

What is most salient about such changes is that they were essentially contingent on other goals. To the extent they involved changes in the powers of individual agencies, they were not directed at "bureaucratic reform" in any coherent sense. At best this was merely a side issue among a diversity of other disparate problems. Reforms were certainly not directed at the recalibration of the balance of power between bureaucracy and other organs of government.

One of the few exceptions was the result of a very early and very low-level examination of all government ministries conducted by John Maki. Maki was charged with compiling such basic information as the physical location of the various government agencies, their internal structure, their methods of operation, and the like. Part of his final report on July 18, 1946, went further and made explicit suggestions for bureaucratic reorganization. Many of his recommendations were adopted almost verbatim by SCAP, supporting the thesis that, at least during the earliest years of the Occupation, initiatives for action were often highly decentralized and resulted in major policy-making power being invested in comparatively junior officials.[27]

A few of the elements in Maki's report warrant special note. He states that his work was conducted to provide reference information on the Japanese bureaucracy and, on that basis, "to recommend changes to eliminate the militaristic and authoritarian characteristics of Japanese government."[28] In several instances, he gave explicit attention to political assessment. This is most noteworthy in the case of the Home Ministry, which apparently was the first agency he investigated. Claiming that "the contributions of the Ministry to the militarism and authoritarianism of Japan are perhaps second only to those of the War and Navy Ministries," he went on:

> Because of the former extremely important policy and political functions carried on by the Ministry of Home Affairs, it is recommended that close supervision be maintained over its reorganization, that basic changes in its structures be demanded, and that many of its functions be removed entirely from the central government. The reorganization of the Home Ministry . . . is a fundamental problem connected closely with the attainment of the political objectives of the occupation.[29]

He also recommended decentralization in various functions of the Ministry of Education. On the other hand, no recommendations for change were offered for the Ministry of Finance or the Ministry of Foreign Affairs. In the case of the former, the reasoning was that technical administration precluded political relevance. The Ministry of Finance was seen as "non-political and technical in nature [having] to do with the fundamental problem of financing the operations of the state."[30]

Maki's report led to a SCAP request that the Japanese government submit a plan for the reorganization of the Home Ministry. Following Japanese efforts to minimize the scope of the ministry's reorganization, "inevitably it became apparent," as one SCAP official involved in these discussions noted, "that the ministry could and should be abolished."[31] A cabinet recommendation to this effect was secured on June 27, 1947, and a dissolution bill was passed by both houses of the Diet in early December. The various functions of the ministry were widely dispersed through other national-level agencies, including among others the Prime Minister's Office, the Police Agency, the Local Autonomy Agency, the Labor Ministry, the Construction Ministry, the Health and Welfare Ministry, and the Education Ministry. This dissolution of the Ministry of Home Affairs deserves to be recognized as a significant step in the area of bureaucratic reorganization. It was also, however, the high point of structural reform within the Japanese bureaucracy.

Efficiency and Conservatism: The Route to Bureaucratic Reform

In the absence of any central high-level American commitment to a fundamental recalibration of the weight of the bureaucracy in the Japanese political equation, the efforts of middle- and lower-level SCAP officials were short-lived and comparatively ineffective. Personnel rotations alone eliminated much of the impetus to a political conception of bureaucratic reform, and by the time that a commitment to the principle of "civil service reform" was gained, the conception of what such reforms should involve had become freighted with American notions of efficiency and scientific management. Furthermore, even as such reforms were pushed forward an additional complication arose, namely that the American Occupation, initially committed to Japan's "demilitarization and democratization" in 1945, had by late 1947 begun to shift certain of its overall goals. Numerous critical changes took place in U.S. domestic and foreign policy during this period. The New Deal coalition fell from power in Washington; the State Department came under the control of militant anti-Communists; and the Republicans gained control of Congress following the 1946 elections.[32] Internationally, it became clear that China would not be unified under Chiang Kai-shek and hence serve as America's key military ally in the Far East; Communist control had been consolidated in eastern Europe; and the Truman Doctrine bespoke a drastic change in relations between the United States and the Soviet Union.[33]

In addition, American business and American public opinion became restive about an Occupation that appeared to be growing extremely costly and that many began to charge was directed, not at the democratization, but at the "socialization" of Japan. Only, it was argued, if the Japanese economy were returned to sound principles of capitalism and free market competition could the costs be reduced, and only if the democratic "excesses" of New Dealers and socialist-leaning do-gooders were checked could a left-wing political takeover be avoided. In this way, also, a pro-American ally would be guaranteed in the Pacific.[34] As a consequence of such broad shifts, early American efforts at "democratization" gradually gave way to policies aimed at "economic rehabilitation" and support for Japanese conservatives. Or, as it is generally referred to in the argot of Japanese history, American policy entered upon a "reverse course."[35] The consequence of this reversal was that many elements of American policy shifted abruptly, and even those that did not had at least to be justified in terms markedly different from whatever original relationship they may have borne to the democratization of Japan.

The American tradition of an apolitical, efficiency-oriented bureaucracy was by no means hostile to the dominant perceptions of the bureaucratic role in Japan, where the social liberalism that had informed the politics of Western Europe and North America was viewed more as a threat to national unity than as a guarantee of fundamental human rights and political democracy. "Politics" was seen as excessively particularistic and manifested its worst side in the chaos of elections and parliamentary activity. As such it was barely tolerated as a frustrating but inevitable handicap to government in the national interest, the interpretation and protection of which was primarily assigned to the national bureaucracy. Japanese political parties never acquired any significant control over patronage in the executive branch, largely as a result of efforts to insulate the bureaucracy from the turbulent currents of party politics. Thus virtually from its inception the Japanese bureaucracy stood separate from and above such politics, with administration treated as the rational, value-neutral, and scientific analysis and handling of critical national problems.[36] As a consequence, during the prewar and wartime periods various agencies within the Japanese government had put forward many suggestions for structural and personnel changes in the national bureaucracy that were highly congruent with American notions of scientific management.[37] After some initial efforts to resist any alterations in the national bureaucracy, it was just such conceptions of "reform" that Japanese government leaders and bureaucrats began to press.

During April 1946, for example, Government Section considered proposing a formal SCAP directive on civil service reform. At that time, however, the use of such directives would have represented a departure from the policy of relying on Japanese governmental initiatives. A SCAPIN was nevertheless prepared, calling for the appointment of a Japanese commission of seven or fewer individuals to be approved in advance by SCAP "to prepare . . . specific and detailed recommendations for the modernization and democratization of the Japanese Civil Service system." Guidelines were included and a penciled note over the SCAPIN reads: "Same directive previously prepared in January. Action postponed. Efforts to win voluntary acceptance by Japanese failed entirely."[38]

On May 3, 1946, the Ministry of Finance, under pressure from GHQ, requested that a commission of American experts be sent to Japan to study the Japanese civil service. But the commission was only to provide suggestions for the revision of the salary and allowance system, a far cry from total reevaluation.[39] Even this raised doubts among some Japanese agencies, and internal disputes concerning the wisdom of tampering with the central bureaucracy were not resolved until a cabinet meeting of May 14, 1946, when the Japanese government went on record officially as requesting a U.S. advisory commission on civil service reform.[40]

In addition, in October 1946 the Japanese government through Imperial Ordinance Number 490 created the Administrative Research Bureau (ARB) (later the Administrative Management Agency) in the Prime Minister's Office, an agency charged explicitly with drafting plans for the reformation of administrative organization in the national government. Its role was, however, limited to ensuring rational and efficient management.[41]

The generally low priority assigned by SCAP and the American government to bureaucratic reform is clearly suggested by the fact that the United States Personnel Advisory Mission was not sent to Japan until November 1946, fully fifteen months after the Occupation had begun. Indeed, selecting commission members alone took six months from the time the Japanese government had been induced to invite the mission. Not until August 23 did Washington send a list of probable members to SCAP and, of the six names then noted as probable, only two eventually went. By mid-September, Washington had lined up four probable members (three of whom eventually were sent), but there was delay in getting a chairman. Robert Barnett, director of personnel in the Department of Labor, was the first choice, but by November it was clear that he would not be available. Only then, at the recommendation of Henry Hubbard, executive vice-chairman of the Federal Personnel Council, was the eventual chairman of the mission, Blaine Hoover, chosen.[42] What is most striking about the character of the mission is that all members were involved in personnel work and civil service of a technical nature. Reflective of the dominant U.S. administrative tradition, all were well grounded in apolitical management. Hoover was president of the Civil Service Assembly of the United States and Canada; Manlio De Angelis was chief of the Program Planning Staff of the U.S. Civil Service Commission; Robert Hare was chief of the Field Classification Section of the same commission; W. Pierce MacCoy was director of personnel at the Department of State. Their backgrounds indicated a high probability that the Occupation's major approach to bureaucratic reform in Japan would follow technical rather than political lines, a probability that became reality as the mission's investigations proceeded.

Drawing on preliminary studies of the Japanese civil service prepared by Government Section, and after several months of autonomous investigation in conjunction with the Japanese Administrative Research Bureau, the mission issued a preliminary report in late April 1947 and a final report in June.[43] As a residue of some of the political rhetoric that had become current in early American discussions of bureaucratic democratization, a few explicitly political evaluations of the Japanese civil service can be found in the preliminary report. In talking of Japan at the time of surrrender, for example, the report notes that Japan was in many respects a feudal state.

> During the occupation amazing progress has been made in the democratization of Japan thru the revision of the constitution, economy and education system. Today, however, as much as ever before, the bureaucracy of Japan is feudal. . . . The upper ranges of the Japanese official hierarchy are populated almost exclusively by men who have been raised and educated in a concept of rendering service to the Emperor as a sovereign who enjoyed all rights, including that of governing others, yet had no responsibility for accounting to the people for his acts. . . . [The] upper bureaucracy, thousands in number, basked with the Emperor in the enjoyment of irresponsible sovereignty with all the special privilege that implies within a state which was frankly characterized as government by men rather than government by laws. These men are here today. Whatever their incompetence as public officials . . . they in fact constitute the bureaucracy at its controlling levels. They are intrenched [sic]. They have money, influence, legal training and little understanding of and a distaste for democratic processes. They want desperately to hold their jobs and official status. At the present time they are unquestionably in a position to sabotage any attempt at reform through existing administrative channels. . . . Reform of the Japanese bureaucracy involves the complete transition from the feudal to the democratic type of bureaucracy.[44]

Despite such a manifestly political rationale, the preliminary report proposed few correctives to such alleged malfunctions.[45] The final report substantially softened such passages as did exist, while the recommendations of both reports were almost exclusively technical and oriented toward the creation of a more *efficient* civil service. Like its counterpart in Germany, the mission urged the establishment of a central personnel authority (based presumably on the model of the U.S. Civil Service Commission and following its tripartite and nonpartisan formula).[46] It went on to call for the introduction of "specialization and scientific management" so as to develop "an efficient system of personnel administration for the Japanese Government." The bulk of the report was devoted to proposals concerning the establishment of detailed standards for recruitment, training, position classification, compensation, employee evaluation, health, safety, welfare, recreation, employee relations, retirement, employment statistics, and the like. These changes were to be brought about through the passage of a National Public Service Law (NPSL), a tentative draft of which, along with justification of specific elements of the law, comprised the bulk of the report.[47]

As its subsequent legislative history indicates, the draft law contained a number of politically contentious measures. Yet very few were contentious because they contained politically significant proposals for restructuring the bureaucracy. Rather, the contentiousness arose because of certain antileftist, antiunion provisions congruent with the growing political conservatism of the Occupation. Two of the more explicit took as their targets something quite the opposite of the previously castigated "feudal elements." Section IV, Standard 1, Part 8 made ineligible for examination or appointment any person who "advocated or belonged to an association or political party which advocated the overthrow by force of the Constitution of Japan." The same section, Standard 5, Part 2 would have prohibited strikes by any member of the government service and would have subjected strikers to loss of all rights to employment; the major effect of this measure would have been on the recently organized and increasingly militant civil servants' unions.

The subsequent controversial history of the NPSL is well documented.[48] When the proposed law was presented to the Diet, Japan was being governed by its only Socialist prime minister, Katayama Tetsu, and Hoover was in the United States. The government had a slim plurality in the Diet, and its major backing was from the national labor union federations. The bill came under attack from diverse political persuasions. By the time it passed, its scope had been drastically reduced, and the stature and power of the proposed National Personnel Authority had been seriously circumscribed.[49] Even more significant for its subsequent history, its provisions concerning the prohibition of strikes by public officials had been eliminated, an outcome supported not only by Japan's political left, but also by the Labor division of SCAP's Economic and Scientific Section. This defeat was not to last long in the face of the changing emphasis of SCAP policies.

Hoover was deeply upset with the NPSL as passed and, when he returned to Japan as head of the Civil Service Division of Government Section, he was in a position to ensure its revision. There was growing resistance by top American officials in Japan and top politicians in the United States to the increased strength of labor and the political left in Japan. Interest had also shifted to regenerating the Japanese economy through balanced budgets and fiscal conservatism and by cultivating a political leadership group that would ensure Japan's becoming a Cold War ally of the United States. Thus on July 22, 1948, General MacArthur wrote a letter to Prime Minister Ashida ordering him to enforce the provisions of the original U.S. proposal. This draft distinguished between labor in the public and private sectors, and prohibited the former from using the strike as a weapon of collective bargaining. On July 31,

1948, bypassing the Diet, the Japanese government put the Hoover program into effect through Cabinet Ordinance 201. Strikes by public employees were banned, and increased powers were given to the National Personnel Authority.[50] Over the next three years Hoover and the National Personnel Authority continued to focus their attention on restricting union activity by government employees.[51]

A key element in efficiency-based approaches to administration and bureaucratic reorganization has traditionally involved bureaucratic retrenchment. Scientific management, if carried out effectively, would, it was argued, allow for a more streamlined administrative structure from which unnecessary dead wood had been pruned.[52] The idea of such cuts had been percolating semiofficially in both the National Government Division of Government Section and in the Japanese government for at least two years. The operational basis for these cuts came with a cabinet decision of February 22, 1949, that initially called for a 30 percent cut in the size of all ministries and agencies. The purported rationale for the cuts was that the size of the national government had expanded drastically during and after the war, and that efficiency and administrative rationality could be improved by a force reduction. The specifics of the reduction were worked out by the Administrative Management Agency of the Prime Minister's Office in a series of plans put forward during 1949 and 1950. These were designed to reduce the number of government personnel in each agency by a uniform percentage. The reductions were to be effected through early retirements, transfers, not filling vacancies, and the like. Most, however, would involve the actual discharge of government personnel.[53]

Several points deserve particular attention. First, the reductions were justified in terms of government economies and in cutting back on excess agencies, boards, advisory commissions, and the like. Virtually all discussion justified the proposed cuts in terms of meeting the criteria of "scientific management," "improving government efficiency," "cutting out dead wood," and the like. Still, as noted, the plans for reductions had been circulating for at least two years prior to the cabinet decision of February 1949, making it clear that at least the original motivations for the cuts were unrelated to the new economic policies represented by the Dodge Line and the Nine-Point Economic Stabilization Program. Yet when the cuts were proposed they were intimately linked to these programs, presumably to provide stronger justification.

Second, the reductions when they came most affected blue-collar government workers. The biggest absolute cuts in both 1949 and 1950 came from the National Railways Corporation, the Ministry of Postal Services, and the Ministry of Telecommunications. Not insignificantly, all three had also been hotbeds of union activity, and the cuts served as a means of reducing public-sector union power.

Moreover, the discharges were made as a consequence of a cabinet decision and thus were not subject to individual or collective appeal despite the fact that individuals employed by the government normally had such job protection. Made in this way, the dismissals legally abrogated existing union contracts and established employment procedures. Finally, although the Japanese government originally proposed to offer four months' severance pay to those dismissed, SCAP rejected this proposal on budgetary grounds.

The force reductions, consequently, did not serve as a device to reduce the political power of "the bureaucracy" in the abstract. Rather, they were justified on grounds of economy and efficiency while serving in fact to undermine union strength within government. In this sense the measure was intimately linked to SCAP's "reverse course" and to the antileftist orientation of the conservative Yoshida government.

What this analysis suggests is that a certain minimal effort to make explicitly political reforms of the central bureaucracy did percolate, primarily at low and middle levels of SCAP, and that some of these reforms took shape in realistic political changes, such as the dissolution of the Home Ministry. Nevertheless, any initial efforts directed at such changes were more than offset by the tendency to equate bureaucratic reform with scientific management and to bypass political change in favor of administrative streamlining and technical management measures. Politics and administration were to be separated. Neither the National Public Service Law nor the cutbacks in the number of government employees drastically altered the prewar powers of the bureaucracy. In fact, with the overall recalibration of U.S. goals from a primary emphasis on "demilitarization and democratization" to one on "economic recovery" and with the creation of a pro-American and anti-Communist government in Japan, even elements of scientific, apolitical management lost their initial neutrality and became weapons aimed against the political left. This is a major factor in explaining the limited nature of the bureaucratic changes that occurred under the Occupation. But another feature is important as well, namely the functional feudalism that characterized most aspects of the U.S. Occupation.

Cross-National Institutional Infighting: Impediment to Bureaucratic Reform

In discussing the Occupation with various participants, I was once told of an experience that seems illustrative of a much broader problem. At one point during the Occupation most of its operations were moved from downtown to the outskirts of Tokyo. Most of the Americans, however, remained billeted in the central city. On the first day of the move an incredibly complex schedule was established to transport the Americans from downtown to their new work areas. In some instances individuals due at work by 8:00 A.M. were scheduled to be picked up at their hotels at 5:30. Buses and trains criss-crossed in a convoluted pattern that seemed to have absolutely no rationality. The person who related the story claims to have gone on the third day of the chaos to see the lieutenant colonel in charge, demanding that something be done to rationalize the system. "Virtually anyone," he charged, "could organize this system more efficiently." In what must be one of the more candid self-assessments ever made, the officer in charge readily agreed, claiming that he could easily move everyone with half the equipment in half the time. "But," he noted, "my power, influence, and promotion chances are not based on cutting *down* the number of personnel and equipment I control. They rest on how much I can *expand* them." In short, the officer's vested interests lay not in streamlining the system, but in making it as complex as possible.[54]

In analyzing the internal memoranda of the Occupation, one is forced to ask just what percentage of time top officials devoted to "reforming Japan" and what percentage to resolving jurisdictional disputes by elements of the Occupation arguing about their respective spheres of responsibility for such reforms. Although formal power lay unquestionably in the hands of the Americans, the Occupation rarely, if ever, involved a united American occupier attempting to reform a united (and presumably opposed) body of Japanese. Familiarity, constant contact, and the emergence of compatible goals between particular groups of Japanese and Americans led rather to a large number of functional and organizational alliances that crossed national lines.

Strong organizational loyalty—rather than programmatic or ideological orientation—has been frequently remarked upon as a characteristic of U.S. bureaucratic behavior.[55] Similar behavior was by no means foreign to Japan. Both institutional and cultural interpretations of Japanese behavior agree on the strong claims for loyalty that an organization can exert over its members.[56] Within the national bureaucracy hiring and promotional patterns tied most individuals to lifetime careers within a single ministry, thereby bolstering such cultural predispositions to group loyalty as might also have existed. Biographical, anecdotal, and analytic studies of the prewar Japanese bureaucracy are equally well laced with stories suggesting that institutional loyalty commanded greater devotion than any ideological or programmatic concerns.[57] Thus, the historical ground was well prepared on both the American and Japanese sides for the creation of a series of cross-national alliances between organizations seeking to maximize or protect their own institutional spheres.

As early as January 1946 Courtney Whitney, chief of Government Section, was engaged in a major dispute with G-3 over the allocation of SCAP staff responsibilities.[58] Economic and Scientific Section and Gov-

ernment Section spent most of the seven years of the Occupation at log-
gerheads. Each usually was supporting, or mustering support from,
counterpart Japanese agencies. The Local Government Division and the
Local Autonomy Board were pitted against a half-dozen or more SCAP
divisions and their counterpart Japanese ministries in regard to problems
of governmental decentralization.

Close ties existed between James Killen, chief of SCAP's Labor Division, and Japanese labor unions (which ties led eventually to Killen's resignation); Blaine Hoover was the perennial SCAP spokesman for the
interests of the National Personnel Authority; Cecil Tilton, chief of the
Local Government Division, was an outspoken advocate of decentralization of governmental functions; Alfred Oppler, who was extensively
involved in legal reform, notes in his memoirs the alliance he formed with
Hosono Chōryo, president of the Japanese Supreme Court: "Soon we felt
and acted as international colleagues in law."[59] In his chapter in this volume Kurt Steiner has noted how essential his Japanese allies in the Civil
Liberties Union were in getting certain measures passed in this critical
area. Similar alliances emerged in many fields, including education,
health, journalism, broadcasting, and transportation. Commonality of
functional or organizational interest and, in not a few cases, common
self-interest drew individuals and organizations together in ways that
came to make a dramatic overhaul of the bureaucracy much more difficult.

Jurisdictional disputes continually arose even between the two agencies most directly charged with the task of bureaucratic reform. When
the Administrative Management Agency (AMA) was proposed in mid-
1948 with the support of the Administrative Management Division
(AMD) of Government Section, for example, Pierce MacCoy of the Civil
Service Division (CSD) called in the deputy chief secretary of the cabinet,
Mr. Fukushima, and informed him that CSD would disapprove of the bill
unless the National Personnel Authority, with which CSD was most
closely associated, was exempted from the new agency's jurisdiction.
Carlos Marcum, chief of AMD, strongly opposed this. In a memo to the
deputy chief of Government Section he "seriously objected to the pre-
sumptive arrogation of responsibility by the Civil Service Division,"
claiming that the jurisdiction of CSD did not permit it any control over
the content of the new law.[60] Yet the NPA was successful in gaining
exemption from the AMA's jurisdiction. This and similar particularistic
alliances in turn served as the precedent for the subsequent exemption of
the Attorney General's Office and the Board of Audit.[61]

For most of the Occupation, CSD in alliance with the National Personnel Authority continued to confront AMD in alliance with the
Administrative Management Agency over the precise nature and direction of any and all proposals affecting the national bureaucracy. At the

time of the proposed cutbacks in bureaucratic personnel, for example, CSD sought initially to remain completely isolated from this highly unpopular move. Subsequently, it sought to gain complete control over key aspects of the program, including reviews of all dismissals and control of severance pay. It also complained that the AMA plan had no provisions to establish bureau-level personnel offices with the various agencies, a move that, if accomplished, would not only have worked against the reductions in personnel, but would have centralized personnel functions within the NPA.[62] Simultaneously, CSD argued that the NPA should itself be exempted from personnel cuts because it was such a new agency and so central to bureaucratic reform.[63]

A similar maneuver, which interfered with a key element in bureaucratic reorganization, concerned the overall efforts made to decentralize certain ministerial functions from Tokyo to either prefectural or local bureaucratic agencies. On the basis of a series of investigations by Paul J. Kent of the National Government Division, for example, a wholesale dissolution of field offices maintained by national government agencies was proposed by the Administrative Research Board (ARB) of the Prime Minister's Office. A coalition among ARB, Guy Swope in National Government Division, and Cecil Tilton of Local Government pressed for a reduction in the number and functions of such field offices. Swope charged that the existence of the branch offices prejudiced the basic purposes of the local autonomy laws.[64] Tilton argued that if the branch offices were allowed to continue "the program will be stifled, vitiated and made hollow."[65] These field offices remained a target of joint attack by the Local Government Division, the Local Autonomy Board, and the ARB and its successor, the Administrative Management Agency, for the duration of the Occupation.

Virtually every SCAP agency charged with responsibilities dealing with national agencies, however, came forward with explanations as to why "their" particular agency's field offices should be exempted from curtailment. The argument of Alfred Hussey, chief of Government Powers Division, was most sweepingly against the proposed decentralization.

> It is my opinion that we are now operating under a basic misconception of the meaning of local self-government in a modern democracy and that our present insistence upon complete political decentralization may well result in the effective hamstringing of the national government in Japan . . . The local official serving his own community cannot at the same time serve the nation at large. . . . National affairs must be administered by national officials . . . and . . . the nation at large must have the sole power of determining the extent of the national interest . . . We cannot ignore the fact that the complexities of modern life and the ease of modern communications render anything near complete autonomy or full decentralization archaic and dan-

gerous . . . The will of the people of the Japanese nation must be directly
and immediately enforceable in each and every local area through the direct
agents and representatives of the people at large.[66]

National Government Division also proposed a series of reversals in
the local autonomy program in January 1948 seeking to preserve many
of the branch offices originally scheduled for cutbacks.[67] The Industry
Division of ESS meanwhile contended successfully that, while the goal of
decentralization was sound, the proper allocation of raw materials and
intermediate products for which it had oversight responsibilities necessitated "tight economic controls . . . in an economy of shortages. Tight
controls can be administered only through a centralized authority."[68]
Other sections within SCAP pressed with similar success for the retention
of various branches, functions, and personnel in their counterpart agencies in the Japanese government. Thus, as a result of opposition of
interested ministries and their Occupation supporters, the detailed plans
for decentralization failed to gain cabinet approval, and field-office
reduction declined sharply from the original proposals.[69] Consequently,
only a small portion of the cutbacks in national governmental scope and
responsibilities at the local level ever took place.

Similar opposition developed at the time of the so-called Kambe report
in late 1950. Kambe headed the Commission to Investigate Local Government Administration designed to implement the Shoup Mission's
report. The commission proposed the decentralization of a number of
national governmental functions. As would be expected, virtually every
agency dug in to resist implementation of these proposals. Again they
were joined in their resistance by officials of various counterpart sections
of SCAP. Public Health and Welfare, for example, opposed any decentralization of health and welfare functions. Labor Division, ESS, stated
officially that it would "not stand for any further decentralization of
labor administration." Natural Resources Section opposed any relin-
quishment of fisheries control by the national government. Public Safety
Division, G-2, was opposed to any modification of existing maritime
controls. The reaction was uniform and widespread.[70]

The same pattern developed in opposition to the reductions in force
proposed for 1949 and 1950. Although few opposed the reductions in
principle, almost all agencies sought to make the case for specific exceptions in their own particular case. Because of the strong impact the cuts
would have had on unionized government workers, Labor Division was
especially strong in its opposition; when it was clear that the cuts would
be carried out anyway, Killen and others resigned in protest.[71]

Floyd L. Whittington, chief of the Price and Distribution Division of
ESS, argued that since the Price Board and the Economic Investigation
Agency both had key responsibilities in the area, the proposed cuts, if

applied to them, would be in conflict with the Nine-Point Stabilization Plan.[72] Harold Moss, chief of the Internal Revenue Division, opposed any reductions that would cut Japanese tax personnel: "It is the position of this Division that a cut of more than 5 percent would seriously hamper the work of the tax service and possibly cost billions in lost revenues."[73] Economics was offered by W. F. Marquat, chief of ESS, as the justification for keeping the regional offices of the Ministry of Commerce and Industry and for postponing reductions in the statistical agencies of individual ministries.

The top levels of SCAP, including the Chief of Staff and General MacArthur, rejected such exceptions in principle, contending that GHQ should not intervene to alter the details of Japanese government proposals except where some specific objective of the Occupation was jeopardized. Nevertheless many of the protests proved successful within both SCAP and the Japanese government. A series of cabinet decisions in 1949 and 1950 exempted a number of agencies and divisions from all or part of the proposed personnel cuts. In addition, many agencies that were unsuccessful in limiting personnel reductions at the cabinet level were able to rely on a different mechanism to bypass the cutbacks. They increasingly resorted to so-called daily laborers. A September 30, 1949, memo notes an increase between January and September of over 350,000 in the number of such daily laborers, suggesting a significant bypass of the reduction plan.[74] Heads of other agencies took advantage of the reduction program to rid their organizations of undesirable personnel. With the relaxation of regulations concerning appeals of discharges, they cut back well below their authorized number of personnel in certain areas with the expectation of subsequently hiring new personnel as cheaper, more efficient, and/or more ideologically compatible replacements.[75] Again SCAP counterpart agencies tended to support such measures. The result was that true cuts in personnel were much closer to 10 percent than to the called-for 30 percent, and the number of national government employees at the end of the Occupation was significantly higher than it had been in 1945.

Finally, one can point to a roughly comparable pattern of opposition surrounding National Personnel Authority efforts to conduct extensive civil service examinations. The exams sought to have members of the Japanese higher bureaucracy—from assistant section chief to administrative vice-minister—compete with fellow officials, subordinates, and private citizens for their positions. These exams were necessitated by Article 9 of the first supplementary provisions of the NPSL. CSD interpreted these provisions to mean that all top officials would be deemed temporary employees until they had passed an appropriate civil service exam to be given within two years. When these tests were initially proposed, the clear objective was to diversify the educational backgrounds of the senior ranks of the civil service and thereby provide a more socially representative national bureaucracy.[76] The same pattern of cross-national bureaucratic opposition developed: many SCAP divisions argued that for one reason or another "their" agencies and "their" officials should be exempted. When the exam was finally held over the objections of virtually all Japanese and American agencies, it proved to be a rather hollow shell devoid of its original political purposes. Officials were given unlimited time to complete their examinations; tea breaks were frequent; pressure was limited; and, most significantly, resulting personnel changes were almost nil. Nearly 80 percent of the incumbents were retained, and at the uppermost level the retention rate was 88 percent.[77]

In short, therefore, limited as the political content of most proposals for bureaucratic reform proved to be, not only Japanese opposition had to be overcome. There was also internal opposition from numerous components of SCAP with different perceptions of how reform efforts should be carried out. Such cross-national alliances usually proved difficult to defeat, and therefore neither the structures nor the personnel of the national bureaucracy were fundamentally revised as a consequence of the Occupation. Most of the changes that did occur came about largely as a result either of very early efforts by middle- and low-level officials or as a by-product of other goals. The predominance of this pattern of functional feudalism preserved most of the central powers of the prewar bureaucracy intact from even some of the minimally consequential reforms associated with "scientific management."

Conclusion

The U.S. Occupation of Japan (as that of Germany) has been treated by most historians and social scientists as a unique episode, and indeed it is unlikely to be repeated. Despite this, questions concerning its impact on Japan are of interest in terms of the historical continuities and changes involved: how much of a difference did the Occupation make to the working out of Japanese history both generally and in specific areas?

The Japanese bureaucracy before, during, and after the Occupation was powerful. Whether the Occupation incrementally or fundamentally added to or detracted from its powers is not a trivial problem. I have argued that, although the bureaucracy was indirectly affected by political changes in other areas, few direct attacks on the political powers of the Japanese national bureaucracy were attempted during the U.S. Occupation. I have contended that this was true largely because the goals of bureaucratic "reform" were not conceived in terms of new structures, new personnel, or new relations to other political units. Bureaucratic "reform" was interpreted almost exclusively in terms of improving the efficiency of Japanese administration. Additionally, the realities of institutional infighting also impeded even minimal reorganization and change. These interpretations and realities grew naturally out of the pre-war and wartime administrative theories and experiences of both Japan and the United States. They were not unique to the Occupation; rather, the Occupation provided laboratory conditions under which they could be realized to their fullest.

Even more significant than the issue of continuity and change in bureaucratic power are questions relating to a bureaucracy's proper role in a democratic society and to the political realities implicit in the sorts of cross-national bureaucratic alliances depicted above. What are the long-run implications for democratic governance of the combination of efficiency, scientific management, rationality, organizational clarity, and hierarchy as dominant bureaucratic goals? What are the consequences of endowing bureaucratic institutions with politically irresponsible hegemony over entire fields of public interest?

There can be little doubt that a modern state bureaucracy is a far more powerful organization than its historical predecessors. The increased reliance on technical expertise and rationality combined with the increasing complexity of the problems faced by modern states gives national bureaucracies and national-level bureaucrats a constant push toward accumulating more power. Such accretions of power have increasingly been taking the form of ever more narrowly focused agencies to deal with ever more specific problems. The rationality, efficiency, and scientific management glorified by Americans from the Mugwumps through the Pentagon "whiz kids" are not drastically different from that represented by Japanese civil servants from the Meiji era to the 1983 proposals for administrative reform.[78] Numerous internally rational agencies compete with one another to insure the acceptance of increasingly narrow and specific solutions to increasingly complex problems. Politics becomes a matter of institutional infighting in which terms such as "public interest," "citizen control," and "democracy" are public relations missiles hurled at one's organizational opponents.

What happens to individual and group liberties in the face of such "rationality" and "efficiency"? Whose rights and privileges suffer in the quest for the ultimate logical solution to increasingly complex problems? Bureaucratic competition can conceivably be viewed as pluralistic in nature and hence as democratic. Lots of agencies linked to lots of groups means lots of competition, with the added presumption that bureaucratic infighting may simply be a modern democratic substitute for the clash of legislators or editorialists. Indeed, such competition does impede the imposition of any single-minded societal arbitrariness and hence should not be lightly dismissed. But not all interests in society can be reduced to functionally specific organizational formats. Many individuals, groups, and interests are not organizationally represented; others are misrepresented. Corporatism, even of a competitive variety, is no substitute for democracy.

In the present case the national bureaucracies of both the United States and Japan seem to have been moving in the same direction. Do they represent a broad historical trend toward increased rationality and functional specificity? Certainly very different models could be suggested for the central bureaucracies of other countries. The French have their various *grands corps,* expert indeed, but composed of experts who move across agencies rather than becoming firmly entrenched in a single ministry. The presumed result is scientific management without a narrow functional specificity that operates against the general interest. The British have their administrative class with its cavalier disdain for expertise and rationality but a presumed dedication extending beyond the institutions they serve and a reputation for nonpartisan political responsiveness. Though hardly democratic, the Soviet civil service is also generally conceded to be politically responsive. Although it is a thought-provoking question, this is not the place to debate what today's Japanese bureaucracy would have looked like had the French, the British, or the Soviets rather than the Americans been in charge of the Occupation. Nonetheless, my suspicion is that there would have been rather different meanings given to "bureaucratic reform" involving much greater conflict between competing bureaucratic traditions than was the case between the Americans and the Japanese. In all probability the ultimate composition and responsiveness of the bureaucracy would also have been more drastically reshaped.

Thus, in examining bureaucratic reform, one must ask whether the unquestioned search for rationality and efficiency may not have been the wrong goal and whether organizational politics may not have been the wrong means. If democracy is to have meaning in the contemporary world, it may well require less of an apotheosis of rationality and efficiency. And if politics is to be democratic, it must surely involve more than institutional struggles among hierarchic hegemonies.

Notes

1. See, for example, Tsuji Kiyoaki, *Nihon kanryōsei no kenkyū* [Study of the Japanese bureaucracy] (Tokyo: Tōkyō Daigaku Shuppan, 1969); Ide Yoshinori, "Sengo kaikaku to Nihon kanryōsei" [Postwar reform and the Japanese bureaucracy], in *Sengo Kaikaku,* vol. 3; *Seiji katei* [The political process], Tōkyō Daigaku Shakai Kagaku Kenkyūjo, ed. (Tokyo: Tōkyō Daigaku Shuppan, 1974), pp. 143–229; Kusayanagi Daizō, *Kanryō ōkokuron* [The bureaucratic monarchy debate] (Tokyo: Bungei Shunjū, 1975); Honda Yasuharu, *Nihon neo-kanryōron* [The neo-bureaucracy debate in Japan] (Tokyo: Kōdansha, 1974); Chalmers Johnson, "Japan: Who Governs? An Essay on Official Bureaucracy," *Journal of Japanese Studies,* vol. 2, no. 1 (Autumn 1975), pp. 1–28; Johnson, "MITI and

Japanese International Economic Policy," in Robert A. Scalapino, ed., *The Foreign Policy of Modern Japan* (Berkeley and Los Angeles: University of California Press, 1977), pp. 227–279; Haruhiro Fukui, "Policy-Making in the Japanese Foreign Ministry," in ibid., pp. 2–35; T. J. Pempel, "The Bureaucratization of Policymaking in Postwar Japan," *American Journal of Political Science,* vol. 18, no. 4 (November 1974), pp. 647–664.

2. Tsuji, *Nihon kanryōsei no kenkyū,* esp. pp. 242–288.

3. Arnold Wolfers and Lawrence W. Martin, *The Anglo-American Tradition in Foreign Affairs* (New Haven: Yale University Press, 1956).

4. Paul Kecskemeti, *Strategic Surrender: The Politics of Victory and Defeat* (New York: Atheneum, 1964).

5. Among the more useful studies that outline the broad changes see SCAP, Government Section, *Political Reorientation of Japan* (Washington, D.C.: GPO, 1949) (hereafter *PRJ*); Kazuo Kawai, *Japan's American Interlude* (Chicago: University of Chicago Press, 1960); and John D. Montgomery, *Forced to Be Free* (Chicago: University of Chicago Press, 1957).

6. The best example of this position is Tsuji, *Nihon kanryōsei no kenkyū.*

7. Taylor Cole, "The Democratization of the German Civil Service," *Journal of Politics,* vol. 4, no. 1 (February 1952), pp. 3–18; Ralf Dahrendorf, *Society and Democracy in Germany* (New York: Anchor, 1969), esp. chap. 14; Karl Hochschwender, "The Politics of Civil Service Reform in West Germany" (Ph.D. thesis, Yale University, 1962).

8. A point made to me in conversation with Borton.

9. See most obviously "United States Initial Post-Surrender Policy for Japan," August 29, 1945; but virtually any overview documents of this time reflect the same bias.

10. *PRJ,* vol. 1, p. 12.

11. Hans Baerwald, *The Purge of Japanese Leaders Under the Occupation* (Berkeley and Los Angeles: University of California Press, 1959), p. 80.

12. At the time, the Japanese government proposed to elevate the Board of Communications to a cabinet-level ministry, largely as a means of allowing the vice-president of the board to become a cabinet member. Debate developed within the ranks of SCAP over whether this should be allowed and whether SCAP should decide a policy and require Japanese compliance. Finally, Courtney Whitney recommended that the question be left to the Japanese. His statement at the time contended that unwarranted restrictions upon the government's own discretion in the conduct of internal affairs would be destructive to the government's dignity and would be a hindrance to Occupation policy. U.S. Government Archives, Record Group 331, Box 2046, "Memo for the Record," dated June 13, 1946. (Subsequent references to archival material will all be to Record Group 331 and will indicate box number, date, and heading of memo where available.) Whitney's memo became the basis for a series of subsequent top-level efforts to prevent various reform and reorganization efforts undertaken at the initiative of lower-level and middle-level officials of SCAP, e.g., see Box 2046, March 11, 1949, "Memo from F. R. [Frank Rizzo]," with reply from Whitney, March 11, 1949; similarly, an effort in April 1948 to require the Japanese government to adopt a particular form of organization for the Ministry of Commerce and Industry was stopped by reference to the original Whitney memo, Box 2046, memo dated April 20, 1948.

13. Herbert Kaufman, "Emerging Conflicts in the Doctrines of Public Administration," *American Political Science Review,* vol. 50, no. 4 (December 1956), pp. 1057–1073; Stephen Skowronek, *Building a New American State* (New York: Cambridge University Press, 1982).

14. Samuel Haber, *Efficiency and Uplift: Scientific Management in the Progressive Era, 1890–1920* (Chicago: University of Chicago Press, 1964), *passim,* but especially chaps. 2–3.

15. Grant McConnell, *Private Power and American Democracy* (New York: Vintage, 1966), chap. 2.

16. Kaufman, "Emerging Conflicts," pp. 1059–1062.

17. Richard Polenberg, *Reorganizing Roosevelt's Government, 1936–39* (Cambridge: Harvard University Press, 1966).

18. The President's Committee on Administrative Management, *Report of the Committee with Studies of Administrative Management in the Federal Government,* p. 53.

19. Polenberg, *Reorganizing Roosevelt's Government,* p. 19.

20. My thanks to Stephen Skowronek for sharing with me his unpublished work on this subject. See also Samuel Huntington, *The Soldier and the State* (New York: Vintage, 1964), pp. 193–221.

21. *PRJ,* vol. 2, p. 578.

22. This was in response to a February 1946 reform proposal from the Cabinet Bureau of Legislation that had been deemed inadequate. Box 2187, undated memo of approximately April 1946 for Japanese Government, "Re: Reform of Japanese Civil Service," tab entitled "The Japanese Bureaucracy."

23. Box 2187, January 25, 1946, memo for Assistant Chief of Staff, G-3.

24. *PRJ,* vol. 1, p. 246.

25. In addition there were many other structural changes seemingly without any single guiding purpose or directive. In certain instances, such as the dissolution of the Imperial Household Ministry or the Court of Administrative Litigation, the new constitution and ancillary legislation provided the basis for change. In others, such as the Board of Audit, specific legislation provided for an increase in functions. The Ministry of Labor was established on September 1, 1947 in part as a result of SCAP initiatives to strengthen the labor sector in Japan, one of the Occupation's early intentions, and in part as a result of the electoral defeat of the conservative Yoshida government and its replacement by the socialist coalition government of Katayama. In other cases, the Bureau of Paper Allocation for Newspapers and Publications was created in the Prime Minister's Office by an October 26, 1945 SCAP Memorandum (AG 461) concerning the elimination of control by the Newspapers and Publishers' Association over the distribution of paper. A Securities and Exchange Commission was created in the Ministry of Finance as a result of a memo from the Economic and Scientific Section. Individual SCAPINs (SCAP Instructions to the Japanese Government) were issued for the creation of such offices as the Disease Prevention Bureau in the Ministry of Welfare and the Electrical Communication Equipment Bureau in the Ministry of Commerce and Industry. A letter from MacArthur to the prime minister dated September 16, 1947 was the basis for transforming the Ministry of Justice into the Attorney General's Office.

26. Box 2046, April 20, 1949, memo for Major Napier.

27. Box 2045 contains the bulk of the Maki reports and numerous memo-

randa surrounding them. Many of Maki's ideas on the subject are more easily available in John M. Maki, "The Role of the Bureaucracy in Japan," *Pacific Affairs,* vol. 20 (December 1947), pp. 391–406.

28. Box 2045, July 18, 1946, memo from John Maki.

29. Box 2045, document no. 25, Government Organization, 1945–1946 folder.

30. Box 2045, July 18, 1946, memo from John Maki.

31. Box 2046, July 20, 1947, report by Guy Swope entitled "Summary of Activities of National Government Division during the Second Year of the Occupation."

32. The change in perspective that resulted can be seen, for example, in the following statement by George Kennan, then a relatively new power within the State Department, in speaking of the pre-1947 guidelines for U.S. Occupation policy.

> They reflected at many points the love for pretentious generality, the evangelical liberalism, the self-righteous punitive enthusiasm, the pro-Soviet illusions, and the unreal hopes for great-power collaboration in the postwar period which . . . had pervaded the wartime policies of the Allied powers. . . .
>   . . . The nature of the occupational policies pursued up to that time by General MacArthur's headquarters seemed on cursory examination to be such that if they had been devised for the specific purpose of rendering Japanese society vulnerable to Communist political pressures and paving the way for a Communist takeover, they could scarcely have been other than what they were. (*Memoirs,* pp. 372, 376)

On the broad changes see among others Montgomery, *Forced to Be Free;* John Dower, "Occupied Japan and the American Lake, 1945–1950," in Edward Friedman and Mark Selden, eds., *America's Asia* (New York: Vintage, 1969), pp. 186–206; Walter LaFeber, *America, Russia, and the Cold War, 1945–1966,* 3rd ed. (New York: Wiley, 1976), pp. 30–100; Harry S Truman, *Memoirs* (New York: Doubleday, 1955), *passim.*

33. These matters are discussed in all the books cited in n. 32 above, but especially the last three.

34. See, for example, the speech by Senator William F. Knowland given in Congress December 19, 1947 and that of Secretary of the Army Kenneth C. Royall on January 6, 1948 before the Commonwealth Club, San Francisco. Both are reprinted in Jon Livingston et al., eds., *Postwar Japan* (New York: Pantheon, 1973), pp. 113–119. See also Charles S. Maier, "The Politics of Productivity: Foundations of American International Economic Policy After World War II," in Peter J. Katzenstein, ed., *Between Power and Plenty* (Madison: University of Wisconsin Press, 1978), pp. 23–49.

35. See, for example, Yanaihara Tadao, *Sengo Nihon shoshi* [Short history of postwar Japan], vol. 1 (Tokyo: Tōkyō Daigaku Shuppan, 1958), pp. 40–48; Fujiwara Hirotatsu, *Kanryō no kōzō* [Structure of the bureaucracy] (Tokyo: Kodansha Gendai Shinsho, 1974), pp. 84–85.

36. Much of this was the result of explicit efforts by those such as Yamagata

Aritomo to insulate the Japanese governmental structures from what were viewed as the evil influences of political parties. Parties made many efforts to improve their bases of support through patronage, particularly in the instance of the Sei-yūkai under Hara Kei. But aside from a few peripheral successes in recruiting bureaucrats and in a few areas such as police the only significant links between parties and bureaucrats came when the latter joined the parties after having established careers based on criteria of merit and actually retired from service. On Hara, see Tetsuo Najita, *Hara Kei in the Politics of Compromise 1905-1915* (Cambridge: Harvard University Press, 1967).

37. Ide, "Sengo kaikaku," pp. 149–158.

38. Box 2187, undated memo of approximately April 1946 for Imperial Japanese Government, "Re: Reform of Japanese Civil Service."

39. *PRJ,* vol. 2, p. 579.

40. Ibid., vol. 1, p. 248.

41. Ibid., pp. 125–126.

42. Message from Washington to CINCAFPAC dated September 15, 1946 and message dated November 1, 1946 (WCL 25948).

43. Box 2038, April 24, 1947, "Report (Preliminary) on the United States Personnel Advisory Mission to Japan"; Box 2038, June 16, 1947, "Report (Final) of the United States Personnel Advisory Mission to Japan, Volume 1."

44. "Report," April 24, 1947, pp. 7–8. Much of this phrasing was changed in the final report dated June 16, 1947.

45. Virtually the entire report is devoted to specific proposals for the introduction of various components of scientific management.

46. The authority was to have three commissioners; explicit provisions prevented anyone from serving who had been an officer or a member of a political committee, an officer of a political party, or a candidate for public office within the previous ten years. Moreover, no two commissioners of the authority could be members of the same political party or, interestingly, graduates of "the same school, college, or department of the same university or institution of higher learning." "Report," April 24, 1947, pp. 14–15.

47. "Report," June 16, 1947.

48. Among the most useful sources is Satō Tatsuo, "Kokka komuinhō seiritsu no keitei" [Establishment of the National Public Service Law], *Refarensu* 138, 139 (July and August 1962), pp. 1–15, 11–31. See also Zadankai, "Kokka komuinhō seitei hitsuroku" [Records of the establishment of the National Public Service Law], *Jinji Gyōsei,* vol. 4, no. 1 (1953); Ehud Harari, *The Politics of Labor Legislation in Japan: National-International Interaction* (Berkeley and Los Angeles: University of California Press, 1973), pp. 63ff.

49. See n. 48 above.

50. The ordinance is included in Jinji-In, *Kokka komuinhō enkakushi* [History of the National Public Service Law], vol. 1 (Tokyo: Sanno Purinto, 1969), p. 305.

51. Box 2037 has a file labeled "NPA—Rules, General," which includes multiple drafts of rules governing political activities by government officials and Civil Service Division reactions. A memo in January 1948 for the file, for example, explicitly indicates that Hoover instructed Dr. Asai of NPA not to give approval to the organization of a union within the National Personnel Authority. See also

Box 2046, January 29, 1948, memo from Hoover to Whitney entitled "Activities of Organized Labor in the Government of Japan"; Box 2041, January 27, 1948, memo to Whitney from Hoover explicitly opposing the activities of Labor Division of ESS as, among other things, "un-American in pattern"; and Box 2041, February 18, 1949, memo from Hoover to Pierce MacCoy of CSD asking for information regarding U.S. efforts to eliminate Communists from public service that might serve as a guide for actions in Japan.

52. Haber, *Efficiency and Uplift,* pp. 113–116; Kaufman, "Emerging Conflicts," pp. 1065–1066.

53. The history of these reductions is based on a multitude of documents in boxes 2044, 2045, and 2046. See also GHQ, SCAP, *Historical Monographs 1945–1951, History of the Nonmilitary Activities of the Occupation of Japan,* vol. 5, no. 13, "Reorganization of Civil Service."

54. A story related to me by Patrick Benner.

55. In this context it is also worth noting that the State Department's plans for the Occupation of Japan were explicitly held back from the Treasury Department to prevent them from becoming a target of attack by Henry Morgenthau, an observation made to me by one of the chief American planners, Hugh Borton.

56. See, for example, Nakane Chie, *Japanese Society* (Berkeley and Los Angeles: University of California Press, 1970), for the most prevailing cultural argument.

57. See in particular Imai Kazuo, *Kanryō* [Bureaucracy] (Tokyo: Yomiuri Shinbun, 1953); Fukumoto Kunio, *Kanryō* (Tokyo: Kōbundo, 1959); Kusayanagi, *Kanryō ōkokuron;* Tsuji, *Nihon kanryōsei no kenkyū.*

58. Box 2187, January 25, 1946, memorandum for the assistant Chief of Staff, G-3, from Courtney Whitney.

59. Alfred Oppler, *Legal Reform in Occupied Japan: A Participant Looks Back* (Princeton: Princeton University Press, 1976), p. 82.

60. Box 2046, May 14, 1948, memo from Marcum to deputy chief, Government Section.

61. These three agencies had a rather ambivalent organizational status that provided the legal basis for their claim.

62. Box 2044, April 5, 1949, memo from Hoover to J. P. Napier, chief, Public Administration Division.

63. Box 2044, n.d., memo from Maynard Shirven, chief, Examination Branch, to Blaine Hoover; Box 2188, September 13, 1951, memo from Edgar N. Jay to Frank Rizzo.

64. Box 2045, November 20, 1947, "Memo for the Record" from Guy Swope.

65. Box 2045, December 30, 1947, memo "Establishment of National Agencies in the Prefectures."

66. Box 2187, December 12, 1947, memorandum for the chief, Government Section; Subject: "Local Autonomy."

67. Box 2046, January 22, 1948, memorandum to chief, Local Government Division.

68. Box 5979, July 7, 1948, file, "Local Autonomy Issue" memo for chief, EES, from W.S.V.

69. Box 2143, October 1950, "Opinions of Various Ministries Concerning the Recommendations of the Revision of National Structures, etc."

70. Box 2143, December 20, 1950, memorandum for the chief, Government Section.

71. Kawai, *Japan's American Interlude,* p. 164.

72. Box 5977, May 7, 1949, memo "Economic Investigations Agency" file.

73. Box 5978, April 7, 1949, memo for the file.

74. Box 2044, September 30, 1949, memo by J. D. M. (McWherter) for Major Napier.

75. Box 2046, August 10, 1949, memo for Major Napier from J. D. McWherter.

76. Maynard N. Shirven and Joseph L. Soeicher, "Examination of Japan's Upper Bureaucracy," *Personnel Administration,* vol. 14, no. 4 (July 1951), pp. 48–49.

77. Ibid., p. 57.

78. In 1983 the Provisional Administrative Reform Commission established by Prime Minister Suzuki issued a series of reform proposals largely aimed at consolidating agencies, simplifying procedures, and cutting personnel.

7

The Occupation and the Reform of the Japanese Civil Code

Kurt Steiner

In the legal history of countries within the civil law tradition, the establishment or reform of basic codes is an epoch-making event. During the Occupation every one of Japan's basic codes was revised to a greater or lesser degree, which makes the period a landmark in the country's legal development.[1] Little in the planning for the Occupation would have led one to expect such a result. Some planning documents referred to the "nullification of obnoxious laws," and the Presidential Policy Statement of September 6, 1945, called for an early reform of "the judicial, legal, and police systems." But the context of these statements indicates that the actions contemplated were to be essentially negative and limited in scope to the elimination of restrictions on civil liberties.[2]

The impetus for the revision of the civil code came from the new constitution.[3] Article 24, stating that laws pertaining to marriage and the family were to be enacted "from the standpoint of individual dignity and the essential equality of the sexes," necessitated a thorough revision of Book IV (Relatives) and Book V (Succession). We shall concentrate on that revision.

The process of the revision provides insights into the process of legal reforms during the Occupation more generally. To what extent did earlier indigenous developments serve as precedents? To what extent did the Japanese participants in the reforms agree or disagree among themselves? And finally, to what extent was the relationship between the American and Japanese participants cooperative and to what extent coercive? Using the civil code reform as a case study, we attempt answers to these questions in the final section of this essay.

The Family System and the Development of Family Law before 1945

Oliver Wendell Holmes described the law as "a great anthropological document" to be studied "as an exercise in the morphology and transformation of human ideas."[4] This holds emphatically true for Japanese family law. To view it merely as a set of rules regulating interpersonal relations is to miss its significance. This significance lies in its connection with the core concept of the official ideology of the Japanese state before 1945, *kokutai,* usually translated as "national polity." A rather vague concept, supposedly constituting "the unique essence of Japanese society," *kokutai* included two interrelated components: the emperor system *(tennōsei)* and the family system *(kazoku seido).* The former was based on the mythology of state Shinto, according to which the imperial family ruled in a lineal succession "unbroken for ages eternal"; the latter was based on traditional Japanese morality, strongly influenced by Confucian precepts. The two components were linked in the family-state symbolism surrounding the emperor. Loyalty to the emperor and filial piety were considered to be one and the same; filial piety was a civic and not merely a private duty. This linkage is evident, for example, in the Imperial Rescript on Education, issued in 1890, which enumerated the values and obligations of the family system as virtues peculiar to Japan.[5]

The legitimation of state authority in family terms and, more generally, the fusion of morality and politics provided a powerful tool for the governing elite. The rulers were very much aware of the importance of the family as a socialization agent. In the family, successive generations of the emperor's subjects were to learn acceptance of a hierarchical structuring of social relations as a moral norm. Equally important was the stress on collectivity. Individualism and egalitarianism were firmly rejected as immoral and un-Japanese ways of thinking. Duties to the collectivity were to take precedence over individual desires, interests, or rights. In this sense the family was also considered a model for other social units, both in the public sphere—from village to state—and in the private sphere—including groups in such areas of life as education and work.

The basic institution of the family system was the *Ie,* or House, a patrilineal unit of social organization built around a vertical axis of ancestors descendants and thus continuing through time. The head of the House—usually the oldest male—represented the House, served as trustee for its interests, and exercised wide powers of control over its members. The interests of the House had priority over those of its individual members. The head was normally succeeded by the eldest son. Women played a distinctly subordinate role. This House, then, was considered the state in microcosm; the state was the House writ large.

When the civil code in force at the beginning of the Occupation was originally drafted, the question whether the family system should be reflected in it, and to what degree, became the focus of heated discussion. A code was enacted in 1890 and was to be put into operation in 1893. But before this could be done, controversies about the parts dealing with relatives and succession arose between two schools of jurists. One group, trained in French law, favored immediate enforcement, while another group, trained in English law, demanded postponement. The "postponement group" argued that law should be an expression of the national character, that the original draft was deficient in this regard, and that, if it were to be adopted, the virtues of loyalty and filial piety would be undermined. In this context Hozumi Yatsuka stressed the importance of the House and the Househead's control of it. The leader of the group favoring immediate enforcement, Ume Kenjiro, saw in the family system a relic of feudalism. He wanted to replace the headship of the House with parental authority, abolish the right of "succession to the House," and establish the principle of equal division of inheritance. His rationale was essentially that the freeing of the individual from the constraints of the House was necessary to facilitate social improvement and economic development. The postponement group was victorious in two ways: the entire civil code was redrafted and the first three books were enacted in 1896, while the books on relatives and succession were not enacted until 1898. The latter books clearly showed the impact of Japanese customs— most prominently in the provisions regarding the institution of the House.[6] The entire code was put into effect in 1898.

The controversies surrounding the family system as an institution of law that started with the enactment of the old civil code continued. As the reality of family relations changed under the impact of industrialization and urbanization, however, court decisions alleviated some of the hardships that were increasingly felt. Thus, the Great Court of Judicature (Daishinin) decided that Househeads could not exercise their control rights arbitrarily or unreasonably; that a divorce registered without the wife's consent was to be considered void; and that, although the code imposed this duty only on the wife, the husband also had a duty of marital fidelity. In 1922 the Nagasaki Court of Appeals decided that parents who had tried to sell their daughters into prostitution forfeited parental power.[7] Jurists and publicists, too, espoused the liberalization of family law, including loosening the Househead's control and improving the status of women. Some scholars of family law felt that the family system, centering on the head of the House, should be transformed into a system in which husband, wife, and children would form the core.

A traditional countercurrent was spearheaded by educators who established a committee to "inquire into educational matters" in 1917. They were shocked by the deviant behavior of the younger urban generation—the "modern boys" *(mobo)* and "modern girls" *(moga)* of the time —and they viewed with great alarm the breakdown in the "harmony of the classes of society" as organized workers failed to "observe propriety and decorum and to maintain due order in the relations of superior and inferior." For them, the answer to these social problems was a reemphasis on the family as socialization agent and model unit. To "preserve the good ways and beautiful customs of the nation" *(jumpū bizoku)*, they advocated strengthening the family system by revising the civil code. The government thereupon established in 1919 a Temporary Deliberative Council on the Legal System (Rinji Hōsei Shingikai). The council was deeply split. Despite its terms of reference, which charged the council with bringing the civil code provisions more into line with the family system, some of the recommendations presented in 1925 were surprisingly progressive. The powers of the Househead over members of the House in regard to their domicile and marriage, for example, were to be restricted; his removal in case of misconduct was to be provided for; the legal incapacity of married women was to be modified, and the mother's parental rights were to be extended; and under certain circumstances, habitual infidelity on the part of the husband was to become grounds for divorce.[8] These recommendations were not put into effect, however.

As Japan descended into the "dark valley" of authoritarianism, the shrillness of demands to bolster the family system increased. All factions of Japanese fascism shared a dedication to *kokutai,* including the family system. Kita Ikki called Japan "an organic and indivisible great family." Tsuda Kōzō stated that Japanese nationalism should be "an extension and enlargement of the family system principle," the keynote being "not the demand for individual rights but service to the family as a whole and, by extension, to the emperor."[9]

In this respect the sentiments of Japanese fascists were quite similar to those of a broad spectrum of the political elite of the day, including some people who—in other contexts—considered themselves liberal. Thus, it could happen in 1933 that Professor Takikawa Yukitatsu of Kyoto University was dismissed, in part because he had criticized the existing criminal code for making adultery on the part of the wife, but not on the part of the husband, criminally punishable.[10] In 1940 Home Minister Hiranuma Kiichiro went so far as to propose that the franchise be limited to Househeads. Nothing came of this proposal. In 1941 the civil code was indeed amended. But this amendment reduced the powers of the Househead to determine the domicile of the members of the House. The war economy needed young workers from the countryside, and it was considered dysfunctional to give rural Househeads the power to recall these war workers to the farm.[11]

The Constitution of 1947 and the Civil Code Reform

The inclusion of an article dealing with family relations in the constitution of 1947 may be considered a reaction to the antiindividualistic and antiegalitarian thrust of the family system that seemed incompatible with the democratic ideology that the Occupation wanted to foster. An early impetus may have come from a constitution draft published on December 26, 1945, by a private group, the Constitution Investigation Society (Kempō Kenkyū Kai), which stated: "Men and women have, officially and privately, equal rights." In a memorandum to the Chief of Staff dated January 11, 1946, General Courtney Whitney, the chief of Government Section, commented that the prohibition of "discrimination of birth, status, sex, race and nationality" belonged to the "outstanding liberal provisions" of the draft.[12]

On February 4, 1946, Government Section began its own draft of a constitution after rejecting the Matsumoto draft. The drafters were given a statement of three points that General MacArthur considered "musts" of constitutional revision. One of these started with the vague sentence: "The feudal system of Japan will cease." The committee that drafted the civil rights section of the constitution made this sentence the beginning of a draft article that continued: "All Japanese by virtue of their humanity shall be respected as individuals." This was followed by a statement of the general principle of equality before the law, including a prohibition of discrimination "in political, economic, educational or domestic relations on account of race, creed, sex, social status, caste, or national origin." A subsequent article—which in somewhat altered form became the present Article 24—was clearly a reaction to certain features of the family system, stating:

> The family is the basis of human society and its traditions for good or evil permeate the nation. Hence marriage and the family are protected by law, and it is hereby ordained that they shall rest upon the indisputable legal and social equality of both sexes, upon mutual consent instead of parental coercion, and upon cooperation instead of male domination. The laws contrary to these principles shall be abolished, and replaced by others viewing choice of spouse, property rights, inheritance, choice of domicile, divorce and other matters pertaining to marriage and the family from the standpoint of individual dignity and the essential equality of the sexes.

It was essentially in this form that the provision appeared in the draft constitution of the Government Section presented to the Japanese government on February 13, 1946. The attached explanatory note stated: "Certain of the provisions are specifically aimed at eliminating anachronistic family customs which tend to perpetuate the feudalistic institutions in Japan."[13]

In the first Japanese government draft of March 4 the relevant article was short. It read: "Marriage shall be based only on the mutual consent of both sexes and it shall be maintained through mutual cooperation, with the equal right of husband and wife as a basis."[14]

In succeeding drafts, however, another sentence was added: "Laws shall be enacted considering choice of spouse, property rights, inheritance, choice of domicile, divorce and other matters pertaining to marriage and the family from the standpoint of individual dignity and the essential equality of the sexes." In this form the article (then numbered 22) was part of the bill for the amendment of the constitution presented to the Diet. It ultimately became Article 24 of the constitution.

Debates in the Diet reflected the concern of conservatives about the future self-image of the nation. Was the "national essence" to be swept away? Were the "good ways and beautiful customs of the nation" to be discarded? Was the family system, one of the pillars of the national polity and a bulwark against the excesses of individualism, to be abandoned together with the idea of a family state presided over by a benevolent emperor? Should filial piety cease to be part of the value system of the national society? Nothing less than the soul of the nation seemed at stake. A few characteristic conservative arguments may be quoted by way of example. In his interpellation in the House of Representatives, Hara Fujiro stated first the official doctrine of the close relationship between the family system and the emperor system. He then asked how the laws to be enacted in accordance with the draft article would affect the rights of Househeads and the succession to the headship of the House. Kitaura Keitaro viewed the draft as "aiming at the wholesale destruction of the family system, centered on the rights of the head of the House, to be replaced by the individualism based on the idea that husband and wife are the center of the family." He expressed his fear that this would "greatly affect the filial piety which forms the foundation of all morals," and that under the new laws sons would be able to marry, to divorce their wives, and to change their domiciles without the consent of their parents.

After approval by the House of Representatives, the bill was sent to the House of Peers. There Sawada Ushimaro expressed the view that the bill established two large bridgeheads for the destruction of the national character in its provisions regarding the emperor and regarding the family. The destruction of the emperor system and the family system, he stated, would reduce the national character of Japan to nothing.[15]

Professor Makino Eiichi had introduced in committee an amendment according to which the article on the family was to begin with the sentence: "The cooperative life of the family shall be maintained." The amendment had been rejected by a few votes. Now he rose to a lengthy interpellation in the House of Peers itself. He wanted the constitution to clarify "the community of family members which has a long history and which exists in our life." From his interpellation it seems clear that he envisioned a family unit larger than the conjugal family, which he wanted to retain the collective character that the House had possessed. Thus, in discussing the implementation of the desired constitutional statement of principle, he referred to duties "to adopt the surname of the family," to "support and cooperate with family members," and even "to obtain proper understanding from the community of family members" in case of marriage or choice of domicile. In regard to succession, he wanted distinctions recognized between "the one who is responsible for the unity of the community of family members and others" on the one hand, and "between persons who continue to belong to the community of family members and those who left it" on the other hand. The echoes of the family system are unmistakable.[16]

Later Makino introduced the amendment that had been rejected by the committee. He admitted that many feudalistic features of the family system were "inconsistent with the actual conditions of society," but insisted that a provision regarding family life was important to avoid popular misunderstandings of the spirit of the constitution. Viscount Ōkochi Kiko nevertheless suspected that the amendment was aimed at the maintenance of the family system. As Makino had done before him, he quoted with approval the words of the Imperial Rescript on Education: "Be filial to your parents, affectionate to brothers and sisters, as husbands and wives be harmonious." But, he stated, the idea of the family system had faded among the great majority of the people. To enforce it was "unreasonable and unjustifiable." He ended in an obvious mood of resignation: "It is not a matter of good or bad, it simply cannot be maintained. . . . If we try to preserve it, we are obliged to make a law that will be entirely apart from the actual situation." He opposed the amendment because he felt that the issue should be dealt with in the civil code "according to the trends of the time," rather than in the constitution. The amendment was then put to a vote. With 165 votes in favor and 135 opposed, it failed to reach the two-thirds majority necessary for passage. The draft constitution was then passed with various amendments that had originated in the committee.[17]

In the debates the question whether Article 24 required the abolition of the House was raised repeatedly, and over time the response of the government representatives to such questions showed a marked discrepancy. Thus, in response to Hara's interpellation in the House of Representatives, Prime Minister Yoshida stated on June 27, 1946, that the principal objective of Article 24 was "to sweep away what might be regarded or interpreted as a so-called feudalistic relic." But, he continued, "no denial is made of the right of the Househead, House membership, inheritance, and other matters." This was corroborated by Minister Kanamori Tokujiro, who was in charge of constitutional reform. He stated that the changes in the family system and the inheritance system were not planned to lead to the loss of the rights of the Househead or parents.[18] When the chairman of the Constitution Amendment Committee, Ashida Hitoshi, presented the committee's report to the House of Representatives on August 25, 1946, he referred to the government's response to questions raised in the committee regarding the family system's future. This response had made it clear that the purpose of Article 24 "was not necessarily to do away with the House inheritance, the rights of the Househead, the right of demanding divorce, etc., but that, because family life always required a center, it was desired to place a strong man in the position of the Househead and to enable him to succeed to the House."[19]

Four days later, however, Minister of Justice Kimura responded to Makino's question in the House of Peers in a different vein. Referring to the feudalistic character and undesirable effect of the family system, he declared that the government intended to "eliminate the so-called family system centering on the head of the House in the light of the dignity of individuals and the fundamental equal rights of both sexes."[20]

The inconsistency of these statements regarding the fate of the family system and, in particular, regarding the fate of the House may be explained by the progress of the work on civil code reform that had been going on simultaneously with the debates on the constitution.

Establishing the Principles of Civil Code Reform

The first indication of any interest on the part of SCAP in family law reform was a somewhat ambiguous report by Lieutenant Commander R. L. Malcolm of Government Section to his chief, General Whitney, on December 28, 1945. On the one hand, the report noted that "there are certain laws in the Japanese Civil and Criminal Codes which seem to obstruct democratic development in Japan" but, on the other hand, it found that "most of the laws, as they are written up in the codes, are fair enough in considering the rights of the individuals of either sex," and that only the application of these laws led to "feudalistic oppression." The only proposal was that, inasmuch as "the whole problem of the family system and its relationships are basic to the problem of democratizing Japan," meetings of representatives of various SCAP sections "as well as especially chosen Japanese" should continue with a view to developing "certain concrete recommendations for action." It appears that this early initiative was stillborn.[21]

On the Japanese side, consideration of the revisions of the civil code required by the new constitution began as soon as the constitution draft was published. Okuno Kenichi, chief of the Civil Affairs Bureau of the Ministry of Justice and thus the official in charge of the matter, found the basic problem to be the continuation or abolition of the institution of the House. The constitution draft provided no clear answer. Okuno considered two plans, one limiting the rights of the Househead severely without, however, abolishing the House, the other calling for abolition of the House and revising code provisions and other laws accordingly. The document that emerged was entitled "Various Problems to be Considered in

Connection with the Amendment of the Volumes of the Civil Code on Relatives and Succession"; it started with the question "What should be done with the House system?" followed by the alternatives "how the system of Househeads and their rights should be reformed, or whether the various control rights of the Househead should be abolished." Numerous problems relating to marriage (including divorce) and succession were enumerated. These problems were dealt with in another document of the Justice Ministry's Civil Affairs Bureau, constituting a "Tentative Draft of Provisions in the Books of the Civil Code on Relatives and Succession, which Should Be Amended on the Basis of the New Constitution." This document started out with the consideration that the House had become a concept, based only on the Family Registration Law (Kosekihō). The concept no longer corresponded to the realities of family life, and the relevant civil code provisions gave the impression of a remnant of feudalism. The proposal to be discussed was, therefore, the "abolition of the House in the Civil Code." Specific proposals regarding amendments of the code, implementing that principle, were offered. These two documents served as references in the drafting process that officially began in July 1946.[22]

Whereas legal reform was under the jurisdiction of Government Section, the Civil Information and Education Section of SCAP (CI&E) had a particular interest in the status of women. Thus, on March 11, 1946, the Research and Information Division of CI&E wrote a special report, "Women's Legal Status in Japan."[23] Lieutenant Ethel Weed, an energetic champion of the rights of women, collected opinions on this subject from party representatives and women lawyers as well as from other knowledgeable persons, including professors Wagatsuma Sakae and Kawashima Takeyoshi. She also had contacts with Okuno and discussed with him, among other things, the future of the institution of the House. When Okuno raised the question whether the position of Househead might remain as a symbol and center of the House, she countered that this might be in violation of the equality clause of the constitution, but—as Okuno was to state later—made it clear that this was only her personal opinion, not the official position of GHQ.[24]

In the meantime, unofficial contacts regarding civil code revision also took place in Government Section. There, Dr. Alfred Oppler, a former German judge who had joined the section in February, was to play the most important role in the legal reforms. On March 15, 1946, five women lawyers presented a memorandum on the family law in a meeting with Oppler, Lieutenant Colonel Pieter Roest (who had chaired the civil liberties committee during the drafting of the constitution in Government Section), and Captain Goodrich, who represented CI&E. The memorandum referred to the family system as "one of the grave remnants of feudalism," cited the hardships it imposed on women, and called for its "abolishment, or, at least, a great revision." It stated that the family should consist of parents and underaged children, all treated as independent individuals, "not as a member of a family whose happiness is only considered in connection with the interests of the family."[25]

These unofficial contacts served as preparations for a task that was to be taken up in the near future. In a memorandum of April 11, 1946, Oppler remarked that a program to deal with some areas of law was needed, including private law; he noted that "it will be the task of the Governmental Powers Branch [of Government Section] to take up those fields of law which apparently have not yet been touched, such as administrative law and family law."[26] Unofficial contacts regarding family law increased during May, soon followed by discussions with judges and representatives of the Justice Ministry, in which Oppler was joined by Thomas Blakemore, one of the few recognized American experts on Japanese law at the time. In March 1946 the Japanese government established a Provisional Legislative Investigating Committee (Rinji Hōsei Chōsakai) to recommend to it changes in law necessary to implement the constitution. The committee, however, did not begin its work until July.[27]

The Provisional Legislative Investigating Committee, given the acronym PLIC by SCAP officials, was formed at the cabinet level and headed by the prime minister. It consisted of government officials, judges, Diet members, lawyers, and law professors. It was divided into five subcommittees, and matters pertaining to the reform of the judiciary and of the main codes were assigned to Subcommittee III. On the level of the Ministry of Justice another committee, the Legislation Deliberation Committee (Shihō Hōsei Shingikai), headed by the minister of justice, was formed. It dealt with the same matters as Subcommittee III of PLIC, and some members served on both committees. A professional staff of so-called secretaries *(kanji)* was appointed to both committees; the "secretaries" had the same background as the "members," but they were younger and less prestigious.

Within Government Section, a Secretariat for the Provisional Legislative Investigation Committee—dubbed SPLIC—was created "to maintain surveillance over and liaison with the activities of PLIC and to advise when appropriate action should be taken." Among the four members of the secretariat, Oppler was assigned to perform this function vis-à-vis PLIC Subcommittee III. At Blakemore's suggestion, liaison with the Justice Ministry committee—which was closer to the drafting process—was established "to secure advance information regarding problems in connection with particular codes."[28]

The first meetings of PLIC and of the Justice Ministry's Legislation Deliberating Committee were held on July 11 and July 12, respectively. The latter body was subdivided into so-called small committees, and the reforms in the field of civil law were assigned to the Second Small Committee. It was to the first session of this Second Small Committee on July 13 that Okuno presented the documents mentioned above. Also at that session professors Wagatsuma Sakae and Nakagawa Zennosuke together with Okuno were appointed as members of the drafting committee, and a number of secretaries were assigned to them. The drafting committee met on the same day, and the secretaries were divided into three teams, of which Team A had to deal with the House, succession, and family registration. This team consisted of a judge of the Great Court of Judicature, Yokota; Professor Kawashima of Tokyo University; and Murakami Tomokazu, then an official of the Justice Ministry.[29] It was on the shoulders of these relatively young men and their counterparts in teams B and C that the responsibility for the drafting process rested in the first instance.

Actually, two tasks were involved. The first consisted in making decisions on the principles of the revision, written down in the form of a draft outline *(Mimpō kaisei yōkōan)*. The second task consisted in drafting the actual provisions of the code, as revised in accordance with the draft outline. Logically, the first task should have preceded the second, but in fact both tasks were undertaken more or less simultaneously, so that the drafting of provisions proceeded before the final approval of the draft outline was given. The three teams, working intensely for a week, were ready with their draft outlines on July 20.

The outline of Team A opened with an unequivocal statement of the basic principle: "The House in the Civil Code shall be abolished. Chapter II of Book IV shall be deleted."[30] The team drafts were then discussed between July 22 and 27 in the full drafting committee, where the basic decision to abolish the House, the rights of the Household, and the succession to the House were advocated heatedly. As Wagatsuma stated later, this was a point the drafters were ready to defend at all costs and on which they did not intend ever to yield. The draft, retaining this basic decision, was brought before the Second Small Committee on July 30. Wagatsuma and Nakagawa had to respond to rigorous criticism by conservative members. Finally, the draft, revised in some particulars, was adopted by the committee. Although the drafting process continued until the end of 1946, Wagatsuma felt that the major principles were definitively decided on July 30.[31]

The formal mechanisms established in Government Section did not impede the continuation of the informal individual contacts initiated earlier. Of course, some of these individual contacts gave Oppler a better look behind the scenes of the drafting process then going on than did others. Thus, according to an entry in his diary dated July 30, 1946, he dined on that day in the Ministry of Justice with Minister Kimura, Vice-Minister Tanimura, and members of ministerial committees. He used the occasion to discuss the impending family law reform individually with some of those present. Finally, he addressed a question about the future of the House to Kawashima. The response was surprisingly unequivocal: "It should be completely abolished." Oppler declared that no one present had expressed this view to him, but he agreed with it, and said he would be glad if Kawashima could find others who held such clear opinions. Kawashima retorted that the view was held by many younger scholars.[32]

The Justice Ministry's Legislation Deliberating Committee met between August 14 and 16 to consider the draft outline of principles, and the proposed abolition of the House was the focus of extended debates. Did the family system in general and the institution of the House in particular still reflect the feeling of the people, or had the House become no more than a legal unit reflecting the arrangements for family registration and kept alive by the civil code provisions? Would the abolition of the House destroy the nation's traditional morality? Would it remove the hardships long felt particularly by women and symbolize a new morality based on the rights of individuals? Inevitably the question of SCAP influence on the drafters was raised, and it was proposed that in the absence of a SCAP order the abolition of the House be reconsidered by the drafters. At this point the representatives of the drafting committee—especially professors Wagatsuma and Nakagawa—had to make good on their determination to defend the principles of the draft. Wagatsuma denied the existence of SCAP orders and stressed the proposal's indigenous character, pointing out—as he was to do many times subsequently—that the abolition of the family system in the civil code was a long-standing desire of Japanese family law experts. Avoiding a direct attack on the family system as a moral concept, he advocated its abolition only as a legal concept. His strategy was not to insist on any specific wording, as long as the principles of the draft were maintained. Thus, when the straightforward wording of the first point of the original draft outline (that "the House in the Civil Code shall be abolished") proved a handicap to the approval of the draft outline, and when Professor Makino, searching for a compromise, suggested it be watered down, the point was redrafted to read: "The regulations concerning the head of the House and members of the House in the Civil Code shall be deleted, and such rules as conform to the actuality of the cooperative life of relatives shall be established." This version, which left the phrase regarding "the actuality of the cooperative life of relatives" open to varying interpretations, was accepted.[33]

On August 19 Oppler sent a memorandum to General Whitney reporting the Committee's decisions. He mentioned the passionate arguments on the abolition of the House, and he referred in particular to the vigorous fight by two women members for the replacement of the House by the conjugal family. Quoting the first point of the draft outline in its revised form, he stated that "this epoch making resolution means actually the complete abolition of the existing family system" and then added:

It was pointed out by the under-signed, as well as by Lieutenant Ethel Weed of C.I.&E., to representatives of the Ministry of Justice that SCAP would not insist on the complete abolition of the family system, although he would welcome it. According to our statements, SCAP was primarily interested in those reforms of the family law of the Civil Code which were necessary to conform with the new Constitution. This would have meant, particularly, to strip the Head of the House of all powers which restrict the individual freedom of the members of the House, and to establish legal equality of women. The fact that the Committee went even beyond these requirements is all the more gratifying.[34]

The draft outline, adopted by the Legislation Deliberation Committee as its intermediary report, was then discussed by PLIC on August 21 and 22, 1946. Some members of the Legislation Deliberation Committee who were also members of PLIC repeated their arguments before this larger forum. Representatives of the drafting committee responded "in a hundred ways" to this "attack of the 'family system ideologues'" *(Kazoku seido ronsha),* and women members of the committee argued passionately for the retention of the principles of the draft outline, which promised to improve the position of women within the family. In the end no significant changes were made in the draft outline, and the issue of the abolition of the House seemed to have been settled.[35]

If we put these developments into the time frame of the Diet debates, we find that the House of Representatives approved the constitution draft on August 24, 1946, that is, two days after the PLIC session. In the debates such government representatives as Yoshida, Kanamori, and Ashida had indicated that Article 24 did not require the abolition of the House. The contrast between their statements and the content of the draft outline for the civil code had been pointed out in the Legislation Deliberation Committee. The drafters—who in the meantime had proceeded to revise the actual provisions of the civil code—felt that the government's attitude called their work into question. It appears that at this critical moment Wagatsuma and Nakagawa, accompanied by Okuno, visited Justice Minister Kimura to clarify the situation. They told him that they could not continue their work and would resign their committee membership if the government's policy was to retain the House.[36] As noted in the previous section, the subsequent statements of government representatives in this regard before the House of Peers were remarkably different from their earlier statements before the House of Representatives.

On September 11, 1946, the Legislation Deliberation Committee met in Tokyo in its third plenary session to discuss the draft outline. Soon after the opening of the session the "family system ideologues" moved to invite the chief of the Cabinet Legislation Bureau, Irie Toshio, to state the government's position on Article 24 of the constitution. As expected, he expressed the view that the constitution did not necessarily require the abolition of provisions regarding headship of the House and succession to the headship. This gave the conservatives an opportunity to move for reopening the issue of the abolition of the House. In supporting their motion, they argued again that if the draft outline in this regard was not based on a SCAP instruction, the drafting committee should reconsider the basic principles of the outline. The representatives of the drafting committee pleaded strenuously against that motion, which would have jeopardized the work they had already done. In a vote the conservatives were unable to muster a majority, and because this was the last session of the Legislation Deliberation Committee, its approval of the draft outline became definitive.[37]

At the final session of PLIC on October 24 Professor Makino criticized the draft outline for failing to conform to the requirement, already decided on at his suggestion, to establish "such rules as conformed to the actuality of the cooperative life of relatives," arguing that the draft over-emphasized the relations between husband and wife and neglected to stress equally the obligation of children to their parents. Counterarguments by Okuno, Nakagawa, and Wagatsuma proved of no avail. Makino hastily drafted three items he desired to be inserted in the draft outline, emphasizing family life and reverence to ancestors. In the heated discussion that followed, two women members of the committee showed keen awareness of the symbolic issues behind some of the innocuous sounding words. One item drafted by Makino read: "Lineal relatives by blood and relatives living together shall mutually cooperate." This item was adopted into the draft outline and ultimately became Article 730 of the present civil code. Other conservative proposals to revise the draft outline failed to pass, and the outline was approved by PLIC with its main principles intact.[38]

Temporary Adjustments and the Drafting and Adoption of Amendments

While the members of the drafting committee defended the draft outline against conservative critics in the two superordinate committees, the secretaries worked on the revision of the code itself, assuming the approval of the draft outline without major changes. They moved from Tokyo to the quieter atmosphere of Numazu where they completed the so called Numazu draft of the bill on August 20, 1946. A third draft was completed at the mountain resort of Yamanaka on October 18, a few days before the final session of PLIC. A fourth draft was readied by December 2, 1946, and a fifth, reflecting the input of the Cabinet Legislation Bureau, on January 4, 1947. The fifth draft was submitted formally to Government Section but it was soon replaced by a sixth draft, submitted in a complete English translation on February 21, 1947.[39]

In the meantime the new constitution had been promulgated on

November 3, 1946. It was to be enforced as of May 3, 1947, and on that day all laws contrary to its provisions were to become invalid. The Japanese drafters desired to have the civil code revision enacted before that deadline. Considering the great number of laws—such as those reforming the judicial and procuratorial systems—that had to be enacted immediately, Oppler felt that the revision of some of the basic codes, including the civil code, would not receive an adequate examination during the ongoing session of the Diet. He thus advised the Japanese to prepare a provisional bill containing only a skeleton of the revision. Okuno and his staff in the Justice Ministry did so within a few days. The bill consisted of only ten brief articles.

Articles 3 and 7 of this makeshift legislation stated that "provisions relating to the head of the House and members of a House and all other regulations of Houses" as well as "provisions relating to the succession of the headship of a House" were not to be applied. Although in committee as well as the plenary session of the House of Representatives concern was expressed about the effect of these provisions on family life, the bill was adopted in short order. In the House of Peers Wagatsuma addressed a lengthy interpellation to the prime minister and members of the cabinet who were present, rejecting the view that abolition of the House was "a measure that the Japanese as a defeated nation must take against their will" and pointing out that the bill was following the same direction as the report of the Temporary Deliberation Council of the Taishō period. This, he stated, was "the most eloquent proof that it is not a measure adopted against our will as a result of the defeat." Taking note of the contradictory statements by Yoshida, Kanamori, Kimura, and Ashida during the debates on Article 24 of the constitution, he exhorted the government as follows:

> If the government which takes the leadership in this reform should feel any attachment to the past system, or should have a mind to minimize the reform, or should take a negative attitude to acquiesce in the reform as if it were forced upon it by the recommendation of the Provisional Legislative Investigating Committee, the objective of this reform will on no account be attained.

In their response the government spokesmen preferred not to explain their earlier vacillation. They stated briefly that the revision was necessitated by Article 24 of the constitution and expressed their belief that, whatever became of the family system in law, actually existing good traditions would not be destroyed by the enactment of the bill. On March 31, 1947, the temporary bill was passed without objections. It was to remain valid until January 1, 1948.[40]

By the end of March, too, the sixth draft of the bill for the revision of the civil code itself had been published. Various provisions reflected the conservative efforts to lessen the impact of the reform. This, of course, did not escape the attention of younger scholars of progressive views. One group, calling itself the Civil Code Revision Draft Study Committee (Mimpō Kaiseian Kenkyūkai), held eight meetings and then explained their misgivings to Oppler. He suggested that they submit to him a report with their proposals for amendments. They did so on May 27, 1947, criticizing the existing draft bill as a veiled attempt to maintain the family system; in particular, they pointed out those provisions that they felt used the family name to keep alive a collectivity in many ways similar to the House.[41]

Over the next two months there were almost continuous discussions between Japanese drafters and Government Section representatives about various articles of the draft. In retrospect Wagatsuma stressed that the participation of the latter took the form of suggestions rather than orders.[42] It appears that Oppler insisted, however, that the draft bill should not deviate basically from the principles of the draft outline. An example in question was a provision regarding parental power. The old code (Article 877) had stated that parental power was to be exercised by "the father *who is in the House*" or, if the father was unable, by "the mother *who is in the House*." Some drafters proposed to bestow parental power on father and mother, "*provided they have the same family name.*" Other drafters felt that this proposal aimed at reestablishing the House under the guise of the family name. Oppler opposed the proposal for the same reason. The version of Article 818 finally adopted reads simply: "A child who has not yet attained majority is subject to the parental power of its father and mother."[43] On the other hand, Oppler did not side with the more progressive drafters in their opposition to the above-mentioned Article 730, nor did he oppose a number of other articles that retained traces of the family system. In such details the eighth and final draft had the character of a compromise.[44]

On June 4, 1947, Blakemore submitted a memorandum to General Whitney asking for immediate SCAP permission to submit the draft bill to the Diet.[45] But discussions of the bill continued for another month. The coalition cabinet under the socialist prime minister Katayama—which had replaced the conservative Yoshida cabinet in May 1947—approved the bill on July 15 and submitted it to the first session of the National Diet (that is, the Diet constituted according to the new constitution) on July 25. Public hearings—then an innovation—were held on August 20 and 21. Among the groups submitting their views to the Diet in writing was the League for Realizing the Democratization of Family Law (Kazokuhō minshūka kisei remmei), composed of progressive university professors, officials, women lawyers, members of the Diet, and the heads of the women's departments of the Democratic party and the Communist party. Their statements called, among other things, for the deletion of certain articles—including some dealing with the family name —that were considered remnants of the family system.[46]

After approval by the House of Representatives, the bill was forwarded to the House of Councillors, where it passed with one amendment on November 21, 1947. The amendment, introduced by Tanaka Kotaro (who previously had been minister of education and who later became chief justice of the Supreme Court), required the attestation of the Family Court before divorces by agreement could be entered in the family register and thereby become legally valid. Referred back to the House of Representatives, the bill was adopted by that house in its original form (that is, without the amendment).[47]

The law became effective on January 1, 1948, the date on which the temporary adjustments lost their validity. In the wake of its enactment more than sixty other laws had to be repealed or revised. These covered a broad spectrum of legislation, from the Family Registration Law to such special statutes as the Law Concerning Control of Fire Arms and Explosives and the Electrical Industry Law, most of which contained references to the House system.

In Retrospect

In the foregoing outline of the process of civil code reform we have touched on certain themes that we now want to make more explicit. They deal with three related complexes of questions, namely, questions about continuity and discontinuity; about the homogeneity or heterogeneity of view among Japanese participants; and about the relationship between Japanese and Americans engaged in the reform.

If we restrict our consideration of continuity and discontinuity to a comparison of provisions of the old code and the new one, we find elements of both. The abolition of the chapter "The Head and the Members of the House" in the book on relatives and of the chapter "Succession to the Headship of a House" in the book on succession clearly breaks with the legal tradition stemming from 1898. On the other hand, many specific provisions retained a certain continuity. We mentioned in passing certain traces of the family system in provisions dealing with the family name. Thus, Article 739 of the old civil code stated that "a person who has entered another House by reason of marriage . . . returns to the original House in case of divorce." This is echoed in Article 767 of the new code, providing that "a husband or wife who has changed his or her family name by reason of marriage resumes, by reason of divorce by agreement, the family name he or she had before the marriage."[48] Another example is Article 897, which exempts the ownership of genealogical records and utensils for religious rites and of tombs and burial grounds from the general rules of succession, providing instead that this ownership devolves upon the person "who according to custom is to preside over the worship to the memory of the ancestors."[49] These and other "echoes of the family system" provide a counterpoint of continuity to the discontinuity that may be seen in the abolition of the House.

If we enlarge our perspective we find a strong element of continuity in the general debate on the institutionalization of the family system. The issue had already been basic to the debates on the immediate or postponed enforcement of the original draft of the old civil code, and it was later kept alive during the Taishō period by court decisions and by the writings of jurists and publicists. Although it is true that the recommendations of the Temporary Deliberation Council, established in 1919, stopped far short of the abolition of the House, the late Professor Wagatsuma was essentially correct when he stressed that the postwar reforms "proceeded in the same direction" as these recommendations.

The salience of the issues underlying the reform continued even beyond the Occupation. In 1955, when some of the Japanese participants met to discuss the process of the revision of the civil code and to record it for the benefit of posterity in a book,[50] endeavors were under way to undo the reform at least in part. The Liberal party's Constitution Investigation Committee under the chairmanship of Kishi Nobusuke—who later became prime minister—proposed a revision of Article 24 to provide for the duty of filial piety, thus establishing that "great principle of humanity" in the constitution. Kishi stated his view in terms reminiscent of earlier debates. He regretted that "the concept of *Ie* is completely nonexistent in the present Civil Code" and that "the ideas of commemorating one's ancestors, of respecting one's lineage, and of passing this on to one's children and grandchildren are all gone forever." He questioned whether "such an individualistic approach" as viewing marriage as a union between a man and a woman could be considered proper. And he concluded: "I believe that the existence of the *Ie,* which so well befits Japan's traditions, its customs, and its national conditions, is essential. It is based on the spirit of the *Ie* that the state is constituted, while at the same time it forms the foundation for the state's advance internationally."[51] In this connection a revision of the civil code was also advocated, and the government actually brought the question of such a revision before a legislative inquiry committee. The proposals ran into heated opposition centered in women's organizations, which saw them as efforts to reestablish the family system ideology. In the end nothing came of them. Extreme revisionism declined under the leadership of Ikeda Hayato, Kishi's successor as prime minister. Thus the Liberal Democratic party's platform of July 1962 specifically rejected the idea of a constitutional revision aimed "at restoring the principles of Imperial sovereignty or the prewar family system."[52]

The passage of time and the decline of revisionism should not obscure

the fundamental importance of the reform. As noted above, the significance of family law in Japan goes beyond that of a mere set of rules, regulating relations within the family, and this significance was recognized by
conservatives and progressives alike. It was seen in the manner in which
the family system, institutionalized in law, shaped attitudes toward a
hierarchical structuring of society, toward authority based on such a
structure, and toward the relations between the individual and collectivities to which he or she belonged. Conservatives fought to retain the existing family system because of its impact on society beyond the family.
This is clear, for example, when we consider the nexus between family
system and emperor system that was the core of the prewar orthodoxy.
The educators who called for a strengthening of the family system in
1917 did so because they hoped thereby to stem the breakdown in the
"harmony of the classes of society" and "to maintain due order in the
relations of superior and inferior," as noted above.[53] Equally important
as the stress on a hierarchical structuring of society as a moral norm—
and the implicit rejection of notions of "essential equality" as immoral—
was the stress on collectivity and the rejection of individualism as
immoral. If, as was frequently asserted in prewar days, "individualism is
the greenhouse for all radical ideas," the loosening of the individual from
the ties of existing collectivities had to be combated, above all in that
model collectivity, the family. The fear of conservatives that the conjugal
family unit would be seen as a relation between individuals rather than as
a collectivity; their efforts to insert provisions stressing the duties of family members; and their search, even after the abolition of the House was
decided, for a larger collectivity to which such duties were owed—all of
these have to be seen in this light. The juxtaposition of views on collectivity and individualism is thus another theme that runs through the debates.

Having noted this marked continuity of basic issues in the debates, we
have already taken an important step in answering the question about the
homogeneity or heterogeneity of the views of the Japanese participants in
the postwar reform. Clearly, a distinction can be made between the views
of "conservatives" and those of "progressives." Although these labels are
commonly used in Japanese politics, it is not easy to agree on their meaning. Dealing with "Patterns of Politics in Present Day Japan," Joji
Watanuki in 1967 coined the term "cultural politics" or "value politics,"
by which he meant "politics in which the cleavages caused by differences
in value systems have more effect on the nature of political conflict than
the cleavages caused by economic or status differences."[54] He noted that
the salient issues of this type of politics center on the value questions
involved in maintaining or revising the 1947 constitution and the Occupation's reform measures in such fields as education, police, and labor
relations—to which we may add, as the proposals of Kishi indicate, the

field of family law. The cleavages apparent after the end of the Occupation on the issue of constitutional revision and the partial undoing of Occupation reforms, that is, the "reverse course," were, however, already present at the time of the creation of these reforms, as this essay has demonstrated in regard to the family law reform.

Yet a closer consideration of the process of the family law reform will indicate that a dichotomy between "conservatives" and "progressives" is too simple. It is more accurate to locate participants along a continuum of views. Some may be grouped close to the "progressive" endpoint of such a continuum—for example, the young drafters of the first outline, the representatives of some women's organizations on PLIC and on the Justice Ministry committee, and some members of the Diet, including some women members. They saw in the family system an outdated feudalistic remnant or a prop to a specifically Japanese type of fascism. Their concern was to make it clear that the reform constituted a break with the past, and they therefore opposed provisions that would foster the notion among the population that the House system would continue under the revised civil code.

Others can easily be grouped close to the "conservative" end of the continuum. There we may find, for example, such Diet members and members of the two legislative committees as Hara, Kitaura, and Sawada (whom we quoted above), some officials of the Cabinet Legislation Bureau, and some representatives of the bar associations. Prime Minister Yoshida and most members of his cabinet, including Minister of Justice Kimura, also belonged to this group. They considered the existing family system not only a time-honored and good custom but also an essential ingredient of the national identity and a prerequisite for Japan's moral and political survival. Some like Makino, who played an important role in the committee and in the Diet, wanted to salvage as much of the principles underlying the family system as seemed possible in the circumstances, while they deplored the "feudalistic features" of the system, such as the excessive rights of the Household.

In between we can recognize a third group. Typical of them was a positive attitude toward the reform, coupled with a lingering distrust of individualism and a desire to maintain the family system in the life of the society as a moral concept fostered by the state through school education. As disciples of the "progressive" jurists of the Taishō period, they were sincerely committed to continuing and broadening the reform efforts of their erstwhile teachers, but they also felt a certain affinity to conservative viewpoints, such as those expressed by Makino, without fully sharing them. They, therefore, welcomed compromises. The older members of the drafting committee, such as Wagatsuma and Nakagawa, may be located within this middle range of the continuum.

In retrospect Wagatsuma talked about a "division of labor" between

the secretaries and the members of the drafting committee.[55] Whereas the
secretaries produced drafts in accord with the progressive views that they
held, although perhaps with some gradations even among them, it fell to
the members who attended the sessions of the two large legislative committees to present and defend those drafts. They did so to the extent dictated by the need to achieve the adoption of the basic principles in which
they believed. Thus, they agreed to the change of the unequivocal formulation of the first item of the draft outline ("the House in the Civil Code
shall be abolished"). But when they perceived that adoption of the basic
principles was jeopardized by the statements of the government representatives before the Diet, they used the threat of their resignation to put
pressure on Minister of Justice Kimura. Clearly, divergence rather than a
monolithic homogeneity of views existed among the various Japanese
participants.

Questions dealing with the relations between Japanese and American
participants in the reform are the most complex. Unfortunately, many
observers of the Occupation deal with this relationship in overly simplis-
tic terms because they assume a degree of homogeneity among Japanese
views that in fact did not exist. The very form in which the questions are
often asked is an impediment to understanding. Did "the Americans"
coerce "the Japanese"? Or were the reforms a cooperative effort between
"the Americans" and "the Japanese"? The view that nationality and only
nationality determined the participants' views is often reinforced by reference to the fact that, after all, one group constituted the occupiers and
the other the occupied.[56] There is also a tendency to identify the views
and attitudes of the government in power with those of the nation as a
whole.

An exclusive concentration on nationality as the only significant variable neglects a multitude of human factors that are involved. It leads not
only to the assumption of a homogeneity of views and attitudes on the
part of the occupied population that is very dubious but also to a similar
assumption regarding views and attitudes within the Occupation. In the
case of the Occupation of Japan there were in fact differences among various SCAP sections as well as differences over time as—in MacArthur's
words—the stern control of an occupying power gave way to the friendly
guidance of a protective force. Mechanisms for the reforms enacted during the Occupation for purposes of democratization give a first indication of such differences. Professor Takayanagi Kenzō distinguishes
among three categories, namely: (1) legislation based on SCAP orders,
such as the Shinto Order, in which there was no room for any Japanese
contribution; (2) legislation based on drafts made by the Japanese government, reviewed and approved by SCAP, such as that revising the civil
code; and (3) drafts made by SCAP but amended by the Japanese government or the National Diet, such as the antimonopoly and labor legisla-

tion and the amendment to the commercial code, in which revision of SCAP drafts was allowed if considered reasonable and proper by SCAP, thus allowing Japanese contributions.[57]

Professor Takayanagi's categorization is based on a simple juxtaposition of SCAP and the Japanese government. It nevertheless reflects differences among SCAP sections in that the legislation mentioned as examples for category 3 originated in various parts of the Economic and Scientific Section rather than in sections (first Government Section, later Legal Section) that had primary responsibility for legal reforms and that normally used the mechanism of category 2. Since the different mechanisms reflect roughly degrees of coerciveness in the order 1, 3, and 2, we may state that preferences for one or the other mechanism by SCAP sections are indicative of differences in attitudes toward the Japanese participants among sections within SCAP.[58]

However, differences did not stop at the level of sections or even divisions. Although the views and attitudes of the chiefs of these units often created the general atmosphere within which the interaction between their subordinates and their Japanese counterparts took place, considerable differences among individuals existed along several dimensions. Prime Minister Yoshida indicated some of these dimensions in his memoirs when he discussed different groups in GHQ and their mutually incompatible attitudes toward their tasks. He was highly critical of the "idealistic" reformers of the early Occupation phase, of the "civilians in uniform" and "New Dealers" with their zeal for democratizing Japan, whom he contrasted unfavorably with the "soldiers," such as General Willoughby and General Eichelberger, who were more "practical" and who recognized the dangers of social unrest and the need for order.[59] Indeed, some occupationnaires saw their task as inducing a social revolution, others as a sort of technical assistance operation in which they provided the American know-how; some were concerned with removing what they perceived as evils of the past, others with the danger that an unstable social situation would open the door to communism or socialism; some felt that "democratization" was identical with "Americanization," while others rejected that view.[60]

On a more basic philosophical level, attitudes of staff members of SCAP toward the reform efforts were influenced by two mutually contradictory views regarding the nature of culture in general and the nature of Japanese culture in particular. Those who had a more static view saw Japanese culture as different from Western culture in its very essence. They considered this essence to be immune to the effects of social change and thus fixed in perpetuity; they assumed that "the Japanese" were homogeneous in their adherence to the traditional value system that was part of their culture. From this vantage point, some Occupation reforms seemed to be ethnocentric attempts to force alien values on a defeated, helpless nation. They also seemed to be inherently futile because they could lead only to superficial and ephemeral results.

Those who held a more dynamic view saw the value system of a society as intimately related to its social development. They felt that social change engendered changes of values in various population groups, leading potentially to a breakdown in whatever cultural homogeneity may have existed previously. To them the developments in Japan during the interwar period—including the sometimes frantic efforts of conservatives to bolster the traditional value system—were indications of the effects of social change. The heterogeneity in attitudes toward the traditional value system apparent at that time was now reinforced by the trauma of defeat and the resultant "reevaluation of all values." It was to be expected that Japanese attitudes toward the reform endeavors would reflect this heterogeneity. To the extent that the reforms were congruent with existing or emerging social realities, as indicated by previous trends in their direction, they were likely to find Japanese supporters. These supporters were the "clientele groups" for specific reforms who would defend these reforms after the Occupation ended.[61] It was natural that a certain affinity existed between reform-minded Occupation officials and equally reform-minded Japanese. At times these Japanese, working for their own goals "through GHQ," tried to influence the Americans in the direction of more radical reform endeavors against the resistance of more conservative Japanese.[62]

A more thoroughgoing analysis of the relations between Japanese and American participants will have to await another occasion. These preliminary observations permit us, however, to approach the question of the relation between Japanese and Americans engaged in the reform of family law. It should be stressed at the outset that the case cannot be considered typical for such relations in general. Broadly speaking, it should be possible to place the relations in individual cases along a continuum according to the degree of coercion and cooperation present, as indicated by Takayanagi's three categories.[63] If so, the reform of the civil code clearly is to be placed toward the cooperative end point of the continuum.

There are two principal reasons for this cooperation. First, GHQ showed great restraint because it considered the topic particularly sensitive. In this regard Oppler noted in *Political Reorientation of Japan* that the abolition of the House "was not directed by SCAP, whose policy was that apart from the principle of equality of sexes and individual freedom, how to modernize and reform the family law should be left to the Japanese people themselves." He added: "This policy was based on the consideration that it would be unwise to impose on an oriental country Western ideas in the field of domestic relations."[64] It is true that this report of Government Section has, in general, a self-serving character. But Oppler's statement is supported by his memorandum of August 19,

1946, to Whitney, quoted above. Whenever the question of SCAP instructions was raised in PLIC and in the Justice Ministry committee, it was always answered in the negative by Wagatsuma and Nakagawa. In an article in *Asahi Evening News* in 1959 Okuno remarked: "I want to make it clear that we did not receive any instructions or directives on the matter," and, when asked about the degree of coercion by SCAP in an interview in 1977 he stated that there was none, adding: "I have always said so."[65] The second reason was noted by Wagatsuma, when he stated that the intentions of the drafters coincided with the preferences of SCAP as far as the abolition of the House was concerned. To Oppler's gratification, the drafters took this step with complete independence. It appears that both sides made the same appraisal of the social changes that had occurred.[66]

Wagatsuma refers in this context to the difficulties in overcoming conservative opposition to the abolition of the House, illustrative of the divergence of Japanese views. It is entirely possible that some conservatives felt "coerced" into agreeing to a proposition with which they were not in sympathy. But this "coercion" was the result of the atmosphere of the times, of the need to reach a consensus on the committees, and of the necessity to avoid loss of face on the part of the prestigious members of the drafting committee who earnestly argued in favor of the proposition, and—in the case of Justice Minister Kimura—of the threat of resignation by Wagatsuma and Nakagawa. It was not the result of SCAP threats or pressure.[67]

After the main principle of the reform was established, its implementation in dozens of provisions of the civil code raised new problems. As we noted, conservatives were able to achieve certain compromises considered an emasculation of the reform by some of the young scholars involved and other progressives. In regard to these compromises Oppler in general favored "a middle of the road course," because he felt that "both extremes, doing too much as well as not enough, had to be avoided."[68] He was clearly in sympathy with the efforts of "the progressive men and women of Japan to lay the foundation for a different, and, as they expected, better society."[69] But, above all, it seemed imperative to him that the reform would be of such a nature that it could find sufficiently broad acceptance as fitting contemporary social realities to ensure its permanence. For these reasons he did not always use his influence in favor of the progressive views. He sided with them when proposed draft articles clearly threatened major principles already agreed upon, as in the above-mentioned case of the proposals to restrict the exercise of parental power to the parent who had "the same family name." But sometimes he brushed aside progressive opposition to specific provisions, although he was aware that these provisions were indeed "echoes of the family system."

We noted that there were differences in attitudes among SCAP officials in the same section or division. Thus, Oppler's attitude was certainly different from that of his first associate and deputy, Thomas Blakemore, who had studied in Japan before the war and thus could be considered an "old Japan hand." Notions of "inducing a social revolution," of "tilting" SCAP's influence in favor of progressive views, and of interfering with the activities of Japanese governmental agencies because of preconceived ideas of what was necessary or desirable were uncongenial to him. His counsel, therefore, was against the Occupation's "doing too much" and in favor of giving the Japanese a free hand to work things out for themselves when clearly stated Occupation objectives, including the implementation of the 1947 constitution, were not obviously involved.[70]

This attitude is illustrated in the memorandum that Blakemore sent to General Whitney on June 4, 1947. In it he asserted that the cleavages of opinion in the drafting committee could "not be explained by identification of views of one group as being 'reactionary,' 'progressive,' or 'bureaucratic,' " but were rather honest differences of opinion between individuals "as to the proper nature of social institutions (as, for example, adoption or divorce), or on highly technical legal mechanisms (such as, for example, classification of property rights)." This interpretation could hardly have been shared by Oppler. Blakemore's memorandum also gives some insight into the differences of attitude within the division by referring to some members who "may favor the views of minority elements on the legislative committee, or of nonparticipating individuals and groups" on certain issues. Blakemore counsels against the substitution of the "views of individual members of Government Section for the recommendations of a widely selected and fairly constituted committee of over a hundred legal scholars who patently are far closer to Japanese social and legal realities than alien observers." In the end Blakemore expresses the division's opposition "to the issuance of SCAP's directives which order changes" in the absence of obviously unconstitutional or undesirable articles in the draft—and on this latter point Oppler was certainly in agreement. It was a matter of pride for him that he rarely "had to resort to the fiat of the conqueror."[71]

The question whether the reform accorded with social reality runs like a red thread through many of the discussions. Japanese progressives were convinced that the family system was outdated. Even moderate conservatives wondered at times whether the House had not become simply an artifact of the arrangements in the Family Registration Law without much support among wide segments of the population. Conservatives wanting to retain the institution of the House admitted that some of the rights of the head of the House were inappropriate for an industrializing society. Blakemore thought that the reform may have come too soon. Oppler, too, wondered at times whether the House system was still a vital ingredient of Japanese society or had already become obsolete. He concluded that it was, at least, moribund.[72] He may have taken consolation from a metaphor that was sometimes used comparing the reform to a garment for a growing boy that was tailored just a little too loose in the expectation that the boy would grow into it in short order. But no one could have expected the massive demographic and sociological changes that rapid industrialization and urbanization were to bring about within the next few decades. They reduced drastically the size of the agricultural and rural population, among whom the former system once had its strongest rationale in the larger family as a productive unit. Under the impact of these changes the "new family system" has attained full "citizenship" in the consciousness of the people. Polls indicate, for example, that by 1965 roughly two-thirds of the population approved of it. Moreover, affirmative responses are not limited to the younger generation but are given by members of all generational groups.[73] The permanence of the reforms—which in time may have come about even without the Occupation—is no longer open to question.

Notes

Soon after arriving in Japan in 1945, I first met the late Judge Alfred Oppler and Professor Kawashima Takeyoshi, who were then engaged in the civil code reform. Years later, when I was working on the present essay, they shared their recollections with me and gave me the benefit of their comments on earlier drafts. For this I am most grateful. I also interviewed Murakami Tomokazu, Okuno Kenichi, and Naito Yorihiro, all officials of the Justice Ministry at the time of the civil code reform. Professors Bai Koichi and Chiba Masaji of Tokyo Metropolitan University, Sato Isao of Sophia University, and Ukai Nobushige of Senshu University, also aided me in many ways.

On this side of the Pacific Ocean I am indebted to Charles Kades and Beate Sirota Gordon, both formerly of Government Section, and to James Hastings of the National Record Center at Suitland, Maryland. Of the participants in the present volume, comments by professors Tanaka Hideo, Susan Pharr, Theodore McNelly, and Sakamoto Yoshikazu were particularly helpful. My research assistant, Carl Walter, facilitated my use of the Japanese material on which much of this study is based. I am deeply grateful to all of them. Their contributions should not obscure my responsibility for errors of interpretation.

1. These codes are the Civil Code, the Criminal Code, the Commmercial Code, the Code of Civil Procedure, and the Code of Criminal Procedure. Together with the constitution they are the principal content of the Compendium of Six Laws *(Roppo Zensho),* that is, the vade mecum of every Japanese jurist and law student.

2. Some relevant planning documents are the memorandum "Preliminary Political and Policy Questions Bearing on Civil Affairs Planning for the Far East and Pacific Areas," prepared in the War Department and Navy Department on February 18, 1944, in *Foreign Relations of the United States—Diplomatic Papers, 1944,* vol. 5, p. 1190; Memorandum on Nullification of Obnoxious

Laws, prepared by the Interdivisional Area Committee on the Far East, March 22, 1944, in ibid., pp. 1214–1216; Report of SWNCC Subcommittee for the Far East, June 11, 1955, in ibid., vol. 8, pp. 549–555. The phrase in the presidential policy statements quoted in the text goes back to the SWNCC draft (SWNCC 150/2) of August 12, 1945, in ibid., pp. 609–611. It appears under the heading "Encouragement of Desire for Individual Liberties and Democratic Processes."

3. The connection with the constitution was most direct in the case of the Code of Criminal Procedure (because of the safeguards for the rights of the accused in articles 31 to 40 of the constitution) and in the case of the civil code. It was most tenuous in the case of the commercial code, revised in 1950. A series of articles written at the time appeared in the *Washington Law Review* between 1949 and 1951. These were republished in 1977 in a special edition "Legal Reforms in Japan during the Allied Occupation." See also Alfred C. Oppler, *Legal Reform in Occupied Japan: A Participant Looks Back* (Princeton: Princeton University Press, 1976).

4. In "Law in Science and Science in Law," *Harvard Law Review,* vol. 12 (1899), p. 99.

5. In his *Kokumin Kyōiku: Aikokushin* [Educating a nation: Patriotism] (1897), Hozumi Yatsuka stated the linkage as follows: "The Sun Goddess is the founder of our race. If father and mother are to be revered, how much more so the ancestors of the House; and if the ancestors of the House are to be revered, how much more so the founder of the country. . . . For the same reason one is filial to his parents and loyal to the throne." Textbooks such as the Education Ministry's *The Way of the Subject* (1941) impressed this idea on school children.

6. See, e.g., Wagatsuma Sakae, *Ie no seido* [The family system] (Tokyo: Kantōsha, 1948), pp. 85–88, and Wagatsuma, "Democratization of the Family Relation in Japan," *Washington Law Review,* vol. 25 (November 1950), pp. 405–426. Kurt Steiner, "Post-War Changes in the Japanese Civil Code," *Washington Law Review* (August 1950), pp. 286–312, and Steiner, "The Revision of the Civil Code of Japan: Provisions Affecting the Family," *Far Eastern Quarterly,* vol. 9 (February 1950), pp. 169–184, refer to some of the more important provisions of the old civil code. See also Ronald P. Dore, *City Life in Japan* (Berkeley and Los Angeles: University of California Press, 1958), chap. 8; Watanabe Yozō, "The Family and the Law: The Individualistic Premise and Modern Japanese Family Law," in Arthur von Mehren, ed., *Law in Japan: The Legal Order in a Changing Society* (Cambridge: Harvard University Press, 1963), pp. 364–398; and Oppler, *Legal Reform,* pp. 111–120.

7. Some of these decisions as well as others of similar import are noted in Watanabe Yozō, "The Family and the Law," pp. 371–372.

8. Other proposals could be read as strengthening the power of the Household, thus indicating the compromise character of the recommendations. See Wagatsuma, *Ie no seido,* pp. 88–103; also Dore, *City Life,* pp. 93–118. The council was evenly split on the adoption of the recommendations so that the vote of the chairman, Hiranuma Kiichiro, had to break the tie.

9. Quoted in Maruyama Masao, *Thought and Behavior in Modern Japanese Politics,* expanded ed. (London: Oxford University Press, 1969), p. 37.

10. Takikawa Yukitatsu, *Kenkyū no jiyū* (Tokyo: Seikatsusha, 1947), pp. 107–109.

11. Interview on November 8, 1976 with Murakami Tomokazu, one of the drafters of the revised civil code, who subsequently became Chief Justice of the Supreme Court (1973–1976). See also Watanabe, "The Family and the Law," p. 372.

12. The memorandum, prepared by Lt. Col. Milo Rowell, may be conveniently found in Takayanagi Kenzō, Ohtomo Ichiro, and Tanaka Hideo, *Nippon koku kempō seitei no katei* [The formulation of the Japanese constitution] (Tokyo: Yuhikaku, 1972), vol. 1, pp. 26–40.

13. Ibid., pp. 218, 222, 272–273, 276, 310. The sentence regarding the family as the basis of human society was subsequently eliminated at the urging of Japanese participants in the drafting. Ibid., vol. 2, p. 170; interview with Professor Sato Isao, November 12, 1977.

14. For other Japanese proposals aimed at diluting the effect of Article 24 and, therefore, rejected by Government Section, see Susan Pharr's contribution to this volume.

15. *Official Gazette Extra*, 90th Session of the Imperial Diet, House of Representatives, no. 6, June 26, 1946, pp. 1 and 8; and House of Peers, no. 23, August 26, 1946, p. 12. (Quotes are from the official English edition and page references are to that edition.) In committee, Hara argued that the "individual dignity," provided in the draft article, meant "the renunciation of the family system and the adoption of individualism." Washington National Records Center (Suitland, Maryland), Record Group 331, Box 2088, File: Minutes of the Subcommittee on the Bill for the Revision of the Imperial Constitution, July 26, 1946. All future references to material at the Washington National Records Center (WNRC) are to Record Group 331.

16. *Official Gazette Extra*, 90th Session of the Imperial Diet, House of Peers, no. 24, August 27, 1946, pp. 23–24. Later, Matsumoto Manabu expressed his regret about the committee's vote, stating that "the foreign style family life" based on marriage compared unfavorably with the Japanese family life around a vertical axis. Ibid., no. 4, October 6, 1946, p. 7. Ultimately, Makino's efforts led to the inclusion of a similar article (Article 730) in the Civil Code (see below).

17. Ibid., pp. 19–23.

18. Ibid., House of Representatives, no. 6, June 27, 1946, p. 3.

19. Ibid., no. 35, August 25, 1946, p. 5.

20. Ibid., House of Peers, no. 25, August 29, 1946, p. 3. Kimura added that the constitutional provision did not mean that the family system in Japan in its good sense would be abolished, and he urged that worship of ancestors and respect for lineage, being virtues and good traditions of the Japanese nation, be carried over to posterity. Minister of Education Tanaka made a similar point, stating that if the family system as a legal concept disappeared, the morality "in accordance with our history and tradition from ancient times should be still more stressed from now on."

21. WNRC, Box 2142, File: Memos for the Chief of Government Section, vol. 1.

22. Much of this section is based on Wagatsuma Sakae, ed., *Sengo ni okeru mimpō kaisei no katei* [The postwar revision of the Civil Code] (Tokyo: Nihon Hyōronshinsha, 1956). This volume (hereafter cited as *Mimpō kaisei*) is the record of retrospective discussions by participants in the revision process,

together with relevant documents. The statements in the text are based on pp.
12–13, and the two documents referred to are reprinted on pp. 211–213. Okuno
later became an Associate Justice of the Supreme Court (1956–1968).

On the Family Registration Law (perhaps more properly called "House Registration Law" before its revision, although the Japanese title has not changed) and
on its revision, see "Post-War Changes," pp. 309–310.

23. WNRC, Box 1503, File: Civil Legislation, Civil Code, 1946 (1).

24. Ibid. For the Okuno statement see *Mimpō kaisei,* p. 13. On the activities
of Ethel Weed as a promoter of women's rights policies, see Susan Pharr's contribution to this volume.

25. WNRC, Box 1500, Chronological File 1946; the memorandum is also
part of the papers of Commander A. R. Hussey in the Asia Library at the University of Michigan, where it is numbered 58-A-2. It calls attention to one of the
ramifications of the House system and of its abolition, stating that the family system provided some social security in the absence of appropriate measures by the
public and private sector. To substitute for this function, it would be necessary to
enact social welfare laws. Conservative attitudes in this regard were illustrated a
few months later when the government responded to the grave housing problem
of the time by urging the homeless to "seek protection in the family system."
Mainichi Shinbun, November 17, 1946.

26. Memorandum to the Chief of the Public Administration Division [Colonel
Kades], "Steps to be taken by the Government Section in connection with the
Legal Reforms Planned by the Japanese Government," Hussey Papers, 58-A-4.
See also Oppler, *Legal Reform,* pp. 83–84.

27. Draft memo by Oppler, May 24, 1947, and, in revised form, memo to
the Chief of Legal Section, August 30, 1948, both in WNRC, Box 1497, File:
General Administration, Courts and Law Division. See also Government Section, *Political Reorientation of Japan* (Washington, D.C.: GPO, n.d.), vol. 2, pp.
791, 812.

28. WNRC, Box 2142, File: Memos for the Chief, Government Section, Book
2 (April–July 1946).

29. *Mimpō kaisei,* pp. 6, 9, 205–213. A special Research Room for Civil
Code Reform was also established within the Civil Affairs Bureau of the Justice
Ministry.

30. *Mimpō kaisei,* pp. 6, 213–225.

31. Ibid., pp. 4, 41–49; the draft emerging from the Second Small Committee
is on pp. 230–233.

32. Oppler, *Legal Reform,* p. 156; interview with Kawashima Takeyoshi,
October 23, 1977; Bai Koichi and Takeshita Shiro, "Shinmimpō no seiritsu,"
[Establishment of the New Civil Code] in Nakagawa Zennosuke et al., *Kazoku:
kazoku mondai to kazoku hō* (Tokyo: Sakai Shoten, 1959), vol. 1, pp. 378–379.
Apparently, Oppler was not informed about the decision of the Second Small
Committee reached on that very day.

33. *Mimpō kaisei,* pp. 50–63, and, for the revised draft outline, pp. 233–237;
see also Nakagawa Zennosuke, *Shinmimpō no shihyō to ritsuan katei no tembyō*
[A profile of the characteristics and drafting of the New Civil Code] (Tokyo:
Asahi, 1949), pp. 6–10. On the day before the plenary meeting of the Justice
Ministry's committee, Oppler and Lieutenant Weed had met with Okuno, Naito

Yorihiro (then both officials of the Justice Ministry), and Kawashima. According to an entry in Oppler's diary all three told him "that they were *personally* all in favor of the complete abolition of the old family system." Oppler, *Legal Reform*, p. 156 (italics in text).

34. WNRC, Box 2142, File: Memos for the Chief, Government Section, Book 3.

35. *Mimpō kaisei*, pp. 63–66; the minutes of the PLIC meeting are contained in full in ibid., pp. 243–263. See also Nakagawa, *Shinmimpō no shihyō*, pp. 13–14. In a memo of August 29, 1946, Oppler stated that he was now receiving documents containing reform proposals, and he suggested that PLIC should be informed about SCAP views on major points before its final meeting (which was held in October). WNRC, Box 1500, Chronological File 1946.

36. Interview with Okuno on October 27, 1977; Okuno Kenichi, "Kizentaru Sensei" in Ariizumi Toru, ed., *Tsuisō no Wagatsuma Sakae* [Reminiscences of Wagatsuma Sakae] (Tokyo: Ichiryūsha, 1974), pp. 242–243; *Mimpō kaisei*, pp. 15–16.

37. *Mimpō kaisei*, pp. 70–74; Nakagawa, *Shinmimpō no shihyō*, pp. 18–22.

38. *Mimpō kaisei*, pp. 79–83; the minutes of the third and last session of PLIC are on pp. 263–290. On Article 730 see Wagatsuma, "Democratization," pp. 407–408, and Steiner, "Post-War Changes," pp. 297–299. For a subsequent controversy on related issues, see the articles by Makino and Kawashima, published under the title "Oyakokō hōritsuka ze-hi ronsō" [The controversy over the merits of the Family System Law], in *Chūō Kōron*, September 1950, pp. 78–101.

39. *Mimpō kaisei*, pp. 110–111; the Numazu and Yamanaka drafts are on pp. 316–342.

40. See *Mimpō kaisei*, pp. 111–112; Memorandum for the Chief of Government Section of May 1, 1947, subject: Gist of the Ministry of Justice Laws passed by the last Diet, WNRC, Box 1500, Chronological File 1947 (March–July); *Official Gazette Extra*, 92d Session of the Imperial Diet, House of Representatives, March 18–28, 1947, and House of Peers, March 29–31, 1947. See also Saiko Saibansho Jimu Sōkyoku, *Mimpō kaisei ni kansuru kokkai kankei shiryō* [Parliamentary materials relating to the revision of the Civil Code] (Tokyo: 1953), pp. 1–75. An English translation of the law is in "Post-War Changes," pp. 294–296.

41. WNRC, Box 1500, Chronological File 1947 (March–July) and Box 1503, File: Civil Legislation: Civil Code, Temporary Adjustment—1947.

42. See, e.g., *Mimpō kaisei*, pp. 114–116.

43. Ibid., and pp. 163–169; interview with Kawashima Takeyoshi, October 24, 1947 (emphasis added). For a critique of the viewpoint that the compromise character of the revised code was due to a partial yielding to conservatives, see Wagatsuma, "Amerika ni okeru kaisei mimpō no shōkai" [The presentation of the Revised Civil Code in America], *Shihō*, no. 4 (1951), pp. 45–49, and by the same author, "Democratization," pp. 409–414.

The issue of certain provisions regarding the family name that was likely to keep the House alive in the consciousness of the people had already surfaced at the time of the so-called Numazu draft. At that time, Oppler asked pointedly whether the term "family name"—the Japanese word *uji* has connotations of lineage and was used in this sense in the old code—was not actually replacing the term House or *Ie*, thus bringing back the House system "by the back door." It appears that this criticism created great consternation among the drafters when Kawashima and Okuno reported the conversation back to them in Numazu. See Bai, "Shinmimpō no seiritsu" [Formulation of the New Civil Code], p. 380, and on the issue more generally, his "Sengo no mimpō kaisei katei ni okeru 'Uji' " ["Uji" in the revision of the postwar Civil Code], in Nippon Hōshakai Gakkai, *Kazoku seido no kenkyū* [Study of the family system] (Tokyo: Yuhikaku, 1956), vol. 2, pp. 75–140. The provision on parental power in the Numazu draft is to be found in *Mimpō kaisei,* p. 321.

44. On criticisms of the reforms as being not thoroughgoing enough and Wagatsuma's reaction to them, see his "Democratization," pp. 410–412.

45. WNRC, Box 1500, Chronological File, 1947 (March–July). The contents of Blakemore's memorandum are discussed more fully below.

46. *Mimpō kaisei,* pp. 342–349. Nosaka Sanzō had submitted the Communist party's opinion to Okuno already on May 12, 1947. See ibid., pp. 349–350.

47. In the debate the bill was criticized in part for failing to establish full equality of the sexes. See, e.g., *Official Gazette Extra,* First Session of the National Diet, House of Councillors, November 19–21, 1947. *Kokkai kankei shiryō* (see footnote 40), pp. 75–619, also contains a report of the committee meetings and of the public hearings.

48. At the urging of women's organizations, Article 767 was amended in 1976 to the effect that the divorced person may keep the married family name upon application. Traces of the House remain in the revised Family Registration Law. Thus in case of marriage of a woman "appearing first in the family register," the husband who assumes her family name is to be entered into her family register. This provision continues notions of an "incoming husband" (nyūfū) marrying into a House with a female head and assuming the position of head of the house, unless a contrary intention was expressed at the time of marriage.

49. "Post-War Changes," p. 308; *Mimpō kaisei,* p. 175–180. Although apprehension was expressed by some Japanese that the provision, and especially its recognition of existing "custom," would perpetuate ancestor worship as one of the pillars of the family system, Government Section acquiesced in it.

50. This is the volume, edited by Wagatsuma, to which we have referred frequently above as *Mimpō kaisei.* See n. 22 above for a full citation.

51. See Jiyūto Kempō Chōsakai, *Nihonkoku kempō kaiseian yōkōan* [Gist of proposals for amendment of the Japanese constitution], November 5, 1954. Kishi's statement is quoted in Watanabe Yozō, "The Family and the Law," p. 379. These efforts were part of the more general "reverse course." A related effort aimed at the reestablishment of "morals courses" in the schools.

52. H. Fukui, "Twenty Years of Revisionism," *Washington Law Review,* vol. 43, no. 5 (June 1968), p. 957; see also Kenzo Takayanagi's "Some Reminiscences of Japan's Commission on the Constitution" (Appendix), ibid., p. 990, for the negative opinion of the chairman of that commission on the proposed inclusion of constitutional provisions relating to the family.

53. Professor Wagatsuma in his interpellation in the House of Peers on March 29, 1947, referred to above, quoted this statement of the educators.

54. In Seymour M. Lipset and Stein Rokkan, eds., *Party Systems and Voter Alignments: Cross Cultural Perspectives* (New York: Free Press, 1967), pp. 447–466.

55. *Mimpō kaisei,* pp. 10–11.

56. Observers who hold such notions neglect the existing evidence from other countries, including those occupied during World War II by the Axis powers, that groups in occupied countries often show sharply divided views and attitudes toward the occupiers. There were those who collaborated freely and often out of ideological conviction with the occupiers and those who risked their lives in resistance to them for the same reason.

57. Takayanagi, "Some Reminiscences," p. 970.

58. In regard to the revision of the commercial code, two participants stated that the committee procedures were "of a character unknown to Robert's Rules of Order." See Thomas L. Blakemore and Makoto Yuzawa, "Japanese Commercial Code Revision Concerning Corporations," *American Journal of Comparative Law,* vol. 2, no. 1 (January 1953), pp. 12–24.

59. Yoshida also criticized two types of "particularly obnoxious" Japanese, the "advantage seekers" and the "progressives" or "radicals," who got together with "leftist elements" in GHQ. See Shigeru Yoshida, *Memoirs* (Boston: Houghton Mifflin, 1962), pp. 38–39, 43–46, 53–55, and 287, and (for the criticism of Japanese), pp. 59–61, 151.

60. With particular reference to the legal reforms Oppler wrote in his memorandum of April 1, 1946: "Although we may be inclined to consider the Anglo-Saxon legal system superior to the Continental, we should resist any temptation to replace hastily one by the other." (See footnote 26)

61. The more static view was often held by persons who considered themselves "old Japan hands" or felt that they had a superior understanding of the "Asian mind." For an elaboration of these issues, see my foreword to Oppler, *Legal Reform,* pp. vii–xiii. See also Robert E. Ward, *Japan's Political System,* 2d ed. (Englewood Cliffs, N.J.: Prentice-Hall, 1978), p. 21, for a list of Japanese interests that benefited from various reform programs.

62. Bai, "Shinmimpō no seiritsu," p. 399–400.

63. In a comment Professor Sakamoto Yoshikazu stressed the imbalance of power between Americans and Japanese that put the Americans in the role of superiors. Taking into account Japanese behavior patterns in relations between inferiors and superiors, the absence of externally observable resistance was not necessarily an indication of cooperation. Thus, in discussing the general problem from the Japanese vantage point, one may have to distinguish among spontaneous cooperation, nonresistance, and resistance.

64. *Political Reorientation of Japan,* vol. 1, p. 215.

65. For Okuno's confirmation of Oppler's statement in *Political Reorientation,* see *Mimpō kaisei,* p. 14. On the general subject see also ibid., pp. 13, 15, 58, 102, 114. The *Asahi Evening News* article is cited in Oppler, *Legal Reform,* p. 116. I interviewed Okuno on October 27, 1977.

66. *Mimpō kaisei,* p. 102. Wagatsuma speculated whether SCAP would have interfered if it had been the intention of the drafting committee to retain the House, but the question never arose.

67. The atmosphere of the times is sometimes characterized as that of the "Revolution of August 15," this being the date of the Japanese surrender. See Bai, "Shinmimpō no seiritsu," p. 373. In regard to the constitution socialist leader Katayama made the point more bluntly, stating that it was imposed on the reac-

tionaries but not on the people of Japan. See Theodore McNelly, "The New Constitution and Induced Revolution in Japan," in L. H. Redford, ed., *The Occupation of Japan: Impact of Legal Reform* (Norfolk, Va.: MacArthur Memorial, 1977), p. 159.

68. Alfred C. Oppler, "The Reform of Japan's Legal and Judicial System Under Allied Occupation," *Washington Law Review,* vol. 24 (August 1949), p. 291.

69. Oppler, *Legal Reform,* p. 38.

70. Oppler mentions that Blakemore's moderation was criticized by "the most fanatical reformers," but that he (Oppler) appreciated Blakemore's familiarity with Japanese attitudes. *Legal Reform,* p. 66.

71. Blakemore's memorandum is in WNRC, Box 1500, Chronological File 1947 (March–July). Blakemore acted as Oppler's deputy during his absence on two weeks' leave following the arrival of his wife and daughter in Japan. See Oppler, *Legal Reform,* pp. 183, 186. In his memorandum Blakemore also warned against "a reliance for information upon individuals or groups who themselves advocate changes of one form or another," because "unconsciously their representations could come to be regarded as reflecting a more general support than the facts warrant."

In a subsequent interview Blakemore admitted that, as a private person, he had some doubt about the reform because it had been carried out by a minority and under the influence of a foreign country inasmuch as GHQ encouraged the Japanese government. He also stated: "GHQ may have had the power to force it, but I did not want to use it. Whether I used it indirectly I don't know." Bai, "Shinmimpō no seiritsu," p. 383–384. Japanese participants recalled, however, that Blakemore himself started meetings by stating with particular reference to the civil code that he was giving advice not orders. Other Americans also repeatedly made statements to that effect. Ibid., pp. 381–382. Oppler was "conscious of the danger that even 'advice' given by members of the occupation . . . might easily be misinterpreted as a milder form of direction." See his "Reform of Japan's Legal and Judicial System," p. 303. On Oppler's attitude toward the issuance of SCAP directives, see *Legal Reform,* chap. 7 ("The Legal and Judicial Reform: A Cooperative Effort").

72. Bai, "Shinmimpō no seiritsu," p. 383; Oppler, *Legal Reform,* pp. 114–116. Oppler was aware of the differential hold of the family system on various population groups in urban and rural Japan. On March 28, 1947, he submitted a memorandum to General Whitney, summarizing the findings of a national public opinion poll on the civil code conducted by *Mainichi Shinbun.* Whereas 57.9 percent of the respondents declared themselves in favor of the abolition of the House, only 43.3 percent of the farmers and fishermen did so. See WNRC, Box 1500, Chronological File 1947 (January–March).

73. See, for example, Nippon Hōsō Kyōkai (NHK), *Zusetsu sengo yōronshi* [Postwar public opinion] (Tokyo: NHK Books, 1975), pp. 30–32. On the progressive nuclearization of the family see, e.g., Bando Mariko, *The Women of Japan: Past and Present* (Tokyo: Foreign Press Center, "About Japan" Series, no. 5, n.d.), pp. 14–15. Until 1955 families had consisted of an average of 5 members; by 1975 the average was 3.444. The ratio of nuclear families to all households surpassed the 60 percent level.

8

The Politics of Women's Rights

Susan J. Pharr

> Equality on the face of the law does not always mean equality
> in actuality . . . The fact that such a thing is openly declared
> in the fundamental law will, however, mean that the unequal
> position in which women were placed heretofore will be
> greatly rectified. Of course, equality [must not] stop there in
> the law . . . it must be won through hard fighting. And that,
> I think, is our future duty.
>
> Kume Ai, lawyer, Tokyo, March 15, 1946

During the past century, issues of women's rights have been the subject of worldwide policy debate. It was not until the end of the nineteenth century, less than one hundred years ago, that women in any country gained the right to vote. Most laws and policies designed to benefit women have emerged, not as the self-evident confirmation of a widespread belief in the equality of the sexes, but as the result of acrimonious debate. The bitter struggle for women's suffrage in Britain; the vigorous opposition even today of secular and religious leaders in many Arab countries to extending full political rights to women; the current resistance in Catholic Europe to a wide variety of changes, from the liberalization of divorce laws to provisions for public daycare for children; and the reluctance of Soviet and Chinese leaders to implement profeminist laws and policies that emerged in the aftermath of revolution—such instances serve as reminders that, everywhere, securing women's rights has been fraught with controversy.[1] In the United States, the century of struggle that preceded the extension of suffrage to American women, the bitter conflict over ratification of the Equal Rights Amendment to the constitution, and the widespread opposition to the implementation of affirmative action policies indicate that debate over women's rights measures has been no less rancorous here than elsewhere.[2]

To recall the stormy history of women's rights reform in other countries is a fitting way to begin an analysis of the truly radical set of laws and policies introduced in Japan by the Americans during the period of Allied Occupation from 1945 to 1952. Standard accounts of the Occupation's policy-making activities in the area of women's rights consistently have failed to put these changes in a meaningful context. Most analysts have chosen to focus on how radical the changes were in relation to the status quo in Japanese society in 1945.[3] But none has acknowledged what is far more startling: that the reforms were progressive in relation to views in Western societies as well. Indeed, laws introduced in Japan by an American occupying force more than thirty years ago in some cases went far beyond what the U.S. Congress, the state legislatures, and many Americans are willing to accept in their own country, even today, in the area of legal guarantees for women's equality and rights.

How and why a U.S. occupying force chose to make Japan a laboratory for one of the world's most radical experiments with women's rights are complex questions. The most obvious answer, widely accepted in previous accounts, is that such measures were seen by the Occupation as part of a larger effort to reform an antidemocratic family system considered by the Americans to be a root cause of the militarism and fascism that had led to the war. Adjusting the status of women in the family and in society was thus a basic step toward the goal of democratizing Japanese society. The present analysis does not challenge this general explanation for what happened in Japan, but maintains that it hardly goes far enough. After all, women's rights reforms have met massive and well-organized resistance in most countries of the world, including the United States and other democracies. Even in those countries where the greatest gains for women have been achieved, such as Sweden, policy change has been preceded by widespread public debate in which none of the participants, profeminist or antifeminist, saw their positions as "undemocratic" or "antidemocratic" in any way.[4] Thus, there is no reason to believe that an American commitment to democracy led automatically to the door of women's rights reform in Japan or that it somehow dictated the particular set of reforms that was actually adopted.

Extraordinarily little has been written about the U.S. experiment with women's rights in Japan. Few have tried to penetrate the facade of American policy consensus on women's rights goals during the Occupation to explore the bureaucratic politics within the Occupation administrative structure that gave rise to the radical experiment. Similarly, little attention has been paid to the role played by Japanese women leaders as advocates of reform or to the opposition of Japanese officialdom to the changes. This chapter takes up precisely these tasks in examining two case studies, analyzing how the radical experiment got under way in Japan, what resistance it faced, and why it was ultimately successful.

In this analysis, it will become apparent that the real impetus for

women's rights measures in Japan emerged from a policy alliance between a group of low-ranking American women serving in the Occupation and a core group of Japanese women leaders who worked closely
with them to formulate and advocate women's rights policies. This "alliance for liberation" faced two sets of hurdles in winning approval for the
reforms: opposition from high-ranking Occupation personnel to a number of their proposals, and opposition from Japanese officialdom to virtually all of them. There were no women at top decision-making levels in
either administrative hierarchy, Japanese or American, so, in effect, the
policy alliance sometimes encountered a solid wall of male resistance to
measures it advocated. A number of its most radical proposals died early
in the face of such opposition. But the women's policy alliance nevertheless was able to push through a whole series of measures that were highly
progressive in relation to the mainstream of thought in most Western
societies in the 1940s. How the policy alliance was organized in the setting of a military occupation is suggested by the diagram in Figure 1.

Each of the two case studies analyzed focuses on a landmark reform.
The first case, dating from the earliest months of the Occupation, exam-
ines the steps by which guarantees of women's equality found their way
into the postwar Japanese constitution. This reform in basic law was of
paramount importance, for it laid the groundwork for all subsequent
change. The second case traces the developments leading up to the formation of the Women's and Minors' Bureau (WMB) in the Japanese Min-

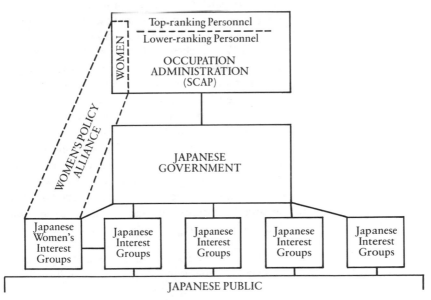

Fig. 1. Women's policy alliance within the Occupation structure

istry of Labor when it was organized in 1947. This second reform was crucial for the long-range success of the radical experiment, for it created a watchdog agency to protect women's gains once the Occupation period ended. Beyond the analysis of the policy-making process itself, the larger issue is why the radical experiment enjoyed such success in Japan. Not only did women's rights measures win the backing of the U.S. military and of the Japanese government during the Occupation period, but virtually all the women's rights measures enacted during that period survive today, more than a quarter of a century later.

Women's Rights Laws and the "Japanese ERA"

A catastrophic war between Japan and the Allied countries came to its official end with the Surrender Ceremony on September 2, 1945. A month later, U.S. forces began arriving in Tokyo to set up an occupation that was to last until April 1952. Although officially designated "Allied" Occupation, it was almost wholly an American undertaking, under the leadership of General Douglas MacArthur, Supreme Commander for the Allied Powers. The acronym SCAP was soon used to refer not only to the commander himself, but to the complex bureaucratic structure set up under him to guide the demilitarization and democratization of Japan.

Some of the Americans' boldest initiatives were taken in their earliest months in Japan, when they set out to overhaul the country's legal structure. The program of legal reform included at every stage measures offering new guarantees to Japanese women, but the signal event was the decision to include explicit women's rights guarantees in Japan's highest law, the Japanese constitution of 1947, which was drafted by the Americans and finally approved by the Japanese before the first year of the Occupation had ended. From these first steps in the area of legal change flowed all subsequent measures designed to upgrade the status of Japanese women, so it is natural that our attention focuses there when we set out to determine how the radical experiment began.

At the heart of the constitutional revisions affecting women are two articles found in the constitution of 1947. Article 14, which might be called the "Japanese ERA," is an explicit guarantee of women's equality: "All people are equal under the law and there shall be no discrimination in political, economic or social relations because of race, creed, sex, social status or family origin." The second is Article 24, which states:

> Marriage shall be based on the mutual consent of both sexes and it shall be maintained through mutual co-operation with the equal rights of husband and wife as a basis.

> With regard to choice of spouse, property rights, inheritance, choice of domicile, divorce and other matters pertaining to marriage and the family,

laws shall be enacted from the standpoint of individual dignity and the essential equality of the sexes.

To many Americans in the 1980s, still locked in a national controversy over a constitutional amendment that in wording and intent is not very different from the "Japanese ERA," inclusion of Article 14 in a constitution promulgated more than thirty years ago may seem quite progressive.[5] But this type of equal rights provision, still subject in 1987 to debate in the United States, is an accepted part of most European constitutions (see Table 1). Article 24 is the more radical of the two measures, for by extending a guarantee of women's equality beyond the public sphere into the private domain of the family, it goes well beyond what most constitutions of the world provide, even today.[6] Only in the constitutions of Communist countries such as the USSR and Poland does one find provisions aimed at guaranteeing equality between the sexes in marriage and in family life.[7]

To trace the impetus for the inclusion of women's rights measures in the Japanese constitution of 1947 is an ideal way to begin to explore the Occupation as a setting for feminist reform. Not only were these consti-

Table 1
Constitutional Guarantees for Equality of the Sexes in Selected Countries

Japan:	"All people are equal under the law and there shall be no discrimination in political, economic or social relations because of race, creed, sex, social status or family origin." (Article 14, Japanese Constitution of 1947.)
U.S.:	"Equality of rights under the law shall not be denied or abridged by the United States or by any state on account of sex." (Proposed Amendment to the U.S. Constitution, passed by Congress in 1972 but still unratified.)
Germany:	"Men and women have equal rights." (Article 3, Basic Law of the Federal Republic of Germany of 1949.)
Italy:	"All citizens have equal social dignity and are equal before the law, without distinction of sex, of race, of language, of religion, of political opinion, of personal and social condition." (Article 3, Constitution of the Italian Republic of 1949.)
France:	"The law shall guarantee to women equal rights with men in all domains." (Preamble, Constitution of the French Republic of 1946.)
USSR:	"Women in the U.S.S.R. are accorded equal rights with men in all spheres of economic, government, cultural, political, and other public activity." (Article 122, Constitution of the USSR of 1936.)

SOURCE: Constitutions of Germany, Italy, and France: Arnold J. Zurcher, *Constitutions and Constitutional Trends Since World War II* (New York: New York University Press, 1951); Constitution of the USSR: Steven Muller, ed., *Documents on European Governments* (New York: MacMillan, 1963).

tutional provisions an especially good example of the radical experiment, but coming as they did in the early months of the Occupation, they offer a window on how the radical experiment got under way. At the outset of this research, a number of possibilities presented themselves as to how the measures might have originated. One possibility was that the impetus might have come, not from anyone, Japanese or American, in Japan, but from U.S. policy makers back in Washington. As chapter 1 of this book indicates, preparatory work for the Occupation of Japan, as for that of Germany, was being done in Washington for several years before the war ended in 1945. It was reasonable to postulate that the U.S. State Department or other agencies in charge of presurrender planning might have drawn up a master plan for feminist reform in Japan or, at least, might have targeted that area as an appropriate one for action. An investigation, however, turned up no evidence to substantiate that theory. The major State Department directive (SWNCC-228) formulated to guide the work of the Occupation was cast in very broad terms, and it made no specific recommendations that could have provided a basis for the far-reaching women's rights measures that were adopted. Furthermore, an examination of the minutes of the State-War-Navy Coordinating Committee (SWNCC), the interagency policy-making body for the Occupation, indicated that at no time between December 1944 and November 1947, when SWNCC ceased to meet, was the subject of Japanese women's rights ever discussed.[8]

A second possibility was that the Japanese leaders and private citizens, male and female, who were in communication with the Occupation in the months before the drafting of the constitution began might have pressed for the inclusion of the measures. The data, however, did not support this theory either. In the fall of 1945, a number of groups, official and private, were engaged in drawing up and proposing constitutions for the consideration of the authorities. Amid all these drafts, however, only one, submitted by a private group known as the Constitution Investigation Society (Kempō Kenkyū Kai), included any reference, however passing, to women. Although this single provision was duly noted by officials in the Occupation, there is little basis for believing that it set in motion the radical experiment. Indeed, by the time the Occupation got around to writing an official history of the constitutional drafting process, the provision was apparently forgotten. Surveying the stacks of drafts submitted by various Japanese groups, the chronicler noted the "curious omission" of "any suggestion either of the extension of the suffrage or the admission of women to equal political status with men," and stated flatly that none of the proposals had really provided for "the removal of the constitutional and legal disabilities under which women suffered."[9]

If these various drafting efforts had little effect on the legal reforms soon to come, the next question was whether Japanese women, singly or in groups, had an impact. As I suggested at the outset, Japanese women leaders played a crucial role in policy making on this subject over most of the Occupation period, so it was natural to speculate that the impetus for constitutional revision might have come from them. This theory did not stand up, however. A number of Japanese women—most of them leaders of a women's movement that had struggled unsuccessfully for suffrage in the prewar period—were engaged in lobbying activities directed at the Occupation forces and at the Japanese government in the fall of 1945.[10] All accounts indicate, however, that their efforts in the area of women's rights reform were targeted almost solely at gaining the vote, and not at constitutional revision. Women's suffrage, a milestone achievement in its own right, was gained, in part through their efforts, with the revision of the Election Law in December 1945. Important as this reform was to all subsequent change, it is not the focus of this inquiry because, in comparison with the truly radical women's rights reform effort that was soon under way in Japan, it was not a controversial reform in the context of the Occupation period. Women's suffrage, after all, had been achieved in most major countries of the world by 1945; the Occupation forces, from MacArthur on down, were committed to the principle of universal suffrage, and thus it was only a matter of time before this reform was instituted.

The investigation described so far led to the conclusion that the Occupation's radical experiment began not in the United States or at the instigation of the Japanese, male or female, but as the handiwork of Occupation personnel in the field. To locate the actual source of feminist reform among Occupation personnel was not an easy task. The obvious place to begin was with General Douglas MacArthur, Supreme Commander for the Allied Powers. During the Occupation and today, many Japanese regard MacArthur as the liberator of Japan's women.[11] MacArthur himself, in his autobiography, indicates that women's rights measures had his full support: "Of all the reforms accomplished by the occupation in Japan, none was more heartwarming to me than [the] change in the status of women."[12] One student of MacArthur's history and psychology holds that the general's close relationship with his mother, who resided with him through the many years of bachelorhood prior to his marriage and who played an active role in advising him and advancing his military career long after he had become a general, may have predisposed him to lend a sympathetic ear on issues relating to women.[13] But to ask whether MacArthur approved of women's rights reforms, once they had been instituted, is different from asking whether the general played a key initiating role in this particular policy area. The fact is that it is quite difficult to establish his leadership role in this, as in many other areas of policy change. None of the early directives issued by the Supreme Comman-

der in 1945 or early 1946 made reference to the problems of women. A
SCAP directive issued on October 4, 1945, forbade discrimination on
grounds of race, nationality, creed, or political opinion, but made no reference to sex as a possible basis of discrimination.[14] MacArthur's directives in February 1946 to Government Section—that section of the Occupation ultimately assigned the duty of drafting the constitution—made
no mention of women's rights or even of the need to reform the Japanese
family system. He directed his subordinates to assure that remnants of
the feudal system, to the extent that they existed in Japan, would be eradicated, but this order was sufficiently broad to have been interpreted in
any number of ways.[15] Although MacArthur's support for women's suffrage is well known and his general support for women's rights measures
well established, it is difficult to establish his leadership role in the radical
experiment.

If MacArthur did not provide the impetus, another possibility to consider was that the Occupation forces as a whole underwent some type of
conversion experience in Japan that made them willing to use their full
military powers to extend to Japanese women far-reaching legal guarantees that were not in force for women in their own country. This explanation was suggested to me by persons who served with the Occupation
and who claim that something akin to a love affair went on between the
American military collectively and the women of Japan, whereby the
Occupation forces came to see themselves as the heroic rescuers of
Japan's downtrodden women. This monolithic view of the Occupation
as women's rights advocates quickly breaks down, however, upon examining relevant materials from the period 1945–1951. An analysis of
memoranda, directives, documents, speeches, records of meetings, press
clippings, and field reports from the several branches of the Occupation
concerned with women's affairs established that among Occupation military and civilian personnel were many competing views of where wom-
en's rights should rank among Occupation priorities. Some within the
Occupation clearly saw women's rights activities as a low priority, and a
number of key persons involved in the drafting of the constitution itself
sought to contain the radical experiment rather than to advance it, as will
be shown below.

Each of the forces discussed so far—the U.S. State Department, Japanese women's groups, the political parties and other citizens' groups,
General MacArthur himself, and the Occupation in a collective sense—
helped to shape the general environment in which feminist reforms
occurred in Japan. If the State Department had taken a hard line *against*
the reforms, if the Americans serving in the Occupation had *not* been
predisposed to the idea of raising the status of Japanese women, if
MacArthur himself had not been sympathetic, then it is unlikely that any
change could have occurred. Similarly, if Japanese women leaders,

through their struggle for suffrage in the 1920s and their pursuit of it again in the fall of 1945, had not made the Occupation aware of a broad constituency in support of measures to benefit women, then the radical experiment might never have begun. None of these factors, however, alone or in combination, explains how the constitutional reform effort originated.

The investigation led at last to one woman serving in the Occupation forces who, in the end, must be credited with setting an extraordinary set of reforms in motion. The general circumstances under which the constitution came to be written are by now well known. On February 3, 1946, MacArthur and other key figures in the Occupation hierarchy concluded that the Japanese were either unwilling or unable to produce a document sufficiently democratic to satisfy either them, the Americans back home, or the Far Eastern Commission. Therefore, on the following day, the division of the Occupation concerned with public administration was called together and assigned the task of writing a new model democratic constitution for Japan. Twenty-one persons, seventeen men and four women, were the primary actors in this task. They were divided into nine small committees, with one to four members each, to write the various parts of the constitution. The job of drafting the section on civil liberties fell to two civilians (Harry Emerson Wildes and Beate Sirota) and one army officer (Lieutenant Colonel Pieter R. Roest) who made up what was referred to as the Civil Rights Committee.[16]

As were all the committees, the Civil Rights Committee was given two ground rules: time was of the essence and they were to conduct all their drafting activities in complete secret. In the limited time available, the first chore was to divide up the work load. During discussion, it was somehow decided that Beate Sirota, the only woman in the group, would draft some measures to improve the status of Japanese women as well as take on a number of other issues, such as academic freedom.[17] A key question is whether the idea of drafting women's rights measures came down to the Civil Rights Committee as a specific assignment from higher up or whether the idea for singling out that particular area for reform originated within the committee. The question is critically important, for upon it hinges the matter of whether the Occupation's radical experiment began as a matter of high-echelon policy, the product of top-level discussions and debate, or whether it was set in motion from below, by the values and policy preferences of a small group of lower level decision makers assigned responsibility in a given general policy area. Based on what is known about prior developments, as outlined above, about the ad hoc nature of the policy-making apparatus set up to produce a constitution, and about the time constraints operating, all available evidence points toward the latter conclusion. The evidence examined so far suggests that the impetus for constitutional reforms to benefit women did originate with the three members of the Civil Rights Committee and grew out of the particular interests of one of its members, Beate Sirota, in issues relating to women.

Born in Vienna in 1923, Sirota was twenty-two when she was asked to write, with two other people, a bill of rights for Japan.[18] Compared with many members of the Occupation force who in 1946 were new arrivals in Japan and were struggling to adjust to a wholly alien environment, she had a special advantage. She had grown up in Japan. From the time she was five and a half until she was fifteen and emigrated to the United States, her father had headed the Piano Department of the Japanese Imperial Academy of Music in Tokyo. As a result of her experience Sirota was fluent in Japanese and hence had been given an important post in the Occupation despite her youth. More important for our purposes, she was deeply familiar with a special slice of Japanese life that had flourished in the 1930s, despite the turbulence of the period—the urban world of artists and performers, which included many talented and highly educated young Japanese women whom she had come to know in growing up. Sirota thus brought to her Occupation tasks a set of impressions and convictions about the conditions surrounding the lives of Japanese women. Her prior knowledge of the country and her Japanese-language skills undoubtedly gave her authority beyond that which she otherwise could have commanded as a female civilian in a military structure.

Be that as it may, Sirota, a twenty-two-year-old woman, was designated the person within the committee who would prepare measures aimed at guaranteeing Japanese women's social, political, and economic equality. When we consider her age and the fact that she had only recently emerged from a U.S. college world of term papers and reports, the way she approached her task comes as no surprise. She went off to the library—not to one, in fact, but to several libraries in Tokyo, where she collected as much information as possible on the current legal provisions, constitutional and otherwise, offering guarantees to European women. Of those she examined, the constitutions and lesser laws of the Weimar Republic and the Scandinavian countries offered the best guidelines. Back in the Dai-Ichi Building, where the Government Section of the Occupation was situated, she began to put together a list of women's rights items for inclusion in what was to become "Chapter III. Rights and Duties of the People" of the Japanese constitution of 1947.

By February 8, four days after she had begun, much of the work was behind her. The Civil Rights Committee had produced a working draft by that date and met with the Steering Committee, the group monitoring the drafting process, to discuss it.[19] It was at this point that lines of conflict within Occupation ranks over the issue of women's rights began to emerge. Many of the social welfare measures drawn up by Sirota and her colleagues came under attack at the meeting. "Meritorious though they may be," the Steering Committee argued, many of the proposed measures belonged in the province of "statutory regulation and not constitutional law." The members of the Civil Rights Committee rallied to the defense, arguing "that inclusion of social welfare provisions was accepted practice in modern European constitutions." The minutes of the meeting reveal that the members of the Civil Rights Committee stood together in the exchange with the higher committee. Roest argued that the low estate of Japanese women necessitated that they be granted full protection in the new constitution. Wildes backed him up by noting that it was crucial that the Japanese government "go on record for these things." It appears to have been understood fully by both sides in the debate that a truly radical set of changes was being discussed. Lieutenant Colonel Milo F. Rowell of the Steering Committee opposed the measures by arguing that "you cannot impose a new mode of social thought upon a country by law." Wildes retaliated in words reflecting the deep sense of mission apparently shared by the members of the Civil Rights Committee: "We . . . have the responsibility to effect a social revolution in Japan."[20]

In the end, the views of the higher level prevailed to some extent, and the measures advocated by the Civil Rights Committee were shortened and streamlined. Certain social welfare measures that Beate Sirota had drafted were deleted, such as a provision for the care of nursing mothers. This and several others measures were regarded by the Steering Committee and the Chief of Government section, General Courtney Whitney, who was brought in to resolve the dispute, as "minutiae of social legislation."[21] When Article 24 and other related articles emerged from the drafting process, what remained was nevertheless a remarkably progressive piece of social legislation. Article 24 still goes well beyond anything found in most constitutions of the world today.

In March 1946 the draft constitution was put before the Japanese. Little has been written about the opposition of Japanese officials to the women's rights measures that appeared in the SCAP draft of the constitution, which is strange considering how pronounced and consistent the opposition was. In the months between February 13, 1946, when the Americans gave their draft to the Japanese for their consideration, and November 3, 1946, when the new constitution was finally promulgated, Japanese authorities made a persistent effort to dilute, omit, or change the intent of SCAP's women's rights provisions.[22] Their main target was Article 24, guaranteeing the equality of women in family life, which was seen to threaten the basis of male domination and female subordination in the family. An early Japanese rewrite of Article 24 dropped all its concrete guarantees of equality for women in matters of divorce, inheritance, and so on (in other words, the entire second paragraph of the two-paragraph article seen in the extract above).[23] A later attempt at revision was even more antagonistic to the spirit of the women's rights measures.

This time both Article 14 and Article 24 came under attack. The new version of Article 14 allowed the original wording to stand, but drained the guarantee of women's equality of any meaning by adding that "due regard must be given to differences of capability, physical and moral, and of social function."[24] In the same Japanese draft, Article 24 was transformed into a measure (proposed as Article 25) that not only upheld the traditional family system, but that, if adopted, would have had devastating consequences for the freedom and opportunities of married women.

> *The state guarantees to protect the family in its constitution and authority, as the primary unit of society, as the necessary basis of social order and as indispensable to the welfare of the nation.* Marriage shall be based on the free consent of the spouses. Choice of spouse, property rights, inheritance, choice of domicile, divorce and other matters pertaining to marriage shall be regulated by law *so as to safeguard the institution of marriage* and to uphold the individual dignity and essential equality of the partners.
>
> *Because of [by] her life within the home, woman gives to the State a support without which the common good cannot be achieved, the State shall endeavor to ensure that mothers shall not be obliged by economic necessity to engage in labor to the neglect of their duties in the home.* (Emphasis added.)[25]

These proposed revisions of articles 14 and 24, along with numerous others put forward by the Japanese government, were rejected by SCAP in lengthy negotiation sessions held during March and April 1946. Previous writers have examined in great detail the powers and methods used by the Americans to force or persuade acceptance of their draft by the Japanese.[26] In the end relatively few changes initiated by the Japanese actually made their way into the document. Once they left American hands, articles 14 and 24, along with most of the "bill of rights" section of the constitution, passed more or less intact into the document that was ultimately endorsed by the Japanese government and approved by the Diet. When the constitution was debated in the Diet in the summer of 1946, articles 14 and 24, especially the latter, once again met resistance. There were lengthy discussions, for example, about what "essential equality of the sexes" really meant. In meetings of the House of Representatives all-male Subcommittee on the Bill for Revision of the Imperial Constitution, a number of members argued that men and women were fundamentally unequal and that the constitution should be revised to stress the essential differences between the sexes, rather than their equality. With quotations from such Western philosophers as Schopenhauer, a strong defense was made of the superiority of the male. Kita Reikichi of the Liberal party even went so far as to argue that women were dominated by sexual passions and were therefore inferior to men, morally and spiritually.[27] In the end, however, the resistance failed, and the constitution of 1947 was promulgated on November 3, 1946, with its women's rights measures intact.

It is important to examine, in view of the next case study, the role played by Japanese women themselves in the events described so far. We must distinguish three steps in the policy-making process as it operated in Japan: first, in which SCAP came to agreement over a law or policy; second, in which the measure was hammered out in closed sessions between SCAP and Japanese governmental authorities; and third, in which the measure was made public and was formally approved by the Diet. By means of this analysis we see that Japanese women leaders played very little role in the actual policy-making process (the first two steps) at this stage of the Occupation. Beate Sirota, by her own account, had no contact with Japanese women regarding women's rights reform before taking up her task of drafting the relevant articles.[28] The subsequent streamlining of Sirota's versions of the articles took place entirely within Government Section, without Japanese participation of any kind. Thereafter, in the three weeks between the time that the SCAP draft was turned over to the Japanese and the point at which the proposed constitution was made public, private groups had no input into the negotiation that went on between SCAP and Japanese officials. Key women leaders of that period, such as Kato Shidzue, have stated that they played no role at all before the proposed constitution was released to the public.[29]

Only during the final step of the approval process did the influence of Japanese women make itself felt. The first postwar election, held on April 10, 1946, brought thirty-nine women into the Diet. Quickly they organized a club made up of women Diet members that, among other things, functioned in strong support of the proposed constitution.[30] Meanwhile, virtually all major women's organizations, from the Japanese League of Women Voters to the Women's Democratic Club that had formed in March 1946 and to the women's sections of the political parties and unions, backed it. By the time the proposed constitution was debated in the Diet, it can be said that Japanese women leaders were functioning effectively to win popular support for the document and the women's rights guarantees it contained.

The bare outlines of the process by which most major women's rights initiatives were made during the Occupation period were visible in the case study just offered. The impetus for women's rights reforms in most cases can be traced to a small number of women serving with the Occupation who, like Beate Sirota, were prepared to press for such measures. Their more radical proposals, as in the case just cited, were generally rejected at higher decision-making levels within SCAP, but the measures that were ultimately approved were nonetheless progressive for their day. Winning approval for the measures from Japanese authorities was generally successful for reasons to be discussed more fully below, but it was a long and arduous process in which the fate of the proposed reforms was often uncertain until the end. In our case study, Japanese women leaders can be seen at work in the aftermath of the policy-making process, warding off attacks on the measures by arguing their merits before the public. What we will now show is how, as the Occupation proceeded, the efforts of these American and Japanese women came to be welded together into an effective policy subsystem that operated in strong support of women's rights reforms at all stages from inception to implementation.

Finding a Home for Women's Affairs in the Japanese Bureaucracy

In September 1947, after more than a year of debate and preparation, a ministry of labor was established in Japan. Within the ministry, as one of the five bureaus of which it was comprised, was the Women's and Minors' Bureau, charged with responsibility for promoting the status of Japanese women. The steps on the way to the creation of the bureau from the spring of 1946 to September 1947 illuminate the politics of women's rights reform. Studying the events allows us to see how women's issues fared as the policy-making setting itself changed. In the case just discussed—in which women's rights guarantees found their way into Japan's highest law—American and other foreign participants in the policy-making process were new on the scene. Policy positions within SCAP were not yet well formulated. There was less of a sense, compared to the later one, that there were policy choices to be made, and that pressing hard in one area of reform might endanger other Occupation goals. The approach to policy formulation was ad hoc. But as the first six months of the Occupation receded, policy positions on all sides hardened. The women's policy alliance referred to at the outset took shape and began to coordinate its efforts on behalf of reform, forcing SCAP's top decision makers to respond to its initiatives. Meanwhile, the Japanese government's resistance to a variety of unwanted measures being pressed upon it by the Americans became better organized.

In the spring of 1946, a great many activities were under way in occupied Japan. The constitution was soon to go to the Diet for debate and approval. The first postwar election had been held on April 10, bringing women to the polls and into the Diet for the first time. Revision of the Civil Code was in preliminary stages.

During that same period, Labor Division of SCAP initiated consultation with officials of the Japanese Ministry of Welfare, which up until that time had been charged with responsibility for dealing with the problems of workers as only one of its many tasks. The aim was to get Japanese agreement and cooperation for the formation of a ministry of labor. In these early discussions the Americans assumed that, although the specifics had not been spelled out, any new ministry would "deal with certain aspects of women's social and economic status" as one of its assign-ments.[31]

From the beginning, quite apart from the issue of what was to be done for women, the SCAP initiative for the creation of a ministry of labor met with considerable resistance from the Japanese. Not only was there opposition to the idea in principle from a bureaucracy then and now known for its close relations with the business community, but there was bureaucratic resistance as well from those whose job definitions, power bases, and promotion prospects were threatened by the prospect of change. Few bureaucrats are eager to desert the known for a leap toward the dark and uncertain future represented by reorganization, and it is lit-tle wonder that negotiations between SCAP's Labor Division and the Ministry of Welfare proceeded slowly. A year or so later, in fact, Japan's cabinet-level officials were to claim ignorance of the fact that discussions had taken place at all.[32] The stage was set, then, for struggle, and in the midst of this larger battle occurred the skirmish over a place for women's affairs in the emerging bureaucratic structure.

The skirmish itself evolved in two stages. In the first, SCAP officials debated among themselves what type of bureau or agency should be instituted in the Japanese government to oversee the implementation of women's rights measures. The bureaucratic politics of this struggle culminated in a SCAP policy decision in August 1946 to support the for-mation of a women's bureau within the Ministry of Labor. In the second stage, SCAP officials, united behind their objective, became locked in a struggle with Japanese officials to get the measure adopted.

That there was to be disagreement within SCAP over bureaucratic arrangements to meet the needs of Japanese women became apparent fairly early on. In May 1946 a memo surfaced that set off a major inter-nal debate over the issue. Directed to the heads of both the Civil Informa-tion and Education Section (CI&E) and Government Section and ori-ginating from lower down in the ranks of CI&E, the memo called for the formation of a women's bureau within the Home Ministry.[33] The pro-posal itself would not have been feasible, for the powerful Home Minis-try was soon to be abolished as part of the Occupation's bureaucratic reorganization. But the memo made clear that some personnel in the lower ranks of SCAP wanted far more in the way of a bureaucratic arrangement to handle women's affairs than anything that had been dis-cussed up until that time. The memo called for the creation of a single agency charged with sweeping responsibility for improving women's sta-tus in Japanese society, empowered to deal with everything from issues of concern to housewives, such as consumer problems, problems relating to home economics, and adult education, to the problems of farm women, business and professional women, and female civil servants. It would offer vocational guidance to Japanese women and initiate "studies concerning women's place in Japanese society—new fields of endeavor—new problems—new solutions." The memo noted that bureaucratic arrangements in Japan up until that time were sadly inadequate for this task. Those persons charged with responsibility for women's affairs in the Japanese bureaucracy were "so far down the scale of organization that they [had] no real power." Meanwhile those "petty government officials" in charge of planning activities and initiatives relating to women were men who had "no real training for their work." As the CI&E memo made clear, the proposals in it had emerged from "conferences with, and recommendations by, Japanese women leaders." The message of the memo stood out boldly: SCAP should join hands with Japanese women leaders in their struggle with "petty government officials" to forward the cause of women in the new Japan.

It can be argued that many of the reforms proposed in the memo were realized in the ultimate establishment of the Women's and Minors' Bureau. The bureau has broad responsibility in the area of women's rights beyond the specific problems of working women, despite its home in the Ministry of Labor. It is made up of three sections: Women Workers Section, Minor Workers Section, and Women's Section, the latter of which is charged with many tasks not bearing on the problems of working women.[34] But it is apparent that a mere section below the bureau level, assigned the task of dealing with the problem of discrimination and inequality faced by more than half the Japanese population, hardly tackles its chores from a position of strength. The memo was attempting to establish a special bureau in Japan's most important domestic ministry that would oversee the efforts of other ministries (including the Ministry of Welfare and the new Ministry of Labor, as the memo made clear) on behalf of women. Rather than make the promotion of women's status a subsidiary task of a bureau charged with primary responsibility for the problems of women workers—a situation, now in effect in both Japan and the United States, in which the mouse directs the elephant—it was proposing that the elephant be given due recognition and a place of importance in Japan's most prestigious domestic ministry.

For reasons that are not fully clear, the memo was not taken up for discussion at higher levels of SCAP for several months. It may well have been that the arrival of a high-level U.S. advisory group brought in to look at Japan's labor problems in the summer of 1946 delayed consideration of the issue of bureaucratic measures to be taken on behalf of women. In July, the twelve member advisory committee, which had one woman, included in its recommendations the proposal that Japan follow the course set down many years earlier by the United States and establish a women's bureau in the Labor Ministry.[35] This recommendation, along with others made by the committee in their 148-page document, was approved as SCAP policy on August 21, 1946.[36] In mid-August, however, a few days beforehand, the higher ranks of SCAP officialdom took up the question of the CI&E memo and its more ambitious plan. A handwritten memo from Commander Alfred R. Hussey, Jr., Special Assistant to the Chief of Government Section, dated August 17, 1946, states his response, which was developed, according to the memo, after consultation with Charles L. Kades, another key decision maker in Government Section. On the specific issue of the creation of a women's bureau in the Home Ministry, the response is cut and dried: "The organization of a Women's Bureau in the Home Ministry or a quasi-independent Cabinet Board of Women's Affairs is not believed to be advisable."[37] His memo offers three reasons for his opposition: (1) the creation of such a bureau or board would "point up differences" and "tend to encourage separation of interests" between women and men; (2) it would cause "needless complications"; and (3) it would cause "serious resentment and reaction." Responding directly to the implication in the CI&E memo that SCAP should join hands with Japanese women against Japanese men in an effort to improve the situation of women, he then went on to elaborate his own ideological position on the appropriate strategy for women's rights reform: "Certainly, women should be represented on important administrative boards in all phases of activity in the fields of labor, welfare, and education. The participation of women in the Diet, not as women but as responsible representatives, should be given every encouragement. But the formation of a women's block [sic] or the encouragement of a feminist movement in Japan must be avoided."[38]

In the memo, Hussey strongly supported the idea that "coordination and cooperation" were called for in achieving women's rights, rather than "independendent special action." He acknowledged the gravity of the problems facing women but then took a firm stand against feminist militance: "True as it is that women in Japan have always been and are now in an inferior and completely dependent position, the solution is not to be achieved by direct assault on the male position, or the male." He concludes with a reference to a satirical theme in works of James Thurber popular in the 1940s, in which men and women have it out to determine, once and for all, which is the superior sex: "We cannot have any suggestion or threat of Thurber's Battle Between the Sexes here."[39]

The memo is an important one, for in it Hussey sets out an ideological view that is seen in more fragmentary form in numerous other memos originating from high-ranking men in the Occupation. It reflects the classic liberal democratic view of the rights and prerogatives of oppressed groups. On the one hand, it vigorously opposed the idea that any group should be denied full equality under the law. Hussey's reference to women's "inferior and completely dependent position" suggests his empathy with women's plight and his conviction that status inferiority is morally wrong in a democracy. On the other hand, he rejects the right of oppressed groups to organize in support of their objectives and to press their claims against those in relation to whom they are in this "inferior and completely dependent position"—that is, men. To Hussey, and to many other men of his time, social remedies for disadvantaged groups could be achieved only through "coordination and cooperation," rather than through "independent social action." Hussey's position on this fundamental issue appears to have been fully shared by General MacArthur, who is well known to have expressed doubts about the appropriateness of collective action by those with social grievances.[40] When the general met in June 1946 with the women who had been elected to the Diet in the first postwar election, reportedly he "strongly cautioned" them "against the temptation to form a women's bloc to influence legislation."[41] The views of these men predate a pluralist view of democracy, which by the 1960s had gained currency in the United States, that it is legitimate for social groups to form "blocs" to press their "independent special claims" as long as their methods are legitimate.

There is a definite duality in the rationale Hussey offers for the policy stance he adopts in the memo. His reference to the "battle of the sexes" suggests that he dismisses the seriousness of Japanese women leaders' attempts to press their claims. Their effort, he seems to be saying, is only part of the traditional sparring that has gone on in every country between men and women in everyday life. He appears to be lightheartedly shaking his finger at those in the lower ranks of CI&E who would drag the Occupation into this eternal comedy. At the same time, however, the concrete reasons he gives for not backing Japanese women leaders' objectives reflect quite a different view of the matter, in which the seriousness of the struggle and its implications are fully acknowledged. To support the women in their demands would not only mean "needless complications" for the Occupation, in terms of carrying out its policies and objectives, but it would stir "serious resentment and reaction" on the part of Japanese men. He appears to harbor no illusions that Japanese male officialdom would take a lighthearted view of the women's demands, scoring them as no more than one more round in the battle of the sexes. Instead, he fully acknowledges that backing women against those male officials in power would involve extremely high costs in relation to other Occupation objectives.

The CI&E memo to which Hussey was responding heralded the presence of a core of lower-ranking SCAP personnel that by this time had emerged in support of women's rights measures. When Beate Sirota had made her contribution to the constitutional revision process in February 1946, she had acted more or less independently, although she was backed by the two male members of the drafting committee on which she served. By August, when Hussey wrote his memo, however, quite a number among SCAP personnel had come to be identified with the promotion of women's rights policies. At the heart of this group was a Women's Army

Corps lieutenant, Ethel B. Weed. A former public relations specialist from Cleveland, Ohio, Lieutenant Weed had arrived in October 1945 in the first shipment of WACs to occupied Japan and was quickly designated "Women's Information Officer" when she expressed an interest in being involved in some way with the education of Japanese women.[42] Interpreting her mandate broadly, she gradually became involved in virtually all Occupation efforts on behalf of Japanese women. Eminent Japanese legal authorities, for example, were told in 1946 that Lieutenant Weed was to be consulted in the revision of the Civil Code.[43] On a day-to-day basis, she was in constant communication with Japanese women leaders both in Tokyo and, through her many field trips, in other parts of Japan. She promoted the development of women's clubs and organizations on a democratic basis to replace the state-led organizations that had enlisted women's support in the war effort. She developed extensive materials in the form of films, pamphlets, and displays to promote the idea of equal employment opportunity for women.[44] In virtually all discussions and debate on Occupation policy making affecting women, Lieutenant Weed was on the scene and in most cases she was a central participant. Only in the drafting of the constitution, which went on in closed sessions within Government Section, was she not a party.[45]

By the spring of 1946 Ethel Weed had become the central figure in a loose informal network of American women serving in the Occupation who, because of their assigned duties or because of their personal interest, stood in strong support of women's rights policies. Although several of the key members were in the Civil Information and Education Section where Weed worked, others were in Labor Division, Economic and Scientific Section, and Government Section, and a few were on temporary assignment in Japan to look into a specific area of policy relating to women.[46] Collectively, these women formed the American wing of the "women's policy alliance," or policy subsystem, referred to at the outset of this essay. Few of them, of course, would have conceived of themselves as members of a "subsystem" of any kind. Scattered throughout the SCAP administrative structure in Tokyo and in field posts in various parts of Japan, they never met as a group. But all were involved in promoting women's rights policies during the Occupation period, frequently in consultation with one or more members of the group and with members of the Japanese wing of the same subsystem.

Not all the women assigned to the Occupation were part of the subsystem; indeed, there were some women who had little sympathy for or interest in its objectives.[47] Nor did the subsystem exclude men. Members of the network, all of whom were low-ranking personnel, often formed alliances with male personnel at their own or slightly higher levels to help win support for specific measures from SCAP's top policy makers. But it was primarily an undertaking by and for women.

The subsystem may be envisioned as a wheel. At the hub was Lieutenant Weed, along with the other women who made up the American wing. The "spokes" were the six or so Japanese women who, from 1945 to 1952, served as assistants to Ethel Weed. To call these talented young women "assistants," however, is to underestimate their contribution to the policy-making and policy implementation process. All were college graduates with an ability to use English that was rare in Japan then. Old school ties united the group, for most were graduates of one top women's school, Tsuda College. Their intellectual caliber is suggested by the fact that most of them went on to hold prominent positions in law, teaching, journalism, and in the bureaucracy after the Occupation ended. In effect they served as policy advisors as well as secretaries to Weed. Many times they came to her with opinions on what was needed by women in Japan; even more often, they served as sounding boards for Weed's own ideas. They offered advice on which Japanese women leaders should be sought out to cooperate with SCAP in the formulation of policies, in the political process of gaining approval for them from the Japanese government, and once approved, in implementing them. In the particular psychological setting created by a military occupation of a defeated nation, these women, because they were Japanese nationals, were referred to by the Americans as "Weed's girls" and were excluded from SCAP policy discussions. But their policy advice quietly steered the direction taken by Weed and other American female personnel, and their English-language ability linked Weed, who knew very little Japanese, to the great outer circle of the wheel—the Japanese women leaders who represented the interests and concerns of large numbers of Japanese women of all walks of life.[48]

When Lieutenant Weed had set to work in the fall of 1945, she had known none of these women. Unlike Beate Sirota, she had no previous exposure to Japan other than six months of training in East Asian Studies at Northwestern University on the eve of her departure for Tokyo. Upon arrival, she had sought out Japanese women leaders who were strong advocates of women's rights measures. Most of the first recruits were women who had been active in the women's suffrage and other movements in the 1920s or 1930s, whose names were known to other Occupation personnel. One by one, these women were sent for or appeared at Occupation headquarters. A prominent example was Kato Shidzue, a former baroness turned socialist well known for her role in Japan's birth-control movement, who had been jailed for her antimilitarist views during the war. Mrs. Kato was sought out in Tokyo by an American of Japanese descent serving with the Occupation, who took her by military jeep to meet Weed.

From an original cluster of Japanese women assembled over the first months of the Occupation, the group gradually expanded to include dozens of women leaders in Tokyo, such as Kume Ai, a lawyer who was the first woman to be admitted to the bar in Japan; Tanaka Sumiko, later a distinguished socialist member of the Diet; Watanabe Michiko, another prominent attorney; and Fujita Taki, later head of the Women's and Minors' Bureau and president of Tsuda College.

One of Weed's early tasks, that of promoting the growth of club and organizational life among Japanese women, had the indirect effect of providing a great many of these women with an organizational base, for a number of them became presidents or officers in the newly formed groups. After the first Diet election in April 1946, in which thirty-nine women (including Mrs. Kato) were elected, the policy subsystem came to include this group as well which, as noted earlier, had quickly organized itself into a club within the Diet. By the period May–August 1946, when the CI&E memo emerged, an impressively large subsystem had developed to promote measures benefiting women. In a given week, Lieutenant Weed was likely to be in contact with anywhere from five to several dozen women leaders to discuss issues relating to women's rights.

The feminist ideology of this group—that is, their view of women's proper role in the family and society—was not radical by today's standards. The word "feminist" was not in vogue in the 1940s and certainly not among female military or civilian personnel attempting to carry out their responsibility in a male-dominated military hierarchy. Their basic view was a multirole ideology. That is, they accepted the idea that woman's primary role in adult life is to be a wife and mother, but believed that married women simultaneously could and should play other roles as well, such as citizen, worker, and participant in civic and social groups, and urged that daycare facilities and household conveniences be introduced to make such participation possible. This role ideology, which was shared by the American and Japanese wings of the subsystem, stops far short of what may be called a radical egalitarian view of women's role, widely accepted among feminists in the advanced industrial democracies today, which holds that no roles (other than the biological role of childbearer) should be allocated to women on the basis of sex, and takes strenuous objection to the notion that housekeeping and childcare are, by definition, women's work. On the other hand, their view was quite progressive in relation to the "one-role" ideology dominant in Japan of that day, which held that women, unless forced to do otherwise out of economic necessity, should devote themselves to the wife-mother role to the exclusion of all other pursuits.[49]

The development of a policy subsystem in support of women's rights measures went on under the noses of SCAP's top decision makers and, indeed, with their full approval. When Lieutenant Weed received an Army Commendation Ribbon from the War Department in September 1946, she was cited explicitly for helping Japanese women to organize themselves.[50] It was well accepted that her primary task, as Women's Information Officer, was to cultivate her ties with these women and to work through them—so much so, in fact, that her office was thought by GHQ to require almost no program budget, and the question of increasing its budget apparently never arose over the seven years of its existence.[51] It can be said, then, that the policy subsystem that grew up in support of women's rights measures was an indirect result of official SCAP policy. What happened, as the CI&E memo indicated, is that the policy subsystem soon came to pursue an independent course. Its American and Japanese members advocated measures that often went beyond what SCAP's top leadership was willing to accept, and they were prepared to lobby within SCAP as well as outside it for women's rights reforms.

In the bureaucratic politics of this military Occupation, the low rank of the SCAP personnel in the policy subsystem dictated the outcome of any policy debates, such as this one, in which top decision makers had a strong opinion. The leadership rejected the CI&E proposal in the same way that, many months before, they had drastically revised Beate Sirota's earliest draft of the constitution's women's rights provisions. By throwing their support behind the idea of creating a women's bureau in the Ministry of Labor, they laid to rest more radical alternatives. At other times during the Occupation, when those at the top did not have a well-defined position or when their attention was engaged in matters of greater urgency to them than women's rights issues, the women's policy subsystem was more likely to see its proposals rubberstamped as SCAP policy. Even in the two cases dealt with here, however, in which the initial proposals of the subsystem were rejected, the pressure for more radical steps on behalf of women undoubtedly had an impact on the policy outlook of SCAP's key decision makers. Willing in principle to support women's rights reforms so long as other Occupation objectives were not jeopardized, the men cheerfully approved measures progressive for their day but which—in comparison with the reforms advocated by the women's policy alliance—looked moderate indeed.

In analyzing how the bureaucratic politics of women's rights reform operated within SCAP, we must ask a key question: what efforts were made by top policy makers to check the internal lobbying activities of the women's policy subsystem? As the strongly worded memo from Hussey indicated, decision makers responded indignantly when they felt themselves goaded from below toward support for a "feminist revolution." The question is whether or not they backed their words with action. There is much evidence that they did, and that SCAP's top policy makers on occasion took concrete steps to contain the activities of the women's policy alliance. Hussey's strategy in the case in point appears to have been to "divide and conquer." First he brought Weed, the chief figure in the subsystem, to task by dispatching an assistant to check up on her loyalties. The assistant confronted her with a press report indicating that

Japanese women leaders, contrary to SCAP policy, were linking their demands for a women's bureau with other unrelated demands, and asked, in effect, if Weed had put them up to it.[52] Weed's reply was an emphatic dismissal of the suggestion that she would defy SCAP policy in the course of her dealings with the Japanese wing: "Lt. Weed says, apropos to this article (she hadn't seen it) that in all her meetings with this group—[the] Women's League—and with Women Diet members—that she has urged strenuously that Diet pressure for a Women's Bureau must be kept separate from . . . extraneous matters."[53] The inquiry itself, however, surely represented pressure on Weed and those in her circle to toe the line.

Meanwhile, Hussey dealt separately with the Japanese wing. The action came after a number of Japanese women leaders, headed by Mrs. Kato in her capacity as a Diet member representing the Social Democratic party, came out in support of an even more ambitious bureaucratic arrangement for women's affairs than the one proposed in the CI&E memo. In the summer of 1946, they spoke out in favor of forming a women's bureau not under the roof of either the proposed Labor Ministry or the Home Ministry, but as "an independent Cabinet Board."[54] This plan, which would have elevated women's affairs to the highest level in the Japanese government and given the proposed board's head a cabinet post, was totally unacceptable to SCAP, as Hussey's memo had made clear. Hussey stepped in to deliver the message in person. Summoning the Japanese women leaders in September, he told them, with Weed present, that their plan was "administratively unsound and unlikely to have SCAP approval."[55] At the end of this round, SCAP's top leadership had brought the women's policy alliance in line behind SCAP's official position on this particular question, and at the same time had attempted to constrain the activities of the subsystem.

As the case study up until now has shown, the women's policy alliance at this point in the Occupation was deeply involved in SCAP's internal politics relating to the formulation of women's reform measures. The alliance was even more active in the policy stages that followed, in which SCAP put the plan for a women's bureau in the Ministry of Labor before the Japanese authorities. Both wings sprang into action almost as soon as SCAP's position on the issue took shape. Women members of the Social Democratic party, following their meetings with Hussey and Weed in September, quickly secured party endorsement for the SCAP-backed plan. Not only did the Japanese wing of the alliance work within their political parties and organizational bases to get official endorsements for the proposed Women's Bureau, but they also took the idea to the public. In the interlude between Diet sessions in the fall of 1946, women Diet members campaigned throughout Japan for the proposal.[56]

Then in February 1947 the Yoshida cabinet submitted to SCAP a proposal for a ministry of labor that included no provision for a women's bureau and made no mention at all of any bureaucratic arrangements for dealing with women's affairs.[57] At this point the American wing of the subsystem became especially active. SCAP, with Ethel Weed involved in virtually every stage of the discussions, moved promptly to inform the Yoshida cabinet that any acceptable plan for a ministry of labor would have to deal with the problems of women.[58] A Memorandum for Record on the meeting states that SCAP's suggestions "were stubbornly opposed . . . on the grounds that (1) the Ordinance should not deal with 'unimportant and minute' bureaus and (2) that there would be too great opposition from other Cabinet sources."[59] It is ironic that the Japanese response should reflect precisely the same duality that had marked Hussey's own reply to the earlier policy initiatives of the women's policy subsystem. On the one hand, Japanese officials discounted the importance of a women's bureau, dismissing it in much the same way that Hussey had minimized the seriousness of the earlier proposal with his reference to the "battle of the sexes." On the other hand, they acknowledged, as Hussey had, that any plan to create such an "unimportant and minute" bureau would stir major opposition and have serious political consequences.

The road from this February 1947 session to the creation of the Women's and Minors' Bureau in September of the same year was a rocky one. Each time the Japanese submitted a new version of the Ministry of Labor proposal, the idea of a women's bureau was either omitted or given short shrift. A revised proposal submitted by the Ministry of Welfare on April 14 provided for the establishment of a women's and children's division as part of the Labor Standards Bureau in the proposed ministry, an arrangement that would have downgraded the program substantially and was opposed by SCAP on those grounds.[60] Even in late June, only weeks before a final proposal won SCAP approval, a Japanese draft submitted to SCAP still held back from specifying in detail what the functions of the new Women's and Minors' Bureau would be.[61] In the end, it appears that SCAP, with members of the American wing of the policy subsystem active throughout the long process, simply wore down the Japanese on the Women's and Minors' Bureau issue by challenging every attempt at omission and evasion and by constantly submitting suggestions that spelled out exactly what was sought. Through the entire period, Weed and other members of the American group were in regular communication with the Japanese women leaders who were lobbying for the women's bureau outside the policy-making arena. By late spring and early summer, Weed was in consultation with them over the question of the staff for the bureau. She is credited by many Japanese women leaders with having taken steps to make sure that a woman was picked to head the bureau and with having tapped its first director.[62]

The work of the subsystem did not end with the establishment of the bureau. The bureau faced a long and arduous struggle in the internal politics of the new Ministry of Labor to keep its foothold in the ministry, both in terms of budget and staff. At each annual budget round, the question of its value was reopened by those Japanese officials who had opposed its formation in the first place.[63] Until the Occupation ended, the American wing of the policy subsystem brought SCAP influence to bear to defend the bureau from its critics. Thereafter, the Japanese wing, which by then had expanded into a large and effective network of women's organizations, managed the task alone. Its survival today as an important and active bureau within the Ministry of Labor is a tribute to their efforts.

Women's Rights Reform in the Setting of the Military Occupation

The importance of the role played by the women's policy alliance as it operated in occupied Japan is consistent with much that is known about the way that social policy has been developed in other settings. Heclo, studying Britain and Sweden, found that radical experiments with social policy in those countries mainly were spearheaded not by top-ranking policy makers but by persons of lesser rank with a personal interest (often amateurs rather than professionals or experts) in the given subject area, who were able to use their access to top people to put social policy questions on the policy agenda.[64] Indeed, the pattern in Japan is strikingly like the one that operates today in the United States in the making of women's policy, in which a network of low- and middle-ranking female personnel in federal and state bureaucracies with links to leaders of interest groups act as key advocates of change.[65] What is perhaps most distinctive about the politics of women's rights reform in the Occupation was the binational character of the policy subsystem, the active role initially played by the "insiders" (the American wing) in creating an external constituency in support of the measures they sought, and finally, the astonishing success of the reformers.

Nevertheless, the success of the radical experiment is still a perplexing matter. Most of the American advocates of women's rights reforms— such as Beate Sirota, only twenty-two when she drafted women's rights measures for the Japanese constitution—were young and inexperienced in bureaucratic politics. In addition, the low rank of all the women in a command structure in which rank was a particularly crucial ordering principle was clearly a formidable hurdle in getting their views adopted as SCAP policy. Furthermore, a military occupation is hardly most persons' notion of an ideal incubator for feminist reform. Finally, Japan itself, with its long history of sex discrimination and its lack of virtually any guarantees of women's equality or rights at the point when the Occupation began, could hardly have been a more unlikely place for an experiment with women's rights reform. To explain why the reformers were successful in the face of such obstacles requires a closer look at some of the special factors that operated. Four explanations stand out.

First, the reformers benefited from a particular ideological pairing between democracy and feminism that occurred during the Occupation. As noted at the outset, many people worldwide who consider themselves wholly democratic are bitter opponents of women's rights reform and would be shocked if told that their views involve a contradiction in terms. But in Japan, democracy and feminism became linked. Commentators on the Occupation often have noted that Americans who served in it tended to operate on a high plane of idealism. Where women's rights were concerned, there was a strong tendency to portray the United States as the home of the world's most liberated women, overlooking the debate and struggle that had preceded every major women's rights measure taken there. The desire to promote democracy in Japan created a predisposition to adopt a number of policies that otherwise might have been dropped on pragmatic grounds, such as aiding the reestablishment of the Japanese Communist party and backing the labor movement. Women's rights reform, a highly controversial area of social policy in all democracies, benefited similarly. Guided by democratic idealism, top SCAP policy makers generally saw only the human rights issue inherent in promoting the status of women, and not the controversial redistributive issue it raised.

A second factor has to do with the immunity enjoyed by SCAP's leadership from the effects of their own policies. Historically, perhaps only colonial contexts have provided policy makers with such immunity. Outsiders to the system, American men in the Occupation could tinker with the balance of power between the sexes in Japan and know that they, unlike Japanese men, would not suffer a loss of male privileges as a result. It is perhaps worth noting that the one area of women's policy that did affect American male personnel directly—proposals to control prostitution—had few supporters among the Occupation's top leadership.[66] This is not to say that the insulation of the Occupation policy makers from the effects of women's rights reforms in Japan was a conscious consideration in their policy deliberations. One need only read accounts of debates over women's rights issues in other countries, however, to realize how deeply the life of everyone is affected by measures to promote the status of women. It is only natural that men who might lose inheritance rights to female relatives, husbands who might have to pay alimony or child support in the event of divorce, employers who might have to promote and give raises to female workers, and politicians who might lose seats to female candidates, will not look at women's rights issues in quite the same way as men whose lives will not be touched in the least by any changes. It may be added that not only were SCAP's leaders protected from the effects of their policies; they also were insulated from the costs of making them. Because feminist issues are so controversial, the career risks can be very high to policy makers if they come out on the losing side. Occupation personnel, foreigners in Japan secure in their own reward-and-promotion structure, incurred no such risks. It can be concluded, then, that many of the constraints that have limited policymakers' support for women's rights measures in other countries did not operate in the setting of the Occupation.

A third factor, important for understanding how resistance to the reforms on the part of Japanese officialdom was overcome, was the nature of the power wielded by the Americans in the Occupation context. With almost total authority in Japan for nearly seven years, SCAP had the power to push through even those reforms that were strenuously opposed by Japanese officials. As a result, Japanese officials were forced to be selective in choosing where to concentrate their opposition. Women's rights measures almost certainly benefited from being considered alongside many other laws and policies—such as those involving the powers of the emperor and Japan's future military capability—that loomed much larger in the concerns of the Japanese goverment. Nevertheless, it is unlikely, with official opposition to women's rights provisions so entrenched, that anything short of an alien military presence with full coercive power behind it could have forced the measures through.

Finally, the vigor and commitment of the women's policy alliance remain an important explanation for why the radical experiment succeeded. The alliance between American and Japanese women in the context of a military occupation was not an easy one to maintain. Not only were the policy positions of the two sides not always congruent, as the second case study illustrated, but as time passed differences of political ideology among Japanese women leaders made cooperation and the formation of a consensus on feminist goals difficult. On the American side, female personnel, to the extent that they became too closely associated with their external constituency and with women's rights issues, ran the risk of criticism and censure from their SCAP superiors and of psychological harassment, in the form of malevolent joking behavior, from their male colleagues. What held together this unlikely alliance of occupiers and occupied undoubtedly were the rewards it brought to each side. Cooperation with the American women in SCAP gave Japanese women a chance, for the first time in Japanese history, to have meaningful access to the policy-making process. It offered them an opportunity to establish themselves as leaders and as representatives of other women in a period when the postwar political system was taking shape. The phenomenal personal success of many well-known Japanese women today who were active in the policy subsystem during the Occupation bears witness to the advantages of being close to power during an era of great change. On the American side, the rewards were less obvious but were nonetheless real. Working for women's rights in Japan gave SCAP's female personnel a chance to play an important role in policy making in a setting in which virtually all significant positions were held by men. Even today, women in most societies of the world play only a minor role—if they play any—in policy formulation and political decision making; thus the women in SCAP were confronted with a rare opportunity. The marriage of democracy and women's rights in the minds of most Occupation personnel heightened the significance of their contribution and increased the amount of recognition that accrued from it. Finally, we can only speculate on what it meant to them as women to have a hand in drawing up a blueprint for the lives of Japanese women in what they, along with the men in SCAP, hoped would be a peaceful and more just world.

Notes

Funding from the National Endowment for the Humanities made this research possible. An appointment as Visiting Research Scholar in the Faculty of Law, University of Tokyo, which was kindly arranged through the good offices of Sakamoto Yoshikazu, greatly facilitated the Tokyo portion of the research. I would like to thank Dale Hellegers, Margaret McKean, Sodei Rinjiro, and Ito Kazuko, along with numerous members of the Occupation Project, for their comments on previous drafts, and Richard Meher and Sato Ikuko for their able research assistance. Finally, thanks go to Kato Mikio of International House in Tokyo, James Hastings of the National Records Center, Suitland, Maryland, and Naomi Fukuda of the Asia Library, University of Michigan, for their help at various stages of the research.

1. See Janet Z. Giele and Audrey C. Smock, *Women: Role and Status in Eight Countries* (New York: John Wiley, 1977); and Kay Ann Johnson, "The Politics of Women's Rights and Family Reform in China" (forthcoming).

2. Among the best accounts of the women's suffrage struggle in the U.S. and the many problems that remained in its aftermath are Eleanor Flexnor, *Century of Struggle* (New York: Atheneum, 1974); and William Chafe, *The American Woman: Her Changing Social, Economic, and Political Roles, 1920–1970* (New York: Oxford University Press, 1973). Recent controversies over women's rights policies in the U.S. are covered in Jo Freeman, *The Politics of Women's Liberation* (New York: David McKay, 1975).

3. For this point of view see, for example, Kawai Kazuo, *Japan's American Interlude* (Chicago: University of Chicago Press, 1960).

4. Edmund Dahlstrom, *The Changing Role of Men and Women,* trans. Gunilla and Steven Anderman (Boston: Beacon Press, 1962).

5. Susan J. Pharr, "A Radical U.S. Experiment: Women's Rights Laws and the Occupation of Japan," in L. H. Redford, ed., *The Occupation of Japan: Impact of Legal Reform* (Norfolk, Va.: The MacArthur Memorial, 1978), pp. 124–151, for further discussion of the proposed Equal Rights Amendment to the U.S. Con-

stitution as it compares with Article 14 of the Japanese Constitution of 1947. First approved by the U.S. Congress in 1972, the proposed amendment as of 1987 had not been ratified by the requisite number of states.

6. The constitutions of France and Germany carry no provisions comparable to Article 24. The Italian constitution provides (in Article 29) that "marriage is founded on the moral and juridical equality of the parties," but the provision is weakened by the qualifying phrase "within the limitations established by law to guarantee the unity of the family." For texts of the French, German, and Italian constitutions, see Arnold J. Zurcher, *Constitutions and Constitutional Trends Since World War II* (New York: New York University Press, 1951).

7. It should be noted that the civil codes and lesser laws (in contrast to constitutional provisions) in the Scandinavian countries and most of the Communist countries offer a fuller range of guarantees to women in many areas than do the Japanese constitution, the Japanese Civil Code, and other laws in combination.

8. Minutes of SWNCC meetings held December 17, 1944–November 4, 1947, Microfilm box T-1194, National Archives, Washington, D.C.

9. SCAP, Government Section, "Chapter III: Unofficial Proposals for Revisions," Draft on Revision of the Japanese Constitution (79-page document prepared by Commander Alfred R. Hussey), p. 34, National Records Center, Record Group 331, Japanese Constitution File.

10. Murosawa Yōko, *Onna no senzenshi* [A history of women in the prewar period] (Tokyo: Miraisha, 1975), pp. 58–66; and Shukan Shincho, ed., *Makkasa no Nihon* [MacArthur's Japan] (Tokyo: Shinchosha, 1970), pp. 266–272.

11. For a typical statement of this view, see Victor Boesen, "MacArthur Frees Mrs. Moto," in *Liberty*, May 18, 1946.

12. Douglas MacArthur, *Reminiscences* (New York: McGraw Hill, 1964), p. 305.

13. See "Discussion" by Sodei Rinjiro in Redford, *Occupation of Japan*, p. 137.

14. U.S. Dept. of State, SCAP Directive, October 4, 1945, "Japanese 'Bill of Rights' " in *Occupation of Japan: Policy and Progress,* Publication 2671, Far Eastern Series 17 (Washington, D.C.: GPO, 1946).

15. SCAP, Government Section, "Three Basic Points stated by Supreme Commander to be 'Musts' in Constitutional Revision." GS paper prepared about February 4, 1946, in Takayanagi Kenzō, Ōtomo Ichirō, and Tanaka Hideo, eds., *Nihonkoku kempō seitei no katei* [The making of the constitution of Japan] (Tokyo: Yūhikaku, 1972), p. 100.

16. National Records Center, Record Group 331, Constitution File, Boxes 2085–2088, SCAP, Government Section, Memorandum on composition of constitutional drafting committees, about February 4, 1946.

17. Interview with Beate Sirota Gordon, March 22, 1977, New York City.

18. Data for this section on Beate Sirota are from my March 22, 1977, interview with her.

19. SCAP, Government Section, "Preliminary Government Section Conferences on Preparation of Draft Constitution," section headed "Meeting of the Steering Committee with Committee on Civil Rights, February 9, 1946," pp. 9–12. National Records Center, Record Group 331, Japanese Constitution File.

20. Ibid. This and other quotations in paragraph are from page 12.

21. Ibid.

22. The Japanese drafts are found in the Papers of Alfred R. Hussey, Jr., Asia Library, University of Michigan, Microfilm Reel 5.

23. Ibid., Document No. 26-C-16, p. 6. Draft dated March 4, 1946.

24. Ibid., Document No. 28-B-5, p. 4. Undated draft submitted before April 8, 1946.

25. Ibid., pp. 7–8. Underlined passages indicate wording added by the Japanese that altered the original intent of the article.

26. See Takayanagi, Ōtomo, and Tanaka, *Nihonkoku kempō seitei no katei,* pp. xxiii–xxxii.

27. Minutes of the Subcommittee on the Bill for Revision of the Imperial Constitution, House of Representatives of the Japanese Diet, July 19, 1946 (official English translation), pp. 54–55. National Records Center, Record Group 331, Japanese Constitution File.

28. Interview with Beate Sirota Gordon, March 22, 1977, New York City.

29. Interview with Kato Shidzue, March 23, 1978, Tokyo.

30. Morosawa Yōko, *Onna no senzenshi* [A history of women in the prewar period] (Tokyo: Miraisha, 1975), pp. 58–66.

31. SCAP, Government Section, Memo to Chief of CI&E and Chief of Government Section dated May 8, 1946, entitled "Proposal to Establish a Women's Bureau in the Home Ministry," Papers of Alfred R. Hussey, Asia Library, University of Michigan.

32. SCAP, Government Section, Memorandum for Record signed by Ruth A. Ellerman, dated February 5, 1947, entitled "Proposed Organization of Ministry of Labor," ibid.

33. SCAP, Government Section, Memo to Chief of CI&E and Chief of GS, May 8, 1946, entitled "Proposal to Establish a Women's Bureau in the Home Ministry," ibid. All quotations in this paragraph are from this source.

34. Ministry of Labor, *Rōdō gyōsei sanjūnen no ayumi* [Thirty years of progress in labor administration] (Tokyo: Rōdōshinbunsha, 1977), p. 187.

35. SCAP, GHQ, *Final Report of the Advisory Committee on Labor Policies and Programs in Japan,* Tokyo: July 29, 1946, pp. 116–117. Papers of Alfred R. Hussey, Asia Library, University of Michigan. The committee's woman member was Helen Mears, listed as a specialist in labor legislation and women's problems. She is the only one of the twelve-member body designated as knowledgeable about women's problems, so it is quite possible that she was responsible for the committee's recommendation that a women's bureau be established in the proposed Ministry of Labor.

36. SCAP, Labor Division, Memorandum for Record, dated November 16, 1946, initialed by Ted Cohen, Papers of Alfred R. Hussey, Asia Library, University of Michigan.

37. SCAP, Government Section, "Memo 1," initialed by Hussey, dated August 17, 1946, Papers of Alfred R. Hussey, Asia Library, University of Michigan.

38. Ibid.

39. Ibid.

40. See D. Clayton James, *The Years of MacArthur, Vol. 1, 1880–1941* (Boston: Houghton Mifflin, 1970), pp. 382–414, for an account of MacArthur's han-

dling of the Bonus Marchers, a group of protesting veterans, when he was Army Chief of Staff in Washington, D.C., in 1932.

41. *Nippon Times,* "SCAP Lauds 'Magnificent Response' by Women," June 22, 1946, p. 1.

42. Data on Ethel B. Weed, now deceased, are from her private papers, which were graciously made available to me in June 1977 by her cousin Thelma Ziemer, New Town, Connecticut.

43. Interview with Kawashima Takeyoshi, March 18, 1978, Tokyo.

44. These fascinating materials are found in the National Records Center, Record Group 331, Women's Affairs Activity File.

45. Interview with Beate Sirota Gordon, March 22, 1977, New York City.

46. In Tokyo, the group appears to have included, at a minimum, Golda Stander of Labor Division; Margaret Stone of Economic and Scientific Section; Beate Sirota of Government Section; Doris Cochrane, a U.S. State Department liaison officer who for a time served as a women's affairs consultant in GHQ; and Lulu Holmes, Jean Pauline Smith, Elizabeth Spence, Esther Waddell, and Maryellen Glerum, all of CI&E.

47. This was confirmed in interviews in Washington, D.C., held December 7–9, 1977, with Elizabeth Jorzick, Frances Foote, and Eleanor Hadley, all of whom served with the Occupation but were outside the subsystem.

48. Interviews in Tokyo with Ito Kazuko, March 10, 1978; Kobayashi Kazuko, March 9, 1978; Kabashima Toshiko, March 15, 1978; and Utsumi Yoshiko, March 20, 1978. All four of these women served as Ethel Weed's assistants.

49. Susan J. Pharr, "The Japanese Woman: Evolving Views of Life and Role," in Lewis Austin, ed., *Japan: The Paradox of Progress* (New Haven: Yale University Press, 1976), pp. 303–304.

50. *Cleveland Plain Dealer,* "Cleveland Wac Cited for Help to Jap Women," 1947 (otherwise undated), in Papers of Ethel B. Weed.

51. Interview with Don Brown (who served as Chief of Information Section, CI&E, during the Occupation), in Tokyo, April 6, 1978. The costs of making films and displays came out of the budgets of the operational branches (e.g., the Motion Picture Branch in the case of films on women). The salaries of the Japanese assistants, like those of all Japanese nationals working for the Occupation, were paid by the Japanese government.

52. SCAP, Government Section, Memo from Ruth Ellerman to Alfred R. Hussey, dated August 20, 1948, Papers of Alfred R. Hussey, Asia Library, University of Michigan.

53. Ibid.

54. SCAP, Government Section, Memorandum for the Record by Ruth Ellerman, dated September 30, 1946, entitled "Conference with Labor Division and members of the Social Democratic Party relative to establishment of a Labor Ministry," Papers of Alfred R. Hussey, Asia Library, University of Michigan.

55. Ibid.

56. Copy of letter from Ethel B. Weed to Frieda S. Miller, Director, Women's Bureau, U.S. Department of Labor, December 2, 1946, Papers of Ethel B. Weed.

57. "First Draft of Proposed Ministry of Labor," submitted by the Yoshida

Cabinet to the Government Section, SCAP, February [5], 1947, National Records Center, Record Group 331, Women's Affairs Activity File.

58. SCAP, Government Section, Memorandum for Record from Ruth Ellerman, dated February 5, 1947, Papers of Alfred R. Hussey, Asia Library, University of Michigan.

59. SCAP, Government Section, Memorandum for Record from Alfred R. Hussey, dated February 12, 1947, Papers of Alfred R. Hussey, Asia Library, University of Michigan.

60. SCAP, Labor Division, Memorandum for Record by P. L. Stanchfield, Acting Chief, Labor Division, dated April 16, 1947, Document No. 61-A-25, Papers of Alfred R. Hussey, Asia Library, University of Michigan.

61. SCAP, Labor Division, Memorandum for Record from James Killen, Chief, Labor Division, dated June 23, 1947, entitled "Functions and Organization of Proposed Labor Ministry," Papers of Alfred R. Hussey, Asia Library, University of Michigan.

62. This is verified by Kabashima Toshiko, who was serving as Ethel Weed's assistant during the period when the appointment was made. (Interview with Kabashima Toshiko, March 15, 1978, Tokyo.) The appointment of Yamakawa Kikue, a noted Marxist, as first head of the Women's and Minors' Bureau, surprised many people at the time. Mrs. Yamakawa herself appears to credit Kato Shidzue with having had a hand in her appointment. Yoda Seiichi, Sakai Harumi, and Shigeto Miyako, "Yamakawa Kikue and the Founding of the Women's and Minors' Bureau, Ministry of Labor," in Journal of Tokyo College of Economics, no. 92 (September 1975).

63. Yamakawa Kikue, "Otoko no koku Nihon" [Japan, a man's country], Fujin to nenshosha, Special Anniversary Issue, no. 42 (1977), p. 15; also, interview with Tanino Setsuko, formerly head of the Women's and Minors' Bureau, March 10, 1978, Tokyo.

64. Hugh Heclo, Modern Social Politics in Britain and Sweden (New Haven: Yale University Press, 1974), pp. 308–311.

65. Freeman, The Politics of Women's Liberation, pp. 221–229.

66. According to one distinguished woman leader, those Japanese women involved in lobbying at GHQ for prostitution-control measures during the Occupation period ran up against a wall of silence on the subject. Interview with Tanaka Sumiko, Member, House of Councillors, Tokyo, March 16, 1978.

9

The Making of the Postwar Local Government System

Amakawa Akira

Japanese laws relating to local government underwent considerable change during the Occupation period. The chapter entitled "Local Self-Government" of the new constitution and the unified Local Autonomy Law (hereafter cited as LAL), both of which became effective on May 3, 1947, are basic to these legal reforms. But did they bring about the expected changes in the local government system in Japan? The purpose of this paper is to answer this question.

Given this goal, the analysis proceeds from two different viewpoints: historical and structural. First, I will focus on the historical process of the local government reforms during the Occupation. The greater part of the Occupation reforms involved the enactment of new laws. These reforms were promoted by both SCAP and Japanese government officials operating with different purposes and perceptions. My second major concern is with intergovernmental relations rather than local government per se. This requires an analysis of "bureaucratic politics" both within SCAP and within the Japanese government. Combining these two perspectives will help us to illustrate the processes of both continuity and change in the postwar local government system.

The Prewar Local Government System

To understand the background of local government reforms during the Occupation it is necessary to understand something of the prewar local government system.[1] The basic laws involved were enacted about the same time as the Meiji Constitution (1889). The City Code (Shisei) and the Town and Village Code (Chōsonsei) were promulgated in 1888; the Code for Urban and Rural Prefectures (Fukensei) and the County Code (Gunsei) followed in 1890. We refer to these collectively as "the local government codes." The County Code was abolished in 1911, and the Code for the Tokyo Metropolis (Tosei) was enacted in 1943, but these changes did not basically alter the multiple structure of the whole.

The core of the prewar local government system was formed not so much by the local government codes, however, as by imperial ordinances *(chokurei)*. Article 10 of the Meiji Constitution gave the emperor authority to establish governmental organs and appoint their officials; thus, the administrative organs were created through imperial ordinances and their officials were appointed by the emperor. One ordinance, known as the Local Government Organization Regulations (Chihōkankansei, hereafter cited as LGOR), which was proclaimed in 1887, fixed the structure, powers, and duties of prefectures as national administrative units. This gave the prefectures a special status among local governments.

Every local government, whether prefecture or municipality, served two functions. Local governments, while directly responsible for the affairs of local communities, were also expected to perform national administrative functions within their areas. The system had, therefore, both local and national administrative functions. All of Japan was divided into prefectures and municipalities which performed national administrative services for the whole country. Power to adjust the boundaries of prefectures and municipalities was reserved to the home minister. The allocation of these dual national and local functions differed according to the type of local government. The prefectures, although autonomous under the Prefecture Code, were primarily units of national administration controlled by the LGOR. Municipalities, however, were supposed to be more autonomous, while still conducting national functions on a delegated basis.

The prefecture was constructed as a comprehensive local branch of national administration by the LGOR. The governor, a national official, occupied a pivotal position in central-local relations. He performed national functions under the general supervision of the home minister and the specific supervision of other ministers whose affairs he conducted. He was also made responsible for "administrative affairs within the district," which meant that all national functions within the prefectures were reserved to him unless explicitly excluded from his jurisdiction. This allowed him both to integrate various national functions under his direction and, at the same time, adjust them to local conditions. Such adjustment to local conditions was an important responsibility, since the governor was, according to the Prefecture Code, the chief executive of his prefecture.

To implement national policies at the municipal level, two forms of delegation were used. One was delegation to the mayor. The City Code, for example, stipulated that the mayor "shall administer the affairs of the nation, prefecture, and other public entities prescribed by law and ordinances" and "shall bear the necessary expenses." In performing delegated functions, the mayor was regarded as an agent of the national organ that delegated the authority and supervised its administration.

The second form of delegation was delegation to the local entity itself. The City Code said that the city was to "perform duties prescribed by existing laws and precedents, and by such laws and ordinances as shall be made in the future" and was "responsible for disbursing the necessary funds." The same statements were found in the other local government codes as well. This made it possible for national policies to be carried out at the local level and at local expense. The more functions delegated to local governments, therefore, the more they had to pay.

The nature of the autonomous powers granted by the local government codes revolved around the powers of citizens and local assemblies. This illustrates the influence of the Prussian theory of *Selbstverwaltung* as *ehrenamtliche Verwaltung* and *korporative Verwaltung*. Only "citizens," as distinguished from "residents," could vote and run in local assembly elections. The assembly was a legislative body with fixed powers to draw up by-laws and budgets and to deliberate on local affairs. These powers differed according to the type of local government. In cities and prefectures, for example, councils were established that served as substitutes for an assembly. The executive branch was more powerful than the assembly in all types of local government. The mayor, who was elected by the assembly and not directly by the citizens, had the power to convoke the assembly and introduce bills as well as to execute the decisions of the assembly.

Finally, all local governments were under the general control of the home minister. Thus municipalities were under the supervision of, first, the prefectural governor, and second, the home minister, while prefectures were overseen by the home minister. If a municipal assembly passed illegal or extralegal legislation, the supervising agency, acting through the mayor, could have it reconsidered. The power of the mayor extended to the budget as well; when funds were not sufficient to meet necessary expenses, he could impose a mandatory budget. Just as the local government had dual functions, so did the Home Ministry. While the home minister was a supervisor of local governments in executing national functions, he was also the protector of local governments' interests in national decision making. When in cabinet meetings demands were made by other ministers concerning the local execution of their respective policies, the home minister coordinated and adjusted these demands on behalf of the local governments. His powers of coordination, however, rested more upon a de facto than a de jure base.

Such was the basic structure of the "local self-government" system of prewar Japan. Local governments were constructed as cost-sharing bodies for national administration and in return were allowed some autonomous power. The Janus-faced Home Ministry and the dual functioning prefecture were the core linkages of central-local relations.

Since local government served two masters, local residents and the national administration, it was pulled in two directions. On the one hand, the local residents and local assemblies sought to enlarge their autonomous powers set forth in the local government codes. Specifically, they wanted to broaden the qualifications for citizenship, extend the powers of the assemblies, and lessen supervision from the executive. On the other hand the central ministries, with their expanding special functions, kept calling for a stronger national administrative system at the local level. They asked for an expansion of prefectural administrative organizations in the LGOR and a stronger executive in the local government codes. The job of reconciling these conflicting demands fell to the Home Ministry, especially to its Local Affairs Bureau.

The Home Ministry responded with various patchwork revisions of the multiple local government codes and the LGOR. As democratic tendencies became stronger, especially after World War I, "citizenship" was extended at both the local and national levels to all males over the age of twenty-five. Local assemblies were also given additional power. The Prefecture Code came to resemble the City Code, which granted more autonomous powers than the former. All these revisions toward increased autonomy, however, were balanced by a strengthening of the executive powers of the home minister.

The Home Ministry had to cope with the demands of other central ministries as well, and this produced some conflicts between them. The local enforcement of national policies through the channels of local governments posed a problem of uniformity and diversity. Although the expansion of special functions uniformly throughout the country was a benefit for the residents as a whole, it also imposed burdens on the local governments. Chief among these were difficulties in coordinating local functions and the burden of cost-sharing. In addition, some central ministries began to establish their own local branch offices instead of delegating functions to the local government. This threatened the basic structure of local government as a comprehensive branch of national administration. To cope with these problems it was essential for the Home Ministry to devise measures of financial adjustment among local governments.

Efforts were made to secure a stronger national administrative system when the government moved to put the nation on a war footing. The Home Ministry initiated the local tax reform of 1940, which established a Local Distribution Tax system to ensure adequate local revenues and adjust financial inequalities among the local governments. This distribution tax system took the following form: three of the national taxes—those on land, houses, and businesses—were returned to the prefectures in which they had been collected. In addition, a fixed portion of four national taxes was distributed to the prefectures (62%) and municipalities (38%) by the Home Ministry. This system increased the local tax revenues as a whole, but it also made the local governments increasingly dependent on these tax allotments.[2]

Administrative regimentation of local government kept pace with the financial reform. The Home Ministry Instruction Number 17 of 1940 ordered local authorities throughout the country to establish neighborhood associations to assure the penetration of national policies to the grass roots. The reform of local government codes in 1943 empowered the mayors to control these associations within their areas. The same reform made it possible to delegate national functions by executive order. In the meantime regional administrative reorganization was also undertaken.[3] Nine regional administrative councils were set up in 1943 to secure overall liaison and coordination among the prefectures within the region. Finally, in June 1945, in preparation for the expected American invasion, these administrative councils were reorganized into regional superintendencies general.

"Local Self-Government" in the New Constitution

Japan's defeat and the Occupation could not but have a major impact on this system of local government. The Government Section (GS) of SCAP, which founded its occupation policies upon the demilitarization and democratization of Japan, emerged as a driving force for political reforms. The Occupation, however, was conducted by using the existing Japanese government, so the Home Ministry and other ministries were not excluded from reform politics. In effect, the process of local government reforms during the Occupation unfolded through the interactions of the existing governmental bodies with the addition of a new powerful foreign actor—the Government Section.

Just after the war the Local Affairs Bureau of the Home Ministry, without waiting for instructions from GS, began to review the local government system. At the end of September it decided to abolish the regional superintendencies-general in order to dismantle the wartime government apparatus. The Home Ministry also set about the democratization of local government, using the familiar strategy of revising the local government codes while leaving the LGOR as it was.[4] Specific measures for increased autonomous powers included a broadening of the qualifications for citizenship, corresponding to a broadening of the national suffrage, a system of direct demands by the people for the enactment of by-laws and the recall of office-holders, the expansion of assembly powers, and the selection of governors by prefectural assemblies. The Home Ministry thought that reform could be accomplished by revisions of the local government codes without recourse to constitutional reforms, a topic that was then just emerging as a political issue.

The sudden announcement by the Shidehara Cabinet of the Outline of the new Constitution on March 6, 1946, had a profound influence on the course of the Home Ministry's reform plan, for the outline included a chapter of four articles entitled "Local Self-Government." The outline was drafted completely outside the Home Ministry. Let us turn our attention to the origins of this new chapter before examining its impact on the Home Ministry's strategy.

The origin of chapter 8 of the outline can be traced to the GS draft of the constitution.[5] Since the GS officials used SWNCC-228 "as a control document," we shall first note the policy recommendations of this document. SWNCC-228 stated that "the popular election or local appointment of as many of the prefectural officials as is practicable would lessen the political power formerly possessed by the Home Minister as a result of his appointment of governors of prefectures. At the same time it would further encourage the development of genuinely representative local government." Thus by February 3, 1946, when the GS began its draft of the constitution, the inclusion of an article concerning the local division of responsibility and the popular election of governors was already pretty well decided upon. The determination of the substance of this policy was, however, left to the drafters in GS, and there were differences of opinion among them.

The first draft, prepared by the Local Government Committee chaired by Major Cecil G. Tilton, "was discarded as inadequate," for "it established a form of local sovereignty." Tilton, who had a strong inclination toward home rule, drew up a draft to give all types of local government, from prefectures to villages, broad powers of government.[6]

The Steering Committee, which consisted of three lawyers, Colonel Charles L. Kades, Commander Alfred R. Hussey, and Lieutenant Colonel Milo E. Rowell, prepared a new draft. A record of the committee's deliberations stated "the final draft of the Chapter on Local Government is a reconciliation of two opposing views—one represented by Colonel Rowell, a strong home rule man, and the other by Colonel Kades, a warm central government man."

A close examination of the handwritten drafts in the Hussey Papers, however, shows us that Hussey was a warmer central government man than Kades. Hussey, as the first drafter, wrote, "All laws governing the administration or organization of local government shall be uniform in their application," while emphasizing that "the right of suffrage shall not be denied." Kades deleted these sentences and gave the local people more powers "to manage their property, affairs and government . . . and to frame their own charters." Rowell, as an anchor man, rewrote it to permit "limited home rule . . . within the structure of parliamentary democracy."[7]

The final GS draft written by Rowell consisted of three articles. The first stipulated that the governors, mayors, and chief executive officers of all local governments, as well as assemblymen and some local officials, "shall be elected by direct popular vote." The second gave to the inhabitants of metropolitan areas, cities, and towns the powers that Kades had suggested. The third required the consent of a majority of the electorate for any special act applicable to a metropolitan area, city, or town. The last two articles obviously gave a special status to metropolitan areas, cities, and towns and tried to secure for them greater powers than prefectural or municipal home rule.

This conception, however, was to be obscured after negotiations with Japanese government officials. Satō Tatsuo, a legal expert of the Cabinet Legal Bureau, was the key person in converting the GS's conception of chapter 8 into something different from its original intent.[8] Satō prepared the Japanese draft of chapter 8 and was the only Japanese official to go over the outline draft with the GS officials on March 4 and 5. The conception Satō held was symbolized in his request to change the title of the chapter from "Local Government" to "Local Self-Government." As a former Home Ministry official, Satō endeavored to link this chapter to traditional Japanese conceptions of "local self-government."

He drafted as a general principle of this chapter a new article, which stated that "regulations concerning organization and operations of local public entities shall be fixed by law in accordance with the principle of local autonomy." This article guaranteed a uniform local government system by national law as before, corresponding by chance to Hussey's idea, and could have threatened Rowell's idea of separating prefectures from other levels of government. Satō ingeniously revised the GS draft along traditional lines of empowering local residents and assemblies, while inserting in every article phrases like "in accordance with," "determined by," or "within" the law. To this legal expert, translating from English drafts to Japanese and vice versa afforded an opportunity to water down the GS conception of local government. Despite Satō's new article, the provision relating to home rule charters, the essence of Rowell's idea, was left untouched in the outline of March 6. The text stating "their right to manage their property, affairs, and government and to frame their own charters," however, was to be revised later to "affairs and administration and to enact their own regulations" in accordance with the Japanese text of March 6.

Thus Satō's work changed the basic conception of chapter 8 from the "constitutional guarantee of municipal home rule," envisioned by the GS, to "a rule of law based on the principle of local autonomy," although minute inconsistencies still remained in the outline draft. The American draftsmen, as Steiner wrote, "failed to grasp the potential implications that the articles as a whole held for their aim of permitting 'home rule.'" This failure should be attributed to haste of composition, the language barrier (which Satō intentionally used), and the misconception within the GS of "local self-government" within the Japanese system.

Enactment of the Local Autonomy Law

The announcement of the outline draft of the constitution put the work of the Home Ministry officials into a new context. At first, they explored the possibility of revising the text of the outline to allow for the indirect election of governors. The Home Ministry officials, accompanied by Satō, made contact with the GS officials, but their efforts were in vain. The text of chapter 8 was left nearly intact except for some readjustments of translation.

Because the outline had been made public, the Home Ministry was forced to integrate the principles of the new constitution into the plan of legal reform it was preparing. The ministry submitted its drafts of local government codes to the GS for consideration in late March and early April 1946.[9] The popularly elected governor was the central focus. The Home Ministry had strongly opposed the popular election of governors because they formed the pivot of the traditional system for local administration of national affairs, and their election would destroy that system. But the Home Ministry now could submit draft bills that presupposed the popular election of governors because it had invented a skillful device: popularly elected governors as national officials. Viewed from the standpoint of either the old constitution or the new, this was a compromise. This device answered the demands of public opinion for the popular election of governors on the one hand while preserving the existing national administrative system on the other. The latter was necessary in part for implementing the Occupation policies. The Home Ministry's strategy seemed to be an attempt to deal with the problem temporarily on the basis of the existing Meiji Constitution. However, it also aimed to make that system permanent under the new constitution by taking the position that this system did not violate the "principle of local autonomy."

It was only after the Diet had begun its deliberations that the GS began to intervene positively in the Home Ministry's reform bills. The necessity of aligning positions within the GS in regard to local government reform was one reason for the lateness of this response. Tilton, as the chief of the Local Government Branch, wrote a memorandum on the Home Ministry amendments in which he said that "these amendments are in the right direction, but fall far short of providing for the changes which are necessary for the accomplishment of SCAP policy. The basic pattern of centralized control is not changed, nor is there any significant increase in the authority and responsibility of local representative bodies. There is no marked curtailment in Home Ministry control of local affairs."

Hussey, again, was the man to criticize Tilton's memo as "it is lacking of the basic principles." Hussey held that (1) it was necessary to lay down certain principles to govern the division of power between central and local authorities and (2) there had to be a clear principle as to whether the job of coordination between the two rested with the executive branch of the central government as before or with the Diet and the courts. He noted that "the requirements of efficiency and economy in some fields demand national operation without local interference" and that "the Diet should exercise the real control" in coordination. The conflict involved the basic character of the GS's local government policy. A compromise was reached at a GS conference on July 1 to keep pace with the rapidly moving Home Ministry. Tilton's contact with the Home Ministry officials, which had been suspended since April, was resumed.[10]

It was at this conference that the GS decided that "the governor was not to be a national official of the Civil Service as provided for in the Home Ministry bill." The Home Ministry, informed by the GS that the above policy was a "must," was forced to revise its original bill, which had stipulated that "the governor shall be a national official." A revision, to make the governor "a national official for the present," seemed to pass the Diet. But the Home Ministry's joy was short lived, for the final amendment read at the House of Representatives made him "a national official until the day the new constitution goes into effect."

The Home Ministry's original intention to maintain the existing administrative system even after the new constitution was frustrated by this amendment. The ministry was driven into a second-round reform plan, within a fixed time limit, to reconstruct the administrative system on the premise of governors as local officials. This needed a rewriting of the LGOR as well as the local government codes. The revision of the LGOR was necessary for another reason as well. Since the draft constitution deprived the emperor of his powers, Imperial Ordinances, as a legal form, would cease to exist. Therefore, a Special Legal Investigation Commission, established in July 1946, was made responsible for reviewing all laws and ordinances and adjusting them to the new constitution. In this commission, it was anticipated that the LGOR would become a Local Administrative Offices Law while remaining nearly intact in its substance. The Home Ministry's second-round reform thus had to take account of this commisison.[11]

If the Home Ministry was unhappy with the first round of reforms, so was the GS. Since the initiative for the first-round reform was taken by the Home Ministry, the GS was not completely satisfied despite amendments made in the Diet. Tilton, who still hoped to have the home rule provision and to lessen the Home Ministry's influence, needed to reconcile his intentions with Hussey's criticism. So even before the first round of reforms was over, Tilton took his initiative for the second round.

On July 26, 1946, Tilton wrote a memorandum for a news release that would appear as a statement by the Home Minister. In this memo Tilton emphasized that the reform bills then before the Diet "represent only a first step toward the democratization of local government" and that the government expected to have "a new set of laws" in the next session. Tilton divided the expected bills into two classes, ones that "affect the structure of local government" and others "to cover matters in related fields." On the latter, he wrote,

> Local police, education, health and sanitation, local finance, and local labor matters shall be placed under the exclusive control and supervision of the local government. In these fields the tasks of the national government will be restricted to establishment of national standards, coordination, and the collection and dissemination of information.

On the revision of structure, he enumerated nine points, among them:

> The status of the governor will undergo a fundamental change. Only in exceptional cases and for special purposes, covered by Diet laws which do not contravene the principle of local autonomy, shall he be made responsible to the central government.
>
> All judicial decisions affecting local governments and their organs shall be made by the appropriate courts.
>
> Provision will be made for variations in the form of governmental organization at local levels in order to permit the inhabitants of *shi, chō,* and *son* [cities, towns, and villages] to select for themselves the form of government they desire in their own communities. The *shi, chō,* and *son* will be empowered to manage their own affairs without minute supervision from above.
>
> A complete revision will be made in regard to supervisory and disciplinary matters on the part of the Ministry of Home Affairs in local government.[12]

Some points included here could be easily traced back to Hussey's two principles.

The home minister released the statement pledging a second round of reforms on the same day the House of Representatives passed the first reform bills. The statement listed nine provisions, basically those requested by Tilton, but in slightly watered down tone from the ministry's viewpoint. To the Home Ministry, the most important issue was how to establish a new prefecture system with governors as local officials. The ministry set up a Local Institutions Inquiry Council to advise and prepare a blueprint for the second-round reform.

The council went to work in October 1946 and reported back to the home minister on December 25.[13] Their report began with a discussion of the "form of legislation" in which they requested abolishment of the old, multiple local government codes and enactment of a new, unified Local Autonomy Law. This unified form of legislation, which had been decided upon without any searching debate, restricted the provisions of the new system of local government. The substantive part of their proposals were as follows.

Concerning municipal home rule, Tilton's chief concern, the report said that "the local entities shall be permitted to determine their organization independently, within certain limits set by the law." Decisions concerning the creation and abolition of local entities were to be reserved to the home minister, and the relationship between prefectures and municipalities was to be "as it is, with the prefectures the high-ranking government" affording the governors a "right to supervise the municipalities."

A special cities system for five big cities was introduced, since these big five had long desired special treatment. This would "apply the prefecture system to these special cities," that is, they would perform more national functions than before.

Concerning the ways of conducting national functions at the prefectural level, the Home Ministry's chief concern, the report said that "the governors, even after they are made into local officials, would conduct the national affairs they currently perform" and that "the national affairs would be in principle transferred to the prefecture. Those functions that would be difficult to transfer would be delegated to the prefectures or governors" by laws and cabinet orders. The latter part was meant to expand the existing delegation system involving municipalities to the prefectures as well. In the case of transferred functions, "national control shall be specified in each law and ordinance." The report also proposed "to integrate the national branch offices to the utmost into prefectural administration." However, it did not mention "judicial decisions affecting local government" or the Home Ministry's control, as these had been dropped from the council's agenda from the start.

In short, the organization of local governments was to be determined by a unified Local Autonomy Law (LAL) despite the existence of different types of local governments, while their functions and supervision were to be covered by a multitude of individual laws and ordinances. The prefecture's ranking position over the municipalities, as well as Home Ministry supervision, would be maintained even under the governors-as-local-officials system.

With this report in hand, the Home Ministry sat down to draft the new Local Autonomy Law. Their outline of January 7, 1947, however, set forth a new character for the LAL by in effect unifying the LGOR with the local government codes. Since the Special Legal Investigation Commission, which dealt with the LGOR, had given up the plan to enact a Local Administrative Offices Law, certain provisions of the LGOR were slipped into the LAL. This gave the prefectures a stronger and more stable character than the council report had originally expected. The prefectures were now "compound local entities comprising cities, towns, villages, and wards." They had vice-governors and treasurers, and their basic departments would be provided by the LAL. The outline also included two separate tables showing the national functions to be transferred to and national branch offices to be abolished or absorbed by the prefectures.

This outline, however, inevitably drew fierce opposition from various central ministries. To them, the transfer of functions to and absorption of branch offices by prefectures meant that powers and authority were being taken away from them and placed under the supervision of the Home Ministry. In the infighting the other ministries had the advantage over the Home Ministry. By invoking their distrust of popularly elected governors and raising the fear that the prefectures would be led into administrative revolt, they emphasized the national character of their functions that should be performed uniformly throughout the country. They combined against the Home Ministry at cabinet meetings, for example, to decide once again to maintain branch offices as they were instead of transferring them to the prefectures. In addition, they sought support from the Occupation authorities with whom they shared a common interest in performing specific national policies. The Home Ministry's outline also drew fire from the GS. The GS insistently demanded, among other things, the curtailment of the home minister's power to supervise local government and to initiate certain judicial measures to coordinate intergovernmental disputes.

Faced with these two-front attacks, the Home Ministry was forced to make concessions if it wanted to enact the LAL before the constitution became effective. As the Home Ministry needed to get cabinet approval of the bill first, they revised the outline into a new bill that leaned toward the line of the other ministries. In this new bill, the idea of transferring national functions to prefectures was abandoned, while allowing the delegation of work from the other ministries to local governments by laws and cabinet orders. The prefectural administrative organization was strengthened again following the LGOR, and certain kinds of officials would continue to be "national officials for the present." To cope with other ministries, the Home Ministry provided for the governor's power to perform "administrative affairs within the district," which would enable him to integrate various national functions under himself as before. The home minister's authority to dismiss governors was also provided.

As these arrangements simply meant a continuity of the old system, the Home Ministry had to forestall GS criticism. The technique used here was to dazzle the GS by inventing new legal concepts and articles. Both prefectures and municipalities were made "ordinary local public entities," as set forth in Article 1, despite their hierarchical relations as before. "Supervision" *(kantoku)* by the home minister over local governments was replaced by "jurisdiction" *(shokatsu)*. And the new LAL "shall come into force as from the day of the enforcement of the Constitution of Japan," as it embodied "the principle of local autonomy."

The local autonomy bill was introduced in the last Imperial Diet on March 15. As had happened with the first-round reform bills, GS demands were introduced in the form of Diet amendments during the brief period of deliberation. In the second round the GS was not so innocent as to be swindled easily. A strong attack was made on Article 146, which defined the home minister's powers of "jurisdiction." The Home Ministry, seeing its raison d'être threatened, fought back in various ways, only to be driven into a tight corner while trying to prevent elimination of this article from the draft LAL. An attack on the Home Ministry depriving the home minister of his power to dismiss governors was also successful. The article was revised to introduce impeachment by the courts. The GS, however, went no further than to request a slight change of Article 150, which specified the competent minister's authority to supervise and guide the heads of local government in performing the national functions delegated to them. With these amendments in the Diet, the Home Ministry lost its fight both against the GS and against other ministries, which retained their powers of supervision and guidance under the new local government system.

The LAL was promulgated on April 16 and went into effect on May 3, 1947, together with the new constitution. The multiple arrangement of local government codes and the LGOR passed away with the Meiji Constitution, while retaining their substance in the new LAL. Thus, the start of the LAL did not necessarily mean the start of an entirely new system of local government. To be sure, the popular election of governors and the elimination of the home minister's powers were major changes; but there was no change in the character of local government with respect to its performing dual functions for its inhabitants and the national administration. In this latter regard, local governments were soon to be overwhelmed with delegated and supervisory assignments from the central ministries. There was no means of regulating such delegations "in accordance with the principle of local autonomy." Furthermore, the device of making both prefectures and municipalities "ordinary local public entities" left unsolved the problem of reconciling the historical and actual differences between the two. The prefectures, in particular, now had to find a new justification for existence in their relations with the municipalities, for they had lost their legitimate role as organs of national administration.

Changes in the Local Government System

The third round of reforms initiated by the GS focused on organizational matters. The neighborhood associations, or *tonari gumi* system, regarded as a "feudalistic quasi-governmental institution" and "a serious danger to the successful democratization of local government" by Tilton, had attracted his attention since 1945.[14] The attempt to abolish the *tonari gumi* system went along with the extension of the purge to the local level, effected on January 4, 1947. As the GS persistently urged the abolishment of the system, the Home Ministry was forced reluctantly to rescind its Instruction Number 17 of 1940, thus discontinuing *tonari gumi* as an administrative organ after April 1.

In April 1947 the first elections for governors, mayors, and local assemblymen were held. The official report of the GS concluded that "the local election of 1947, based on universal suffrage, brought a new breath of life into the many communities of Japan." The changes in prefectures, however, were not so sweeping. Among the forty-six newly elected governors, twenty-six had had previous careers as appointed governors in the same prefecture, and two had served in another prefecture. Four other governors had had careers in the central government or prefectures. The influence of the bureaucrats, especially those of the Home Ministry, was thus still powerful in the prefectures.

On April 30, the day the elections for local assemblymen were held, the GS, in the name of its chief Whitney, issued a memorandum on "decentralization of the Ministry of Home Affairs." The memorandum labeled the Home Ministry as "the focal point for centralized controls within the governmental structure of Japan" and requested "a plan for the reorganization of that Ministry" not later than June 1, 1947. The process which led from this demand for "reorganization" to one for "dissolution" of the Home Ministry at the end of that year is so complex that a thorough analysis would require another whole essay. We shall focus our attention here only on the major points from the Home Ministry's viewpoint.[15]

In this process of "reorganization" two major actors in the local government reforms, the Local Government Division of the GS and the Local Affairs Bureau of the Home Ministry, played but a minor role. As the functions of the Home Ministry covered many fields such as police, construction, and local finances, other sections of GHQ and other ministries of the Japanese government were involved. The leading actors were Deputy Chief Kades and Guy J. Swope of the National Government Division of the GS and the officials of the Administrative Research Bureau of the cabinet. Although the memorandum of April 30 came as a shock to the Home Ministry, a reorganization plan for the ministry had been prepared long before in the GS.[16]

The Home Ministry's first response to the request of the GS was to try to maintain a ministry that would be in charge of local government and finances. The Home Ministry claimed that because the local governments performed functions of national administration, it was necessary to have a ministry that would represent and defend the interest of local government as a whole at the central government level. Without this kind of ministry, "even if the LAL is executed in form, it will be devoid of content of local autonomy within a few years, local areas being harassed by conflicting branch offices of other ministries." Along this line, the Katayama cabinet approved a reorganization plan on June 20 that would "preserve most of the present structure of the Home Ministry, while changing its name to 'Popular Government Ministry' (Minseisho) and the name of its Local Affairs Bureau to 'General Affairs Bureau' (Sōmu-kyoku)."

When this plan was revealed by the press the next day the GS immediately responded to the Japanese officials, indicating that "the Cabinet completely and utterly misunderstood the purpose of the original memorandum" and requesting "a full and final" plan. Then the GS worked directly with Maeda Katsumi, an official of the Administrative Research Bureau, to ensure that the GS's point of view would be taken into account when he reported back a new plan. With the GS officials Maeda devised a plan to dissolve the Home Ministry, just as Satō had in the constitution-making process fifteen months before. In this new plan the Home Ministry would be abolished along with its Local Affairs Bureau. Its functions relating to local governments would be transferred to a proposed Local Affairs Commission, while those relating to local finances would be transferred to the Finance Ministry. Faced with dissolution, the Home Ministry proposed that the commission should be comprised of a minister of state as chairman representing the national government and two other members representing local governments and the public. The commission should also be aided by a secretariat to handle affairs relating to the LAL. With the approval of GS, this scheme was adopted at the cabinet meeting on June 27, but with a revision that left the question of local finances unsettled.[17]

The Japanese government drafted a bill to dissolve the Home Ministry along the lines of this agreement and proposed it to the Diet. In mid-September while the Diet was deliberating the bill, the GS presented strong objections to the commission plan. Why the GS abruptly changed its position is not clear. Perhaps the reorganization plan for the police system had some effect upon its changing its previous position. (In his letter of September 16, 1947, MacArthur recommended that Prime Minister Katayama adopt a drastic decentralization of the police system.)

In any case, the Home Ministry defended its position, referring to the previous approval of GS, but had to withdraw the bill under protest. In a new bill designed to ensure Home Ministry dissolution, the functions of the Local Affairs Bureau would be transferred to a provisional Domestic Affairs Bureau which would last only ninety days and, additionally, to a newly established National Election Management Commission and a Local Finance Commission. On December 31, 1947, the 75-year history of the Home Ministry came to a close. The GS report stated that "the date will be a significant one in Japanese history because it marked the end of an institution which had long been the Japanese Government's central policy and control agency for the oppression of the Japanese people." In actuality, however, the new Local Finance Commission with a minister of state at its head became a means for the revival of the influence of the former Home Ministry officials.

Along with the ministry reorganization, the GS urged the Home Ministry to revise the LAL. In scrutinizing the text of the LAL, one official of GS found that "the Home Ministry changed the wording after approval by" the GS. Another official was irritated by the "reactionary attitude" of Home Minister Uehara, stating that "the spirit of cooperation with SCAP which characterized the Home Ministry was swiftly replaced by a passive resistance which at times amounted to obstructionism."[18] Most of the demands of the GS, as before, centered on broadening the scope of powers of local government and eliminating those of the Home Ministry. Some demands, however, were new. One related to the introduction of the special cities system provided in the LAL. The GS requested, contrary to the petitions from the big cities, that the laws to designate special cities be submitted to the entire electorate of the prefectures concerned. This requirement would frustrate the big cities' attempt to become independent of the prefectures.[19] Other new requests related to local branch offices and local finances. The GS demanded that the Diet be given the power to ensure against the arbitrary creation of branch offices and that financial support for delegated functions be provided in the national budget.

These requests from the GS were incorporated in the revision plan prepared by the Home Ministry, in part because they coincided with the intent of the ministry in curtailing the local powers of other central ministries. The basic aim of the ministry in the revision, however, was to maintain its power through the proposed Local Affairs Commission, even to the extent of giving it supervisory power over local governments. The Home Ministry, as stated before, ultimately had to give up this commission plan and to accommodate itself instead to a new local government system that lacked any central agency responsible for local self-government. This situation came about through the abolition of the governor's power to conduct "administrative affairs within the district" and through the bestowal upon local governments of the authority to conduct "administrative affairs" within their own areas. Thus the local governments, instead of the governors, became the principal agents of the general administration of their respective areas. In conjunction with this change, the local government was required to "prescribe its disposition of administrative affairs by its bylaws, unless otherwise provided for in laws or ordinances." Prefectural by-laws took precedence over municipal ones. Thus administrative supervision that had formerly run from the Home Minister to the governor to the localities was replaced by legislative supervision running from national laws and ordinances through prefectural by-laws and municipal ones. Furthermore, the impeachment procedure in the original LAL was replaced by a mandamus procedure for supervising governors and mayors in their roles as national agents. With these revisions, a new system of local government without the Home Ministry was inaugurated, while still leaving local governments performing their dual functions as before.

On the day when the revised LAL was promulgated, Hussey wrote another memorandum on "Local Autonomy" and expressed his concern over the "principles" of local government policy held by the GS.[20] He wrote that "we are now operating under a basic misconception of the meaning of local self-government in a modern democracy." "Complete political decentralization may well result in the effective hamstringing of the national government." He continued that "the local official serving his own community cannot at the same time serve the nation at large," emphasizing the principle that "national affairs must be administered by national officials and local affairs by local officials." This criticism led eventually to still another revision of the LAL.

Referring to the home rule system in the United States, the GS officials enumerated nineteen specific functions to be delegated to local assemblies. With this request, the officials of the Domestic Affairs Bureau assigned these functions, with some alteration, not to local assemblies but to the local public entities, adding "except in cases where they have been provided for in laws and cabinet orders." This restriction would frustrate the expected separation of functions between central and local governments. Furthermore, they extended the hierarchical relations of laws and ordinances, prefectural by-laws, and municipal by-laws, which originally covered only "administrative affairs," to cover all affairs of local government, allowing their chiefs veto powers over assemblies.

In June 1948, when the third round of reforms came to an end, the Local Government Division of the GS was transferred to the Military Government Section of the Eighth Army. This seemed to indicate a recognition that GHQ's reforms had come to a halt. Stress in local government policy now shifted from calls for structural reforms to on-site guidance and dissemination of the reforms. In apparent response to this development, there was a wave of enactments of local by-laws under the guidance of the Military Government Section, starting around July 1948.[21]

In order to function independently, the local governments needed more than just the power to enact by-laws. They needed a financial base. At that time, local finance was in a state of chronic distress, with a shortage of financial resources out of all proportion to rising expenses. The decentralization of functions aggravated the financial burden. Nine years of compulsory education and the introduction of local police and fire departments increased the burden, too. The local tax system underlying these new expenses was basically the same as the one created in 1940, although some interim measures had been taken. A sweeping reform of the local financial system corresponding to that of the administrative system was now required.

When the Home Ministry was abolished, a Local Finance Commission was formed to draft a plan that would create "local finance autonomy," balanced with national interests. It was required to submit a draft of the necessary legislation within ninety days. Under this time limit the commission, the core of which consisted of former Home Ministry officials, set to work on a new local finance system.[22]

In January 1948 the commission decided on targets of local financial reform to provide "thorough local financial autonomy" and "to meet present economic conditions." Following this line the commission completed the outline of a reform plan. The commission proposed putting a basic provision concerning local financial structure into the LAL and then enacting a new Local Finance Law (hereafter cited as LFL) in which the principles governing fiscal relations between the central government and local governments would be set forth. The basic principle of the LFL was to separate as much as possible national expenses from local ones. All functions performed by the local government were classified as national, local, or combined in character, and their costs were to be borne nationally, locally, or in combination as the case might be. The rate of national subsidies for functions of a combined character would be fixed by relevant laws, while the general principle involved was to be stated in the LFL. Hearings before the Local Finance Commission would be required in connection with any laws, cabinet orders, or national budget items that might incur local expenses.

As had been the case with the transfer of functions on the enactment of the LAL, a good deal of opposition came from various central ministries. The Finance Ministry, holding that "healthy local finance" rather than "autonomy" was the real issue, looked askance at the commission's plan for reform and sought support from the Economic and Scientific Section, their counterpart in GHQ. As a result, the commission's draft of an outline for the LFL was not completed until just before the expiration of the ninety days and took a somewhat weaker stance on the issue of national subsidies.

Submission of the LFL was further delayed because of a cabinet reshuffle caused by problems of budget reorganization. The new Ashida cabinet could not reconcile the conflict between the Local Finance Commission and the Finance Ministry over the 1948 local budget. This dispute gave time for other ministries to become involved. Furthermore, the issue of local branch offices became entangled with that of local financial problems. Consequently, the final version of the local finance bill was adopted at a cabinet meeting only in early June. After adjustments with other ministries, the bill's provisions differed drastically from the commission's original outline.

The purpose of the law was "to ensure healthy local finance" and "the development of local autonomy." Local governments were prohibited from adopting "policies that would upset national finances in contravention of national policies." The general concept of financial responsibilities that accorded with functions was still there; the rates would be fixed by ordinances as well as laws. Hearings before the commission were provided, and the law also allowed the national government to order a reduction or repayment of its share of the expense if a local government violated these laws and ordinances. As had been the case with by-laws, the vertical relationship between prefecture and municipalities was incorporated in this bill. The LFL based on this bill was passed in July 1948.

The relation between GS and the Japanese government on the enactment of the LFL is not clear from the Japanese sources. While infighting within the Japanese government continued on the problem of local finances, a keen rivalry sprang up within GHQ over the issue of local branch offices. In dealing with this, the GS found itself in a situation similar to that of the Home Ministry within the Japanese government, that is, in conflict with other special staff sections of GHQ. The problem arose after prefectural governors became local officials. The central ministries, distrusting the governor's ability to work effectively for them, began to establish their own local branch offices staffed by their own national officials. Seen from the perspective of local governments, these branch offices represented not only a duplication of functions but also a source of obstructions. The Home Ministry as well as the GS took this position in the revision of the LAL in 1947.

A prime minister's letter of May 17, 1948, set off the infighting within GHQ.[23] In this letter Ashida proposed an "absolute minimum" plan for the readjustment of local branch offices, abolishing some of them and transferring their functions to the governors. A meeting of interested section chiefs discussed the proposed plan, and strong objections were raised from each section, just as if each was representing its counterpart Japanese ministry. The Public Health and Welfare Section, for example, "does not concur in the proposal" to eliminate a section of the Welfare Ministry. The Natural Resources Section, along with the Agriculture Ministry, "was definitely interested in any change which might adversely affect the distribution of critical materials needed by farmers." The ESS, representing many ministries relating to economic controls, said that local branch offices "should remain." Coping single-handed with these objections, Whitney, chief of the GS, brought forth a counterargument, stating that "the efficiency of the Japanese governmental administration is not *per se* a concern of the Occupation" and that "these statements disclose a serious misconception of the nature of the readjustment plan, a lack of understanding of the status of prefectural governors under the LAL, and a disregard of the events of the last two years under the Occupation." With MacArthur's approval, Whitney wrote a letter to Ashida advising him to have the matter determined by the Japanese government. While this might have been a victory for GS within the GHQ, it did not awaken any sympathetic echo in the Japanese government, since there was no central ministry that could act for the local governments as the Home Ministry had done before. The problem was left pending.

Changes in the Environment

While these struggles over local government policy were developing in Tokyo, Washington officials were reviewing U.S. policies toward Japan. A new policy aimed at economic recovery and calling a halt to further reforms was adopted by the president as NSC-13/2 in October 1948. A nine-point economic stabilization program was given to MacArthur to be transmitted to the Japanese government in December. And Washington dispatched Joseph Dodge to act as an advisor in carrying out the new program.

Arriving in February 1949, Dodge began his work with the Finance Ministry to restructure the 1949 budget, then in the process of preparation, as an "ultra-balanced budget." This had a very considerable effect on local finance.[24] The stipulated rate of the Local Distribution Tax, a source of local revenue, was cut in half, and the issuance of local bonds was severely restricted since this was considered a source of inflation. Faced with a financial crisis, local governments and their associations arranged an alliance with the Local Finance Commission against the Finance Ministry. Although their fight was in vain, the former Home Ministry officials found supporters here in their struggle for survival as an agency in the central government.

In May 1949, while Dodge's fiscal reforms were being carried out, a mission led by Dr. Carl Shoup arrived to investigate the Japanese tax system and to make recommendations for its reform. The idea to invite a tax mission was first conceived in 1947 by the Finance Ministry, which expected the mission to defend it against Tilton's demands for local finance reforms.[25] Now the Finance Ministry, which was to receive the Shoup Report, expected the mission to support its position; the ministry had already planned to reduce taxes as had been publicly promised by the Yoshida cabinet. The Shoup Report, however, which was prepared after two months of intensive investigation, proved to be a greater boon to the Local Finance Commission than to the Finance Ministry since it emphasized local autonomy.[26]

The report began with the introductory statement that,

> local autonomy is one of the announced goals of the Occupation and of the Japanese government, but local autonomy is far from being fully achieved at the present moment, and has little chance of being achieved unless the fiscal powers of the local governments are strengthened, including a more equal division of power among the richer and poorer areas.

Making its chief aim "to provide adequate and independent sources of revenue for local government," it proposed (1) a strengthening of independent local taxes, (2) the elimination of all except "promotional" subsidies, (3) the establishment of a general equalization grant system in place of the Local Distribution Tax, (4) a relaxation of controls over the issuing of local bonds, and (5) the establishment of a permanent Local Finance Commission to adjust fiscal relations between the central and the local governments.

Acknowledging that the allocations of functions and finances were inseparable, the report recommended the establishment of a commission to investigate and perform a reallocation of functions among the various levels of government. This commission was to operate under the principles that (1) the functions of the three levels of government should be clearly demarcated, and each specific function should be assigned exclusively to one level of government; (2) each function should be allocated to that level of government equipped by virtue of its size, power, and financial resources to perform it efficiently; and (3) in the interests of local autonomy each function should be given to the lowest appropriate level of government, with municipalities having first priority.

When the Shoup Report was made public, Prime Minister Yoshida said that it should be adopted not piecemeal but in toto if it was to become a basis for a rational and fair tax system. The finance minister, however, accepted the report with some reservation. While rejoicing in the recommended tax reductions, he felt it was "too theoretical to be realized" in respect to the local finance system. Even the former Home Ministry officials, who welcomed and supported its "bold philosophy of local autonomy," were not in favor of adopting the report in its entirety.

The major stumbling block to the Japanese was its "too clear" principle of delineating functions and responsibilities. The report took the view that a clear separation of functions and responsibilities among the three levels of government, giving priority to the municipalities, would lead to local autonomy. This view, however, was incompatible with the theory and practice of traditional Japanese local self-government. Japanese officials believed that local government should serve dual functions both for its community and for the national administration and that the prefectures should be the cornerstone of the system. This basic clash of views led to the selective adoption of the report's recommendations.

The report recommended the abolition of subsidies based on the "theory of dual responsibility" and advocated the equalization grant system for purposes of fiscal adjustment. Fierce opposition to the Local Finance Equalization Grant Law came from various ministries, which held that the replacement of subsidies with equalization grants would endanger the performance of national affairs under their jurisdiction. Accordingly, incorporated in the bill was a provision for the withholding or return of grants in cases where a local government did not follow the orders of the competent ministers. The Education Ministry, with support from CI&E, even introduced a special law for compulsory education expenses. Although a letter by MacArthur dated April 11, 1950, decided against these attempts to water down the equalization grant system, more than 170 different subsidies continued after the new system had been established.[27]

Another problem was the method of determination of the total amount of the equalization grant. The report recommended that the total amount be determined by adding the differences between the sums required by the local governments and their tax revenues. But to determine the amount annually in the budget-making process caused uneasiness among local finance officials, since they had seen the Local Distribution Tax cut in half in the previous year. The final method introduced in the law conformed basically to the Shoup Report, leaving the task of measurement of amounts and their distribution to a newly proposed Local Finance Commission.

Thus the organization and powers of a Local Finance Commission became still another focus of attention.[28] After the enactment of the LFL, the former Local Finance Commission was integrated into a Local Autonomy Agency which was established in June 1949. This agency was to facilitate liaison between the central and local governments in both administrative and financial matters with a state minister at its head. The Shoup Report recommended the establishment of a new Local Finance Commission in place of the Local Autonomy Agency. The officials of the agency accordingly drafted a plan to create a Local Autonomy Commission combining the functions of the agency with those of the Finance Commission proposed by Shoup. This proposal met with opposition from the Finance Ministry on the Japanese side and also from the GS. In the end the Local Autonomy Agency was allowed to continue along with the Local Finance Commission, which was made independent of the cabinet.

The last problem raised by Shoup was the review and reallocation of functions among the three levels of government. The Local Administration Investigation Committee (commonly known as the Kambe Committee) was established in December 1949 to draw up such a reallocation plan.[29] The Kambe Committee referred to the three principles of the Shoup Report as the principles of clarification of administrative responsibility, of efficiency, and of municipal priority, and applied them as broadly as possible within the framework of a Japanese system.

The main issue was, as expected, the principle of clarifying administrative responsibility. The Kambe report took the line that "as far as possible, the affairs within the boundaries of a local public entity should be allocated to that local government" and that the affairs of the central government should be limited to those "directly necessary for the state's continued existence." The report enumerated twenty-nine functions for the central government, leaving all others to local governments. The Kambe Committee also noted the "complexities of modern life," although somewhat differently from the way Hussey did in his memo of 1947.[30] The report recognized the existence of "a large number of functions that, while of national significance, should be performed by local government close to the people in accordance with their will" and held that it was "natural for the state and local government to work together toward a common goal, while clarifying their responsibilities." One need hardly point out that this did not fulfill the principle of separation of functions set forth in the Shoup Report. The Kambe report recommended the continuance of the agency delegation system with some reservations.

Although the report admitted the dual functions of local government, it was not a mere reiteration of the old concept of "local self-government." While the system of delegation of functions would continue, it was proposed that their scope be stated in the LAL so as to put an end to their limitless expansion by central ministries. Following the Shoup Report, the Kambe report recommended that "affairs belonging to local government should, as a rule, be allocated to the municipalities." It also recommended allowing a variety of local government organizations, while suggesting the amalgamation of municipalities to make them stronger. Thus the Kambe report made a complete restudy of the nature of local administration and finance, and attempted to draw up a new blueprint for them. The report, however, was in effect shelved and fated to become, as Steiner wrote, the "flowering of the last rose in the Indian summer of local autonomy reform."[31]

Changes in the environment brought about this fate. In implementing the new Occupation policy of NSC-13/2, MacArthur had displayed a positive attitude toward economic recovery but a negative one toward the reversal of reforms already initiated. While the coordination of policy with respect to a peace treaty had been carried on within the U.S. government,[32] MacArthur gradually shifted his position to allow the Japanese government to proceed toward a "de facto peace." The outbreak of the Korean War in June 1950 accelerated this shift in his attitude.

Keeping pace with this shift by MacArthur, Prime Minister Yoshida prepared a letter to SCAP in which he tried "to seek your advice concerning the problem of repealing or revising certain laws and ordinances promulgated during these past years of Allied occupation." Yoshida continued further, "Of course, my government has no intention to alter the fundamentals of democratic government. The proposed measures are calculated to secure democracy more firmly by adapting the existing legislation to the actual conditions of the country." He enumerated several laws and ordinances to be reviewed, including the LAL.[33]

With the sudden dismissal of MacArthur, the Yoshida letter was handed over to the new SCAP, General Matthew Ridgway, who marked Constitution Day in May 1951 by giving the Japanese government the right to review existing laws and ordinances. An Ordinance Review Committee, established in response to Ridgway's statement, undertook a large-scale review of Occupation legislation from the standpoint of "adapting to the actual conditions of the country" and "rectification of excesses."[34] The report on administrative reforms prepared by this committee in August 1951 provided new guidelines in place of those of the Kambe report.

It elevated the doctrine of "simple and efficient administrative organization, based on the principle of democracy," thus leading toward administrative streamlining. It recommended that the Local Finance Commission be combined with the Local Autonomy Agency and that the Public Safety Commissions and Boards of Education of municipalities with populations under 150,000 be abolished. No positive statements concerning "local autonomy" appeared in this report at all. Since its recommendations restored a Japanese coloring and were supported by the personal leadership of the prime minister, it goes without saying that they had a better chance for adoption than the Kambe report. From them came a bill amending the LAL which was passed in September 1952.

Continuity in Changes

The reforms during the Occupation marked a new stage in the development of the Japanese local government system. This does not mean that a complete new system was born out of these reforms; many legacies of the past continued in modified form. However, an overstressing of this inheritance from the past obscures the real changes that centralized control suffered under the Occupation reforms. We shall now consider the legacy of Occupation reforms from the standpoint of change and continuity.

The process of reform explains to some extent the character of the reforms. The reforms during the Occupation were not carried out by the Occupation authorities alone, but by using the existing Japanese government, if not always supporting it. This "indirect rule" made it easy to preserve existing central-local relations.

The local government reforms during the Occupation were promoted by four actors. The first main actor was the GS. Expecting to plant "local autonomy" in Japanese soil, the GS tried to introduce a type of home rule system first into the constitution and then into the LAL. It also tried to deprive the Home Ministry of its powers over local governments. Differences of opinion within the GS, however, hindered it from achieving a strong and consistent policy. The second main actor was the Home Ministry and its successors. The Home Ministry as well as the GS advocated the strengthening of "local self-government." To the ministry it was already an established policy to allow more latitude to local governments, as long as the ministry kept ultimate control over them. The ministry identified itself as a defender of local governments against the other central ministries. Its main goal was to preserve its dual functions in the central government. The third actor was the other central ministries of the Japanese government that delegated functions to local governments and claimed preference for them. They were rivals of the Home Ministry, since they demanded priority for their functions without respect to local conditions. The last actor was other staff sections of GHQ, which were sometimes in conflict with GS in implementing their own Occupation policies. As time went on, the last two actors allied themselves with their respective counterparts against the decentralization policies of the GS and the Home Ministry. In this process local governments themselves played only a subordinate role. This was the reason why the GS emphasized local autonomy and the Home Ministry acted as sponsor for local governments' interests. The Diet's role also was limited, although it was ostensibly established by the GS as "the highest organ of state power."

The first round of reforms was initiated by the Home Ministry and proceeded at its pace. After the adoption of the new constitution, the GS caught up with the Home Ministry and took the lead in the second and third rounds. Although it was able to integrate the old LGOR into the new LAL, the Home Ministry lost its power over local governments and was finally abolished by the GS. The conflict between them derived from their conflicting perceptions of "local autonomy."

Keeping pace with these reform politics, another conflict developed between the Home Ministry and other national ministries. This centered on the issue of how to perform national functions at the local level. The

Home Ministry advocated local performance under the comprehensive supervision of the governors or mayors, but the other ministries wanted to preserve their own specific controls over them. The LAL removed the power of the Home Ministry while providing for the continuance of the powers of other ministries. The other ministries, additionally, could establish their own branch offices despite opposition from the Home Ministry.

After the dissolution of the Home Ministry, the issue of the other ministries' relations to local government came to the fore in the GS. The former Home Ministry officials were in search of a new local government system without the Home Ministry. In this phase the GS and the former Home Ministry officials were allies sharing a common goal of "local autonomy." But this goal was superseded by the new goal of "economic recovery." To achieve economic recovery the Dodge plan would have sacrificed local finances to national reconstruction; the Shoup Report, in contrast, sought to revitalize the philosophy of "local autonomy"; and the Kambe report, following Shoup, proposed a new idea of "local self-government" from a Japanese point of view.

Were these reports too late? They were in the sense that there were not strong enough supporters to reform the existing system along the lines of these comprehensive plans. However, if the Home Ministry had been strong enough to reform the system, it would not have produced a plan like the Kambe report. That report was produced after a third round of reforms, during which the Japanese officials had learned a good deal about the process of interacting effectively with GS.

What were the legacies of the Occupation reforms to the local government system in Japan? The Occupation officials tried to introduce American institutions into Japan—as an American observed, "in our image and likeness." But it is too hasty to characterize their attempt as an "Americanization of Japan,"[35] since this view neglects too many legacies of the past inherited by the LAL and does not explain adequately the failure of the GS's attempt to introduce a home rule system in Japan. On the other hand, it would be a half-truth to discern the LAL as the only heir of the LGOR and conclude therefrom that the essence of the prewar centralized system is nearly intact despite some modifications in form.[36] Emphasizing the continuity in the administrative laws, such a view makes light of the changes in the constitution and of the significance of changes of legal forms in the unified LAL. We need another view to evaluate accurately continuity and change in the postwar local government system.

The Occupation reforms accelerated a trend toward decentralization that had already existed under the prewar local government system. The expansion of the powers of local residents and the local assemblies was an already established goal in the process of reorganization from wartime administration to postwar administration. To the Home Ministry officials these were familiar issues in encouraging "local self-government." Through these measures the power of local governments was strengthened beyond what it had been in the prewar system.

The Occupation went much further when it made the prefectural governor a local official and dissolved the Home Ministry itself. Without initiatives from the Occupation, these reforms would not have been accomplished, at least under Home Ministry auspices. Even so, such trends existed in prewar experience. The popular election of governors had been advocated since the 1920s, and "reorganizations" of the Home Ministry, too, had taken place as national functions became more complex. The history of the Home Ministry was, in a sense, a history of transferring its functions to other and newer agencies. Its dissolution brought this trend to completion.

As a consequence of these reforms, central-local relations in the postwar system underwent great change in the direction of local autonomy. This does not mean, however, that control by the central government was completely eradicated. Although the Home Ministry was "the focal point for central control," it was only one point for such control. Other ministries' local relationships were left nearly intact, since local government performed national functions as before. In performing national functions delegated to it, local government is still under control of the respective ministries and financially dependent on national subsidies. Where coordination of national-local relations is concerned, it might be said that general control by the Home Ministry was replaced by treasury control by the Finance Ministry upon a de facto basis. Under the postwar system, a popularly elected governor or mayor could play a real leadership role, but he would have to find the financial resources to support it.

As local governments continued to perform dual functions, it was natural that an agency like the Local Autonomy Agency should be established. Local government needed a "representative" in the cabinet to protect its interests as a whole, otherwise it would be left at the mercy of the various central ministries. The establishment of the new Ministry of Home Affairs (Jichishō) in 1960, although the culmination of this effort, did not amount to a revival of the old Home Ministry.

A phrase in the new constitution—"the principle of local autonomy"— was helpful in assisting the postwar system to take roots in Japanese society. It served as a bulwark for postwar reforms against a restoration of the prewar system. Since this phrase permitted various "misconceptions" of its meaning, people could refer to it freely in defending their own concept of "local autonomy."

Although the drastic changes originally intended by the GS were not completely implemented by the Japanese government, the Occupation accelerated changes that already existed in previous Japanese experience.

Some of these reforms would not have been introduced without the influence of the Occupation, while others were not able to take root in Japanese soil despite the influence of the Occupation. This selective adoption was made possible not only by Japanese officials but by the Japanese people as well. Throughout these changes the Japanese people chose decentralization, which made for continuity in the changes.

The postwar local government system therefore, while not according with the plans of either the GS or the Home Ministry, is a product of the Occupation's reforms. This leaves us with a still more fundamental question about the legacy of the Occupation: Can a result of this sort be termed "planned political change?"

Notes

1. For specific information on what follows, see Kurt Steiner, *Local Government in Japan* (Stanford University Press, 1965); Kikegawa Hiroshi, *Jichi gojūnenshi* [Fifty-year history of local self-government] (reprinted by Bunsei Shoin, 1977); Tsuji Kiyoaki, *Nihon no chihō jichi* [Local autonomy in Japan] (Iwanami Shoten, 1976).

2. Usui Mitsuaki, "Chihō zaisei no tenkai to Shoup kankoku" [The Shoup recommendations and the development of local finances], in *Shoup kankoku to wagakuni no zaisei* [The Shoup recommendations and our finances], Nihon sozei kenkyū kyōkai, 1983.

3. Amakawa Akira, "Regionalism and Autonomy: The Continuing Debate in Japan" (Paper presented at a conference on Local Institutions in National Development, Bellagio, Italy, March 15–19, 1982).

4. For details on what follows, see Amakawa Akira, "Senryō shoki no seiji jōkyō" [The political scene in the early Occupation period], *Shakai kagaku kenkyū*, vol. 26, no. 3; "Chihō jichi seido no kaikaku" [Reform of the local government system], in *Sengo kaikaku 3: seiji katei*, Tōkyō Daigaku Shakai Kagaku Kenkyūjo, ed. (Tōkyō Daigaku Shuppankai, 1974).

5. On the draft of the constitution, see Government Section, GHQ/SCAP, *Political Reorientation of Japan*, 2 vols. (GPO, 1949); Takayanagi Kenzō, Ōtomo Ichirō, and Tanaka Hideo, eds., *Nihonkoku kempō seitei no katei* [Formulation of the Japanese constitution], 2 vols. (Yuhikaku, 1972; hereafter cited as *Rowell Papers*); Tanaka Hideo, *Kenpō seitei katei oboegaki* [Notes on the establishment of the Japanese constitution] (Yuhikaku, 1979).

6. For the committee draft, see *Rowell Papers*, No. 11 H1. Concerning Tilton, see Harry E. Wildes, *Typhoon in Tokyo* (George Allen & Unwin, 1950), pp. 150–152; Justin Williams, *Japan's Political Revolution under MacArthur* (University of Tokyo Press, 1979), pp. 59–61. On the drafting of chapter 8 of the constitution, see Amakawa Akira, "Chihōjichihō no kōzō" [Structure of the Local Autonomy Law], in *Senryoki nihon no keizai to seiji* [Economics and politics in occupied Japan], ed. Nakamura Takafusa (Tōkyō Daigaku Shuppankai, 1979).

7. For the drafts by Hussey and Kades, see Tanaka, *Kenpō seitei katei oboegaki*, pp. 166–167 (although both are cited as written by Rowell). The author obtained a copy of the handwritten draft courtesy of Professor Tanaka.

8. Satō Tatsuo, "Kempō daihasshō oboegaki" [Memorandum on chapter 8 of the Constitution], in *Chihō Jichi ronbunshū* [Documents on local government], ed. Jichichō (Chihō Zaimukyōkai, 1954). The Satō Papers are located at the National Diet Library; Kurt Steiner analyzes the confrontations between GS and Satō in his *Local Government in Japan,* pp. 81–84.

9. For details on the following events, see Jichi Daigakkō, *Sengo jichishi II (shōwa 21 nen no chihō seido kaisei)* [History of postwar self-government (the 1946 local government reforms)] (Jichi Daigakkō, 1947); Takagi Shōsaku, "Chiji kōsensei to chūō tōsei" [The popular election of prefectural governors and central control], in *Gendai gyōsei to kanryōsei* [Contemporary administration and the bureaucracy], vol. 2, ed. Taniuchi Yuzuru et al. (Tōkyō Daigaku Shuppankai, 1974).

10. Memorandum for Chief, Government Section (referred to below as m/c, GS), no title (Tilton) April 30, 1946; m/c, GS "Commentary on Report on Local Government Branch, dated 30 April 1946" (Hussey) May 29, 1946; m/c, GS "Local Government Recommendations, Public Administration Division Concurrence" (Tilton) July 9, 1946. National Records Center, Record Group (RG) 331.

11. For the Special Legal Investigation Commission and the Local Administrative Offices Law, see Amakawa Akira, "Shinkempō taisei no seibi" [Consolidation of the new constitutional system], in *Taiheiyō sensō* [World War II], ed. Kindai nihon kenkyūkai (Yamakawa Shuppansha, 1982).

12. m/c, GS "News Release for the Ministry of Home Affairs re Local Government Reform Bills" (Tilton) July 26, 1946.

13. For material from the Local Institutions Inquiry Council concerning enactment of the Local Autonomy Law, see *Kaisei chihō seido shiryō dai-san bu* [Part 3, materials on the reform of the local government system] (Naijikyoku, 1948); *Sengo jichishi V (chihō jichihō no seitei)* [Volume 5, history of postwar local government (Establishment of the Local Autonomy Law)] (Jichi Daigakkō, 1963).

14. *Political Reorientation,* vol. 1, pp. 284–288; m/c, GS "Dissolution of Feudalistic Quasi-Governmental Institution" (Tilton) June 9, 1946 [?]; m/c, GS "Questions Re Tonari Gumi System" (Tilton) November 5, 1946; *Sengo jichishi I (tonarigumi oyobi chōnaikai, burakukai nado no haishi)* [History of postwar self-government I (Abolition of neighborhood associations)] (Jichi Daigakkō, 1960).

15. *Political Reorientation,* vol. 1, pp. 135–138; Steiner, *Local Government in Japan,* pp. 75–77; *Sengo jichishi VIII (Naimushō no kaitai)* [History of postwar self-government 8 (Dissolution of the Home Ministry)] (Jichi Daigakkō, 1966); Hirano Takashi, "Sengo kaikaku to naimushō no kaitai" [Postwar reforms and the dissolution of the Home Ministry], in *Shuyo shokoku no gyōsei kaikaku* [Administrative reform in the major powers], ed. Taguchi Fukuji (Keisō Shobō, 1982).

16. m/c, GS "Recommendations Regarding the Ministry of Home Affairs" (J. M. Maki) July 19, 1946; J. M. Maki, "The Role of the Bureaucracy in Japan," *Pacific Affairs* (December 1947); Dr. Maki "made [a] systematic survey of the entire administrative structure and of the personalities involved." Wildes, *Typhoon in Tokyo,* p. 94.

17. Memorandum for the Record (m/r), "Dissolution of the Home Ministry" (G. J. Swope), June 30, 1947; interview with Maeda Katsumi, December 14,

1977. The Home Ministry officials were suspicious of Maeda, a former Finance Ministry man, when he proposed the transfer of local financial functions to the Finance Ministry.

18. m/c, GS "Abolition of Regional Administrative Affairs Bureaus" (F. E. Hays), April 30, 1947; m/c, GS "Home Minister Uyehara" (Pieter K. Roest), May 1, 1947; m/c, GS "Mr. Uyehara, Home Minister" (Roest), May 24, 1947. For the process of the revision of the LAL, see *Sengo jichishi VII (shōwa 22–23 nen no chihō jichihō kaisei)* [History of postwar self-government (The 1947–1948 revision of the Local Autonomy Law)] (Jichi Daigakkō, 1965).

19. On the movement by big cities, see Steiner, *Local Government in Japan,* pp. 178–181. Governor Uchiyama Iwatarō, a former diplomat working then as the governor of Kanagawa Prefecture, endeavored to influence the GS attitude on the prefectures. He petitioned Tilton and General Eichelberger, commander of the Eighth Army in Yokohama. The Diary of Uchiyama Iwataro, November 4, 1946; December 23, 1946; and September 23, 1947. The author had access to the Uchiyama Diary with the approval of the late governor's family.

20. m/c, GS "Local Autonomy" (Hussey), December 12, 1947; *Sengo jichishi VII.*

21. Memo for Chief of Staff, "Transfer of Local Government Division of Government Section" (Whitney) May 13, 1948; Headquarters Eighth Army, Office of the Commanding General, "Information Plan for Local Autonomy Law," June 17, 1948. For the enactment of ordinances, see Oppler to Hauge, "The Unchecked Local Legislation," January 8, 1948; Steiner, *Local Government in Japan,* p. 128; Ozaki Osamu, *Kōan jōrei seitei hishi* [Secret history of the establishment of the Public Safety Regulations] (Tsuge Shobō, 1978).

22. Ōkurashō zaiseishi shitsu, ed., *Shōwa zaiseishi, shūsen kara kōwa made 16—chihō zaisei* [Financial history of the Shōwa period, from the end of the war to the peace, 16—Local Finance] (Tōyō Keizai Shimpōsha, 1978); *Sengo jichishi XII (chihō zeizaisei seido no kaikaku, I)* [History of postwar self-government (Reform of the local tax and finance system, I)] (Jichi Daigakkō, 1969). Shibata Mamoru, "Chihō zaisei seido no kaikaku to chihō zaisei iinkai" [Reform of the local finance system and the Local Finance Commission], in *Jichi jihō* II; Shibata Mamoru, "Chihō jichihō to chihō zaiseihō" [The Local Autonomy Law and Local Finance Law], in *Jichi kenkyū,* vol. 25, nos. 6 and 25; and Shibata Mamoru, *Jichi no nagare no naka de—sengo chihō zeizaisei gaishi* [In the wake of self-government—an unofficial history of postwar local taxes and finances] (Gyōsei, 1975).

23. *Political Reorientation,* vol. 2, pp. 711–714; on branch offices, see Steiner, *Local Government in Japan,* pp. 318–321. Memorandum for Deputy Chiefs of Staff, "Readjustment of Local Offices of the National Government" (Whitney) June 2, 1948, and memos attached to this paper.

24. *Sengo jichishi XII (chihō zeizaisei seido no kaikaku II)* (Jichi Daigakkō, 1972).

25. Ōkurashō zaiseishi shitsu, ed., *Tai senryogun hiroku Watanabe Takeshi nikki* [The Watanabe Takeshi Diary, an anti-occupation secret memoir] (Tōyō keizai, 1983), esp. October 2, 1947, and October 4, 1947. Watanabe was a liaison official of the Finance Ministry.

26. *Shōwa zaiseishi 16,* chap. 3, and *Sengo jichishi XIII (chihō zeizaisei seido*

no kaikaku III-1) (Jichi Daigakkō, 1975) give detailed information on the Shoup Report.

27. Concerning the discussion within GHQ, see m/r, "Conference Re National Government Aid to Local Government" (Osborne Hauge), October 11, 1949; m/r, "Inter-SCAP Conference Re Interpretation of Shoup Tax Mission Recommendation Concerning National Equalization Grants" (Nicholas Cottrell), October 14, 1949.

28. Steiner, *Local Government in Japan*, pp. 109–110, 302–305; m/c, GS "Local Finance Commission Establishment Law" (A. O. Carpenter), February 28, 1950; m/r, "Article 5, para 3, of the Local Finance Commission Establishment Law" (Kurt Steiner) May 26, 1950. The author obtained these copies courtesy of Professor Steiner.

29. On the Kambe Committee, see Sakuma Tsutomu, "Chihō gyōsei chōsa iinkaigi no tanjō" [The birth of the Local Administration Investigation Committee], *Jichi kenkyū*, vol. 26, no. 1. This committee submitted its first report on the redistribution of administrative affairs in December 1950.

30. Hussey wrote in his memo cited in n. 20 above: "The modern trend has everywhere been toward greater centralization as well as toward greater uniformity of administration. . . . we cannot ignore the fact that the complexities of modern life and the case of modern communication render anything near complete local autonomy or full decentralization archaic and dangerous."

31. Steiner calls the Kambe report "a constructive and careful blueprint for a system of genuine local self-government." Steiner, *Local Government in Japan*, pp. 112–113.

32. Chihiro Hosoya, "The Road to San Francisco: The Shaping of American Policy on the Japanese Peace Treaty," *The Japanese Journal of American Studies*, no. 1 (1981).

33. Yoshida's letter to MacArthur, April 9, 1951. In the attached sheet the LAL is cited as follows: "Because of the emphasis placed on the importance of local autonomy, a considerable number of affairs which intrinsically belong to the State have been delegated to local public entities. Under the existing system the Cabinet's position is too weak without adequate authority for unified execution of these affairs. It is desired to render more effective the Cabinet's directive authority over local public entities with respect to these State affairs."

34. John Dower, *Empire and Aftermath: Yoshida Shigeru and the Japanese Experience, 1948–1954* (Harvard University Press, 1979), pp. 356–361; S. Sidney Ulmer, "Local Autonomy in Japan since the Occupation," *Journal of Politics*, vol. 19 (February 1957).

35. George A. Warp, "In Our Image and Likeness," *National Municipal Review*, vol. 42 (April 1953), p. 178; Warp, " 'Americanization' in Japan," ibid., vol. 41 (October 1952). In these articles Warp criticized the Occupation policies on local government. The former Home Ministry officials joined in chorus with him after regaining their power after the Occupation.

36. Akagi Suruki, *Gyōsei sekinin no kenkyū* [A study of administrative responsibility] (Iwanami, 1978), chap. 2.

10

The U.S. Occupation of Okinawa and Postwar Reforms in Japan Proper

Ota Masahide

It is interesting to note the way researchers have treated postwar Okinawa in their studies of U.S. postwar policy toward Japan. Considering Okinawa in this context raises questions about the so-called postwar reforms, while not doing so raises questions about the researcher's own views of Okinawa. Because both the Japanese and United States governments treated Okinawa as if it were not a part of Japan, there has been a general tendency to look upon the decision to separate Okinawa from Japan as natural or inevitable. This has led many researchers to overlook the importance of comprehensively evaluating and interpreting U.S. postwar policy toward Japan in the context of the Okinawa question.

It is not true, as is often claimed, that the separation of Okinawa was an unavoidable consequence of Japan's unconditional surrender. The tendency to consider it as such, however, has diverted researchers from scrutinizing the separation itself and determining whether or not it was indeed as inevitable as is generally assumed. Consequently, the factors underlying the separation have never been adequately clarified, nor has its legality ever been seriously questioned.

This chapter will examine the U.S. occupation of Okinawa and attempt to relate it to general U.S. postwar policy toward Japan by clarifying the factors that lay behind the separation. Because of space limitations, discussion will be limited to events prior to 1952, when the peace treaty took effect.

U.S. postwar occupation policy toward Japan and toward Okinawa are essentially two sides of the same coin. At first glance, the U.S. occupation of Japan seems to be one in which the "occupier" (the United States or the Allied nations) and the "occupied" (Japan proper) interacted directly. Schematically expressed, however, Okinawa stood between the occupier and the occupied, and the occupation of Okinawa made the occupation of Japan proper easier for the Allied forces. The United States thought of Okinawa as a "means" of maximizing the effectiveness and success of its occupation policies in Japan proper. On the other hand, for its own advantage and the eventual strengthening of its position as a defeated nation, Japan was perfectly willing to have part of its territory detached and used as a military base by the foreign occupying power. As a result of this coincidence of interests between occupier and occupied, Okinawa was not only detached from Japan proper but, against the will of its people, was compelled to play the role of a military and political pawn. In short, the separation of Okinawa was a product of U.S.-Japanese collaboration, albeit collaboration between somewhat unequal partners.

Planning the Occupation of Okinawa

It is possible to divide the postwar U.S. military administration of Okinawa into three phases: (1) planning, (2) assault or combat, and (3) garrison. The planning phase lasts from the start of planning by the Tenth Army staff in Hawaii until the actual landing of U.S. forces on Okinawa; the second phase runs from March 26, 1945, when the Kerama landing took place, to the end of organized resistance by Japa nese forces on June 21; the third phase terminates with the reversion of Okinawa to Japan in May 1972.

The drafting and adoption of plans and policies for the military government of Okinawa began in conjunction with the planning of the Okinawa campaign some time in the summer of 1944. The plans were drawn up by the military affairs section of the Tenth Army, which was the principal force in the Okinawa campaign. This military affairs section was later transformed into a civil affairs section with headquarters at Schofield Barracks on Oahu Island. Fifteen navy and four army officers were dispatched from Washington to plan the military government of Okinawa. Since the Okinawa campaign was to be a joint operation of the army, navy, and Marine Corps, all three shared responsibility for the actual drafting and adoption of the policies.[1] The planning for the U.S. military government of Okinawa, therefore, differed greatly from that for Japan proper in that the actual combat forces involved assumed the central role.

In addition to the career military personnel of the assault unit, former professors and others assisted in the work. About the same time that military government personnel of the Tenth Army were working on the planning, a handbook entitled *The Civil Affairs Handbook: Ryūkyū (Loochoo) Islands* was being prepared by Dr. George P. Murdock, a navy lieutenant commander and former professor of anthropology at Yale University, working with some graduates of Columbia University's Naval School of Military Administration. A similar handbook was also prepared by the survey analysis department of the Office of Strategic Services (OSS), but this was primarily for use in all prefectures of Japan proper.[2]

In addition to the *Civil Affairs Handbook,* a document entitled *The Okinawa of the Loochoo Islands: A Minority Group in Japan* was published by the Office of the Chief of Naval Operations. This is an important source for information on the perceptions on which U.S. military policy toward Okinawa was based. While the former describes external conditions of Okinawa, the latter focuses on the ways of thinking and behavior of the Okinawans. Many of those who participated in military government activities say that it was very helpful and widely used in the actual administration of the islands. The book consists of three parts: Part 1 analyzes Okinawa's position in the context of Japanese history; part 2 describes the past and current (1943) living conditions of Okinawan immigrants in Hawaii and touches upon their social and psychological characteristics; and part 3 clarifies the unique characteristics of Okinawans and Okinawan society. It specifically discusses the possibility of using this knowledge in psychological warfare against the Japanese on the mainland and in Okinawa.[3]

Although space does not permit a close examination of this important document, its basic message is that in any Japanese communities, whether in Hawaii, South America, or the South Seas, the mainland Japanese have always discriminated against and looked down upon Okinawans as not "real" Japanese. The Okinawans, for their part, have always resented such treatment. This navy document emphasizes the existence of a clear-cut cleavage between the two groups and recommends playing upon this antagonism of the Okinawans to the maximum extent possible to turn the tide of war in favor of the American forces. In other words, the authors of this document believed that the underlying dislike between Okinawans and people from Japan proper was of a nature that could be readily exploited for psychological warfare purposes on the battlefield and that this cleavage was "a natural phenomenon rooted in ethnological differences."[4]

The U.S. military acted accordingly in its psychological warfare campaigns against the inhabitants of Okinawa and tried to fuel their feelings of estrangement from Japan. Although the existence of "ethnological differences" between Okinawans and people in Japan proper is dubious scientifically, this view was later bluntly reiterated by General MacArthur in regard to the draft of a treaty of peace with Japan on September 1, 1947: "The draft provides for the retention of the Ryūkyū Islands by Japan. Control over this group must be vested in the United States as absolutely essential to the defense of our Western Pacific Frontier. It is not indigenous to Japan ethnologically, does not contribute to Japan's economic welfare, nor do the Japanese people expect to be permitted to retain it. It is basically strategic, and in my opinion, failure to secure it for control by the United States might prove militarily disastrous."[5]

MacArthur's remarks might have been intended to justify a strategy of "divide and rule" for Okinawa. Those who planned U.S. policy toward Japan during the war attempted at one time to start a "free Japan movement" based on people like Ōyama Ikuo, a noted liberal, and others who lived abroad and were critical of Japanese militarism.[6] *The Okinawa of the Loochoo Islands* records that the U.S. military actually considered the possibility of promoting a "free Okinawa movement" by mobilizing anti-Japanese Okinawans in South America. According to this document, since 60 percent of the Japanese community in Peru consisted of Okinawans critical of Japanese from the mainland, the "free Okinawa movement" would have a good chance of success if the situation could be skillfully exploited. Furthermore, since Okinawans had had to emigrate abroad because they were conquered, destroyed, and driven from their homeland by mainland Japanese, "a publicity campaign could remind them of their past glories as an independent kingdom as well as their traditional role as the bearer of the great Chinese civilization." The authors of this document also reasoned that if the Okinawans in Hawaii and Brazil could be organized behind a "free Okinawa movement," not only would the nearly 200,000 Okinawans living in Japan proper rise up against the Japanese Empire but the Chinese in Peru and other Latin American countries, who were sympathetic to the Okinawans, might cooperate with them in support of their movement.[7]

The Establishment of U.S. Military Government

Unlike U.S. occupation policy toward Japan proper, which was put into final form after a variety of specialists from different departments of the government had been duly consulted, the occupation plans for Okinawa seem to have been drafted and put into final form by a combat unit. Strictly speaking, however, the Tenth Army did not do it alone, since its policy making was guided by clearly stated principles. The Inter-Divisional Area Committee on the Far East in Washington on March 21, 1944, issued a document entitled *Japan: Military Occupation. Proclamations (Postwar Programs Committee [PWC]-120)*, which contains instructions that *The United States Army and Navy Manual of Military Government and Civil Affairs (Field Manual [FM] 27-5)*, chapters 35 and 36 of section 6, should be used as a guideline in drafting proclamations concerning the occupation of Japan.[8] Judging from their contents, the proclamations issued in Okinawa were guided by this manual.

Moreover, PWC-123, *Japan: Mandated Islands: Status of Military Government,* dated March 22, 1944, discusses the legality of setting up a military government and establishing military bases in the mandated territories of the Pacific.[9] These arguments were also applied to Okinawa. The document that provided the actual framework for the plan to establish military government in Okinawa, however, was a directive issued by

C. W. Nimitz, Commander-in-Chief, Pacific Ocean Area, dated November 3, 1944. Apparently based on JCS 1231, *Directive for Military Government in the Japanese Outlying Islands,* Nimitz's directive, *A Proposed Political Directive for Military Government of the Japanese Outlying Islands,* was sent to the Tenth Army on the same day that he was ordered by the Joint Chiefs of Staff to secure one or more tactical positions on the Ryūkyū Islands.

As soon as the military affairs section of the Tenth Army received Nimitz's directive, they began to give special training sessions for military government officers to familiarize them with Okinawa. And, in consultation with Section 1 of the General Staff, they started to prepare concrete proposals for the establishment of military government. The actual planning for military government on Okinawa was triggered by a strategic switch from Taiwan to Okinawa—a previously planned attack on Taiwan was canceled. As a result, numerous revisions and last minute changes had to be made before the plan was finally adopted. The military affairs section is said to have had considerable difficulty because of its low standing within the Command Headquarters. Lieutenant Commander Malcolm S. MacLean, a former professor, who served as head of the military affairs section until mid-November 1944, had originally been involved in planning for the occupation of Taiwan but was then shifted to head the planning for a military government on Okinawa. MacLean soon fell ill, however, and Brigadier General William E. Crist replaced him.[10]

With the appointment of a general officer as its chief, the military affairs section, which had until then been under Section 1 of the General Staff, became more independent. It was designated C-5, that is Section 5 of the General Staff, and had equal ranking with the other major sections in the Command Headquarters. In this manner the importance of military government in the overall war strategy came finally to be recognized.

By December 1944 the staff was increased and, reflecting the fact that the Okinawa campaign was a joint army-navy operation, the military affairs section was made responsible to both the army and the navy.[11] However, rivalries between these two branches caused considerable difficulty, and the Tenth Army military affairs section had to expedite its planning for the military occupation of Okinawa while simultaneously striving to strike a balance between the two rival branches.

By the end of November the Tenth Army's military affairs section had received *The Civil Affairs Handbook* and *The Okinawa of the Loochoo Islands* from the Office of the Chief of Naval Operations. These documents considerably facilitated the work of the military affairs section. In January and February 1945, the Tenth Army Command distributed its *Technical Bulletin,* which contained the operational directive and general plan of implementation for military government. On March 1, 1945, *The Political, Economic, and Financial Directive for Military Government in the Occupied Islands of the Nansei Shotō and Adjacent Waters* was issued by Chester W. Nimitz, Fleet Admiral, United States Navy, Commander-in-Chief, United States Pacific Fleet and Pacific Ocean Areas. It was this directive that determined the substance of military government in Okinawa, containing as it does, among other things, the all-important Proclamation 1 (popularly known as the Nimitz Proclamation).[12]

It was on the basis of this directive that the military government of Okinawa was established at the same time as the operational strategy against Okinawa was being developed and carried out. In this respect the occupation of Okinawa was inherently different from the occupation of Japan proper.

What were the aims of this early military government? The answer is found in a radio broadcast beamed to the United States by Brigadier General William Crist, the man responsible for the military government project and, after the landing, Deputy Commander for Military Government, Okinawa. Crist explained: "The first aim of the military government is to make it possible for combat units to concentrate on the war without having to worry about non-combat personnel." Along with this paramount aim, Crist said, "The military government will take measures to provide the minimum relief needed for civilian survival under international law," and he added that he wanted to "minimize the economic burden on the United States by promoting economic self-sufficiency in the occupied territory."[13]

In short, the basic purpose of military government on Okinawa was to accomplish military ends at minimum cost to the United States. To realize that purpose it adopted a harsh policy as reflected in Crist's blunt remark: "We have no intention of playing Santa Claus for the residents of the occupied territory."[14] Such a policy might be understandable under wartime conditions, but it was characteristic of military government on Okinawa that it continued this harsh policy even after the war. For example, military government tried to separate the Amami Oshima Islands, Miyako Islands, and Yaeyama Islands from Okinawa because of their uselessness as military bases and the costs of administering them.[15]

Military government on Okinawa, based on the principle that military rule should be effected in such a manner as to minimize the financial burden on the United States, not only worked against the interests of the local residents but also hampered the activities of the military government staff. Its difficulties were by no means limited to a lack of food, clothing, and shelter. For instance, the confusion that surfaced in the command arrangements for military government on Okinawa had dire consequences. While the U.S. Joint Chiefs of Staff in 1943 had assigned

Admiral Nimitz responsibility for capturing the small islands in the Pacific and establishing military government over them, the larger land masses were assigned to the Supreme Commander of the Southwest Pacific Area, General MacArthur. Supreme authority was thereby divided according to the geographic features of the area, with both MacArthur and Nimitz in command of the army, navy, marines and air force in their respective territories. This arrangement was abruptly changed in late July 1945 on the very eve of the assault on Japan proper, when Nimitz was given command of the entire navy in the Pacific region and MacArthur command of the army in the same region. In addition, the tactical air force was newly established as a combat unit on an equal footing with the army and navy with General Carl A. Spaatz at its head, and all three branches were brought under the direct command of the Joint Chiefs of Staff. In short, when faced with the climactic invasion of Japan, the Joint Chiefs of Staff attempted to unify the command channels.[16]

But in Okinawa, which was on the receiving end of this command channel, the changes at the top caused only confusion. Moreover, the rapid demobilization following Japan's surrender added to the confusion in the military government. Space does not permit a detailed treatment of the problem, but there was a bewildering transfer of military government control between the army and the navy, illustrated by the fact that the U.S. occupation of Okinawa had some 22 different individuals at its head during 27 years of military administration.[17] It was thus impossible even to hope for consistency in government policies (particularly in civil affairs), let alone to think of formulating any long-range economic policy for Okinawa.[18] As noted by those who actually ran the military government, this situation was in part caused by the United States government's and in part by General MacArthur's indifference toward Okinawa.[19]

On June 21, 1945, the United States announced that the Japanese forces on Okinawa had ended their organized resistance and that Okinawa had been secured. With the fall of Okinawa, control of military government was transferred to the Island Command. Considering that the original function of the Island Command was to care for noncombat personnel and to supply them with goods, the transfer meant that responsibility for running the military government on Okinawa was finally placed in the right hands.

When the Island Command, also called the Army Garrison Forces, assumed complete control, military government on Okinawa entered its third or garrison phase. The new situation, however, was worse than in the combat phase. In addition to haphazard and makeshift policies resulting from confusion in the military government command channels, the situation also deteriorated because local military government specialists were being rapidly discharged. There was an especially costly departure of former university professors and others who had been involved in Okinawa's military government from the planning stages. Not all of their successors took their responsibilities seriously. The military government came to be dominated by people who had neither sympathy for nor understanding of military government, people who were simply killing time until their tours of duty ended. Their presence had most adverse effects on the Okinawan's perception of the United States. Thus, Okinawa soon became notorious even among Americans as "the logistical end of the line," "a Botany Bay for bad bureaucrats and colonels," or "a 'dumping ground' or place of exile for American personnel unwanted at GHQ in Japan proper."[20] Harlan Youel, who worked with the military government on Okinawa's economic recovery, states that within the command hierarchy Okinawa was placed under the jurisdiction of the Ryūkyū Command (RYCOM), which was under the Philippine-Ryūkyūs Command (PHILRYCOM), which in turn was under the Far East Command (FEC). Youel goes on to say that it was common practice for undesirables and useless individuals in the Far East Command to be sent to the Philippine-Ryūkyūs Command, and for the dregs of the Philippine-Ryūkyūs Command to be sent to the Ryūkyū Command.[21]

Under these circumstances, it did not take long for military government on Okinawa to slip into a period of what George Kerr has termed "indifference."[22] This state of indifference on the part of the U.S. government and military lasted until the end of 1949, when the program for transforming Okinawa into a permanent military base went into high gear. This led to a gradual change in U.S. policy toward the residents of Okinawa. Until then, however, as we have seen, numerous problems beset the military government: (1) lack of trained personnel, (2) lack of communication between U.S. military personnel and local residents caused by lack of a common language, (3) confusion caused by the division of authority between the army and navy, (4) ambiguity over the ultimate political status of the Ryūkyūs, and (5) lack of essential provisions and equipment. After noting these problems, Leonard Weiss, who had been directly involved in running the military government, concludes that these negative factors combined to make the military government a total failure[23]—a view widely shared by those familiar with the situation in Okinawa.

Thus far, we have briefly summarized the problems that beset the men who ran the military government. Let us now turn to the military government as seen by the local inhabitants.

Changes in Okinawan Views of the United States

It was obvious that the long-term success of the U.S. military government would depend largely on how the residents of the occupied territory reacted. From the standpoint of the residents, as long as the occupation policy toward Okinawa, unlike that toward Japan, did not aim at "democratic reform," the suitability of the actual policy was of secondary importance to the military occupation itself. Besides questioning its legality, Okinawans had doubts about its political and humanitarian aspects. People resented the fact that Okinawa was the only part of the Japanese Empire, aside from the northern territories, to be detached and placed under foreign military forces. They were not satisfied with justifications such as "Japan lost the war," "tension persists in the Far East," or "there is a need to ensure the security of the United States and Japan including Okinawa."

Many residents of Okinawa, having been completely brainwashed by anti-U.S. propaganda before the American landing, naively believed that capture by American troops would mean instant death for men and rape followed by death for women. Indeed, the brainwashing was so thorough that some 700 old people, women, and children actually committed mass suicide rather than be captured when U.S. forces landed on the Keramas. By contrast, practically all those who were rescued from the horrors of war by American troops were astonished and gratified at the way the American soldiers treated them. Their treatment was completely different from what they had been taught to expect. It was altogether human for Okinawans to feel deeply indebted to the Americans who had saved their lives and who had provided them with food, shelter, and clothing even in the midst of war. It was particularly so since many of the Japanese troops had not only acted thoughtlessly, but in not a few cases had indiscriminately committed atrocities. Among the Japanese soldiers were those who claimed to be protecting the residents but who actually stole food, who chased residents out of places of refuge so that they could have them to themselves, who massacred innocent natives on groundless charges such as spying, and who otherwise acted most brutally toward those local residents who had sacrificed everything they had to the war effort.

The Okinawans were the more moved by the Americans' kindness by comparison, and the Japanese soldiers more feared than the Americans.[24] The U.S. forces quickly launched a psychological campaign to take advantage of this situation and to alienate the local residents from Japan by playing up every atrocity committed by the Japanese troops.

Directive 1, which the Tenth Army promulgated on May 3, 1945, as a guideline for the officers and men in charge of military government, illustrates this with instructions that "the military government staff shall deal firmly with the residents, but must at the same time avoid cruel and incompassionate acts which would only lower them to the level of the Japanese forces." Nevertheless, the Okinawans were extremely friendly and cooperative toward the U.S. military at the beginning of the military government not because U.S. propaganda was effective but rather—and more importantly—because the people caught up in the war had no choice but to rely upon the American soldiers for their very survival.

Unlike some Okinawan intellectuals (particularly those critical of the establishment), who at first considered the U.S. military an army of liberation, the average Okinawan learned through direct contacts on the battlefield to accept the Americans on an emotional level as friendly people. In fact, unlike the intellectuals, who measured the military government against the principles of democracy, the average man reacted toward the United States in terms of what benefited him most in his daily life. But this initially positive popular opinion, based as it was on emotion and pragmatism, could be easily swayed by a change in the situation. Thus, the masses were rapidly disillusioned by the onset of confusion and indifference within the U.S. military government. Moreover, although the attitude of the Okinawan people toward the United States shifted from "favorable" to "unfavorable" seemingly as a result of the everyday behavior of the U.S. troops, this change was inevitable sooner or later, given the essential nature of military government.

Time after time, the U.S. military authorities declared that they would turn Okinawa into "a showcase of democracy." But for the staff of the military government, charged with the task of building a major base in the Pacific, trying to democratize Okinawa was like trying to square a circle.[25] Under the rationale of turning Okinawa into a permanent base, the U.S. military expropriated land in a manner that defied description.

For the Okinawans who live on it, land is never a mere plot of dirt. Frequently, it is something precious, something tied up in their affection for their ancestors. It is insurance, something they can always fall back on to eke out a subsistence. Since the U.S. military ruthlessly expropriated the land at bayonet point or even by using tanks from time to time, it is no wonder that popular attitudes toward the United States were reversed. There were times when people were not even paid for their land, and times when bulldozers leveled houses and cultural treasures that had somehow survived the war.[26] As these and other similar acts showing a complete disregard for the people's feelings became more frequent, the American troops were inevitably compared to the Japanese troops who had acted so ruthlessly during the war. Under such circumstances, it was only natural that the people should come to look upon the United States not as a liberator but as an oppressor as the military moved to turn Okinawa (beginning with the most important central areas) into a vast military base. This anti-American antagonism against the U.S. military for usurping the land was further aggravated when the military government took possession of 51 percent of the stock of the Bank of the Ryūkyūs and took over the management of key local economic organizations such as water resources, electricity, and public finance corporations.[27] Furthermore we should not overlook the fact that turning Okinawa into a military base completely changed the traditional local economy and created an economic structure utterly dependent upon the military bases.

Even in its broad outlines, then, it is clear that the occupation of Okinawa was completely different from the occupation in Japan proper. However, the Okinawan people worked on their own initiative for a "democratic reform" despite the separate rule imposed by Article 3 of the treaty between Japan and the victorious powers, an article that even Prime Minister Kishi had to admit in his Diet testimony was of a legally dubious nature despite the fact that Okinawa was thereby placed outside the scope of the Japanese constitution.[28] It is worth mentioning that the reforms that the people of Okinawa achieved were different from the "democratic reforms" of Japan proper. It is one of history's ironies that, by serving as a "negative model," the U.S. occupation forces helped the Okinawan people achieve self-reliance—something they had never had before.

By the same token, the undemocratic situation in Okinawa had the unexpected effect of calling into question the real significance of the "postwar reforms" in Japan proper. What is one to think of a Japanese government willing to detach part of its own territory and cede it to foreign military rule in blind pursuit of its own narrow interests? Questioning such heartless acts, one Japanese constitutional scholar has stated: "To the extent that the Japanese Constitution permits the security arrangements with the United States, it cannot but be inadequate as the constitution of an independent country. The most visible consequence of this flaw is the presence of U.S. military bases on Okinawa and elsewhere, for neither the Japanese Constitution nor the sovereign will of the Japanese people can exert any influence inside these bases."[29]

Okinawa's Detachment and Postwar Policy toward Japan

In order to examine the relationship between the postwar policy toward Japan and the separation of Okinawa from Japan, it is necessary to trace the two policies back to their planning and drafting stages. With regard to Okinawa's detachment, it is useful to analyze the process in terms of both military strategy and political objectives, since detachment became inevitable when the military and political exigencies converged and the Japanese government simultaneously supported it.

In early 1942 the United States began drafting the terms of Japanese surrender. Later, in August 1942, after Japan had been defeated in the battle of Midway, the United States began deliberating the question of Japan's postsurrender territorial boundaries.[30] At about the same time China declared that it would demand the return of the Ryūkyūs, Man-

churia, and Taiwan.[31] Shortly afterward, in October and November, the
drafting of postwar policy toward Japan accelerated, but it was not until
the beginning of 1943 that the problem of Okinawa came up. It is noteworthy that demands portending Okinawa's detachment appeared at
about the same time that substantive work on postwar policy toward
Japan proper began.

Following the March 1943 establishment of the Civil Affairs Department (CAD) within the Department of the Army, the Joint Chiefs of
Staff, directly responsible to the president, began to involve themselves in
the problem of establishing military governments on enemy soil.[32] This
concern affected equally Okinawa and Japan proper, although it was to
have a particularly strong influence on the future of Okinawa. When the
Allied forces captured the Solomon Islands in August 1943, U.S. policy
toward Japan began to assume concrete and clear form, and the United
States' plan to detach Okinawa from Japan proper began to crystalize.
The Cairo Conference in November 1943 was a fateful turning point for
Okinawa, for it signaled important changes both militarily and politically. On the military level, while Churchill and Roosevelt were determining the timetable for the Pacific war, they also discussed Okinawa as
one of their strategic targets.[33] On the political level, Roosevelt and
Chiang Kai-shek had dinner together during the conference and ex-
changed ideas on some ten topics, including China's international status,
the treatment of Japan's imperial family—and the problem of Okinawa.[34] Roosevelt asked Chiang whether China wanted the Ryūkyūs under
joint U.S.-Sino occupation and, later, under a mandate controlled by an
international organization with a joint U.S.-Sino administration. This
episode cannot be taken lightly in its bearing upon Okinawa's detachment. A president's statements and thinking can have an enormous influence on American foreign policy, and Roosevelt's personal diplomacy is
said to have been particularly decisive at Cairo.[35] Thus if it was true that
Roosevelt saw Okinawa not as an integral part of Japan but as a territory
destined to be separated from Japan proper, such a view could have easily
served as the basis for fundamental U.S. policy toward Okinawa.

In fact, there is no reason to believe that Roosevelt's views failed to
affect the decision-making process. The Cairo Conference is particularly
important in connection with Okinawa because the Cairo Declaration
released just after the conference is closely tied to the Potsdam Declaration and to Article 3 of the peace treaty between Japan and the Allied
forces. The Cairo Declaration states that "Japan will also *be expelled*
from all other territories which she has taken by violence or greed"
(emphasis added unless noted otherwise). To this the Potsdam Declaration adds, "The terms of the Cairo Declaration shall be carried out and
Japanese sovereignty shall be limited to the islands of Honshu, Hokkai-
do, Kyushu, Shikoku, and such minor islands as we determine." It is

commonly believed that Okinawa *was not included* among the Cairo Declaration's "territories which she has taken by violence or greed" and *was included* among the Potsdam Declaration's "such minor islands as we determine." While some scholars disagree on the latter point,[36] both the Japanese and U.S. governments took the position that Okinawa *was included* among the "minor islands" in the Potsdam Declaration. While there is no really clear and authoritative statement as to the Japanese attitude on the Cairo Declaration, it is at least possible to speculate that at some point the four heads of state may have looked upon Okinawa as a territory that Japan had annexed by force.[37] Such speculation is reasonable because even the Soviet Union, which later came out against the separation of Okinawa, went along with the other Allied powers at the Pacific War Conference of January 1944; and Stalin, having been thoroughly briefed on the history of the Ryūkyūs, told Roosevelt that he would agree if China wanted the Ryūkyūs back.[38]

There is no clear statement concerning the Ryūkyūs in the Cairo Declaration, just as there was later to be none in the Potsdam Declaration, because vagueness was politically preferable at that stage. As for the Potsdam Declaration, even though both Japan and the United States later stated that Okinawa *was included* as a "minor island," the noted specialist in international law, Yokota Kisaburo, for instance, says that Okinawa *was not included* because the term "minor islands" meant those islands in the vicinity of Japan's four major islands, and thus Okinawa did not come under Japanese jurisdiction.[39] The present writer agrees that Okinawa *was not included* simply because the crucial U.S. secret documents cited previously indicate that Okinawa *was not included and was to be treated separately from Japan.* Okinawa was not included at first because the military influence was sufficient to exclude it, but it was later included because U.S. policy changed during the conclusion of the peace treaty and because Okinawa was used as bait to draw Japan into the American camp. There is, in fact, evidence that the United States at the beginning adopted a policy that did not recognize Okinawa as belonging to Japan.

The Cairo Conference is also important because the concept discussed by Chiang Kai-shek and Roosevelt, that the United States and China share administrative authority in Okinawa under the trusteeship of an international organization, was later embodied in Article 3 of the peace treaty, unaltered except for China's role. Although it is not clear how influential Chiang Kai-shek's opinion was, it was at least an important bit of background. In other words, although most scholars have ignored the Cairo Conference because it does not contain any explicit reference to Okinawa, the historical importance of the Cairo Conference for Okinawa is clear.

In July 1943, prior to the Cairo Conference, the Territorial Subcommittee of the U.S. State Department drafted a document proposing a U.S. policy toward Okinawa that was independent of policy toward Japan. After going out of its way to refer to Okinawa by its old name as the "Liuchiu" (Ryūkyū) Islands, the document points out that the question of detaching the Ryūkyūs from Japan would be included in the forthcoming discussions of postwar territorial arrangements in the Far East and establishes 30° N as the line of demarcation. The document then discusses the history of Japan's acquisition of Okinawa and notes that the local Okinawan people strongly resent the appointment of people from the other Japanese prefectures to all appointive positions in the prefectural government. Given this historical background, the document then presents for consideration three concrete policies as alternative solutions: (1) transfer to China, (2) international administration, and (3) conditional retention by Japan.[40]

As far as this writer has been able to discover, this is the earliest document to deal with policy toward Okinawa. It is safe to conclude that the detachment of Okinawa was modeled after the alternative policies it presents. It can also be surmised that this document influenced the Cairo Conference. Since the document refers to the fact that China had demanded the Ryūkyūs' return on several occasions even before the Cairo Conference, it can be argued that Roosevelt was at least in part responding to this when he asked Chiang Kai-shek if he wanted Okinawa. In addition, the Cairo Declaration was drafted by the Regional Committee and the Territorial Subcommittee, which had participated in drafting this document.

Furthermore, this document is interesting in that it reveals the real aim involved in the separation of Okinawa. It also provides partial support for this writer's hypothesis that the postwar reforms of Japan proper were drafted and adopted on the premise of Okinawa's detachment. The document reasons that, since Japan would be defeated, disarmed, and deprived of its territories in Taiwan, Korea, and other mandated regions, Japan would not pose an immediate threat to other countries even if it were to retain Okinawa; but it might pose a long-term threat if it did so. Thus before Japan could be allowed to retain Okinawa, certain restrictions needed to be established to ensure that Okinawa would never again be used for military purposes. Periodic inspections of Okinawa by an international body over a long time could provide such assurance. Those who viewed the long-term threat as serious argued that future international security demanded that Japan be completely disarmed and Okinawa either be placed under the surveillance of an international body or be detached from Japan.

But why would Japan constitute a threat if it retained Okinawa? Although the said document does not make direct reference to this question, there are clear statements concerning this point in other records.

Simply stated, the justification for this argument is that Japan did, in fact, use Okinawa and the islands under its mandated rule as stepping stones for attacks on other nations. This is also the reason why Okinawa is always discussed in the same context as the mandated islands under Japanese control.

As is generally known, those who drafted U.S. occupation policy toward Japan were anxious to make full use of the lessons learned from the Versailles peace treaty. In pouring over voluminous documentation, this writer has been most impressed by United States regrets that Japan had been given free rein in the territories under its mandated control. This free rein is referred to as one of the most important causes of World War II. The United States clearly felt that Japan used Okinawa and the regions under its mandated rule as staging points from which it ultimately threatened U.S. security. As John Emmerson has pointed out, the United States began to take an interest in Pacific bases after World War I when the League of Nations gave Japan a mandate over these islands.[41] Ever since, the U.S. military have wanted never again to permit foreign powers, particularly Japan, to threaten the United States and other countries by ruling and fortifying Okinawa and other Pacific islands of strategic importance.

Although it is not possible here to analyze the basis of the American insistence that Japan would again become a threat if it were allowed to retain Okinawa, one historical fact must be cited. In the Meiji period, the Japanese government forced through the so-called Ryūkyū disposition to consolidate Japan's boundaries under the excuse that "in the past, as a neighbor of Japan and China, the Ryūkyū *han* (fief) was given protection by Japan while taking orders from the emperor of China. Thus it was never clear which country the Ryūkyū *han* belonged to."[42] After carrying out the "disposition," the Meiji government announced: "It goes without saying that the Ryūkyū *han* is geographically, traditionally, linguistically, and historically part of Japan."[43]

However, no sooner had this announcement been made than the Japanese government proposed its notorious *"bunto kaiyaku"* (cut up the islands and revise the treaty). Under this proposal, the Japanese government intended to offer China the Miyako and Yaeyama islands in the southern Ryūkyūs in return for commercial privileges within China. In other words, the Japanese government proposed to pursue its economic interests by partitioning territory that it had just annexed and obtain in return most-favored-nation treatment in its trade with China. History shows, however, that the real significance of this move lay elsewhere.

While the *"bunto kaiyaku"* proposal came to naught, the Chinese minister to Japan, Li Hung-chang, in a memorandum written to Ho Ju-chang during his negotiations with the Japanese, accurately predicted that once Japan had absorbed the Ryūkyūs, it would then invade Korea, Taiwan, and eventually China. What comes to mind in this connection is the point made by Ding Ming-nan in postwar *Chinese Imperialism: Its History of Violence*. The author considered the 1879 abolition of Okinawa's fief status and its establishment as a prefecture an act of "annexation" and pointed out that it was the first important step in Japan's foreign aggression against Korea and the Chinese mainland. Another author referred to the *"bunto kaiyaku"* proposal in the following manner:

> The Japanese plan was a very serious plot. The plot was to cut up the Ryūkyūs and to bribe the Ch'ing dynasty with the two most barren groups of islands into recognizing Japan's annexation of the Ryūkyūs. Another important point is that Japan wanted to take advantage of this opportunity to further its ambition of invading China by obtaining a foothold in China identical to those which the imperialistic nations of the West had already achieved. Thus this plan integrated Japan's hopes to annex the Ryūkyūs and to invade China.[44]

Thus there was historical justification for considering Japan's retention of Okinawa as a threat. Even apart from this, the various records available indicate that it was actually proposed during the course of drawing up the policy toward Japan that the earlier plan to place Okinawa under international supervision be extended to the whole of Japan and that this international surveillance be continued for 25 to 30 years to ensure Japan's complete disarmament.[45] In short, it must be borne in mind that, although the policy calling for Okinawa's separation was drafted and adopted independently of the policy toward Japan, the two were closely interrelated nearly from the beginning. In addition, the previously noted document by the Territorial Subcommittee of the U.S. State Department states that while the Okinawans were bitterly resentful toward the Japanese, it was inconceivable that they would welcome the prospect of being placed under Chinese rule. This view doubtless influenced the policy toward Okinawa that was finally adopted and may well be one of the reasons the concept of transferring Okinawa to China was dropped.

In the final analysis, there is no denying that the separation of Okinawa was conceived well before the beginning of the Okinawa campaign and implemented as soon as the fighting commenced.[46] The purposes of the separation were: (1) to establish a base from which to invade Japan proper, (2) to use Okinawa as a monitoring station from which to ensure that Japan abided by the surrender terms of the Potsdam Declaration, and (3) to prevent Japan's rearmament and ensure that Japan would not again pose a threat to the security of the United States and other countries.

Concerning the first of these aims, MacArthur, just after he captured Manila, declared that Tokyo would be his next target and that Okinawa was the natural invasion bridge for the attack on Tokyo. Indeed, the work of turning Okinawa into a base started as soon as the U.S. troops landed on Okinawa. It is important to keep in mind that MacArthur, who assumed complete control of Okinawa in July 1945, consistently adhered to the idea that the United States should have sole control of Okinawa.

The second objective is the main focus of this chapter. The present writer views the separation of Okinawa as, among other things, a pre-condition for the postwar reforms of disarmament, demilitarization, and democratization in Japan proper. One quick way to prove this point is to ask if the Allied forces stationed in Japan proper were sufficient to enforce the terms of surrender—in other words, was it perhaps necessary to transform Okinawa into a monitoring base in order to disarm and demilitarize Japan proper as one of the two pillars of postwar reforms? According to available records, the Joint Chiefs of Staff and MacArthur at first lamented the lack of occupation troops.[47]

Before the Occupation it was estimated that there were 2.5 million Japanese troops in Japan proper and about the same number abroad. By contrast, there were about 1.8 million U.S. troops in the planned occu-pation force. Although United Nations forces were to be sent to help, this was little consolation because 1.5 million U.S. troops were sched-uled to return home by the middle of 1946. Even though this was suffi-cient Allied strength to carry out the earlier phases of the Occupation, U.S. government leaders shared a belief that it would be necessary to retain U.S. bases in the vicinity of Japan proper to prevent rebellion and the like.[48] Since the actual number of occupation troops was only 117,580,[49] MacArthur termed occupied Japan a military vacuum and requested reinforcements. Moreover, in order to establish his historical role in the postwar reforms, MacArthur strongly urged that all occupa-tion troops be withdrawn from Japan proper once the treaty was con-cluded. The more MacArthur was committed to the demilitarization of Japan proper, the more inevitable it was that Okinawa should be detached. Not only did MacArthur urge the withdrawal of American troops, he also emphasized that the position of the United States in Asia would be seriously jeopardized if it relinquished Okinawa. It is therefore easy to understand why MacArthur echoed Perry in proclaiming that Okinawans are not Japanese and that they would be happy under the United States' rule.[50] Since few studies have dealt with MacArthur's role in the detachment of Okinawa, this should certainly be an important subject for future research.

In conclusion, there is no denying that Japanese government since the Meiji era has seen Okinawa not as an indispensable part of Japan but rather as a tool to be used in pursuit of Japan's (i.e., Japan proper's) interests. That the Japanese government conceived the defense of Okinawa as a necessary sacrifice to delay the assault on Japan proper and thus willfully caused the death of approximately 170,000 Okinawans, or more than one-third of the island's total population, but has never reflected upon the gravity of this act is only one example of its basic attitude toward Okinawa. Just before the Potsdam Declaration was put into effect, the Japanese government made several proposals regarding its provisions, among which were requests to have the occupation forces stationed away from Tokyo, to have only a symbolic occupation, and to have food and medicine sent to the Imperial Japanese forces stranded on Pacific islands. Not only did the Japanese government make no request on behalf of Okinawans caught in the horrors of the war but, at least as far as American records indicate, it did not even take notice of a telegram that Ambassador Saito sent from Moscow after he had heard the terms of the Potsdam Declaration on the radio expressing concern that Okinawa might not be included among the "minor islands" belonging to Japan.

Far from acknowledging the telegram, the records show that Konoe Fumimaro's draft of conditions for the peace negotiations with the United States and England indicates his willingness to have Okinawa, Ogasawara, and Karafuto excluded from Japanese "national territory."[51] Moreover, Prime Minister Yoshida Shigeru asserted before the peace negotiations that Japan would not be opposed to leasing Okinawa to the United States and England under the so-called Bermuda formula[52] for ninety-nine years. Right after the peace treaty went into effect, a well-known scholar in Japan proper expressed appreciation for the way the occupation of Japan had been carried out in that, unlike Germany and Korea, neither the Japanese *homeland* nor *people* were divided.[53] Both of these views reveal that Okinawa was not considered as an integral part of Japan and symbolize the Japanese attitude toward Okinawa. It is thus no exaggeration to say that, contrary to the widely held belief that the detachment of Okinawa was an unavoidable consequence of Japan's having lost the war and accepted the surrender terms of the Potsdam Declaration, its detachment was actually the consequence of a joint effort (direct and indirect) by the governments of Japan and the United States acting in their respective national interests.

Conclusion

The following conclusions may be reached on the basis of the materials discussed and other materials too numerous to be examined adequately in the space available.

1. Although researchers have tended to overlook the importance of the Cairo Declaration in its relation to the detachment of Okinawa, it was at the Cairo Conference that this policy was largely decided. The ini-

tial inclusion of Okinawa among the territories of Japan "taken by violence and greed" is particularly significant.

2. Okinawa was not initially included among the "minor islands" in the territorial clause of the Potsdam Declaration. Detachment did not result from Japanese acceptance of the terms of surrender but was conceived well before Japan surrendered.

3. The plan to divorce Okinawa from Japan, place it under exclusive U.S. control, and make it into a permanent base was virtually decided before the U.S. military forces landed on Okinawa. This was, however, left ambiguous until around 1949 because of the lack of legal and political consensus among the victorious nations regarding territorial rearrangements.

4. The principle of "divide and rule" applied to Okinawa was not a unilateral decision by the United States but had the active support of the Japanese government, and, at least to that extent, was the product of a joint U.S.-Japanese effort.

5. Throughout the entire occupation of Okinawa, the U.S. and Japanese governments consistently adhered to the principle that "sometimes the greater good requires the lesser evil." Accordingly, the Okinawa minority was systematically ignored in the name of majority interests.

6. The principle of "divide and rule" was both directly and indirectly applied to Okinawa, and was inseparably tied to U.S. postwar policy toward Japan. Therefore, any evaluation of the postwar reforms in Japan proper must take account of the postwar situation in Okinawa.

Notes

1. John T. Caldwell, "Military Government Planning, Xth Army, August 1944–February 1945" (Unpublished manuscript), p. 1.

2. One reason why the manuals of civilian government for Okinawa and for Japan proper were prepared separately was that the authority to direct the campaign was also divided. This is why the *Manual of the Civilian Government of the Ryūkyūs* was published by the Department of the Navy.

3. For details, see Ota Masahide, "Senryōka no Okinawa" [Occupied Okinawa], in *Iwanami kōza Nihonshi* [Iwanami lectures on Japanese history], vol. 23, *Modern History II* (1977), pp. 297–301.

4. *The Okinawa of the Loochoo Islands: A Minority Group in Japan*, pp. 80–83, 85.

5. MacArthur's telegram to the secretary of state. See U.S. Department of State, *Foreign Relations of the United States, 1947*, vol. 6, *The Far East* (Washington, D.C.: GPO, 1972), p. 512. Hereafter cited as *FRUS*.

6. John K. Emmerson, *The Japanese Thread: A Life in the U.S. Foreign Service* (New York: Holt, Rinehart and Winston, 1978), p. 225.

7. See the appendix to *The Okinawa of the Loochoo Islands: A Minority Group in Japan*.

8. For example, the same document cites a few basic statements which, it says,

should be included in the first proclamation. *FRUS, 1944,* vol. 4 (1965), pp. 1209–1210.

9. Ibid., p. 1218.

10. Following Crist's appointment, Colonel William B. Higgins (in charge of provisions) and Colonel Frederick B. Wiener (in charge of administration) were appointed from the army, and Captain Lowe N. Bibby (acting department head) and Commander James N. Varnaman, III (in charge of administration) from the navy to complete the staff.

11. The so-called Watkins Papers, unpublished documents at Stanford University, contain very useful information concerning military government on Okinawa.

12. See National Archives, "Military Government Report" of June 10, 1945.

13. Policies were adopted also to restore a money-based economy. The U.S. military government experimentally restored a money economy on Zamami, one of the Kerama Islands, in 1945, and Wiener, who administered the project, remarked to the Deputy-Commander for Military Government: "There is no room for long-range programs, for pampering of any sort, for economic utopias. The plan must show that it meets the cold-blooded requirements of minimizing imports. . . . We must hold their wants down and may not supply their needs above minimum humanitarian level."

14. National Archives, Reports on Military Government activities, March–August, 1945 (unpublished).

15. It was only after February 1946 that the navy's military government assumed control of the Miyako, Yaeyama, and Amami islands.

16. *New York Times,* July 20, 1945.

17. Even the U.S. military records with regard to the changes in the command structure are incomplete.

18. On this point, a former staff member of the military government on Okinawa states: "Reorganizations within on-the-spot military government staff on Okinawa have occurred with demoralizing frequency throughout the occupation. Changes in commanders, because of the Army's rotation policies, have been such that the average military governor has lasted little longer than a postwar French premier. Consequently, maintenance of coherence and continuity in plans and programs has proved an almost impossible task." See James N. Tull, "The Ryūkyu Islands, Japan's Oldest Colony and America's Newest: An Analysis of Policy and Propaganda" (M. A. thesis, University of Chicago, 1953), p. 33.

19. Ibid. There are also other records that document this.

20. For instance, Lawrence Olson states, "Okinawa came to be regarded as a kind of Siberia to which mediocre or undesirable personnel in the occupation of Japan were exiled." Lawrence Olson, *Okinawa Perspective* (American University Field Staff Publication, Lo-5-59, May 25, 1959), pp. 2–4.

21. See the record of Harlan Youel, who worked for the military government on Okinawa in 1949–1950, at Columbia University's Oral History Department.

22. According to George Kerr, Okinawa was important first as a base from which to launch an assault on Japan, next as a "dumping ground" for undesirables from Japan proper and GHQ (in the "period of indifference"), and last as a permanent base to combat communism's expansion. George H. Kerr, *Okinawa: The History of an Island People* (Rutland, Vt.: Tuttle, 1958).

23. Leonard Weiss, "U.S. Military Government on Okinawa," *Far Eastern Survey*, vol. 15, no. 15 (July 31, 1946), pp. 234–238.

24. The war records on the battle of Okinawa, which can be found in *Okinawa-ken shi* [The history of Okinawa Prefecture], contain a good number of accounts of this kind.

25. In this regard, MacArthur comments, "It is a truism that democracy is a thing of the spirit which can neither be purchased nor imposed by the threat of application of force." *FRUS, 1947,* vol. 6, p. 455.

26. In this connection, one military government staff member commented: "This complete topographical transformation, frequently including senseless destruction of private property, was common throughout the war. Bulldozer operators have a psychology all their own. In clearing an area, any obstacle in the neighborhood is a challenge and must be knocked down. Native buildings not destroyed in the fighting suddenly disappeared. These practices were rationalized on the grounds that 'It's all Jap stuff, anyway.' No appeal by the military government officers to the combat forces that such activities were unwarranted had any effects." Tull, *The Ryūkyū Islands,* p. 45.

27. For example, Senaga Kamejiro gives specific figures in denouncing the way the military government pillaged Okinawa. See *Okinawa kara no hokoku* [Report from Okinawa] (Iwanami Shinsho, 1966).

28. Prime Minister Kishi, responding to a question from a Socialist Dietman in the House of Councillors' Standing Committee on Foreign Affairs, remarked that Article 3 should be understood as a temporary measure, and expressed doubt about its legal validity. *Asahi Shinbun,* April 4, 1957.

29. Kobayashi Naoki, "Kenpō seiji no tenken" [Review of constitutional politics], *Sekai,* June 1967, p. 34.

30. See National Archives, Advisory Committee on Postwar Foreign Policy, *The Minutes of the Twentieth Meeting of the Political Subcommittee,* dated August 1, 1942.

31. For details, see Kerr, *Okinawa,* p. 464.

32. In this regard, see Hugh Borton, *American Presurrender Planning for Postwar Japan* (The East Asia Institute, Columbia University, 1967).

33. Benis M. Frank, *Okinawa: Touchstone to Victory* (Purnell's, 1969), p. 8.

34. According to Hugh Borton, the Cairo Declaration was drafted jointly by the Territorial Subcommittee and the Area Committee. Borton, *American Presurrender Planning,* p. 13.

35. Yokota Kisaburo asserts that the Cairo Declaration has no direct relevance to Okinawa and contains no provisions concerning it on the grounds that the phrase "territories which she [Japan] has taken by violence and greed" does not apply to the history of Okinawa under Japan. Yokota, "Okinawa to Nihon no shuken" [Okinawa and Japanese sovereignty], *Okinawa no chii* [Okinawa's position] (Yuhikaku), p. 108. In contrast, Professor Higashionna Kanjun, a noted specialist on Okinawa, suggests that the Japanese government's statement of having used force in annexing Okinawa might have led the United States to believe that this was indeed "taken by violence." Higashionna Kanjun, *Higashionna Kanjun zenshū* [Collected works of Higashionna Kanjun] (Daiichi Shobō, 1978–1981), vol. 8, p. 60.

36. Professor Yokota comments, "Because this provision can be understood to

mean the four islands and the small islands adjacent, it is wrong to include Okinawa and Chishima. At the minimum, it is not possible to claim on the basis of this provision that Okinawa belongs to Japan." Yokota, "Okinawa to Nihon no shuken," p. 108.

37. Refer to the memorandum that the United States government sent to the Soviet Union on May 19, 1951, and to the records of the question and answer period for the 12th Session of the Diet in 1951. During deliberation in the House of Councillors, Dietman Horigi Kenzo asked if the Nansei Shotō were included among the "minor islands," to which Nishimura Kumao, Director-General of the Treaty Bureau responded, "We think they were."

38. Izuno Shigemitsu, "Nanpo Shotō no chii to hensen" [The position and changes of the Nansei Shotō], in *Okinawa fukki no kiroku* [Records of Okinawa's reversion] (Tokyo, Nanpo Doho Engokai, 1972), p. 2.

39. Yokota, "Okinawa to Nihon no shuken," p. 108.

40. Record Group 59, General Records of the Department of State—Records of Harley A. Notter, 1939–1949. (This document consists of eight single-spaced typewritten pages.)

41. J. K. Emmerson (Iwasaki Toshio et al., trans.), *Nihon no Dilemma*, vol. 1 (Tokyo, Jiji Tsushinsha, 1972), p. 26.

42. *Meiji bunka shiryō sōsho* [Records of Meiji culture], vol. 4, pp. 77–88.

43. Ibid., "Ryūkyū shobun" [Ryūkyū disposition], vol. 2, p. 94.

44. For details, see Kinjo Seitoku, "Chugoku kindai-shi to Ryūkyū shobun" [Modern Chinese history and the Ryūkyū disposition], *Shin Okinawa bungaku*, vol. 38 (1978), pp. 33–47.

45. See the Draft Treaty on the Disarmament and Demilitarization of Japan which the U.S. Secretary of State sent to Kennan, U.S. Ambassador to the Soviet Union, on February 28, 1946.

46. Comparison of the military government proclamation in Manila and Article 1 of the proclamation on Okinawa is enlightening in this regard. The latter states that occupation of Okinawa was necessary to ensure Japan's demilitarization.

47. For instance, MacArthur comments: "The Joint Chiefs of Staff considers it appropriate to point out that effectiveness of the United States Army and Navy has already been reduced incident to demobilization, and that continuance of demobilization under current plans will, in the course of the next twelve months, further reduce the fighting strength of the United States armed forces to a point where it will be difficult to deal with any serious unrest in Japan." *FRUS, 1946*, vol. 8, pp. 102–103.

48. *New York Times*, August 19, 1945.

49. *Report of General MacArthur, MacArthur in Japan, Vol. I, Supplement* (Washington, D.C.: GPO, January 1966), p. 266.

50. *FRUS, 1948*, vol. 6, pp. 700–701.

51. Ota, "Senryōka no Okinawa."

52. Shiso no Kagaku Kenkyukai, ed., *Kyodo kenkyu Nihon senryogun sono hikari to kage* [Joint research on occupation troops in Japan: The good and the evil], vol. 2 (Tokuma Shoten), p. 145.

53. Ibid., p. 138.

11

Japan's Postwar Conservative Parties

Uchida Kenzō

On August 14, 1945, Japan accepted the terms of the Potsdam Declaration. On the following day the emperor broadcast an imperial edict accepting this proclamation, thus ending the Pacific War. On September 2 Japan formally surrendered.

On the previous day, September 1, the 88th Extraordinary Session of the Imperial Diet had been convoked. On that day, the composition of the lower house of the Diet (which totalled 466 members) was as follows: Dai Nippon Seijikai (Greater Japan Political Association), 377; Yokusō Giin Dōshikai (Association of Imperial Assistance Dietmen), 21; independents, 25; and vacancies, 43.

Another wartime group, the Gokoku Dōshikai (Comrades for Defense of the Nation Association), had dissolved on August 15 and merged with the Dai Nippon Seijikai. Moreover, the Yokusō Giin Dōshikai was in reality an arm of the Dai Nippon Seijikai. Thus the Diet at the end of the war was for all practical purposes composed of a single party, the Dai Nippon Seijikai. Shortly thereafter, on September 6, the Yokusō Giin Dōshikai dissolved itself, followed on September 14 by the Dai Nippon Seijikai.

In place of this unified wartime Diet, a movement for the creation of new political parties soon developed. Between July and August 1940 all of the prewar parties had dissolved themselves in order to participate in the Imperial Rule Assistance Association, a national unity program under the auspices of Konoe Fumimaro. Prior to this dissolution, the major parties had been the Rikken Minseitō (Constitutional Democratic party); the Kuhara, Nakajima, and independent factions of the Rikken Seiyūkai (Friends of Constitutional Government Association); the Jikyoku Dōshikai; and the Shakai Taishutō (Social Masses party). After the war the intricately interrelated successors to these prewar parties formed new political parties. In addition, a movement was launched to rebuild the Japan Communist party, which had been outlawed in the prewar period. Finally, plans for the organization of new parties unrelated to the prewar parties were also set in motion.

From these movements emerged the major postwar political parties: the Nihon Shakaitō (Japan Socialist party) on November 2, 1945; the Nihon Jiyūtō (Japan Liberal party) on November 9; the Nihon Shimpōtō (Japan Progressive party) on November 16; and the Nihon Kyōdōtō (Japan Cooperative party) on December 18.

The circumstances at the time of the formation of these parties were still chaotic and the interrelationships of their members complex. One notes the following:

1. The awareness among politicians of the political changes that defeat and occupation would bring was weak, but their sense of continuity with the prewar and wartime eras was strong.
2. Consequently, prewar party circumstances and personal relationships were conspicuous in both the policies and membership of the new parties.
3. Perhaps because of these factors, one finds almost no foreknowledge or presentiment of the wide-scale purges that were shortly to be launched by the Occupation authorities. (The Kyōdōtō, the last party to be formed, was an exception on this score.) Consequently, the purge directive of January 4, 1946, aimed at public officials was a severe blow to the new parties and had major consequences for all of them. Although there were certain differences, the character and membership of all parties underwent substantial changes. Before January 4 the continuity with and inheritance from the prewar period had been great in all cases, but after this there emerged for the first time a discontinuity between the prewar and wartime eras. In this sense, therefore, for Japanese political parties the turning point dividing the prewar from the postwar period is neither August 15 nor September 2, 1945, but January 4, 1946. The circumstances of the formation of these conservative parties prior to this turning point and the changes thereafter are the subjects of this chapter.

The Issue of Responsibility for the War

On August 17, immediately following the end of the war, the Suzuki cabinet was replaced by the cabinet of Higashikuni Naruhiko. The 88th Diet Session opened on September 4 and closed immediately thereafter on September 5. Prime Minister Higashikuni, in his September 5 speech stated: "The results of defeat will be many. Both the battlefront and the homefront, the army, the officials, and each and every one of the people must reflect and repent at this time. . . . We must make the past a lesson for the future; cleansing our hearts, each must exert himself to the utmost to fulfill his own duty."[1] This was Higashikuni's so-called concept of 100 million repentences, which he had strongly advocated earlier, at his first press conference on August 28, along with "protection of the national polity."[2]

This extraordinary session of the Diet had been convened to report the end of the war. Its term was a mere two days, and the only interpellation on the prime minister's speech came from Tōgō Minoru of the Dai Nippon Seijikai. Essentially this Diet was a formality; it unanimously passed the resolution to "respectfully receive the imperial edict ending the war." However, an independent member, Ashida Hitoshi, made use of this opportunity to raise a question as to responsibility for the war.

Ashida, in a lengthy, written summary of his question, put the following harsh questions. "Why does the government think the Pacific War ended to our disadvantage? Where do they think the responsibility lies for leading us to this unfavorable conclusion? What measures is the government taking to make clear the causes and responsibility for this?" Strictly speaking, rather than "responsibility for the war" this was a question concerning "responsibility for the defeat." However, the government's response completely avoided any concrete discussion of responsibility and presented instead an abstract argument: "In every aspect of the execution of the war, both organization and policy, there were many regrettable points. We endeavored in all respects to remedy these. The fact that we did not attain our ideal and arrived at the inevitable conclusion of the war is extremely regrettable."[3]

Thus in the extraordinary Diet of early September, the domestic issue of responsibility for the war ended inconclusively. Gradually, however, the emerging Occupation policies of the Allies began to clarify the consequences of defeat.

The sixth clause of the Potsdam Proclamation required the elimination from power for all time of the militarists who had deceived and misled the people of Japan into embarking on world conquest. Its tenth clause ordered the punishment of war criminals and the elimination of all obstacles to the revitalization and strengthening of democratic tendencies in the Japanese government. On September 11, 1945, GHQ arrested former prime minister Tōjō Hideki and ordered the Japanese government to turn over 38 other alleged war criminals as well.[4]

On September 24 all newspapers published the official text of the "United States Initial Post-Surrender Policy for Japan." This made clear the basic direction of future Occupation policy: "The Japanese people shall be encouraged to develop a desire for individual liberties and respect for fundamental human rights, particularly the freedoms of religion, assembly, speech, and the press. They shall also be encouraged to form democratic and representative organizations. Democratic political parties, with rights of assembly and public discussion, shall be encouraged." It also announced that "persons who have been active exponents of militarism and militant nationalism will be removed and excluded from public office and from other positions of public or substantial private responsibility."[5] In this fashion quite rigorous limitations were placed on who would be allowed to lead the new Japan.

The response of the Japanese government to this policy was viewed as unsatisfactory by the Occupation authorities, and on October 4 GHQ issued its "Memorandum concerning Removal of Restrictions on Political, Civil and Religious Freedom" and simultaneously demanded the resignation of Home Minister Yamazaki Iwao. On the following day, October 5, the entire Higashikuni cabinet resigned, and on October 9 the Shidehara Kijūrō cabinet was formed.[6] This also was not a party cabinet. On October 11 MacArthur instructed Prime Minister Shidehara to execute the following five major reforms:

1. emancipation of women through enfranchisement
2. encouragement of the unionization of labor
3. opening of the schools to a more liberal system of education
4. abolition of systems through which secret inquisitions and abuses kept the people in constant fear
5. reform of monopolistic control of industry and democratization of the economy

Parallel with the development of these strict Occupation policies, the formation of "democratic political parties" was promoted. Almost all of those who took the initiative in this movement had been wartime political leaders. The new conditions of defeat and occupation raised for such leaders the issues of responsibility for defeat and for the war, hindering their ability to serve as suitable leaders in the new postwar era. Moreover, under these conditions of defeat and occupation, with GHQ on the one hand asserting the responsibility of "persons who have been active exponents of militarism and militant nationalism," and on the other, the need of settling the issue of domestic responsibility for the war and defeat vis-à-vis the Japanese people, these early leaders soon found themselves in very difficult circumstances.

The Formation of the Nihon Jiyūtō

In his memoirs Hatoyama Ichirō, founder of the Nihon Jiyūtō, had this to say about the party's formation:

> It was at the urgings of others, rather than on my own, that I came to consider the formation of a new political party. I felt that it was necessary to take time to ponder and sufficiently refine one's thoughts on the indepen-

dence and rebuilding of Japan, and not to do so hurriedly. Because I felt this way, I somehow thought that the meeting of the informal group which Ashida and Andō had planned a day or two after the defeat was too soon, and so didn't want to go. It was a week after the end of the war, on August 22, when I left the mountains of Karuizawa for Tokyo.

This meant that several of my colleagues, such as Andō Masazumi, Ashida Hitoshi, Uehara Etsujiro, Makino Ryōzō, Kita Reikichi, Hoshijima Niro, Yano Shōtarō, etc. were waiting for me in Tokyo. Of these, Andō and Ashida seemed to be the main ones responsible for persuading me, and after them the next most enthusiastic were Uehara and Kita.[7]

Certainly, as Hatoyama states, it was Ashida who first foresaw Japan's defeat and who was the first to conceive of and act upon a postwar political structure.

The chapter on the Liberal party in the report on Japanese political parties, prepared by the Government Section of GHQ, stated:

> The initial suggestion for the formation of a Liberal Party (Jiyūtō) came from Ashida Hitoshi . . . who, while the war was still in progress, held frequent conferences at his Kamakura home with Katayama Tetsu and Hara Takeshi, both now of the Social Democratic Party. . . . after surrender, the circle widened and new men were drawn into the group. These included: Saitō Takao, Kawasaki Katsu, Yoshida Shigeru, Ushiba Toratarō, Okubo Tomejiro, Arita Hachirō, Shimanaka Yusaku, Hatoyama Ichirō, Matsuno Tsuruhei . . .[8]

This suggests that in June 1946, when this report was written, GHQ's Government Section thought highly of Ashida. It can also be regarded as related to its support of the "Katayama-Ashida coalition government" of 1947–1948. In this report Ashida himself was seen as the first to conceive of a postwar democratic party, while Yoshida and Hatoyama were perceived as mere sympathizers and participants.

In contrast to its assessment of Ashida, the Government Section report was not very favorable toward Hatoyama. At the time the report was written, Hatoyama had already been purged from public office. However, the purge of Hatoyama was largely motivated by political expediency. It is questionable whether the political beliefs and past career of Yoshida Shigeru, who was then in power, and those of Hatoyama were so disparate that one should have become prime minister and the other purged from public office. At least one could probably say that, among the members of the Imperial Rule Assistance Diet, Hatoyama's course of action during the war made him, after Ozaki Yukio, the most qualified to become a postwar political leader. Hatoyama did not participate in the Yokusan Giin Dōmei (Imperial Rule Assistance Representatives' League) under Konoe's new order, but organized a group critical of it. In the Imperial Rule Assistance election, he ran and was elected without official recommendation and, although for about a year following the election he had to belong to the Yokusan Seijikai (Imperial Rule Assistance Political Association), in the end he criticized Tōjō's politics and withdrew. From that point until the day of defeat he remained an independent.[9]

Even the above-mentioned Government Section report recorded that Ashida had met with Katayama and Hara of the Socialist party. From the first, therefore, there was a close connection between Nishio Suehiro, Hirano Rikizō, and Mizutani Chōzaburō, who later formed the Socialist party, and the Hatoyama group. Nishio, in his book *The Political Memoirs of Nishio Suehiro*, stated: "On the day the war ended I visited my old colleague Mizutani immediately and impatiently asserted that the formation of a socialist political party and of labor unions was an urgent matter." On the morning of August 18 Nishio arrived in Tokyo, followed shortly by Mizutani. They contacted Hirano and the three at once began preparations for the formation of a new party.[10]

Hirano, the only one of the three still living, recollects that toward the end of the war these three plus Hatoyama, Ashida, and others formed an independents' group. These three from the old proletarian parties had often discussed the matter of forming a social democratic party and trying to take power as soon as the war ended. Accordingly, on the morning after the end of the war, August 16, Hirano rented a room at the Kuramae Industrial Association building near Shimbashi Station in Tokyo, established an office, and urged Nishio and Mizutani to come to Tokyo from Kansai. Hirano spoke quite explicitly about the shared political consciousness of these three close friends at that time. "We were all aware that Japan was defeated and would be occupied by America. America would rule Japan with democracy. Democracy is parliamentary politics. Parliamentary politics means the taking of power by controlling the majority. . . . Then with the end of the war we were able quickly to take decisive action."[11]

The circumstances of the formation of the Socialist party are not the concern of this article. However, in this recollection by Hirano one detects more than a concept for the formation of a socialist party. There is also a strong and naive belief in the arrival of an era of general democratic parliamentary politics. This was quite similar to the views of Hatoyama and the others who organized the Jiyūtō. Any sense of conflict between conservative and progressive, between right-wing Jiyūtō and left-wing Shakaitō was weak at this time. Instead, as a result of their shared experiences in the wartime Diet, there was a strong feeling of commonality and closeness as forces joined in opposition to those who were trying to preserve the wartime system of cooperation and who in due time would form the Shimpōtō.

This interpretation is also supported by the fact that on August 23 the Nishio and Hatoyama groups met to discuss the formation of a new party. Hatoyama felt at that time that, if they formed a new party, it should be one large, progressive party including the prewar proletarian party forces. Correspondingly, he attempted to strike a bargain with them. He conveyed these views to Hirano, with whom he had previously been in contact, and on August 23 a meeting between the two groups took place. In Hatoyama's words, "[b]ecause our own faction and Nishio, Hirano, and the others had fought together against Tōjō, there was a common bond of sentiment linking us." "Us" included Hatoyama, Andō, Uehara, Ono Banboku, Nishio, Hirano, and Mizutani. But in contrast to Hirano, who favored one large concentration of political power, Nishio, who had already decided to organize a socialist party, was lukewarm. Nishio said: "I replied that I thought that we leaders, being adults, could perhaps consider the general situation and cooperate, but that it would be very difficult for the various forces that were behind us to act in harmony. Then Hatoyama, laughing, said: 'Ultimately our upbringing is different from yours, so it is probably impossible to act together,' and on this note the meeting broke up."[12]

It must be noted, however, that both Hatoyama's and Nishio's memoirs record that the two groups parted with a lingering sense of commonality. In fact, the friendly relationship between these groups continued until the purge of Hatoyama in 1946, and even after that these personal linkages continued to influence the relationship between the parties.[13]

The next problem in connection with the formation of a political party by the Hatoyama group was the variety and nature of the forces arrayed within the conservative camps. As long as the leaders were to be sought from the ranks of the prewar and wartime leadership of the old parties, it was difficult to avoid feelings of conflict based on these former party affiliations.

From the beginning, in addition to Hatoyama's faction, the old Minseitō-line liberals—Saito Takaō, Kawasaki Katsu, Ichinomiya Fusajirō, and others—also participated in the efforts to create a new party. Finally, however, unable to settle their differences arising from prewar conflicts between Seiyūkai and Minseitō, Hatoyama and Saitō, who during the war had jointly opposed Tōjō, parted company. Iwabuchi Tatsuo, a man who had been close to Konoe Fumimaro, Hatoyama Ichirō, and Yoshida Shigeru during the war and postwar period and was well-versed in politics, stated in his *Seventy-Year History of Japanese Politics:*

> The movement to form a new party that centered on Hatoyama rallied those who had defended the isolated ramparts of liberalism and parliamentary politics during the long period of the war, and who, while subject to oppression and persecution by the military, consistently opposed both the Imperial Rule Assistance Association and the new order. It gathered those who, opposing the forces of the old Yokusan Seijikai, were attempting to build a new liberal democratic party. However, the personal relations involved were

neither disinterested nor open. Saitō harbored anti-Seiyūkai sentiments from his old Minseitō days and did not want to be absorbed into Hatoyama's ranks. This was probably also due to Saitō's feeling that, in terms of experience in the Diet, he was senior to Hatoyama.[14]

In this way the old Minseitō faction drifted away from Hatoyama's vision of a new party. Partly to fill the resulting vacuum, "Hatoyama decided to draw into his party critics, journalists, scholars, businessmen and the like who had criticized the parties from the viewpoint of outsiders. Accordingly, he approached such men as Minobe Tatsukichi, Kuwaki Genyoku, Kikuchi Kan, Ishibashi Tanzan, Ishii Mitsujirō, Hiratsuka Tsunejirō, and others, sought their entry into the party, and obtained their agreement."[15]

On October 7 a preliminary meeting for the establishment of the new party was held, and on November 9 the Nihon Jiyūtō was formed. The party platform read as follows:

1. voluntary enactment of the Potsdam Proclamation, eradication of militaristic elements, and construction of a new Japan in accordance with universal principles
2. maintenance of the national polity; establishment of a democratically responsible political system; and the unimpeded flow of ideas and speech through freedom of learning, art, education, and religions
3. stabilization of financial administration through encouragement of free economic activities, and perfection of the national economy through the rebuilding of agriculture, industry, and commerce
4. promotion of political and social morality and cleansing of the national life
5. respect for human rights, elevation of the status of women, execution of an extensive social policy, and stabilization of a prosperous standard of living

Hatoyama Ichirō was selected as president and the young Kōno Ichirō as secretary-general. Given the circumstances of the party formation, it would have been natural for Ashida to become secretary-general, and Hatoyama himself thought this. However, because Ashida had entered the Shidehara cabinet (formed October 9) as welfare minister, this expectation was not realized. Hatoyama commented: "Thereupon we made Kōno, who had worked most ardently, secretary-general." However, it has now become clear that behind the appointment of Kōno lay a flow of funds that linked Kodama Yoshio, Tsuji Karoku, Kōno, and Hatoyama. According to a report on Diet parties and factions as of November 26, the Nihon Jiyūtō had forty-six members.

It is true that the principals involved in the formation of the Jiyūtō had been critical of the wartime system that had led to the Pacific war. This is clear from a comparison of the platforms of the two parties as well as from their differing responses to the issue of responsibility for the war. However, it is also true that, as their memberships increased, the Shimpōtō came to be largely composed of former Minseitō-members and the Nakajima faction of the old Seiyūkai. At the same time, many of the former Kuhara faction of the Seiyūkai entered the Jiyūtō. Both inherited sizable elements from the prewar parties.[16]

The Emergence of the Nihon Shimpōtō

Compared to the immediate reactions of the Hatoyama group and the old proletarian parties—including not only the Nishio group, but also Suzuki Mosaburo, Kato Kanjū, and others of the old Rōnōtō (Labor-Farmer party)—the response of the mainstream conservative forces that had belonged to the Dai Nippon Seijikai was extremely slow. The Seijikai, which had been the official organization for wartime political cooperation, was dissolved on September 14, 1945. But desirous of preserving its position as the major political power and its status as a composite grouping of heterogeneous elements, there emerged from its membership a variety of plans for the formation of a new political party. Iawabuchi Tatsuo stated:

> The Shimpōtō was an extension and transformation of the old Dai Nippon Seijikai and the Yokuso Dōshikai. Saitō, having been linked with the old Minseitō, joined Machida Chūji's Shimpōtō. For the old Yokusan Seijikai faction, given the general criticism of their opportunistic wartime response to the military, the inclusion of Saitō who from first to last advocated parliamentary government was partially attributable to their need for camouflage and partially to a desire to prevent his joining Hatoyama. Consequently, when Saitō as a member of the old Minseitō joined the new party formed from old Yokusei elements, other former Minseitō members such as Ichinomiya Fusajirō also, because of their long-time close relationship with Saitō, broke with Hatoyama and joined the Machida faction. In this way the various divisions within the old parties became the starting point for the new parties. They took the form of a conflict between the Shimpōtō on the one hand—which was old Yokusei and Dai Nippon Seijikai and particularly the Machida Chūji faction of the old Minseitō and the Nakajima Chikuhei and Maeda Yonezō factions of the old Seiyūkai—and the Jiyūtō on the other which centered on the Hatoyama faction of the old Seiyūkai.[17]

Within this movement for the formation of a new party by mainstream elements of the old Dai Nippon Seijikai, the activities of the Shin Nihon Kensetsu Chōsakai (Research Committee on the Building of a New Japan), a group of younger dietmen who had been elected fewer than three times, merits attention. This group, represented by Inukai Takeru, agreed upon its basic policies for the formation of a new party in a meeting on September 28. They emphasized the "rejection of former political bosses" and opposed the formation of a party that would be a mere extension of the Dai Nippon Seijikai. In time, after the upsets occasioned by GHQ's purge, this position led them to support the activities that transformed the Shimpōtō into the Minshūtō (Democratic party). At this earlier stage, however, they also attacked those "who were proud of having been idle spectators of the war" and exhibited hostility toward Hatoyama's new party. One can perceive in this development some of the problems that beset the followers of the old Dai Nippon Seijikai.

Because of such views on the part of the young dietmen's group, the plans to select as a candidate for the party presidency a prewar leader such as Konoe Fumimarō or Ugaki Kazushige encountered obstacles.[18] When the Nihon Shimpōtō was finally formed on November 16, Tsurumi Yūsuke became secretary-general, but the issue of the presidency was still unresolved. The party platform provided for

1. protection of the national polity and establishment of responsible parliamentary government based on thoroughgoing democracy
2. respect for freedom of the individual, perfection of character based on cooperation and self-government, and devotion to the establishment of world peace and human welfare
3. promotion of active production and equitable distribution through an "independent work-for-all system" and the regulation of industry; creation of a new economic system and security for the people's livelihood

If one compares the platforms of the Shimpōtō and the Jiyūtō, their similarities and differences are apparent. Both spoke of the maintenance and protection of the national polity and advocated democracy and freedom. Both were abstract in expression and left vague the question of the contradictory and tense relationship between the so-called national polity and democracy as well as the extent to which they recognized a break between the prewar and postwar eras.

They also differed in several respects. In contrast to the specific demand by the Jiyūtō for voluntary "enactment of the Potsdam Proclamation and eradication of militaristic elements," the Shimpōtō's platform was totally devoid of planks relating to the war. Second, in contrast to the Jiyūtō's emphasis on the promotion of free economic activity and its clear advocacy of a liberal economy, the Shimpōtō called for "regulation of industry" and "equitable distribution," thus manifesting a tendency toward economic control.[19]

According to a report on party membership in the Diet on November 24, there were 273 dietmen belonging to the Shimpōtō. On December 16 former Minseitō president, Machida Chūji, was finally selected to fill the vacant presidency. Within the Diet, the financial assets of the Shimpōtō gave it great power, but the fact that it was composed of the leaders of the wartime Diet was the party's Achilles' heel. This weakness centered on the issue of responsibility for the war.

This problem once again flared up in the 89th Extraordinary Session of the Diet convoked on November 26. Prime Minister Shidehara stated in his speech on November 28: "It is necessary to clarify the causes and true facts of the defeat in the Greater East Asian War so that the grave mistakes that this occasioned will not be repeated in the future." He also announced the establishment of a Cabinet Committee to Investigate the Greater East Asian War. However, when questioned about responsibility for the war he said: "With regard to the identification of those responsible for the war, it is not desirable to do so by methods that will result in internecine conflict among the people."[20]

For the newly-formed parties, however, as long as they aimed at an active expansion of their strength prior to the approaching general election, the issue of responsibility for the war could not be avoided. In this respect the Shimpōtō, which included many of those who had cooperated with the military during the war and which was attempting to define this issue as narrowly as possible, was certainly no exception. Consequently, a motion for the passage of a "Resolution concerning the Responsibility of Diet Members for the War" introduced by the Jiyūtō and supported by the Shakaitō and a "Resolution concerning Responsibility for the War" introduced by the Shimpōtō came into active conflict on the floor of the Diet.

The Jiyūtō resolution asserted that it was intolerable that the political realm alone should be permitted to evade confronting this issue when, since the end of the war, every other sphere had engaged in deep and serious reflection on this score. It held that those who from the beginning of the Greater East Asian War had supported the government and led the Diet should now recognize their personal responsibility and voluntarily resign their seats.

The Shimpōtō's resolution, however, took as its premise the view that "responsibility for the war" meant only responsibility for starting the war and for crimes and offenses against international law during the war and did not extend to the general populace who volunteered to assist the conduct of the war under legal sanctions following the official declaration of war. It went on to assert: "Although manifestly it was the tyranny of the military cliques and the bureaucrats which brought about this defeat . . . those in political, financial, and intellectual circles who slavishly cooperated with them also cannot escape responsibility. . . . Further, we officials of the legislative branch must calmly reflect on the actions of the past, seriously discipline ourselves, and thus press forward in the building of a new Japan." This resolution thus surreptitiously substituted a question of general morality for that of responsibility for the war.

Both resolutions were introduced into the plenary session of the Diet on December 1, 1945. The Jiyūtō resolution, although supported by the Shakaitō, was defeated and the Shimpōtō resolution carried, thus demonstrating the strength of the majority party.[21] However, the Shimpōtō had really not been able to dispose in this fashion of the issue of responsibility for the war. On the following day, December 2, GHQ issued a further list of fifty-nine alleged war criminals containing the names of six incumbent Diet members (Nakajima Chikuhei, Sakurai Hyōgoro, Ōta Masataka, Ikezaki Chuko, Shiōden Nobutaka, and Sasakawa Ryōichi). This extension of the pursuit of war criminals into the ranks of party leaders (Nakajima, Sakurai, and Ōta) foretold that GHQ's definition of "militarists" would strike directly at the Shimpōtō.[22]

The Birth of the Nihon Kyōdōtō

Both the Jiyūtō and the Shimpōtō were heirs of the prewar Seiyūkai and Minseitō, and the Shakaitō was also a successor to the prewar proletarian parties. In contrast, only the Kyōdōtō was a new party originating in a defeated Japan. Its ideals and platform marked a new phase in Japanese politics. Even this new party, however, had to depend on the wartime Diet for its origins and personnel.

In the fall of 1945 the Nihon Shakaitō with 15 members (November 2), the Nihon Jiyūtō with 46 members (November 9), and the Nihon Shimpōtō with 273 members (November 16) were formed. When the 89th Extraordinary Diet was convoked on November 26, the ninety-two Diet members who had joined none of these parties organized and reported the formation of a Nonpartisan Club. Among its members one finds Akagi Munenori, Ino Hiroya, Funada Naka, Ikezaki Chūkō, Ikeda Masanosuke, Hashimoto Kingorō, Nakatani Takeyo of the old Gokoku Dōshikai;[23] Rōyama Masamichi, Kanno Wataro, Uda Koichi, and Nagano Mamoru of the old Yokusō Dōshikai; and Ozaki Yukio, Kurosawa Torizō, Miki Takeo, Kawashima Shōjirō, and Tanaka Isaji.

Many of the members of this Nonpartisan Club were either adherents of the view that all Diet members should resign, thus taking responsibility for the war (following December 1, 17 had announced their resignation), or they were opposed to joining new parties that were simply successors of the prewar parties. Some of these nonpartisan members began to work for the formation of the Kyōdōtō.

The circumstances involved have, until now, been unclear. For example, there is the following account:

It was the Kyōdōtō that proclaimed itself from the extreme left of the conservatives. Shortly after the emergence of the Jiyūtō and the Shimpōtō, on December 7, Sengoku Kōtarō [former Minister of Agriculture and Commerce], Kurosawa Torizō [a dairy farmer], Yoshiue Shōsuke [poet] and Ikawa Tadao [Konoe's secretary] formed the Kyōdō Kumiai Kenkyūkai [Cooperative Union Research Committee] and mutually agreed to form a party that would take as its guiding political principle "cooperative unionism." Funada Naka, Akagi Munenori, and Nakatani Takeyo of the group that toward the end of the war had split off from the Dai Nippon Seijikai and joined the Gokoku Dōshikai were all participants. Because executives such as Sengoku and others had been purged from public office, they installed Yamamoto Sanehiko, president of the magazine *Kaizō*, as chairman and Ikawa as secretary-general, thus forming the Kyōdōtō in considerable haste.[24]

The following is Funada Naka's account of the formation of Kyōdōtō:

The first to broach the matter of the formation of the Kyōdōtō were Sengoku Kōtarō and Kurosawa Torizō. It began with these two suggesting, in the light of the industrial association cooperative movement, the advisability of a cooperative movement for poor farmers who should also have a voice in the new politics. They, therefore, recommended the formation of a farmers' party involving those who had been connected with the industrial union movement. Because it was in this sense a party of cooperativism, they decided to call it the Kyōdōtō.[25]

At that time, Funada, as well as being a Diet member, was a director of the Tokyo Chamber of Commerce and Industry, a position he had held since August 1943. The president of the chamber was Fujiyama Aiichirō. In due time as the war developed, the Chamber of Commerce and Industry was reorganized through the collaboration of Minister of Commerce and Industry Kishi, President Fujiyama, and Director Funada and became the Association of Commercial and Industrial Economy. Funada was appointed Chief Director of the nation-wide organization, the National Association of Commercial and Industrial Economy. Sengoku and Kurosawa proposed to Funada that, because the members of the Association of Commercial and Industrial Economy were small and medium-size businesses and their employees, they should form a party so that these small and medium-size merchants and industrialists, joining with the farmers, would have a voice in the new politics. Funada agreed to this and thus participated in the new party movement. It has also been said that Fujiyama was an important participant, but Funada claimed that Fujiyama did not participate directly and Fujiyama himself denies having done so.

Funada continued:

My friends, Akagi and Yoshiue Shōsuke, as well as Prince Konoe's private secretary, Ikawa Tadao, were close to the American State Department group and were fluent in English, so I asked them to join as well. Yamamoto Sane-hiko, as president of *Kaizō*, had been critical of the wartime system, so I asked him to join, too. Then, borrowing the home of a sympathizer, Toku-gawa Yoshichika, we held several conferences. Ikawa and I went nearly every day to GHQ and explained our plan and sought their approval. The Political Section of GHQ agreed that it was a fine plan. They said also that cooperativism was a plank of the British Liberal party.

One can understand that the originators of a new party which, unlike the Jiyūtō and the Shimpōtō, was relatively unafflicted by a prewar gene-alogy might naturally be expected to take great interest in and devote much energy to sounding out the view of the Occupation authorities.

However, just before the formation of the party, those Diet members who had been officially recommended candidates in the election of Showa 17 (1942) were all purged. A directive was not issued, but it was suggested that they withdraw voluntarily. Thus, Sengoku, Kurosawa, Akagi, Yoshiue and myself were all affected, and only Ikawa and Yamamoto remained.[26]

On December 18 the Nihon Kyōdōtō was formed, with Funada Naka and Kurosawa Torizō as private sponsors. Its platform advocated (1) preservation of the Imperial lineage and establishment of a democratic political system in which the Diet reflects the will of the people and (2) reconstruction of industry, economy and culture, and the creation of a democratic, peaceful Japan by means of cooperativism based on service, autonomy, and fraternity.

The use of the phrase "preservation of the Imperial lineage" in the first plank was clearly different from the "maintenance of the national polity" used in the Jiyūtō platform and "protection of the national polity" found in the Shimpōtō platform. The Kyōdōtō plank, while recognizing the existence and continuation of an emperor, did not necessarily advocate the continued existence of the sort of emperor system enshrined in the Meiji Constitution. Compared to the positions taken by the Jiyūtō and the Shimpōtō, it was a more passive stance.

The "cooperativism based on service, autonomy and fraternity" es-poused in the second plank was the fundamental political ideal of the Kyōdōtō. This also differed from the conservative political concepts of the Jiyūtō and Shimpōtō.

Even the Kyōdōtō, however, which differed somewhat in character and predisposition from the other two conservative parties, had among its central members Sengoku from agriculture (leader of the industrial association movement) and Funada from commerce and industry (direc-tor of the National Association of Commercial and Industrial Economy and chairman of the Policy Affairs Research Council of the old Gokoku Dōshikai), both of whom had been promoters of the wartime coopera-tive system. Thus the limitations of an incomplete break with prewar

Japan and of insufficient awareness of the modes of behavior and organization in postwar Japan were made clear.[27] Consequently, once the storm of the purge of officials by GHQ hit, the shock to the Kyōdōtō almost rivaled that to the Shimpōtō, which suffered a fatal blow. The Kyōdōtō then embarked upon a path of reconstruction focusing on Yamamoto and Ikawa, who had escaped the purge. In time, by adding new members such as Miki Takeo, it once again set out to form a new party.

Pre-election Developments

Thus far we have examined the process of the formation of the three postwar conservative parties. While there had been unofficial actions and advice by GHQ authorities, the founders of each party acted autonomously, at least until the actual formation of the parties. From today's perspective the insensitivity of their judgments to the political changes occasioned by defeat and occupation is surprising, but this was a common feature of political leaders at that time. This phenomenon can also be seen in the response of the party leaders to the impending election.

The breakdown of Diet members by party as of November 26 when the 89th Imperial Diet was convoked was Nihon Shimpōtō, 272; Nonpartisan Club, 92; Nihon Jiyūtō, 45; Nihon Shakaitō, 15; independents, 2; and vacancies, 40. The major issue confronting this Diet, which was composed of members elected in the Imperial Rule Assistance election of April 1942, was to reform the election law of the House of Representatives and, as stated by Prime Minister Shidehara, "to make the Diet function so as properly to reflect the will of all the people. . . . This is, in fact, the main reason that I have petitioned the emperor to convoke this extraordinary session of the Diet."[28]

The government's bill for reform of the election law vastly expanded the electorate and the numbers of those eligible for elected office through such measures as women's suffrage and the lowering of the voting age qualification from 25 to 20. In place of the existing medium-size electoral districts, it adopted a system of large electoral districts with a limited plural ballot. It also abolished the prohibition on pre-election campaigning and simplified the other regulations controlling election campaigning. It intended in this manner to destroy the former fixed electoral bases, create a new, broader foundation, and increase the possibility of electing national figures and so-called new men who would truly enjoy public confidence.[29]

Separate reform bills were also introduced by the Shakaitō, the Jiyūtō, and the Shimpōtō. As in the case of the resolutions concerning the responsibility for the war, the major conflict was between the Shakaitō and the Jiyūtō on one hand and the Shimpōtō on the other. The Shakaitō and Jiyūtō introduced bills that would have changed the government's proposal to divide large prefectures and cities such as Tokyo and Osaka into two electoral districts to a system of one electoral district per prefecture; changed the voting method to a single-entry ballot system; and adopted a system of single, transferable, proportional representation. In contrast, the Shimpōtō's bill adopted a limited plural ballot system in all electoral districts (in the government's proposal only districts with five or fewer seats had single-entry ballots; those with six to ten seats had plural-entry) and gave electoral districts with ten or fewer seats a dual-entry ballot system. However, with regard to the liberalization of election campaigning—for example, the abolition of the restriction on pre-election campaigning—the Jiyūtō agreed with the government bill. In contrast, the Shakaitō, arguing that the need for election funds constituted a major obstacle to the emergence of new figures, demanded the continuation of these restrictions and hence fell into line with the Shimpōtō. Ultimately, the reform bill proposed by the Shimpōtō, which held a numerical majority, was adopted. It tended more toward preserving the status quo than did the government's bill.

On December 16 when the election reform bill was passed, the government dissolved the lower house. Since during the session there had been resignations of members and the formation of the Kyōdōtō, the breakdown by party of the 466 members as of the day of dissolution was Nihon Shimpōtō, 270; Nihon Jiyūtō, 45; Nihon Kyōdōtō, 26; Nihon Shakaitō, 17; independents, 51; and vacancies, 57.[30]

On the day of the dissolution Shimada Toshio, speaker of the house, stated to a reporter of the *Asahi Shinbun:* "I think that the relative strength of the Shimpōtō, Jiyūtō, and Shakaitō will, in general, remain at about the same ratio as at present."[31] Shimada predicted that of the approximately 400 members at the time of dissolution, about half would be reelected. Further, he assumed that the Shimpōtō would remain the majority party and the other parties, minority parties. In other words Shimada, a typical Diet member of the time, having experienced the severe shock of defeat and occupation and given a new election law under which changes in the former electoral constituencies were foreseen, believed nonetheless that the character and make-up of the wartime Diet would continue in the postwar period.

Shimada's view was in its general outlines shared by most of the leadership of the era. The *Asahi Shinbun,* which had reported Shimada's comments, began on the same day to carry reports and analyses of conditions in each electoral district called "Pre-election Skirmishes." Although asserting that the election was an epoch-making event on a scale and with implications never seen before, the paper reported as follows:

> Overall, the majority of the people, oppressed by the present national standard of living, are disinterested in the election. In particular the conscious-

ness of women is extremely low. As for relative party strengths, the Shakaitō got an early start through its organization and activities among the farmers and is developing its campaign and exhibiting superiority in several cases. The Shimpōtō, hampered by its internal situation, has not yet surmounted its state of confusion. The Jiyūtō is not expected to advance. The Communist party is carrying out a campaign aimed at obtaining the votes of war victims and intellectuals and to a limited extent is cutting into these votes. The present total number of candidates has already reached twice the number of seats.

Although recognizing the political realignments among the people after the defeat, leaders of each party differed somewhat in their predictions of the number of seats they expected to obtain and the nature of the ensuing government. Okura Kinmochi, who had been active in promoting Ugaki as president of the Shimpōtō, foresaw: "As a prediction based solely on my intuition, I think the Shimpōtō will get approximately 160 to 170 seats, the Jiyūtō between 40 and 50, the Shakaitō 50 to 60; the Communist party will get several seats, and the rest will be independents." As he wrote in his diary, "Anyway, it is certain that the Shimpōtō will become the first party. Should, however, it ultimately fail to obtain a majority, it will probably cooperate with the Jiyūtō and form a coalition cabinet. Ultimately it can be predicted that a cabinet with capitalistic tendencies will be formed."[32]

On the other hand, according to a memorandum of the GHQ Government Section, in the view of the Jiyūtō's Hatoyama,

the Liberal party (Jiyūtō) . . . will probably become first in party strength but will not have an absolute majority in the Diet. He counts on about 150 Diet members. If he becomes responsible for the formation of a government he would set up a coalition government, preferably with the Socialists. Expecting the Social Democrats to have some 70 or 80 seats in the new Diet, a coalition with them would assure an absolute majority. The Communists may win more seats than most people think. At a recent rally Mr. Hatoyama noticed that a considerable number of young people voted Communist on a trial ballot.[33]

The alignment foreseen by Hatoyama was an extension of the "political aftereffects" remaining from the time of the formation of the party. The watershed in this trend was the issue of responsibility for the war. The memorandum states: "The big problem, Hatoyama said, was to find out how far this headquarters would go in its definition of war guilt, since he does not want to have members in his party who may be apprehended as war criminals." Hatoyama stated that only six of the twenty members of the Shimpōtō who wished to join the Jiyūtō were allowed to do so because the party gave serious consideration to the presence or absence of war crimes or ultranationalist tendencies on the part of these twenty applicants.

The Purge of Officials and Its Effect

The intentions of GHQ in which Hatoyama had been interested soon became clear. They far exceeded the expectations of the party leaders. The day after the dissolution of the Diet the government selected January 22, 1946, as election day and was about to announce this when GHQ prohibited its doing so. The *Asahi Shinbun* of December 21 reported:

> General MacArthur feels that, unless the Allies take steps, Japan's wartime political structure will completely dominate the election and he is seriously considering strong measures to prevent this. As one such measure he is considering announcing that any politician who was connected with a wartime totalitarian organization such as the Imperial Rule Assistance Association, who joined a secret patriotic group, or who collaborated substantially with the militarist faction is ineligible to run for election. If this is carried out, the majority of former Diet members will become ineligible for election.

On January 4, 1946, GHQ ordered the purge from office not only of war criminals but also of ultranationalist and militarist leaders and the dissolution of right-wing organizations.[34] Following this, the three hastily formed conservative parties were all compelled to undergo major alterations. On January 12 GHQ issued a directive approving a general election after March 15. The Shidehara cabinet, which included persons who came under the purge directive, was on the verge of a crisis; but following a reconstitution of the cabinet, it began to rebuild the system and move toward the enactment of the purge directive.

The purge was aimed at the removal of militarists from positions in government service. The government therefore, faced with an imminent election, was obliged to determine quickly the scope of application of the GHQ directive and the necessary criteria of eligibility for candidacy. Accordingly, on February 9 it excluded from candidacy individuals falling in Category C (influential members of extreme nationalist or terrorist groups or of secret patriotic organizations) and Category D (persons influential in the activities of the Imperial Rule Assistance Association, the Yokusan Seijikai, or the Dai Nippon Seijikai). At the same time, because of its fear that persons who ran in the election of 1942 as so-called recommended candidates would fall within the scope of Category G (militarists and extreme nationalists), it recommended that such individuals refrain from running in the coming election.[35]

The Shimpōtō was the hardest hit by these developments. Since all executives of the wartime Imperial Rule Assistance Association, the Yokusan Seijikai, the Dai Nippon Seijikai, and, in particular, all Diet members who ran as "recommended candidates" in the Imperial Rule Assistance election of 1942 were automatically subject to purge, it was inevitable that the blow to the Shimpōtō would be severe. Of its 270 Diet

Table 1
Candidates by Party, First Postwar Election (April 10, 1946)

Party	New	Former	Previous*	Total
Shimpōtō	337	19	22	378
Jiyūtō	432	14	42	488
Shakaitō	308	7	17	332
Communist party	143	0	0	143
Kyōdōtō	91	2	1	94
Minor parties	568	0	3	571
Independent	749	4	13	766
Total	2,628	46	98	2,772

*Candidates who had served in earlier Diets but had not been successful or had not run in the 1942 election

members at the time of dissolution, a mere 27 escaped the purge. Nearly all important party leaders from President Machida Chūji and Secretary-General Tsurumi Yusuke down were purged. The few remaining leaders, such as Saitō Takao and Inukai Takeru, applied themselves to rebuilding the party and to devising a strategy for the approaching election.

For the Jiyūtō the effect of the purge was relatively slight. Of its 45 Diet members at the time of dissolution, only 10 were purged, and President Hatoyama Ichirō and Secretary-General Kōno Ichirō escaped the purge at this time. Consequently, the Jiyūtō's preparations for the election were far less affected than the Shimpōtō's. Shimada's earlier prediction turned out to be wide of the mark, and the relative strengths of the Shimpōtō and the Jiyūtō were reversed.

Although the purge swept away so many of the old politicians, new men appeared to fill the political vacuum. The breakdown of candidates by party in the first postwar election, held on April 10, 1946, is shown in Table 1.

The Jiyūtō, which fielded more candidates than the Shimpōtō because the purge had not affected it so severely, was generally predicted to become the leading party after the election. Nevertheless, because the Shimpōtō had been the major political force during the war and possessed a firm electoral base from the days of the old Minseitō and Seiyū-kai, it was able to attract new young candidates to replace its purged Diet members. The Jiyūtō, boasting of its image as a party that would support and develop a new era for Japan, did its best to exploit the electoral base and personal ties of the Hatoyama faction of the old Seiyūkai and, whenever possible, selected influential candidates. The same was true of the third major conservative party, the Kyōdōtō.

On the other hand, as can readily be seen from the fact that minor parties and independent candidates accounted for half the total number, many candidates represented small, local, or personal parties unrelated to the three conservative parties, the Shakaitō, or the Communist party.[36] By election day, April 10, the total number of parties had reached 363. These minor party and independent candidates were a heterogeneous group, but many were of the younger generation which rejected the established politics of the old Japan and aspired to the democratic politics of a new Japan.

Of the new Diet members, 375 were elected for the first time in this election. Some were "second generation" members; that is, they ran as substitutes for purged members, but even they wished to bid farewell to the old era and create a new one. The following cases illustrate the conditions of the election of April 1946, and the bitter struggle between old and new faces that was waged in the midst of the storm of defeat, purge, and democratization that beset postwar Japan.

At the end of the Pacific war, Ide Ichitarō was engaged in the family sake manufacturing industry in his native place of Saku in Shinshu. His family belonged to the Hatoyama Ichirō faction of the Seiyūkai. But Ide's father-in-law, Koyama Kunitarō, was a Minseitō Diet member who toward the end of the war belonged to the Dai Nippon Seijikai. Ide was sought as a candidate by all the parties that were formed in the fall of 1945. Koyama, who had decided to retire from politics, encouraged him to enter the Shimpōtō as his own successor, while Uehara Etsujirō and Takeuchi Shigeyo of the Hatoyama group urged him to join the Jiyūtō. Ide described his frame of mind as follows: "At this time I felt that it was not the time for the emergence of the corrupt parties of the prewar and wartime eras. A completely new political force had to emerge. So I refused. And yet I could not go so far as to join the Shakaitō. I felt I couldn't join a party so removed from my own life."[37]

At this point Ide's poetry teacher, Yoshiue Shōsuke, encouraged him to join the Kyōdōtō, which he himself was planning to form. Ide gave this a great deal of thought but ultimately decided that the Kyōdōtō was weak. Further, he felt that there was no need for haste in determining his political course. Therefore, in the election of 1946 he ran as an independent. After the election the Diet members from Nagano—Ando Hatsu, Ikegami Takasuke, Ogawa Ippei, Kosaka Zentarō, and Ide—formed a temporary group within the Diet.

Hayakawa Takashi, who entered politics from the bureaucracy, is another example of these independent candidates; he was also elected for the first time in 1946. Hayakawa graduated from Tokyo University in the spring of 1941 and entered the Home Ministry. After a mere two weeks as a Home Ministry official, however, he became a short-term volunteer paymaster in the navy and served in the military until the defeat. In the summer of 1945 he was discharged but did not return to the Home Ministry. Hayakawa spoke of his state of mind at that time as follows:

Since the time when I was in the navy I had discussed starting out completely fresh when the war was over. I thought that following the defeat Japan would not be a continuation of prewar Japan but would have made a major, revolutionary break with the past. I, therefore, thought that we should rebuild Japan from a clean slate. When one looks at what happened afterwards, however, prewar party members as well as those who had been purged returned, and the postwar reconstruction which we had envisioned did not develop.[38]

In Tokyo after the war Hayakawa and his colleagues published a magazine, *Democrat,* but in time he returned to his home in Tanabe, Wakayama Prefecture. The April 1946 election was held during this period.

Naturally I stood for election. In this election the entire prefecture constituted a single electoral district and there were 46 candidates for the six seats. At this time there was an old leader of the Minseitō, named Koyama. Koyama, having been purged, was unable to run. He offered to give me total support if I entered the Shimpōtō, but I flatly refused, saying that it was they, the old parties and politicians, who had ruined Japan. I ran as an independent. Koyama ran his younger brother but he lost and I was elected.[39]

When asked his thoughts about the formation of the parties in the fall of 1945 and the purge directive of 1946, Hayakawa replied: "The old political parties were finished. I recognized that the old politicians were responsible for the war, so I was opposed to the formation of these parties. As for the purge directive, well, I think I accepted it as natural, because I had been critical of behavior which evaded responsibility for the war."[40]

We can thus clearly see that among the independent candidates were new politicians who were conscious of a break with the established parties.[41]

The results of the April 1946 election are shown in Table 2. In this table "former member" indicates one elected in the Imperial Rule Assistance election of 1942. In that election 81.8 percent or 381 of the total 466 members elected had been IRAA-recommended candidates and only 85 nonrecommended candidates were elected. In the 1946 election all such recommended Diet members were purged. Of the 85 nonrecommended incumbents, 38 were reelected. This was 8.2 percent of the total and 44.7 percent of the nonrecommended candidates elected in 1942. Of these 38, Hatoyama Ichirō, Kōno Ichirō, and Miki Bukichi were purged shortly after the election, and the strength of the prewar and wartime leaders was thereby weakened still more. Of course, if one combines these former members with those successful in the Diet elections prior to 1942, that is, "previous members," the total number of those who had served in the Diet comes to 89, but even this is a mere 19.1 percent of the total. The new Diet was thus one in which the 375 new members held an overwhelming majority (80.5 percent).

Table 2
Results of First Postwar Election (April 10, 1946)

Party	Prior to Dissolution	After Election (Women)	Elected for First Time	Former Members	Previous Members
Shimpōtō	274	93 (6)	70	13	10
Jiyūtō	46	139 (5)	102	14	23
Shakaitō	17	92 (8)	70	7	15
Kyōdōtō	0	14 (0)	13	0	1
Communist party	0	5 (1)	5	0	0
Minor parties	0	38 (8)	37	0	1
Independents	72	83 (10)	78	4	1
Unfilled seats	57	2	0	0	0
Total	466	466 (38)	375	38	51

SOURCE: *Political Reorientation of Japan*, vol. 1, p. 321. The results from Tokyo's second district and from Fukui Prefecture were not clear, resulting in two vacancies. There are some differences in the breakdown by party of election results depending on the source.

As these figures indicate, it was only as a result of a democratization of the system involving the expansion of the suffrage, the shift to large electoral districts, and the purge of numerous individuals from official positions that a break between the political forces of the prewar and wartime eras and the new forces of postwar politics became possible.

Changes in the Parties

The April 1946 election was characterized by (1) the emergence of the Jiyūtō as the leading party and the creation of a tripartite conflict among the Jiyūtō, Shimpōtō, and Shakaitō; (2) the overwhelming number of new Diet members (376 including one elected in the Fukui recall election); and (3) the large number of minor party and independent members elected (121).

The result was a period of constant realignment of forces between the old politicians, who, though lacking decisive power and now a minority still had strong political roots, and the new Diet members, who lacked political expertise. A complicated political situation developed involving the reorganization of many small parties, the independent members, and the leadership struggles and maneuvers of the many factions within the major parties which were trying to absorb both minor parties and independent members. This continued until the election of April 1947. During the intervening year the three conservative parties were caught up as well in a further purge of a highly political nature, and each underwent significant changes. Hatoyama's Jiyūtō became the Yoshida Jiyūtō; the Shimpōtō became the Minshūtō (Democratic party); and the Kyōdōtō became first the Kyōdō Minshūtō (Cooperative Democratic party) and finally, the Kokumin Kyōdōtō (National Cooperative party). Seen from another perspective, this was also a process whereby the conservative parties, which had heretofore displayed a high degree of continuity with the prewar parties, now emerged, under pressure from the purges, as new postwar political parties.

In the case of the Jiyūtō the shock caused by the initial purge directive had been minimal. Consequently, in the 1946 election it was able to obtain 143 seats, some forty more than the ninety-odd seats held by both the Shimpōtō and Shakaitō. Later, however, the purge of May 4 confronted it with a new situation just prior to the formation of the incoming cabinet, and it hastily brought in Foreign Minister Yoshida Shigeru as its new president. Next, both Miki Bukichi, who had been elected speaker of the house, and Secretary-General Kōno Ichirō were purged, and the founding Hatoyama faction thus received a further major blow. Thereafter, the new president, Yoshida, gradually took over the leadership of the party. In the January 1948 election many high-level bureaucrats joined the Jiyūtō and were elected, and these began to form a Yoshida Jiyūtō which, compared to the Hatoyama party, had a far stronger bureaucratic element. In time this led to a conflict with the members of the Hatoyama group who were later depurged and returned to politics, but this was still several years in the future. At the time, the change of presidents from Hatoyama to Yoshida was accomplished without major strife in the party, as is clear from the fact that it was Ōno Bamboku who replaced Kōno as secretary-general.

The realignment of the 38 minor party Diet members and 83 independent members elected in the general election of April 1946 was associated with the reorganization and factional maneuverings of the four major parties, the Jiyūtō, Shimpōtō, Shakaitō, and Kyōdōtō. From them four principal minor groupings gradually emerged. At the time of the convocation of the 90th Diet in May 1946, their situation was as follows: Nihon Minshūtō Junbikai (Japan Democratic Party Preparatory Committee), 38; Kyōdō Minshū Club (Cooperative Democratic Club), 33; Shinkō Club, 29; and Nonpartisan Club, 25.[42]

The Nihon Minshūtō Junbikai was formed by Miki Takeo, Tanaka Isaji, and others who had run without the recommendation of the IRAA during the war plus such newly elected members as Sasamori Junzō and Okada Seiichi. They planned to form a new party, but Sasamori and his colleagues as new politicians chose to adopt a policy of party "purification," and Miki, Tanaka, and Kasai Jūji (all former Diet members) ultimately became alienated from them.

The Kyōdō Minshū Club was formed when the Nihon Kyōdōtō, which had elected only 14 of its 92 candidates, gained the support of two minor parties, the Nōhontō (the Agrarian party) of Uda Kunie and the Hyūga Minshūtō (Hyūga Democratic party) of Itō Iwao plus some independent members. Shortly thereafter, on May 24, they formed the Kyōdō Minshūtō with Yamamoto Sanehiko as chairman. On June 15 Miki Takeo and Matsumoto Takizō, who in time became an influential adviser, left the Nihon Minshūtō Junbikai and joined the Kyōdō Minshūtō.[43]

The Shinkō Club was formed under the sponsorship of Matsubara Kuzuhiko. Many of its members had had careers in education. In addition, it included the independent members of Nagano Prefecture (Ide Ichitarō, Kosaka Zentarō, and Ogawa Ippei) and a young officials group including Hayakawa Takashi, Ishida Ichimatsu, Hososako Kanemitsu, and Matsutani Tenkoko.

In addition to the "architect of constitutional government," Ozaki Yukio, the Nonpartisan Club was composed of Ishiguro Tadashige, Nakano Shirō, Hozumi Shichirō, and eight women members including Togano Satoko.

Following a period of severe postelection instability occasioned by maneuvers of the Shidehara cabinet to stay in power, plans for various coalition cabinets, the purge of the Jiyūtō's Hatoyama, the appearance of a new president, Yoshida, and the food-shortage demonstration of May 19, the Yoshida cabinet was finally formed on May 22. The realignment of small parties in the Diet, however, continued.

On July 19 forty members from the Nihon Minshūtō Junbikai, the Shinkō Club, and a part of the Nonpartisan Club formed the Shinseikai. In August there was talk of a merger between the Shinseikai and the Kyōdō Minshūtō, but nothing came of it. Then on August 25, 33 members of the Shinseikai formed the Kokumintō (People's party). This group decided not to select a president immediately but to manage its affairs through a standing committee whose members included Sasamori Junzō, Nomoto Shinakichi, Okada Seiichi, Ogawa Ippei, and Hayakawa Takashi. The chairman of its Dietmen's Conference was Matsubara Kazuhiko; its youth bureau, Ide Ichitarō; and its organization bureau, Hozumi Shichirō. Kosaka Zentarō, also a member of the Shinseikai, did not join the Kokumintō but shifted to the Shimpōtō.

Following these realignments, the breakdown of party strengths on October 11, 1946, when the 90th Diet closed was Jiyūtō, 148; Shimpōtō, 110; Shakaitō, 96; Kyōdō Minshūtō, 45; Kokumintō, 33, Nonpartisan Club, 23; Communist party, 6; and independents, 5. The following February, the Kyōdō Minshūtō chairman, Yamamoto, was purged and actual power shifted to Miki. According to Hayakawa, "Miki came to me suggesting a merger of the two parties." Consequently, on March 8, 1947, the Kokumintō merged with the Kyōdō Minshūtō, forming the Kokumin Kyōdōtō (National Cooperative party) with 78 members.[44] The party chairmanship remained vacant but the executive positions were filled by Miki Takeo (secretary-general), Funada Naka (chairman of the Policy Affairs Research Council), Okada Seiichi (chairman of the Central Standing Committee), and Sasamori Junzō (chairman of the Dietmen's Conference).

The Kokumintō disappeared after only six months, but it was virtually the only purely postwar party to emerge from the confusion and uncertainty of Japanese politics immediately after the war. Many of its members had middle-class backgrounds as educators, officials of agricultural groups, or entrepreneurs of small or medium-size businesses. According to Hayakawa, who was the party ideologue, "There were many educators such as elementary school principals, and intellectuals such as myself and Ide. We were not from the established parties, but were complete amateurs who emerged out of the defeat." Since Hayakawa was later involved in a political conflict with Miki, he may have exaggerated here, but his interpretation of the merger with the Kokumin Kyōdōtō saw Miki, the professional politician from the established parties, as muscling his way in. It is, of course, true that the founders of the Kyōdōtō were to a far greater extent prewar professional politicians than were the members of the Kokumintō.

The founding statement and the platform of the Kokumintō were written entirely by Hayakawa. The former stated:

> We are firmly in sympathy with the working classes, the intellectual classes, and the young masses who are dissatisfied with the existing ideology and the old political parties. . . . Japan formerly had many martyrs in political movements of the extreme right and extreme left but the lack of martyrs in the politics of the center is a fundamental cause of the present tragedy. . . . We promise to be martyrs for the politics of the center.

The party platform consisted of six planks. Beginning with such lofty phrases as "Our party advocates a humanistic world view which harmonizes materialism and idealism and whose keynote is the practice of brotherly love," it was fraught with an amateurism not encountered in the established parties. As might be expected, when it developed into the Kokumin Kyōdōtō the tenor of its platform changed: (1) establishment of national parliamentary politics; (2) reconstruction of the Japanese economy by cooperativism; and (3) contribution to world peace and culture on the basis of humanistic principles.

Thus, the third major conservative party, the Kyōdōtō, which had obtained a mere 14 seats in the April 1946 election, managed to rally a group of unknowns who had made their appearance only in the postwar era, and in May 1946 became the Kyōdō Minshūtō. In March 1947 this merged with the Kokumintō to form the Kokumin Kyōdōtō which under Hayakawa Takashi and Ide Ichitarō gradually strengthened its foothold as a major postwar party.

The Shimpōtō, which had lost most heavily in the purge and the election of April 1946, turned first to Prime Minister Shidehara and Chief

Secretary Narahashi Wataru, and made Shidehara its president. Shortly thereafter, however, it turned to Yoshida Shigeru, and on May 22 the Yoshida cabinet was formed. It included four Shimpōtō executives, among them party president Shidehara and the chairman of the Executive Board, Saitō Takao. The party management was entrusted to Secretary-General Tanaka Manitsu and Chairman of the Executive Board Inukai Takeru.

The 90th Extraordinary Diet lasted for four months during which the new Japanese Constitution was promulgated. Developments within the Shimpōtō proceeded apace. Shidehara's biography describes them as follows:

> The Shimpōtō at the time of its formation had advocated protection of the national polity. However, since a new constitution had been promulgated and would be put into effect on May 3, 1947, it was argued that, unless they announced a new platform, the formation of the party would be meaningless. This view was forcefully advocated and became a major issue among party members. At this point the Shimpōtō's Dietmen's Conference on December 26 framed and announced a new platform and policy based on the concept of modified capitalistic social solidarity. At the party convention of January 31 the following year, a demand for the public election of party executives and public disclosure of party finances grew. Furthermore, the call to rehabilitate the party in order to establish its new posture as a sound conservative force, to rally like-minded people throughout the land, and to change the abstract party name became widespread.[45]

This movement was inevitable in a party that had undergone such major alterations. The driving force within the party was now Inukai Takeru, and Ashida Hitoshi and Yano Shōtaro of the Jiyūtō responded to this call. There ensued a movement to develop a new party that would unify the entire conservative camp. Accordingly, in March 1947 the Shimpōtō issued a statement dissolving the party.

Narahashi, although himself an independent, was active from outside the party in maneuvers to promote its alteration and recognized at once the true goal of this dissolution: "A conservative party such as the Shimpōtō which lacked principles had to try to surpass the Jiyūtō, wedge itself between the Jiyūtō and the Shakaitō, muster those not belonging to any party or faction, and become a sound centrist party with a progressive democratic character."[46]

The plans for a new party proceeded smoothly. In March, Narahashi joined the Shimpōtō; Ashida Hitoshi and Yano Shōtaro left the Jiyūtō and became independents; Hayashi Heima left the Kokumin Kyōdōtō and became independent; and all watched and waited. Then on March 31, 1947, they formed the Minshūtō (Democratic party). The new party did not adopt a presidential system; Shidehara was given the honorary position of highest adviser while the management of the party was entrusted to seven chief executive committeemen—Saitō Takao, Ashida Hitoshi, Hitotsumatsu Sadayoshi, Kawai Yoshinari, Kimura Kozaemon, Inukai Takeru, and Narahashi Wataru. Ishiguro Tadashige, who had entered the Shimpōtō from the Nonpartisan Club in September 1946, became secretary-general, and Yano Shōtaro became chairman of the Policy Affairs Research Council. Of the 466 Diet members, 145 joined the new party, which thus became larger than the Jiyūtō. The Lower House was dissolved on the day the Minshūtō was formed. At that time the distribution of party strength after the formation of both the Kokumin Kyōdōtō and the Minshūtō was Minshūtō, 145; Jiyūtō, 140; Shakaitō, 98; Kokumin Kyōdōtō, 63; others, 19; and vacancies, 1.

The new Minshūtō—as indicated by the selection of Ashida, Inukai, and Narahashi as chief executive committeemen, Ishiguro as secretary-general, and Yano as chairman of the Policy Affairs Research Council—was dominated by the Ashida-Inukai faction, which had advocated a new party and which favored a modified capitalism. The platform of the new Minshūtō was reformist, differing from the earlier Shimpōtō's "Protection of the National Polity" platform. It advocated

1. preservation of the spirit of the constitution; establishment of a democratic political system; and resolute execution of a major new policy for the establishment of a peaceful nation
2. democratization, speedy rehabilitation of production, and stabilization of the masses' standard of living on the basis of a comprehensive economic plan
3. promotion of education which aims at the perfection of individuality; cultivation of religious sentiment and elevation of popular culture; and contribution to world enlightenment
4. restoration of international morality and cooperation in the establishment of a peaceful world.

Just when it seemed that this new platform and structure would dissipate the image of the old Shimpōtō and the party would be able to run well in the April election, its central figures—Inukai, Narahashi, and Ishiguro—were all purged from public office, a staggering blow to the new Minshūtō. This purge was even more politically suspect than the purge of Hatoyama the previous year. Hori Shigeru, who had been active with Inukai in the formation of the new party and was purged along with him, in later years described it as follows: "Instead of a backward-looking party which remained unchanged, embracing Mr. Ashida we had tried to create a fresh, new party and to turn it into the mainstream of postwar conservativism. Then all of the group who had worked for the formation of the Minshūtō were purged. This was known as the 'Y' purge."[47]

Hori also told of an interesting experience. In February 1947 he became parliamentary vice-minister of Commerce and Industry. When he met Tsuji Karoku, who was active behind the scenes in Hatoyama's Jiyūtō, the following conversation took place:

TSUJI: Congratulations on becoming parliamentary vice-minister. By the way, is there talk of the formation of a new party?

HORI: I'm working at it very hard.

TSUJI: You will need great determination. You're being watched, so be careful. Yoshida seems to be getting ready.

In this fashion the purge gradually became a political instrument strongly influencing the fortunes of particular parties and showed signs of deviating from its original goal as the instrument of genuine democratization. Despite this setback, the shift from old to new within the Minshūtō progressed and, to a certain extent, succeeded.

In the election of April 1947 the Minshūtō fell to the rank of third largest party in the Diet. At its party convention on May 18, however, a compromise was reached that resulted in Ashida becoming party president, Shidehara, honorary president, and Saitō, the highest adviser. Ashida's presidency meant that the young Shinshinkai group of Kitamura Tokutaro, Kawasaki Hideji, and Kosaka Zentarō, who had replaced the purged Inukai as leaders, had seized the initiative within the party. The Minshūtō accordingly acquired the image of a centrist party "to the left of the Jiyūtō and to the right of the Kokumin Kyōdōtō and the Shakaitō." It then set about the creation of a coalition government of the three parties—the Shakaitō, Minshūtō, and Kokumin Kyōdōtō.

Notes

1. Shūgiin [House of Representatives] and Sangiin [House of Councillors], eds., *Gikai seido shichijūnenshi seitōkaihahen* [Seventy-year history of the parliamentary system: Party and faction volume] (1961), p. 657. All figures concerning the party affiliation of Diet members, unless otherwise stated, are based on this work.

2. Prime Minister Higashikuni stated at his press conference on August 28: "At this time I believe that the entire nation of military, bureaucracy, and civilians must thoroughly reflect and repent. I believe that for all the people of the nation to repent is the first step in rebuilding our country and the first step toward national solidarity." Higashikuni Naruhiko, *Watakushi no kiroku* [My record] (Tōhō Shobō, 1947), p. 184. For the complete text of the prime minister's speech of September 5, see *Gikai seido shichijūnenshi, teikoku gikaishi* [History of the Imperial Diet], vol. 2 (1962), pp. 1021–1025.

3. "Ashida shitsumon shuisho" [Question by Mr. Ashida], *Gikai seido shichijūnenshi, teikoku gikaishi*, pp. 1027–1028. In this question Ashida noted: "If at

this point one says that the responsibility for the defeat lies with the masses of the people, it will surely earn their resentment."

4. The fact that GHQ intended to give serious consideration to the issue of war crimes had been inferred earlier by the Yokohama Liaison Office for Ending the War. Accordingly on September 11 the Japanese government decided on an emergency policy of proposing its own voluntary investigation and punishment of those responsible, but failed in fact to follow through on this. Concerning the situation at this time, see Suzuki Tadakatsu, *Nihon gaikōshi* [History of Japanese diplomacy], vol. 26, *Shūsen kara kōwa made* [From the end of the war to peace] (Kajima Kenkyūjo Shuppankai, 1973), pp. 33–47.

5. "Kōfuku ni okeru Beikoku no shoki no tainichi hōshin" [The initial postsurrender policy of the United States toward Japan], in Tsuji Seimei, ed., *Shiryō sengo nijūnenshi* [A 20-year documentary history of the postwar period], vol. 1, *Seiji* [Politics] (Nihon Hyōronsha, 1966), pp. 16–18. (Concerning the encouragement of democratic political parties, however, it is well known that this was "subject to the necessity for maintaining the security of the occupying forces.")

6. Higashikuni described his reasons for resigning as follows: "Although General MacArthur stated in a meeting with me a few days ago that there was no need to change cabinet ministers, the fact that several days later he issued this directive is probably because he does not have confidence in the cabinet. I thought that I would issue a general amnesty order and, in the name of the emperor, release persons who had been harshly punished in the name of the emperor as Communists, for treason, or for lese majesté, etc. However, these procedures were delayed, and the fact that these people have not been released in the name of General MacArthur cannot be justified to the emperor." Higashikuni Naruhiko, *Higashikuni nikki* [The diary of Higashikuni] (Tokuma Shobō, 1968), p. 246.

7. Hatoyama Ichirō, *Hatoyama Ichirō kaikoroku* [The memoirs of Hatoyama Ichirō] (Bungei Shunjū Shinsha, 1957), pp. 23–24.

8. Political Parties Branch, Government Section, GHQ, "Liberal Party," in *Japanese Political Parties,* vol. 1, ed. Government Section, GHQ. This compiled the results of several surveys on the Jiyūtō, the Shimpōtō, the Kyōdōtō, the Shakaitō, the Communist party, minor parties, women Representatives, and Diet groups and independents. It was written between June and August 1946. H. E. Wilds was responsible for the section on the Jiyūtō.

9. The Dōkōkai was a group that was critical of the Imperial Rule Assistance system and the "one nation, one party" trend. Its principal members were Ozaki Yukio, Hatoyama Ichirō, Andō Masazumi, Kawasaki Katsu, Ashida Hitoshi, and Katayama Tetsu, several of whom later became founders of the Nihon Jiyūtō. Furthermore, during the Tōjō cabinet, Hatoyama, Miki Bukichi, and Nakano Seigo formed a "three-man anti-Tōjō league" and attacked Tōjō's politics. See Hatoyama Ichirō, *Aru daigishi no seikatsu to iken* [The life and views of a Diet member] (Tokyo Shuppan, 1952), and *Watakushi no jijoden* [My autobiography] (Kaizōsha, 1951).

10. Nishio Suehiro, *Nishio Suehiro no seiji oboegaki* [The political memoirs of Nishio Suehiro] (Mainichi Shinbunsha, 1968), pp. 32–34. See also Mizutani Chōzaburō, *Mizutani Chōzaburō den* [Biography of Mizutani Chōzaburō] (1963), pp. 174–179.

11. Hirano Rikizō, interview, March 7, 1978. This view of the United States, rather than being based on a detailed analysis of its probable Occupation policies, seems to have been inferred from the "lessons of the past" of the experience of Germany after the First World War.

12. Hatoyama, *Aru daigishi*, p. 25. Nishio, *Nishio Suehiro*, pp. 39–40. Andō Masazumi, who together with Hatoyama played a major role in the founding of the Jiyūtō, in his diary entry for August 23 wrote: "We finally met at 2:00 as a discussion group. Hatoyama, Uehara, Ōno, Yano, Hirano, Mizutani, and Nishio were there. We discussed such major issues as the relationship between the high command and national affairs; a liberal economy versus a controlled economy; social policy versus socialism; and the basic underlying tone of education. We then separated, having decided to meet again on the 30th." The *Andō Masazumi nikki* [Diary of Andō Masazumi] is in the Constitutional History Documents Room of the National Diet Library. Nishio places the date of this meeting as August 25, but here I rely on the date given by Andō.

13. This "friendly relationship" between Hatoyama and Nishio was perceived by the Government Section as well. See Government Section, *Japanese Political Parties*, p. 5.

14. Iwabuchi Tatsuo, *Nihon seikai shichijūnenshi* [Seventy-year history of Japanese politics], in *Iwabuchi Tatsuo senshū* [Collected writings of Iwabuchi Tatsuo], vol. 1 (Seiyūsha, 1968), p. 568.

15. Hatoyama, *Aru daigishi*, p. 26. Hoshijima Niro recalled: "I became a member of the Standing Committee in October. At that time we had many join who were not politicians, but in the long run we could not interest such men professionally and, before we knew it, they drifted away." Andō Yoshio, ed., *Showa keizaishi e no shōgen* [Testimony for an economic history of the Showa era], vol. 2 (Mainichi Shinbunsha, 1966), p. 96.

16. Leaders of the Jiyūtō, such as Hatoyama and Andō, had their first contact with Major Roest and other staff members of the Government Section on November 25. As a result of this meeting, Roest felt that "it seems likely that his [Hatoyama's] party will play a moderately conservative role in the earlier stages of Japan's political rebirth, with a good chance of holding the balance of power if the Progressive party splits up. Its strength will be derived from the people's political inertia rather than from any leadership in ideas or plans. . . . The widely current impression that Mr. Hatoyama is a pure 'laissez-faire' type liberal appears incorrect. He might pass rather as a well-educated Tory." Memorandum for the Record, "Interview with Hatoyama Ichirō" (P. K. Roest), pp. 4–5.

17. Iwabuchi, *Nihon seikai shichijūnenshi*, pp. 568–569. One can also view the activities connected with the formation of the Shimpōtō as divided among four groups: an elder politician group; the central executive group composed of the Machida and Nakajima factions; the young Dietmen's group; and the Maeda-Oasa-Miki group, which had taken the initiative during the Imperial Rule Assistance era. Gikai Seiji Kenkyūkai, ed., *Seitō nenkan* [Political party yearbook 1947] (Nyususha, 1946), p. 10.

18. Ugaki cited three conditions for progress in Japanese domestic politics: (1) the ability to recruit men of talent from all over the country, (2) the ability to raise the necessary funds, and (3) the issue of whether or not the United States could be relied upon to prevent the political resurgence of the former military (September

20). He believed that "if one synthesizes information with regard to the third point, we will scrape through; the second point (funds) for the most part looks promising; but where the recruitment of men of talent is concerned, the third prerequisite, there is still some pessimism" (October 19). He planned to run for election after resigning his honors. *Ugaki Kazushige nikki* [The diary of Ugaki Kazushige], vol. 3 (Misuzu Shobō, 1971). See also Naiseishi Kenkyūkai, Nihon Kindai Shiryō Kenkyūkai, ed., *Ōkura Kinmochi nikki* [The diary of Ōkura Kinmochi], vol. 4 (1975).

19. "The Progress Party (Shimpōtō) began as a frankly tentative organization. To a degree greater than those of other contemporary Japanese political groups, its history has been opportunistic. This leads to the party's insincerity of principle." Government Section, "The Progress Party," June 22, 1946, in *Japanese Political Parties*, pp. 8, 15.

20. *Gikai seidō shichijūnenshi, teikoku gikaishi,* vol. 2, pp. 1041–1044.

21. The Nonpartisan Club's resolution stated: "It is extremely regrettable that [in the resolutions of both parties] as Dietmen they hasten to pursue the responsibility of others, but lack an attitude that feels strongly their own political responsibility for the defeat and apologizes to the people for their crimes. We . . . appeal to the judgment of the people from a position of independence." Ibid. Although this resolution was not adopted, ten members including Rōyama Masamichi resigned on December 1.

22. Of the Shimpōtō executives, it was Tsurumi Yūsuke who maintained contact with GHQ. On December 1 Tsurumi requested that the Counter-Intelligence officer clarify the situation concerning the preparation of a directive purging 200 incumbent Diet members. Government Section, GHQ, SCAP, *Political Reorientation of Japan,* vol. 1 (Washington, D.C.; GPO, n.d.), p. 13.

23. In March the Gokoku Dōshikai was formed by those Diet members who had left the Yokusan Seijikai. It included Ino Hiroya as representative, and Funada Naka, Akagi Munenori, Nagayama Tadanori, and Nakatani Takeyo as executives. This group was regarded as the personal party of Kishi (Nobusuke). Its main constituents were proponents of racialism and right-wing activists, and it included such heterogeneous elements as Miyake Shoichi and others from the proletarian movement. It advocated completion of the war and opposed the movement to terminate the war. See Nakatani Takeyo, *Senji gikaishi* [History of the wartime Diet] (Minzoku to Seijisha, 1970).

24. Tominomori Eiji, *Sengo hoshutōshi* [A history of postwar conservative parties] (Nihon Hyōronsha, 1977), pp. 5–6.

25. Funada Naka, interview, April 12, 1978. For another interview with Funada, see Nakamura Takafusa, Itō Takashi, Hara Akira, eds., *Gendaishi o tsukuru hitobito* [Creators of modern Japanese history], vol. 2 (Mainichi Shinbunsha, 1971).

26. Ibid.

27. "The Co-Operative Party is largely an agrarian party representing the larger landowners. It is a conservative group supporting traditional Japanese ideas while cloaking those ideas in modernized terminology. The key-word 'Co-Operation,' in actuality, is the same phrase used by Japanese totalitarians to justify the unification of the nation under Imperial supervision." Government Section, "Co-operative Democratic Party (Kyōdō Minshūtō)," July 15, 1946, in *Japanese Political Parties*.

28. *Gikai seido shichijūnenshi, teikoku gikaishi*, vol. 2, p. 1038. Other important bills addressed the reform of the agricultural land survey law and the labor union law.

29. Concerning the process of reform of the election law, see Jichi Daigakko, *Sengo jichishi* [A history of postwar self-government], IV, *Shūgiin giin senkyohō no kaisei* [Reform of the lower house election law] (1961); Zenkoku Senkyōkanri Iinkai, *Senkyo seidō kokkai shingiroku* [Records of the Diet deliberation on election systems], first ed. (1951).

30. Figures are based on *Jiji Nenkan* [Current affairs yearbook] (1947). Figures in *Gikai seido shichijūnenshi, seitōkaiha* are slightly different, showing Shimpōtō, 274; Nonpartisan Club, 72; Jiyūtō, 46; Shakaitō, 17; Absentee, 57. The Kyōdōtō did not organize a parliamentary group.

31. *Asahi Shinbun* [Asahi News], December 19, 1945.

32. *Ōkura kinmochi nikki*, vol. 4 (December 18), 1945, pp. 365–366.

33. Memorandum for Record, "Report of Interviews with Political Leaders on 18 and 20 December 1945." December 24, 1945 (Roest). This memorandum is a record of questions asked of the Jiyūtō's Hatoyama, the Shakaitō's Mizutani, the Shimpōtō's Tsurumi, and the Communist party's Shiga Yoshio concerning their attitude toward the major bills of the 89th Diet (i.e., election campaigning and so forth). In this connection, Mizutani predicted that the Shakaitō aimed at one-third of the seats in each electoral district and would ultimately run 200 candidates including the 17 incumbents. He stated that the average age of those already informally selected was 45. Tsurumi noted that the reputation of the Shimpōtō had declined in the 89th Diet and gave as the reasons for this the problem of the selection of a president; the fact that the Diet members' speeches, except for Saitō's, were weak; and the clumsy handling of the war responsibility issue. He stated that the Shimpōtō would run 400 candidates, including the 219 incumbents, and that there would be 20 female candidates.

34. M. Gayne, in his diary of December 20, wrote: "Two or three days ago there was a top secret meeting concerning the draft directive to purge war criminals from Japanese politics, and representatives from each section of GHQ attended. However, a split immediately developed." *Nippon nikki* [Japan diary], vol. 1 (Chikuma Shobō, 1951), pp. 35–38. Concerning the official purge, see Hans Baerwald, *The Purge of Japanese Leaders under the Occupation* (University of California Press, 1959), and Jichi Daigakko, *Sengo jichishi*, VI, *Kōshoku tsuihō* [Purge of public officials] (1964).

35. Where the scope of the purge was concerned, categories B and E were agreed upon on February 14 and category G on March 10. All parties were concerned about the relationship between category G and IRAA-recommended Diet members and about other issues such as whether or not a party president should be considered a public official. In mid-February, however, all such questions were temporarily settled. See *Sengo jichishi*, VI, pp. 100–112.

36. "The minor parties' representatives are in general a conservative group; some of them are 'fronts' for influential interests, others are political opportunists, and still others are sincere but confused proponents of some plan for rehabilitating Japan. They have been, and will continue to be, quite easily influenced by whatever conservative group seeks their support." Government Section, "Minor Parties Represented in the 90th Diet," in *Japanese Political Parties*. For an analysis of the Nihon Mintō (Japan People's party), see Itō Takashi and Morita

Yoshichida, "Taishō chūki-Shōwa sanjūnen no hankiseiseito seiryoku-Ibaraki-ken no baai" [Antiestablishment party forces from mid-Taisho to the Showa thirties, the case of Ibaraki Prefecture], *Shakai Kagaku Kenkyū,* vol. 29, no. 2 (1977).

37. Ide Ichitarō, interview, April 11, 1978.

38. Hayakawa Takashi, interview, May 8, 1978.

39. Ibid.

40. Ibid.

41. A similar analysis is also possible of the women candidates who became eligible for candidacy for the first time in this election. See Government Section, "Japan's Women Representatives," August 23, 1946 (Beate Sirota), in *Japanese Political Parties,* vol. 2.

42. Government Section's *Japanese Political Parties* contains an eleven-item memorandum of July 24, entitled "Diet Groups and Independents." The discussion here takes this memorandum into account but with some discrepancies due to the scale and rapidity of changes in the minor party scene. According to the Government Section memorandum, at the time of the opening of the 90th Diet there were the Minshū Club (Nihon Minshūtō Junbikai), the Shinkō Club, and the Nonpartisan Club. These groups accounted for the majority of Diet members who did not belong to a major party.

43. In the view of the Government Section, a conflict between the urban faction of Yamamoto, Ikawa, et al. and the agrarian faction of the Kita brothers led to problems in the recombinations of the minor parties. The agrarian factions of the Kyōdō Minshū Club favored the entry of the Hyūga Minshūtō (Hyūga Democratic party) dominated by Ugaki and the Nōhontō (Agrarian party), while the urban faction favored Miki, Matsumoto, and Tanaka Isaji. Ultimately Tanaka was refused entry. Government Section, "Cooperative Democratic Party," in *Japanese Political Parties,* pp. 8–13.

44. For the founding of the Kokumin Kyōdōtō, see Asahi Shinbun Seitō Kishadan, *Seitō nenkan* [Political party yearbook], 1948 (Nyūsusha, 1948), p. 243 *et seq.*

45. Shidehara Heiwa Zaidan, *Shidehara Kijūrō* (1955), p. 721.

46. Narahashi Wataru, *Gekiryū ni saosashite* [Boating in a swift current] (Yokushoin, 1968), p. 135. See also *Seitō nenkan,* 1948, p. 206 *et seq.*

47. Hori Shigeru, *Sengo seiji no oboegaki* [Memoirs of postwar politics] (Mainichi Shinbunsha, 1975), pp. 21–22.

12

Early Postwar Reformist Parties

Takemae Eiji

It is the purpose of this essay to examine the impact of Occupation policy upon the reconstruction and restructuring of political parties, especially the "reformist parties" in the immediate postwar Occupation era from the perspective of continuity and discontinuity in the development of party politics in Japan.

The prewar proletarian parties (Labor Farmer party, Japan Labor-Farmer party, and Social Democratic party) and especially the socialist parties (Japan Communist party [JCP], Japan Socialist party [JSP], and Democratic Socialist party [DSP]) were virtually incapacitated under the prewar Imperial political system. They were unable to coordinate or consolidate either public opinion or popular interests. The very foundations of party political functions—parliamentary democracy, freedom of political activity, women's suffrage—either had not been established or were inadequately provided in the constitution, the Elections Law, and the Political Parties Law. It was the Occupation's policies with regard to *zaibatsu* (financial combines) dissolution, political party liberalization, and universal suffrage that made possible the rapid economic growth, the expansion of the role of reformist political parties, and other basic features of postwar Japan.

In this sense, there is clear discontinuity between the prewar and postwar periods in the history of Japanese political parties. It is my thesis that Occupation policies were a major cause of this discontinuity. Yet the use of the term "Occupation policies" should not be taken to imply that these policies were uniform throughout the entire period of the Occupation. In fact, the force and direction of the Occupation's progressive policies varied from time to time within the Occupation period. The first six to eight months had the greatest impact upon the democratization and liberalization of Japan's political parties, for at this time the authority of Japan's wartime rulers reached its nadir and popular enthusiasm for reform peaked, while the reformist zeal of the Occupation forces themselves was at its height, and they brought strong pressures to bear on the Japanese government for reformist actions of real substance. In effect, conditions were just right for reshaping the "substance" of Japan's traditional institutions and culture under the "pressure" of forceful Occupation directives in the "heat" of a favorable public opinion. In later stages of the Occupation, however, countervailing forces (the reverse course) emerged and negated the effect of many of the initial reforms, thus weakening the impact of earlier Occupation policies and enhancing continuity with Japan's prewar traditions and practices. With this shift in mind, the present chapter is primarily an analysis of the initial Occupation period from the end of the war in August 1945 through the postwar revival and reorganization of political parties to the start of parliamentary activity in April 1946.

This period was transitional to the full-fledged establishment of Occupation institutions, and it was the time when the policies of demilitarization and democratization so important to overall Occupation policy were formulated. From the standpoint of political dynamics within the Occupation's General Headquarters (GHQ), this period coincided with the Office of the Political Advisor's extremely important role in such areas as the release of political prisoners, the designation of war criminals, the purge of wartime leaders, and the liberalization of political parties. It largely preceded the time when the Office of the Political Advisor transferred its work on the purge and political parties to the Government Section (GS) and its prosecution of war criminals to the International Prosecution Section, keeping for itself only its diplomatic responsibilities centering on liaison with the Allied Council for Japan. Also, it was not until late February 1946 that the Far Eastern Commission in Washington, D.C., began to function, in theory at least, as the ultimate policy-determining authority for the Allied Occupation of Japan.

Within Japan, this period witnessed the determination of the contents of the new constitution (in February–March 1946) and the holding of the first postwar general election in April under conditions that barred purgees from running for public office and resulted in a new Diet, 80 percent of which consisted of first-term members. This was thus an extremely important period in the development of postwar parliamentary politics in Japan.

In the following pages, I shall examine (1) the neglected area of GHQ Occupation policy toward political parties, especially the JCP and the JSP, and (2) the postwar restructuring of the reformist parties, concluding with a consideration of factors of continuity and discontinuity in the development of postwar political parties in Japan. On the assumption that early Occupation policies were a major cause of discontinuity, this essay will examine the nature of these early Occupation policies and the JCP and JSP reactions thereto. Consideration of the 1946 election, the

new Election Law, and the stillborn Political Parties Law will, unfortunately, not be possible within the space available.

GHQ's Initial Occupation Policies

The dissolution of ultranationalistic and militaristic political bodies and
the liberalization of activity by "all political parties" in order to restore
and strengthen democratic processes lay at the heart of GHQ's policies
with respect to political parties. However, a problem arose as to whether
or not socialist political parties, especially the JCP, should be included
within this phrase "all political parties." The Department of State and
State-War-Navy Coordinating Committee (SWNCC) documents contain
no explicit instructions on this point, directing simply that political prisoners are to be released in keeping with the basic policy of guaranteeing
civil rights. The October 4, 1945, GHQ directive freeing large numbers
of political prisoners, including the JCP leadership, and legalizing Communist party activity was especially significant. It was, in fact, a decisive
blow to the old ruling clique's efforts to maintain the Imperial institutions (polity) intact and to retain the policy of outlawing the JCP. Input
from such Japan specialists as E. Herbert Norman and John K. Emmerson contributed to this October 4 directive. Supreme Commander
MacArthur's decision is thought to have been especially influenced by the
"positive policies toward the JCP" advocated by Emmerson as one of his
political advisors. This raises the question of GHQ's initial expectations
and policies with respect to the JCP and JSP.

GHQ's Assessment of Japanese Liberals

The February 18, 1944, memorandum entitled "Preliminary Political
and Policy Questions Bearing on Civil Affairs Planning for the Far East
and Pacific Areas," sent to the State Department jointly by the War
Department's Civil Affairs Section and the Navy Department's Occupied
Areas Department, poses two questions relating to political parties: "Are
there any political agencies or political parties of the enemy country with
whom we can deal to assist in the restoration of essential authority in
Japan and in its subsequent administration?" and "Are there any political
parties, organizations or groups in enemy country that should be dissolved? If so, which ones?"[1] The State Department's response was contained in its March 23, 1944, document "Japan: Political Parties or
Agencies."

After cogently analyzing Japan's prewar and wartime political parties
and political organizations and discussing the ultranationalistic, militaristic character and dangerous potential of such organizations as the
Imperial Rule Assistance Association, Imperial Rule Assistance Political

Society, House of Peers, Japan Martial Virtues Association, and Black Dragon Society, the State Department memorandum makes the following recommendations: (1) the dissolution of the Imperial Rule Assistance Association and Imperial Rule Assistance Political Society as well as their member organizations, the closure of the House of Peers' clubhouse and the banning of meetings there (albeit permitting the continued existence of the House of Peers itself), (2) the dissolution of such nationalist organizations as the Reservists' Association, (3) the termination of other quasi-cultural organizations that would impede democratization, and a ban on their meetings, (4) utilization of the neighborhood associations for such purposes as the maintenance of public order, hygiene, and relief activities, and (5) a cautious attitude by military government officals toward so-called liberal political forces.[2] This last recommendation notes that the liberal camp also included many people sympathetic to the militarists and ultranationalists to the extent that it would be a mistake to view all those in the liberal camp as truly liberal.

At this time, then, U.S. policy on political parties centered on the elimination of ultranationalistic and militaristic parties and political organizations, while explicit policies toward the reformist parties were not yet in evidence. Still, the advocacy of caution in dealing with liberal political forces is nonetheless noteworthy in that a separate document, also drawn up by the State Department, listed the 1920s pro-American liberals in Japan as one of the groups that should be assisted, along with political parties, labor unions, cooperative associations, and other grass-roots organizations in keeping with the overall policy of abolishing militarism and strengthening democratic processes.[3] This discrepancy is the result of differing assessments by the two authors involved of the fact that some of the 1920s liberals had cooperated with the military, were loud in their praise of militarism and ultranationalism, and had become apostles of these creeds as the military became dominant and the winds of militarism blew stronger in the 1930s.

The Emmerson Plan

In July 1944 the U.S. assault on Saipan breached Japan's last line of defense (the Marianas–Carolines–West New Guinea line as decided upon at the September 30, 1943, Imperial Conference) and brought Tokyo within range of B-29 raids. This position of military superiority once achieved, the U.S. State Department turned its attention to political and psychological means of hastening the Japanese government's surrender and to an analysis of the kinds of potentially favorable forces that existed in Japan and how they could best be used in the postsurrender occupation to foster Japan's political and economic reconstruction.

Within Japan the Communists and some religious groups such as

Ōmoto-kyō and Tenri-kyō had consistently opposed the military's fascism. The drafters of State Department policy were concerned with how to minimize U.S. military losses by using such groups to oppose the war and promote its early end, as well as with the role they could play in the postwar democratization of Japan.

When the Dixie Mission headed by Ambassador Patrick J. Hurley visited China in September 1944, one of its members was John K. Emmerson. In China Emmerson met Nosaka Sanzō (then using the alias Okano Susumu) in Yenan as well as Kaji Wataru in Chungking and questioned them about the antiwar movement in China and their thoughts on postwar Japan. These contacts with Nosaka, Kaji, and others led Emmerson to conceive a design for unifying all of the antiwar, antimilitarist, antifascist, and prodemocratic forces inside and outside Japan. In effect, this was a psychological warfare plan that would bring together such U.S.-resident Japanese and Japanese-American pacifists as Ōyama Ikuo and Fujii Shūji with the Japanese People's Liberation League group led by Nosaka in Yenan and the antiwar propagandists headed by Kaji in Chungking.[4]

Soon after his return from China to the United States, Emmerson sounded out the Office of Strategic Services (OSS) and the Office of War Information (OWI) on the possibilities of collecting information about Japanese Communists from Communists in the United States, including Japanese-Americans, with a view to cooperating with them. He contacted Ōyama Ikuo and obtained valuable information from him through a Northwestern University political science professor, Kenneth Colegrove.[5] This initial program to bring Ōyama, Nosaka, and Kaji together later (March 1945) developed into a plan for supporting the Japanese Communists, strengthening the antiwar underground in Japan, and sending operatives into Japan from abroad.[6] Although this plan was not finally implemented, Emmerson's Yenan interview with Nosaka on his plans for postwar revolution had a major influence on U.S. policy vis-à-vis the Communist party immediately after the war.

In the program that he outlined for Emmerson, Nosaka divided the revolution into three stages: (1) the end of the war, (2) the democratic revolution, and (3) the socialist revolution. Nosaka's expectation was that the democratic revolution would take a long time and would probably not be completed within his own lifetime. On the question of the emperor system, an issue central to political reform, Nosaka said that Emperor Hirohito could not escape responsibility for the war, since he was responsible for the military's actions since the Manchurian Incident of September 1, 1931, and that he should therefore abdicate. However, he also thought that it would be possible to maintain the imperial institution with diminished powers. Because adulation for the emperor was still strong among the Japanese people, he felt that the final resolution of this issue would be decided by the popular will as the truth about the imperial institution became known. The JCP should not, however, initiate a campaign to overthrow the emperor system for the time being. Still, it would be dangerous for the Allied powers or the Japanese people to try to use the emperor system, since there was a danger that reactionary groups might turn such an effort to their advantage. Nosaka also favored diminishing the powers of the *genrō*, the Privy Council, and the House of Peers; having the government buy up the farmlands of parasitic landlords and open these to impoverished tenant farmers; and instituting government controls over the giant capitalist corporations.[7] Especially noteworthy is the fact that Nosaka, like the Chinese Communist party, opposed the confiscation of private property and instead proposed a joint front bringing together all antifascist and antimilitaristic democratic forces, including capitalists, and the establishment of a popular democratic government by the liberals and Communists. Also notable is Nosaka's welcoming of the dissolution of the Soviet-dominated Comintern, and the JCP's consequent escape from Comintern control and freedom to pursue its own independent activities.[8]

Emmerson was, in effect, advising the Secretary of State that a positive policy of assistance for the JCP was to be preferred to a negative policy of repression in light of U.S. strategy vis-à-vis the Soviet Union. This analysis of Emmerson's later came to be very influential when he came to Japan soon after the war's end as one of General MacArthur's first political advisors and was put in charge of GHQ's initial policy toward the political parties.[9]

The State-War-Navy Coordinating Committee (SWNCC) and GHQ's Initial Policy

In June 1945, SWNCC, established on December 1, 1944, as the highest decision-making organ for Occupation policy on Japan, began its study of the United States Initial Post-Surrender Policy for Japan (SWNCC-150 series). This document, later released on September 22, 1945, as a White House directive, says that "democratic political parties with rights of assembly and public discussion shall be encouraged, subject to the necessity for maintaining the security of the occupying forces," thus guaranteeing freedom of political activity in principle.[10] This was in keeping with the Potsdam Declaration's call for "the revival and strengthening of democratic tendencies." The Joint Chiefs of Staff's Basic Policy Directive transmitted to General MacArthur on November 1 that same year (JCS-1380/15), which was drawn up virtually in parallel with this initial policy paper, was even more specific than the SWNCC paper, stating that "(1) the Political Association of Great Japan, the Imperial Rule Assistance Association, the Imperial Rule Assistance Political Society, their affiliates and agencies of any successor organizations, and all Japanese ultra-nationalistic, terroristic and secret patriotic societies and their agencies and affiliates" were to be dissolved, and that (2) the existing political parties and political organizations would be placed under the control of the Supreme Commander for the Allied Powers (SCAP), that those supportive of the needs and objectives of the military Occupation would be assisted, while those in opposition thereto would be dissolved, that the formation and activities of democratic political parties would be supported and they would have rights of assembly and of public debate to the extent that such did not interfere with the maintenance of public order by the Occupation forces.[11]

Quite aside from this policy decision made in Washington, GHQ, shortly after landing in Japan, issued its own "Proposal for Political Reform in Japan." In this, GHQ foresaw an important future role for political parties. In light of a situation wherein the Diet had not in the past served as a legislature truly representative of the popular will and the political parties had not been able to maintain their independence, the proposal states that "much of the attention now being devoted to the question of civil liberties is intimately linked with discussion of the future role of political parties and the Diet. General agreement on the future importance of the Diet and the desirability of freely organized political parties is evident."[12]

This thrust was made more specific in a paper entitled "The Revival of Political Parties in Japan" issued one week later on September 28. In this the authors note that the end of the war made a revival of political parties possible, and that the dissolution of the Political Association of Great Japan, Society of Patriotic Comrades, I.R.A. Youth Corps Diet Member Society, and other organizations was followed by an eruption of political organizations of all types but whose positions and future directions remained uncertain. Consequently, the period preceding the general election to be held in early 1946 (four to six months hence at the time of the paper) would be of critical importance not only for the role the political parties could play in a provisional Diet immediately after the war but even more as an indication of the various parties' strengths and directions for the future. The thrust of the paper lies in its assertion that postwar political parties were emerging in Japan under extremely difficult conditions, being forced to organize rapidly to prepare for a proposed general election only four to six months away. They were almost entirely dependent on old political leadership, which was essentially conservative and out of touch with current popular trends, and their apparent adherence to prewar political affiliations might lead to the revival of the factional differences that weakened party unity in the past. The limitations imposed on the effective action of political parties and on the powers of the Diet by the Meiji Constitution still existed, and it remained to be seen whether the present political leadership would work for radical change or whether they could evoke popular support for such action. Furthermore, the inability of political parties to solve Japan's pressing internal economic problems, which were largely beyond their control, might well weaken their popular support.[13]

It was the view of GHQ, therefore, that the existing political groupings should probably be considered as only interim parties. Their continuance was dependent upon the re-election of their leaders, the quality of new members elected to the Diet, and the degree to which they would be able to organize their parties and programs to overcome past weaknesses and offer constructive solutions to current problems. However, such factors as the diversion of public interest from politics to more urgent problems of food and shelter, the slowness of antiparty forces outside the Diet to organize, and the continuity of leadership in Japanese party organizations afforded some respite.

At the time the Socialist party appeared to have an advantage over the other political groups. Its organization was consolidating more rapidly than others and its members seemed to have a unity of purpose lacking in other more heterogeneous groups. Also, the socialist solutions to the prevailing economic problems may have been more realistic and more popular than the more conservative policies of the other parties. On the other hand, the future strength of the new Socialist party would depend not only on its ability to attract new Diet members but also on its ability to maintain its current unity of purpose and thus to avoid a repetition of former factional strife.

Notable also were the facts that GHQ (the Office of the Political Advisor) had already planned to hold Japan's first general election in early 1946 and that, since the political parties that were revived immediately after the war were in the traditional conservative mold, it strongly favored the formation of more democratic opposition parties and political organizations.

The Release of Political Prisoners

It was this situation that was responsible for the release of political prisoners and the ensuing favorable climate for the rebuilding of the Japan Communist party. Notwithstanding the loss of the war on August 15, 1945, and strong appeals both from within and outside the prisons for the release of prisoners,[14] Japan's old ruling clique refused to repeal the Public Order Preservation Law (Chian-iji-hō) or to release political prisoners. As late as October 3, 1945, the authorities were maintaining that "the *Tokkō* [Special Higher Police] are still operative, and [that] anyone who advocates abolition of the emperor system [would be] viewed as a Communist and arrested under the Public Order Preservation Law."[15]

This adamant policy of the Japanese government even after "liberation" not only disturbed the foreign reporters but was also a great shock to GHQ. At the time, Miki Kiyoshi, Tosaka Jun, and a number of other well-known philosophers and antiwar figures had died in prison, the political prisoners were in a state of high anxiety,[16] and it was reported in the press that the prisoners had reached their limit both physically and mentally.[17]

There had already been a State Department document on the release of political prisoners dated June 14, 1944. The general policy of releasing political prisoners having already been adopted, this paper recommended that (1) the military government establish principles and procedures for the release and restoration of civil rights to all people being held unjustly or illegally and review all relevant cases, and (2) all people arrested in connection with violations of laws unjustly restricting political or religious belief be released whether they were already serving their sentences or awaiting judgment.[18] Although this paper on the treatment of political prisoners is at one with another State Department paper[19] that recommended the repeal of the Public Order Preservation Law, the Law for Protective Surveillance of Ideological Criminals, and other repressive legislation, the policy involved did not support communism per se or specifically direct that Communists be released from prison. It simply provided that Communists be released as an indirect and inevitable result of its guarantee of civil liberties and freedom of thought and belief for all, including the Communists. This State Department stand was reflected in the thinking of people within GHQ and the Office of the Political Advisor, the State Department's branch within the Occupation command organization.

GHQ was occupied throughout September with disarming the Japanese military and putting down right-wing anti-Occupation activity, and thus had virtually no time to spare for dealing with the release of political prisoners until late September or early October. Acting upon information from the prisons,[20] the final decision on the release of political prisoners was made by MacArthur, Chief of Staff Sutherland, and Government Section Chief Crist with the assistance of the Civil Intelligence Section (Brigadier General E. R. Thorpe), Counter-Intelligence Division (E. H. Norman), Civil Information and Education Section (Brigadier General Kermit R. Dyke), Office of the Political Advisor (Ambassador G. Atcheson and J. K. Emmerson), G-2 (Major General Charles A. Willoughby), Crist's Government Section, and others.[21]

The following circumstances lay behind this decision and the issuance on October 4 of the "Memorandum Concerning the Abolition of Restrictions on Political, Civil, and Religious Freedoms." Three foreign reporters—R. Guillain, J. Marquise, and H. Isaacs—visited Fuchū Prison on October 1; correspondents for United Press, Associated Press, Dōmei, and other wire services visited Fuchū Prison and Toyotama Detention Center on October 2; and the UP Japan Bureau Chief and people from the Acme Film Company visited these two facilities on October 3,[22] with the result that news of these political prisoners was cabled world-wide,[23] thus sensitizing GHQ to the possibility of negative public opinion in the United States, the Soviet Union, Britain, China, and elsewhere. Emmerson obtained the Isaacs report and other reports of these visits to Fuchū and Toyotama and concluded that GHQ should release the political prisoners as soon as possible.[24] Additional urgency was imparted by the above mentioned October 3 policy decision of the Japanese government, the deaths of several imprisoned political prisoners, and other factors in this complex and shocking situation.[25] Accordingly, GHQ decided that "the Japanese government must release these prisoners by October 10. A detailed report on all action taken to comply with the directive must be submitted by October 15." GHQ was alert to the possibility of covert resistance to the implementation of the Potsdam Declaration by the Japanese old guard and was worried about what might happen to these political prisoners. Commenting on the significance of this memorandum, "Col. Ken R. Dyke, Chief of Civil Information and Education, pointed out [that] for the first time in their entire history the Japanese people are actually free to think, to talk, and to worship as they see fit. He indicated that the order is a spectacular demonstration of the United Nations' willingness to foster democracy in defeated Japan."[26] These events constituted a symbolic curtain-raising in the drama of the transfer of power from the old to the new guard in Japan.

The shock of GHQ's October 4 order was considerable as GHQ demanded not only the release of the political prisoners but also the abolition of the Tokkō, the suspension of the minister of Home Affairs and the police leadership, the repeal of the Public Order Preservation Law, and more. In effect, the order destroyed the Higashikuni cabinet's efforts to serve as an apologist for the old guard and also provided a new and legal status for the JCP, which had been forced to operate illegally ever since its founding in 1922.

GHQ Policy toward the JCP

However, even as an America (GHQ) premised upon liberalism (essentially of a strongly anti-Communist nature) thus recognized the effectiveness of utilizing the Japanese Communists to dismantle the old militaristic and ultranationalist power structure, GHQ continued to be very concerned about the policies the JCP would adopt and actions it might take. On October 3 the chief of staff, Lieutenant General Sutherland, sent a message to the Office of the Political Advisor requesting studies of the backgrounds and characteristics of all political parties, including the

JCP, and weekly reports on their activities. JCP members and other political prisoners were also interviewed and questioned by GHQ staffers several times before being released on October 10.[27] In these private interviews each individual was questioned primarily about such topics as the
treatment he received in prison and his own and his party's plans for the
future. As far as can be seen from the GHQ documents, the responses
were very much along the lines of the "Appeal to the People" *(Jinmin ni
uttō)* and "Party Policy for the Immediate Situation" as these appeared on
October 20 in the first issue of the revived *Akahata.* The GHQ officers
were particularly impressed by the prisoners' indomitable fighting spirit
and the fact that, despite prolonged internment, they were informed in
accurate detail about the current situation of the secret societies (National Foundation Society, National Essence League, Dark Ocean Society,
and so on), the Imperial Household, the justice and home affairs ministries, and the Mitsui and other *zaibatsu,* as well as on wartime economic
and political developments, other political parties, and other such
topics.[28] The statements by Tokuda, Shiga, Yamabe, and others are particularly noteworthy as expressions of the views of one of the JCP's two
leadership centers at the time—Fuchū (the domestic center) and Yenan
(the overseas one).

There were two points of particular interest to GHQ in these interviews. The first was the relationship between the JCP and the Soviet
Communist party, and the second the issue of the emperor system. On
the first point, Tokuda Kyūichi is reported to have said:

> The JCP should have no relations with Soviet Russia. The Russian Commu-
> nist Party is so large that the Japanese party would lose its identity and inde-
> pendence should it affiliate. Tokuda states that he believes it dangerous to
> depend too much upon Russia and that, if such should happen, the strength
> of the Japanese party would decrease. He emphasizes that the party would
> refuse any military assistance from Russia and that there is no need whatso-
> ever for it to look for help in that direction. One of the objectives of the Jap-
> anese party will be to satisfy the United States that there is no connection
> with Soviet Russia. Communism will not be established in Japan in the near
> future. Democracy should prevail for a long time, perhaps for a hundred
> years. Communists believe, however, that after that period the system they
> advocate will be accepted by the people as the best. Now Japan must decide
> between democracy and the emperor system. The Communists will support
> fully the policy of Great Britain and the United States.[29]

On the emperor system, Tokuda said, "The Emperor and the Imperial
Household Minister have responsibility for the enactment of the Public
Order Preservation Law, and the Emperor has responsibility for the outbreak of the war and for defeat. The emperor system is incompatible
with democracy. The emperor system must be overthrown."[30]

With the exception of some minor differences on the emperor system, the policies voiced by Tokuda and the other prisoners were largely in agreement with the postwar revolutionary concept expressed by Nosaka at Yenan.[31] Because these views very nearly coincided with the U.S. basic policy directions for Japan's occupation, they lent added momentum to the promotion of the sort of "positive policies toward the JCP" advocated by GHQ and, especially, the Office of the Political Advisor (Emmerson).

This positive policy toward the JCP favored by Emmerson did not, however, enjoy the full support of the G-2 section of GHQ or even of Government Section (GS) or of Atcheson, the chief of the Office of the Political Advisor. Their doubts are evident in letters written by Atcheson to the Secretary of State and to General MacArthur. This divergence of views between Emmerson and Atcheson over the JCP gradually widened, beginning around October 1945, until by January 1946 there was little chance of Emmerson's ideas being put into practice. Thus it was that Emmerson returned to the United States in February 1946 and was reassigned as assistant chief of the Division of Japanese Affairs in the Department of State. With the reorganization of the Office of the Political Advisor into the Diplomatic Section and the completion of GS's work on revising the Japanese Constitution, GHQ policy toward the political parties became more wary of the JCP and the overall mood of GHQ became more openly anti-Communist[32] as the JCP proved a poor vote-getter in the April 1946 general election, the Cold War intensified, and other factors came to the fore.[33]

GHQ Policy toward the Socialist Party

While initially perceiving the JSP as in principle a "liberal party," GHQ was sharply critical of its defense of the national polity, its factionalism, and other prewar features. Nevertheless, GHQ had high hopes that the JSP would, like the JCP, grow into a major force for democracy. Even as it recognized problems within the JSP, GHQ noted: "However, if it can avoid an open break among its diverse elements, it stands to gain widely in popular support. It still lacks an outstanding leader. Some circles believe that if Ikuo Ōyama were to return from Chicago, he would immediately be accepted as head of the party."[34] Especially as the "positive policy toward the JCP" waned, hopes built within GS for the JSP as the central promoter of postwar democratic politics.[35] Thus when, despite a lackluster performance, both right and left wings of the JSP made major advances (capturing 93 seats) in the April 1946 election, this was hailed as "democracy has thus demonstrated healthy forward advance."[36]

This GHQ policy toward the JSP was not unrelated to the fact that the prewar Seiyūkai and Minseitō parties (reorganized during the war into the Imperial Rule Assistance Association, Imperial Rule Assistance Political Society, and the Political Association of Great Japan) were revived as three conservative parties (Liberal party, Japan Progressive party, and Cooperative party) after the war and, still adhering to their former policies in defense of the national polity *(kokutai)*, rapidly became more influential than the JSP. This policy was further reinforced when the Japan Progressive party, the group most closely associated with the old Imperial Rule Assistance Association, increased its adroit resistance to Occupation policies. GHQ's Office of the Political Advisor then revised its November 9, 1945, memorandum ordering that measures be taken to include blanket restrictions on the candidacies of former Imperial Rule Assistance Association dietmen, and recommended to SCAP and the chief of staff that "the Japanese Government should be informed (orally) that no person should be permitted to become a candidate for the Diet in the coming election who has been an influential member of one of the organizations specified in the Directive."[37] The Office of the Political Advisor further recommended to SCAP that the election then scheduled for January 22, 1946, be postponed at least one month until standards for screening candidates' qualifications could be set and other measures taken.[38] Through these and other moves GHQ approved the April 1946 election while restraining the ultranationalist parties so as to favor the development of the truly liberal or socialist parties.

Rebuilding the Political Parties

As seen above, GHQ policies had established a framework guaranteeing freedom of action for political parties. Within this framework, Japan's reformist parties worked to rebuild and reorganize their power on the basis of their prewar legacy. During this period they received no specific organizational guidance or financial support whatever from GHQ.

However, a number of questions remain about the postwar rebuilding of the political parties. In the reemergence of socialist parties, for example, why did the JSP get the jump on the JCP, and why did the JSP make such spectacular advances in the first general election after the war? Conversely, why did the JCP fail to take advantage of the "period of liberation" to expand its strength through that same election? And why was the JCP unable to develop the People's Liberation League (Jinmin Kaihō Renmei), which seemed so promising a means of constructing a popular front movement? What were the limits and significance of this format?

Rebuilding the Japan Socialist Party

The first party to launch a postwar rebuilding campaign was the JSP. These moves began while the conservative parties which had cooperated with the wartime military were still suffering from the shock of defeat and while the JCP was unable to mount a similar campaign because its leadership was still in prison. The JSP was based on a coalition of three prewar elements—the Social Mass party, the Japan Labor-Farmer party, and the Japan Proletarian party. It was the Social Democrats who took the initiative. The Labor-Farmer party—embarrassed that Kawakami Jōtarō, Kōno Mitsu, Miyake Shōichi, Asanuma Inejirō, Tahara Haruji, and others of its members had sympathized with the military and the Imperial Rule Assistance movement during the war—was in a poor position to take the lead. The Japan Proletarian party leadership—including Katō Kanjū, Suzuki Mosaburō, and Kuroda Hisao—were still on trial for their part in the popular front incident and this delayed its rebuilding.[39] By contrast, Nishio Suehiro, Hirano Rikizō, and Mizutani Chōzaburō (socialist dietmen not affiliated with the Imperial Rule Assistance movement) had been close to the seats of power but had steadfastly maintained their antimilitary, anti-Tōjō, anti–Imperial Rule Assistance position,[40] with the result that they had good access to information,[41] knew of the inevitability of Japan's defeat before it occurred, and had already held secret talks on the postwar rebuilding of the Proletarian party. Having heard in Osaka the Imperial broadcast announcing the end of the war, Nishio rushed to visit Mizutani in Kyoto and proposed that they begin work immediately on rebuilding the party. In Tokyo, Hirano rented a fifth floor office in Shinbashi's Kuramae Kōgyō Kaikan for a preparatory meeting for the Socialist party's formation the next day (August 16). On August 21, these three met in this office to discuss the basic issues in forming the new party. This advance preparation is one of the reasons they were able to respond so quickly to postwar conditions.

In forming the new party, Nishio, Hirano, and Mizutani shared a common awareness that "there were a number of places in Europe where communists or socialists came close to governing or actually governed after World War I. In this sense, the end of the war offered favorable conditions for our gaining power. Japan would be occupied by America. America practices democracy. Democracy means parliamentary government. In a parliamentary government, it is the majority that rules. The question was how to gain a majority within the Diet."[42] Given these premises, they concluded that the new party had to encompass as wide a spectrum of opinion as possible and that they could not afford to indulge prewar factionalism. Even so, the new party's character would be defined by where it set its limits on the left and on the right. Thus they decided to try sounding people out on a spectrum going from the left-wing social democrats (the old Japan Proletarian people), but excluding the Communist party, to liberals and right-wing social democrats (the old Japan Labor people) on the right, but excluding extreme conservatives. It was as a result of this decision that Nishio, Hirano, Mizutani, and others met with Katō Kanjū, Suzuki Mosaburō, and their group at the Tokugawa Yoshichika residence on August 24, and with Hatoyama Ichirō, Ashida Hitoshi, Uehara Etsujirō, Ōno Banboku, and their group on

August 25.[43] Although the Japan Labor people were obviously opposed to the participation of Katō and the leftists, as were some of the socialists (e.g., such people as Matsuoka Komakichi and Yonekubo Mitsusuke), the leftists were allowed to take part because: "The people want a broad union. The leftists are a minority, and they can be adequately controlled by the majority. We should not forever hark back to prewar events. The best way to win a majority is to set petty differences aside and to form a broad-based union under the banner of socialism."[44] Similar arguments were used to counter left-wing opposition to the participation of the Japan Labor people. On the question of allying with Hatoyama, Uehara, and the other Liberal Party members, however, no agreement could be reached capable of rebutting the argument that "we agreed in opposing Tōjō, but we were brought up differently and live in different worlds." As a result, the social democratic left and right wings joined to form a single socialist party.

Labor movement elders Takano Iwasaburō, Abe Isoo, and Kagawa Toyohiko designated some twenty people to spearhead the call for the new party's formation, and invitations were sent out on September 14 inviting them to a preparatory meeting to be held on September 22. At this September 22 preparatory meeting, it was decided to hold a mass meeting to establish the party on November 2, 1945. Thus was the Japan Socialist party officially launched.[45]

The party platform and postmeeting communiqué were drafted by Hara Hyō and Mizutani Chōzaburō, and the party policies by scholars, bureaucrats, labor union leaders, farm cooperative leaders, and other policy experts. Although these policies can be faulted for their lack of consistency, in that they were largely a hodge-podge without any systematic or logical formulation, they were notable for their detailed and strongly liberal proposals for political reform (including abolition of the House of Peers and direct election of the heads of local governments), economic reform (nationalization of important industries and the like), labor reform (establishment of a Labor Ministry, enactment of legal provisions for labor's basic rights, establishment of internationally accepted labor standards, and so on), agricultural reform (land reform, the spread of cooperatives, and similar changes), and educational and cultural reforms. On the question of the emperor (the national polity), however, they were unable to reach agreement within the party and this was left blank, perhaps out of deference to public opinion or to the Communist party. Nishio has explained this by saying, "There were those within the party who opposed the emperor system as incompatible with socialism, but the issue of the emperor system is more an issue of national mood than one of logic. When you think that it was the Emperor's intervention which made it possible to avert chaos at the end of the war, stressing opposition to the emperor system was not the best way to advance the party's growth."[46] Hirano has explained, "Party policies, platform, name, and other things were secondary and even tertiary issues. Our primary concern was how to gain a majority in the Diet and how to prepare for the upcoming election."[47]

The people who took the initiative in the formation of the JSP were occupied first with gaining a majority to win political power; policy questions, therefore, took a back seat to such questions of election strategy as whom to run in which electoral district. As a result, Nishio was put in charge of Diet policy and Hirano of election policy (including raising campaign funds). Because Hirano was influential in rural villages throughout Japan as a leader of the prewar farmers' movement and also had many friends in business and politics, he was able to use his abilities to best advantage and to become one factor accounting for the major victories scored by the JSP in that and the next election.

With all of the intraparty quarrels, the mass meeting was unable to decide who should be party chairman. The party started, therefore, with Katayama as secretary-general and the post of chairman vacant.[48] At the close of the meeting Asanuma Inejirō, who was seated with the presiding officers' group, bowed in the direction of the Imperial Palace, and Kagawa Toyohiko shouted *"Banzai!"* The resultant clamor of protest from the left threw the meeting into an uproar. Even though this genuflection and *banzai* were a normal ritual in the Diet and political party conventions until the end of the war, to some it seemed unimaginable from that day's perspective.

The first foreign national to approach the JSP during the process of the party's formation is said to have been Nicholas Arjigakhen. According to Hirano, this Soviet citizen visited the party's preparatory office soon after the war's end and before the U.S. military arrived, and suggested in fluent Japanese, "Put this new party that you are going to start on the Soviet side. The Soviet Union will certainly be for Japan's own good." However, Hirano and the others rejected this overture because they had already decided to follow an American-style democratic course. Arjigakhen visited the party's offices several times after that, but stopped when he was rebuffed.[49] The next approaches were from the U.S. Occupation forces. On September 3, a Nisei First Lieutenant, T. Tsukahara, and Mr. Arthur Behrstock (both from GHQ's Civil Information and Education Section) asked for an interview with Katō Kanjū, showed him a list of some 500 people in the Japanese socialist and labor movements, and asked him for his views on the list's accuracy. Katō was also asked at that time to become an advisor to GHQ. In reply, Katō recommended Suzuki Bunji, Matsuoka Komakichi, and Nishio Suehiro, and the four of them subsequently met secretly with Behrstock. Likewise, after the JSP was formed and the Allied Council for Japan began work, Lieutenant General Derevyanko of the Soviet delegation to the council came to the Tokyo Shisei

Kaikan at Hibiya and provided information to Katō, Suzuki, Kuroda, and other JSP leftists.[50]

Finally, there is the question of joining fronts or alliances with other parties around the time of the JSP's founding. Both the question of an alliance with the Liberal party (Hatoyama Ichirō, president) and the question of a joint front with the JCP (Tokuda Kyūichi, secretary-general) came up, but I will discuss only the latter.

Although the JCP suggested a joint front four times (October 19, December 4 and December 27, 1945, and January 15, 1946)[51] the JSP— feeling that it was too early for a joint struggle, that there was insufficient mutual trust, and that it might be "a maneuver to hurt the JSP" whereby the JCP would brand refusal to cooperate as reactionary and then attempt to split the JSP from its following—turned it down every time.[52] Within the party, the left-wing group of Matsuoka, Yonekubo, Kuroda, Morito, and others were sympathetic to the Democratic People's Front (Minshu Jinmin Sensen) proposed by Yamakawa Hitoshi, but Nishio, Hirano, Kōno, Asanuma, Tawara, Sunaga, and others opposed it.[53] However, it is worth noting that some prefectural branches, such as Aomori, Gifu, and others where the conservative forces were strong and the JSP weak, opposed this decision and petitioned the central headquarters to form a joint struggle or joint front with the JCP and come out clearly on issues such as opposition to the emperor system. GHQ evidenced interest in the fact that in Kyoto the prefectural JSP organization actually formed a people's front with the JCP even though they recognized that it was a JCP maneuver. In conservative Yamanashi Prefecture, by contrast, the prefectural headquarters expelled JSP members who participated in joint struggles with the JCP in violation of the central headquarters decision.[54]

Rebuilding the Japan Communist Party

Unlike the JSP, the JCP was unable to rebuild for some time after the war's end. The party's leadership did not get out of prison until the October 1, 1945, directive on the release of political prisoners and the October 5 notice from the Japanese government (Ministry of Justice) to all prosecutors' offices and prisons that political prisoners were to be released. With a few exceptions such as Miyamoto Kenji and Hakamada Satomi,[55] approximately 3,000 political prisoners were released on October 10, including Tokuda Kyūichi, Shiga Yoshio, and Kim Chon-He.[56] Prior to this, Tokuda, Shiga, and ten other JCP members in the Fuchū Prison Tokyo Preventive Detention Center heard reports of the war's end on August 15 and immediately called a meeting of their group at which Tokuda said: "Strengthening our solidarity so as not to fall prey in word or deed to the devices of our enemies, all cell members must now arrange their personal affairs so that we can act in complete unity in order to be prepared for whatever unexpected situation may develop in the postwar chaos."[57] This statement may have arisen from Tokuda's memories of the strangulation of Ōsugi Sakae in Kosuge Prison, the Kamedo incident, the massacre of Koreans, and other incidents of "white terrorism" that followed in the wake of the great Kantō earthquake in 1923. When Tokuda subsequently wrote his tract "A New Policy for Struggle: What Does the New Situation Demand of Us?"[58] as a policy guide for postrelease activity, it was passed around the cell and agreed upon. Along with consolidating cell solidarity, the members of the cell also addressed a request to Justice Minister Iwata Chūzō on September 12 petitioning for their release.

About this same time nationwide moves were initiated to gain contact with JCP members out of prison. The October 4 evening directive for the release of political prisoners was followed by ambitious moves to secure the prisoners' actual release, to prepare for this, to revive *Akahata,* and so on. *Akahata* was not in fact revived in time for the prisoners' October 10 release, and the "Appeal to the People" had to be printed separately, as *Akahata*'s first postwar issue was not put out until October 20, 1945.[59]

The fact remains that it was the occupying army and not the Japanese masses that set Japan's political prisoners free. Why was this? Among the reasons that come readily to mind are the fact that Japan's old power structure (including the Public Order Preservation Law and the *Tokkō*) did not crumble with wartime defeat, the fact that the "Communist majority movement" did not find its rightful place, and the fact that the people were still under the influence of their wartime anti-Communist education (that Communists are extremely evil and immoral). This failure to win their own liberation despite objective conditions in their favor may also be attributed to the movement's inexperience and to such strategic mistakes in the prewar reform movement as the erroneous assessment of the "Communist majority movement" and the failure to establish ties with the social democratic movement. It is noteworthy that, under these conditions, the first people to stand up for liberation were the Koreans who had been suppressed and discriminated against before and during the war.[60]

The rebuilding of the JCP after the political prisoners were released began at the suburban Tokyo Kokubunji Self-help House (Jiritsu-kai).[61] A Committee to Promote Party Expansion and Strengthening was first established (Kamiyama, Kim, Kuroki, Shiga, Tokuda, Hakamada, and Miyamoto) and a national conference held on November 8 to prepare for the Fourth Congress, at which a de facto central committee was elected. The party's financial needs were to be met by contributions from party members and sympathizers,[62] party dues, subscriptions to and sales of *Akahata* and other publications, and so on. The rumors then current of financial assistance from the Soviet Union appear to have been simply rumors.[63] Among the policies set forth were the overthrow of the emperor system and establishment of democracy, dismantling of the military–bureaucratic–parasitic landlord–monopoly capital complex, agrarian land reform, trade union freedom, freedom of belief, rescinding of wartime controls, universal suffrage for all men and women 18 years or older, repeal of the lèse majesté and the Public Order Preservation Laws, constitutional reform, and discontinuance of wartime compensations. It is worth noting that the party put forth very detailed policy proposals on such items as controlling inflation, effecting agrarian land reform, combatting unemployment, rationing food and other necessities (including distribution of hoarded goods), and reforming the tax system.

Although the JCP was rebuffed in its frequent appeals for a joint front with the JSP, it was JCP policy to seek to form joint fronts with anyone who would agree to "overthrowing the emperor system and establishing a people's republic," or even to form partial joint fronts with parties that disagreed on these two points if they agreed on such issues as foodstuffs, unemployment, or wage hikes. The establishment of the People's Liberation League as an organization to promote popular fronts is particularly notable.[64] The first characteristic of this league was its decentralized nature as a broad-based coalition of joint-struggle forces taking advantage of local circumstances and independent initiatives to deal with concrete problems.[65] Because the various regional people's liberation leagues were so organized as to be able to act independently of central control, they were able to score considerable successes at the local level even though the JCP and JSP were unable to work together at the national level. It is this experience which may be said to have laid the foundations for the postwar reformist local governments.

The second characteristic of the People's Liberation Leagues was their attempt to form people's councils (jinmin kyōgi-kai) in the different areas of popular struggle by bringing together labor councils at places of production (including factory councils, employee unions, trade unions, and the like), farmer councils in agricultural villages, and citizen councils concerned with the rationing of foodstuffs and other daily necessities. Although these efforts did not always go smoothly, they are worth noting in that the labor councils developed into factory representatives councils and regional labor councils and the citizen councils had considerable impact at the neighborhood committee level. This People's Liberation League concept could well have had a major impact if it had been more organized and more specific. However, since it represented social revolution from below and was in direct opposition to the exercise of authority by the existing power structure, it came into conflict with GHQ and Japanese government policies, and could not have succeeded without the most thorough preparations and the broadest popular understanding. In practice, the advocacy of "overthrow of the emperor system" and "attack on the tenets of social democracy" were not the most expedient policies to advocate. That these policies served more to repel than to attract popular support is demonstrated by the April 1946 election, in which the JCP received only a very minor share of the votes cast despite objective conditions being in its favor.

GHQ and the JCP sought to make use of each other for their own purposes. The JCP designated the Occupation army as an "army of liberation," while there were those within GHQ who considered the JCP an important bastion of Japanese democracy. This underlay the so-called liberation army debate. In their "Appeal to the People" upon their release from prison, the domestic JCP party leadership wrote: "We express our profound gratitude for the fact that the foundations will be laid for a democratic revolution in Japan through the stationing in Japan of Allied forces to liberate the world from fascism and militarism." Tokuda and Shiga publicly stressed their support for the Occupation army and Occupation policies. There were also suggestions that the Occupation army make use of the JCP.[66] By contrast, today such views are defended on the grounds that "the adoption of this attitude on the part of Tokuda, Shiga, and others in the JCP leadership represented support for the antifascist and democratic policies of the Allied countries including the Soviet Union and does not imply support for the policies of American imperialism." However, the documents of the period do not bear out this disclaimer. In view of the process by which the initial democratization policies were established (that is, formulated by the U.S.) and the constitution of the Occupation army (composed almost exclusively of U.S. forces), these statements by Tokuda and Shiga were unquestionably expressions of support for U.S. policy.[67]

Is it possible then that Tokuda and Shiga did not then know that the U.S. was an imperialist country? It seems to me that they were fully aware of this. Yet I suspect they did not necessarily conclude that an imperialist country would inevitably adopt antidemocratic policies. Rather they moved to use the power of the Occupation army to make it easier for the JCP to act. In view of conditions at the time, they did not really have any choice but to adopt this strategy. There may have been some who argued that the JCP should promote its own campaign of liberation without relying upon the Occupation army, but Tokuda, Shiga, and the others instead adopted a two-pronged strategy of promoting an independent campaign of liberation on their own power and, simultaneously, using the Occupation army to further their ends. In this sense, this so-called liberation army strategy was a decision resulting naturally from conditions at the time, and it is doubtful if it can really be branded an error.

Conclusion: Continuity and Discontinuity, Prewar to Postwar

Japan's socialist political parties were splintered and severely repressed by the authorities before the war. Despite this, the JCP was able to survive by forming cells in the prisons and through its "Communist majority campaign" outside of prison even though it was declared illegal and harshly repressed almost from its beginning in 1922. Likewise, the postwar JSP displayed strong prewar-postwar continuity through its incorporation of the three prewar proletarian groups. Of course, the banding together of these three factions was due to a desire to avoid the prewar divisiveness and to use the postwar situation to best advantage.

This liberalization of political party activity, including the legalization of the JCP and the formation of a socialist-led government, albeit only briefly, were unimaginable before the war and thus represent a sharp discontinuity between the two eras.

The main factor for discontinuity lay in Occupation policy, especially GHQ policy toward the socialist political parties. This aimed at using the socialist parties, and especially the JCP, to eliminate the militaristic and feudal elements of Japanese capitalism and to create instead an American-style capitalism with democracy as its political mode. To this end, GHQ liberalized political party activity, issued its October 4, 1945, memorandum guaranteeing freedom of speech, assembly, and association, and embarked upon constitutional revision to make the legislature more independent and to enhance the Diet's powers. While these policies were in keeping with the Potsdam Declaration, the U.S. Department of State had recommended the release of political prisoners and the encouragement of political parties, labor unions, cooperatives, and the like as independent democratic organizations one year earlier in 1944. The release of political prisoners would have been impossible or at least much delayed without GHQ compulsion, which in turn would have made for a very different postwar political process.

In the traditional Japanese ideological and cultural context the litmus test of postwar democracy has been the degree to which Communist or JCP activity was permitted. In this sense, the positive initial GHQ policy toward the JCP may be termed very "healthy." With the intensifying of the Cold War, however, GHQ policy became increasingly anti-Communist, culminating in the "red purge," thus retreating from the "healthiness" of initial Occupation policy; Japanese intellectuals, labor unions, reformist political parties, and others replaced GHQ in maintaining and encouraging democracy's health. Behind GHQ's red-purge policies lay a fear of the Soviet threat, especially after the September 1948 secret meeting of the Cominform Far Eastern Section in Pyongyang, Korea, which was intended to strengthen the ties between the Japanese and Korean

Communist parties and step up their antiimperialist activities. However, when the Japanese government (the Yoshida cabinet) drew up a bill to outlaw the JCP and took it to GHQ for approval, the GHQ Legal Section, drawing upon the bitter experience of Australia and adopting a protective stance toward civil rights, rejected the bill. For this, GHQ is to be praised. The shift in GHQ support from the JCP to the JSP and then to the Liberal party is best understood in light of the changing power relations within GHQ as authority shifted from the Office of the Political Advisor to the Government Section and then to G-2.

Notes

1. Department of State, *Foreign Relations of the United States, 1944,* vol. 5, pp. 1190–1194, 1262–1263. (Hereafter cited as *FRUS.*)

2. "Japan: Political Parties or Agencies" (CAC-111a; PWC-113), March 23, 1944, *FRUS, 1944,* vol. 5, pp. 1219–1221.

3. "Abolition of Militarism and Strengthening Democratic Processes" (CAC-185b; PWC-152b), May 9, 1944, *FRUS, 1944,* vol. 5, pp. 1257–1260.

4. Yamagiwa Akira, "America gunji shisatsudan no En'an hōmon" [The American military mission to Yenan], *Iwanami kōza sekai rekishi geppō 29* [Monthly Iwanami lectures in world history 29], September 1971, supplement to vol. 29, pp. 9–12. Stein, *Yenan 1944,* pp. 74–76. Matsuba Hidefumi, *Beikoku no Chūgoku seisaku* [America's China policy], p. 274.

5. U.S. Senate, Committee on the Judiciary Subcommittee to Investigate the Administration of Internal Security Act and Other Internal Security Laws, 91st Cong., 1st Sess., *Amerasia Papers,* vol. 2, p. 1702.

6. John K. Emmerson, "Plan to Permit Overseas Japanese to Organize for Political Warfare Against Japanese Militarism," PR-6, March 14, 1945, in the National Archives.

7. "Programs of the Japanese Communist Party: Interview with Nosaka, September 13, 1944," *Amerasia Papers,* vol. 2, p. 1738, pp. 1728–1729.

8. *Nosaka Sanzō senshū (senji-hen)* [Selected works of Nosaka Sanzō (The war years)], pp. 380–386.

9. J. K. Emmerson, "The Japanese Communist Party," January 5, 1945. This paper is included in a letter sent by John Davis, Jr., to Secretary of State Stettinius dated January 17, 1945. *Amerasia Papers,* vol. 2, pp. 1736–1738.

10. Division of Special Records, Foreign Office, Japanese Government, comp., *Nihon senryō oyobi kanri jūyō bunshoshū* [Documents concerning the Allied Occupation and control of Japan], vol. 1, p. 100.

11. "Basic Initial Post-Surrender Directive to Supreme Commander for the Allied Powers for the Occupation and Control of Japan," November 1, 1945, Office of Political Advisor, ibid., pp. 123, 131.

12. "Proposal for Political Reform in Japan," September 21, 1945 (POLAD File), Office of Political Advisor, p. 8.

13. "The Revival of Political Parties in Japan," September 28, 1945, ibid.

14. Calls for improved treatment of prisoners and for their release were frequent immediately after the war's end. Outside of the prisons active campaigns

were waged by the Korean Committee to Campaign for the Release of Political Prisoners and by the Appeal for Political Prisoners' Release led by the lawyer Kuribayashi Toshio, Hattori Mugio, Takahashi Katsuyuki, Fujiwara Haruo, and others. See Matsumoto Kazumi, " 'Shutsugoku zengo' jyūgatsu tōka no omoide (chū)" [Before and after release from prison: Remembrances of October 10 (pt. 2)], *Akahata,* no. 68 (October 5, 1946); Yamabe Kentarō, *Aru shakai-shugi-sha no hansei* [Interim autobiography of a socialist] (Iwanami Shoten, 1971); Kamiyama Shigeo, *Waga yuigon* [My testament] (Gendai Hyōronsha, 1978); and Hakamada Satomi, "Tō to tomo ni: 17" [My years with the party: 17], *Zen'ei,* no. 275 (February 1968).

15. As told to Reuters' Tokyo correspondent Robert Ruben by Minister of Home Affairs Yamazaki Iwao on October 3, reported in *Stars and Stripes* on October 4, and subsequently reported in *Asahi Shinbun* on October 5. See also Justice Minister Iwata Chūzō's reply to a question from China Central News Agency reporter Song Tsou-Ho that "we are not considering releasing political prisoners at this time, nor do the judicial authorities have that kind of authority. This would only be possible with an Imperial amnesty. Nor do we intend to abolish the Police Law, although some modifications might be possible. It may be possible to recognize some communist activity, but anything which constitutes lèse majesté will be strictly clamped down on." *Asahi Shinbun,* October 5, 1945.

16. See Robert Guillain, "Toku Kyū shakuhō shita no wa watakushi da: Fuchū Keimusho de no bōken" [I sprang Tokuda Kyūichi: An adventure at Fuchū Prison], *Bungei Shunju,* October 1955; and Hakamada Satomi, "Watakushi no sengo-shi—shutsogoku zengo: hisoka-ni kesareru koto e no kyōfu" [My postwar history—before and after release from prison: The fear of being quietly eliminated], *Shūkan Asahi,* March 10, 1978.

17. *Yomiuri Shinbun,* October 3, 1945; *Mainichi Shinbun,* October 4, 1945; *New York Times,* October 4, 1945; and *Nippon Times,* October 5, 1945.

18. "Japan Military Government: Treatment of Political Prisoners" (PWC-219; CAC-221), June 14, 1944.

19. "Japan: Nullification of Obnoxious Laws" (CAC-123; PWC-114), March 22, 1944, *FRUS, 1944,* vol. 5, pp. 1214–1216.

20. Takemae Eiji, "Nihon Kyōsan-tō no kaihō sareta hi" [The day the JCP was freed], *Chūō kōron,* July 1978.

21. "J. K. Emmerson chi danwa sokkiroku" [Verbatim record of statement by J. K. Emmerson], *Tōkyō Keizai Daigaku kaishi* [Journal of the Tokyo College of Economics society], vol. 99 (January 1977), p. 72; "Manson-Yamagata kōshi kaidan" [Discussion between Manson and Minister Yamagata], Ministry of Foreign Affairs Public Documents, October 5, 1945.

22. Matsumoto, " 'Shutsugoku zengo,' " pt. 3, *Akahata,* no. 69 (October 13, 1946).

23. *New York Times,* October 4, 1945; *Washington Post,* October 5, 1945; Guillain, "Toku Kyū shakuhō shita no wa watakushi da."

24. See J. K. Emmerson verbatim record; and H. Isaacs, "Notes on Visit to Fuchū Prison," October 3, 1945.

25. For details, see Takemae, "Nihon Kyōsan-tō no kaihō sareta hi."

26. "Statement by Civil Information and Education Section Chief Brig. Gen. Kermit R. Dyke," *Pacific Stars and Stripes,* October 5, 1945.

27. Takemae, "Nihon Kyōsan-tō no kaihō sareta hi"; and *Pacific Stars and Stripes,* October 11, 1945.

28. J. K. Emmerson, "Visit to Fuchū Prison," October 5, 1945. Complete text in Japanese translation in Takemae, "Nihon Kyōsan-tō no kaihō sareta hi."

29. John K. Emmerson, "Interrogation of Tokuda Kyūichi, released political prisoner, conducted at General Headquarters, Tokyo, October 7, 1945, by John K. Emmerson, under the auspices of the Counter-Intelligence Section," Takemae, ibid.

30. Ibid.

31. Emmerson predicted that Tokuda, who emphasized overthrow of the emperor system, would probably ultimately compromise with Nosaka, who emphasized a strategic compromise (leaving the emperor as a ritualistic and religious symbol stripped of political authority). In this case it seemed to Emmerson that Nosaka would have the upper hand in view of the relations between the Comintern (Moscow) and the Chinese Communist party, the experiences of the Japan People's Liberation League (Yenan), relative age (Nosaka was 53 and Tokuda 51), conditions in postwar Japan, the popular situation, and other factors, and that it was likely that things would turn out largely along the lines Nosaka advocated. ("The Japanese Communist Party," October 19, 1945.) In fact at a later date, Nosaka and the Central Committee issued a joint statement on the emperor system, and such a compromise was explored subsequent to Nosaka's January 12, 1946, return to Japan. *Akahata,* January 14, 1946.

32. See, for example, G. Atcheson's May 15, 1946, anti-Communist statement and General MacArthur's statement "Banning Violent Demonstrations" on May 20 of that same year. *Pacific Stars and Stripes,* May 16 and 21, 1946.

33. SCAP/GS, *Political Parties,* vol. 2 (July 24, 1946).

34. Office of the United States Political Advisor, Tokyo, Japan, Secret No. 31: Periodical Report to SCAP, "Developments of Political Parties and Movements for the Week ending October 26," October 27, 1945, Appendix I: Report on the Japan Socialist Party, in the National Archives.

35. Robert A. Fearey, "The Occupation of Japan," enclosure to Dispatch No. 73 of November 26, 1945 (POLAD File).

36. From Commander-in-Chief, American Forces in the Pacific to War Department, Chief of Staff (from Baker for Parks), April 23, 1946, in the National Archives.

37. Office of the United States Political Advisor, Secret No. 74, "Development of Political Parties and Movements for the Week ending November 24, 1945: Recommendation as to Registration of Parties and Prohibitions against Certain Candidates," November 24, 1945.

38. Office of the United States Political Advisor, Secret No. 128, "Political Parties in Japan: Developments during the Week ending December 22, 1945," December 27, 1945.

39. Together with Suzuki Mosaburō, Kuroda Hisao, Fujita Yutaka, and others, Katō had planned to get Marquis Tokugawa Yoshichika to put up 200 million yen to build a Permanent Peace Research Institute to study the directions in which Japan should move to deal with the postwar confusion. Katō envisioned expanding upon these discussions to develop them into a preparatory meeting for the JSP's founding. (Interview, February 14, 1978.) At the same time, Yamakawa

Hitoshi, Arahata Kanson, and others were also thinking about rebuilding. Yama-kawa Kikue and Sakisaka Itsurō, ed., *Yamakawa Hitoshi jiden* [Autobiography of Yamakawa Hitoshi] (November 1961), p. 447; and Arakawa Kanson, *Arakawa Kanson jiden* [Autobiography of Arakawa Kanson], vol. 2 (Iwanami bunko, December 1975), p. 346.

40. Hirano has characterized this stance as one of "(1) opposition to the Imperial Rule Assistance budget, (2) opposition to the wartime special criminal law, and (3) opposition to the expulsion of Saitō Takao." A group of about twenty liberal or socialist anti-Imperial Rule Assistance dietmen joined together to form the Yōkakai (Eighth Day Club) as a discussion group. Among the other members were Hatoyama Ichirō, Ashida Hitoshi, Hoshijima Nirō, and other conservative dietmen as well as Nishio, Hirano, and Mizutani from the proletarian group. Interview with Hirano Rikizō, February 7, 1978.

41. For example, Nishio was in regular attendance at the Bunjin-kai and knew that the Pan-Pacific Labor Conference, International Labor Organization, and others were discussing what to do about postwar Japan (Nishio Suehiro, *Nishio Suehiro no seiji oboegaki* [Political recollections of Nishio Suehiro], p. 33), and Hirano was close to such important people as Konoe Fumimaro and Ugaki Kazushige. Interview with Hirano, February 7, 1978.

42. Interview with Hirano, February 7, 1978.

43. Nishio, *Nishio Suehiro no seiji oboegaki,* p. 39.

44. "Interview with Kōno Mitsu," in Nakamura, Itō, and Hara, eds., *Gendaishi o tsukuru hitobito* [Men who make contemporary history], vol. 1, p. 103.

45. The draft proposal put before the founding mass meeting calls it the Social Democratic party. Katō Kanjū and others argued vigorously for calling it the Japan Socialist party so as not to have it confused with the distinctive image of Western European social democratic parties, an argument that spilled over into disagreements about Katayama Tetsu's election as secretary-general. After fierce debate, a compromise was reached whereby the party would register with GHQ under the English name Social Democratic party but would be the Japan Socialist party (Nihon Shakai-tō) in Japanese.

46. Nishio, *Nishio Suehiro no seiji oboegaki,* p. 44.

47. Interview with Hirano, February 7, 1978.

48. Funada Naka, Arima Yoriyasu, and others were considered, but to no avail. As for the reports that Katō Kanjū championed Tokugawa Yoshichika, Katō himself denies them. Interview with Katō, February 14, 1978.

49. Interview with Hirano, February 7, 1978.

50. Interview with Katō, February 14, 1978.

51. For some details see *Akahata,* no. 2 (November 7, 1945).

52. According to Hirano, "When the four of us—Nosaka, Tokuda, Nishio, and I—met when it was still cold in early 1946 to discuss the possibilities of a joint front, Tokuda asked what the JSP policies were and I told him that we wanted to get a majority in the Diet and take over political power, to which Tokuda immediately exclaimed that that was no good because it was social democracy. To this, Nishio jumped in with an angry 'What do you know? While you were under surveillance or in Yenan, we were placing our lives in jeopardy fighting for the working masses.' And that was the end of the joint front." Interview with Hirano, February 7, 1978.

53. GHQ/GS, "Social Democratic Party," June 29, 1946.

54. Ibid.

55. In response to GHQ's October 4 directive, the Justice Ministry tried to limit its application to purely political prisoners and to exclude political people imprisoned on other charges. Shiga's October 5 protest of this Justice Ministry policy was one factor behind the release of Miyamoto (October 9 from Abashiri Prison) and Hakamada (October 19 from Miyagi Prison). "Shiga-shi, 'Miyamoto, Hakamada' mondai de hajimete hatsugen" [Shiga breaks his silence on the Miyamoto and Hakamada question], *Sandē mainichi,* February 26, 1978.

56. Ministry of Labor, ed., *Shiryō rōdō-undō-shi* [Documents on the history of the labor movement], vol. 1945–1946. See also Takemae, "Nihon Kyōsan-tō no kaihō sareta hi."

57. Matsumoto, " 'Shutsugoku zengo,' " pt. 1 *Akahata,* no. 67 (October 2, 1946).

58. *Akahata,* first issue after republication (October 20, 1945).

59. The printing of this "Appeal to the People" and the first issue of *Akahata* were handled by Itō Ken'ichi at a friend's Katsurayama Printing Plant. The appeal was sold for 80 *sen* (0.80 yen) and the first issue of *Akahata* for 2.50 yen. On the question of how large a printing to order, Itō argued for 3,000 and Matsumoto for 10,000. For details on how this printing was handled during that time of turmoil, see Itō Ken'ichi, *Kaihō senshi betsuden: Nankatsu kara Nanbu e* [Lives of freedom fighters: from south Katsushika to Tokyo's Nanbu industrial district] (Iryō Tosho Shuppan Sha, 1974); also, interview with Itō, February 10, 1978, and with Matsumoto, March 28, 1978.

60. Of the approximately 700 who gathered outside Fuchū Prison on October 10 to greet the prisoners as they were released, 400 are said to have been Koreans (Matsumoto, " 'Shutsugoku zengo,' " pt. 3), as were half of the approximately 1,000 people who attended the October 10 People's Mass Rally to Welcome Free Fighters (Ministry of Labor, *Shiryō rōdō-undō-shi: Shōwa 20–21 nenban* [Documents on the history of the labor movement: vol. 1945–1946], p. 890). Graphic witness of this is also provided by Ernest Childer's October 11 *Pacific Stars and Stripes* photograph of the demonstration parade after this mass rally, a photograph in which the Communist red flag and the flag of the Korean independence movement are clearly visible.

61. This Self-help House was actually a correction dormitory attached to the prison, but Tokuda negotiated with the Fuchū Prison warden and got permission for the political prisoners to use it for accommodations after their release. Thus the Self-help House served as temporary headquarters for the national party until it moved in October 1945 to the party headquarters in Yoyogi donated by Iwata Eiichi.

62. For example, Hasegawa Hiroshi, Hosaka Hiroaki, and others contributed 50,000 yen each. Hakamada, "Tō to tomo ni: 18."

63. Nor does SCAP have any evidence on this point. SCAP/GS, "Communist Party," in *Political Parties,* vol. 2, July 24, 1946.

64. "Jinmin kaihō renmei no soshiki to katsudō hōshin" [The organization and action policies of the People's Liberation League], in Tokuda Kyūichi, *Tennōsei no datō* [Overthrowing the emperor system] (Bun'ensha, February 1946).

65. There were regional organizations such as the Kansai Region People's Lib-

eration League, the Ibaragi Prefecture People's Liberation League, and the Aomori Prefecture People's Liberation League.

66. For example, Tokuda spoke of "using the Occupation army to force the Japanese government to comply fully with the Potsdam Declaration" and "supporting fully the U.S. and U.K. democratization policies" ("Tennōsei no datō," *Akahata,* first issue after republication). An Occupation report notes that "Shiga called at GHQ to suggest that SCAP use Communist Party facilities to make its wishes known to the Japanese people; it was his idea that the Communists should be accepted as the mouthpiece of the Occupation army" (SCAP/GS, "Communist Party," *Political Parties,* vol. 2, July 24, 1946).

67. For example, Tokuda in the GHQ interview cited earlier denied any connection with the ˙Soviet Union and supported Anglo-American policies fully, while Shiga in his interview with the U.S. Army First Cavalry Brigade immediately after his release from prison rejected a (Soviet-style) violent revolution and said that the JCP was hoping for an American-style political structure. *Pacific Stars and Stripes,* October 11, 1945.

13

The *Zaikai* under the Occupation: The Formation and Transformation of Managerial Councils

Ōtake Hideo

The early reforms introduced by the Occupation produced a vacuum of authority and power due to the dismantling of the traditional order. With regard to the economic order, such reforms stigmatized the *zaikai* (economic elite) as advocates of or collaborators in an aggressive war policy by designating some of them as war criminals and purging them from public service. These reforms also deprived big enterprises of their social legitimacy through the dissolution of the *zaibatsu* (financial combines). At the same time, labor reforms seriously threatened the prewar and wartime system of labor management. This dismantling of the old system by the Occupation reforms seriously endangered not only the authority of old economic elites but also the authority of management, indispensable for capitalistic enterprises, and the right of ownership, which provided legitimacy to the system, and thus threatened the very foundations of modern industrial production. On what sort of legitimacy could the authority structure within an enterprise be rebuilt: some reorganization of capitalist management, the sort of discipline offered by the Communist party, or the nationalization of industry together with an invitation to labor to participate in management? Furthermore, since the issue of the structure of corporate authority is fundamentally related to the nature of the political regime, this issue had to be debated in a way that was inseparable from the ongoing struggle about the nature of that regime. Was it to be liberal, democratic socialist, or communist? Inevitably, a serious power struggle resulted.

The postwar reforms were, however, aimed not only at dismantling the old order but also at providing guiding principles for the new order. At this early stage the chief principle was "democratization." But since the national value system was in ferment as a result of the abolition of the traditional emperor system, "democratization" was invoked by some not only as a means of denying the authority of the old order but also of denying any authority whatsoever. The term "democratization" thus acquired in some quarters an extremely radical content, quite contrary to the intentions of the Occupation. Especially with respect to the economic order, it was variously used to legitimize "enterprise democratization," management participation by labor, and even management exclusively by labor (a syndicalistic form called "production management").

Modern factory production, like modern bureaucracies, is based upon an organizational form in which the majority is subordinated to decisions made by a minority. Furthermore, the majority does not have a right to elect this minority, whose authority is usually legitimized on the basis of principles different from those of a political democracy. Consequently, the authority structure within an enterprise may be in conflict with the principles of modern democracy. In point of fact, liberal political regimes explicitly limit the principle of democratic control to the sphere of politics. Thus, when it is introduced into the world of production and distribution, it naturally gives rise to serious problems.

The Occupation reforms both denounced the basic concepts of the prewar and wartime labor management system and, through their ambiguity, threatened the legitimacy of bureaucratic control under capitalist management. It is not surprising, therefore, that the slogan of "democratization," introduced in such circumstances, lent itself to use as a means of legitimizing management control by labor and the mass public instead of management control by a limited number of capitalists and executives.

In this chapter the issue of how business managers dealt with the resulting "management crisis" will be examined mainly by focusing on the question of labor's participation in management. This will be explored primarily in terms of the responses of business and management associations to the threats posed by labor's participation. Particular emphasis will be placed on the efforts of these associations to legitimize management in ideological terms. The author believes that the postwar "management crisis" was, above all else, an ideological crisis. Needless to say, dealing with this "management crisis" was an important issue for the Japanese government as well. Therefore, both the Occupation authorities and the Japanese government played extremely important, and in some cases decisive, roles in the reorganization of the authority structure within private economic enterprises. It should be noted, however, that the analysis in this chapter will focus exclusively on business managers, and especially the activities of the *zaikai*. Very few analyses have been undertaken from this perspective.

A Plan for Managerial Councils Prepared by "Progressive Managers"

Lacking confidence, most business managers in the early postwar period did nothing about the problem of management control. The Keizai Dō-yūkai (Economic Comrades Association), however, advanced "A Plan for

Managerial Councils" that tried to institutionalize labor's participation in management and, in so doing, attempted to justify the continuation of capitalistic business management. Behind this plan lay an acute perception of a crisis in a capitalistic system that, because of labor's offensive, had been strained to the breaking point and might soon be replaced by a communist order. The plan attempted to protect capitalism by recommending serious modifications, which meant in effect that business managers themselves were advocating a revised capitalism. The following sections examine, first, the formation of the Dōyūkai and its early activities and, then, its plan for a revised capitalism.

Formation and Early Activities of the Keizai Dōyūkai

Two groups of young businessmen joined to form the Dōyūkai.[1] One group was composed of businessmen who belonged to the Kayōkai (Tuesday Society) of the Nihon Kogyo Kurabu (Japan Industrial Club). The Kayōkai had been organized by Shibusawa Keizō, Fujiyama Aiichirō, and others who met every week to discuss politics, economics, or the war situation on the basis of presentations by military officers and high-ranking government officials.[2] It was Moroi Kan'ichi, Managing Director of Chichibu Cement Company, a central figure in the Kayōkai, and a man who had played an important role in the formation of other postwar economic associations, such as Keidanren (Federation of Economic Organizations) and Nikkeiren (Japan Federation of Employers' Associations) who became the nucleus in the formation of the Dōyūkai. Because of their relationship with Moroi, more than ten members of the Kayōkai—including Aoki Kin'ichi, Suzuki Michiyo, and Shōda Hidesaburō—also participated in its formation.

The second group consisted of young managers involved in the Jūyō-Sangyō Tōsei Dantai Kyōgikai (Jūsankyō, the Council of Key Industry Control Associations). The Jūsankyō's main goals were to provide assistance to the activities of the control associations and to petition the authorities with respect to the operation of industrial controls. It is said that during the war the Keizai Renmei (Economic Federation) and the Chamber of Commerce were dormant politically because the influence of the *zaibatsu* had markedly declined with the outbreak of hostilities and that the Jūsankyō alone continued effectively to represent the interests of business.[3] The Jūsankyō thus was providing leading young business managers with both opportunities to consider economic activities in macro-perspective and a means of promoting personal relations among them. In this way, the Kayōkai and Jūsankyō bred in young business managers a concern for political and economic problems that transcended their individual enterprises.

Gōshi Kōhei, who was secretary-general of Jūsankyō at the end of the war, working with Hoashi Kei, a former secretary-general, began to form the Dōyūkai by establishing contact with businessmen connected with the Kayōkai. From Jūsankyō, Noda Nobuo, Fujii Heigo, Horikoshi Teizo, Ōtsuka Banjō, Nagano Shigeo, and others joined the organizers of the Dōyūkai.

Thus in terms of lineage, a strong continuity with wartime business circles can be detected in the Dōyūkai. Ideologically speaking, this indicates that the Dōyūkai's "left-wing" proposals for a "revised capitalism" really reflected a national socialist approach to the problem. Despite this, the 80-odd business managers who took part in the formation of the Dōyūkai couched their proposal in terms of "democratization," in this way trying to cope with the new postwar ideological situation. They reinforced this position by severely criticizing the old economic elite. This stance can clearly be seen in the Dōyūkai's prospectus and the addresses at the inaugural rally.

While Moroi played an important role in the formation of the Dōyū-kai, he was a typical mediator type of leader in that he attached great importance to moderation and group consensus. Accordingly, the early activities of the Dōyūkai were exclusively initiated by its left wing (especially Noda, Ōtsuka, and Gōshi), consisting of members of the Jūsankyō group and the secretariat. Other members such as Nagano Shigeo and Hotta Shōzō, who later became leading figures in the *zaikai,* also expressed very radical opinions and supported this trend at the time. For example, in early July 1946 approximately two months after the formation of the Dōyūkai, its Research Committee on Labor Problems, with Noda Nobuo as chairman, put together and submitted to the executive committee a statement noting that "it is not altogether appropriate to deny entirely production control [workers' seizure and operation of plants]." One month prior to this the Yoshida cabinet had announced a policy that "production control cannot be recognized as lawful." Business managers were thus expressing a view that was in direct conflict with the government's. Some Dōyūkai members, with Aoki Kin'ichi as the central figure, strongly opposed this stand. After a heated debate the executive committee decided not to publicize the statement. However, it appeared in the next day's newspapers as a resolution of the Dōyūkai.[4] Aoki and others of the right wing criticized the secretariat, saying that it had acted arbitrarily. The right wing's opinion, however, was ignored by the mass media. In October of the same year, Noda's Research Committee on Labor Problems followed similar procedures in issuing to the press "An Opinion Concerning Counter-Measures against Unemployment." Because of its timing this gave the impression that Noda's committee supported labor's "October Offensive." This, too, was severely criticized by senior *zaikai* leaders. Gōshi himself was even thought to be a Communist.[5]

At this time the "moderate" faction within the labor movement showed a strong interest in this sort of "progressiveness" on the part of the Dōyūkai and tried to get in contact with them. As a result a move for the formation of a Keizai Fukkō Kaigi (Economic Recovery Conference), based on cooperation between labor and management, got under way. In this context the left wing of the Dōyūkai made an effort to clarify its ideological standpoint. A plan for managerial councils resulted, and it was Ōtsuka Banjō who played the central role in this turn of events.

At the end of January 1947, Ōtsuka organized within the Dōyūkai a group to study enterprise democratization. It started its research with a paper on "Economic Democratization and the Specific Measures Involved" prepared by Ōtsuka himself. Furthermore, referring to the plan for managerial councils developed by Tōshiba's labor unions and the Nihon Denki-Sangyō Rōdō-kumiai (Densan, the Japan Electrical Workers' Union), the study group drew up "A Tentative Plan for the Democratization of Enterprises" based on some twenty meetings held over about half a year.[6] While this plan was not adopted as an official view of the Dōyūkai, because other members judged it premature, everyone basically agreed on the principles of the plan.[7] The plan was published in the form of a pamphlet and as a Committee Plan, and it evoked a variety of responses in many quarters. The progressive business managers' perceptions of the existing situation and their ideas for a new regime based on this plan will be examined in the following section.

The Plan for Managerial Councils

There is no doubt that the Dōyūkai's revised capitalism was intended as a countermeasure to a socialist nationalization of enterprises. However, the Dōyūkai's grounds for denying socialism are not entirely clear. It is characteristic of the arguments for a revised capitalism that the liberal business managers do not make clear whether their case rests on a guarantee of freedom as an essential social value or upon the need for economic efficiency. In any case, they reject the concept of nationalization, which was then thought to be one possible measure of economic democratization and, in so doing, necessarily limit the question of democratization to labor's participation in enterprise management.

This argument is based on the separation of capital and management, and assumes that a business manager is the mediator between the workers and the capitalists. Accordingly a managerial council, consisting of workers, capitalists, and managers, is the highest decision-making organ within an enterprise. In other words, this argument gives to such a council the authority to elect the highest responsible person in an enterprise, its president, and the additional responsibility of distributing the profits *equally* among the three parties. It expects that the adjustment of each party's interests will be accomplished through the exercise of "mutual restraint" within the council.

> Namely, if the demands of the workers went to an extreme, or if such demands endangered the foundations of an enterprise by descending to class utilitarianism, the managers and the capitalists would resist it in concert. On the other hand, if the capitalists . . . tried to make an enterprise a sheer tool for making profits, the managers and workers together would be able to resist. Furthermore, if the managers ignored both the welfare of the workers and the interests of the capitalists, and thus carried out a self-complacent management, or tried to use an enterprise as a tool to expand the influence of the managerial class, the capitalists and the workers would be able to prevent this by a concerted effort. (Tentative Plan, p. 61)

To put it another way, the purpose of the managerial councils would be to enable each party—workers, capitalists, and managers—to pursue its interest within an enterprise. It is clear that the most important aim of the proposal was to induce the labor unions to take a moderate stand by giving them a role in management. The tentative plan frankly states: "While traditional labor unions basically tried to protect their interests from outside the enterprise, in the new business system they would assume a positive role in enhancing their interests by placing themselves within management and thus improving the efficiency of management" (Tentative Plan, p. 164). Here, one can see a clear intention to preserve and strengthen the intraenterprise union system, whereby each company has its own union.

The plan set forth above has an indispensable condition that severely limits the control of an enterprise by capitalists in order to achieve a balance of power among labor, capital, and management. This is the provision that establishes a role for management independent of that for capitalists, a provision that the Dōyūkai borrowed from J. Burnham's *Managerial Revolution.* It should not be forgotten, however, that this notion is simply a variation on the thinking of so-called progressive bureaucrats during the war who tried to free management from the constraints of private capital in order to achieve an approved social or national status for production.

The Dōyūkai were aware that it was not possible to reorganize the authority of management without making some serious concessions to labor that recognized the power relationship between workers and managers. In their conception, labor's participation in management could substantially affect the policy making in an enterprise, if labor's will was strong enough. Thus they based their justification of the existence of private enterprise on the concept of "democratization" and labor's participation in management rather than on the concept of private property rights.

There was, however, an important prerequisite if the Dōyūkai's Tentative Plan for Democratization was to be realized. This was that "labor would not be influenced by political motives that have no direct relationship with the management of a specific enterprise" (Tentative Plan, p. 166). Thus, the sine qua non was that labor should abandon any policy of regime change and, working within the framework of capitalism, try to increase its share by increasing the productivity and profit of the specific enterprise it worked for. This was both the premise and the ultimate goal for the managerial councils plan. When in practice the labor movement turned out to be both "influenced by political motives" and guided by the Communist party and the Zen-Nihon Sanbetsu Kaigi (Sanbetsu, the National Congress of Industrial Unions), it became necessary, in order to realize a managerial councils plan, to turn to the theme of "production recovery."

Managerial Councils and the Economic Recovery Conference

Ōtsuka's attempt to utilize managerial councils as a consultative and decision-making organization for both labor and management was not new. Similar councils had already been established in various forms at many factories and enterprises. At the time they were highly regarded by the general public as well as labor and management as a demonstration that the democratization of enterprises was actually possible. The first managerial council was established in the Yomiuri Newspaper Company at the time of the settlement of the First Yomiuri Dispute. Soon thereafter, many others were set up in various enterprises throughout Japan. According to a survey conducted by the Ministry of Labor, by the end of June 1948 "the number of unions having managerial councils amounted to 15,055, or 44.3 percent of the total number of unions."[8] Both Sanbetsu and the Nihon Rōdō Kumiai (Sōdōmei, the Japan Trade Union Federation) from their different standpoints valued highly this management participation through managerial councils. They held that such councils should be efficiently used and strengthened.[9] Moreover, business managers and the government as well expected such managerial councils to play a role in preventing labor disputes and in increasing production, and they showed a strong concern for the "healthy fostering" of these councils.[10] In many cases the managerial council was set up as a result of initiatives by the company.[11]

The fact that both labor and management had great expectations for the managerial councils resulted in each attempting to control them. This created a struggle for power between labor and management with regard to the structure and operations of the councils. Consequently, in practice the structure of the managerial councils reflected the actual balance of power between labor and management, and one encounters a great variety of forms. For example, in the case of the Keisei Dentetsu Company (a private railroad) it was stipulated that the managerial council "has authority over the overall management, not only of labor conditions, welfare, and technology, but even over general operational plans, personnel management, and accounting, which have to be brought before the council. . . . As for personnel management, the approval of the union is necessary for recruitment, dismissal, changes, and so forth of all employees including executives. As for accounting, everything, including the distribution of profits, must be approved by the union."[12] On the other hand, in the case of the Japan Corundum Company the managerial council was established to provide a forum where the company could explain to labor the situation of the company and convince labor that a wage increase was impossible and a personnel cut was necessary. In this fashion the managerial council provided labor with a means of understanding the company's policies.[13]

With respect to the democratization of enterprises, however, it can hardly be said that the managerial councils fulfilled their role as originally conceived. Even in the case of the Keisei Dentetsu Company, where the union was endowed with strong authority, the union's participation in management tended to be restricted to negotiating labor conditions. The other issues of management were so specialized that the unions' "managerial capability" was seriously limited in terms of any effective participation in management. Furthermore, except at a time of labor disputes when morale was temporarily very high, it was difficult to keep the union members interested in daily management, even during the "democratization fever" in the early stages of the postwar period. Although many of the managerial council meetings were open to the average workers, "there were few observers."[14]

Some leaders of the Sōdōmei were, however, giving serious consideration to participation in management through the managerial councils and to the democratization of enterprises as a means of structuring labor's authority. Takano Minoru in particular planned to organize the managerial councils of each enterprise into a nationwide network and to establish solidarity by having labor initiate industrial reconstruction measures. It was in this way that he began his activities in the industry reconstruction movement.[15] As we have seen, the Dōyūkai's left wing responded to these initiatives, developing the Tentative Plan.

In those cases where the managerial councils were actively utilized and labor's creativity and will mobilized, the result was often improved efficiency and increased production. In the case of the Toyota Automobile Company, for example, the managerial council reportedly took up the issue of productivity increases as well as wage increases. "Since the union also fully recognized that, without a production increase, an improvement of the employees' lives would not be possible, serious discussions

were conducted to decide new production targets" and "the union submitted its own materials to supplement insufficient and inaccurate points
in the company's materials and made various necessary proposals to the
company."[16] It was said of even the radical unions connected with Sanbetsu that, while they were very firm in dealing with management on
some points, on others involving negotiated production increases they
were more willing to make concessions.[17] It can be said, therefore, that,
although each side's goals differed, the slogan of economic reconstruction created a situation favorable to management.

In coping with the production increase movement that had developed
as a result of rising competition among enterprises, however, the unions
in general, including Sōdōmei as well as Sanbetsu, tried to prevent mere
capitalistic reconstruction and to solidify labor's strength by organizing
unions that transcended individual enterprises. The left wing of the Dōyūkai also believed that the democratization of enterprises meant more
than just cooperation by the unions. This was the basis upon which both
of these groups began to cooperate to formulate the Economic Recovery
Conference. In the following section, the formation of the conference
will be examined with particular reference to the Dōyūkai.

The Economic Recovery Conference

The movement to form the Economic Recovery Conference solidified in
the middle of the "October offensive."[18] On October 19, 1946, the Dōyūkai held an urgent meeting of the executive committee to discuss their
policy with respect to the coming general strike. At this meeting it was
decided to oppose the general strike and to declare that managerial rights
should be respected. With regard to the proposal for an industrial reconstruction movement advanced by both the radical Sanbetsu and the moderate Sōdōmei, the committee also decided to publicize the view that
industrial reconstruction could not be achieved without the business
managers' cooperation and that the managers were ready to cooperate
with the reconstruction movement.[19] The Sōdōmei, which had been
planning for the Economic Recovery Conference proposed by Takano
Minoru, quickly responded to this appeal and invited the Dōyūkai to the
preliminary meetings. Thus from late October until November representatives of the Dōyūkai, the Sōdōmei, and the neutral Zen-Nihon Rōdō
Tōitsu Kyōgikai (National Labor Unification Council) all worked together to decide basic policy through a preparatory committee.

In this basic policy, some of the arguments that would later be system-
atized in the "Tentative Plan for the Democratization of Enterprises"
were foreshadowed. For example, it was decided that "during the present
period of solving the economic crisis, restrictions on the dividends to be
distributed to capital" should be imposed, and that "with regard to pro-

duction exceeding normal standards, a remuneration system for labor based on an established ratio" should be employed.[20] Furthermore, the organizational basis for the economic reconstruction movement was placed within the managerial councils and, at the same time, it was decided that the managerial councils should serve as a means of opening and explaining to the workers the accounting systems used by the enterprises. Based on this information, labor conditions, the level of wages, and the terms of pay systems were to be discussed and decided. This policy became one of the major concepts for the "thorough democratization of management through the healthy fostering of managerial councils."[21]

When the recovery conference began to deal with specific issues, however, this focus on the democratization of enterprises shifted drastically, and the actual focus centered only on increasing production and reconstruction. Specifically, it attempted to "develop a movement to break through the production crisis by calling together both business managers and labor union representatives from each industrial sector" who would then "attempt to improve the working-level or regional-level solutions for bottlenecks in production by means of their originality and ingenuity."[22]

In the process of organizing the recovery conference, the question arose as to whether the Communist-led Sanbetsu, which was preparing for the impending February 1 general strike, should be invited to participate. Sanbetsu had criticized any reconstruction movement based on labor-management cooperation and, especially, the idea of giving rights of decision to managerial councils. They feared that such a move might restrict collective bargaining and create a deadlock between labor and management. Nevertheless, it was difficult for them openly to oppose such a move, since there was a public demand for economic reconstruction. Furthermore, since Sanbetsu at that time regarded its prime objective to be the defeating of the "financial monopoly of capital and its proxy, the government," they were suspicious of a recovery conference initiated by "industrial capital."[23] On the other hand, although Gōshi Kōhei and others were strongly opposed, the majority of the managers favored requesting the Sanbetsu's participation, largely because many of the business managers who wanted to participate in the reconstruction movement had Sanbetsu-influenced unions in their enterprises, and they thought that without Sanbetsu's participation in the movement it would be meaningless. The managers hoped to induce the radical unions to adapt themselves to the moderate Sōdōmei line of thinking through their participation in this movement.

The negotiations with Sanbetsu were conducted through the leaders of the Dōyūkai. After some delay, the Economic Recovery Conference was officially inaugurated on February 6, 1947, with Sanbetsu participating. The organizational statute adopted at that time followed the line taken by the preparatory committee. The participating parties included, from labor's side, Sōdōmei, Nichirō-Kaigi, and Sanbetsu, and from the management side, Nissankyō, Kankeikyō, Kansaikeikyō, and Dōyūkai. The unions of each industry and various industrial organizations also participated. Furthermore, in parallel with the Economic Recovery Conference, other smaller recovery conferences for each industry or region were formed, such as the National Coal Industry Recovery Conference, the National Steel Industry Recovery Conference, the Kanto-Shin'etsu Regional Metalliferous Mines Recovery Conference, among others.

The managers recommended Miki Takashi of Nissankyō and, together with Sakurada Takeshi, he assumed the office of vice-chairman. The Central Permanent Committee members, however, were mostly members of Dōyūkai. After the reelection of officers in October, 17 of the 18 Central Permanent Committee members representing managers were members of Dōyūkai. The six executive officers representing management included Ōtsuka Banjō, Noda Nobuo, Fujii Heigo, Gōshi Kōhei, Hoashi Kei and Mizuno Shigeo—all of whom were leading members of Dōyūkai. In the background was the expectation that the good offices of the "progressive" managers of Dōyūkai would help to moderate Sanbetsu. The Dōyūkai was expected to persuade Sanbetsu of the merits of their "high efficiency/high wages" approach to industrial problems. As the forum for this strategy, the Economic Recovery Conference gave rise to many hopes on the part of management.

The Failure of the Economic Recovery Conference

Although there was considerable public support for the Economic Recovery Conference, at least in the beginning, there was little cooperation between labor and management. The central organs were hamstrung because Sanbetsu was "uncooperative." Whenever the executive committee met or rallies were held, the representatives of Sanbetsu made speeches featuring ideological propaganda and the theme of struggle, rather than constructive contributions concerning policy decisions. Consequently, few meaningful decisions were made. Even in the few cases in which a decision was reached, such as the case of the rice relief movement, Sanbetsu hampered its implementation instead of cooperating with the majority decision. In addition, unnoticed, many Communists joined the secretariat, thus causing serious problems in the smooth operation of the conference. Consequently, the percentage of management representatives attending fell, meetings were rarely held, and the central organs became a fiction.[24]

On the other hand, cooperation between labor and management made some progress at the industry level. For example, the Coal Industry Recovery Conference held its third nationwide committee meeting in

May 1947 to discuss coal prices, financing, and food problems. Based on such discussions, the following resolutions sent to the government were adopted. With regard to financing, the resolutions included decisions such as "the minimum amount of physical plant capital should be fixed first and should be financed as planned." As for food, the resolutions requested, for example, that, because "the report from the field said that no prospect can be seen of securing food after June, concrete plans should be urgently made." Concerning production increases, it is reported that the conference decided to consider a coal production plan of 30 million tons, using actual figures from the mining sites.[25] However, since the connection between the central organs of the coal conference and the production sites was by no means adequate, even at the industry level the reconstruction movement can hardly be said to have been organized on a nationwide scale.

With the formation of the Katayama cabinet, a movement to reorganize the conference began, and in the fall of 1947 it made a new start with financial support from the government. The cabinet decided that the Economic Recovery Conference should take the initiative in a production recovery movement to solve the present crisis and that the government should reward industries for their achievements in recovery from a 4,000,000,000 yen fund allocated by the Ministry of Labor. Accordingly, an executive office was established, with Takano Minoru as the central figure. Although this policy was tied to a "priority production system" and although an increase in production of coal and steel was achieved through government investments, there was no significant effect in other areas. Since the central organs of the recovery conference were making such a poor show, the managers finally decided to dissolve them. Seizing an opportunity provided when Sōdōmei announced that they wanted to "dissolve the conference and make a new start involving those whose opinions are in agreement," the managers finally dissolved the Economic Recovery Conference on April 28, 1948, despite Sanbetsu's opposition. Thereafter, the Dōyūkai showed no enthusiasm for establishing a new "organization of those whose opinions are in agreement," and the reorganization did not materialize, notwithstanding much fanfare about it. Thus the national-level recovery conference ended without any significant products during its one year and two months' existence.

At the enterprise level, however, it seems that the birth and the existence of the National Recovery Conference possibly served an ideological function as the symbol of a movement. Although it is difficult to back up this statement with empirical evidence, judging from achievements in the recovery of production during this period the statement is reasonable.[26] In this regard, the reconstruction movement in general had some achievements, in spite of the failure of the central conference. Progress was made in forming managerial councils as a means for production cooperation.

Furthermore, the very fact that the reconstruction movements at individual enterprises were not thoroughly integrated on a nationwide scale made it easier for recovery to be achieved within individual enterprises by capitalistic reconstruction measures, thus strengthening the managers' positions. This was the reason why Takano Minoru later criticized his own position, saying that the reconstruction movements "were confined within an enterprise's consciousness," "quietly stirred up competition among enterprises," and ended up with "being company-controlled movements."[27]

As far as the pacification of radical unions was concerned, however, the movement failed. The managerial expectations that had been entrusted to Dōyūkai were betrayed. Because of this, the revised capitalist and labor-management cooperation line rapidly lost influence within business circles, and carefully planned attacks against radical unions began. Behind this development lay the managerial class's assessment of the Cold War and their related expectations of GHQ support. The fact that Nikkeiren was established in April 1948, the same month in which the recovery conference was dissolved, symbolically expresses this policy shift. Thereafter, the central activities of the *zaikai* featured the "liberal" business managers who were the chief executives of Nikkeiren.

The Establishment of Nikkeiren

Nikkeiren (Nihon Keieisha Dantai Renmei, the Japan Federation of Employers' Associations) is an organization resulting from the joining of two currents: an organizing effort from above by the central *zaikai* and an expansion of horizontal connections at the industry and regional level by the people in charge of labor management for each enterprise. Both currents were direct successors to the personnel and organizational traditions of prewar and postwar employers' organizations, such as the Zenkoku Sangyō-dantai Rengōkai (Zensanren, the National Federation of Industrial Associations) and the Sangyō Hōkoku-kai (Sanpō, the Industrial Patriotic Society).

In the prewar period, the business organization that especially dealt with labor problems was Zensanren. Fujiwara Ginjirō was the central figure in this organization, and Zen Keinosuke, originally from the Ministry of Commerce and Industry, was in charge of its actual operations.[28] Until Zensanren was dissolved and absorbed into the Sangyō Hōkoku-kai in 1942 it had maintained "close contacts" with the Social Affairs Bureau of the Ministry of Home Affairs and, "in the case of drafting new legislation or amending laws, Zensaren's secretariat always received unofficial drafts in advance and offered its opinions after thoroughly studying these."[29] It is reported that men such as Kawada Shige, Maeda Hajime, and Morita Yoshio, who later played important roles in Nikkeiren, had served as a brain trust for Zen Keinosuke in Zensanren and were later also active as "masterminds" of the industrial patriotic movement.[30]

While most of the central figures of the prewar *zaikai,* such as Fujiwara, retreated into the background in postwar times, Zen became very active in coping with postwar labor problems. He participated in legislative consultative organs as a member of the Labor Legislation Council and the Inquiry Commission on Social Insurance Programs. He also joined the Central Labor Committee as the first representative of the employers, and confronted Tokuda Kyuichi, the Communist leader.[31] Furthermore, while most business managers either lost confidence or assumed a "progressive posture," he consistently maintained his open opposition to labor, for example by denouncing the illegality of workers' control of production and appealing to public opinion through open debates on the radio.[32] Zen also began laying the groundwork for reconstructing the managers' organizations with the cooperation of Adachi Tadashi, a subordinate of Fujiwara Ginjirō.[33] This move was successful, and in February 1946 some *zaikai* were invited to a meeting on labor problems. Reportedly it was difficult to choose which *zaikai* to invite since, there were not at that time many business managers who were interested in or had experience with labor problems.[34] For business managers who had depended on governmental regulations to cope with labor movements during the prewar and wartime periods, it was a new experience to deal directly with labor unions. Therefore, their hopes centered on the Zensanren-related businessmen, who had studied and made suggestions on labor management.

In any case, at this meeting it was decided to establish a nationwide employers' organization which would be primarily in charge of labor problems. And in March of the next year (1947), based on a draft plan prepared by Zen which outlined the organization's structure and operations, a preparatory committee was established with Zen as chairman.[35] This plan later became the organizational basis of Nikkeiren.

The preparatory committee adopted a plan to establish an employers' association for each prefecture, then to integrate such associations at the district levels, such as the Kantō and Kansai areas, and then to organize a nationwide federation. Zen provided energetic leadership in contacting each district. The network of people established by the local organizations of the prewar Zensanren was fully utilized in such approaches. Simultaneously, liaison organizations among business managers for the purpose of coping with union movements were reviving at many places around the country through the reorganization of institutions associated with the wartime industrial patriotic movement. Such local entities were ready to respond to invitations from the central business circles.[36]

In parallel with the central *zaikai*'s move to form local organizations, the business managers' organizing efforts in individual industries were progressing, at first seemingly independently. These efforts were characterized by horizontal connections among people in charge of labor management at the working level who were trying to cope with the emerging unions. An example is provided by the coal industry, whose managers' organization was the earliest formed.[37]

Maeda Hajime was the central figure in formulating the managers' organization in the coal industry. Maeda had been active in the Jūsankyō and the Sangyō Hōkoku-kai in the prewar period, and at the end of World War II he was in Hokkaidō as director of labor affairs for the Hokkaidō Mining and Steamship Company. To cope with the coal miners' unions, he planned around October 1945 to create a coal industry managers' organization. Maeda realized that if regulation by the government was impossible, the only way to cope with the union movement was through the solidarity of management in an effective organization. Consequently, Maeda formed the Hokkaidō Coal Mining Industry League at the end of 1945 with the cooperation of Fukagawa Masao, director of labor affairs at the Mitsui Mining Company. As if in response to this move, similar organizations were established in January 1946 in many places—Kyūshū, Jōban, Yamaguchi, Ube, and Tokyo—and these were subsequently integrated into the Nihon Sekitan Kōgyō Renmei (Japan Coal Mining Industry League), a nationwide organization. Maeda appointed Hayakawa Masaru, who had been with Mitsubishi Mining Company and who was then the organizational director of the Sangyō Hōkoku-kai, as managing director of this league, with himself assisting.

In this process of organizing a managers' organization on a nationwide level, each businessman on the preparatory committee informally consulted GHQ's views through several channels. GHQ's response in each case was that the time was premature for the forming of a managers' organization on a nationwide scale.[38] Accordingly, Zen and others decided to strengthen local organizations instead, and three months later, in June 1946, established the Kantō Keieisha Kyōkai (Kankeiren, Kantō-area Employers' Association) with Adachi as chairman and Moroi as vice-chairman.

Only shortly thereafter, Zen took office as secretary-general of the Economic Stability Center (Keizai Antei Honbu) in the Yoshida cabinet, and then was purged from public office along with Adachi. Many members of Dōyūkai, however, joined Kankeiren. Except for its left wing, those who were active in Dōyūkai—such as Isomura Otomi, Sakurada Takeshi, Imazato Hiroki, Mizuno Shigeo, and Shikanai Nobutaka—as well as those businessmen of the postwar generation—such as Aoki Kin'ichi and others—who had temporarily left the Dōyūkai because of their confrontation with its left wing, all joined Kankeiren and became its central force. Shikanai, in particular, later became one of the central figures in Nikkeiren's secretariat, together with Maeda Hajime and Satō Masayoshi.

Dōyūkai thus became a means of recruitment for Kankeiren. This group of businessmen had been involved in the earlier activities of the Economic Recovery Conference and, when the conference was dissolved, had become the nucleus of Nikkeiren and had led the "capital offensive." Thus, the two-year delay in the formation of Nikkeiren caused by the Occupation authorities made Nikkeiren clearly an organization of businessmen of the postwar generation, despite its prewar antecedents. This fact is worthy of attention, since some businessmen of the prewar generation in the field of labor affairs, such as Zen, rose rapidly in the immediate postwar period. This GHQ-imposed delay had an important influence on the ideology of Nikkeiren and, as will be pointed out shortly, resulted in strengthening its liberal rationalism, which had replaced its prewar paternalism.

When Kankeiren was founded in 1946, it mainly dealt with research and information exchange concerning labor problems. It started to publish a monthly magazine, *Keieisha* (The Manager). But it was difficult to collect dues, and the organization could not afford adequate salaries for the staff. Moroi and others even had to sell the magazine themselves.[39] With General MacArthur's prohibition of the February general strike as a turning point, however, GHQ's attitude toward managers' organizations changed. Captain Korb of the Labor Section handed Moroi a memorandum notifying him that the time had come to form a nationwide employers' organization.[40] Accordingly, in May 1947 Kankeiren formed the Keieisha Dantai Rengokai (League of Employers' Associations) as a liaison facility for local organizations. On April 12 of the next year the organization was upgraded from "union" to "federation" status as it became a genuine nationwide organization; it was renamed the Nihon Keieisha Dantai Renmei (Nikkeiren, Japan Federation of Employers' Associations). The federation included employers' organizations of all industries, as Maeda Hajime had suggested.

Although the "hawks" of the *zaikai* had started preparatory work right after Japan's defeat in World War II, they were in this fashion forced to delay their organizational activities for two years, during which time Kankeiren conducted research and information exchanges only. Meanwhile the Dōyūkai took the initiative and attempted to establish and maintain a policy of labor-management cooperation. In contrast, Zen participated in the Yoshida cabinet and took charge of its labor policies, working with the minister of health and welfare, Kawai Yoshinari, who was also originally from the *zaikai*. The formation of the Economic Recovery Conference by the Dōyūkai was, in effect, a declaration of distrust of the Zen-Kawai line in the Yoshida cabinet. The criticism repeatedly voiced at that time by the postwar generation members of the *zaikai* that the "government lacks flexibility" was directed at the *zaikai*'s prewar generation who produced Nikkeiren.

However, by the time Nikkeiren was established in April 1948, GHQ's

policy had changed. Furthermore, Dōyūkai's attempt at labor-management cooperation had failed, and management was beginning to change
its policies. Thus, Nikkeiren started its activities with new expectations.

While Kankeiren, like the other business organization, had initially
undergone a financial crisis when Nikkeiren was formed, it received
strong support from business managers throughout the country. Within a
year it became the most active and also the most wealthy of all the business organizations.[41] Nikkeiren set out to strengthen its local branches
by means of "propaganda activities." It also organized a group of lawyers
specializing in management in an effort to cope actively with labor movements. It was very active, indeed, as the following statement demonstrates: "Business managers who had troubles in coping with labor problems one after another consulted Nikkeiren to learn about tactics and
techniques for dealing with labor unions, and the number of such cases
already amounted to 5,000. In March [1949], when the summer labor
offensive began, 301 cases needing consultation rushed in from all over
the country."[42]

The Ideology of Nikkeiren

Nikkeiren consisted of the following elements: (1) its chief executives—
Moroi, Miki Takashi, and Katō Masato; (2) the "militant business managers," who were mainly company presidents and members of the right-
wing faction of the *zaikai;* (3) the people in charge of labor affairs in each
company; and (4) members of the secretariat, which included managing
directors and secretaries-general of regional managers' associations or of
a particular industry's managers' association. Each of these groups had
its own ideology and debated with one another within Nikkeiren.
Among the people in charge of labor affairs and the members of the secretariat, there were supporters of a revised capitalism. In general these
people took stances relatively favorable to labor unions.[43] It was not
these elements, however, that took the initiative in the policy making of
Nikkeiren, but the group of "militant business managers" of the company president class. The most active were Sakurada Takeshi (director-
in-chief of the Nisshin Spinning Company), Aoki Kin'ichi (Shinagawa
White Brick Company), Isomura Otomi (Hodogaya Chemical Company), Okano Yasujirō (Mitsubishi Heavy Industry Company), Kobayashi Ataru (Fukoku Life Insurance Company), Imazato Hiroki (Nihon
Precision Company), and Nagano Shigeo (Kokusaku Pulp Company).
Except Okano and Kobayashi, all were originally from the Dōyūkai and
were former executives of the Economic Recovery Conference.

These managers were committed to the classic principle of free enterprise and the economic rationalism that stemmed from this commitment.
Sakurada and Aoki, for example, had implemented a policy of "cost

reduction by means of the complete elimination of waste" within their own companies,[44] and they coped with their labor problems by a policy of "high efficiency, high wages."[45] With regard to the dismissal of employees, paternalistic business managers generally disliked the formation of unions because of their enterprise-as-a-family conception and were reluctant to discharge workers even during slow times. "Liberal" managers, on the other hand, approved of the formation of unions and participated in contract negotiations with labor as equals. They felt free to dismiss employees when business was slow and were quite cold-hearted in their assertion of economic rationality. In other words, while denying traditional upper class–lower class status relationships, they also denied any sense of noblesse oblige.

Furthermore, contrary to the advocates of a revised capitalism, the liberals denied labor's rights to participate in management. They set out to clarify business managers' prerogatives and responsibilities by rejecting labor's participation in management; by so doing, they thought to safeguard the principle of market competition within the enterprise. This demand for complete control of labor by management caused the union movements to limit their goals to demands for wage increases. This line of thinking on the part of the liberals was an attempt to introduce Taylor's labor-management system to Japan under the slogan of "high efficiency, high wages." This is the real meaning of the "establishment of managerial prerogatives."

These liberal managers also had a distinct political style. Their statements were very frank, almost provocative, and their actions demonstrated their willingness to attack even at the risk of a confrontation with labor. This attitude was revealed in many of their actions such as, for example, their rejection of any effort "to ingratiate the mass media," their repeated and severe criticisms of the government's inefficiency, and their denunciations of the corruption of the political parties. More than anything else, they maintained an exhaustive opposition in labor disputes, thus reflecting their aggressive rationalism, a policy that denied the traditional enterprise-as-a-family type of paternalism. Nikkeiren in its role as advisor to management in labor disputes frequently used the tactic of dividing unions by assisting the organizing of second unions, thus causing serious trouble in the internal relationships of labor.

The liberals based this insistence on the prerogatives of management on the proprietary rights which ultimately support the existence of any private enterprise.[46] This was the basis for their "hawkish" argument for the mobilization of judicial powers, such as provisional disposition, to cope with labor's infringements on ownership rights. Accordingly, they advocated the judicial settlement of labor disputes, rejecting "political" compromises. It was inevitable, therefore, that they would come to rely on the physical enforcement powers of government. Having abandoned a

policy of conciliation toward labor movements, they needed strengthened police powers. But here they encountered the weakness of the postwar Japanese police system, and repeatedly they were obliged to rely on
the enforcement powers of the Occupation forces. This consideration,
coupled with their fear of the Communist party, made it natural for
them, as the conclusion of a peace treaty drew near, to advocate both the
strengthening of police powers and the rearmament of the country as a
means of maintaining public order. Consequently, their concrete policies
exhibited many characteristics similar to those of the conservative parties' extreme right wing, which dreamed of the revival of the emperor system. They were, in effect, proposing policies that made it difficult to
regard them as "liberal."[47]

It is interesting to note that many of these *zaikai* liberals had been
black-listed as dangerous liberals by the Japanese authorities during
World War II.[48] However, their wartime criticisms of the government
were mainly based either on their judgment that "there [was] no way to
win a war against a big power such as the United States" or on their criticisms of wartime bureaucratic controls that "neglected the actual situation of the economic sector." Both criticisms were based on grounds of
economic rationality. Thus, although their attitude contrasted to that of
the Sanpō-related nationalist group who became members of Nikkeiren's
secretariat and who had earlier been strong supporters of Japan's wartime nationalism, the liberals were not really directing their criticisms at
the Japanese political system itself. And in the postwar period, these economic liberals were really indifferent to the issue of political freedom.
This was clearly revealed at the time of the "Red purge." Judging from the
published materials, these so-called liberals were totally insensible to the
implications of their aggressive anti-Communist attitude for liberal principles.[49]

Business managers throughout Japan, faced with labor disputes, derived both spiritual and material support from the energetic activities of
these dogmatic liberals. And, just as the Dōyūkai in its early period stood
much farther to the left than did its members in general, so, too, did
Nikkeiren adopt more rationalistic and aggressive policies than the positions held by its membership would have warranted.[50]

Nikkeiren's "Capital Offensive"

It is not quite clear exactly how Nikkeiren extended its support and guidance in labor disputes. On the premise that Nikkeiren's becoming a
highly visible actor would strengthen the solidarity of the union movement and create a nationwide confrontation between capital and labor,
its activities were often carefully concealed. This secretiveness in turn
caused the unions to suspect that Nikkeiren was hatching plots. Togeth-

er, Nikkeiren's secretiveness and the unions' suspicions resulted in an exaggerated image of Nikkeiren as a bastion of capitalists. This makes a valid analysis quite difficult. Nonetheless, based on the available materials, the following points can be affirmed.

1. Since the managers of an enterprise never transferred their rights to settle labor disputes to managers' associations, except in those few industries where collective bargaining was conducted by an all-industry organization, it can be surmised that Nikkeiren's guidance never exceeded the provision of support and advice. Each enterprise manager was free to decide whether or not he should accept such advice. In this sense, Nikkeiren was playing the role of consultant. However, since labor disputes were struggles in which proper timing and tactics were nearly always decisive, its advice on such matters could have a serious impact upon the course of the dispute and on the nature of the power structure within an enterprise after the dispute. Therefore, the role Nikkeiren performed through giving tactical advice was significant.

2. The degree of Nikkeiren's intervention varied significantly depending on the size of the enterprise. In the case of small and medium size enterprises, which often lacked an adequate labor relations staff, the secretariat members of Nikkeiren or its local branches "often participated directly in collective bargaining and disputes."[51] For example, in the case of the Shinagawa White Brick Company where a "revolutionary anarchic situation existed for about five days" in the town of Katayama in Okayama Prefecture, the secretariat members sent by Nikkeiren took charge and were busily engaged in many activities including contacting the police and hiring guards. It was reported that "the people of the company followed the direction [of the secretariat members] constantly and closely."[52]

On the other hand, big enterprises in general were much less dependent on Nikkeiren in times of labor disputes. For example, in the case of the Hitachi Company, President Kurata was criticized on the score that he neglected even to contact Nikkeiren.[53] Still, the fact of the criticism indicates that it had become a practice to report to Nikkeiren even in cases of large-scale disputes. In other labor disputes in big enterprises, such as the 1949 dispute at the Tōshiba Electric Company, the advice of Nikkeiren was sought and utilized.[54]

3. Even in the case of a big enterprise, Nikkeiren played a central role when it came to requesting cooperation from outside organizations such as presenting demands to the government, contacting the law-enforcement authorities, or receiving financial support. For example, when the dispute at the Ōji Paper Manufacturing Company became serious, it was reported that the chief executives of Nikkeiren discussed the measures to be taken with the law-enforcement authorities.[55] In a dispute at the Nissan Automobile Company, Nikkeiren reputedly enabled the company to

persist in its "Struggle Formula" by persuading financial organizations to make additional loans to Nissan, which had fallen into debt.[56] On numerous other occasions Nikkeiren became engaged in activities designed to appeal to public opinion or provided management representatives for conciliation committees in times of dispute.

4. Since labor disputes cause serious financial losses for an enterprise, it is natural for the company to try to reach as early a settlement as possible. But Nikkeiren, thinking of the spill-over effect on other enterprises or industries, often urged companies to reject "easy compromises" and to fight tenaciously. When enterprises that were doing well tried to raise their wages to a higher than average standard in an effort to improve relations with their own unions, they were apt to be criticized by Nikkeiren. In such cases when Nikkeiren attempted to intervene in an individual company's policy making, it would claim to represent the "position of capital as a whole."

Nikkeiren also assisted individual companies' labor policies by establishing advisory institutes on legal affairs and by compiling "exemplary" labor agreements. It is not an overstatement to say that, on the basis of these activities, Nikkeiren's ideology spread to business managers throughout the country.

The Transformation of Managerial Councils

One of the activities in which Nikkeiren engaged immediately after its foundation was the revision of labor agreements. It was these agreements, concluded immediately after the war, that had provided the basis for establishing managerial councils as institutional symbols of the democratization of the enterprise. In revising these labor agreements, Nikkeiren flatly denied the Dōyūkai's concept of the democratization of enterprises and thus transformed this basic concept.

Nikkeiren first made public its "Fundamental Policies of Revised Labor Agreements"[57] in June 1948, and then its "Guidelines on the Adjustment of Labor-Management Relationships"[58] in June of the following year. These offered an overall concrete reform plan for managerial councils. This plan rejected the previous tendency for management participation and proposed instead to divide managerial councils into three organs: a negotiation committee (collective bargaining), a grievance committee, and a production committee.[59] The production committee was given the function of obtaining the union's cooperation in the smooth implementation of production plans made by the company. Thus the *zaikai* acknowledged the actual conditions then emerging in unions that were influenced by the right wing of Sōdōmei and endorsed the unions' efforts to cope with radicals.

In the meantime, with the revision of the Labor Union Law in 1949, labor agreements, which had heretofore been automatically extended, were arbitrarily abrogated. Consequently, in the "capital offensive" known as "enterprise readjustment" (which gained momentum after 1949), one of the most important issues, beyond mere personnel cuts, was the revision of labor agreements in such a way as to alter the power relationship of management and the unions. Enterprises started an all-out attack on radical unions based on the standard plan for labor agreements written by Nikkeiren. Nikkeiren, of course, fully supported this trend. This series of disputes led to a stalemate in many enterprises which naturally resulted in the drastic decrease in the number of managerial councils. Thus, labor's participation in management gradually lost its institutional foundation.

However, after the radical unions were dissolved and Communist party–influenced labor leaders dismissed with the settlement of disputes, labor-management consultative organs reappeared in new roles. The increase in the number of "managerial councils" that began in 1950 demonstrates the trend.[60] There is no question that these new labor-management consultative organs were based on Nikkeiren's guidelines. Although the name of these organizations was the same, their actual role was the "mobilization" not the "participation" of labor.

Conclusion

Success in dealing with the "management crisis" immediately after the end of World War II depended on management's success in coping with labor's demand for the democratization of enterprises. Business managers successfully evaded this crisis by giving priority to the issues of "reconstruction" and "recovery" as a means of opposing the demand for "democratization." They regained their "managerial prerogatives" by utilizing the slogan of production increases for purposes of "reconstruction," and thereby reestablished the authority of management. The symbol of "reconstruction" was later replaced by the symbol of "economic growth." Thus, power structures within the enterprise were maintained as they had been, and this continuation of the status quo supported the high economic growth of the 1960s.

This transformation from "democratization" to "reconstruction" and then to the "establishment of managerial prerogatives" was accompanied by a transfer of initiative within the *zaikai* from the left wing of Dōyūkai to the "militant business managers" of Nikkeiren. However, after its successful attacks on radical unions and "political" labor movements, Nikkeiren changed its policies and acted in concert with Dōyūkai. The fact that Gōshi Kōhei and others established the Japan Productivity Center in 1955, again appealing to the necessity for labor-management cooperation, symbolizes this conversion. On this occasion the interaction

between Dōyūkai and Sōdōmei, which had initially been established at
the time of the Economic Recovery Conference and then was maintained
during the period of the "capital offensive," once more came into play.
The Japan Productivity Center was a means of studying and developing
measures to obtain positive cooperation from labor within the scope of
established managerial prerogatives. The fact that the center was made
possible by former leaders of the left wing of Dōyūkai is a splendid demonstration of the transformation of the movement for enterprise democratization. With its establishment after an intense power struggle and in
spite of "the excesses of the Occupation," the sort of "healthy" labor-
management relationship anticipated in 1946 by the United States finally
emerged.

Notes

1. Hazama Otohiko, *Keizai Dōyōkai jūnenshi* [A ten-year history of Keizai
Dōyūkai (Economic Comrades Association)] (Keizai Dōyūkai, 1956), pp. 19–
23; "Keizai Dōyūkai no hitobito" [Members of Keizai Dōyūkai], parts 1–5, *Tōyōkeizai shimpō,* January 25–February 22, 1947.

2. *Moroi Kan'ichi tsuisō bunshū* [Essays in memory of Moroi Kan'ichi] (Chichibu Cement Co., 1969), pp. 59, 230.

3. Nakamura Takafusa, ed., *Gendaishi o tsukuru hitobito* [Makers of modern
history], vol. 3 (Mainichi Shinbunsha, 1971), pp. 25–30. For the activities of
zaikai groups during World War II, see *Keizaidantai Rengōkai zenshi* [The prehis-
tory of the Federation of Economic Organizations] (Keizaidantai Rengōkai,
1962).

4. Aoki Kin'ichi, *Watakushi no rirekisho* [My curriculum vitae], vol. 11
(Nihon Keizai Shinbunsha, 1960), p. 63.

5. Nakamura, *Gendaishi o tsukuru hitobito,* p. 34.

6. The activities of this committee were reported in detail in *Keizai Dōyūkai
kaihō* [Keizai Dōyūkai bulletin] on and after February 1, 1947. Ōtsuka's proposal, "Keizaiminshuka to sono gutaisaku" [Economic democratization and its
concrete proposals] first appeared in *Keieisha* [The Manager], March 1947. In
addition, Ōtsuka published several essays, including "Shūsei shihonshugi no
kihon kōzō" [Basic structures of a revised capitalism], *Tōyōkeizai shimpō,* May
10, 1947; "Keizaiminshuka to shūsei shihonshugi" [Economic democratization
and revised capitalism], *Keieisha,* December 1947; "Kigyōminshuka towa"
[What is the democratization of enterprises?], *Keieisha,* January 1950; "Chūkan
antei to sangyō no tachiba" [Temporary stability and the industrial standpoint],
Ekonomisuto, August 11, 1948.

7. The author's interview with Gōshi Kōhei (November 1978). As will be
pointed out shortly, the labor-management negotiations in the Economic Recovery Conference as well as in the managerial councils at the factory level were
about to fail in late 1947, and most of the business leaders were too busy organizing the Nikkeiren to deal with the coming confrontation. Thus, the publication
of the pamphlet had already lost proper timing. Nevertheless, some members
insisted on publishing it, arguing that they should be prepared to cooperate with

the moderate unions in the event of a defeat of the radical unions. This argument was accepted and the pamphlet was published.

8. Rōdōshō [The Ministry of Labor], *Shiryō rōdō undōshi: Shōwa 23* [Documents on the history of labor movements: 1948] (Rōmu Gyōsei Kenkyūjo, 1952), p. 1055.

9. For the policy change from production control to managerial councils in the Communist party, see Yamamoto Kiyoshi, *Sengo kiki ni okeru rōdōundō* [The labor movement in the postwar crisis] (Ochanomizu Shobō, 1977), sect. 3, chap. 2.

10. See Rōdōshō, *Shiryō rōdō undōshi: Shōwa 20–21* [1945–1946] (Rōmu Gyōsei Kenkyūjo, 1951), chap. 7, for different views on managerial councils on the part of business, labor, and the government.

11. In the Yuasa Storage Battery Co., for example, the president of the company took the initiative in establishing a labor-management conference and gained both a harmonious resolution of labor disputes and improvements in production. Yuasa Yuichi, "Waga sha no rōmu kanri no tokuchō" [Characteristics of labor management in our company: Emphasis on management democratization], *Keieisha*, November 1949. Yuasa was one of the leading members of the Kansai Keizai Dōyūkai (Keizai Dōyūkai in the Kansai area) and a prominent ideologue of a revised capitalism, as was Ōtsuka.

12. Rōdōshō Rōseikyoku [The Labor Policy Bureau of the Labor Ministry], ed., *Keiei sanka seido* [Participation in management] (Rōmu Gyōsei Kenkyūjo, 1954), p. 165.

13. "Kigyō seibi to keiei no gōrika" [Readjustment of enterprises and the rationalization of management], *Keieisha*, September 1973, p. 6.

14. Rōdōshō, *Shiryō rōdō undōshi: Shōwa 23*, p. 1063.

15. Cf. Takano Minoru, *Chosakushū* [Collected works], vol. 1 (Takushoku Shobō, 1974), chaps. 4, 5.

16. *Tōyōkeizai shimpō*, March 29, 1947, p. 19.

17. Comment by a manager of Nissan Chemical Co. in a round table discussion, in *Keieisha*, December 1947, p. 12.

18. See Rōdōshō, *Shiryō rōdō undōshi: Shōwa 22*, chap. 3, and *Shiryō rōdō undōshi: Shōwa 23*, chap. 6; "Sangyo fukko kaigi no kōsō" [A plan for the Industrial Recovery Conference], *Ekonomisuto*, March 15, 1947.

19. Attending this executive committee were Moroi, Kanai, Asano, Sukurada, Fujimoto, Koike, Hoashi, Shikanai, Noda, and Gōshi. *Keizai Dōyūkai kaihō*, November 1, 1946, and *Asahi Shinbun*, January 22, 1946. It is noteworthy that this list includes all the business leaders who became active members of the Nikkeiren.

20. "Keizai Fukkō undō no kihon hōshin" [Basic policies of the Economic Recovery Movement], in *Shiryō rōdō undōshi*.

21. Ibid.

22. Ibid.

23. *Asahi Shinbun*, December 4, 1946.

24. This author's interviews with Gōshi (November 1978) and Noda.

25. *Asahi Shinbun*, May 17, 1947.

26. See the following articles for the realities of economic recovery conferences at the factory level: "Genba ni miru keizai fukkō" [Economic recovery on the

actual spot], articles serially appearing in *Keizai Fukkō* [Bulletin of the Economic Recovery Conference], and Nakamura Takatoshi, "Kigyōnai seisan fukkō undō ni tsuite" [On production recovery movements within enterprises], *Keieisha,* nos. 1–2 (July–August 1947).

27. Takano Minoru, *Nihon no rōdō undō* [Japanese labor movements], in *Chosakushū,* vol. 5, p. 56.

28. For Zensanren, see Morita Yoshio, *Nihon keieisha dantai hattenshi* [The development of the Japanese managers' associations] (Nikkan Rōdō Tsūshinsha, 1958); for Zen, see *Zen Keinosuke tsuisō roku* [Reminiscences of Zen Keinosuke] (Nihon Dantai Seimei Hoken, 1959).

29. *Zen Keinosuke tsuisō roku,* pp. 79–80. See also Yoshida Shigeru Denki Kankō Hensan Iinkai, *Yoshida Shigeru* (1969).

30. Maeda Hajime, "Tōshō ichidai" [The life of a fighter], Bessatsu *Chūō kōron, Keiei Mondai,* Autumn, 1969.

31. *Ekonomisuto,* August 15, 1946, p. 7.

32. *Zen Keinosuke tsuisō roku,* p. 94.

33. *Moroi Kan'ichi tsuisō bunshū,* p. 52.

34. *Zaikai kaisō roku* [Reminiscences of the economic elite], vol. 1 (Nihon Kōgyō Kurabu, 1967), pp. 136–137. The nine people present at this meeting were Asano Ryōzō, Adachi Tadashi, Ishikawa Ichirō, Uemura Kogorō, Zen Keinosuke, Terai Hisanobu, Noda Nobuo, Maeda Hajime, and Moroi Kan'ichi.

35. Katsuta Kazuo, *Keizai dantai monogatari* [A narrative of economic associations] (Shin Keizaisha, 1956).

36. See the nearly fifty chronicles of local employers' associations that are in the collection of the library of Nikkeiren.

37. Cf. Maeda, "Tōshō ichidai," vol. 1, Summer 1969; Nakamura, *Gendaishi o tsukuru hitobito,* pp. 150–156.

38. The Organizing Committee consulted the following people of the GHQ staff: C. Whitney, J. G. Liebert (Anti-Trust and Cartels Division of ESS), A. Constantino (Labor Division of the ESS), P. L. Stanchfield (Labor Advisory Committee).

39. *Moroi Kan'ichi tsuisō bunshū,* pp. 212, 510–511.

40. "Zadankai: Nikkeiren hossoku tōji no kotodomo" [Round-table discussion: Episodes in the early days of Nikkeiren], *Nikkeiren taimusu,* April 12, 1953. See also Moroi Kan'ichi, *Watakushi no rirekisho* [My curriculum vitae] (Nihon Keizai Shinbunsha).

41. *Tōkyō Shinbun,* July 24, 1949.

42. Ibid.

43. *Zaikai,* January 1954, p. 107; "Zadankai: Wakaki jidai no keieisha ni kiku—kumiai undō to rōmu tantōsha no kushin" [Round-table discussion by managers of the younger generation: Union movements and the hardships of those in charge of labor control], *Keieisha,* January 1949; Shikanai Nobutaka, "Sangyō anākī to sono saikisei" [Industrial anarchy and its readjustment], *Keieisha,* June 1947.

44. Nakagawa Keiichiro and Yui Tsunehiko, eds., *Keiei tetsugaku to keiei rinen/Shōwa-hen: Zaikaijin shisō zenshū* [Managerial philosophy and managerial ideals/Shōwa era: Collected works of the thoughts of *zaikai* leaders], vol. 2 (Daiamondosha, 1970); Aoki Kin'ichi, *Watakushi no rirekisho;* Takeyama Ya-

suo, "Aoki Kin'ichi ron" [An essay on Aoki Kin'ichi], in *Gendai Nihon no keieisha* [Managers in contemporary Japan] (Nihon Seisansei Honbu, 1961).

45. Sakurada Takeshi, "Keiei no kinō" [The functions of management], in Nakagawa and Yui, *Keiei tetsugaku to keiei rinen;* Aoki Kin'ichi, "Tōsei keizai kara jiyū keizai e no michi" [The road from a controlled economy to a free economy], *Keieisha,* November 1949.

46. It should be noted, however, that these managers legitimatized their property rights by appeals to the democratization of stockholding (people's capitalism) or to the social functions of production. (See Sakurada, "Keiei no kinō.") Obviously, these ideas were inherited from Dōyūkai's ideology of a revised capitalism.

47. It is well known that Sakurada often advanced provocative arguments for rearmament. Aoki also surprised the GHQ staff when he was appointed to the National Public Safety Commissions in 1950, when he commented that public safety could not be maintained without the suppression of Communists and the repatriation of Koreans (*Zaikai kaisōroku,* vol. 2, pp. 353–354). See also Aoki Kin'ichi, "Chian taisaku to keisatsu seido" [A measure of public safety and the police institution], *Keieisha,* August 1952.

48. *Zaikai kaisōroku* vols. 1 and 2 include many episodes of this kind.

49. This insensibility is also common in the anti-Communist liberalism of business circles in the United States and is not, therefore, a phenomenon peculiar to Japanese business circles.

50. It is reported, however, that the titular chief executives of Nikkeiren—Moroi, Miki, and Kato—occasionally restrained "excessive moves" by the liberals (*Zaikai,* September 1953, pp. 16–18, and January 1954, pp. 104–108). These three businessmen, judging from both their personalities and ages, held managerial views affected by prewar paternalism and the enterprise-as-a-family concept. They seem not to have been as dogmatic as the postwar so-called militant managers.

51. Kanagawa-ken Keieisha Kyōkai, *Kanagawa keikyō nijū-nen no ayumi* [Twenty years of the Kanagawa Managers' Association] (1968), p. 107.

52. "Sōgi gakuya banashi" [Inside stories of labor disputes], *Keieisha,* November 1950, p. 41.

53. *Zaikai kaisōroku,* vol. 2, p. 157.

54. Maeda, "Tōshō ichidai," p. 357.

55. "An Interview with Imazato Hiroki," in Nakagawa and Yui, *Keiei tetsugaku to keiei rinen,* p. 425.

56. *Asahi Shinbun,* August 8, 1953; *Yomiuri Shinbun,* August 13, 1953; *Sangyō Keizai Shinbun,* September 17, 1953; *Mainichi Shinbun,* August 22, 1953.

57. Appeared in *Keieisha,* July 1948.

58. Rōdōshō, *Shiryō rōdō undōshi: Showa 23,* pp. 1024–1027.

59. The Labor Ministry made a similar proposal.

60. Rōshi Kankei Chōsakai, *Rōshi kankei to ningen kankei* [Labor-management relations and human relations] (Rōshi Kankei Chōsakai, 1963), chap. 1.

14

Conclusion

Robert E. Ward

Japan is commonly viewed as the most precocious examplar of a historical process that has been variously described as "westernization," "industrialization," "modernization," or "development." Further interest and
significance attach to the Japanese case by virtue of the facts that its cultural antecedents are totally non-Western and that the process of change
involved has to an unusual extent been the product of deliberate planning
and adaptation.

We know now that the roots of the societal changes involved in this
process of "development" are deeply and complexly buried in Japan's
past and that the earlier accounts that looked upon the Restoration
(1867–1868) as a watershed demarcating premodern—or, to use the
more commonly employed term—"feudal" Japan from "modern" Japan
were both grossly oversimplified and erroneous in many respects. Making due allowance for the importance of such pre-Restoration antecedents, however, it is still the case that a very high proportion of the basic
institutional innovations and changes that characterize what has frequently been termed "the Japanese miracle" cluster in two historically
brief periods: the thirty-eight years from 1868 to 1905 (from the Restoration to the end of the Russo-Japanese War) and the almost seven years
of the Allied Occupation of Japan (1945–1952).

We have been concerned only with the latter of these two nodal clus-
ters of change and, in particular, with a selection of major political and
legal changes that occurred during these six years and eight months. Prewar Japan had a notably authoritarian political system while postwar
Japan, by any realistic standards of judgment, must be considered democratic. In a world where democratic political systems constitute a rare
and endangered species, this transition is remarkable enough in its own
right. But added interest and significance flow from the further facts that
practically all of the basic institutional changes involved—and many of
the associated attitudinal and behavioral changes—originated during the

Occupation period and that the initiatives underlying these changes, and a very substantial proportion of their content as well, stemmed from American officials who in fact, though not in theory, controlled what was ostensibly an Allied undertaking.

This coincidence of factors—extensive and basic political change of a democratic sort, a high degree of compression in time, and a critical degree of subjection to immediate foreign direction and control—is historically very unusual. The closest analogue is probably the Allied Occupation of what is now the Federal Republic of Germany or, if one were to accept the Soviet Union's definition of its political institutions as democratic, the Russian occupations in Eastern Europe. So unusual and so important a development naturally poses questions of great interest to all students of social and political change.

To what extent was this particular sequence of political and legal changes planned by American or Japanese agencies? Who did the planning? And to what extent do the outcomes conform to the plans? What was the role of historical accidents in this process? Were there notable omissions in the planning process?

To what extent were developments in Japan during this period affected by the general international context in which the Occupation took place? The so-called reverse course, for example, was in some still controverted degree obviously a product of developing tensions between the United States and the Soviet Union. What was this "reverse course" and how did it develop?

To the degree that sociopolitical changes during the Occupation period were a product of planning, what were the strategies of change employed? How can one describe the "social engineering" of the Occupation? To what extent are the outcomes a result of coercion by the Occupation authorities, and to what extent are they a product of cooperation between American and Japanese agencies?

In what degree did varying legal perspectives and traditions between Americans and Japanese involved in this process of change affect the outcomes of the Occupation in Japan?

Finally, to what extent do the particular political and legal changes under survey in this book introduce a significant measure of discontinuity into the history of postwar as distinguished from the history of prewar Japan? Or, alternatively, can it be claimed that they are in significant degree a product of earlier endogenous developments, that is, that continuity rather than discontinuity is involved?

These are difficult and complicated questions. We are not so presumptuous as to imagine that we can provide fully satisfactory answers to any of them. We do believe, however, that the preceding essays make new and substantial contributions to the current state of scholarly knowledge on these problems. Let us then examine and comment in more general terms on what the preceding chapters have to tell us.

The Occupation as an Exercise in Planned Political Change

Any comparison of the contents and recommendations of the multitudinous presurrender planning documents produced by the State-War-Navy Coordinating Committee (SWNCC) and its predecessors in Washington, D.C., with the political institutions and practices of post-Occupation Japan cannot help but tempt one to conclude that there is a cause and effect relationship between them. An all-powerful American Occupation armed in advance with a prescient and complete set of plans simply carried out the Washington planners' recommendations and, in doing so, transformed Japan from an authoritarian to a democratic society. There is some truth in such a view. But there is also a great deal that is lacking and, in any serious effort to understand what actually transpired, the missing elements are of substantially greater importance. But let us consider first the elements of truth involved in such a Washington-centered view of the Occupation and its effects on Japan's political system.

There is no gainsaying the fact that the prewar Japanese political system was by the standards of the time predominantly authoritarian. Despite some institutions possessed of democratic potential and a gradual process of liberalization from the Restoration to about 1932, its performance was notably not democratic. It is equally obvious that both the institutional and the performance characteristics of post-Occupation Japan compare favorably with those of any of the other major contemporary democracies. In this respect Japan has undergone a profound change in a relatively brief time. What happened between August 1945 and April 1952 to cause this change?

The only viable candidates for the causes of the change are defeat and the Occupation. The consequences of defeat in terms of Japanese national attitudes, values, and behavior are undoubtedly vast and still not very well explored or understood. They are also diffuse and unfocused. No one has suggested, moreover, that by themselves or in any comparable time-frame they would have led to the particular political outcomes that characterize post-Occupation Japan. This is not to deny, however, that they were prerequisite to those outcomes. On the other hand, the Occupation did in general terms share the views espoused by the Washington planners and in particular cases, most notably the new constitution, is known to have acted specifically on the basis of the Washington planning documents. Furthermore, it had the power to enforce them, temporarily at least, and it undoubtedly played a vigorous and active role in initiating the changes involved. It does not seem amiss, therefore, to conclude that to this degree at least a relationship does exist between the presurrender planning in Washington and the new democratic regime in post-Occupation Japan.

But to stop there would leave the most interesting and important parts of the story untold. Consider the following qualifications to the preceding viewpoint.

First, the extent to which the contents of the Washington planning documents—or even their existence—were either known to or actually utilized by the working-level officials of SCAP is in most cases still uncertain. They were routinely forwarded to General MacArthur in their final form and often in preliminary versions as well. The State Department also sent copies to SCAP's Political Advisor. Occasional officers such as Government Section's Colonel Kades, when assigned to duty with the Occupation, secured and brought with them personal copies of some planning documents—clandestinely, it might be added. But the state of the official SCAP records is such that it is presently impossible in most instances to tell what actual use was made of the few copies that reached Japan.

In at least three cases, however, it can be said that they had a critical influence. The two most obvious instances are the United States Initial Postsurrender Policy for Japan (August 29, 1945) and the Basic Directive for Postsurrender Military Government in Japan Proper (November 3, 1945). Despite the postsurrender dates of these final versions, both documents were the products of a planning process initiated in May 1942. Between them, they stipulated the overall goals of the Occupation and, in general terms, some of the means by which these goals were to be achieved. For the most part SCAP followed their injunctions closely. The third case related to the constitution. The Government Section, in drafting a new constitution for Japan, operated under formal orders to insure that all of its provisions were in accord with the recommendations of SWNCC 228. Beyond these three, no other such cases come to mind. Indeed, the available evidence suggests that copies of the presurrender planning documents may have been restricted to General MacArthur's personal use and possibly made selectively available also to a few of his closest advisors such as General Whitney. There is testimony that Colonel Kades kept his set of the early papers in his private safe and normally did not share them with any of his colleagues. The Political Advisor was intentionally and systematically isolated from the operations of the so-called civilian sections of SCAP after the opening months of the Occupation, and there is little reason to assume that his State Department copies became generally accessible.

While the evidence is not conclusive, there is reason to believe that relatively few of the multitude of carefully prepared Washington planning documents that assumed their final form as numbered SWNCC papers ever reached more than a handful of General MacArthur's closest associates and a few others who had private and irregular channels of access. They could still, of course, have been influential through the medium of those few who did have either official or private access, but there is no evidence that such mediated influence either occurred with any regularity or was transmitted in terms that accurately reflected the intent of the original document. Normally, General MacArthur and his associates displayed a strong preference for doing their own thinking and planning, and they invariably claimed the credit therefor.

Second, as the preceding paragraphs suggest, there was an additional set of planners involved in shaping the Occupation's policies toward a defeated Japan. This consisted of General MacArthur, his immediate advisors, and an astonishing number of subordinates usually situated in one or the other of the so-called civilian sections of the Supreme Commander's headquarters. None of these were completely free agents. All functioned and did their planning within the limits of policies for the governance of Occupied Japan set forth in the two basic documents cited above—the United States Initial Postsurrender Policy for Japan and the Joint Chiefs of Staff's Basic Directive for Postsurrender Military Government in Japan Proper. But the direction provided by these documents was necessarily general in nature and related more to goals than to means for their achievement, especially where Japanese political institutions and changes therein were concerned. In practice, therefore, the SCAP planners, while scrupulously obeying these general directives, enjoyed considerable freedom of choice. They were in effect commanded by the president and the Joint Chiefs of Staff to democratize and demilitarize Japan. Devising specific means to achieve these ends was largely left to SCAP and his staff. The preceding chapters lavishly demonstrate this situation in a variety of contexts. The obvious conclusion is that the foreign or external portion of the planning for political changes in Occupied Japan largely originated on the spot from the Supreme Commander and his staff, at least insofar as the specific institutional and procedural structure and content were concerned.

The precise degree of this independence from external influence enjoyed by SCAP is, however, subject to partial qualification on several scores other than the general requirements of the presurrender planning documents. In a very few instances the Far Eastern Commission, representing the Allied Powers in general and sitting in Washington, was able to exert a modest influence on particular decisions by SCAP. It is also possible that on occasion SCAP policies may have been influenced by General MacArthur's well known sensitivity to media commentary at home. A more fundamental external determinant, though, was doubtless the degree of ideological consensus that characterized American society in general at that time and the personnel of SCAP as well. For most

Americans victory was a vindication of their own political institutions and ideals. It was also a justification for sharing these with—or imposing them upon—others. When it came to devising the basic political institutions for postwar Japan, therefore, there was not a very wide spectrum of real choice either among the American people in general or, more specifically, the Americans who staffed the Occupation. The gap that separated the "New Dealers" from the "conservatives" at General MacArthur's headquarters was in many respects not that wide and, in this sense, there was a high proportion of predetermination to the decisions made about how postwar Japan should be democratized.

This self-righteous bias in favor of American political institutions and practices may well have been reinforced by the ignorance of most higher ranking Occupation officials where Japanese history, society, and politics were concerned. It is worth noting that, while the presurrender planning in Washington was done by a small group of the outstanding American specialists on Japan, the Occupation itself was, with few exceptions, administered by Americans who had little, if any, preestablished knowledge of Japan. What they knew was largely learned on the job and, often, from highly selective associations with the Japanese with whom they had business. This difference between the pre- and postsurrender planners as individuals is reflected in the plans they produced. The presurrender plans display a far greater consciousness of the obstacles to the successful democratization of Japan posed by Japan's past experiences and culture. They were in this sense more diffident, more limited, and less optimistic. The SCAP staff, on the other hand, might with only slight exaggeration be characterized as "rushing in where angels fear to tread." It might equally be said, however, that had they known more, they might have accomplished less.

As one reflects on this particular case of advance planning in Washington and what actually happened to those carefully wrought plans in Japan in the light of the general literature about social planners and their plans, it loses many of its seemingly special characteristics. In instances of this sort where there is a sharp and decisive break in institutional sponsorship and authority, in the personnel directly involved, in the physical and geographic setting, and between the stage of planning and the stage of action, it is to be expected that a new set of actors will become dominant and refashion or particularize the preexisting plans as seems best to them.

This is what happened in the case of the Allied Occupation of Japan. A wartime situation characterized by the primacy of a small set of State Department planners knowledgeable about Japan, operating at a distance of thousands of miles from the subjects of their planning, and necessarily ignorant of the circumstances and attitudes that would actually prevail in a defeated Japan gave way to a postwar situation characterized in theory by the primacy of the Joint Chiefs of Staff but in fact by the dominant authority of General MacArthur and his staff. They were on the spot, faced with realities rather than hypotheses, and possessed of guidelines in the form of the Joint Chiefs' November 3 directive that spelled out the general directions in which they were to travel. Under these circumstances and largely ignorant of the detailed Washington plans, they interpreted their directive along lines basically predetermined by their American experience and heritage, given added focus when necessary by General MacArthur. The results were generally quite similar to those proposed in the Washington plans. This was not accidental in two senses. The Washington planners shared the same national heritage and biases as the Tokyo planners. And the November 3 directive was a distillation of the Washington planners' work phrased in more general terms.

Third, it would be a serious error in this planning context to regard SCAP as a unitary agency. Professor Pempel has used the phrase "functional feudalism" to describe the internal structure and relationships of the Supreme Commander's headquarters. We find it appropriate. Apart from the strictly military portions thereof, SCAP was divided into a number of civilian sections each charged with overseeing and conducting a particular set of functions such as political reforms, economic reforms, labor reforms, and the like. Short of explicit intervention by General MacArthur or the chief of staff, there was no means of coordinating the plans or activities of these sections. General MacArthur never held staff conferences that brought together representatives of these sections; their chiefs seldom, if ever, met collectively. The result was great practical autonomy for the individual sections and, inevitably, frequent disagreements and rivalries among them. Under these circumstances the loyalties of individual members of SCAP normally lay with their sections or subunits thereof and with the particular plans that their section or unit had embraced. Some notable feuds resulted that stemmed from bitter clashes between both personalities and sectional policies about the details of how best to democratize Japan. SCAP's planning for the Occupation of Japan is, therefore, best perceived as the product of a number of sometimes conflicting and largely autonomous planning agencies and agents rather than as deriving from any single or coordinated source.

Fourth, it is important to note the existence and importance in this planning exercise of what might be called "wild cards" or, more pretentiously, "historical accidents." We have in mind the remarkable and historically important influence of particular individuals of low or medium rank on the outcome of the Occupation. The preceding chapters document at least three such cases on the SCAP side. Beate Sirota was a very junior, twenty-two-year-old member of the Government Section who had lived in Japan and spoke fluent Japanese. More than any other single individual, she was probably responsible for the incorporation of provi-

sions for far-reaching women's rights into Article 24 of the Japanese constitution. The influence of Ethel Weed, a lieutenant in the Women's Army
Corps attached to the Civil Information and Education Section, was similarly prominent in the establishment of a Women's and Minors' Bureau
in the new Ministry of Labor. Finally, the terms of Japan's new Civil
Code were in a number of instances heavily influenced by Alfred Oppler,
a middle-ranking member of the Government Section. All three were
planners and all three, as individuals, had a profound and organizationally improbable effect on the shape and content of Japan's new democratic system.

Finally, SCAP in theory, and frequently in practice as well, preferred to
react to Japanese initiatives for political or legal change that were compatible with its own predispositions rather than to launch a plan of its
own devising at the start. The manner in which the new constitution was
finally drafted by SCAP has tended to obscure this important point. Yet
even then SCAP would have greatly preferred to react to some Japanese
initiative, provided that it was substantially more liberal than the Matsumoto drafts. In fact, it was only after the Japanese cabinet failed to
produce such a draft that the Government Section proceeded unilaterally.
Practically all of the preceding Japanese-authored chapters and several of
the American ones demonstrate admirably the extent and importance of
Japanese contributions to the planning process that underlies the political
and legal changes effected during the Occupation. Contemporary Japan
is by no means an exclusively American creation. Japanese, too, had a
great deal to do with its form and substance.

The real issue in this instance, however, is "which Japanese?" The Japanese populace was divided in many ways in its attitudes toward the
Occupation and toward particular Occupation programs. This was true
also with respect to Japanese political parties, politicians, academics, and
bureaucrats. As the SCAP staff became more aware of this, they made
more systematic use of such rifts in Japanese opinion to advance their
own reform programs and, in so doing, give more credibility to the
injunction in the November 3 directive that "it is not the responsibility of
the Allied Powers to impose upon Japan any form of government not
supported by the freely expressed will of the Japanese people."

They took both positive and negative steps. The massive categorical
purge of those suspected of supporting the old regime, the war crimes
trials, and the rigorous censorship exemplify negative steps. They were
intended among other things to debar access to the political arena to
those who might most effectively oppose SCAP's "reform" programs.
The release of political prisoners, the new election law, the early encouragement of labor unions, and the favoritism shown some political parties, politicians, and scholars as opposed to others exemplify a more positive strategy. It was "friendly" initiatives from these latter groups that

SCAP sought, listened to, and was frequently influenced by. In this qualified sense, it is fair to say that some Japanese had a great deal to do with
the form and substance of the Occupation and that they played an important role in its planning. But they were "friendly" Japanese—collaborators in a constructive sense, if one approves the goals of the Occupation.
Their numbers, in terms of those actually exercising effective influence,
were probably not very great, and they often owed a good deal of their
domestic status and influence either directly or indirectly to the Occupation and the changes it brought to the Japanese political scene. In many
cases they could not have become influential had not SCAP removed
them from the arena or silenced their domestic rivals. The process thus
involves elements of both selective coercion and selective favoritism and,
depending on one's standards, this aspect of the Occupation can accordingly be viewed as "discriminatory coercion" or "discriminatory cooptation." Both phenomena were undoubtedly present. The precise propor-
tions of the mix are still a subject of lively controversy, but there can be
no doubt that the total environment of the time was shaped—in part by
the accident of defeat and Occupation and in part deliberately by U.S.
policy—to place powerful pressures on Japan and the Japanese to accommodate themselves to SCAP's programs.

Special note should be taken of two aspects of this cooptation process.
First, it was not one-sided. Japanese politicians, bureaucrats, or scholars
who chose to collaborate actively with the Occupation invariably had
their own agendas to accomplish and frequently took the initiative in
seeking and establishing an Occupation contact. Second, it was through
such associations that SCAP's staff gained much of their knowledge
about Japanese society and politics. Many of the resulting insights were
undoubtedly distorted or inaccurate in their reflection of actual Japanese
conditions or opinions. But they were influential. Most of the Occupation's major reform programs resulted in laws that represent an amalgam
of components based in part on American official policies and individual
experiences and preferences and in part on the inputs of "friendly" Japanese with access to SCAP. One suspects also that most of the legal and
administrative details connected with these laws and their associated regulations, which are often of critical importance where the actual execution of laws is concerned, especially in highly bureaucratized states such
as Japan, were of Japanese provenance.

Structurally and institutionally speaking, there is a good deal of similarity between prewar and postwar Japan. We will spell out some of the
details when we shift to the topic of continuity versus discontinuity later
in this chapter. Briefly, however, what Professor Amakawa, for example,
has to say about the SCAP-sponsored reforms in the Japanese system of
local government and the resemblances between the old and the "reformed" system can be duplicated in many other spheres. This should

come as no surprise to anyone familiar with the nature and requirements of the modern administrative state. It is not easy—even given total legal authority—to intervene from the outside in structures and processes of this complexity and interrelatedness. This is especially true when the outsiders involved are almost totally ignorant of the working details of the Japanese legal and political systems. When it came to the precise formulation of particular reform programs and writing the specific and detailed legislation and regulations that really give substance and meaning to the "new Japan," the Occupation authorities were forced to rely heavily and continuously on Japanese advice and assistance. In this sense at least, whatever "success" may be attributed to the Occupation owes a great deal to Japanese participation. It was the availability of Japanese collaborators willing—and often eager—to provide both ideas for change and the technical knowledge as to how they might best be implemented in statutory, regulatory, and administrative terms that made these changes possible. The Japanese contributions to this volume testify clearly and eloquently to this effect.

We began this section with a question about the role of planning and planners in bringing about the political and legal changes that distinguish post-Occupation from prewar Japan. We end with a complex answer. The Allied Occupation of Japan was perhaps the single most exhaustively planned operation of massive and externally directed political change in world history. Some of the earliest and most cogent planning—the Washington-based component—appears to have had only generalized or indirect consequences with respect to actual changes in Japan. The effective planning was mostly done in Japan very shortly in advance of, or almost simultaneously with, the particular programs of change involved. There were no really meaningful overall plans involved beyond the general specification of major goals and programs contained in the U.S. Initial Postsurrender Policy and the Joint Chiefs' November 3 directive, unless General MacArthur himself, or he and a few top advisors, had some full-blown plan in mind at the outset. There is no creditable evidence that this was the case. The real plans, therefore, were the product of a number of SCAP sections, their leading officials, occasional low-ranking individuals, and a very important element of Japanese planners and advisors. The relative importance of these elements and their contributions to a particular program of political or legal change varied from case to case. One of the least representative, but most important, cases was the initial drafting of the new constitution. Unfortunately, this has received a disproportionate amount of attention that has seriously distorted the general view of the planning process that really underlay the emergence of the "new Japan."

A question was also posed as to the degree to which the actual results in post-Occupation Japan conform with those anticipated by the above-described planning process. Any extensive linkage between the Washington-based plans and the political institutions of post-Occupation Japan would have been a truly notable event in the annals of large-scale sociopolitical planning. However, while there is a strong resemblance, there seem to be very few cases in which direct causation is involved. Usually the planning operations of SCAP and its Japanese associates intervened. In terms of the actual nature of the outcomes, however, it is doubtful that this intervention made much difference. There is little essential difference between SCAP's plans and the plans originating in Washington, except that the former cover more topics and are much more specific.

Accordingly, if one drops from consideration the Washington-based plans and considers only the SCAP plans, the degree to which they accurately describe the principal characteristics of the contemporary Japanese political system is remarkable. While there are deviations, one is on balance much more impressed by the similarities than by the differences. The basic institutional and procedural changes survive without essential change. There are, of course, controversies over some of the uses to which the new institutions and political processes have been put. A number of the chapters in this volume make clear the position of many Japanese that the "reverse course" involved a major perversion of the democratic goals of the Occupation and a serious invasion of constitutionally guaranteed civil and political rights. The issues are complex, and we will revert to this matter later.

How can one explain this preponderant similarity between the SCAP plans and the institutions and practices of contemporary Japanese politics? At first, given the seemingly enormous gap that separates the authoritarian politics of prewar Japan from the democratic politics of postwar Japan, this may seem like an unprecedented example of historical discontinuity, of a nation turning its back upon its own political traditions and doing so primarily as a result of external pressure. In some respects this is true, but there is much more to be said on this score, most of which will be reserved for later treatment under the rubric of continuity versus discontinuity.

In the narrower context of planning and the consequences of planning however, it is possible to conceive of a scenario wherein Japan's general and remarkable cooperativeness during the Occupation was motivated primarily by a grand strategy of compliance as the speediest means of bringing the Occupation to an end and thereby regaining national sovereignty and the capacity to do as it pleased. Prime Minister Yoshida occasionally gave this impression. Under such a scenario the end of the Occupation would probably entail a large-scale reversion—perhaps sudden, perhaps gradual—to more traditional modes of governance. In some degree such a calculation undoubtedly figured in the private views of numerous highly placed Japanese. Several post-Occupation attempts to amend the new constitution point in this direction. But other more potent forces were also involved.

First, there was a genuine and massive revulsion of popular feeling against the war, the losses and suffering caused thereby, and the leaders and policies that had led the nation to these distressing circumstances. In this sense the Occupation coincided with an unusual potential for change in Japan. Second, the purge brought about a more extensive shift in both public and private leadership than has generally been recognized. While connected with the older prewar leadership, many of the new leaders were not mainstream figures. A large proportion came from political party backgrounds where there had always been an aspiration to increase the power of the parties and politicians at the expense of the military, the peerage, and, in some cases, the civil bureaucracies as well. Now they had an opportunity to do so and, in effect, the public was ready to support such an endeavor. Third, this new leadership in time discovered that the Occupation broom was not really seeking a clean sweep. Its wielders were talking about sorts of political change that had in many cases long been advocated by prewar Japanese parties and liberals. In this sense the Occupation provided opportunities as well as problems. Professor Takemae has provided a few telling examples. Fourth, after the early months of the purge and the shock of a new and prefabricated constitution, SCAP policy in the political sphere generally became more cooperative and more receptive to Japanese ideas and initiatives, even with respect to the later stages of amending and enacting the first draft of the new constitution. Most of the preceding chapters testify to the extent and meaningfulness of Japanese participation, usually official but not infrequently private, in the development of these plans for change. To the extent to which this practice prevailed, it is not so surprising that the Japanese government, *faute de mieux*, was willing to live with its results. Japanese had a good deal to do with determining the nature and content of these plans. Also, time is a great healer. Given time and practice, people and governments learn to live and work with institutions that in the first instance they may strenuously have opposed. It is one of the oldest and wisest adages of politicians that existing systems usually operate on behalf of the party in power. In Japan the party in power did not really change after the early purges. The Katayama cabinet was not actually a socialist government. All governments were of a conservative persuasion. In other words the party in power had some six years of experience with the new forms of governance and manifest success in learning to use them to its own advantage. Under such circumstances why should they want sweeping changes when the Occupation finally came to an end in April 1952? It should also be remembered that while the Occupation formally ended in 1952, Japan's dependence upon the United States did not. This depen-

dence argued strongly against any dramatic reversals of Occupation programs calculated seriously to offend the American government or people.

One further comment is in order. As Professor Amakawa in particular
makes clear, the Japanese government did not hesitate to eliminate completely and at the earliest possible moment those Occupation-imposed
reforms that it found particularly obnoxious and that were at the same
time not central to American concerns. The fate of the Shoup Mission's
recommendations for tax reform is an excellent example. This did not
even await the formal end of the Occupation. In effect the Japanese government regained its autonomy for most domestic purposes with the outbreak of the Korean War and expanded it still farther with the advent of
General Ridgway as Supreme Commander. In 1951, acting with SCAP's
explicit permission, the Japanese government conducted an extensive
review of the changes effected during the Occupation under the authority
of the so-called Potsdam ordinances. This led to a number of "retrogressive" changes and made it still easier for some Japanese to live with the
programs effected during the Occupation.

Finally, where the planning process is concerned, a number of interesting gaps should be noted. Professor Pharr, for example, makes clear the
absence of prior attention in Washington to the entire field of women's
rights. The relevant planning originated in Japan. This was also true of
the Occupation's somewhat dilatory efforts where reforms of the Japanese bureaucracy were concerned. In such cases, however, postsurrender
planning initiatives in Japan did assure some action in these fields. There
are other areas, however, where no action at all occurred and, in some
cases, these were of substantial importance.

For example, after a certain amount of internal controversy, the Government Section decided to limit its intervention into the Japanese electoral system to requiring the enfranchisement of women, lowering the
ages for voting and eligibility for office-holding, increasing the numbers
of elective officers, ordaining a purge, and providing for direct legislation
and recall at the local and constitutional referenda at the national level.
In retrospect, some Japanese might well regret that the Occupation
neglected this opportunity to endow the country with a more representative and satisfactory electoral system. Once established, it has proven
especially difficult for any modern democracy to change the dispensa-
tions of its electoral laws that relate to such fundamentally sensitive matters as districting, balloting, reapportionment, and the financing and regulation of election campaigns. Japan has been no exception to this rule.
The Occupation could have performed an unwelcome but useful service
in this respect rather than simply assenting to the reintroduction in 1947
of the substance of the 1925 election law. No Japanese government since
then has found it possible to introduce any really meaningful changes.

Much the same is true of political parties and labor unions. SCAP chose to regard both as essentially private organizations, the structure, membership, financing, internal procedures, and authority of which should be left to the determination of its members, which is to say to their leaderships. The same was true of employers' organizations. The public importance of these organizations is such that SCAP may have foregone an opportunity to perform a function that democratic governments invariably find very difficult to accomplish for themselves.

The External Context of the Occupation

It has taken a substantial literature of protest in Japan against the malefactions of the "reverse course" plus, more recently, the writings of revisionist historians in the West to focus an appropriate degree of attention on the interactions between the general international environment during the years from 1945 to 1952 and developments within Japan. Since this was the period that witnessed the birth and development of both the Cold War and the real war in Korea and since, in global terms, the United States and the Soviet Union were the principal protagonists involved, it is highly improbable that the course of international events would not have some influence on the policies of the Occupation. No one seriously denies this. But there agreement ends. There is a great deal of controversy over the extent, type, and effectiveness of external influence, the particular motivations involved, their relative weight, and the manner and extent to which foreign forces interact with domestic ones to explain contemporary developments in Japan. Viewed from the Japanese standpoint, these issues come to focus in the debate over the so-called reverse course on the part of the Occupation authorities.

A principal problem involved in this polemic has been the lack of a generally accepted definition of the very term "reverse course." Professor Sakamoto's chapter provides a systematic insight into the true complexity of this issue. The phrase is Japanese in origin and was coined probably in the mid-1950s by elements opposed to both the Japanese government in power and to reversals of earlier policies that they discerned in SCAP itself. It has become an omnibus term that in various usages and contexts incorporates some or all of the following notions. Basically the conception is one of periodization linked fundamentally to alleged policy changes on the part of SCAP. According to this view, the Occupation may be usefully divided into two principal stages: a first or "New Deal" phase where the thrust of Occupation policy was predominantly reforming, progressive, and democratic, and a second or "Reverse Course" phase where it shifts and, in some controverted but notable degree, becomes reactionary, conservative, and selectively punitive and repressive in its policies toward the truly democratic elements of the Japanese populace.

When does this second stage begin? A variety of dates and events have been cited.

General MacArthur's intervention to prohibit the planned general strike on February 1, 1947

Secretary of the Army Draper's San Francisco speech of January 1948 in which he called for an end to the anti-*zaibatsu* campaign in Japan and a speedy rehabilitation of the Japanese economy

The visit to Japan in March 1948 by George Kennan, chief of the State Department's Policy Planning Staff

The adoption in October 1948 of the National Security Council's paper on the redirection of the United States' strategic policy toward Japan (NSC 13/2).

The removal from the public service in Japan of elements suspected of radical sympathies in 1949–1950, the so-called red purge.

All these and more are critical dates in the chronology of the "reverse course," but opinions differ widely as to how seminal and diagnostic particular dates are with respect to the inception of this period.

There is a similar question about the basic cause of the "reverse course." Was it an American effort to rescue and rehabilitate the capitalist system and economy in Japan in order to get the costs of the Occupation off the backs of the American taxpayer and in the longer run provide the United States with lucrative trading opportunities—as the Draper speech would suggest? Was it responsive to the growing hostility—the Cold War —between the Soviet Union and the United States and the consequent need of the American government for a reliable ally and a base for its Containment Policy in Eastern Asia since China could no longer be expected to play that role—as Kennan's views and the NSC paper indicate? Was it simply a case of exporting to SCAP and to Japan the anti-Communist frenzy that arose in the United States at about this time? Had the Occupation decided that the opposition elements in Japan were subversive of its goals for that country and, therefore, extended further the policies foreshadowed by its treatment of the 1947 general strike? Or was there really a "reverse course" at all in the sense of a dominant shift in SCAP policy toward Occupied Japan? Granting the existence of some significant discontinuities of policy, did these really outweigh the underlying consistencies involved? Could some of the discontinuities be more simply explained as incidental to the gradual and planned return of real administrative authority to the Japanese government and to that government's well-known distaste for some of its allegedly radical domestic opponents?

And, finally, there is the question of consequences. If, indeed, there was a "reverse course," did it really mark the end of SCAP's role as a democratizing force in Japan and the succession thereto of those native elements in Japan that resisted the influence of Cold War forces? Or has SCAP's democratizing mantle passed to the party in power and its supporters?

These are complex issues rendered more so by the heavy loading of political interest that some of them have acquired, especially in terms of domestic Japanese politics. They also happen to be a subject of substantial current interest to students of the Occupation, both Japanese and foreign. Under these circumstances it is inevitable that there should be disagreements on some of the scores noted above. These will be noted in the following account.

The weight attached by revisionist historians to the Cold War as the prime, if not exclusive, determinant of certain policy alterations during the latter stages of the Occupation, the "reverse course," seems excessive. An earlier chapter addresses this issue by nominating for a share of the blame the United States' alleged failure to plan for a "postreform" or "post-Occupation" phase of its activities in Japan in which advance provision would have been made for the transfer of authority to some warrantably democratic leadership group that would assume responsibility for carrying on and indigenizing the reform programs. It regards this failure as perhaps of equal importance to the Cold War among the factors responsible for the reverse course in Japan. Some would maintain, however, that the issue is much more complicated than that and attempt to demonstrate the added complexity by reference to both pre- and postsurrender planning in this respect.

The basic intent of the presurrender planners was to equip Japan with the best possible democratic institutions and processes. Having established these in the broadest possible sense—not only politically but socially, educationally, and economically as well—it was always their intention to turn this apparatus over to Japanese management, with SCAP supervision and intervention in the earlier stages replaced by increasing Japanese autonomy in the latter. The American presurrender planners were not oblivious to longer term problems where their reform programs were concerned, but not knowing at the outset how long the Occupation was going to last, they placed their faith in this respect on two developments, both of which they considered probable. First, they believed that the Occupation would be successful in introducing and in staffing a responsible and democratic form of governance in Japan and that this would acquire substantial inertial force in the course of the Occupation. Second, they believed that after the Occupation this new Japanese government would continue to be friendly to the United States and in important respects dependent upon American support and good will. In combination it was felt that these circumstances would provide a reasonable long-term guarantee of the stability of the reform programs.

Once the Occupation was underway, the problem of the post-Occupation treatment of Japan did not really emerge for some time, except at
lower levels of the Department of State where a small group that included
some of the presurrender planners was charged with studying the terms
of an eventual treaty of peace with Japan. Their activities received small
attention either publicly or within the government until General MacArthur on March 17, 1947, in an interview with the foreign press in Tokyo
stated that he favored a peace treaty with Japan "as soon as possible."
The subsequent exchanges between Washington and SCAP leave little
doubt as to General MacArthur's sentiments in this respect. They are
best summed up in the words of his memorandum of March 21, 1947.

> As I have previously stated, it is my considered view that the Japanese
> nation and people are now ready for the initiation of negotiations leading to
> a Treaty of Peace—ready in the sense that Japan's war-making power and
> potential is destroyed, the framework of democratic government has been
> erected, reforms essential to the reshaping of Japanese lives and institutions
> to conform to democratic ideals have been instituted, and the people have
> been accorded the fundamentals of human liberty. And ready in the sense
> that there is "a peacefully inclined and responsible government" which can
> pledge Japan to the undertakings incident to such a treaty.
>
> Such a treaty, however, must be designed effectively to restore peace—not
> merely to extend in modified form the foreign military controls now exist-
> ing. For it is a truism that democracy is a thing of the spirit which can nei-
> ther be purchased nor imposed by the threat or application of force.[1]

General MacArthur was still of this view when George Kennan interviewed him on March 5, 1948:

> As for the other reform measures, he [MacArthur] thought they were almost
> completed. Another three or four months should see the process substan-
> tially wound up. The Civil Service reform was the only important outstand-
> ing measure. When this had been implemented, we might indeed be able to
> relax and permit the measures already taken to be assimilated.[2]

These statements were not intended to assert that Japan had already
become a fully and reliably democratic nation but only that it had been
given the means of attaining such a condition, had shown promising
progress along these lines, and that the nature of democracy was such
that foreign agencies like SCAP had done all that was possible or desirable to assist Japan along this path. The rest was up to the Japanese government and people, subject to some quite modest degree of continuing
foreign scrutiny, preferably by the United Nations. The general's views
about the limited utility of foreign occupations are well known: "History
points out the unmistakable lesson that military occupations serve their
purpose at best only for a limited time, after which a deterioration rapidly sets in."[3]

Against this background, it was quite logical for SCAP to conclude that by 1948 the time had arrived to turn increasing authority over to the freely elected government of Japan. The primary responsibility for the future of democratic government in Japan now belonged to the Japanese government. There was no further need to plan for postreform or post-Occupation Japanese democracy. General MacArthur believed that what could be done along these lines had been done. His government did not object.

This decision, taken cumulatively and informally by many of the higher-ranking American officials during 1947 and early 1948, marks the most basic shift in U.S. policy toward the Occupation itself. It also inaugurates on SCAP's part the developments that are loosely termed the "reverse course." It should be noted, however, that this particular decision was in turn part of a much larger complex of policy changes occurring at roughly the same time.

For example, where the internal conduct of the Occupation was concerned, there were notable exceptions to this phased return of authority to the Japanese government and retirement to a less active role by SCAP. It notably did not apply to the economy. Indeed, the reverse was true. It was in 1948 that SCAP, with pressure from Washington, began actively and aggressively to work on the massive rehabilitation of the Japanese economy by means that were highly interventionist. Also, as General MacArthur made clear to George Kennan in the above-noted interview in March 1948, he continued to have some concern as to the extent occupation policies had been influenced by academic theorizers of a left-wing variety, at home and in Tokyo. He also indicated an intention to conduct a housecleaning of SCAP on this score. There were, therefore, areas of unfinished business where SCAP intended still to be active and assertive despite the general decision to begin returning greater authority and initiative to the Japanese government. And two of them were specifically identified as the Japanese economy and left-wing influence on Occupation policies—both areas that lay at the heart of the "reverse course." General MacArthur's views expressed to Kennan in March 1948, therefore, foreshadow in general terms the impending changes of SCAP policy with respect to the treatment accorded business and labor in the course of the economic rehabilitation program and the events of the "red purge" of 1949–1950. Similarly, the associated policy of returning greater authority to the Japanese government in the political sphere made it possible for the conservative party in power to play a more active and influential role in the "reverse course" than would otherwise have been the case.

These developments do not, of course, invalidate the view that, given different or better planning for the terminal stages of the Occupation, the "reverse course" might not have taken place at all. They do, however, explain why this alternative sort of planning did not in fact occur and, in part at least, why the changes in SCAP's policy toward big business, labor, and alleged "radicals" in the public service did. Added to these considerations, of course, was the factor of increasing concern and uncertainty on the part of both SCAP and Washington about the role the Soviet Union might play with respect to Japan when a peace treaty was negotiated, especially if this were to lead to the withdrawal of American forces from Japan. There is no doubt that such contingencies were very much on SCAP's mind at this time and that they played a part in the policy changes involved in the "reverse course." They were by no means, however, a sufficient cause for those changes.

It has also been argued earlier that the "reverse course" and the Cold War play a critical role in engendering and defining those elements in Japan that should, in a better-planned Occupation, have inherited the role of protectors and indigenizers of the democratic reforms. They are described in terms of foreign policy as those who opposed the influence of the Cold War and favored peace, disarmament, and a noninvolved role for Japan rather than rearmament and involvement on the American side. In domestic terms they are those who resisted the "red purges" of 1949–1950 and regarded coexistence with the Communists as the touchstone of true liberalism and democracy.

This is an interesting and important point. It is also one where interpretations can differ, sometimes along national lines. The Japan Communist party (JCP) and the Japanese Communists have a very special meaning in the history of the development of democratic political institutions in Japan. The forceful suppression of the JCP in prewar times also marked the beginning of the suppression of liberal political parties in general. Furthermore, it was largely the Communists and a few religious elements, mostly Christian, that stood firm against governmental repression and, during the 1920s and 1930s, paid the price in prison and elsewhere for adhering to their convictions. Most other liberals and intellectuals capitulated and became real or ostensible converts to the official mythology. In the early postwar years the JCP continued to stand for a variety of very popular causes in Japan: peace, democratization, workers' rights, and opposition to the resurgence of prewar political leaders.

Against this background of retrospective loyalties and shared causes, it is easy to understand the importance attached by many Japanese, including liberal intellectuals, to the "red purges." They were perceived as the replaying of a disastrous episode in the history of Japanese democracy and conducive to a return of prewar institutions and practices. From such a standpoint the "red purges" were far more than an unsavory and discreditable aspect of both the SCAP and the Japanese governmental records. They were a fundamental threat to the survival of democracy in Japan. Similarly, those who resisted the purges and other associated "reverse course" policies were the true defenders of Japanese democracy who, given a better-planned Occupation, should have been the group entrusted with power by the Japanese electorate as the Occupation drew to a close.

Seen from such a standpoint the "reverse course" was a true national disaster. Subsequent events such as partial rearmament, the failure of an omnilateral peace treaty, the security treaty, the continued presence of American forces in Japan, and the persistent ascendency and conservative policies of the Liberal Democratic party and its predecessors in office strengthened this persuasion. Quite logically, the historical stature of the "reverse course" is greatly enhanced by such an interpretation of prewar and postwar Japanese history. It becomes either a critical and adverse turning point in the record of postwar Japanese democracy or, at best, a serious setback to the democratic progress made in the earlier "New Deal" phase of the Occupation. Similarly, the degree to which democratic institutions and processes survive in contemporary Japan is seen as an artifact of the reforms during the earlier stages of the Occupation combined with the continuing influence of a large and at least marginally influential liberal opposition.

Other interpretations that assign less significance to the impact of either the "reverse course" or the Cold War on democratic institutions in Japan are possible. Proponents of these views would agree that the "reverse course" had a great deal to do with the development and policies of opposition political parties in Japan but dissent from the conclusion that the political elements involved were the sole defenders of peace and democracy.

While admittedly the "red purges" were an unsavory and discreditable aspect of both the SCAP and Japanese governmental records, they should not be evaluated as fatal to the survival of democracy in Japan or as the unique touchstone of true liberalism and democracy. There is more than this to a democratic society. By any realistic standards derived either from Japan's own past or the comparative performance of other present-day democracies, the overall record of postwar Japanese governments is creditable. This should not be denied because of shortcomings in particular and limited respects. Nor should the overall record of SCAP be depreciated. The emergence of the new forces of peace and democracy in Japan would not have been possible had it not been for SCAP's earlier reform programs.

A similar case can be made with respect to the economic aspects of the "reverse course." It would be difficult to deny, given the circumstance prevailing in Japan in 1948, the urgent need for economic reconstruction and rehabilitation. Further weight was added, on the one hand, by the rapidly growing desire in the United States to diminish its share of the costs of the Occupation and, on the other, by visions on the part of some Americans of future advantages to be gained through trade with a resuscitated Japanese economy. Finally, concern over the Cold War and Japan's future role therein was undoubtedly involved. The ensuing program of economic reconstruction was in its early stages almost totally the product of Washington and SCAP planning, initiatives, and control. It involved the overt repression of some elements in the labor movement. This policy is not new. It had been emerging since the abortive general strike of February 1947. The program also involved a marked deemphasis—some would say reversal—of earlier efforts to dissolve the *zaibatsu* and a positive encouragement of big business organization and initiatives. Given the circumstances, few Americans would have regarded these developments as antidemocratic. It would certainly have been naive to expect SCAP to preside over the installation of a socialist economy in Japan—or anything remotely resembling one.

There was also an important foreign policy dimension to the "reverse course." In general its opponents in Japan favored demilitarization, a strict interpretation of Article IX of the constitution, an omnilateral peace treaty, the withdrawal of American troops, and a neutralist foreign policy for posttreaty Japan. The Japan that actually emerged from the "reverse course" period was partially remilitarized, committed to a loose interpretation of Article IX, had signed a less than omnilateral peace treaty, and, through the Security treaty, had committed itself at least passively to the American side in the Cold War.

These outcomes differ in important respects from General MacArthur's design for posttreaty Japan. He envisaged a Japan demilitarized by an international treaty to which the Soviet Union would be signatory and which would be monitored by the United Nations. The actual outcome was, therefore, determined in Washington, not by SCAP. And there can be no doubt that it differed dramatically from the pre-1948 plans. In this respect there was real substance to the "reverse course." One should be aware, however, that these changes were for the most part imposed upon the Japanese government by the United States against the objections and, in some cases, the stubborn resistance of that government. They were, in effect, a price reluctantly paid by Japan for ending the Occupation.

This last point about resistance on the part of the Japanese government is important. The Yoshida cabinet was by no means inert in this matter. Influenced in a measure difficult to evaluate by political pressures from the opposition parties, it played an important role in both a cooperative and an oppositional sense and displayed an increasing capacity and readiness over time to resist unwanted changes desired by the Occupation. This culminated in its review of the Potsdam ordinances in 1951. In other words, the disposition to resist the Occupation in important respects was not restricted to either the opposition or the party in power. It was a more general and completely natural phenomenon representing an essential part of what General MacArthur had in mind when he said in effect that all military occupations run downhill.

The "reverse course" and its constituent parts can, therefore, be interpreted in different ways. The concept is most valid when applied to changes in the international and military aspects of Japan's circumstances in and after 1948. When applied to domestic political and economic changes during this period, it requires more qualification. This inevitably poses a question as to whether the changes involved are substantial enough and sufficiently derogatory to the quality of Japanese democracy to merit the title "reverse course."

If one accepts the "liberal" argumentation in Japan, the answer must be in the affirmative: a drastic, although not complete, reversal of course really occurred in Occupation policy, and the consequences were distinctly and massively adverse for the quality of Japanese democracy both domestically and in terms of the nation's international position and policies.

But the same set of circumstances can be interpreted quite differently. The basic goals of the Occupation were the democratization and demilitarization of Japan. When Japan regained its sovereignty in April 1952, judging either by comparison with Japan's prewar past or the current institutions and practices of American or Western European states, its system of government was obviously and creditably democratic. Where demilitarization is concerned, the case is essentially similar, although complicated by much argumentation about the proper interpretation of Article IX of the new constitution. By any meaningful standard of military power, however, Japan itself certainly no longer constituted a threat to the security of any of its neighbors. If democratization and demilitarization were the goals at the outset and were similarly the actual outcomes at the conclusion of the Occupation, it would seem excessive to speak of a "reverse course" that drastically redirected the course and nature of the Occupation. The basic reform programs did not change and no one in authority in either SCAP or the American government urged that they be changed. The one major exception relates to the size and quality of Japan's armed forces. In 1950–1951 the American government did urge that these become significantly larger and more powerful The Japanese government successfully resisted these pressures. Comparable changes in the basic domestic reform programs were not even suggested.

Viewed in terms of their effects on the quality of Japanese democracy, the changes that did occur in the course of the Occupation were specific, not systemic. The most fundamental of these was the extension of the Containment Policy to Eastern Asia, in prospect as early as 1948 but not effectuated until the Korean War. This entailed a fundamental shift in the United States' conception of Japan's role in American global strategy. From a defeated and potentially still dangerous enemy, it became an ally and a major base for U.S. forces in the Western Pacific. Given the prevailing American view of the international scene and the long-obvious absence of any attractive alternative, it is really rather remarkable that this decision emerged as late as October 1948 in the form of the NSC paper 13/2. Even while still a debated prospect, however, it began to have important consequences within Japan. It doubtless facilitated the decision to work more actively and decisively for the rehabilitation of the Japanese economy, although views such as General Draper's and the desire for enhanced U.S. trade probably also played a part, as did the emerging success of the Marshall Plan in Europe. Similarly, the anti-Communist frenzy that was building in the United States was clearly supported by the development of the Cold War and in turn influenced the propensity toward a "red purge" in Japan. In other words, a great variety of domestic and international factors interacted to bring about a shift in particular earlier SCAP policies in Japan. There is no persuasive evidence, however, of policy changes on the part of either SCAP or the American government so sweeping and fundamental in nature as to constitute a reversal of the Occupation's original goals with respect to the democratization of Japan. Essentially what did occur was that an Occupation that had originally lacked any strategic goal more positive than the prevention of further Japanese aggression began to acquire a new and more positive international dimension in 1948, and this contributed to several changes in particular domestic programs of SCAP. But these changes had endogenous causes and were attributable to causes in Japan and in SCAP as well as in the external context of the Occupation.

The Occupation and Planned Political Change

The Washington-based planning for the Occupation of Japan, while very impressive in many respects, notably fails to come to grips with the practical problem of just how SCAP was going to create a democratic and demilitarized society in this "new Japan." The individuals involved were not oblivious to such problems of social engineering. There were factors that simply made it impractical for them to devote much time to so uncertain and conjectural a problem. Chief among these were the following.

No one knew when the war would end or under what circumstances. Yet the situation prevailing at that time would critically affect the Supreme Commander's options with respect to how he would set about accomplishing his mission in Japan. Would the Japanese government defend to the last every inch of Japanese territory against Allied forces fighting their way inland slowly and at great cost, or would it surrender without an invasion? Would there be a Japanese government in being at the end of the war with which the Allies could deal? What would become of the emperor? Was the Occupation to be administered directly by American military government teams as in Germany or indirectly through the Japanese government? If the latter, what sort of Japanese government?

Even given this degree of uncertainty, the Washington planners did not completely ignore these tactical problems. They did discuss the various phases into which an Occupation should be divided, and as early as March 1944 one finds them identifying liberal elements in the Japanese population with whom the Occupation authorities should be able to work constructively. This is a theme that recurs thereafter with some frequency in their planning documents. It was also an article of faith with several of the leading State Department planners that the emperor's prestige and authority should be utilized by the Occupation as a means of insuring Japanese cooperation and compliance with the terms of surrender. All of these tactics were later to play an essential role in the actual operations of General MacArthur in Japan. It is impossible to say, however, whether he owed them to his reading of the Washington documents or reached this conclusion independently. In any event the tactics actually used by the Occupation were predominantly developed on the spot in Japan.

Consider the Supreme Commander's circumstances in this respect. He was faced with certain givens. First, his goals were in general but extensive terms defined for him by the initial postsurrender policy and the November 1945 directive of the Joint Chiefs of Staff. Second, he was given total power over the Japanese government and people to accomplish these goals. Whatever the merits of the current controversy over whether Japan surrendered conditionally or unconditionally, there can be no doubt that MacArthur's orders from the president informed him that the surrender was unconditional and his authority in Japan absolute. Third, whenever possible he was directed to work through the Japanese government. In other words this was to be predominantly an indirect rather than a directly administered occupation, and thus essentially different from its German counterpart. Beyond these three basic prescriptions, General MacArthur was largely on his own.

In practice it is possible to divide SCAP's mission into two parts: demilitarization and democratization. The methods employed to accomplish the short-term aspects of the former require scant comment. What was involved was the rapid and complete disarmament, repatriation, and dissolution of all Japan's armed forces. This was an essentially military operation conducted under orders and with the cooperation of Japan's military authorities and the emperor. It was given the highest priority, was conducted with speed and efficiency and, once well under way, permitted MacArthur to turn his attention to the far more complex matter of democratization. How did the general and his staff set about this? One can examine the question in several ways.

First, there is a question of phasing or periodization. Where the political aspects of the Occupation's program are concerned, this went as follows. There was an initial period of preparing the ground that dominated SCAP's activities in this area from September 1945 until about February 1946. This was the time when the Japanese government was required to rescind a great variety of laws that were considered undemocratic by the Occupation. The revival of political parties was encouraged and a new election law enacted. The period culminated in the purge edicts of early 1946 that ultimately either removed from office or precluded from seeking or holding office upwards of 200,000 individuals falling in designated categories. A second period begins with the drafting and publicizing of the new constitution in February and March 1946 and runs roughly to the end of 1947. It includes the enactment of practically all of the major political reform programs. A third period encompasses the two and a half years from January 1948 to the outbreak of the Korean War in June 1950. It is characterized by sharply diminished initiatives and gradually lessening supervision on the part of SCAP and increasing initiatives and control on the part of the Japanese government. The fourth and final stage runs from June 1950 to April 1952 during which SCAP undertook no significant political initiatives of a domestic sort and exercised little meaningful supervision over the Japanese government, which by this time was largely running its own domestic affairs again, primarily within the framework of the preestablished reform programs but occasionally changing aspects of these, especially following the arrival of General Ridgway after General MacArthur's recall in April 1951.

This fourfold periodization is, of course, approximate. The terminal dates represent central tendencies, not clean breaks. But it does generally reflect the patterning of the Occupation's principal activities in the political sphere. With two major exceptions, it does not differ greatly from the profile of SCAP activity in other fields. The exceptions are economics and rearmament. The basic decisions to make a major effort to rehabilitate the Japanese economy and to press for some rearmament were not taken until 1948 and 1950, respectively. The efforts to effectuate these decisions were, consequently, basically out of synchronization with the pacing of the rest of SCAP's activities.

Was this particular periodization purposeful? Was it planned in advance? The answer cannot be an unqualified "yes" or "no." At some point it seems to have emerged from the actual experience of administering the first and second periods. There was certainly no formal agreement in advance on such a pattern. Interviews with those involved, however, indicate that after the enactment of the new constitution both General MacArthur and SCAP officials were thinking and talking about the necessity of a gradual and supervised transition of authority from SCAP to the Japanese government closely resembling in general outline that of the schema described above.

Where the more detailed planning of particular programs of political reform is concerned, several general matters should be noted. First, none of the programs is a product of long-range planning. All were more or less improvised on the spot, and the planning phase shades imperceptibly into and sometimes actually overlaps the implementation phase. A good deal of feedback and adaptation was involved. These were men—and, in a few cases, women—operating under the pressure of very difficult tasks and of time constraints that, because they were at the outset unknown and unpredictable, had to be construed as exigent. They moved from one undertaking of great complexity to another at high speed. Institutionally speaking, they dismantled Japan's prewar political system and fabricated a new one in the two years and four months between September 1945 and December 1947. There was little time for abstract or long-range planning.

Second, with respect to the civilian aspects of the Occupation, SCAP was exclusively a planning and supervisory, not an action, agency. The Occupation of Japan was indirectly administered. The Japanese government was SCAP's action agency, subject to supervision by SCAP centrally in Tokyo and by the Eighth Army's military government teams locally throughout Japan.

Third, as a matter of general policy SCAP valued Japanese initiatives and cooperation where the devising of specific plans for political change was concerned. They really had no other choice. Effective political planning requires extensive working knowledge of the subject matter concerned, of the general context of law and administration within which it is set, and, ultimately, the cooperation, or at least tolerance, of the agencies and staffs that will implement the plans. Even in a military occupation vested with absolute and unchallengeable authority, basic changes are not simply the product of deciding what one would like to do and issuing orders to that effect. The SCAP staff knew little or nothing about the Japanese system of law or administration in practical working terms. They needed informed Japanese assistance. Occasionally, a particular SCAP official chose to act on authoritarian rather than cooperative terms. The attempt to remake Japan's bureaucracy in the image of the University of Chicago's latest theories of civil service administration is an excellent example. Temporary and minimal changes usually resulted from such tactics.

Fourth, this emphasis on the practical importance of Japanese assistance in planning is not meant to imply that SCAP either sacrificed the initiative or accorded dominant or even equal weight to Japanese participation in the planning process. SCAP officials were aware of the sorts of democratic results they wanted to see achieved by their plans and able to judge in general terms whether a particular formulation would be conducive to that goal. They were quite prepared to require conformity from their Japanese counterparts in cases of disagreement on such scores. The making of the new constitution is a dramatic example of this sort. SCAP would much have preferred that this be the product of Japanese initiatives. Only when a satisfactory draft was not forthcoming from the Japanese government and it was feared that a most unsatisfactory one might be published with the government's official imprimatur did SCAP intervene and produce its own version. In the negotiations that followed, SCAP's stance was rigid, almost totally inflexible, despite strong pressure from the Japanese side. Once the draft was published, however, SCAP's attitude became much more flexible. Professor Tanaka estimates that thereafter, with the exception of the preamble, Government Section accepted some eighty to ninety percent of the Japanese government's suggested revisions of the text. In cases of less fundamental importance than the constitution, the entire planning process was normally much more cooperative from the outset. The chapters on the revision of the civil code or the local government system provide good examples. The Americans had certain basic objectives on which they stood firm, but a number of other goals and most of the means involved were negotiable.

Finally, it is important to note the origins of this much-needed Japanese advice and assistance. Some of it came, of course, from government officials, and came more freely after the carrying out of the purges. The Japanese government and bureaucracy, like their counterparts elsewhere, were not a solidary force. They proved both individually and collectively to be surprisingly cooperative and helpful. But SCAP benefited greatly as well from a wide range of completely unofficial Japanese advisors. Some were leaders of opposition political parties. Others were academic specialists, intellectuals, or professionals of liberal persuasion who viewed the Occupation as an opportunity to achieve changes that they had long but vainly advocated in the past. Some of them had very substantial influence on particular programs of political or legal reform. This combination of official and private advice was very helpful to the SCAP planners.

Against this background there developed in time what might be termed a general strategy that, with some exaggeration, may be said to embody the social engineering element of the Occupation. There is no evidence that it was present from the beginning or that it was the creation of some one individual or section in SCAP. Rather does it seem to have emerged gradually from repetitive experiences. It probably became a conscious strategy sometime in 1946. It may be summarized as follows with respect to a hypothetical political reform program.

Programs for political change normally began either as assignments to or initiatives by an individual or small group in SCAP's Government Section, sometimes at the suggestion of Japanese sources. Often the starting point was some provision or chapter of the new constitution which, once formulated, provided a sort of master plan. Flesh had to be added to the skeleton it provided in the form of a detailed structure and implementing legislation and regulations. The planning process normally began with preliminary thought and conversations within Government Section to sketch rough goals and possible means of effectuating these. This internal procedure would shortly be supplemented by informal consultations with informed Japanese advisers thought to be well-disposed toward the program in question. From these internal and external processes would gradually emerge a schema of sufficient substance to warrant either written or oral transmission to the Japanese government as a matter for official attention and action. Most such transmissions were oral. The government would then constitute an advisory committee to put the proposal into the form of a bill for legislative consideration. This committee would normally include private as well as official experts in the field concerned and would represent a variety of opinions. It would work closely with, and subject to the constant scrutiny of, the SCAP representative concerned. The process that ensued usually contained appreciable elements of bargaining and compromise, the effective limits of which could be informally controlled by the SCAP representative. Ultimately, a bill would emerge for submission to the Dict, which in theory could add further amendments but in practice did not usually do so.

This process was loaded in favor of outcomes desired by SCAP in several ways that may not be immediately obvious. The original initiative and definition of the basic objectives and terms involved lay with SCAP. This was advantageous. At any point in the ensuing process SCAP could intervene either to protect or forthrightly order a particular outcome. The Japanese government could not be certain in advance as to just when or under what circumstances the individual SCAP officer involved would be able to persuade his superiors to do so. While the Japanese government was not totally lacking in either the disposition or capacity to resist, it had limited capital to expend along such lines and wanted to conserve this for use in really critical circumstances. It was, therefore, usually easier to go along with rather than to resist these SCAP initiatives and, in so doing, to temper and qualify them along lines that the government could live with. SCAP was also in a position to insure representation on the government's committee of experts or individuals friendly to the initiative involved, who were also in frequent unofficial contact with SCAP in an advisory capacity. In this way the Occupation staff member involved had informal, continuous, and varied sources of information about the committee's proceedings and decisions. In effect, he was represented on the committee.

Finally, the subjects of SCAP's initiatives where major programs of political change were concerned were usually such as to have a preexisting and potentially expansible base of domestic Japanese support. For example, women and youth obviously stood to gain by the electoral reforms. Political parties in general were enormously advantaged by the increase in the status and authority of all Japanese legislative bodies. Women, youth, and younger sons and daughters were all beneficiaries of the changes in the civil code. In this sense the new constitution, viewed as a political document, represents one of the greatest assortments of political favors crafted in recent history. SCAP rather shortly became aware of both the short- and long-term advantages implicit in these appeals to the self-interest of major cross-sections of the Japanese populace. SCAP's staff worked hard at publicizing them in the most attractive possible terms. This made it much more difficult for relatively weak and uncertain Japanese governments to oppose openly changes that manifestly had at least potential appeal to sizeable parts of the electorate in circumstances where the opposition parties were often willing and eager to take up such causes, and to do so with SCAP on their side.

Under these circumstances there was a strong probability that SCAP would have its way, not entirely, for normally a fair amount of give and take was involved, but in large part, because the essentials of the plan were apt to survive. Furthermore, once enacted into law and applied in practice under circumstances where SCAP remained an attentive spectator and potential intervenor, the new legislation had an opportunity to demonstrate its value to an earlier unaware, ill-informed, or unconvinced public clientele of sufficient size to make it increasingly difficult for the government later to tamper with these new entitlements. The role of the opposition political parties as champions of much of this new legislation provided important additional protection. These are all reasons for the subsequent durability of SCAP's political reforms.

It is highly improbable that much before the summer or fall of 1946 anyone in SCAP thoroughly understood the methodology that we have just described. But in time and on the basis of actual experience they did come to understand and make habitual use of it. Herein resides the "social engineering" of the Occupation.

The Occupation as a Clash of Politico-Legal Perspectives

Insofar as SCAP devised anything like a master plan for the democratization of Japan, it was undoubtedly the new constitution of 1946–1947. The origins and developments of that document are treated at several points in the preceding sections, but Professor Tanaka in his chapter has cast new light on one aspect of the process that has long puzzled scholars. Why did not the Matsumoto Committee produce a draft constitution that stood some chance of acceptance by SCAP?

The facts that the original version of Japan's new constitution was written by SCAP's Government Section, that its final version preponderantly reflects that first draft, and that substantial pressures were applied by SCAP to procure the document's enactment have always constituted a potential threat to the integrity and survivability of the 1946 Constitution. If at some future time there were to be a strong revival of Japanese nationalism accompanied by a government of authoritarian tendencies that felt itself seriously hampered by the provisions of the present constitution, the foreign and constrained antecedents of that document might well lend themselves most effectively to an emotionally charged campaign for its replacement by some more authentically Japanese substitute.

In principle SCAP was aware of this liability. Indeed, this was one of the reasons for which General MacArthur told prime ministers Higashikuni and Shidehara that constitutional revision would be required, that SCAP's Political Advisor provided informal guidance on constitutional changes to Prince Konoe's associates, and that the Government Section long refrained from any more positive action in this area pending the results of the Matsumoto Committee's work on a revised constitution. Both Washington and SCAP preferred that constitutional changes originate from Japanese initiatives. The Matsumoto Committee was officially charged with taking such an initiative. As Professor Tanaka makes clear, the fact that it did not results in substantial part from a difference in its and the American perceptions of Japan's postwar circumstances where constitutional revision was concerned. Had it not been for this, it is quite possible that the procedures underlying the new constitution would have been basically different, that the original draft would have been the product of Japanese initiative, and the final draft a result of Japanese authorship tempered by SCAP "advice" of a substantially less dominant and obtrusive sort. This would certainly have been a more desirable outcome from all standpoints. What went wrong?

According to Professor Tanaka, "The tradition of constitutional scholarship in Japan prevented an adequate understanding of the requirements of the Potsdam Declaration. To GHQ, operating in the American legal tradition, the need for extensive revision of the constitution was self-evident, but it was not so obvious to the Japanese. The adoption of the postwar constitution proceeded in a maze of mutual misunderstanding due to deep-rooted differences in legal culture." More specifically, the Matsumoto Committee appears to have operated under the following misapprehensions. First, it interpreted the terms of the Potsdam Declaration in a literal and highly legalistic sense with little or no appreciation of its essentially political nature or of the international context in which it was shaped and was to be applied. This resulted in its taking literally and with no reference to this larger context the statement in the United States' reply to Japan's qualified acceptance of the Potsdam terms of surrender that "the ultimate form of government of Japan shall, in accordance with the Potsdam Declaration, be established by the freely expressed will of the Japanese people." This led to what most Americans would regard as the naïve assumption that the Japanese government would in effect be substantially free to determine the nature and extent of constitutional changes. Indeed, several members of the Matsumoto Committee doubted that any revision at all was necessary. Second, the Japanese legal tradition attached very little importance to the study of foreign constitutions or legal systems except insofar as these related directly to the interpretation of Japan's legal codes. The result was a rather astonishing ignorance of the prevailing Western standards and precedents by which the Americans were certain to evaluate whatever constitutional changes the Matsumoto Committee might recommend. Finally, the Japanese tradition also predisposed them to conceive of liberalizing political changes as essentially a function of increased power for the legislature. This inevitably led to an almost complete neglect of other forms of liberalizing change highly prized, by Americans in particular, to wit the constitutional protection of civil and human rights and the role of the judiciary as a means of assuring these.

Given a set of basic assumptions of this sort, it was quite reasonable that the Matsumoto Committee should conclude that relatively minor tinkering with the Meiji Constitution was all that circumstances justified or required and that it should produce the sort of drafts that it did. It was equally reasonable that the American authorities should strongly dissent from these results. In the absence of so fundamental a difference in viewpoints, matters might have worked out very differently. The Matsumoto Committee might have recognized that SCAP would expect and require truly extensive constitutional changes and, accordingly, it might have sought the sort of informal and quiet advice that Government Section would have been happy to provide. The result could well have been a draft constitution appreciably different in style, language, and degree of detailed specification from the present document, but perhaps not too different in its practical consequences. It would also have been much more authentically and demonstrably Japanese. It is, of course, impossible to say on substantive grounds whether Japan would have fared better or worse with such a more home-grown product or, indeed, whether it would really have made any difference. On procedural grounds, however, it is regrettable that these differences facilitated the development of a situation in which the Matsumoto Committee was not disposed to solicit informal American advice and Government Section was not inclined to be more positive and less tardy about making these requirements informally known to the Japanese government. This is the more regrettable since there were more positively and liberally inclined groups possessed of the necessary legal skills to which the Japanese government could have turned for advice and assistance. The decision to select Matsumoto rather than such alternates was a political one.

There is a further consequence of this culturally based outcome just described. Failing an acceptable Japanese initiative where constitutional revision was concerned, SCAP was impelled to step in and provide its so-called model constitution. In effect this meant turning over to the staff of Government Section the responsibility for determining the style and contents of what turned out to be substantially the final draft of the new constitution of Japan. Inevitably this was a product of America's traditions, experiences, and political and social values. Indeed, in this particular case, given the accident of the composition of Government Section's staff at the time, the American values represented in the SCAP draft were of a distinctly idealistic and progressive variety. Under no conceivable political circumstances would it have been possible in 1945–1946 to enact the equivalent of, for example, Chapter III on the "Rights and Duties of the People" at either the federal or state levels in the United States.

But, while it is interesting to speculate along these lines about the effects of differences in legal and political perspectives on history, it is the results that really matter. When viewed from this standpoint the thrust of Professor Tanaka's concluding remarks is undoubtedly correct. Given the confusions and cultural misunderstandings that attended the birth of the new Japanese constitution, the truly remarkable facts are that it has worked fairly well in practice and has survived intact so far as formal amendments are concerned.

Continuity and Discontinuity in Recent Japanese History

One of the most fascinating aspects of modern Japanese history is the impression of pronounced discontinuity that it conveys at two points—the Restoration and the Occupation. These seem to be years when enormous and highly discontinuous changes of an institutional and behavioral sort are compressed into very short periods of historical time. Those familiar in any depth with the historiography of the Restoration period will readily recall, however, that the more we have learned of its details, the greater the emphasis that has been placed on the elements of continuity rather than discontinuity. In the light of recent scholarship the Restoration has not turned out to represent so abrupt a break with the institutions, values, and behavior of the past as earlier historians had fancied. Indeed in more general terms, history affords few, if any, examples of real watersheds of that sort. This should make us very cautious about attributing such characteristics to the Allied Occupation of Japan.

Let us begin, therefore, by considering some of the continuities encountered on the postwar political scene in Japan. In doing so the time frame we have in mind for both continuities and discontinuities is the prewar period of the 1920s and early 1930s, not the years from 1932 to 1945 that were characterized by the dissolution of the political parties and the installation of extensive wartime controls. While this was not a time of undifferentiated historical experience for Japan, it offers greater coherence with the past than do the war years proper. Similarly, the terms of comparison we have in mind include both formal institutions and their functions and performance characteristics.

It is helpful at the outset to recall prewar attempts at the periodization of modern Japanese history. Most foreign accounts were keyed to the gradual emergence and development of democratic political institutions and practices in Japan. The central focus was normally on the increasing role and influence of political parties and parliamentary practices of the Western variety. According to this teleology the prewar culmination of this trend occurred between the early 1920s and 1932 when this progressive tide was brutally reversed by a series of coups d'état by ultranationalist and militarist elements.

The American planners in both Washington and SCAP were quite uniformly partial to this view of prewar Japanese history and, indeed, in significant part constructed their plans and based their hopes for the success of the Occupation on the doctrine that the years from 1932 to 1945 were a temporary aberration in the larger course of Japan's political development. Their mission was to redress this deviation from proper democratic norms and restore Japan to what an earlier generation of Japanese scholars was wont to call *kensei no jōdō* (the normal course of constitutional government). Not only was this their hope; it was also a basic strategy. The formal political institutions that had in the 1920s been relatively democratic in performance still existed, and many of the individuals who had manned them in these more liberal days were still alive and, in some cases, even politically active. The problem was to identify, revitalize, protect, and support such individuals while removing their rivals, at least temporarily, from the scene, and at the same time to improve the performance and extend the authority of such potentially democratic institutions as still existed in Japan while adding some new ones. America's plans for the success of the Occupation rested in large degree on the revivability of this earlier liberal tradition and its proponents in Japan while, it was hoped, garnering large numbers of new recruits to the cause in the process of doing so. Viewed in this light the plans and activities of the Occupation have a profound, if selective, continuity with the history of prewar Japan.

A second strand of continuity is to be found in the fact that the Japanese government, unlike the government of Nazi Germany, never went out of existence. The Allied Occupation was an indirect occupation in which the government of Japan survived defeat and continued by its normal means to administer all domestic affairs of state, subject to the authority of SCAP. This situation is of enormous importance. While it is true that SCAP could intervene at will and, when it chose, order particular outcomes, the previous chapters make clear the fact that in practice it

did so only selectively, that in general it was fairly receptive to many Japanese initiatives and suggestions, and that in practice it was heavily dependent upon the Japanese government for both essential working knowledge of the system and the entire process of carrying out all projects of change. These factors plus the related inputs from Japan's private sector meant that in general selected Japanese representatives acceptable to SCAP played a far more positive and more legitimate role in shaping the "new Japan" than was the case in any of the other postwar military occupations. Where the role of the Japanese government in particular was concerned, they endowed it with a very substantial capacity for assisting, qualifying, or frustrating in whole or part the plans and desires of SCAP. This power was inevitably a potent force for a much larger degree of continuity than would otherwise have been possible.

Similarly, it is of great symbolic and psychological importance that the imperial system, following fundamental changes in its substantive and ideological role and status, still survived the war, defeat, and Occupation. It is interesting to observe that the Japanese government, the Washington planners, and General MacArthur were all in wholehearted accord on this score. All identified the emperor as standing at the very core of Japan's political system and as the basic and perhaps only means of eliciting loyalty, obedience, and discipline from the postwar populace at large. All felt that in the physical and psychological tumult and distress that was certain to attend upon an unprecedented military defeat and foreign occupation, the emperor had a vital role to play. The Japanese government believed him essential to the preservation of internal order and, possibly, to the survival of the political system in any terms that they could accept. There was a real fear of a popular revolution in some quarters. The Washington planners and General MacArthur saw him as their best means of insuring Japan's compliance with the terms of surrender and eliciting the obedience and cooperation of both the Japanese government and people in carrying out SCAP's mission. The consequent preservation of the imperial system, although in drastically changed terms, must at the same time, therefore, be counted as a fundamental aspect of both continuity and discontinuity between pre- and postwar Japan.

Then there is the bureaucracy. Modern states are by definition bureaucratic. Japan is no exception. The Occupation did not seriously try to change the prewar role and functions of the Japanese bureaucracy. They enveloped it in a new and more democratic context and hoped that this would engender more democratic attitudes and performance on the part of bureaucrats. But, as Professor Pempel makes clear, the basic concepts of scientific management, recruitment by merit on the grounds of rigorous examinations, and the separation of administration from politics were shared by both the SCAP authorities and the Japanese government. The purge bore lightly on Japan's higher bureaucracy. Consequently, nei-

ther war nor defeat and occupation had any very revolutionary effect on the staffing or the operations and authority of the Japanese bureaucracy. They continued to conduct the daily affairs of government as before and, additionally, assumed the new role of consultants to SCAP and executors of all of the Occupation's reform programs. Several of the earlier chapters describe in some detail the sorts of cross-national bureaucratic alliances that developed between SCAP staffs and their counterparts in the Japanese government. A substantial capacity to influence SCAP plans and decisions and to interpret by their own lights the way and extent to which these programs would actually be carried out at the national and local levels was implicit in this role. This, too, was a conserving force and an important element of continuity in postwar Japan.

There are further continuities to be found on the more explicitly political side of Japan's postwar government. As the chapters on the postwar development of the conservative and progressive or social democratic political parties demonstrate, the relationship between the ostensibly new postwar parties and their prewar counterparts was in practically all cases close and continuous. On the conservative side, prior to the purge and with the exception of some wartime deaths and casualties, the same leaders emerged and began to put together new coalitions of factions familiar from the days of the Minscitō and Sciyūkai. With the exception of the legalization of the Communist party, the situation was not much different on the progressive side. It is not surprising under these circumstances that the postwar governments of Japan and the opposition parties as well bear more than a passing resemblance to their prewar predecessors. They are of the same stock. There is manifest continuity on this front too.

It is important also not to exaggerate the extent of the really novel versus the more continuous elements in SCAP's widely heralded reform programs. One of the principal virtues of the preceding chapters is the clarification that several of them provide in this respect. Their treatments, for example, of the new local government system, of the Diet Law, and of the Civil Code all restore a much needed sense of balance and proportion. The elements of continuity are strong in each case, sometimes even stronger than the innovative elements. The new local autonomy system is a case very much in point. The principal changes effected were the popular election of prefectural governors and the abolition of the Home Ministry. But the decentralizing force of these changes was almost fully offset by the continued power of the national ministries to establish local offices, delegate responsibilities to all local officials, and supervise their execution. To a large extent also the Ministry of Finance assumed the coordinating authority of the former Home Ministry. Thus, while important innovations were involved, the essential powers of the central government to control, coordinate, and supervise all local governments did not really undergo a critical change. This was often the case.

Finally, there was one very important matter that lay beyond even the plenary powers of SCAP. We have in mind the consensual decision-making system that characterizes Japanese government and many other segments of Japanese society. It is relatively simple to change institutions. It is far more difficult to change the attitudes, values, and behavioral patterns that underlie them. And, when it comes to taking collective action, these express themselves through some sort of decision-making system. In the Japanese case the highest possible degree of consensus among all concerned is a principal requirement of "legitimate" decisions. By its very nature this is normally a conserving force. It is biased against any form of drastic change and favors stasis or small, incremental adaptations. One should not lose sight of this fact in evaluating the question of continuity versus discontinuity where the impact of the Occupation on actual practice in Japan is concerned. In this sense the means by which governmental decisions are taken can and does powerfully influence the real content of what are ostensibly radical programs of change.

Against this background it should be obvious that the actual impact of the Occupation on Japan as a force for discontinuous political change can readily be exaggerated. The postwar political scene contains many elements of effective continuity with prewar Japan. It would be foolish to underestimate, however, the discontinuous elements of the postwar scene, the truly innovative developments attributable to initiatives launched or sponsored by SCAP. Let us now turn our attention to these.

Given the multiplication of issues and dissentient groups that characterizes all modern societies, it is risky to speak of national goals widely, if not universally, shared by a populace. In the case of Japan, however, geographic, racial, and cultural homogeneity combine to confer on the Japanese people an unusual capacity for achieving a working consensus on this score. It was perhaps more the shared experience of war and defeat, however, than any purposeful action of the Occupation that engendered a new national goal for Japan. From the beginning this was economic in nature: first "recovery," followed by "economic growth." While prewar Japan was far from indifferent to "economic growth," it also pursued other goals such as imperial expansion and, additionally, defined economic growth in somewhat different terms. In postwar Japan the single-minded and exclusive way in which Japan has focused on a succession of expanding economic goals is certainly one of the country's most notable new characteristics. While only in part and somewhat tardily attributable to initiatives by SCAP, this was a phenomenon born of the Occupation period and in this sense an important element of discontinuity.

Underlying the working consensus on the economic aspects of national goals, however, lay an extensive element of dissension about political ends and means best represented in organized fashion by the opposition parties, the labor unions, and associated interest groups. Beyond such organizations lay the great mass of the Japanese people who were both the ultimate subjects of the far-reaching changes attempted by the Occupation and the ultimate gauge of its success or failure in such ventures. How did they react? Were there extensive changes in popular values, attitudes, and behavior of a democratic and more participatory sort that stemmed from SCAP programs?

Any adequate response would be enormously complex and very dependent on the particular evidence one chose to consult and the time frame within which the answer was sought. But given a time frame that compared such popular attitudes, behavior, and values in the 1920s or 1930s with those in present-day Japan, there is no doubt that the verdict would come down on the side of a pronounced discontinuity. The norms of political attitudes and behavior have undoubtedly changed a great deal in the intervening years.

This change did not happen either quickly or uniformly. Fundamental to the process of change after the war was a sense of widespread disillusion and resentment against the political leadership and system that had led the country into the misery and suffering attendant on a lost war. In this sense few tears were shed for the passing of the old order. But the development of new political commitments took much longer. They emerged first from prewar roots and in this limited sense represent an element of historical continuity. As the chapters by Takemae and Uchida make clear, the surviving leaders of many prewar political parties and factions, both progressive and conservative, lost no time in renewing their prewar associations at the leadership level and arranging for the revival of organized political parties. The same was true of labor unions and employers' associations, both of which had political as well as economic goals. While particular groups of this sort with immediate and urgent political needs and objectives surfaced very rapidly and dramatically after the surrender, they included a relatively small part of the total population.

The years from 1945 to the early 1950s were a time of great difficulty for the Japanese people. The war resulted in about 1,800,000 military and civilian casualties. Twenty-five percent of the national wealth was destroyed. Forty percent of the built-up area of the 66 largest cities subjected to air attack was leveled, involving 20 percent of the nation's residential housing. Thirty percent of industrial capacity was destroyed. At the same time Japan lost its empire—46 percent of its prewar total territory—and had simultaneously to absorb into its domestic economy about six million Japanese soldiers and civilians repatriated from its former empire and from battlefields throughout the Pacific. These circumstances combined with a heritage of acceptance of established political authority in a way that insured the focusing of most mass energies and concern on problems of survival. Since the presence and policies of the Occupation effectively precluded the emergence of any revolutionary political elements that may have been latent in this postwar scene—in fact there seem to have been few anyway—the available channels for mass political action were at first largely restricted to the postwar political parties or the unions. And while they were able to recruit an appreciable following, no Japanese political party has yet succeeded in establishing a strong, committed, and reliable base of mass support. This was especially notable in the early postwar years when the average person was largely preoccupied by problems of food, housing, health, transportation, jobs, pay, and family interests at a far more intense level of concern and need than ever before. With some notable exceptions at the political party and interest group level, therefore, it seems valid to conclude that the masses of the Japanese people did not at first undergo more than a fairly passive adaptation to their country's new postwar political circumstances resulting from the new constitution and SCAP's programs of democratization. The abortive general strike of 1947 was rather exceptional in this respect.

In the early 1950s, however, one begins to find episodes indicating rising and sustained popular interest and concern in national issues that transcended immediate preoccupations with food, jobs, and housing. The national debate over the nature of the peace treaty in 1951 was an issue of this sort. So were the antinuclear demonstrations of 1954. Much more spectacular, of course, were the 1950–1960 demonstrations in connection with the revision of the Security Treaty. This was a nationwide movement that, for a limited time, succeeded in mobilizing and using widespread popular interest and concern in support of a particular national political policy. Of greater fundamental importance, however, was the gradual emergence of local and national interest group associations and citizens' movements with goals that required political action if they were to succeed. During the 1960s and 1970s these grew rapidly in numbers, in influence, and in the sophistication of the ways in which they dealt with and exploited the institutions of Japan's new democratic political system on behalf of their particular causes. Many of them worked with political parties of their choice and, in so doing, added a further element of popular participation in the system. With the passage of time and increasing familiarization with the potentialities of the new postwar system of government, the political parties themselves have become much more assertive and influential in their dealing with the bureaucracy. The revised educational system and the gradual accession of new generations to positions of power and influence have also played an important part. The result today is a far more politically informed, involved, and participant population than existed in the Japan of the 1920s or 1930s. The discontinuities involved are numerous, obvious, and of major importance.

Where the specific democratic content of Japan's postwar political sys-

tem is concerned, there can be no doubt that the elements of discontinuity far outweigh those of continuity or that these changes are primarily
the product of initiatives by SCAP. Fundamentally, this new measure of
democratization was a product of the 1946 constitution, which in turn
was vastly different from its predecessor, the Meiji Constitution of 1889.
This new document in legal terms drastically redistributed power among
the central organs of the state. Most notable of all was the new treatment
of the emperor and the imperial system. While it is true that the emperor
personally had exercised little, if any, meaningful power in Japan for
many centuries prior to 1945, it is equally true that the imperial institution was the ultimate means by which the actual exercise of power in prewar Japan was legitimized for all government at every level. All officials
were agents of the emperor. Their authority derived from and was sancti-
fied by this relationship. The mythology of divine descent and the cult of
emperor worship were deliberately cultivated in post-Restoration Japan
as a means of inculcating his subjects with the virtues of loyalty, patrio-
tism, discipline, and obedience and of endowing his officials with dignity
and unchallengeable authority. Nothing better signifies the centrality of
the imperial institution to the prewar Japanese political system than the
desperate efforts of the last wartime cabinet to salvage it from the ruins
of defeat, regardless of what else had to be sacrificed. The drafters of the
new constitution were well aware of this and, while desirous of retaining
the imperial institution for the reasons noted earlier, were equally determined to strip it of all its divine-right and sovereign attributes. The combination of Chapter I of the new constitution and the emperor's New
Year's speech on January 1, 1946, denying his divinity effectively accomplished these ends. These developments mark a profound discontinuity
with the circumstances of prewar Japan.

In addition to substituting popular for imperial sovereignty, the new
constitution also conferred all legislative authority on an elective bicameral Diet, provided extensive and detailed protection for civil and human
rights, minimized, if not eliminated, the role of the military, created a
powerful cabinet chosen by and responsible to the Diet, gave constitutional sanction to local autonomy, and endowed the judiciary with more
extensive authority. These new institutions in turn brought about pronounced changes of a democratic sort in the performance characteristics
of the Japanese government. While the results are obviously not in all
respects ideal, they compare favorably with the actual standards of performance achieved in other democratic societies of far older lineage.
They are further remarkable in that they were brought about in so short
a time, primarily as a result of foreign intervention, and are so sharply
discontinuous with the dominant thrust of prewar Japanese political
institutions and performance.

Especially notable is the degree to which Japanese politics have been opened to popular participation. The Occupation's innovations in this area were far-reaching. Women were enfranchised and the ages for voting and office-holding were substantially reduced. The upper house of the Diet was made popularly elective. So were the chief executive offices of all local public entities at all levels of subnational government. Provision was made for direct legislation and recall at the local level. Amendments to the constitution were made contingent on the result of a national referendum. The Communist party was legalized for the first time. And the purge opened a large number of public offices to new and popularly chosen political leaders. Changes of these sorts mark the dawn of a new era for popular participation in Japanese politics on a scale vastly exceeding the prewar possibilities. They were, of course, particularly significant for women, who had no legal standing or role in prewar Japanese politics.

It was a new political world also for the reformist or progressive parties that comprise the main opposition in postwar Japan. Their forebears were a sort of endangered species subject to harsh regulations and occasional dissolutions by the Justice Ministry and the police, small in membership, and almost completely lacking in influence. After the war they multiplied in size, acquired equality of legal status with the party in power, and, collectively, were able to exercise a formidable degree of suasion—and, sometimes, of veto—on the government. While with a single rather meaningless exception failing in their efforts to form a government, they were still a far more conspicuous and influential group than they had been before the war and undoubtedly responsible through their existence and influence for numerous important aspects of governmental policy in postwar Japan.

The same is true of Japanese labor unions which in technical terms had not even had a clear legal sanction for their existence in prewar Japan. Despite variations in SCAP policy and treatment where they were concerned, postwar labor unions increased enormously in membership and political influence. Indeed, they became the mainstay of three of the major opposition parties and a substantial force in Japanese politics. The discontinuities with prewar Japan where unions normally tottered on, and sometimes over, the brink of illegality and police tolerance is obvious.

Even the family system was not immune from SCAP's attention. The *ie* or house system in prewar Japan had been characterized by the dominance of the eldest male of the senior lineage, the subordination of its female members, and inheritance by primogeniture. The postwar Civil Code specified the equality of women, favored nuclear rather than extended families, and instituted equality of inheritance among the children of a nuclear family. In these basic respects, abrupt discontinuities were introduced into the system.

Where practical politics is concerned, note must also be taken of the effects of the 1946 purge. These have frequently been underestimated by foreign students of the Occupation. Uchida's chapter on the postwar conservative parties should make clear the fact that its consequences for most of the parties were both extensive and serious. The purge did remove from formal participation in politics a large number of the surviving prewar influentials of conservative persuasion and replaced them by a new generation of political leaders who were by no means reliably subject to the influence of the purgees whom they succeeded. While it is true that an appreciable number of these purgees returned to office after the depurges of 1950–1951 and that others continued to exercise covert influence, they were by this time a minority in the conservative ranks and the entire context of Japanese politics had changed substantially. There is here, therefore, a significant, if partial, break with Japan's prewar conservative political party leadership. A similar situation prevailed where the leadership of Japanese big business was concerned.

Finally, one of the most dramatic and important of discontinuities is to be found in the area of Japan's foreign relations. Japan entered upon the Occupation experience as a bitter, recently defeated, and still potentially dangerous enemy that had to be effectively disarmed, demilitarized, and deprived of any real potential for aggression for all time to come. Japan emerged from the Occupation experience as a major ally of the United States, a forward base for American power in Asia, and in circumstances where the Japanese government was being strongly pressured by the United States to make very substantial increases in its armed forces. It is hard to conceive of a more improbable and sharply discontinuous development than this.

The record is mixed, therefore, when the Occupation is viewed from this perspective of continuities and discontinuities in modern Japanese history. Both factors are present in abundance. Items of major importance are to be found on both sides of the ledger, and often within the same reform program or sphere of activity working dialectically to produce a new synthesis. Personally, we find this diversity and dialectical interaction reassuring in the sense that it conforms to our conception of the process of historical change. History is usually a complex compound of continuous and discontinuous elements of precisely this sort. Under recent and detailed study, few historical periods have proven to be as markedly discontinuous with their predecessors as earlier scholarship has sometimes fancied. Just such a mix of conserving and innovative institutions and practices is normal for most periods of modern history. The Japanese case, while not basically divergent in this sense, is, however, remarkable in several respects.

The changes involved were not segmental; they involved practically every major sector of Japanese society and culture. Historically speaking, they were compressed into a very brief period—some six years and eight months or, if one accepts the beginning of the Korean War as the effective end of most, although not all, of the major reform programs, only four years and ten months. And they were initiated and in important degree shaped by a foreign agency, the civilian sections of the headquarters of the Supreme Commander for the Allied Powers. The fact that the institutions, behavior patterns, and values that the Occupation was trying to transmit to Japan were predominantly Western in provenance whereas the indigenous non-Western institutions, behavior patterns, and values of Japanese society were only partially Westernized might be added to this list.

Given these basic facts, one can only be surprised by the degree of success that attended upon SCAP's efforts. Depending on definitions and theories about what constitutes a democratic society, one can legitimately argue about whether or not SCAP succeeded in democratizing Japan or whether Japanese society is truly democratic today. By any real-world standards of actual practice in any other contemporary democracy, however, it is difficult to sustain such an argument. Japanese institutions and practices compare favorably. Similarly, one can legitimately argue as to whether SCAP succeeded in demilitarizing Japan. Here it is a question of how one interprets the intent of Article IX of the constitution and how one evaluates the aggressive potential of Japan's role in the American alliance system. At the very least one conclusion has to be that, at present and in the near future, Japan has no independent capacity for aggression of any sort and, apparently, very little intention of acquiring one.

Under the circumstances these are truly remarkable outcomes. They argue conclusively for the success of the Occupation in the terms originally set for it by the U.S. Initial Postsurrender Policy and the Joint Chiefs' directive. They testify even more eloquently, however, to the extraordinary talents of the Japanese people and government in adapting these innovations to their national needs and purposes and utilizing them so successfully on their own behalf. Neither ancient nor modern history has seen the equal of their performance in any remotely comparable span of time.

Notes

1. U.S. Department of State, *Foreign Relations of the United States, 1947* (Washington, D.C.: GPO, 1972), vol. 6, pp. 554–555. Hereafter cited as *FRUS*.

2. *FRUS, 1948*, vol. 6, pp. 702–703.

3. Supreme Commander for the Allied Powers, Government Section, *Political Reorientation of Japan* (Washington, D.C.: GPO, n.d.), p. 764.

Appendix I
Draft of Justin Williams Memorandum
of November 5 [4?], 1946*

1. *Standing Committee*
    a. One for each major field of activity.
    b. Each standing committee (and budget sub-committee) to be furnished office space, secretarial assistance, and expert assistance at state expense.
    c. Members of standing committees, once appointed, to remain on such committees ~~from session to session, or as long as they desire.~~ for term.
    d. Set of parliamentary rules to be drawn up for conducting committee hearings, and uniform system of recording and reporting such hearings to be devised.
    e. Standing committees to hold public hearings on all bills of general interest and purport: all persons and organizations having real interest in the bills may attend the public hearings and present their observations and arguments.
2. *Legislative Council*
    a. To be composed of members from both Houses.
    b. Functions: to advise Cabinet and both Houses on legislative needs and problems; to study and propose constant revision of the Diet Law and Regulations of the Houses.
3. *Diet Library and Diet Legislative Bureau and Reference Service*
4. *Plenary sessions and committee hearings*
    a. To be open to general public without discrimination, except for executive sessions.
5. *Debate*
    a. Provision to be made for all members at least once every two weeks to take the floor and speak freely on national policy and important measures (possibly in the Committee of the Whole House).
    b. If a time limit on speaking is fixed, speakers to be privileged to have their remarks extended in the official record.

435

6. *Interpellations*
   a. To be subject to a definite time limit and thus permit more members to interpellate the Government.
7. *Dignity of elected representatives*
   a. Practices, procedures, ceremonies, and rituals that tend to dignify Government officials at the expense of Diet members to be forbidden.
8. *Contingent funds for the Diet*
   a. To be provided in the budget.
   b. To be determined by each House and to be used as each House sees fit.
9. *Franking privileges*
   a. Diet members to be privileged to send through the mails free of charge public documents printed by order of the Diet and all other mail matter of an official nature, under conditions to be prescribed by the Diet.
10. *Office space and secretarial assistance*
    a. To be provided each member at State expense.
11. *Salaries of Diet members*
    a. To be not less than total pay and allowances of highest career officials.

November 5, 1948   [signed]
                                                        T. Yamasaki

---

*This is a complete and accurate reproduction of the contents of the original memorandum sent to Yamasaki.

Index

437